KU-522-091

EARLY
VICTORIAN ENGLAND
1830–1865

GENERAL ELECTION, 1865: A MEETING

EARLY
VICTORIAN
ENGLAND
1830–1865

Omnium rerum aut similitudo aut multitudo
stomachum facit, praeter intelligere. VIRGIL.

VOLUME II

LONDON
OXFORD UNIVERSITY PRESS
HUMPHREY MILFORD

1934

RETURN TO
COUNTY LIBRARY BOOKSTORE
TAMWORTH ROAD
HERTFORD
TEL. 6863

OXFORD UNIVERSITY PRESS
AMEN HOUSE, E.C. 4
LONDON EDINBURGH GLASGOW
NEW YORK TORONTO MELBOURNE
CAPETOWN BOMBAY CALCUTTA
MADRAS SHANGHAI
HUMPHREY MILFORD
PUBLISHER TO THE UNIVERSITY

HERTFORDSHIRE
COUNTY LIBRARY
653580
942·081

C 6106223·5

PRINTED IN GREAT BRITAIN

CONTENTS

VOLUME II

LIST OF ILLUSTRATIONS

Acknowledgements are due in each case to the owner whose name appears below, and in particular to H.M. the King for gracious permission to reproduce Frith's Ramsgate Sands (Plate 126) from the Buckingham Palace Collection.

VOLUME II

IX
THE PRESS

II   B

THE PRESS

By E. E. KELLETT

§ I. THE POWER OF THE PRESS

THE Reform Act of 1832 was at once the Parliamentary recognition of a revolution which had been going on for many years, and the stimulus of a revolution which was, in its turn, to receive recognition by the Reform Act of 1867. On its industrial side much has been written. But almost more important was the educational metamorphosis which took place, gradually but rapidly, during the same time. The middle classes were becoming more and more literary, and the lower classes were learning to read. A few figures will illustrate this process more clearly than a dozen pages. In 1838, in Southwark, 40 per cent. of the population could not read. In Manchester, in the same year, 55 per cent. signed the marriage register, 45 per cent. made a mark. There were schools, but the results did not always last. In Hull, a census of 4,735 ex-scholars showed that 823 could not read a complete sentence, and 1,870 could not write. Nor is this surprising; for, in the census of 1851, out of 29,425 private schoolmasters and mistresses, 708 signed their returns with a mark.[1] In 1845 it was computed that (for the United Kingdom) 33 per cent. of the males were illiterate and 49 per cent. of the females. But in 1851 these figures fell to 31 and 45 respectively; in 1861 to 25 and 35; and in 1871 to 19 and 26.[2] There was thus an enlarging field to be harvested by the publishers of newspapers and magazines.

To continue this educative process was the desire of all reformers, whatever their differences in other respects. Their cry was for a Reading People. A people which read would, *ipso facto*, not only throw off its degrading vices, but become an 'exceeding great army' for the destruction of the tyrants. First, then, teach the people to read, and then provide them with the right reading material. Reform would speedily follow.

[1] F. Smith, quoting from Horace Mann (*Education in Gt. Britain*, 1854).
[2] These figures are given by Graham Balfour (*Educational Systems of Gt. Britain and Ireland*, Appendix) from the Registrar-General's Returns.

THE PRESS

Publishers were not slow to see their opportunity. To the growing interest of the middle classes in politics and social questions they at once appealed. Religious organizations, following Wesley's example, issued books, magazines, tracts, and newspapers for the benefit of their adherents; and publishers of a different type endeavoured to make their profit out of the popularity of sensational literature. Some of them, it is true, like Charles Knight, were reformers as well as publishers; but all alike were sensible of the growing power of the new engine. Nothing strikes the student of the thirty years after the Reform Bill more forcibly than the naïve belief in this omnipotence of the printed word, a belief shared equally by the Press itself and by the public. It is spoken of with bated breath both by those who admire it and by those who detest it. The dangers of 'bad' literature were as profoundly felt as the dangers of illiteracy.[1] On the other hand, what was mighty for ill could be made mighty for good. The soothing draughts of Whiggism and Ricardianism could be dexterously administered to a restless populace by this means, and revolution would be staved off by education. The immense, but cautious, reforming energy of the time conceived that here was the sure means of progress. Horrors might exist; grievances might abound; ignorance might kick against the wage-law and the substitution of machinery for handwork; the dark places of the earth might be full of cruelty; but the Press would let in light,[2] and the pen, more potent than the tree of Moses, would cleanse the waters of corruption. The demagogue and the oppressor would stand revealed together, and the Millennium would be at hand. From Dickens[3] and Reade downwards, all men seem to have felt that ventilation was the cure of every ill, and that the Press was the ventilating agent. Among politicians this

---

[1] See Report of Committee on Public Libraries, p. 85; Hammond, p. 319; and infra, on the 'Salisbury Square' publications.

[2] Of this the career of 'Jacob Omnium' (Matthew Higgins, 1810–68) is an apt illustration. He was perhaps the first of that long line of writers of letters to the Press, exposing every abuse of which they happened to hear. This function of the Press, as receiver and transmitter of such messages, is possibly its most useful one; though, like other good things, it has been abused.

[3] It was no mere oratorical flourish when Daniel Webster told his audience that Dickens had done more by his writings to ameliorate the condition of the English poor than all the statesmen in Parliament (Forster, 1842). In 1853 Baldwin Brown said that the three great social agencies were the cholera, the London City Mission, and Dickens's works.

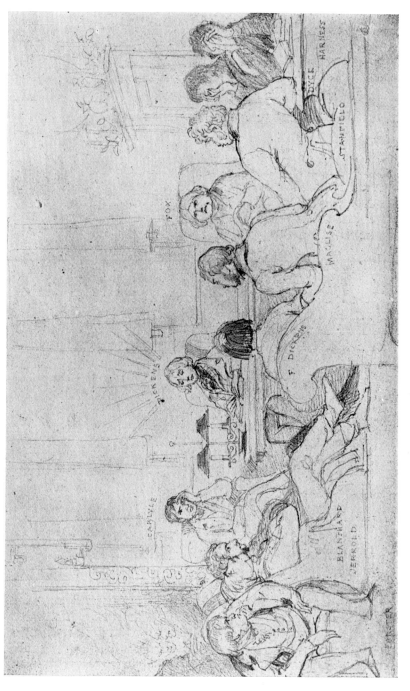

DICKENS AND HIS FRIENDS—*MACLISE*

feeling was perhaps specially strong: they may have harboured an uneasy suspicion that *they* were among the ills the Press might be called upon to cure.[1] Accordingly, they took pains to make friends of the newspapers while in the way with them; and some, like Palmerston, were suspected of a still closer and more sinister association with particular papers, which they, it was asserted, inspired, used for their own purposes, or even subsidized.

It was not only the popular Press which had this power. In the ferment of the time, even the great and expensive reviews had an influence which to us seems strange. The Whig *Edinburgh*, indeed, was not quite what it had been; nothing, in all probability, but the sagacity of Jeffrey in securing Macaulay, in 1825, saved it from decline. 'It would be mere affectation in me', wrote Macaulay to Napier in 1833, 'to pretend not to know that my support is of some importance to the Review';[2] and he knew that people often hesitated to purchase it if there were no article of his in the current number. But the Tory *Quarterly* was and remained powerful;[3] and the effect of James Mill's opening article in the Radical *Westminster* is not in the least exaggerated by his son in his *Autobiography*.[4] The class to which these reviews appealed was the one already in political power, or the one about to seize it.[5]

[1] In the *Croker Papers* (ii, pp. 21, 24) is an account of a plan for controlling the Press in the interests of Downing Street by the agency of Joseph Planta (Letter to Planta, Aug. 21, 1829).　　[2] Trevelyan, popular edn., p. 252.
[3] The *Quarterly* was known in France, and had the honour of being formally answered by Lamartine.
[4] Popular edn., p. 52. The influence of the other great quarterlies, such as the *Home and Foreign*, the *North British*, &c., was limited in range, but probably profound.
[5] They appealed of course to the well-to-do, as they were necessarily expensive, costing usually about six shillings a number; for most of them paid their contributors on a lavish scale, and it was, e.g., the principle of the *Edinburgh* to do so. Macaulay speaks of receiving, or being owed, £90 for a single review, apparently that on Lord Mahon (Trevelyan, popular edn., p. 221). Southey's articles in the *Quarterly* sometimes brought him in £100 (Dowden, *Southey*, 101); and to Sydney Smith, Jeffrey used to write, 'To a very wise and witty article in the *Edinburgh*, *x* sheets, at 45 guineas a sheet' (Russell, *Sydney Smith*, p. 27). As a contrast, it may be mentioned that Leigh Hunt's son John wrote for Cleave's *Gazette* at a shilling a column (Blunden, *Votive Tablets*, p. 217).
The cost of *printing* an ordinary sheet (2,000 copies) was about £8, which might rise to £9 or more if the corrections were numerous; a cost almost prohibitive unless the circulation or the advertisements seemed likely to justify the risk.

It was, of course, at once the duty and the pleasure of the Press to foster this idea of its own importance; and in the newspapers of the time, perhaps more even than in those of to-day, we detect an air of omnipotence and omniscience which strikes us, who know the failures of their policies and the vanity of their forecasts, as somewhat ludicrous. Even Delane, as we shall see, was utterly wrong on some of the most crying questions of the day. But there was much to explain the attitude. The amazing success of Cobbett, with his vigorous and pellucid style of writing, and the earlier lesson taught by Junius, that anonymity can add force to invective, had not been lost on their successors. 'There is', wrote Junius to his brother-journalist Wilkes, 'something oracular in the delivery of my opinions. I speak from a recess which no human curiosity can penetrate; and darkness, we are told, is one source of the sublime. The mystery of Junius increases his importance.' The great Unknown might have added that his importance was further increased by his habit of always talking as if he knew everything.

Editors may therefore be pardoned if they believed that by adding the anonymity of Junius to the popular appeal of Cobbett, and by maintaining a pontifical attitude of infallibility, they might exert an almost unlimited power. They spoke to an audience which believed in knowledge as such, either fearing it like the Tories or rejoicing in it like the Liberals. While a Liberal like Brougham, in his *Observations on the Education of the People*, and in his establishment of the *Society for the Diffusion of Useful Knowledge*,[1] seemed to think that, to build Jerusalem in England, it was sufficient to set up a school, others, in the spirit of Archbishop Moore and the Duke of Wellington, looked with suspicion on all teaching that was not supervised by a safe and moderate Church of England parson. The schoolmaster, said Brougham, was already abroad; it was necessary and desirable to provide him with pistols and holsters. As he was abroad, said the others, and could no longer be entirely suppressed, he must be compelled to teach the right things; and those whom he had taught to read must be carefully restricted to those works which their masters considered harmless and fitting.

[1] Both in 1825. Brougham contributed the first volume to this series, and supported it with his usual formidable ferocity.

§ 2. TAXES ON KNOWLEDGE

Hence, to a great degree, sprang that indirect control of the Press which took the place of the direct censorship abandoned in 1695; a control exercised largely through the stamp duty, the advertisement duties, and the duty on paper. As the fears of Revolution died away, the Press gradually threw off its financial shackles.[1] The history of our period, from this point of view, is the history of the relaxation of these restrictions, and a narrative of the consequent enormous growth of popular ephemeral literature. It is true that the restrictions had not always restrained. Many papers defied the law.

'The belief', wrote Fonblanque in 1831,[2]'that helpless old hags could rule the winds . . . will not seem less (sic) astonishing than the belief that poor scribblers can exercise baneful powers over the public mind, and order at pleasure the rise and fall of institutions. . . . By imposing taxes on newspapers[3] . . . a contraband trade has been called into existence, and cheap illicit spirit, ten times above proof, has been hawked among the working classes. The cheap publications, of whose inflammatory tendency so much is made, are the offspring of the stamp duties.'

That Fonblanque was right could be proved by scores of instances. The Chartists (and extreme Radicals) were not deterred by fines and imprisonments. Cleave, Watson, Abel Heywood of Manchester, were all incarcerated, and all went on with their work. Hetherington was, if possible, even more uncompromising.[4] When, in 1831, he started the *Poor Man's Guardian*, unstamped, at a penny for the liberal measure of eight quarto pages, he opened with the words, 'This is a weekly newspaper for the People, established contrary to Law, to try the power of Might against Right. Defiance', he added, 'is our only remedy.' The result was what might have been expected: he was himself imprisoned; 800 vendors of his papers were prosecuted and 500 punished; but he went

[1] For the earlier history, 1819–32, see Wickwar, *Struggle for the Freedom of the Press*, 1930.
[2] Quoted, from the *Examiner*, by Fox Bourne, ii. 83.
For the increase of the stamp duty by Lord North in 1776, see Lecky, iii. 476. It was further increased during the Great War.
[3] The *Examiner*, in 1830, was headed thus: 'Paper and Print, 3d.: Taxes on Knowledge, 4d.: Total 7d.'
[4] He took his revenge by prosecuting Moxon for publishing *Queen Mab*, and won his case (1841).

on. What added to the fury of the masses was the partiality of the Law. In trying a man for selling Hetherington's paper, the judge asked, 'Why not sell the *Penny Magazine* or the *National Omnibus*, which contain none of the inflammatory trash of the *Poor Man's Guardian*?'

Many papers, in fact, appeared unstamped, but were never prosecuted. This brought out Fonblanque once more. 'The punishment is not for selling unstamped papers, but for expressing opinions offensive to the Government'; and in Parliament itself Bulwer, supported by O'Connell, was impelled to move the total abolition of all taxes impeding the diffusion of knowledge. It is noteworthy that so stubborn an economist as Joseph Hume, though *The Times* alone paid £48,000 in one year in stamps and £16,000 for advertisements, was in favour of abolition.[1] All efforts, however, were as yet in vain.

In 1836 the Whig Government lowered the stamp duty from fourpence to a penny,[2] but the concession, such as it was, met with scant gratitude. The Whigs made the little finger of their penny thicker than the loins of the groat, and administered the law more stringently than their predecessors. The reduction, indeed, did not work as its promoters had expected; for apparently even after it the prices were too high. When Dilke lowered the price of the *Daily News* from 5*d*. to 2½*d*., the increase in circulation did not compensate him;[3] and it was noticed that the circulation of *The*

[1] Joseph Hume was also a firm friend of the British Museum, and championed it against the niggardliness of the Treasury.

[2] 6 & 7 Wm. IV, c. 76. The Act defined a 'newspaper' as follows: 'Any paper containing public news intelligence or occurrences printed in any part of the United Kingdom dispersed and made public. Also any paper printed weekly or oftener or at intervals not exceeding 26 days containing only or partially advertisements. And also any paper containing any public news intelligence or occurrences or any remarks or observations thereon printed for sale and published periodically in parts or numbers at intervals not exceeding 26 days . . . where any of the said papers shall not exceed two sheets of the dimensions hereinafter specified (exclusive of any cover or blank leaf or any other leaf upon which any advertisements or other notices shall be printed)'; &c., &c. (length 21 in., breadth 17 in.). 'Any of the several papers hereinafter described shall be liable to the duties in whatever way or form the same may be printed folded or divided into leaves or stitched'; &c., &c.

The same definition is given in the Newspaper Registration Act, 1881; somewhat different is the Post Office Act, 1908. Legal authorities differ: the Solicitor-General and the Solicitor to the Treasury did not agree as to the interpretation of 6 & 7 Wm. IV, c. 76.

[3] Collet, in M'Carthy's *History of the Daily News*, p. 127 sq., gives a good, brief discussion of the effects of the reduction.

Times, which in 1837 was only a quarter of that of the London papers generally, was in 1851 a half—though it retained its old price, and many of the others lowered theirs. Hopes had been raised too high, and disappointment speedily hardened into hatred. 'Reader,' wrote Feargus O'Connor in the *Northern Star*, which he started at Leeds in 1837, 'behold that little spot in the centre of my newspaper—the Whig *beauty* spot, your *plague* spot. That spot has cost me nearly eighty pounds in money, and nearly a thousand miles of night and day travelling.' 'Chartism, Socialism, and the other heresies that the comfortable classes desired to put down, were promoted, instead of being restrained, by the penny stamp and the wrath it stirred up.'[1] We must, however, remember that certain penny weeklies, like Hetherington's *Poor Man's Guardian*, or the *London Reformer*, in which Livesey advocated temperance, were not newspapers within the meaning of the Act; and the lowering of the tax tended to raise the *number* of publications, some of which contrived to gain, or to keep, large circulations. Nevertheless, as Dilke pointed out, there were in 1846 fewer London papers than in 1750, and fewer dailies in the British Isles than in New York, while the circulation of Paris papers was twenty times that of London.[2]

The advertisement duty perhaps caused equal exasperation. The Inland Revenue authorities certainly interpreted the law very strictly. A favourable review was treated as an advertisement, especially if it mentioned the price of the book; nor was the proprietor of the paper entirely satisfied when, in 1833, the review cost him but eighteenpence instead of three and sixpence.[3] The temptation to bid his band of critics 'slate' the books must have been strong, and was apparently not always resisted. As for general advertisements, they increased enormously as the value of publicity was more and more clearly perceived. The first number of *The Times* contained about sixty advertisements. In early days, about seven of its sixteen columns were taken up with advertisements, which by 1811 had risen to about

---

[1] Fox Bourne, ii. 115, from which some of the above facts are derived. See also Hammond, *Age of the Chartists*, p. 317.
[2] 'A Few Words to the Public,' *Daily News*, June 1, 1846. In 1836 there were: in United Kingdom, 274 newspapers; in France, 234; in Germany, 593. In 1851 the circulations were: United Kingdom, 95 million, or $3\frac{1}{2}$ per head; U.S.A., 420 million, or 20 per head.   [3] In Ireland, half a crown.

150. But in May 1853[1] a single issue of *The Times* contained 2,575 advertisements.[2] The total abolition of the duty later in the year is reflected in a still more rapid increase: in 1861 the 4,000 was passed. After that date *The Times* became a less faithful mirror of the growth of this special trade: the *Telegraph* and other papers were outstripping it in circulation, and, consequently, in attraction to advertisers. A curious feature of our whole period is this, that no self-respecting paper would admit pictorial advertisements.[3] Otherwise, there are probably few devices for humbugging the public to-day of which at least the germ was not known and utilized in the fifties; nor would Carlyle have found much more to denounce, or Peacock to ridicule, in the papers of our time than they found then.[4]

Meanwhile, by the efforts of the Association for the Repeal of Taxes on Knowledge, as well as by silent public opinion, Government was being gradually driven further. Under the presidency of Milner Gibson, with the 'Radical tailor' Francis Place as treasurer, the Association forced Lord John Russell, in 1851, to grant a select committee, and actually performed the miracle of making Parliament attend to the committee's suggestions. Finally, by '16 & 17 Vic., c. 59', on the anniversary of Magna Carta, June 15, 1855, the obnoxious 'beauty-spot'[5] finally disappeared. There remained but the paper duty.[6] The fact that the Exchequer had actually gained by the reduction of the advertisement

---

[1] Quoted from the *Quarterly Review* by Moran, *Business of Advertising*, p. 65.

[2] In 1850, a fairly typical year, 890,650 advertisements appeared in the London 'newspapers'; 875,631 in the provinces; in Scotland, 240,141. It may be noticed that advertisements in *books* and on hoardings, &c., were not taxed. Hence the extraordinary farragoes adorning the fly-leaves of old volumes.

[3] Not at all uncommon before 1830.

[4] Just after, with the Repeal Act, came the Betting Act, 16 & 17 Vic., c. 119, by which any person publishing an advertisement giving information as to betting, was liable to £30 fine or two months' imprisonment. Similarly, in 1845 and 1846, the Lottery Act of 1836 against advertising lotteries in the Press was amended and strengthened.

[5] Number of stamps issued in England:

1825: 26,950,693	1840: 49,033,384
1830: 30,158,741	1845: 56,433,977
1835: 32,874,652	1850: 65,741,271

This list does not include the supplementary halfpenny stamps, which in 1850 were 11,684,423. Haydn's *Dictionary of Dates, sub voce* 'Newspapers', gives a convenient statistical summary.

[6] Varying from $1\frac{1}{2}d.$ to $3d.$ (raised to $4d.$ in 1815).

duty, as it finally did by Rowland Hill's postal policy,[1] was an added argument for the enfranchising plans, though in 1828 *The Times* alone had paid £3,300 to the Government for paper. It was a principle of Peel and Gladstone that, within limits, low taxation assisted Government more than high; but this was not the main reason which weighed when finally, in 1861, after a memorable struggle with the Lords, the last of the 'taxes on knowledge' was abolished. Gladstone was conscious of the importance of his triumph. 'The paper duty is gone,' he said to Sidney Herbert; 'for the full results of its removal men must wait until we of the nineteenth century are no more.' We are certainly feeling the results, both good and evil, to-day. But many were immediately obvious. It is possible that future historians may fix the golden age of the Press as that which immediately followed its emancipation, and may mark its decline as setting in when the nineteenth century went out.

§ 3. THE PRESS AND PUBLIC LIFE

The history of this long conflict shows clearly how strong was that sense of the power of the Press which we noted above. But for the fear of it, the authorities would assuredly not have held on so obstinately to their fancied means of restraining it; and Fonblanque's attacks on the restrictions reveal, in spite of his sarcasms, that he realized the greatness of the force it was sought to check. On the other hand, the papers that appealed to the higher classes felt *their* power. When, in 1834, the Whigs were dismissed, and Wellington was looking out for the means of propping up his temporary and minority Ministry, Barnes, the famous editor of *The Times*, told him plainly the terms on which alone his alliance could be gained. When Wellington refused to answer this new and exacting Blücher, Lyndhurst was approached, and was plainly alarmed; 'so great and dangerous a potentate is the wielder of the thunders of the press.' 'Barnes', said Lyndhurst, 'is the most powerful man in the country.[2]' It was indeed one of the causes of the weakness of Melbourne,

---

[1] It must be remembered that the stamped papers alone went by post (and could be indefinitely re-addressed). In 1857, 71 million papers went through the post—nearly all of which would now require a *postage*-stamp. As their numbers increased, the Exchequer would gain—and it did. The unstamped papers, of course, did not go by post; the gain to the Post Office from these, after 1855, was great.   [2] Greville, under date.

when he returned to office, that Barnes was so furious an opponent.

On the Tory side, this fear of the Press may have been accentuated by the knowledge of the enormous influence exerted by French journalists in the twenties. Polignac, we know, warned Wellington not to permit English journalists to acquire a similar power; and Wellington was always afraid an English Jean Paul Courier might arise.[1] Nor was this fear altogether hidden from view by the real or pretended contempt which, with the inconsistency so characteristic of human nature, often went along with it. Scores of examples of this attitude could easily be adduced, from the days of Defoe to those of Delane. The *Newgate Calendar*, enumerating the crimes of the forger Dr. Dodd, counted it as not the least among them that he had sunk so low as to edit a newspaper,[2] and it seemed to think that after such a degradation a Royal chaplain was *capable de tout*. But the feeling, or the pretence of the feeling, appears much later, and in unexpected quarters. The *Lancet* was founded in 1823 by Dr. Thomas Wakley of St. Thomas's Hospital, who had suffered many things at the hands of the Thistlewood gang.[3] He had, however, almost as much trouble with a man very different from Thistlewood. When his paper reported the lectures of Astley Cooper, the great surgeon proclaimed his regret that he could not publicly resent such an outrage, and loudly asserted that he felt 'disgraced and degraded' by the appearance of his name in the Press.[4] The politicians were not behind the doctors in their professions of contempt, which remind us of the affectations of those Elizabethan noblemen who would write poetry but not put their names to it. An utterance of Lord Althorp in the House of Commons provoked a deserved rebuke from Rintoul in the *Spectator* (September 17, 1831).[5]

---

[1] The social status of the French journalist was so much higher than that of his English brother as perhaps to explain the bitterness of the Blanchards, Thackerays, and Albert Smiths. They suffered from a sense of inferiority. A good instance is given by Bulwer in *England and the English* (see esp. pp. 264–8). When men like Frederic Rogers and Thomas Mozley had shown that journalists could be 'gentlemen', this peculiar acridity of tone begins to disappear. Incidentally, the words *journalism* and *journalist* are of French origin.

[2] This was in 1777. See Knapp and Baldwin, *Newgate Calendar*, iii. 53.

[3] See *D.N.B.* under 'Wakley'.   [4] Squire Sprigge, *Life of Wakley*, p. 85.

[5] I quote from Beach Thomas, *Story of the Spectator*, p. 46.

'The tone in which newspapers are usually mentioned in the House of Commons', wrote Rintoul, 'is absurd. Men who cannot breakfast without one, in the evening pretend to be hardly cognizant of the existence of such things. Men who in private life look to them almost for their sole stock of opinions, are found in public sneering at their contents, thus despising that with which they are crammed to the very mouth, so that they can hardly speak without betraying the source of their information. . . . Newspapers are far above the contempt of Members of Parliament in ability, and in power are scarcely beneath the Honourable House itself.'

Nor were the Lords, in Rintoul's view, any better than the Commons.

This Parliamentary peculiarity was doubtless, like many other Parliamentary peculiarities, a survival from earlier days, when war between St. Stephen's and the Press was furious and unconcealed. Whatever its cause, there is no doubt that men of political eminence were, in their hearts, fully alive to the importance of the rising power, and used it as gladly as Harley had used Swift's pamphlets or Walpole those of his army of Grub Street hacks. Long before our period ended, not a few distinguished statesmen were more or less furtively courting the chiefs of the Press, and some were even writing for them with their own hands.[1] Brougham, for example, wrote in *The Times*, and, characteristically enough, was detected by Barnes with an article in his hands for the *Morning Chronicle*, refuting a *Times* article he had himself written.[2]

To generalize about the newspapers of the thirties is peculiarly difficult and dangerous. Many of them, of course, had already existed for long, and had established their individuality. The *Globe* had been founded in 1803, the *Observer* in 1791, *The Times* in 1788, the *Morning Post* in 1772, the *St. James's Chronicle* in 1769, the *Stamford Mercury*, and the *Leeds Mercury*,[3] in some form or other, still earlier. Papers like the *London Evening Post*, the *Universal Chronicle*, the *York Courant*, had flourished a

[1] Palmerston used the *Morning Chronicle* against the hated *Times*. The *Globe*, which had once attacked Disraeli as a rat, was supposed, in later years, to be inspired by him. Aberdeen, as is well known, kept in close touch with *The Times*. In 1842 a promising attempt was made to induce Palmerston to write for the *Edinburgh*. He declined, not on the ground of dignity (the *Edinburgh* was no daily), but for the thoroughly Palmerstonian reason that he wished to keep his good things for the House of Commons (Trevelyan, *Macaulay*, popular edn., p. 422).

[2] This was ungrateful, as Brougham received from *The Times* £100 a month. [3] 1717. This paper was vastly transformed later at different times.

hundred years before, and, though many had died, each of them had made its contribution to the realization of the idea of a newspaper. But, in the modern sense of the word, there was no newspaper at all till the passing of Fox's Libel Act in 1792, which put the decision as to the character of a publication in the hands of juries. The judges struggled long to retain their old power,[1] and it took some time before editors discovered the change in their position. It may be said, with little exaggeration, that they did not fully realize it till the thirties; and as a result the years between 1830 and 1860 showed a greater advance than the whole previous century. Making full allowance for many exceptions, and for early sporadic adumbrations of later features, we may say that our period exhibited a rapid growth in the self-consciousness of a paper, and in the perception that, if a consistent policy were pursued, a constituency might be gained and kept. The inner soul of this advance was editorial control; the outer expression was given not only in the whole tone of the paper but in the leading articles, over which the editor, even when, like Delane, he wrote none of them, exercised a close supervision. Readers gradually came to know, within limits, what to expect, and the paper was recognized as representing certain principles. These principles a new paper was careful to lay down at starting; an old one took any opportunity that arose of letting it be known what lines it would follow. With the increase of numbers—and the increase was rapid—rivalry naturally intensified;[2] and we begin to note the appearance of what to-day is called a 'scoop' or a 'stunt'. The reporter became an instrument of greater and greater value to the paper. The *Morning Chronicle*, for example, was fully conscious that it had in the young Dickens the best reporter in London. The editor himself was often, to all intents and purposes, a reporter: the manipulation of indiscreet politicians was one of his special tasks, and Delane's supremacy was largely due to his skill in this art. The incident of which Meredith made use in *Diana of the Crossways* [3] is only one of many feats of the

---

[1] The career of Ellenborough provides many examples. See also the trial of Mary Ann Tocker in 1818, before Burroughs, J.

[2] In 1830 there were nine London dailies: in 1865, twenty-two.

[3] Mrs. Norton's supposed guilt in this transaction has often been disproved; but 'someone had blundered', i.e. Aberdeen.

kind. Much earlier, in 1839, *The Times* obtained from Gilbert Wakefield a copy of the Durham Report, with two sections on the Crown Lands which the Government wished to delete. Already Lord Durham had given the Report to Sir John Easthope of the *Morning Chronicle*, with instructions that it was not to be published. 'I wish he had not done so,' said Easthope; 'for I could have got it in a dozen ways, and should then have anticipated *The Times.*' Other devices were not neglected. No sooner had the telegraph been invented than the papers utilized it, but less as a means of acquiring early news than as an advertising show. Thus in August 1844 *The Times* announced the birth of Prince Alfred, adding, 'We are indebted to the extraordinary powers of the Electro-Magnetic Telegraph for the rapid communication of this important announcement.'[1] In 1845 the *Chronicle* received a message from Portsmouth by the telegraph-line of the London and South-Eastern Railway; in 1847 the Queen's Speech was telegraphed; and in 1850, when the cable between England and France was laid, prompt use was made of it; but these were merely feats to boast of. It was long before the cost of transmission became low enough for the telegraph to be used in the ordinary way of business.[2]

Reporters began to seek for news, instead of waiting for it to turn up; and it is wonderful with what speed they got it to the office, even without telegraphic aid, and how well-written, for their special purpose, their reports were. Hardships—as one can read in Dickens—were defied, and no expense of time and labour was spared in the service of the paper and the public. Salient points were seized, and the facts were related in a brief and taking fashion, the merits of which the somewhat heavy language of the forties must not be allowed to disguise from us to-day. Nothing could show this advance more clearly—in one important sphere—than a comparison between the scanty and fragmentary accounts of the trial of Eugene Aram in 1759,[3] or even those of the trial of Corder in 1828,[4] and the almost verbatim

---

[1] A facsimile of this announcement is given in Mr. Stanley Morison's *English Newspaper*, p. 220.

[2] Fox Bourne, ii. 139. It is, probably, the Crimean War which marks the real rise of the telegraph.

[3] *Trial of Eugene Aram*, by Eric Watson, 1913. Mr. Watson's summaries of the newspaper notices are very instructive.

[4] More can be learnt from pamphlets about this famous 'Barn murder'

Times report of the trial of Palmer in 1856. No methods, in fact, of improving the papers and enlarging their circulation were neglected; in some respects they were ahead of their successors of to-day.

It must also, in fairness, be recognized that—with inevitable exceptions—the papers, while of course aware that they must not go too far for their particular band of readers, did strive gradually to enlarge their minds within the obvious limits, and to educate them in something like the manner in which Disraeli 'educated' his party in 1867. They did not always lag in the rear of opinion, but sometimes seriously tried to form it. Even *The Times*,[1] which has never been accused of being too advanced, more than once took a decided line even when it cannot have been certain that its views would be popular. For instance, it strongly advocated the abolition of public executions, and in 1849 admitted Dickens's tremendous letter on the execution of the Mannings;[2] while its account of the horrible scenes at the execution of Müller in 1864[3] had much to do with the Act of 1868, which abolished such exhibitions. As a rule, however, the papers of 1840, like those of to-day, rather reflect public opinion than try to direct it.[4]

§ 4. THE TIMES

Among all these papers, the chief place was held by *The Times*, though its supremacy in some respects was less, in others far more clearly marked than now. The *Morning Chronicle*, founded in 1769, and the *Morning Herald*, founded in 1780, were not likely to yield to a paper of 1788[5] than from the papers. The play on the theme was performed, more or less impromptu, even before Corder was executed.

[1] In 1839 *The Times* began slowly to 'educate' its readers in favour of Free Trade.   [2] Forster, *sub anno*.

[3] Thackeray's article on Courvoisier's execution in 1840 ('Going to see a Man Hanged') shows the feeling of humane persons on this painful subject. Holidays, however, long continued to be given by schoolmasters when this edifying sight was promised. Thackeray's tone may be compared with the calm style in which Thomas Walker (*The Original*, 1835) speaks of his experiences. *The Original*, a paper written by Walker without assistance, is worth reading as presenting the views of an enlightened man on the political and social problems of his time.

[4] 'Cleon,' says Grote (about 1850), '*like leading journals in our times*, appeared to guide the public because he gave vehement expression to what they were already feeling' (*Hist. of Greece*, c. 52).

[5] It grew out of Walter's *Daily Universal Register* (Jan. 1, 1785), and hence *The Times* is sometimes dated from that day.

the reverence due from youth to age; and the fact that *The
Times*, at sevenpence, was for the rich only, told against it
in some quarters. But it had the memory of having faced
a trial for libel before Lord Mansfield, and the glory of
having unearthed the Melville scandals of 1805. It had also,
what it has long since lost, by far the largest circulation in
the country. This was a triumph of machinery. John Walter
the first, a mechanic himself, knew an invention when he
saw one, and by adopting König's steam-press, which turned
out in three hours what no other machine could produce in
ten, he stole a long march on his rivals.[1] It is said that in
1830 a Parliamentary speech could be reproduced in *The
Times* within an hour and a half of its conclusion.[2] But
Walter was never content; he was always introducing improvements, whether his own or another's. The circulation
doubled in five years, and with the circulation the advertisements increased rapidly. True, this machinery[3] was crude
enough compared with that which to-day will turn out
a 'stop-press' within fifteen seconds; but it achieved its
purpose—that of being first in the field—with equal effec-
tiveness. As the paper succeeded, it could afford the means
to ensure greater success. The discovery and transmission
of news could be so well organized that again and again *The
Times* was ahead of the Government itself. Its power grew
with its circulation and its prestige; and was steadily
exerted in one direction. Already the famous leader by
Edward Sterling[4]—'We thundered out the other day an
article on social and political reform'—had given the paper
the half-bantering, half-serious, nickname of the 'Thunderer';
and it was conscious of its Olympian character. John Walter

[1] Better machinery meant also larger size. *The Times* gave nearly twice the
matter of any other journal, so much so that the *News of the World*, 'the novelty
of nations', which came out in 1843, boasted that it was of 'size equal to the
immense double sheet of *The Times*' (Morison, pp. 217, 252. I take this
opportunity of expressing my obligations to Mr. Morison's admirable work,
referring the reader to it for full information as to newspaper typography and
machinery). Even before 1830 both *The Times* and the *Herald* had begun the
practice of issuing occasional special supplements.

[2] Or, which was then much the same thing, within five or six hours of the
commencement of the speech.

[3] Before the end of our period *The Times* had adopted Hattersley's com-
posing machine, of which a description will be found in Southward, *Practical
Printing*, 1892, p. 310.

[4] Carlyle's description of Sterling (*John Sterling*, part ii, chap. i) is classical,
but ascribes to Sterling more power than he really possessed.

the second was the proprietor, Barnes the editor: in both cases the property, like a great family estate, dominated the men connected with it. Barnes, once the friend of Leigh Hunt and Hazlitt, and actually a writer for the *Examiner*, grew more and more Tory with years, and, though he tried, with praiseworthy energy, to keep fanaticism out of the paper, did not fully succeed. *The Times*, in those days, demanded that Radicals should be abused as it had abused Napoleon from 1800 to 1815, and the writers did what the paper bade them; they became subdued to what they worked for. Many of the special contributors, literary, financial, even Parliamentary, such as Thackeray,[1] Bishop Stanley, Grote, and Jones Loyd, the famous banker, were Liberals or Radicals. Even Disraeli, whose *Runnymede Letters* (1836) secured Barnes's friendship, could hardly at that time, if ever, be called a full-fledged Tory.[2] But the savagery of the paper's attacks on O'Connell (from whom it got as good as it gave), on Cobden, on Bright, and on multitudes of others, is almost incredible in these days. 'For weeks together, even in its leading articles, the great newspaper could find no other appellation for Macaulay than Mr. Babbletongue.' When Macaulay and Sheil were sworn of the Privy Council, *The Times* ejaculated, 'These men Privy Councillors! These men petted at Windsor Castle! Faugh! Why, they are hardly fit to fill up the vacancies that have occurred by the lamented death of her Majesty's two favourite monkeys.'[3] When Macaulay made his famous slip, addressing a letter from Windsor Castle, *The Times* kept up a series of scurrilous jests for many months. Its printed rivals it attacked as it attacked its human enemies: the *Morning Chronicle* it called a 'squirt of filthy water'; and they retorted in kind. The *Age*, May 4, 1838, 'found it actually impossible to express the unmixed disgust with which it had read a series of beastly attacks upon the Duke of Cumberland in that most filthy of all filthy papers, the old *Times*'. When, in 1845, *The Times* announced the conversion of Peel to Free Trade, the *Standard* and the *Herald* called the

---

[1] It was in *The Times* that Thackeray reviewed the *French Revolution*. He always thought his *Times* articles the best things of the kind (and the worst paid) he ever did.

[2] Thus later such opposite men as Dean Burgon and Dr. Cumming wrote for *The Times*. It was in a *Times* leader that Burgon, as he boasted, 'killed the Revised Version'.   [3] Trevelyan, p. 387.

announcement an atrocious fabrication, and were dubbed maundering old women for their pains. These amenities, in fact, were almost universal. The *Globe*, to the *Standard*, was 'our blubber-headed contemporary'; and the *Age* agreed. 'Old Jerry Bentham's paper, the *Globe*, is in high dudgeon with us for calling Mr. Peel a rat. It adds that we have designated Lord Lyndhurst[1] a rat also. To the first we answer, no one but such an old dotard as the author of *Chrestomathia*[2] doubts it; and to the last, that it was not we, but Cobbett, Jerry's old friend the bone-grabber,[3] who christened the Lord Chancellor Rat Copley.' Dickens's two Eatanswill papers were scarcely more vigorous. 'It seems to me', said Dr. Arnold, 'that the mischief of our newspapers mainly arises from the virulent language which men use while writing anonymously'; and he tried, by himself writing anonymously but moderately in the *Herts Reformer*, to set an example—which was not always followed.[4]

That challenges, sometimes leading to duels, between journalists and their victims were not uncommon, will not surprise the reader; nor were all as harmless as that between the Rev. Henry Bate, of the *Morning Post*,[5] and Mr. Stoney, or as that between Jeffrey and Moore. The story, if not true, is *ben trovato*, of the visit of Hugh Brontë to the offices of the *Quarterly*, armed with a shillelagh, to punish the author of the venomous review of *Jane Eyre*.[6] We may perhaps have said enough on this subject, but we cannot refrain from alluding to the story[7] of the contest between *The Times* and Alderman Harmer. Bell's *Weekly Dispatch* was founded in 1801, and made itself popular by its vivid descriptions of prize-fights. Later, it fell into the hands of Harmer, a typical Smiles hero, who started life as a Spitalfields weaver

---

[1] Lyndhurst (John Copley) was regarded as a pillar of Radicalism till Eldon gave him the 'Cheshire Cheese'—the sinecure Chief Justiceship of Chester. His old allies never forgave him his instantaneous conversion. (But see Martin's *Life*.) The administration of 1830 was described as a tame Elephant (Wellington) standing on a gigantic Rat.

[2] Bentham's work on education.

[3] An allusion to Cobbett's removal of Tom Paine's bones from America to England.

[4] Stanley, letter of February 14, 1840.

[5] See Croker's note to Boswell, June 11, 1784. Bate did afterwards wound a man in a duel, and rose to be a prebendary, a baronet, and a Dudley.

[6] Who turned out to be a woman, Miss Rigby, afterwards Lady Eastlake.

[7] Often told; e.g. by Fox Bourne and by Bowman (*Story of The Times*, p. 142).

and retired at sixty from his practice as a solicitor with a fortune of £4,000 a year. Under him the *Dispatch* became Radical, and it was in its pages that W. J. Fox wrote the famous articles signed 'Publicola'. The circulation, even when the price was 8½*d.*, was 30,000 weekly, and when, after the reduction of the stamp duty, it was lowered to 6*d.*, not less than 60,000 were sold. The paper *explained* Chartism, and actually declared that there was no more moral depravity in being an infidel than in being a clergyman. In addition to this, it objected to the provision for the Prince Consort. It was therefore blasphemous, atheistic, and a public nuisance.

How many of the upper classes were themselves unbelievers will never be known. Macaulay's famous saying that there were not two hundred men in London who believed in the Bible is an exaggeration, but Mill's more sober expression[1] is worth remembering: 'The world would be astonished if it knew how great a proportion of its brightest ornaments are complete sceptics in religion, many of them refraining from avowal.' All the rulers, however, held that the ruled ought to believe, and the judges still laid it down that Christianity was part of the common law of England. *The Times*, therefore, had its whole constituency on its side in its attack on Harmer.[2] In 1840 it was Harmer's turn to be Lord Mayor, and *The Times* led the opposition from the noblest motives. 'We must stamp with the blackest mark of reprobation the principles of the *Dispatch* in the person of its proprietor . . .,' principles which 'constantly and deliberately reviled the Christian faith'. Harmer was defeated, and the jubilation of *The Times* is a good specimen of Christian charity.

It is fair to say, that just as the 'thundering leaders' of Sterling gave way in 1844 to the quieter style of Thomas Mozley, so, whenever a leader was written by Frederic Rogers, the tone was restrained and entirely free from scurrilities and personalities. It has been well remarked that Rogers was 'the first to write leaders like a gentleman'.[3]

---

[1] *Autobiography*, chap. ii, p. 26.
[2] The law was laid down by Ellenborough at the trial of Hone, December 19, 1817 (*Report of Hone's Trial*, p. 44). See also trial of Carlile, and the *Pooley* case, 1857 (Mill, *Liberty*, p. 54, and Buckle, *Posthumous Works*). It is well known that Palmerston's private views did not differ greatly from those of Carlile.
[3] *Letters of Lord Blachford*, pp. 112–15. Lord Blachford (Frederic Rogers)

It may be asked by people of the present generation, 'What do leaders matter? Who reads them?' But the fact is that, in the forties, the leader contained the news, and presented it in its own fashion. Thus, in 1845, when *The Times* announced Peel's conversion to Free Trade, the information, along with the comments on it, was given in a leading article. Those, therefore, who wanted news had to read it with all the embellishments, alike of flattery and abuse, which the editorial chose to give it.

Barnes's chief enemy, however, though attacked with less open venom than the Irish and the Radicals, was Palmerston; and Palmerston fully returned the hostility, taking care, as we have seen and shall see, to give any official information at his disposal to a rival paper. This did not make Barnes love him more; it helped the rival's circulation. On the stamp question, similarly, the attitude of Barnes was perhaps less political than financial; he assailed the reduction of the duty because, with a prophetic instinct, he feared it might strengthen the democratic papers.[1]

Barnes was of a somewhat retiring disposition; but even he was compelled by circumstances to appear in clubs and in society generally; and his editorial work took on more and more of the character which was soon exhibited by so many editors of all kinds: that of the listener, watching his public, seeing what 'took', and testing the trend of opinion. It is said that he never made a joke in his life; but he coveted earnestly, though rather late in life, the best social gifts— always with a view to the interests of his paper.

When Barnes retired in 1841, Delane,[2] a young Oxonian of twenty-four, succeeded him; and the history of the paper for the next thirty or forty years is the biography of Delane. Inevitably, he was the object of hatred and devotion, of contempt and fear, during the whole of that time; and his character, like that of nearly all distinguished public men, will probably always be a matter of controversy. But

was one of the chief promoters of the *Guardian*, and there, too, remembered what are the marks of a scholar and a gentleman.

[1] Something of the same feeling appears in 1860 and 1861, when the paper duty was under discussion. But *The Times* was now much more cautious. It had become reconciled to Palmerston, and adopted his nonchalant attitude on the question.

[2] See Dasent's *Life of Delane*. The memoirs of the time are full of references to him, favourable and the reverse. How far Trollope's 'Tom Towers' is Delane is a matter of opinion.

certainly he was a great editor. He kept as tight a hold over his writers as Peel did over his Cabinets, and there was never any doubt that every one of his writers wrote for *The Times*, and not for himself. 'A great newspaper', it has been well said, 'is greater than any of its contributors'; and of no paper is this truer than of *The Times* under Delane.

What Barnes had done, at first more or less perfunctorily, Delane did as to the manner born. Never, except perhaps to add a vigorous touch to an article, writing for his paper, he devoted himself to watching his constituency, which was well represented by the London clubs and salons. Of the opinions of the class which haunts these places he became an uncannily accurate judge; and he tended, as was inevitable, to adopt them and make them his own. Hence, when they were right, he was right: when they were wrong, he was wrong. For fifteen years Henry Reeve was his Foreign Correspondent, and was considered by many, including himself, to be indispensable. But Reeve began to show independence in his views. Delane, finding these views unpleasing to the clubs, took pen in hand, told Reeve to be careful, and finally compelled his resignation. The ideas of *The Times* readers were Delane's breath of life; and he would stay up half the night to discover them. He is said to have seen more sunrises than any other man in England; but he felt that even a sunrise was worth seeing if he could read a face by its light. He was determined, long before the phrase was hit upon, to give his public what his public wanted. His private opinions did not matter, nor did it matter that his public was but a tiny fraction of the people as a whole.

In 1853, when Stratford de Redcliffe was gradually urging us into war, Delane was strongly against Stratford's policy. 'Has England', he said—for his leader-writer was but echoing 'his master's voice'—'has England nothing better to do than to support barbarism against civilization, the Moslem against the Christian, slavery against liberty, to exchange peace for war—all to oblige the Turk?' Bright, meeting Delane at this time, found no appreciable difference between the great editor's views and his own;[1] and it is possible that

[1] Bowman, *Story of The Times*: cf. also Dasent, and Trevelyan's *Bright*. 'His opinion as to its non-necessity agrees precisely with my own' (*Diaries of John Bright*, April 29, 1854). For the quarrel between Delane and Cobden in 1863,

at the moment they were the views of the clubs. But the clubs drifted round, and Delane with them, until not Queen Victoria herself could have been a more violent partisan of war than he.

As to the American Civil War there was no drift. From the very first *The Times*, voicing upper-class opinion, was for the South, and malignantly against Lincoln and the North. This prejudice even coloured its presentation of facts;[1] so much so that long after the Southern cause was hopeless it continued to set forth victory as likely and almost certain. The final crash came therefore as a stunning surprise to those who took their views from *The Times*. For that fatal policy, which made an enemy of the North without conciliating the South, Delane must bear a large proportion of the blame.[2]

On one occasion, it is true, Delane did stand out against war. He always boasted that it was he who prevented Palmerston, in 1864, from supporting by arms Denmark's claim to the Duchies. Palmerston, however, did not need Delane to tell him that twenty thousand badly trained British troops, unaided by a single French *poilu*, would have been of little avail against the united forces of Prussia and Austria; and he wisely accepted humiliation in preference to utter disaster.[3]

Delane himself would have cared little if he had been told he was not a great man. His object was to make a great newspaper: this he did; and he was always looking out for

see Morley's *Cobden*, p. 887 sq., where Morley discusses the politics of *The Times*.

[1] Charles Mackay's report, 'the battles prove nothing but the valour of both sides' was mysteriously altered to 'prove *anything*'. Russell also (see *infra*) differed from his chiefs, but his accounts somehow came out Southern in tone.

[2] It would be unfair, however, not to refer here to the Letters of 'Historicus'. Harcourt and Delane had been neighbours and friends in the Temple, but Harcourt, in the *Saturday*, had been a ceaseless critic of the 'diabolical tone' of *The Times*, and had demanded that England should be not only politically but morally neutral. None the less, Delane opened his columns—indeed more of them than he quite liked—to his determined opponent. These famous letters, which made Harcourt's reputation, began in the autumn of 1861, and continued till after the end of the war. On the *Alabama* case, especially, they are classical. The whole episode, as Gardiner says, is 'creditable alike to Harcourt and Delane'. (A. G. Gardiner, *Life of Harcourt*, i. 125 sqq.). Delane was fully conscious of Harcourt's great legal knowledge and journalistic ability.

[3] The attitude of *The Times* to Kossuth expressed with exactness the views of the upper classes. Those of the middle classes were reflected, with equal exactness, by the *Daily News*.

an instrument to make it greater. One of these instruments he may not actually have discovered, but he was the first to use it on the great scale. This was the War Correspondent, whose life, though short, was like that of Achilles, eventful and glorious. He arose through circumstances. To make a war correspondent there must be a war, there must be speedy means of communication, and there must be a paper ready to risk vast sums over what may prove entirely unremunerative adventures. All these conditions were satisfied in 1854. There had been no great European war for forty years. In the short struggle of 1848 between Denmark and Prussia, William Howard Russell had gained a little experience. As soon as the Crimean War broke out, he was ready to put that experience to use. *The Times* gave him almost *carte blanche*; and, meagre as the means of communication were as compared with those of to-day, they were marvellous as compared with those of 1814.[1] Russell had further an advantage in the very hindrances that were put in his way. It was fully understood that the enemy gained information from our newspapers,[2] and the British officers, regarding Russell as in effect an enemy, thwarted him at every turn. Russell, seeing how he was viewed, felt that he was free to get the truth by any means, and to tell it out beneath the heavens. The result was the tremendous revelations which broke the already weakened Coalition Government of Lord Aberdeen to pieces, gave Palmerston ten belated years of glory, and made Florence Nightingale immortal. Incidentally, as Delane well knew, the work of Russell doubled the prestige of *The Times*.[3] But it was Delane's work as well as Russell's. No sooner had Russell's reports reached Printing House Square than Delane, along with Kinglake, visited the Front to see things with his own eyes. When he had seen them, he struck.

During the American Civil War, Russell had difficulties of another kind. Though an enemy of slavery—he had visited the South and seen the horrors of the system—he was an

[1] The armies of Wellington and Napoleon were often as much lost to view as the Ten Thousand Greeks.
[2] There are some good remarks on this in E. T. Cook's *Press in War-time*, especially in chap. ii.
[3] The story is one of the most familiar in history. It is told from varying points of view by Dasent in his *Delane*, by Atkins in the *Life of Russell*, by Kinglake, by Miss O'Malley in *Florence Nightingale*, and by scores of others.

emissary of *The Times*, and that was enough. The Northern armies suspected him, and his very life was in danger. Though he contrived to send stirring reports of the battles, he did not repeat here his amazing Crimean success.

Readers of Russell's reports will notice one omission, which contrasts strangely with certain features in such accounts as Steevens sent to the *Daily Mail* from the battle-fields of South Africa. There are few *personal* touches, though Inkerman gave more chances for details of that kind than any other battle recorded in history. Where sergeants acted as colonels, and lance-corporals as majors, one would have been glad to know their names. But Russell, as he himself owned, 'did not grasp the fact that it was in his power to give a halo of glory to some unknown warrior by printing his name in type'. This 'halo' was given by a lucky inspiration of Queen Victoria,[1] and has since been given, in hundreds of cases, by the humbler hands of nameless newspaper correspondents.

The history of *Parliamentary* reporting is a study in itself.[2] The early struggles to break down the wall of reserve behind which Parliament concealed itself, have been repeatedly described—notably by Lecky; and the slow transition from Johnson's 'reports' of the Debates in the Senate of Lilliput, through the amazingly accurate reproductions which William Woodfall gave the *Morning Chronicle* from memory, down to the comparative freedom enjoyed by Luke and Thomas Hansard, is as familiar as any episode in our history. Luke reported debates from 1774; Thomas from 1803. Thomas was, it is true, prosecuted for 'libellous' reports in Cobbett's *Register*; but in 1820 the victory was practically won. It was still, of course, open to any member to 'spy strangers'; and the House still, at times, appeared to regard reporting as a species of espionage; but on the whole the Press gallery, though terribly uncomfortable, was unshackled—for the London newspapers. In 1847 a great change took place. The telegraph had come into use, and the provincial papers demanded to be supplied with London news by its means. The Telegraph Company applied for, and obtained, admission to the Gallery, which had accordingly to be enlarged for their accommodation. When the Government took over the control of the telegraphs, press agencies undertook to provide the reports; but these,

---

[1] See *Letters of Queen Victoria*, January 5, 1856, June, 1857. The first V.C.s were bestowed, by the Queen's own hand, on June 26, 1857, when many private soldiers received the decoration.

[2] See, particularly, Pendleton, *Newspaper Reporting in the Olden Times and To-day*, 1890.

II   E

as the provincial newspapers increased in importance, were found to be inadequate; and the demand became more and more insistent that these papers should be represented by their own agents. A special Parliamentary committee, in 1879, considered this demand, and reported favourably. Permission was finally granted, and in 1881 the first provincial reporter took his seat with his London brethren.

Readers of the papers of the sixties will be struck with the fullness and apparent accuracy of the reports of speeches—at once the cause and the effect of the intense interest of the time in Parliament and its doings.[1] The scrappy and misleading notes that figure in some papers of to-day were then rare; and attempts were faithfully made to keep up with even the most torrential orators.[2]

Such reporting, in which very ordinary papers often rivalled *Hansard* itself, was due to the increased practice of shorthand. Abbreviated writing, of course, has been known for thousands of years: it is hard, for instance, to believe that Cicero could have produced the enormous mass of his works without the aid of Tiro's stenography. But it was not till the reign of Elizabeth that shorthand, properly so called, was invented—by Timothy Bright; nor was it till the middle of the eighteenth century that anything approaching a sound system was adopted. Very eminent men, such as Doddridge and Wesley, adapted Bright's or Rich's schemes for personal use; but no system obtained a general vogue till Gurney, in 1750, produced a tolerably workable method. Gurney's 'Brachygraphy', as is well known, was the one used for Parliamentary reporting not only by Gurney's relatives during many years, but by Dickens when he was working for the *Morning Chronicle*.[3] Either Gurney's or Taylor's (1786) system was almost universally employed until, in 1837, Isaac Pitman produced his 'Phonography', which has since eclipsed its rivals. As almost all shorthand-writing, if very rapid, tends to become illegible even to the writers, the method of combined writing was often adopted. Half a dozen or more would join, and one would take down the speech for two minutes, thus having ten or twelve minutes to copy it in long-hand, while his brethren, in succession, took down and copied their portions. The whole would in this way be ready for the compositor. Much of this labour has become unnecessary with the decay of interest in Parliament, and all of it will probably soon be superseded by the dictaphone; the reporter will need his shorthand solely for making hasty notes of murders or conflagrations. During

---

[1] The reports were sometimes even too exact. The story is, I believe, true of the politician who attacked *The Times*, which retaliated by publishing his speeches *verbatim* and *stutteratim*, with the 'hums' and ''ers' and dropped *h*'s; thus utterly destroying his reputation.

[2] See Macaulay's preface to his *Speeches*, 1853.

[3] Dickens's description of his herculean labours in mastering the system was used by Pitman as an advertisement for his own system.

our period the shorthand speech-reporter attained an importance to which he will perhaps never again rise.

§ 5. THE *DAILY NEWS*

The story of the *Daily News*[1] is remarkable, and carries a moral. Its first editor was the most famous of all editors, and perhaps one of the worst, as his reign was certainly one of the shortest. Dickens was not without newspaper experience. His work, as reporter first for the *True Sun* and then for the *Morning Chronicle*, was first-rate; and, despite the hardships involved, there can be little doubt that he looked back on it with pleasure. It provided him with some of the best material for his novels, and may be said to have started him on his wonderful career. After retiring from it, he hankered for newspaper work, and applied, in 1844, to be taken on by the *Chronicle* as a contributor. As may be imagined, the terms demanded by the author of *Pickwick* and *Nicholas Nickleby* were higher than those accepted by the author of *Sketches by Boz*; and Andrew Doyle rejected his overtures on the ground of expense. Dickens went away more in anger than in sorrow, and instantly started plans for the foundation of a rival paper. The plans soon matured, and the issue of a dummy number on January 19, 1846, like the warning first shot of a sea-fight, spread consternation in Fleet Street and even in Printing House Square. The result cannot be better told than in the words of Howard Russell:

'The 21st of January, 1846, came at last, and there was a wild rush for the first number. At the sight of the outer sheet, hope at once lighted up the gloom of Printing House Square, the Strand, and Shoe Lane. I am not sure that there were not social rejoicings that night in the editorial chambers, which had been so long beset by dread. Dickens had gathered round him newspaper celebrities, correspondents, politicians, statists. Yea, even the miscalled penny-a-liner was there. But Dickens was not a good editor; he was the best reporter in London, and as a journalist he was nothing more. He had no political instincts or knowledge, and was ignorant of, and indifferent to, what are called Foreign Affairs; indeed, he told me himself that he had never thought about them till the Revolution of 1848.'

All this, and more, was visible to the practised journalistic eye from a single glance at a single sheet of the paper. A

[1] See Forster, Justin M'Carthy, and John Collins Francis, *ut infra* (on Dilke).

well-known anecdote shows that all this was already plain not merely to fear and jealousy, but to friendly perceptions. The coming birth of the paper was celebrated by a dinner, at which Dickens spoke with even extravagant hope of its prospects. On the way home Henry Reeve, who was afterwards (1855) to edit the *Edinburgh Review*,[1] said to Charles Wentworth Dilke, editor of the *Athenaeum*, 'It is your knowledge that will be called upon to remedy the mischief done by Dickens's genius to the new paper.' Even the general public soon became dimly, but fatally, conscious that there was something wrong; and disaster seemed to be all too likely.

The fact is that Dickens could not learn, and he certainly made no effort to master his business. He moaned to John Forster about the fogs of Fleet Street, and pined for the sun of the south. He could toil at his natural work, but editorial drudgery he could not endure. His manager, it is to be feared, was of little use to him. It is creditable to Dickens's filial piety, but hardly so to his worldly wisdom, that he appointed his father to that post. Aeneas might as well have set Anchises to face Diomedes. One can hardly imagine Mr. Micawber in a newspaper office.

Dickens practically resigned in a month, and Mr. Micawber with him. John Forster, first actually, and then for three months nominally also, took the post of editor. When he in turn retired, the difference was soon seen between the genius that can create a David Copperfield and the humbler talent that can attract readers and advertisers. The foresight of Reeve was justified. Dilke became manager and Eyre Crowe editor. They understood their business. Dilke reduced the price from fivepence to twopence-halfpenny, and the size (save on exceptional occasions) from eight pages to four. He and Crowe gave the paper that mysterious something called personality, kept an eye on the reporters, gained a repute for early and accurate news, and finally turned almost certain failure into conspicuous success. But they had a hard task. The first hundred thousand was lost, and they had to obtain from their supporters that large sum over again. They started with a circulation of 4,000,[2] and even when they raised it to 22,000, they found it all but

---

[1] And the Greville Memoirs, 1865.
[2] *The Times*, at the same time, was 25,000.

impossible to make a profit after paying 22,000 pence to the Government. But the reward they deserved came at length. During the Revolutionary year 1848 their information was surpassed by none; readers of the *Daily News* learned of an abdication or a rebellion as soon as, or sooner than, those of *The Times* itself; and the paper was made. Later, it became, in effect, the Government organ when the Liberals were in power. A second immense advance, due to the energy and daring of Archibald Forbes, lies outside our province; but it was gained in the spirit of Dilke.

It must not, however, be forgotten that, if Crowe and Dilke watered the paper, Dickens, despite his failure, had planted it. Without him it would never have come into existence. It was his personal friends that provided the funds. Bradbury and Evans supplied the initial capital; and further contributions were made by Paxton, Sir William Jackson, the leader of North of England Liberalism, and Sir Joshua Walmsley, who regarded Dickens with admiration as the best friend of reform ever seen among English novelists. Walmsley brought to the paper all the knowledge of practical politics which Dickens lacked: he had worked with Cobden through the Corn Law agitation,[1] and had even, to some degree, succeeded in reconciling Chartism with bourgeois Liberalism. Nor did Dickens fail to gather round him a distinguished band of writers. In addition to Reeve, Dilke, and Forster, there were—to mention no others—Harriet Martineau, who contributed from her Westmorland home at least one article a week; 'Father Prout' (Frank Mahony), wittiest of Irishmen; Charles Mackay, most popular of songwriters; and, above all, W. J. Fox, the 'Publicola' of the *Weekly Dispatch*. Fox, even when Bright shared the platform with him, was the most persuasive of anti-Corn Law orators, and his writing was as good as his speaking. No man understood the causes of the unrest of the time better than Fox, and no man could explain them more forcibly. Dickens chose him to write the first leader. Nor must we omit Dickens himself, whose contributions were better than his editing. He sent to the *News* those letters which afterwards appeared as *Pictures from Italy*, and even a poem on the Wiltshire Labourers.

We must remember, also, that Dickens gave the paper its

[1] Morley, *Cobden*, popular edn., p. 521.

programme, and laid down the main lines from which it has never departed. Justly is his name still honoured in Bouverie Street, where a facsimile of the letter in which he sketched his ideas is kept as a Decalogue and an inspiration for his successors.

In the same year the proprietors of the *News* started an evening paper, the *Express*, under the editorship of Thomas Elliott. The price was twopence, at which it had a considerable success. Curiously enough, soon after it had been reduced to a penny (February 1868) the paper came to an end (April 30, 1869). The explanation of this failure is hard to discover; one thing is certain, that the immense vogue the evening paper enjoys to-day was something which would have seemed miraculous in the sixties. The stop-press, for instance, had not been invented.

§ 6. OTHER PAPERS

The rise and fall of newspapers and of periodicals generally,[1] indeed, are often as hard to explain as the rise and fall of the Roman Empire. For a long time the stability of the *Morning Chronicle* seemed as certainly assured as that of Rome in the days of Virgil. It had the prestige of antiquity, having been founded by one of the Woodfalls in the 'Junius' year, 1769; and it had the glory of having stood a triumphant trial before, or rather against, Lord Ellenborough himself. Its aid was sought by politicians, not least by Palmerston; and a famous article denouncing Guizot in 1840 was actually ascribed to the Foreign Minister.[2] But too close an association with statesmen is often dangerous to papers.[3] The public

[1] Some, for no clear reason, if not actually still-born, are sickly from birth and fade out. Such was the *Constitutional*, which started under the auspices of Grote, Molesworth, Joseph Hume, Charles Buller, Roebuck, and others only less distinguished, to be the scourge of Whiggery. A capital of £60,000 was provided, and Laman Blanchard was its editor, Thackeray its Paris representative. It was a Walcheren expedition. Begun on Sept. 15, 1836, it vanished on July 1, 1837, having lived just long enough 'to mourn for the death of William IV and its own'. Apparently, though there were Radicals in plenty all over England, this paper was too 'high-brow' for most of them. (See Fox Bourne, ii. 96.)

[2] Really by Eyre Crowe. See throughout *Palmerston and the Press*, by Kingsley Martin, on this statesman's newspaper activities.

[3] The *Morning Star*, a penny paper, founded (1855) by Sturge in the interests of peace, mentioned Cobden and Bright so often that Cobden himself remonstrated—'an instructive warning', says Morley, 'to leading politicians who meddle with newspapers' (*Cobden*, p. 637). Cobden had no financial

suspects a lack of independence, and the *Chronicle*, which was already feeling the competition of the *Daily News*, was no exception to the rule. In 1848 it was acquired by Cardwell and Stanhope to bolster up the fortunes of the Peelite party. But, despite the brilliancy of the young writers whom the new proprietors gathered round them, prosperity did not follow. The Peelites were themselves gradually absorbed by the Liberals; Cardwell ended by becoming one of Gladstone's best ministers; and in 1862 the Peelite paper, the shade of what once had been great, was quietly purchased by Levy and lost itself in the *Daily Telegraph*.

As with the *Morning Chronicle*, so with the *Standard*. Why has this once so famous paper disappeared—a paper so great that to have written on it was sufficient to gain a poet the Laureateship? Fortunately we have not to answer that question: we deal here but with the time of the paper's rise and maturity of glory. At first it was an evening star, projected from another evening luminary. The *St. James's Chronicle*, founded in 1761, came out on three afternoons a week. In the twenties it was the property of Charles Baldwin. In 1826 the opponents of Catholic Emancipation, after some difficulty, induced Baldwin to start a daily evening sheet to propagate their views. This was just at the time when Lord Liverpool had broken down, when Canning became Prime Minister, and when Peel and Wellington left him to carry on with the help of the Whigs. Fifteen thousand pounds were subscribed by these 'Protestants'; and the new paper appeared under the editorship of Stanley Giffard,[1] formerly editor of the *St. James's*.

The new paper gave its readers its 'groatsworth of wit'. It was lively, pointed, and abusive of its enemies, nay, even of its friends; for, becoming displeased with Wellington, it showed no fear of the great man, and was one of the few that did not run away from him. It gave great pleasure to the Abraham Plymleys and other opponents of the Catholic claims—so much so that the Duke of Newcastle, who did what he would with his own, actually gave Giffard £1,200 of his own money as a token of his regard.[2] Its attacks on the

interest in the *Star*; but his supposed connexion with it injured its repute. (The case was similar with the *Daily Chronicle* when, in 1916, it became a Lloyd George organ.) [1] Father of Lord Chancellor Halsbury.

[2] Giffard accepted it, though not for his private purse; but the incident did him harm.

Catholics were worthy of an early Reformer, but no worse
than its abuse of the 'base and filthy' *Times*. Much of this
vituperation was provided by Maginn, who had had plenty
of practice in the art.

In 1857 a complete change took place. Baldwin's affairs
were at a low ebb, and he sold his papers to a set of men of
whom James Johnstone and Morier Evans were the chief.
Under them the *Standard* was brought out as a morning
paper at twopence,[1] while the *Morning Herald*,[2] which was
under the same management, appeared, with the same news,
for fourpence, but with leaders and other articles adapted
to the presumably higher intellects of the people who could
afford a higher price. In 1860 the company published an
afternoon edition known as the *Evening Standard*, large parts
of which were the same as had appeared in the *Herald* of the
morning. This curious arrangement lasted some time—in
fact till the end of 1869, when the *Herald* died and was
buried.

During the years with which we are concerned, the
Standard was edited by Thomas, or rather Captain, Hamber,
who might have been the model for one of Ouida's *Guards-
men*, and who is still a gorgeous tradition in the newspaper
world. An Oriel man, he was famous for his skill in what
Ouida calls the 'Oxford Science' of fisticuffs, and carried into
journalism his pugilistic vigour, as well as the Balaclava-like
dash which he had learnt in the Crimea. But he had an eye
for ability, and gathered round him not merely hard-hitters,
but men of literary power and accurate knowledge—among
them Thomas Adolphus Trollope, whose acquaintance with
Italy was wide and profound, and Alfred Austin, whose
name would have stood higher to-day if he had never become
Poet Laureate.[3]

Hamber overdid his ferocity; and, as the *Standard* became
more and more the official Conservative organ, the proprietors
thought it well to secure a more responsible editor, and one
who knew better how to retreat with grace from impossible positions. Politicians are not prize-fighters, and are not
expected to continue the struggle till they receive the knock-
out blow. Hamber, however, was still in the ring when our

[1] Reduced in 1858 to a penny.
[2] On which Thomas Beard, 'Dickens's oldest friend', served for many years.
[3] 'Omnium consensu capax imperii nisi imperasset.'

period ends. The Civil War provided full scope for his peculiar talent; neither *The Times* nor *Punch* was more persistently virulent in its attacks on the North. The letters signed *Manhattan* 'sent up the circulation of the paper by leaps and bounds',[1] and materially increased the tension between England and America.

The *Morning Advertiser*, founded in 1794, was in the fifties more or less controlled by the famous and eccentric David Urquhart, whose Turcomania led him not only to introduce the Turkish bath into England, but to suspect everybody, including Palmerston and Bakunin, of being paid agents of the Tsar. This peculiarity made him acquainted with the Russian refugee Herzen,[2] who has thus occasion to mention him more than once in his voluminous memoirs. As a result, we are able to view the *Advertiser* through the eyes of a keen-sighted foreigner. Karl Marx and his friends, says Herzen, needed an honest man to give them some sort of standing, and pitched on Urquhart, by whom they were introduced to the *Advertiser*, and carried on in its columns those quarrels without which Marx found life insipid.

'The *Advertiser*', says Herzen, 'is a paper of a strange kind; not to be found in clubs, nor in the best stationers' shops, nor in the houses of the respectable classes. But it has a greater circulation than the *Daily News*, and only recently have cheap papers like the *Daily Telegraph* and the *Morning Star* reduced it to the second rank. The *Advertiser* is a peculiarly English phenomenon—the journal *par excellence* of the public-house; and there is not a public-house where a copy of it is not to be found.'

In this strange medium Marx fought out his battles with Bakunin. In July 1853 there was a letter beginning, 'Is Bakunin a Russian agent?'; and in August a reply asserting that he was no agent, but a *victim*, of Nicholas I; in September a rejoinder; and later still rejoinders again and sur-rejoinders. These recriminations must have been bewildering to the jovial and not too erudite clientele of the paper; but they gave Urquhart a chance of airing his darling delusion.[3] We

---

[1] Escott, p. 200. Escott is particularly lively on the congenial theme of Hamber.

[2] Herzen, *My Past and Thoughts*, part vi, chap. vii (dealing with 1853 and 1854). The translation above is by Mr. E. H. Carr.

[3] It is interesting to note that, with the help of Trübner the publisher, Herzen started cheap Russian papers in England: *Polyarnaya Zwesda* (the Pole-Star) and *Kolokol* (the Bell)—both of them in or about the central year 1855.

must not, however, forget that in the *Advertiser* appeared Grant's excellent *Random Sketches*, the forerunner of a whole class of newspaper articles.

§ 7. THE *DAILY TELEGRAPH*

Herzen, it will be noted, speaks of the *Telegraph* as cheap; and so it was. Not the least important result of the abolition of the duty was the foundation of this famous paper,[1] which started as one small sheet for twopence on June 29, 1855, but in September lowered its price,[2] and later doubled its size—a feat which it has recently almost exactly repeated. It may thus be regarded as the first *London* penny daily.[3] Established by Colonel Sleigh as hardly more than a rich man's toy, it became, in the jargon of to-day, a 'business proposition' when it was bought by Levy the printer.[4] The purchase in 1862 of the *Morning Chronicle* from Cardwell and Stanhope removed a possible rival, and the paper speedily entered on that course of success which it has maintained, with hardly a lapse, under the Levy-Lawson family. Its politics were at first such as to secure the adhesion of the *Chronicle's* constituency—Liberal with a tendency to the Right, or (to use Strachey's definition of the *Spectator* policy) 'Left-centre, the whereabouts of the heart in the human and political body'; and it may perhaps claim that it still holds its original views, the apparent change being due to the alteration in the nature of Liberalism. Very early it assumed that character of 'leonine adolescence' which Matthew Arnold afterwards satirized in *Friendship's Garland*; and the style of its writers was possibly tainted with the 'middle-class Macaulayese' which revolted Arnold's Oxonian soul. Any one who reads a few *Telegraph* articles of the fifties will easily detect that complacency which has been hastily dubbed Victorian: that 'unconquerable hope' which Liberals then so vigorously nursed, though without 'clutch-

[1] At first the *Telegraph and Courier*. A facsimile of the first page is given in Morison (*English Newspaper*, p. 266), and an account of its typographical features on p. 267 sq.

[2] This was in imitation of the American two-cent. paper.

[3] The *London Evening News* seems to have preceded the *Telegraph* by five weeks, as it came out, price one penny, on Aug. 14, 1855 (Morison, p. 269); but 'an evening paper was then regarded as no better than a Sunday one'.

[4] It invented the 'Box' system (Morison, p. 269; 'replies to be sent to Box No. 120'), and an improved advertising method. In Sept. 1855 its circulation almost overtook that of *The Times*.

ing the inviolable shade'; a hope expressed in a strong, uncompromising, and 'Macaulayese' fashion. Later, we notice a change. The leaders, in 1861, begin to be written by Edwin Arnold; and we can see in them obscure forebodings of the *Light of Asia*, contrasting strangely with the direct hammer-and-tongs manner of George Augustus Sala and the roarings of the 'lions'. Edwin Arnold, though a Newdigate prizeman, was a poet; and there was some poetry even in his leaders. His close acquaintance with Indian subjects strengthened the paper on one important side. But almost more important than the accession of Arnold was the simultaneous appearance of J. M. Le Sage, who later became manager. Early in the sixties the *Telegraph* had become what the *Morning Chronicle* had been in the thirties—the most dangerous rival of *The Times*; nor was it long before it could boast the possession of the 'largest circulation in the world'.

§ 8. THE *MORNING POST*

Readers of Macaulay's Essays will know that in the early thirties the *Morning Post* was under a cloud. 'It seems', says Macaulay in his Essay on Croker (1831), 'almost incredible to a person living in our time that any human being should ever have stooped to fight with a writer in the *Morning Post*,' as Stoney in 1777 fought with Henry Bate. Nor is this one of Macaulay's 'heightened and telling' modes of expression. The days when Coleridge wrote for the paper, when Wordsworth contributed to it his immortal patriotic sonnets, and when Southey completed the connexion of the Lake School with it, were over; and the days of the Borthwicks had not yet begun. What the paper had lost in genius it made up in acrimony. Its mainspring was still, in a measure, that rivalry with the *Morning Herald* which had started fifty years before, when Bate left it and set up the *Herald* in opposition, and when virulence on both sides was the order of the day. But the *Herald* had now reformed. Bate was dead (1824), and the paper, under Baldwin, was deservedly renowned for the excellence of its foreign correspondence, as well as for its general tone. The *Morning Post* was soon to follow suit. Under the guidance of Peter Borthwick,[1] M.P. for Evesham, it at once took its place as one of the best

[1] See Lucas, *Life of Peter Borthwick*.

papers of the day. Sold at threepence, it appealed to a somewhat different audience from that of *The Times*; but it had a comparable influence; and when the stamp duty disappeared it assumed much of the character so familiar to us to-day. In 1850 Peter Borthwick became actual editor; and on his death, two years later, his son Algernon, who had been thoroughly trained for the post by his education in France and by his work as foreign correspondent for the paper, took his father's place with a double portion of his spirit. Algernon survived to our own time (1908), and was one of the best-known figures in the newspaper world, as well as one of the first editors to receive a peerage. As at once editor and chief proprietor, he was to the *Post* almost more than Delane was to *The Times*; and he has stamped a distinct and unmistakable impress upon his paper.

Though professedly Tory, the *Post* supported Palmerston —who indeed wore his Liberalism with a difference—and it certainly benefited by its friendship with him. It was commonly believed that Palmerston actually contributed to the paper, and it was more than suspected, as we have hinted, that in his dislike of *The Times* he gave it official information. On one point only did it show independence. It strongly and consistently opposed his episcopal appointments, which, as is well known, were nearly all in favour of the Evangelical party. Here, as may easily be understood, it had the support of Bishop Wilberforce and Archdeacon Denison.[1]

More sinister than the charge of Palmerstonianism was the suspicion, largely based on Algernon Borthwick's intimate knowledge of French affairs, that the *Post* was not only influenced, but actually subsidized, by Walewski,[2] then French Ambassador in England. Lord Malmesbury, our Foreign Secretary, whose distrust of France in general and of Walewski in particular is well known, and who lived in fear of some Palmerstonian intrigue with France, was convinced that the rumour was true, and showed his belief almost openly.[3]

---

[1] Palmerston's defence of his principles may be seen in *Letters of Queen Victoria*, Dec. 2, 1860. 'If the Bench were filled with men like the Bishops of Oxford (Wilberforce) and Exeter (Phillpotts) there would be no religious peace in the land. . . . Viscount Palmerston can assure your Majesty that though his selection of Bishops has been much found fault with by the High Church Party, they (*sic*) have given great satisfaction to the nation at large.'

[2] Son of the great Napoleon by the Pole, Maria Walewska; in 1858 Foreign Minister in Paris. [3] See Malmesbury's *Memoirs of an Ex-minister*.

Two more London papers, the Castor and Pollux which still rise together every Sunday morning, cannot be passed over; but their names are great enough to speak for themselves. They are the *Observer* [1] (founded 1791) and the *Sunday Times* (1822). They were both mildly Liberal, but their real power was not yet; in fact, as we have seen, they were hardly respectable.

§ 9. THE PROVINCIAL PRESS

London has never been England, and the London papers have by no means always spoken the mind of England. But, as the 'provinces' were more or less inarticulate, the opinion of London was naturally taken as the authentic voice of the country—often with disastrous results. It was in our period that the provinces found their voice, and the voice was the local newspaper. In 1846 there were 200 such papers, of which it is said five were 'worth counting'; in 1865 there were 750, of which at least thirty were of considerable weight. In 1837 they had combined in the Provincial Newspaper Society—an organization which was of immense utility to journalists, both as a protection and as a stimulus. [2] Founded by men like Baines of the *Leeds Mercury*, Blackwell of the *Newcastle Courant*, and others, it did a great work for the removal of the stamp duties and for the reform of the libel laws; more, perhaps, than the London papers put together.

These provincial papers were still (till 1881) kept out of the Reporters' Gallery of the House of Commons; but they contrived to give first-rate news; and the importance of their rapid growth can scarcely be exaggerated, either politically, socially, or journalistically. Their numbers make it impossible to deal with them as they deserve; but let the reader bear always in mind that in the fifties the Liverpool man cared nothing for *The Times*—he had his *Daily Post*; that the Scot had his *Scotsman*, well suited to his needs; the Mancunian his *Guardian*, his *Examiner and Times*, or his *Courier*; the Sheffielder his *Courant*, [3] his *Independent*, and his *Telegraph*; the Leeds man his *Mercury* and his *Leeds*

---

[1] Owned by Bell, of *Life in London*, the *Englishman*, and the *Morning Chronicle*.

[2] See Whorlow, p. 29; and Hunt, *Fifty Years of Newspaper Work*; cp. Frost.

[3] To which Dr. Arnold contributed in 1831. (Stanley, Dec. 6, 1837.)

Times; and that the united influence of these papers vastly outweighed, *within our island*, that of all the London papers put together. It was the error of foreigners, and to a great extent the error of Parliamentarians, to neglect these organs of opinion. There were then few or no means by which the London papers could reach the provinces early enough to compete with these rivals; the northern manufacturer received his northern paper at breakfast, and read no other; and, as a result, his views were often found, too late, to be staggeringly at variance with those of the south. It must suffice here to take two or three typical specimens, and to leave the reader's imagination to do the rest.

The *Scotsman* was already in existence. Founded in 1817 by Charles Maclaren,[1] who edited it for many years, it suffered sadly from the taxes on knowledge. It came out only twice a week, but even so not more than 2,500 Scottish families could afford to purchase it—and that though the manager, James Law, was one of the ablest men of his kind ever known. As soon, however, as the duty was abolished, it became a penny daily, and the effect was speedily manifest. During the Crimean War the circulation touched 6,000; it declined afterwards to 4,000, but in 1859 rose to 10,000, and by 1865 was 25,000. This growth is typical, and may be paralleled in the history of many papers of comparable rank. But the real greatness of the *Scotsman* is due less to outward circumstances than to one man. In 1848 Alexander Russel became its editor. Russel was thirty-four, but he had already had years of editorial experience on the *Berwick Advertiser*; he was young enough to learn, and old enough to know. In a very short time he made his paper, for the north of the Tweed, all, and more than all, that Delane had made *The Times* for the capital. Two-thirds of Scotland was of one political creed, and Russel represented that creed to perfection. The paper penetrated to every corner of the land, and was the oracle of minister, elder, and congregation. Its power can hardly be over-estimated: it controlled elections and dictated policies to candidates,[2] even though it had, during the fifties, a strong rival in the *Edinburgh Courant*,

[1] Maclaren, after the good old style, fought a duel with Dr. Browne, the editor of the rival *Caledonian Mercury*.

[2] Some would ascribe Macaulay's re-election for Edinburgh in 1852 to the *Scotsman*; the paper bore its part, but it was a universal movement, even Tories sharing in it.

one of the oldest papers in the world,[1] and one of great historical importance. The *Dundee Advertiser* will be mentioned later.

The *Liverpool Daily Post*, a journal hardly second to any, began in the fateful year 1855, under the editorship of Michael Whitty, and is said to have been, by a few weeks, the very first penny paper in England. Whitty had at first as his assistant editor Edward Russell, who, after leaving the *Post* to serve under Justin M'Carthy on the *Morning Star*, returned to make the *Post* the admirable paper which it still is. But its first years gave promise of the great things to be.

The *Birmingham Daily Post*, a development of the weekly *Journal*, became a penny daily in 1857. It was founded by John Feeney and Sir John Jaffray, and the editor was Bunce—all three names still remembered in the city. The *Manchester Guardian*, started in 1821 by the two Taylors, had its quarrels with the Government. It may almost be said to have sprung out of the Peterloo Massacre of 1819. This illustrious paper, which in some respects has had no superior, had not yet established its unquestioned position. It had to contend not only with the Tory *Courier* (founded by James and Thomas Sawler), but with the Liberal *Manchester Examiner and Times*.[2] But it was already up to date. In 1855 it became a penny paper, with the usual results.

To think of Plymouth is to think of the *Western Morning News*—and Drake. But this paper was not started till 1860.[3] Before it arose, to eclipse all other Plymouth journals, there was the weekly *Plymouth Mail*, edited by Mortimer Collins as one of the adventures of his variegated life. Collins enlivened his pages by doggerel squibs at the expense of Isaac Latimer, the editor of the rival *Plymouth and Devonport Journal*:

> Isaac the editor, Isaac the ass,
> The sayer of things that don't come to pass.[4]

[1] Founded in 1707, and famous as having been one of Defoe's many organs. Later, it declined, and was scarcely resuscitated even by James Hannay.

[2] So well known for its connexion with the vigorous Henry Dunckley and with Alexander Ireland (author of the *Booklover's Enchiridion*), James Ashcroft Noble, and a whole literary set.

[3] Under Edward Spender and Hunt. In 1863 Spender started at Hull the *Eastern Morning News*, of which Mr. J. A. Spender gives some account in his *Politics and Journalism*.

[4] Escott, p. 299. Such journalistic amenities were not uncommon. In 1874 the *Sheffield Independent*, suspecting the *Telegraph* of stealing its news, wrote

'All these and more came flocking,' attended by a throng of equal or lesser spirits: the *Leicester Mercury*, on which Thomas Cooper served, the *Midland Counties Illuminator*, which he edited, the *Newcastle Chronicle*, the *Brighton Herald*, the *Sussex Daily News*, the *Liverpool Mercury*, and, hoariest of all, the *Stamford Mercury*, which still exists after 200 years. But not less important was the army of Irish papers, which, from the influence they exerted on politics, no historian has been able to neglect. The Irishman's genius for journalism, indeed, unlike his talent for war, has been perhaps more visible in his own country than abroad. Not even the Frenchman has known better how to use the Press as a political weapon; [1] and, like the Frenchman, the Irish journalist has often developed into the statesman. Swift, Burke, O'Brien, T. P. O'Connor, are but conspicuous types of a vast number of men who, beginning by stirring their readers, have gone on to move senates and nations. Thus the names of Irish newspaper men are, far more than those of their English confrères, names familiar in political history. If the Irishman came to England, he might, like Whitty or Sterling, become a distinguished *journalist*; if he stayed in Ireland, he was, like Davis or Mitchel, a political power. This was true from very early times. Lord Edward Fitzgerald was the owner of the *Press*; nor is it a mere figure of speech to call even Swift's *Drapier's Letters* a kind of journal.

In 1842, when O'Connell was ceasing to satisfy the Repealers, the *Nation* was started to oppose him, and Thomas Davis,[2] its first editor, a poet and an enthusiast, bore his full share in pulling down the Dictator after the fiasco of Clontarf. Along with him worked John Mitchel,[3] who, however, *more Hibernico*, soon quarrelled with the *Nation*, and set up the weekly *United Irishman* in 1848, which 'talked incessantly of pikes, barricades, bullet-making, and vitriol'—with the natural result. Mitchel was condemned for treason-felony.[4]

an entirely fictitious and sensational narrative. Great was its joy when the *Telegraph* reproduced the story in absolute good faith.

[1] Bagehot (*Literary Studies*, iii. 332), and in his letters on the *coup d'état* of 1851, remarks on the difference, in this respect, between England and France: a difference less pronounced to-day than in the fifties.

[2] With John Blake Dillon and Gavan Duffy.   [3] From 1845 to 1847.

[4] When Mitchel reached America, he continued his work with the New York *Citizen* (1854) and the *Southern Citizen* (1857). Like so many Irish patriots, he was an anti-Abolitionist.

On other famous papers—the *Freeman's Journal*, founded as early as 1763, the *Cork Examiner*, on which Justin M'Carthy started his distinguished career, or the Murphy papers—the *Independent* (afterwards edited by Harrington), the *Evening Herald*, the *Irish Catholic*—a single word, unfortunately, must suffice. To elderly men, who remember the tremendous storms of the Home Rule struggle, the names are household words, and their editors, many of whom suffered suspension in Parliament or imprisonment in their native country, are part of the thrilling history of that time. Any one who wants to read vituperation at its most violent, and words which led too surely to deeds, can find them to abundance in these papers; nor less forceful is the language of their opponents, the *Northern Whig*, the *Irish Times*, the *Express*, and the *Belfast News Letter*.[1] The Irish leading article was a shillelagh, used impartially against Peel or Derby, and—if it so seemed good—against Sheil or O'Connell.

Finally, we must not omit to notice, all too briefly, the astonishing growth of specialized technical journals, the influence of which, though largely silent, must have been immense. We have already mentioned the *Lancet*, a paper of enormous importance. In 1856 it had to meet a rival, or perhaps rather a coadjutor, in the *British Medical Journal*.[2] Shortly before this, in 1853, Webster the actor founded the *Field*, which afterwards fell into the hands of Serjeant Cox, and speedily took the position which it has ever afterwards held, as the indispensable companion of the 'Country Gentleman'. The *Gardener's Chronicle* started in 1841, the *Farmer* in 1843. Musicians had the *Musical World* in 1836, and the more famous *Musical Times* in 1844. For the theatrical world, there was the *Era*[3] (1837); for teachers, the *Educational Times* (1846); for painters, the *Journal of the Society of Arts* (1852); for skilled workers and men of science, the *Chemical News* (1857), the *Engineer* (1855), the *Industrial Review*[4] (1861), not to mention the *Mining Journal*, which

[1] Sheridan Le Fanu became in 1841 editor and proprietor of the *Warder*, in 1842 of the *Protestant Guardian*; later, part-owner of the *Statesman*, the *Evening Packet*, and the *Evening Mail*: in all of them writing vigorously against the Nationalists. (See S. M. Ellis, *Wilkie Collins and Others*, p. 154.)

[2] The *Medical Press* had appeared in 1838; the *Medical Gazette* still earlier, in 1827.

[3] At first an organ of the so-called 'Trade'.

[4] Known at first as the *Bee*, a slightly fantastic title soon dropped.

had been in existence since 1835, or *Herapath's Railway Journal*, which started in the same year. For understanding of the sinews of industrial war and peace, men could have recourse to the *Economist*, founded in 1843, and then as now a pillar of Free Trade. During the great controversy of the time, the *Economist*, under James Wilson,[1] bore a leading part, and gained a great influence through the triumph of the cause in 1846. This influence it used vigorously during the Railway Mania, endeavouring to check the folly of rash investors. There is no need to add that its repute did not decline when, in 1861, Walter Bagehot became its editor.

Besides these, it may suffice to mention, as a type of technical journals, *Gaslighting* (1849), and as a type of the sporting, Bell's *Life in London* (1820), which survived almost till our own time. It is hardly too much to say that the early Victorian age was the first to discover the utility of the Press as an engine of specialized instruction. Our own age has merely gone further on Victorian lines.[2]

§ 10. IMPROVING LITERATURE

We have thus considered the Press as the disseminator of news, and have seen how, by assuming the right of commenting on the news it gave, it enormously increased its power, and learned how to create, or at least to direct, opinion. We now have to look at it from another point of view, as an engine of moral improvement. Here, again, it was the expression of a dominating idea of the time. England had not yet adopted the Republican watchwords of Liberty, Equality, and Fraternity; but not even the France of Napoleon or the America of Lincoln was more closely wedded to the doctrine of 'La carrière ouverte aux talents'. For every one there was opportunity, and the very jail-birds were 'pri-

---

[1] See Morley, *Cobden*, chap. xiii, p. 291. Wilson was afterwards Financial Secretary to the Treasury. Bagehot's account of him in *Literary Studies* will be known to many. He was, of course, Bagehot's father-in-law.

[2] The influence of 'W. H. Smith & Co.' on newspapers and novels is a subject too large to be dealt with here in full. The firm obtained its monopoly in 1848, and from that year may be dated the start of a special railway literature. It is certain that alike in format and in content thousands of books have adapted themselves to the supposed needs of railway travellers. A whole genre, perhaps, has grown up for the short suburban journey, and another to ease the tedium of a long one. Before the end of our period the well-known 'yellow-back' had made a sporadic appearance; but the vast developments belong to a later time.

soners of hope'. A man must be content with the position
to which God called him; but God's call was always to something higher; and he need not be content till he reached the
highest. His remedy, under Providence, lay in his own
hands. With diligence, with thrift, with the chances of
educating himself now so cheaply provided, to what could
not a man of determination rise? Examples gross as earth,
but sublimated into almost celestial patterns, were there
to instruct him. Stories of self-made men, of office-boys
attracting the notice of their masters by hoarding pins, of
youths turning themselves into scholars by burning the
midnight oil, were flung before the artisan or the labourer,
with the implied injunction, 'Go thou and do likewise'.
Aged persons who can recall the sixties will perhaps remember most vividly the figure of the self-made man on the
platform telling the story of his success for the benefit of his
youthful hearers, or they may recall the tale in the weekly
magazine of the prosperous merchant who had started with
half a crown and ended with half a million. The anecdote of
the burglar who ascribed his fall from virtue to an early mis-
understanding of a Sunday-school lesson on the text, 'God
helps those who help themselves', is but a parable illustrating
a generally accepted doctrine.[1]

The most celebrated exponent of this belief was Samuel
Smiles,[2] once editor of the *Leeds Times*, whose *Self-Help*,
published in 1859, gathered into a long anecdotal sermon the
accumulated experience of the previous thirty years, and,
being the expression of the views of millions, had a circulation which was the envy of the most popular novelists. He
followed it up with *Thrift*, *Duty*, and *Character*, inculcating
these Victorian virtues by showing how often they received
recognition in this world as well as rewards in the next.
But, while giving Smiles his due, I would prefer to take, as
an illustration even more convincing, certain works issued
by William and Robert Chambers. These were themselves
men who had risen from obscurity to eminence by persever-
ing effort. Robert, in fact, is one of the best specimens of

[1] A curious parallel may be found even in ancient Egypt. During the Fifth
Dynasty the vizier, Ptah-hotep, speaks of 'the elevation of humanity through
writing and knowledge' (Schneider, *Civilization*, i. 46).

[2] Smiles has been somewhat unjustly treated. He is far from regarding
more worldly success as a criterion of merit; and some of his examples are
taken from men to whom virtue was its own sole reward.

this class. Some of his books, such as the *Vestiges of Creation*, are real contributions to thought; others, like the *Book of Days*, are valuable helps to knowledge; and he remained, amid all his success, modest and unassuming. William, his elder brother, with less ability, had more of the Bounderby in him; he was vain, didactic, and platitudinous.[1] But both alike were convinced that what they had done could be done by others; that a boy who minded his book could become an LL.D. of St. Andrews, or even rise to be Lord Provost of Edinburgh. And—though not without an eye to the main chance—they were nobly anxious to assist those who desired thus to rise. I shall speak later of their *Edinburgh Journal*; what I desire here to mention is their *Miscellany of Instructive and Amusing Tracts*[2] (1845), followed in 1852 by their *Repository* of the same kind. (This phrase, 'instructive and amusing', with the variant 'entertaining', we shall meet again; it is the hall-mark of a whole class of Victorian literature).[3] The aim of these publications is well expressed in the advertisement of the *Repository*:

'This work, to resemble in some respects the *Miscellany*, will aim at a higher, though not less popular tone, and satisfy, it is hoped, the new requirements of the day in regard to literary elegance. . . . An important object will be to furnish innocent entertainment, mingled with correct information and instruction, under the control of good taste, and free, as far as possible, from controversial matter. The Editors, therefore, trust that the present series will take as prominent a part as the former in the department of the great business of educating the People which is committed to the untrammelled agency of the Press.'

Twenty volumes of the *Miscellany*, which were enormously popular, were issued, not once but many times, each consisting of a dozen thirty-two- or sixteen-page articles of instruction or amusement. Each began with a selection of poetry, such as the *Ancient Mariner*, fragments of Scott, or three or four ballads, which was followed by essays in light science (the *Romance of Geology* or *Earthquakes and Volcanoes*); an historical sketch dealing with Gustavus Adolphus, or, as was inevitable in a Scottish publication, panegyrizing Wal-

---

[1] For a comparison of the brothers, as they struck a man intolerant of priggishness, see the *Literary Recollections* of James Payn, who ceased to edit the *Journal* when Robert died in 1871 (p. 266).

[2] *Amusing* in the sense of 1840: 'interesting'.

[3] *Family Herald*, 'Useful Information and Amusement for the Million', 1842.

COMMON THINGS.

TIME.

CHAPTER IV.

THE PYRAMIDS; AND THE CRYSTAL PALACE

lace and Bruce; some true tale of adventure or out-of-the-
way historic episode; a biography of a successful man like
William Hutton, the Birmingham bookseller, of John Leyden,
the scholar, or of a youth who, by patience and perseverance,
had made himself a successful painter. Finally, there was
always a didactic tale—of a servant-girl of Nancy who, by
putting steadily aside a portion of her earnings, gained at last
a position of independence; or, conversely, of a feckless
Irishman who, refusing to save, came to want. The mere
titles of these tales were often homiletic—'A Tale of Life
Assurance', 'The Three Ways of Living: Below, Up to, and
Beyond one's Means', 'Be Just before you are Generous';
and the catastrophes of the little stories never failed to
point the moral with remarkable felicity. Not Hogarth's
Idle and Industrious Apprentice could preach more clearly.
The implication throughout the work is twofold. First, the
lesson of self-help is taught in scores of ways; and secondly,
it is gently hinted that there is no better means of helping
oneself than studying such books as *Chambers's Miscellany*.
To those who wished to go further, the firm offered, at a
marvellously low price, a whole series of works on all subjects, from Practical Economy (an anticipation of Smiles's
Thrift) to a first-class Latin Grammar by Leonhard Schmitz,
entitled *Chambers's Educational Course*. Nor was this all.
There was, in two large but cheap volumes, an encyclopaedia
of utilitarian knowledge, *Chambers's Information for the
People*.

The evils of the time, in fact, were—if we may loosely
generalize—looked upon from three points of view. There
was the helpless terror of such a man as Greville (1832), as he
contemplated 'the rotten foundation on which the whole
fabric of this gorgeous Society rests; for I call that rotten
which exhibits thousands upon thousands of human beings
reduced to the lowest stage of moral and physical degradation'. No interest was secure. Yet Greville had no remedy.
The other two attitudes are perhaps represented by the
respective views of Southey and the young Macaulay[1] as
shown in the *Essay on the Colloquies*. At the time, it is
probable that Macaulay's view was the prevailing one. The
evils were great, but they were diminishing, and would

---

[1] Macaulay's later opinions show a strong movement away from *laisser-
faire*. See his speeches on Education, the Ten-Hours Bill, and similar subjects.

ultimately be rooted out by a steady application of Whig principles—*laisser-faire*, publicity, self-help, competition, and education. Nobody had seen or felt the evils more intensely than Dickens; but he, too, like the prosperous Macaulay, believed they were curable. His own novels, which were exposures of the injustices, were in their measure a remedy. To aid these men came the whole army of those who had raised themselves. 'Give us the power, and we will show that these ills are curable: the means which have made us what we are will raise others.' The foundations, though rotten, were not destroyed; the righteous might yet do something—by instruction; and one main means of instruction was the Press.

§ II. THE *SPECTATOR*

The Press might not only, as Chambers held, instruct the lower middle ranks of society; it might also instruct their immediate superiors, the upper middle classes. It might teach the teachers. Of the papers which undertook this task, not the least representative is the *Spectator*, which was founded just at the time when the religious tests were being removed,[1] and bore a valiant part in the tremendous struggle of the next half-dozen years. Starting as a 'non-political' journal, it found itself soon drawn into the Reform battle, taking up the quarrel—of course, on the Liberal side—'with a deliberate and deadly seriousness which its occasionally facetious sallies only deepened'.[2] Some of its utterances read curiously to-day. When William IV, in 1831, dramatically dissolved Parliament, the *Spectator* told 'our second Alfred' that he was now really King; he had gained the hearts of his subjects, and thenceforward would be all-powerful for good. But it is not this naïve dithyramb that has made the paper's advocacy of Reform immortal. It boasts more justly that it was the inventor of the slogan, 'The Bill, the whole Bill, and nothing but the Bill', which, like the footsteps of sublime bards, has echoed ever since down the corridors of Time.

Like all successful journals, the *Spectator* owed much to its editor. Stephen Rintoul had served a good apprenticeship.

---

[1] First advertised, July 11, 1828 (Beach Thomas, *Story of the Spectator*, p. 26). In the same year the *Test* and Corporation Acts were repealed; in the next, the Catholics were emancipated.   [2] Beach Thomas, p. 107.

At twenty-four he had become editor of the *Dundee Adver-tiser*, then a weekly, which he soon raised to a position of importance; and later he edited the London *Atlas*. Quarrel-ling with the proprietors, he resigned within two years. But his friends, Douglas Kinnaird and Joseph Hume, supported him, and in 1828 collected sufficient capital to launch him out, with practically absolute powers, on the new venture, called by the historic name of the *Spectator*.[1]

It is quite clear that Rintoul, at least when allowed to have his own way, was a first-rate editor. Having found his work, he threw himself without reserve into his paper, watched over every detail of typography, headings, arrangement, style; keeping an eye also on the sales and on the finances. Starting at sixteen pages for ninepence, he raised, or lowered, the price to a shilling for twenty-four pages. He made a point of paying his contributors well; and as the receipts from advertisements were at first ridiculously small, we can feel little surprise that for some years there was a very heavy balance on the wrong side. But Rintoul, and his supporters, knew that if a paper is to establish a definite character, it must be content for a time to run at a loss; while, when once a high character is established, the circulation will, in a fashion, look after itself. It may even gain a circulation by posing as indifferent to it; and Rintoul was never tired of saying that he made no appeal either to the popular market or to the tastes of the rich vulgar. 'The tone and character of the *Spectator*,' he said, 'the variety of its contents, and even its external form, peculiarly fit it for the use of respect-able families'; and he pointed out that, if it reached those families, its influence could not be measured by the number of copies sold. None the less, the circulation increased regularly, month by month, and almost week by week. Sir W. Beach Thomas gives figures which show that by 1840 it was selling at least 3,500 copies weekly, and that, among the eleven weeklies of the time, only *John Bull* surpassed it in circulation—a defeat which Rintoul probably regarded as better than many victories.

So soon as the *Spectator*, dropping the very pretence of impartiality, took its place openly in the ranks of reform, its circulation at once increased. An 'independent' paper is

[1] For all this, and much more, see W. Beach Thomas's admirable centenary volume, *The Story of the Spectator*.

rarely a success: it can make enemies, but it makes few friends. An Ishmael, with its hand against every man, it finds every man's hand against it. Henceforward, the *Spectator* had a definite policy, and the supporters of that policy gave it their support. If it did much to make Reform, there can be no doubt that Reform did more to make it.

It is not easy for us, as we glance at one of these early numbers, to realize what a new thing it was. Almost all the 'features' to which we are now so thoroughly accustomed were present; but it is certain that they had never, at least in combination, appeared in any paper before. First and foremost, there was always a condensed, but remarkably complete, summary of the events of the week; a summary so complete, indeed, that one finds in it an almost sufficient history of the time. To this was added a discussion of 'interesting topics of a general nature', with a view—is it Rintoul or Chambers that is speaking?—'to instruction and entertainment at the same time'. Then came departments devoted to literary criticism (of course, only of 'the best books'), dramatic and musical subjects, scientific and miscellaneous information. Sir W. Beach Thomas notes that so early began that interest in animal intelligence which, if not of the essence of the *Spectator*, might almost be called, in the old philosophical language, one of its inseparable accidents. One feature, however, would probably strike the devotees of Hutton and Strachey as remarkable. There were occasional illustrations.

The whole was, and boasted of being, a 'family paper'; and there is more in this phrase than may meet the unwary ear. Middle-class Victorian society was still emphatically a society of families. The 'evening' was spent 'at home' as regularly as when Mrs. Barbauld wrote; and, in consequence, the habit of reading aloud was then common. Among the innumerable letters which Dickens received from his admirers, several speak of the enjoyment the writers had received from *hearing* his novels read in the family circle.[1]

---

[1] Forster gives many examples. Mr. Hine, in his *Hitchin Worthies* (most of whom were Quakers), speaks of 'books read aloud in the leisured fashion of that age' (see the chapter on Samuel Lucas). Ruskin (in *Praeterita*) tells us how his parents read Byron aloud.

A man wrote to Macaulay asking him to omit the passage about the Taunton girl's visit to Feversham's camp, because he could not read it aloud. Much of the (largely imaginary) Victorian prudery and reticence is probably due to this

The evening was longer than now, for dinner, or high-tea, was rarely later than five. For multitudes of the respectable population, outside entertainments, such as the theatre or the music-hall provided, were practically non-existent. Dancing was a snare of the devil. Even concerts, though Catalani might be singing and Paganini playing, were not encouraged by the unworldly; and it was not till the undeniable 'goodness' of Jenny Lind conquered the prejudice, that anything but oratorio was considered safe. Nonconformists and Claphamites, therefore, on evenings not set apart for missionary meetings, shunned outside dangers, and spent the time in 'profitable' instruction and 'harmless' entertainment. Cards, of course, were forbidden, and, while a game of bagatelle might be allowed, billiards, even in the home, were never mentioned. While the mother knitted, and the girls sewed or embroidered, an improving book would be read aloud. Authors accommodated themselves to the custom. We are still, in fact, in the age of the family book— as much so as a hundred years before, when Doddridge's *Family Expositor* was to be seen in every other house. Take, for instance, John Kitto's *Daily Bible Illustrations*. This work is a sort of commentary on the Scriptures, consisting of short essays of four or five pages each, for every morning and evening of the year, which, as the author says, can each be read aloud in ten minutes or a quarter of an hour.[1] So careful is Kitto to keep to his plan that he actually makes his Sunday readings—what might be thought impossible— more devotional, and therefore more suitable to the Sabbath, than those of the week-days. Few books have been more popular than this.[2]

But more secular writers followed the same course. No one can read certain novels of the time without perceiving that they were intended, like Dickens's *Household Words* or that once-famous *Family Friend*, for a public not so much of individuals as of 'households'. Some peculiarities in Wilkie Collins's *Woman in White*, and still more in *John Halifax*, point the same way; and I have sometimes thought, perhaps too rashly, that Collins's trick of assigning different parts of

habit. It would take a tough man to read some novels of to-day aloud to his children.

[1] It must have been a sad deprivation to Kitto that he could not join in such an exercise himself. He was totally deaf.

[2] Kitto died in 1854. A new edition appeared in the eighties.

deeply one is steeped in the politics of the forties, the more one admires the force and spirit of those weekly leading articles. They are, in the best sense of the word, Tracts for the Times. Apart from their literary power, however, they would deserve praise for their liberal spirit. They are informed throughout by a hatred of hypocrisy, of oppression, and of indifference to misery; as we have already seen,[1] Fonblanque was the scourge of humbug. The position held by his paper is illustrated by the fact that in 1839 Carlyle chose it as the medium for his famous petition in favour of a law of copyright, which was afterwards (January 29, 1841) sponsored in Parliament by Serjeant Talfourd.

'The Petition of Thomas Carlyle, a Writer of Books, Humbly sheweth, That his labour in writing has found hitherto in money or money's worth small recompense or none: that he is by no means sure of its ever finding recompense, but thinks that, if so, it will be at a distant time. . . . May it therefore please your Honourable House to protect him in said happy and long-doubtful event; and (by passing your Copyright Bill) forbid extraneous persons, entirely unconcerned in this adventure of his, to steal from him his small winnings, for a space of sixty years at least. After sixty years, unless your Honourable House provide otherwise, they may begin to steal.'[2]

A word may here be permitted on American 'pirate-publishers'. How many thousands were lost to English authors by the activities of these gentry can never be known; for they not only published popular English books in their own country, but smuggled them into ours. As the Dublin publishers had done with Richardson, so did the Yankees with Scott, but on a far larger scale. Scott, however, apart from a gentle allusion or two to 'a lack of the sense of public justice in the great Transatlantic community', said little about the business,[3] though a royalty of five per cent. would have paid off his creditors. To Macaulay, Harpers sent a single complimentary copy of their cheap edition of the *History*. 'We have already sold over 40,000 copies . . . there have been three other editions published by different houses. . . . Probably, within three months, the sale will amount to two hundred thousand.' Unless Macaulay sold the copy Harpers sent him, he can have gained little from this immense popularity.[4] Else-

[1] According to Mill (*Autobiography*, p. 99) Fonblanque wrote three-quarters of the paper himself; Mill contributed a weekly article on France, and much besides.

[2] Copyright, at the beginning of our period, was for the author's life, *or* twenty-five years from publication. Talfourd proposed life *and* sixty years; Mahon life *and* twenty-five years. By Macaulay's influence, the period was fixed at life *or* forty-two years. His speech is a classic.

[3] Lockhart, Apr. 4, 1819: a letter to Southey.

[4] Trevelyan, *sub an.* 1849. There can be little doubt that American piracy

where (December 1842), speaking of the republication of the *Essays*, Macaulay says, 'The question is now merely this, whether Longman and I, or Carey and Hart of Philadelphia, shall have the supplying of *the British public* with these papers. The American copies are coming over by scores, and measures are being taken for bringing them over by hundreds.' Tennyson was another victim. He made arrangements with Ticknor and Fields, and announced his desire that, as far as possible, the American rights to his poems should rest with that firm; but this did not prevent other firms from issuing thousands of copies of *In Memoriam* or *Maud*; and, though Ticknor and Fields honestly paid him his share of their profits, these others did not.

But it is, of course, with Dickens that the question is most closely associated. The story is well known of his visit to America in 1842. He found all the best men in the country disgusted with the system, but afraid to say a word about it, and amazed that Dickens should dare to mention it. Mention it he did. 'I wish you could have seen the faces at Hartford when I began about Scott. My blood so boiled that I felt as if I were twelve feet high when I poured it down their throats.'[1] The result was nothing but abuse—anonymous letters comparing him unfavourably to Colt the murderer, threatening him with the tar-brush, or calling him no gentleman. Letters might arrive from England, including one from Carlyle, approving his action; but all failed, as Harriet Martineau's appeal to Congress had failed before, and as other appeals failed later, till justice was at last done, or half-done, when Dickens, Macaulay, and Carlyle had been long in their graves.

Why the *Examiner* ultimately failed is hard to say. It may have been too closely dependent on one man, and when Fonblanque retired in 1847 the loss may have been too severely felt. But its decline has been ascribed to another cause, in which lies a lesson already hinted at. It was suspected of too keen a devotion to Melbourne at a time when he was losing influence not only in the country but with his colleagues.[2]

Surpassing both the *Spectator* and the *Examiner* in circulation was their Tory rival *John Bull*[3]—a most characteristic product of the times. Started, ironically enough, as

---

had something to do with the alienation of English feeling which became so visible during the Civil War.

[1] Forster, *sub an.* 1842: well abridged by Gissing, *Dickens*, p. 100.
[2] See Fox Bourne, ii. 125.
[3] Price 4*d*. For *John Bull* see Barham, *Theodore Hook*, passim. A shorter account in Bourne, *English Journalism*; for a contemporary appreciation, Lockhart's article in the *Quarterly*, just after Hook's death in 1841.

a Sunday paper,[1] it was inspired, in the first instance, by
hatred of Queen Caroline, and gradually developed a furious
antagonism to Whigs and Radicals of all kinds. In 1820
Theodore Hook began the assault with 'Tentamen, or an
Essay towards the History of Whittington and his Cat';
in December of that year the first number of *John Bull*
appeared. It was certainly, despite a number of unveracious
disclaimers, almost entirely written by Hook, who, in fact,
continued to share the profits, till his death, with Shackell the
publisher; and the profits, even when the expenses of libel
actions were deducted, were considerable. Within six weeks
the circulation reached 10,000, and the profits at one time
amounted to £2,000 per annum. At the period of the Reform
agitation it had become a little less virulent, and was established as an important mouthpiece of Toryism. As Hook
tired of incessant writing, other contributors were enlisted:
Maginn, Thomas Haynes Bayly, 'Ingoldsby' Barham, James
Smith (of *Rejected Addresses*).

Hook's character is not unduly travestied by Thackeray
in *Pendennis*: the name 'Wagg' fairly represents him, as
does the 'Lucien Gay' of *Coningsby*. He had wit, which too
often showed itself in feeble practical jokes, or in verbal
puns, such as crowd the pages of his once-famous *Mrs.
Ramsbotham*:[2] jests which, however, were not unsuited to
the tastes of the time. His powers of improvisation were
great, and some of his novels, which were practically impro-
visations, can still give a dubious kind of pleasure. *Gilbert
Gurney* and *Jack Brag* have the vivacity and vigour which
we see also in the novels of Albert Smith: the vivacity and
vigour of a journalist. Hook, in fact, to borrow Macaulay's
terse description, was a 'clever, coarse, vulgar writer'. A
specimen or two may illustrate the accuracy of this criticism.
Writing in 1822 on Leigh Hunt's *Liberal*, *John Bull* remarks:

'Surely the Attorney-General will not suffer this execrable and
idiotic performance to escape the punishment it deserves. The blas-
phemies of Shelley, infamous and infernal as they were, were light,
compared to the detailed burlesque of the heavenly kingdom which

[1] A Wednesday edition was started later, in which Hook was greatly
assisted by Maginn.
[2] e.g. 'The clock is indeed a striking object'; 'many a man who has a stake
in the country goes and has a chop at the House of Commons restaurant';
'The *Duchess of Kent* was in stays, and we were too shy to look at her'.

is contained in this farrago of absurdity. . . . He who has framed this horrible disgusting poem deserves a ten-fold visitation of the law.'

Let us take another passage, from a later date (January 18, 1835):

'Joseph Hume is again Member for Middlesex. After a struggle of almost unexampled severity, the worshipper and slave of faction, the abettor of rebellion, the scoffer at religion, *mis*-represents, *for another Parliament*, the sentiments and the interests of the metropolitan county, with its million and a half of inhabitants.

'Mourn, *to-day*, ye Christians!—Rejoice, *for a season*, ye Jews and Infidels! He who mocks at the mention of the Deity and insults the God of both Jews and Gentiles, by stigmatizing as "cant" and "humbug" all recognition, by a Christian Legislature, of a super-intending Providence, owes his ultimate success, it is said, in a great measure, to the gold of the Children of Israel!'

John Bull's hatred of the Jews—who were then, it will be remembered, making slow advances towards the emancipation which had just been conceded to the Catholics—approached almost to frenzy. When, in 1835, Mr. Solomon was elected Sheriff of London, and the Duke of Sussex was invited to dine with him at the London Tavern, the noble orthodoxy of the paper could not be restrained.

'Against the religious opinions of Mr. Solomon we have nothing to say. No doubt he is right, and all the Christian world is wrong. We know nothing about him personally; and, abstractedly, he may be as good a man as the Grand Seigneur or the King of Timbuctoo:—all we go upon is that Mr. Solomon *is not a Christian*, and we therefore think Mr. Solomon to blame for permitting his subordinate to write a letter to the Duke of Sussex in which, by implication if not in so many words, Christianity is denounced as an absurd and unjust prejudice, and infidelity and disbelief are dignified into liberality of opinion.'

This because the Duke had declared the exclusion of Jews from civic privileges to be inconsistent with Christian charity.

John Bull being such a champion of religion, we are prepared to find it antagonistic to science.

'So long as people', it says, on September 6, 1835, 'simply make fools of themselves, without outraging the feelings of others and violating the decencies of society, it is just as well to permit them to enjoy their conceits and absurdities—but there *are* limits even to folly.

'Among the extensive humbugs which so eminently distinguish this very extraordinarily enlightened age, none, perhaps, is more glaring than the meeting of what is called the British Association for the Advancement of Science, now held annually in different parts of the Empire, at which a crowd of persons anxious only to get their names in the newspapers assist (as they call it) gentlemen who are considerably glorified by being cardinals of a conclave of Pidcockians, dignified as a Zoological Society; their laudable exertions being devoted to the pious and Christian-like purposes of attracting all the well-bred female Sabbath-breakers to the metropolis to see monkeys flirt and elephants wash on Sundays.'

Then follow some sarcastic remarks on the Statistical Society, inspired possibly—if we may impute motives—by the fact that the Whig Lord Lansdowne was its head. After that, one can read with equanimity a series of jeers on phrenology. The Association—which for some reason was then considered fair game [1]—did not retaliate; but *John Bull*, as may be expected, had to stand libel actions from less patient victims.

§ 13. THE *SATURDAY REVIEW*

We, when we think of the *Spectator*, are apt to think of its old equal and opposite, the *Saturday Review*. But the *Spectator* was already full-grown when the *Saturday* was established—in the fateful year 1855; and the real glory of this famous weekly was not fully achieved before the sixties. [2] Curiously enough, the weekly was generated, in a fashion, by the corruption of a daily. When it was plain that the days of the *Morning Chronicle* were numbered, and when Cardwell and Stanhope were meditating its sale, [3] plans were formed for securing the future of the too brilliant band of writers on the staff of the Peelite paper. The chief mover in the scheme was Beresford Hope—and Hope's ecclesiastical position marked the sympathies of the new paper as in a sense High Anglican. But its readers were not troubled with too much religion, except so far as the writers occasionally exercised their sarcastic powers on all religions equally. In point of fact, the *Saturday* is a new phenomenon. It represents that revolt of the intelligentsia against the *bourgeoisie* which is described elsewhere. [4] It voices the

---

[1] It is laughed at in many publications of the time; few treated it with the respect which, as we shall see, it received from the *Athenaeum*.

[2] A lively account of the early days of the *Saturday* is given by Escott, *Masters of Journalism*, p. 230 sq.

[3] See *supra*.   [4] See the Introduction to the present work.

restlessness of the highly educated under the yoke of people they hold to be inferior. The changes in Public Schools, the expansion of the Universities, the Tractarian movement, any number of other causes, had formed a new educated class to combat the dominant middle class. The cause these 'superior' people espoused might be lost; but they were conscious Catos. At any rate, living or dying, they could take their revenge by contemptuous and cultured sarcasm. The *Saturday* was their mouthpiece. Among the writers were the Erastian Vernon Harcourt, the agnostic[1] John Morley, the free-thinking Mrs. Lynn Linton, and the Puseyite Parson Scott—a motley band, but all astonishingly clever. In these pages, also, the future Lord Salisbury exercised his sardonic gifts on the wickedness of Gladstone's finance and the duplicity of Napoleon III. Motley as they were, they were marshalled to one end, under the despotic control of John Douglas Cook, an editor whose office might have been an old naval captain's quarter-deck. 'Mercy on us, what a temper!' said Mrs. Lynn Linton years afterwards. 'Has he not sworn at me? Yes, and actually hit me, if he thought I had not carried out his orders properly in the smallest detail?'[2] Under Cook, the paper soon acquired that character which it maintained, almost unaltered, for fifty years. 'None of the surface brilliancy of the *Saturday Review*,' Oxford dons used to say to their pupils; but they read, and involuntarily enjoyed, the obnoxious brilliancies week by week, and gladly paid their ninepence. 'Every good man', said Spurgeon,[3] who often felt its lash, 'is born for the love of God and the hatred of the *Saturday Review*.'

One very excellent feature of the *Saturday* was not original, but borrowed, at first- or second-hand, from the *Leader*, and has since been adopted, in one form or another, by papers of all kinds. This is what, to steal a title of Wordsworth's, we may call the Descriptive Sketch. Instead of mere reports of speeches, the writer gave

---

[1] This name, of course, was invented a little later, by Huxley about 1869; but the thing was common enough at all times, in England and elsewhere.

[2] Escott, p. 232.

[3] Towards Spurgeon, as towards Nonconformity generally, the *Saturday* often adopted a tone of contemptuous condescension. It was remarkable how well a man with so few educational advantages could contrive to preach and to write commentaries. Nonconformists, as was natural, felt towards the *Saturday* much as they felt towards Matthew Arnold.

but its place was at once taken by *All the Year Round*, which was equally triumphant. 'So well has it gone,' wrote Dickens,[1] 'that it was able to repay me, with five per cent. interest, all the money I advanced for its establishment, and yet to leave a good £500 balance at the banker's.' To this were contributed, as serials, *The Woman in White, The Moonstone, Hard Cash, A Strange Story*, and hosts of less celebrated tales; but the chief attraction was always the *Christmas Pieces*, the most popular of all Dickens's writings, which raised the circulation to nearly 300,000 copies.

But all these, and many others, such as the *Gem, Hood's Own* (1838), *Hood's Magazine* (1844), we must leave with a mere look, and pass on. Almost more expressive of the spirit of the time is *Chambers's Journal*.

'The grand leading principle of this paper', says the editor in its opening number, 'is to take advantage of the universal appetite for instruction which at present exists; to supply to that appetite food of the best kind, and in such form and at such a price, as must suit the convenience *of every man in the British dominions*. Every Saturday, when the poorest labourer in the country draws his humble earnings, he shall have it in his power to purchase a meal of healthful and agreeable mental instruction: nay, every schoolboy shall be able to purchase with his pocket-money something calculated to influence his fate in life—instead of the trash upon which the grown children of the present day are wont to expend it.

'I shall present, but not too hurriedly, papers on Literary and Scientific subjects, articles on the Formation and Arrangements of Society, observations on Education and our Scholastic Institutions, sketches on Agriculture, Gardening, Sheep-farming, the making of Roads, the Increase of Population, the Uses of Machinery—indicative of the vast improvements effected and of what still remains to be accomplished. For the express use of the *poor man*, I shall open a flow of information for his guidance, should he be disposed to emigrate. For the benefit of those who live among the hills, and who cannot come to church, I shall give pithy passages from the great British moralists. For the recreation of those who reflect, I shall present passages from the works of Newton and Bacon, from the Encyclopaedists, and other English luminaries.

'To the ladies and gentlemen of the "old school" I shall relate innumerable amusing anecdotes, not one of which probably they ever heard before. With the ladies of the "new school", and all my fair young countrywomen in their teens, I hope to be on agreeable terms. I will tell them what I intend to do for them: I shall make a point of

[1] Dickens to Forster, July 1859.

giving them every week, if I can find room, a nice amusing tale, either original, or selected from the best modern authors—no trash about Italian coaches and daggers, and ghosts in the blue chamber, but something really good. I will also inform them of a thousand useful little receipts of housewifery, calculated to make them capital wives: and perhaps I may give them new insight into sewing, painting in water-colours, drawing with pencils or chalk, or singing and improving their taste in music.'[1]

This was a sufficiently comprehensive programme; but those who have read the *Journal* will admit that, bold as it was, it was carried out with a large measure of completeness. When we remember that the *Miscellany* and the *Repository*, which appeared in succession a few years later (1848 and 1852), had a very similar design, and must have appealed to nearly the same constituency, we shall be inclined to regard the success of the *Journal* as a credit alike to the publishers and to the public. Even the platitudinous moralizing paragraphs, which William Chambers contributed too regularly, did not deter the purchasers. There was little of the catch-penny in the paper; and almost the only concession to popular feeling is the occasional appearance of wood-engravings. The Chamberses gave good weekly value for three-halfpence, good monthly for fivepence, and good bi-monthly for a shilling.

These illustrations must not be despised. When we look at the cuts in the *Miscellany* and the *Repository*, or at the coloured boards in which their reissues were bound, we are apt to forget that till comparatively recent times the production of illustrations was a slow and somewhat expensive process. Photography had not yet arisen to simplify it; and the super-abundance of pictorial embellishments with which every paper now supplies us was quite impossible. Sporadic cuts might appear in a daily; and a weekly, like *Chambers's* or *Lloyd's*, might venture on them more freely; but, if we pass over such 'monthlies' as *Pickwick* (1836), with its four

[1] See also an article by W. F. Gray in the centenary number of the *Journal*, Feb. 1932. Magazines catering specially for women were not uncommon, and throw a vivid light on the ideas of the time. The *Ladies' Magazine* always gave a song, with an accompaniment of one note for each hand. 'No lady can consider her education completed unless she has produced at least one picture worthy to be framed and glazed.' 'No young lady would be seen running in public.' Young ladies are warned in the thirties not to enter Shillibeer's omnibuses, for fear of rudeness from male passengers. Reading (except of this particular magazine) was not encouraged; novels were pernicious, and solid reading tended to making blue-stockings. (An amusing article on these magazines appeared in the *News Chronicle* of Sept. 24, 1931.)

illustrations a number, we may say that no paper made them a prominent feature till *Punch* began to employ the talent of its famous artists; nor did the illustrated paper proper, as we know it, arise till the following year (1842) when Herbert Ingram, noting, it is said, the success of any number of the *Morning Chronicle* that had an illustration, hit upon the idea of founding a paper for British households, in which the news should be subordinate to the pictures. Ingram, a Nottingham newsagent, was no scholar, but he knew the truth of the Horatian maxim that things seen strike the mind more forcibly than things heard. The result was the *Illustrated London News*,[1] which he produced with the help of his brother-in-law Cooke, and with Mark Lemon to advise him. The paper contained sixteen folio pages, each of three columns, a dozen small pictures, sketches, and humorous drawings. Once again we have a family paper. 'Our business will not be with the strife of party, but with . . . the home life of the empire, with the household gods of the English people and above all of the English poor.' Its success was immediate and immense. Ingram, a middle-class man himself, understood the taste of the middle classes; and he was a first-rate man of business. When David Bogue's *Illustrated Times* under that strange genius Henry Vizetelly [2] (a journalist and an artist) showed signs of becoming a dangerous rival, Ingram bought it up, and his paper remained without a serious competitor till the foundation of the *Graphic* in 1869. It is probable that, as in the case of the *Mirror* to-day, its chief supporter was the British woman, who has always seemed to prefer her newspaper to have about it a tinge of the magazine.

There was one feature of the *Illustrated* which must not be passed over, as it probably gained for the paper at least some readers in almost every country of the world. This was the chess-column, now so prominent in scores of periodicals, but then, if not quite unknown, exceedingly rare. From 1844, for more than twenty years, this column was conducted by the famous chess-player, Howard Staunton,[3] who made it

[1] Described by Fox Bourne, ii. 119.
[2] A lively account of this many-sided man is given by Escott, p. 223 sq. He had already brought out the *Pictorial*, 1843. His subsequent quarrels with Mrs. Grundy over his translations of Zola will be fresh in the minds of elderly readers.
[3] Known also for his edition of Shakespeare, and for his 'Shakespeareana'

not only a centre of interest to enthusiasts for the game, but also, *more suo*, a vehicle for his personal antagonisms. He quarrelled with nearly every one, including even those who had had the misfortune to lose matches he had expected them to win; nor were his sarcasms less painful because they were often pointed with a Shakespearian tag. When Paul Morphy, in the late fifties, came over from America full of eagerness to play him, Staunton, recognizing Morphy's superiority, was afraid to accept his challenge; and his wriggling excuses make his columns, even now, at once painful and amusing to read. But he was a real benefactor of the game; and he will be remembered not merely for his standard chessmen, but for the pioneer work of annotation which he did in the *Illustrated*, and later in the *Era*. To his example, perhaps, we owe the first-rate notes which after-wards enriched the *Field* or the *Observer*.

Whether the name of Eliza Cook is now sufficiently great to rescue the name of her magazine from oblivion may be doubted; but it is certain that it secured for it a magnificent start and a long-continued success. The immense popularity of her verse [1] did for her paper what the renown of *East Lynne* did for Mrs. Henry Wood's *Argosy* [2] a dozen years later. Within a very few weeks of its foundation [3] the paper was selling 60,000 copies,[4] and rivalling *Chambers's* in popularity. Eliza Cook, like Chambers, was moved by the universal impulse. 'I am', she said, 'anxious to give my feeble aid to the gigantic struggle for intellectual elevation now going on'; and she did her part with characteristic seriousness. There was plenty of instruction,[5] amid some amusement, in her pages. Every week the *Journal* begins with one of her morally elevating poems,[6] and the stories

contributed to the *Athenaeum*. Buckle, the author of the *History of Civiliza-tion*, considered Staunton his only superior at chess.

[1] Aided by the voice of Henry Russell, who set to music and sang *The Old Arm Chair, Sir Harold the Hunter*, and many more of her poems.

[2] *East Lynne*, 1861: first number of the *Argosy*, 1865.   [3] 1849.

[4] Select Committee on Public Libraries, 1849, Q. 2790.

[5] In 1851 there is a long review of Spencer's *Social Statics*. It is noteworthy that the book is unfavourably judged, chiefly on the ground that its extreme individualism is out of date.

[6] Hammond, p. 316, quotes one of the poems:

> And when fair Flora sends her butterfly,
>   Painted and spangled, as her herald mummer,
> 'Now for warm holidays,' my heart will cry.
>   'The poor will suffer less!' Thank God for summer.

which follow are never without an improving lesson. The
hero borrows books from the Mechanics' Institute, and the
heroine is rewarded, by a happy marriage, for her devotion
to her parents.[1]

Chambers's was entirely non-political, and even its historical articles leaned to the safe side. Eliza Cook was, if
possible, still safer. But what has been called the 'Rebel
Journalism' was suspect even when it ostentatiously es-
chewed politics. Its public was Chartist, and it was the
object of the fear and scorn of the Grevilles and Crokers.
Even Thackeray attacked it with bitterness.[2] Yet, if certain
of its publications could have been dissociated from their
editors, they might have been thought harmless enough.
John Cleave [3] was an indefatigable writer, who had often
come into collision with the law, and had, like Hetherington
and Abel Heywood, suffered imprisonment, without yielding
an inch to his judges and jailers. In 1837 he brought out his
London Satirist and Gazette of Variety, the name of which
was soon changed to *Cleave's Penny Gazette of Variety and
Amusement.* This paper claimed to be non-political, and to
be 'one of those broadsheets to which the intellectual requirements of the millions, and their appreciation that
Knowledge is Power, gave birth'.[4] It dealt with Natural
History and gardening, and provided anecdotes of eminent
persons, extracts from Dickens, and Dickens-like sketches.[5]
Frost [6] speaks of it highly, and notes that it appealed not
only to the working men, but to their wives and children.
But its cartoons, satirizing the powers that were, its addresses to Working Men's Associations, its accounts of the
Dorchester labourers, and, above all, the mere name of the
editor, aroused fear. It was suspected of being subsidized by
the Anti-Corn-Law League; and it certainly taught politics
indirectly, if not overtly. Its popularity in the Black
Country—a home of disaffection—did not contribute to
favour in Government circles.

---

[1] Cp. the story, Aug. 31, 1856, entitled *The Second Floor Lodgers.* Incidentally, 'Luke Flemming' reads the books *aloud* to 'Alice'.

[2] *Fraser's Magazine,* 1838. (Anonymous, but known to be Thackeray's.)

[3] John Cleave was a 'person of importance in his day'; but he is not mentioned in the *D.N.B.*

[4] Sept. 18, 1841.

[5] There were many Dickens plagiarisms and forgeries, which Dickens, on the
advice of Forster, decided not to notice.   [6] *Forty Years' Recollections,* p. 83.

Such papers as the *London Reformer*, with Livesey's temperance articles as a main feature, might pass unchallenged; but Bell's *Penny Dispatch* was more dangerous. This, in 1842, began to issue translations of Voltaire's *Philosophical Dictionary*, and ran counter to the theory that the poor must be kept religious. A perusal of papers like these provides a good commentary on Carlyle's *Chartism*, Kingsley's *Alton Locke*, or Fox's *Publicola* articles.

Very different alike from Chambers, Eliza Cook, and Cleave was Edward Lloyd, the founder of the 'Salisbury Square School of Fiction'. Lloyd appealed to yet another class, and gave that class what it wanted, with but the pretence of a desire to elevate it in morals and in taste. In September 1841 he started the *People's Police Gazette*, a penny weekly, consisting solely of what to-day are called 'thrillers', or narratives of some sensational crime of the day. He did not touch on politics, and allowed no political cartoons, but made his stories still more horrible by ghastly illustrations. The success of this paper was unprecedented, and Lloyd followed it up with another (1843), *The Weekly Penny Miscellany*, sixteen closely-printed tales and novels, short or serial, saving space for these by omitting the illustrations. This also was enormously popular. There seemed, indeed, to be no limit either to the fecundity of Lloyd's press or to the willingness of his public to absorb its products. In 1843, also, he brought out the *Penny Atlas and Weekly Register of Novel Entertainment*, while in an endless stream he poured forth penny novelettes, either selected from his magazines or quite new; not forgetting the serial, in which the 'To be continued' at an exciting point ensured the purchase of the next number. The style of these works was what used to be called 'elevated and impassioned';[1] and their general character may be gathered from such titles as *Alice Horne, or the Revenge of the Blighted One*,[2] *Ada the Betrayed*.

What the refined classes thought of all this may be easily guessed. In the Report of the Committee on Public Libraries, 1849, are many proofs of the anxiety caused by the popu-

[1] A phrase used by a critic in the forties to describe the 'strain' of the *Scottish Chiefs*.

[2] Hammond, p. 319, gives the headings of chapter 85 (note the length of the novel): 'Strange Odour in the Old House. Finding of the Gamester's Body. A Critical Moment. Sir Charles Horne's Insensibility.'

larity of this 'Saturday trash'. Lovett, who owned, however, that he had not himself read it, considered that, at least in the early stages, Lloyd's publications were immoral and anti-social. The evidence of George Dawson (a name well remembered in Birmingham) may carry still more weight.[1]

'We give the people an appetite to read, and supply them with nothing. For the last many years, in England, everybody has been educating the people, but they have forgotten to find them any books. In plain language, you have made them hungry, but you have given them nothing to eat; it is almost a misfortune to a man to have a great taste for reading, and not to have the power of satisfying it. . . . The penny stamp upon newspapers makes the cost of a good thing dear; and adds facility to the cheap people to circulate trash to an extent which is almost incredible: the rubbish issued every Saturday is very great.'

Dawson, as we may believe, was perhaps overcolouring the picture; but it is not surprising that he spoke strongly. Nor is it surprising that Charles Knight, who attributed the failure of the *Penny Magazine* [2] to the competition of Lloyd's papers, should have felt some indignation. But Lloyd was quite unrepentant. He noted with contempt, in the preface to the *Miscellany* (1846), the wailings of Knight; and he always insisted that his stories had an 'elevating' tendency. Thus, in another of his prefaces, he declares:

'It has ever been our aim, in the management of *Lloyd's Penny Atlas*, to combine as much practical and real knowledge of human life as possible with the "brain-woven" narratives, which from time to time appeared in our pages; for we hold an opinion, which in practice we have had frequent opportunities of verifying, that true morality, sound reasoning, and exalted sentiments may be more easily, more effectually, and more pleasantly conveyed to the mind through the medium of works of fiction than by any other means. . . . We paint virtue oppressed and borne down by the wicked, and then we show the rebound of its energies: while the wild turbulence of vice has brought forth nothing but evil fruits and deep vexation of spirit.' [3]

---

[1] Qs. 1308, 1310. See also *Journal of Statistical Society*, 1838–9, which analyses the books found in small circulating libraries: 'enormous preponderance of Salisbury Square type'; 'Bad Books' kept to be fetched by coffee-house waiters for gentlemen to read at dinner.

[2] To this John Kitto began to contribute in 1833, and from 1834 onwards he wrote weekly, over the signature 'The Deaf Traveller'. At the same time he was contributing 'Answers to Correspondents' in the admirable *Penny Cyclopaedia*. (Ryland, *Memorials of John Kitto*, 2nd edn., p. 354 sq.)

[3] *Penny Atlas*, 1843 (abridged).

'We lay before a large and intelligent circle of readers those same pleasures of the imagination which have hitherto, to a great extent, graced only the polished leisure of the wealthy.'[1]

Nor was Lloyd without his defenders. Thomas Frost, who made an attempt to earn the half-sovereign which Lloyd paid for each instalment of his novels, considered that the Salisbury Square School provided a useful connecting link between the ballads, 'last dying speeches' of murderers, and terrific legends of diabolism, which had been the favourite literature of the 1790's, and the more wholesome reading of his own time.[2] The whole controversy was, in fact, another instance of the eternal quarrel between realism and idealism, with this curious difference, that Lloyd's business-like realism induced him to supply his public with stronger doses of romanticism than the idealists could endure.

Lloyd had but one serious rival. This was G. W. M. Reynolds, a strong Chartist, who thoroughly knew the taste of the people he met day by day. As a novelist, he challenged the supremacy of G. P. R. James, and was equally prolific.[3] In 1846 he started *Reynolds's Newspaper*, in which innumerable stories represented vice as a monster of frightful mien, yet, it is to be feared, not in such a manner as to render it hateful. There is the usual assemblage of bad baronets, designing marquises, and harassed maidens. From time to time there are sheer horrors, outdoing Mrs. Radcliffe at her most horrible.[4] A typical specimen of Reynolds's

---

[1] *Penny Miscellany*, 1843.

[2] Frost, *Reminiscences of a Country Journalist.* The following passage, p. 92, referring to 1849 or 1850, may be worth quoting: 'When the *National Instructor* had gone to limbo, and serial stories were asked for no more, reissues being more popular than new ventures, I called upon Macgowan.

'"Any brilliant ideas that would make our fortunes? Any forgotten novels that you could dig up, and clothe the dry bones with new flesh?"

'"I would rather provide skeleton and all," I replied with a smile.

'"I am afraid the days of novels in shilling or even sixpenny numbers are over," he observed. "I have a notion that all serial literature will come before long to the penny form, and ultimately lower; and I sometimes feel disposed to anticipate the era of halfpenny literature by a bold venture in that direction."'

[3] Several of his novels, in double-column, paper-bound, sixpenny form, were still circulating in the present writer's youth.

[4] A good type of this style is *Varney the Vampire*, a full account of which has been recently given by Mr. Montague Summers. It is remarkable that even in Chambers's *Repository* there was a story of the Vampire, entitled 'The Mysterious Stranger'.

style is perhaps the following, from *Ellen Percy, or the Memoirs of an Actress* (ii. 268):

' "Ah, is it so?" I ejaculated; and the next instant my hands were at the throat of Lady Lilla Essendane.

' So sudden and so powerful was my attack, that she was completely overpowered in the twinkling of an eye; and she fell upon the floor.

' "Let her go, Miss Percy! and don't be a fool!" ejaculated Dame Betty. "Those ruffians will come up and murder us!"

' "Be quiet, dame!" I said in a most peremptory manner. "Listen!"

' And we did listen, while my hands were still upon Lady Lilla's throat,—my looks showing such stern determination that she evidently thought I should strangle her outright at the first indication of an attempt to cry or resist. For several moments we listened, and still all was silent.

' "Now," I said, "you see, Lady Lilla, that thus far the victory is my own, and the momentary conflict has not reached the ears of your myrmidons. Answer me!—for you see I am desperate, in as much as my position was rendered desperate by your menaces. Tell me in what part of the building is the young man confined, who was captured by your ruffians in the middle of the night? Beware how you deceive me, for I must inform you this is not the first time I have been a prisoner in these ruins, and I am familiar with their situations and details."

' "That young man," said Lady Lilla, who was just enabled to speak in a whisper as I loosed to the slightest degree the gripe which I had upon her throat,—"that young man is a certain William Lardner——"

' "Yes, yes, I know it," I ejaculated: "he is a sailor on board the yacht where you used to meet Edward St. Clair and plot your horrible schemes for my destruction." '

It is clear that Reynolds's readers would not only snatch a fearful joy out of his narratives, but also acquire some acquaintance with the polysyllabic resources of the English language. Not the least noteworthy characteristic of all the novels of the time is the way in which the heroes, at the most exciting moments, contrive to retain command of a Johnsonian vocabulary.

Whatever may be said against the 'Salisbury Square' School, it was clean. The production of pornographic literature was carried on by a class of tradesmen whom Lloyd would have despised; and it was carried on systematically, on a vast scale. Travellers regularly visited Oxford and Cambridge with their pernicious wares; and one seizure yielded half a ton of indecent pictures. The common law, relying on the informer and sworn depositions, proved totally in-adequate for dealing with the evil; and in 1857 Lord Campbell brought in the *Obscene Publications Bill* (20 & 21 Vic., c. 83), giving the magistrates power of summary jurisdiction on information from the police. The debate was noteworthy for a lively passage of arms between Lyndhurst and Campbell;[1] but the Bill passed, and was, in its author's opinion, completely successful. Recent notorious applications of the Act tend to justify Lyndhurst's objections; for it was never meant to have any bearing on art or literature, and the *Athenaeum* did not think it worth mentioning.[2]

But of all these 'household words' probably the most typical, in a certain kind, and beyond all doubt the most popular, among a certain class, was the *Family Herald*, the name of which still lasts as a shorthand phrase to save pages of description. Who does not know the sort of story which it produced in endless abundance, and which, devoutly studied by governesses and servant-maids, spread—to use the title of a Victorian work once well known—'Sunshine in the Kitchen'?[3] Stories of the *Fatherless Fanny*[4] genre, of the secrets of convents, of poor girls marrying aristocrats, of young ladies who might have married grandly if they had not shown their bad temper too early to the eligible young man—these, as they pursued their exciting course in weekly instalments, were eagerly waited for and passionately perused. Priced at a penny, the paper was accessible to nearly every one, and within seven years was selling 125,000 copies a week.[5] But stories were far from being the sole pabulum provided. In accordance with its motto, 'Life without mirth is like a lamp without oil,' it gave the million amuse-ment; but it was also careful to give 'useful information'; and it is remarkable that it was as severe on sweated female labour as Hood himself. It may be as well to give here a sum-mary of its first number (December 17, 1842): 'To the Reader.' The paper was to be 'interesting to all, offensive to none'. It was a 'literary curiosity', as it was the first specimen of a publication produced entirely—types, ink, paper, and

---

[1] Campbell's account of this *fracas* is woefully inaccurate; see 'Autobio-graphy' in Mrs. Hardcastle's *Life*.

[2] See Martin, *Lyndhurst, sub anno*; Atlay, *Victorian Chancellors*, i. 164; H. Paul, *Modern England*, i. 83.

[3] By the Rev. Benjamin Smith.

[4] I do not know the author of this enormously popular story.

[5] Lovett's evidence before Committee on Public Libraries, 1849. This is twice the circulation of *Chambers's Journal*.

printing—by machinery.[1] Half a column follows, giving
a description of 'Young's Type-composing Machine'—the
first popular account of a device which was to have a portentous progeny.

'Ill-Regulated Female Labour.' 'It is the bounden duty of public
journals, and more imperatively of a Family Herald, to sternly tell
those who have any pretensions to Christian charity, that their work
is not complete by merely pitying the oppressed and necessitous, by
doling out to them a sympathetic sovereign, and that they cannot,
and must not, satisfy their consciences by having afforded relief in
perhaps only a single instance, and that too from impulse, while there
are thousands of cases equally heart-rending and as eloquently demanding present succour and public amelioration.'

There were, on the average, 5,000 'genteel females' in
London, who, from lack of experience in housework, were
obliged to seek a livelihood by needlework; and the chances
were that not more than one-third would find employment.
To provide the necessaries of life, many of them turned to
crime. Statistics follow as to the wages of shirt-makers and
parasol-makers. The fault, to a great extent, lay in the habit,
not confined to women of the middle class, of boasting about
their bargains, and higgling in the shops. Men were as much
to blame as women—and here the article stopped short; for
to go farther would have involved touching on politics, from
which the *Family Herald* desired to keep itself free.

Then follows a series of short notes, or reviews, dealing with
'Steele's Spelling-Book', 'Parental Affections', 'Honour',
'The Zollverein', and 'The Submarine Telescope'; after
which comes advice to servants as to how to get on with
their mistresses. We are now on page 2, where instruction
for the most part ceases, and amusement begins. Here we
find 'The Shepherdess of the Alps', a short story; 'Castelia
Cronomia'—to be concluded in our next; 'Kirkleven, or
the Pilgrimage of Grace', the first three chapters of a serial;
a life of Confucius; a somewhat lame article on public
grievances, among which is included the overflow of Irish
into England; 'Random Readings'—a collection of so-
called funny stories; a column for 'Youth'; and a single
column for advertisements. There can be no doubt that the
purchaser got good value for his money.

[1] Much of this machinery was the invention of Henry Bessemer. See Bessemer's *Autobiography* and Hine's *Hitchin Worthies*.

Later numbers contained extracts from the Royal Commission Report on the work of women and children. 'The remedies proposed, schooling and shortening of hours, are totally insufficient, and must prove a failure.'[1]

Of the moralizing verses to which the *Herald* accorded occasional space, one specimen may suffice:

The Drunkard's Farewell to his Folly.

Farewell horrors and blue devils;
Farewell dews of midnight revels;
Farewell, shoes that have no soles on;
Farewell, fires that have no coals on;
Farewell, cupboards with no meat in;
Farewell, chairs that have no seat in;
Farewell, landlords and your spouses;
Farewell, spiders and your houses;
Farewell, pockets that are empty;
Farewell, landlords, you have plenty!

It is plain that the *Herald*, in its own sphere, was as intent on doing good as *Chambers's Miscellany* itself. As one turns its pages, one is stirred now to laughter, now to an over-tragic terror, but never to disgust.

It must not, however, be imagined that this kind of literature satisfied all, even in the classes to which Reynolds, Lloyd, and the *Herald* so successfully appealed. Apart from Knight and Chambers, there were authors who had a hold on the best minds of the masses. The autobiographies of men like Thomas Cooper, the Chartist,[2] are sufficient refutation of such an idea. The very growth of Chartism is a testimony to the fact that men read politics and studied sociology. A good example may be found in Jessie Fothergill's novel, *Probation*—a story drawn from the life—in which Myles Heywood is represented as a student of John Stuart Mill, Henry Thomas Buckle, and others;[3] and he stands, though idealized, as a type of many.

Myles Heywood's Bodleian, like Luke Flemming's, was the Mechanics' Institute, a concrete product of the Society for the Diffusion of Useful Knowledge, the dread of old-

---

[1] A popular feature of the *Herald*, which it did not originate, but carried farther than most journals, was the Answers to Correspondents.

[2] Author of that remarkable poem, *The Purgatory of Suicides*, for which Cooper prepared himself by a diligent study of Milton.

[3] *Probation*, though published in the seventies, deals with the fifties and sixties.

fashioned Tories and the hope of Radicals.[1] The London Institute was started in 1823, the Manchester in 1824, the Birmingham and the Liverpool in 1825. Very soon every important town had its Institute, and in 1850 there were 700, with over 107,000 members, and the libraries contained nearly 700,000 volumes. There were, of course, many failures. The lecturers often forgot that their audiences could not be expected to understand the technical terms of science, and some found themselves talking to empty benches. It is certain that Brougham, Birkbeck, and the other founders, were disappointed at the results; and the artisans were often disgusted. 'Many of us', said a correspondent of the *Poor Man's Guardian*, 'are already saturated with as much of what is called science as we can carry.'[2] None the less, it is probable that the unseen and imponderable benefits were great; and that those fit, if few, to profit by these societies gained immensely.[3]

Nor must we forget that, in certain cases, the very difficulty of obtaining knowledge spurred men on to get it. In the early fifties, in an out-of-the-way part of Durham, a little voluntary club of artisans and labourers was formed to study Watts *On the Mind*, Locke *On the Understanding*, and Dugald Stewart. Their only possible place of meeting was the country-inn, and here they met every Saturday evening. Hearing that Mansel was bringing out his *Limits of Religious Thought* (1858) they combined to buy it, and no fewer than ten copies were purchased. This by no means easy work was then discussed by these men, chapter by chapter, for some months.

For the upper-middle classes the pabulum provided was of a very remarkable kind; much of it, indeed, so remarkable that it has survived as a permanent part of English literature; and some of the magazines will be remembered for their connexion with illustrious names. Not many may recall the *Westmoreland Gazette*, which De Quincey edited for two years for a guinea a week; but everybody knows the

[1] See Coates, *Report on State of Literary, Scientific, and Mechanics' Institutes*, 1841 (Society for Diffusion of Useful Knowledge). Hammond, p. 322 sq., has a good, brief account of these institutions.

[2] Quoted by Hammond, p. 324: Dec. 19, 1835.

[3] Isolated cases have come to the present writer's own knowledge, and are quite astonishing. A servant-woman he knew in his youth was a thorough mistress of Browning's poems.

London Magazine, which has the unsurpassed glory of finding space for a few verses of Keats, for many of the *Essays of Elia*, and for the *Confessions of an Opium Eater*.[1] To this magazine Hazlitt was a contributor, as also Cary, the translator of Dante, Tom Hood, George Darley, and—hardly less famous in his own way than these—Wainewright, art critic, dilettante, forger, and murderer. Splendour like this could not last; but the *London Magazine* continued for many years to regale its constituency with first-rate fare. What surprises us, however, is almost more the readers than the writers. The articles, though so brilliant, are often lengthy and elaborate beyond what our degenerate day will stand. As Macaulay could send 104 pages on Bacon to the *Edinburgh*, and be read, so the writers in magazines that did not claim to be reviews could send long and comprehensive essays, and be asked for more. People had no more time then than now, but they seem to have been willing to spend more of it on close study. An essay that took months to write they thought well worth a couple of hours' reading. Of all this, *Fraser's*, *Tait's*, and *Blackwood's* provide proofs in abundance. The career of *Fraser's* is almost as illustrious as that of the *London*; much of it, indeed, is known to all students of literature. James Fraser [2] was a publisher in Regent Street, who started *Town and Country* in February 1830. The name *Fraser's*, which he never himself used, was derived not from him, but from Sir Hugh Fraser, who, with Maginn, had projected the Tory review *Regina*. The paper became almost instantly famous for its 'Gallery of Illustrious Literary Characters'—eighty-one portraits, chiefly by Daniel Maclise, with letterpress by Maginn. But it deserves yet more credit for the daring with which it gave the first chance to *Sartor Resartus*—not indeed printing the whole, but showing enough to bewilder the world. Carlyle himself [3] sardonically quotes the criticism of the *Sun* (April 1, 1834):

'*Fraser's Magazine* exhibits the usual brilliancy, and also the—etc. *Sartor Resartus* is what old Dennis used to call a heap of clotted nonsense, mixed however, here and there, with passages marked by thought and striking poetic vigour. But what does the author mean by Baphometic fire-baptism? Why cannot he lay aside his pedantry, and write so as to make himself generally intelligible?'

[1] Masson, *De Quincey*, p. 71.
[2] See *D.N.B.*: Fraser died in 1841.   [3] *Sartor*, Appendix, p. 212.

II   L

Fraser's Magazine for long gave Carlyle a share of that 'small recompense or none' which he declared was all his literary labours brought him. It published *History* in 1830, *Schiller* in 1831, *Biography*, and the review of Croker's *Boswell* in 1832, *Cagliostro* in 1833, *Edward Irving* in 1835, and the immortal *Diamond Necklace* in 1837, besides others too many to mention. Almost all were full-dress reviews; long and by no means easy to read. It is safe to say that few periodicals would now accept them, and that if they did, very few readers would be found for them.[1] *Fraser*, however, even after James Fraser died, and Nickisson succeeded, continued to give its public strong meat. In 1847 it was transferred to John W. Parker, under whom the same character was maintained. It was in *Fraser* that many of the delightful, though lengthy, essays appeared, which Froude afterwards republished under the slightly misleading title of *Short Studies in Great Subjects*.[2] In 1860 Froude became editor, and could therefore insert what he would; but many of these articles were published *before* he took the omnipotent chair. Their style is, of course, always charming; but their 'subjects' would probably be too 'great' for most magazine readers of our age.

This length and elaborateness characterize almost all the magazines of the class. That there was at least one reader of the time who thought them heavy, is shown by James Payn's daring boast on becoming editor of the *Cornhill*, that he would 'make it readable from cover to cover'; but other papers, even when unreadable, were read. *Blackwood's* is a type. This famous magazine was in the thirties in the full blaze of glory. The irresponsible time of the Chaldee Manuscript was over, and 'Maga' no longer lived by scandal and libel actions. The attacks on Coleridge, on the 'Cockney School of Poetry', and on the immorality of Leigh Hunt's *Story of Rimini* were dim memories only. Ended were the quarrels which had led John Murray to 'declare to God' that

---

[1] While Carlyle was writing these 'lighter' articles in *Fraser*, he was contributing essays on German literature to the *Edinburgh* and the *Westminster*, but chiefly to the *Foreign Review*. Practically every number of this review, from its foundation in 1828, contains an article from Carlyle, each of which fills, on the average, 50 pages in the *Collected Works*.

[2] e.g. 'The Dissolution of the Monasteries', 1857, 40 pages. 'The Philosophy of Catholicism' appeared in the *Leader*, 1851. The famous articles on Biblical Criticism (*Fraser*, 1863, 1864) fill 80 pages of *Short Studies*.

if he had known what was coming he would have had no part
in the magazine. Lockhart had transferred his scorpion pen
to London and the *Quarterly*;[1] and even Christopher North
had softened somewhat. A sarcastic article on Bulwer by
Landor was actually *rejected* as too severe. The stock
writers were men like Alison, who discoursed on Commerce,
Finance, Figures, Currency, Afghanistan, or Population; the
sound lawyer Lord Neaves; the mild Mallalieu; and, of course,
Christopher North with his *Noctes Ambrosianae.* To these
came De Quincey, with his *Revolt of the Tartars* (1837), *Kant,
Dr. Parr,* the *Essenes, Rhetoric,* and *Casuistry,* all first-rate,
and all long. Yet Blackwood told their author, 'Your two
pages appear like the twenty-four of anyone else';[2] and
White, another contributor, cried, 'What a miracle that
little wretch De Quincey is!' All De Quincey's unpunctuality
and uncertainty could not weary Blackwood, or prevent
him from dragging from him article after article, however
abstruse and learned; and apparently the readers lapped
them up with eagerness.

There were, needless to say, lighter features. In 1839
Samuel Warren burst on the world with his amazingly
popular *Ten Thousand a Year*—'worth', according to the
opinion of *Maga,* 'all that Dickens had ever written', and
worth still more in its author's estimation. The vanity of
Warren, indeed, might have provided Isaac Disraeli with
another volume on the eccentricities of authors.[3] When
Maga omitted his 'great election scene', he wrote that Pol-
lock and Thesiger both said that not a tittle should be lost
to posterity. Of his novel *Now and Then,* which Blackwood
contrived to avoid publishing in the magazine, he wrote,
'You might speak of the simple-minded earnestness with
which an established writer like myself has devoted all his
energies on behalf of the cause of Christianity.'

Equally successful were Michael Scott's *Tom Cringle's Log*
and *Cruise of the Midge,* which Blackwood published, despite

---

[1] He ceased to contribute in 1829.

[2] Mrs. Oliphant, *William Blackwood and his Sons,* 1897, i. 424. This book
gives a full history of the magazine.

[3] *Ten Thousand a Year* was anonymous. Warren was eternally referring to
it in conversation, and mischievous friends, who well knew its authorship,
delighted to depreciate it and watch his discomfiture. It is a tribute (perhaps
to the taste of other publishers, but certainly to Blackwood's eye for a sale)
that the book was rejected everywhere before he accepted it.

Scott's terrible handwriting. 'Search out of your pande-monium', said Scott, 'some Champollion of a devil, skilful and patient enough to decypher my hieroglyphics.'[1] These two admirable stories, which rivalled Marryat in contemporary vogue, show Blackwood's flair for merit of a rare kind. Nor less does his acceptance of Bulwer's *Caxtons*, in which that versatile writer struck out a quite new line. Blackwood accepted it, though anonymous, and paid Bulwer £25 a sheet, as well as £1,000 for the complete work. Bulwer, in his usual style, repaid him with a compliment on the 'pyramidal massiveness' of the magazine.[2]

All editors make mistakes; and, clear-sighted as Black-wood was, he, too, sometimes saw wrong. He can hardly be blamed for rejecting Branwell Brontë's voluminous contri-bution, with its passionate appeal 'to condemn, if he must, at least not unheard'; but it was a grievous error to refuse Thackeray's offer to contribute a kind of 'Roundabout Papers'. Possibly politics may have had something to do with it;[3] for *Maga*, then as now, was the monthly hope of stern and unbending Tories, whose ideas were well repre-sented by Alison's naïve remark that William Napier (whose *Peninsular War* he reviewed) '*admitted* that he was a Whig'. When, however, an author was once accepted, Blackwood stuck to him. He retained Warren, though he hated his 'beastly names'; Gleig, whose *Subaltern* came out in 1826, was still contributing sixty years later; Maginn, who quar-relled with everybody, could not wear out the generosity of Blackwood. Reduced, as so often, almost to his last six-pence, he sent his wife to the firm with a set of short tales. 'I gave her ten pounds for them,' wrote Alexander. 'She said she had a school-bill for £25 yet unpaid. Like a fool, I changed the cheque to that amount. She had orders not to leave without some tin.'[4]

Of other writers a word must suffice: Aytoun, whose *Firmilian*[5] appeared in these pages; 'Ingoldsby' Barham,

---

[1] Oliphant, ii. 42. [2] ii. 406.

[3] *Tait's Magazine*, founded in 1832 by an Edinburgh publisher, was Whig in principle, but non-political where literature was concerned. It welcomed in 1834 the Tory De Quincey's *Sketches from the Autobiography of an Opium-Eater*, which ran to thirty numbers, and even *A Tory's Account of Toryism* (1835). (Masson, *De Quincey*, 91.) For some time *Tait* was a powerful rival to *Blackwood*. [4] Oliphant, ii. 286.

[5] Not, as often supposed, the *Lays of the Cavaliers*, nor the *Bon Gaultier Ballads*.

who contributed a wretched serial entitled *My Cousin
Nicholas*, in which the reader will seek in vain for Ingoldsby
wit; the Rev. John Eagles, who, as the 'Sketcher', tried to
combine amusement with instruction in his articles on Art
and Nature; John Sterling; Frederick Hardman, a Mezzo-
fanti who, over the strange signature the 'Amicus of P.', sent
in translations from a score of languages; Mrs. Gore, who
was introduced by Warren, and wrote light pieces from time
to time; Margaret Oliphant, whose *Katie Stewart* appeared
in the magazine, and who in consequence was known as
Katie for years afterwards; and, above all, George Eliot, the
story of whose relations with *Maga* is too well known to need
repetition.[1]

Those who have seen the series of volumes entitled *Tales
from Blackwood* will often be inclined to think that the pages
of *Maga* needed the enlivening given by Alison and Gleig.
Duller stories are hard to imagine. Whatever may be
thought of the long novels, the short stories are, as a rule,
vastly inferior to those poured out to-day in hundreds. It
would appear that true short stories are a later discovery.
One thing is certain, that the art of making them really
'short' was then unknown. With hardly an exception, they
are far too long: explanation takes the place of suggestion,
and dissertation that of simple narrative. Yet they were
certainly popular, and 'took well' both in the magazine and
when republished.

§ 15. THE *ATHENAEUM*

Last, but far from least, among these journals, stands the
clarum et venerabile nomen of the *Athenaeum*—in some respects perhaps the most notable literary achievement of the
Victorian age, and one certainly not surpassed, in its kind,
by any journal of our own.[2] Founded in 1828 by the
eccentric Silk Buckingham, it passed for a moment into the
hands of Frederick Maurice and his friends,[3] but failed so

---

[1] *Scenes of Clerical Life*, 1857; *Brother Jacob* and the *Lifted Veil* later.

[2] For the history of the *Athenaeum* see *John Francis, a Literary Chronicle
of Fifty Years*, by John Collins Francis, 1888. Also the Centenary Number,
1928, with articles by Edmund Blunden and John Randall. To Mr. Randall,
who served the paper for more than fifty years, the present writer is specially
indebted.

[3] It was in Maurice's time that Tennyson's prize-poem *Timbuctoo* was reviewed, and his coming greatness confidently predicted (1829).

sadly under their too delicate care that £80 or £100 was considered a fair price for the property. In 1830, however, Wentworth Dilke became editor and part-proprietor, and showed the same ability which was afterwards to rescue the *Daily News* from a similar plight. With calculated daring he reduced the price from eightpence to fourpence.[1] Dilke's wide knowledge, critical acumen, and business skill were all needed, and all applied. He did not himself write much,[2] but he collected a band of able writers, and watched their work. After an experiment in the lighter style of literature—he inserted some very humorous, but not very illuminating, criticism by Hood, and prose and verse by Lamb—Dilke realized that his public demanded more solid fare, and gave the paper that character which it so long retained. The reviews were to be thorough and fair; brilliancy was to be made subordinate to accuracy, and the readers were to be taught that a statement in the *Athenaeum* was as reliable as a Government report.

In 1831 an advertisement for 'a young man of activity and intelligence' brought John Francis, aged twenty, into the office. In a month or two Francis became business-manager and Dilke's right-hand man, as well as his close personal friend. He continued to serve the paper for fifty years, and the Francis family, for nearly a century, was almost synonymous with the *Athenaeum*. Under Dilke and Francis the paper immediately gained the highest of all reputations—that of honesty; and may almost be said to have been the first literary paper to have made honesty its aim. The *Literary Gazette*, at first its only rival, was certainly not above puffing its own clientele and flattering those whose influence was worth cultivating. 'I could do much', wrote its editor Jerdan to Canning in 1827, 'to modify opinions, heat friends, and cool enemies. I am on terms of intimacy with forty-nine out of fifty of those who direct the leading journals, and I can from time to time oblige them all.' The implication was, 'Help me, and I will help you'. It was not easy for a Radical author to get a good review from *Blackwood* or the *Quarterly*; and, on the other hand, authors had been accustomed to

---

[1] 'Mercy on us!' wrote John Hamilton Reynolds, 'after the cost of writers, printing, duty, and paper, what in the name of the practical part of a farthing remains to report upon as profit?' *Francis*, i. xxiv.

[2] The famous *Papers of a Critic*, with their elucidation of the Pope–Curll quarrel, were only in part contributed to the *Athenaeum*.

expect laudation from their own set. If an author handed his work over to a publisher, it was the business of the publisher to secure a favourable review: nor were the Colburns and the Teggs unskilful in the art of delivering the required goods. This it was which Macaulay had in mind when, in the year 1830, he attacked Robert Montgomery, in an article inspired less by contempt for the unhappy poet than by hatred of the system which had brought him notoriety; and this it was that the *Athenaeum* refused to countenance. Despite obloquy, it maintained its principles on grounds both of morality and of utility. Publishers, it said, might suffer by the censure of a bad book; but the praise of a good book, when known to be sincere, would more than compensate them. Right or wrong, the judgements of the *Athenaeum* were not to be bought; nor was the public slow to recognize their character. To us, many of them may appear woefully ponderous; but we, as well as contemporary readers, can perceive their honesty. One marked feature, which often excuses their length, is their habit of quoting largely from the book reviewed. Whether they praised or blamed, they gave full samples of the wares.

It would, however, be a great mistake to imagine that the *Athenaeum* was exclusively literary. A perusal of a single volume is almost sufficient to put a careful reader abreast of the whole intellectual and aesthetic life of the time. The paper, in fact, sometimes undertook too much. In 1846, W. J. Thoms, under the pseudonym of Ambrose Merton, began a series of articles on popular antiquities, to which he gave the now-famous name *Folk-Lore*: 'it was', he said, 'more a lore than a literature.' This series led to so much correspondence that Dilke suggested to Thoms that a journal should be founded to deal specially with such topics. The result was that remarkable publication *Notes and Queries*.[1] Similarly, in the early days of the paper, much attention was paid to the state of the poor and other social questions; but it was found necessary to curtail the treatment of such subjects, which, indeed, almost entirely drop out after a few years.

To illustrate the wide range covered by the *Athenaeum*, it may perhaps be worth while to take a glance at a few numbers of the year 1851, when Dilke had given up the

[1] First number, Nov. 3, 1849.

editorship to T. K. Hervey, but still occasionally contributed, and when the character of the paper was fully established. In one respect, however, this year is an unfavourable specimen; for it was a year of singularly low mortality among authors, and the journal is therefore less rich than usual in those obituary notices which make it, as a rule, almost a complete biographical history of contemporary literature.

We observe at once the small print, the severe and almost repellent aspect, the three-columned page, with which we are so familiar. Four pages of advertisement open the number, and four close it. On May 17, we find three and a half pages, by Dilke,[1] of a review of 'Walpole and Mason'; liberal quotations in still smaller print give the reader, if he has a 'microscopic eye', a chance of judging for himself. A shorter, but still long, review of an *Histoire des Journaux* follows, by Madame de Peyronnet. Then comes a very full account of the Great Exhibition by Hepworth Dixon, supplemented by H. F. Chorley's criticism of the music in the Crystal Palace. A column or two of 'Weekly Gossip', mainly by Dixon, and musical notes, again by Chorley, conclude the paper.[2]

On May 24, Bulwer's *Not so Bad as we Seem* is reviewed by Heraud, Miss Martineau's *History of the Peace* by Madden, and the *House of the Seven Gables* by Chorley, in a very lengthy and laudatory article. On June 7, five columns by Marston are devoted to *Casa Guidi Windows*, the extracts amounting to more than a hundred lines. Turner's *Domestic Architecture* is dealt with by Cunningham, and again there are many quotations. Babbage on the Great Exhibition falls to Hepworth Dixon; but the most interesting columns are those containing long scientific notices, on the Royal, the Geographical, and other societies.

On June 28, Gladstone's translation of Farini's *Roman State from 1815 to 1850* is severely trounced by Masson; E. Lankester reviews Hooker's Science; the 'Weekly Gossip', to which Hervey, Dixon, Payne, Collier, and others, supply paragraphs, fills a column and a half; but the chief feature

---

[1] All the articles are unsigned; but manuscript editorial notes, in a copy preserved in the office of the *New Statesman and Nation*, often give the names of the contributors.

[2] Music, at this time, is generally discussed by Chorley. Later, much work of the kind was done by that great scholar Ebenezer Prout.

is a full report of the British Association meeting—one mathematical lecture being actually illustrated with diagrams.

There is, in fact, hardly any topic omitted that can by any possibility interest the man of cultivated mind. One omission, however, is noteworthy. Speaking of Dr. Achilli's 'revelations' of Romish intrigue, the *Athenaeum* remarks, 'The theme is entirely one of sectarian strife and bitterness, and therefore unsuited to the calm world in which we live and labour.'

It is plain, not only that the *Athenaeum* provided sound stuff, but that it had no lack of readers willing to give the pains requisite for its enjoyment. To judge by the stamp returns, the circulation steadily grew. In 1851 the paper required 128,000 stamps; in 1852, 140,000; in 1853, 147,000.[1] When, in 1861, the paper duty was removed, the price was lowered to threepence, and the circulation further increased.[2]

§ 16. THE RELIGIOUS PRESS

If not a consequence, yet a sequel, of the reduction of the duties, was the appearance of a host of religious, or at least denominational, publications. Not, of course, that there had not been something of the kind before. Wesley, as so often, had led the way. His *Arminian Magazine*, edited by himself, started in 1778:[3] its lineal descendant, the *Wesleyan Methodist Magazine*, which still exists, appeared under its new name in 1822, and was read by thousands monthly.[4] The Nonconformist *Eclectic Review* began in 1803, and was, in 1830, under the editorship of the bookseller and hymn-writer Josiah Conder,[5] who contributed many of his own hymns to its columns. The poet James Montgomery assisted

---

[1] Francis, ii. 384. It must be noted that the *Athenaeum* was not a 'stamped' paper: the stamps were required only for postage. It was issued both weekly and monthly; the stamps therefore represent only a part of the actual circulation.

[2] In the seventies the proprietor made a clear profit of £7,200 a year.

[3] It was the curious religious anecdotes and biographies in this magazine that roused the wrath of Sydney Smith. 'The circulation is so enormous', says he, 'that it cannot but be an object of curiosity and importance.' (*Essays*, 'Ingram on Methodism', 1807.)

[4] A magazine for children, *Early Days* (in which were many biographies of youthful prodigies of sanctity), and one for their elders, the *Christian Miscellany and Family Visitor*, as well as *Missionary Notices*, issued from the same source.

[5] Conder also produced the *Patriot*, which had some vogue. He died in 1855, and his periodicals only just survived him.

him with a monthly prose article. The circulation was about 3,000. According to the Tory Blackwood, there was much 'black bigotry and cant in its pages'; but, he adds, sadly, 'all Dissenting works have many readers'.[1] The Congregationalist *World* dates from 1826. The Quakers were particularly prolific. The *British Friend*, a monthly paper, was started in 1843, and just reached the Psalmist's span of life. The *Friend*, another monthly,[2] began in the same year. The *Annual Monitor* ran from 1813 to 1920. Till 1842 it was an obituary and calendar, with some literary additions. From 1843 it was almost entirely an obituary list of Friends, with biographies of the more prominent characters; but, though the Friends have always been remarkable for the exactitude of statistical information about their members, they, unlike the Methodists, have not been given to writing elaborate lives of the saints.[3] No learned quarterly was issued till our period had expired.

The famous *Record*, the somewhat dubious organ of the Evangelical party in the Church of England, dates from 1828. Students of the ecclesiastical history of the time will recall the impartial vigour with which this paper struck out right and left, attacking equally the Tractarian Pusey[4] and the Liberal Robertson of Brighton.[5] On the other side, the *British Critic*,[6] which had been in existence since 1814, escaping from the benumbing hands of Dr. Nares,[7] came under the control of Newman, and naturally defended the Oxford views. When Newman retired, the editorship fell into the hands of Thomas Mozley,[8] who walked in Newman's steps, *sed non passibus aequis*.

[1] Oliphant, *William Blackwood and his Sons*, i. 499.   [2] Since 1892 a weekly.

[3] These are only a few of the Victorian Quaker periodicals. I owe this paragraph to Mr. J. L. Nickalls, Librarian of the Friends' House, Euston Road.

[4] It joined Pusey, however, in his assault on Colenso.

[5] See Stopford Brooke's *Robertson* for an account of the relations between the *Record* and the great preacher. The *Life of Maurice*, also, shows how virulently another great Liberal leader was attacked by this paper.

[6] A review, and an ambitious one, rather than a magazine.

[7] So well known from Macaulay's review of Burleigh: a voluminous seventeenth-century writer born a hundred years after his due time.

[8] See *Reminiscences*, ii. 207. In chap. cvii Mozley gives an account of his own contributions. When, in 1843, he resigned, Rivington dropped the paper and brought out the *Christian Remembrancer* (*Rem.* ii. 394), to which very able men contributed. Readers of Acton will remember that Döllinger was much struck with James Mozley's article on Luther, and with Church's on Dante, and, on a visit to Oxford in 1851, asked to be introduced to the authors (*History of Freedom*, p. 403).

No sooner was the stamp reduced than publishers realized that religion, if cheap enough, is popular. In 1843 appeared the *English Churchman*, the aim of which was to counteract the influence of the *Record*. Three years later the *Guardian* was established—Gladstone himself being one of the chief promoters—the general lines of which, despite the alterations of emphasis which time inevitably brings about, have remained much the same throughout its long and distinguished career. Then, as now, the *Guardian* was the spokesman of a moderate and liberal-minded High Anglicanism, of which—to single out one name from scores—the illustrious Dean Church is perhaps the best representative. But other religious organizations were not behindhand; indeed, in certain cases, they led the way. The Unitarian *Christian Teacher*, under the editorship of J. R. Beard, G. Buckland, and others, started in 1835. In 1839 J. H. Thom became editor; and when the journal ceased (in 1844), Thom became one of the editors of its successor, the *Prospective Review* (1845), of which, during the ten years of its existence, the chief pillar was the great philosopher James Martineau.[1] Martineau was further assisted by J. J. Tayler and C. Wicksteed. Among the contributors was Walter Bagehot.[2]

Meanwhile, at the opposite pole of religious belief, the Roman Catholics were bestirring themselves. The first number of the *Tablet* is dated May 16, 1840. Its editor was Frederick Lucas, a man of high character and ability, who, though a convert to Catholicism from Quakerism, showed none of the usual over-zeal of converts. His liberality, indeed, did not suit his associates, and he resigned,[3] to set up the *True Tablet* in opposition to the old. Strange to say, he was completely victorious; the new paper eclipsed its rival, and he went back to the *Tablet*—or rather, the *Tablet* came back to him.[4] On January 1, 1843, he resumed the editorship, enlarged the paper, and re-started it on the career which has since proved so successful.[5]

[1] Readers of F. W. Newman's *Phases of Faith* (edn. 1881, chap. ix) will remember the friendly controversy between the *Prospective* and Newman with reference to that book.

[2] The article on *Oxford* appeared in Aug. 1852; that on (Henry Rogers's) *Bishop Butler* in Oct. 1854.

[3] Feb. 26, 1842.   [4] See *Life of Frederick Lucas*, i. 74.

[5] A too brief mention must suffice for the *Rambler* and the *Home and Foreign Review*, both illustrious for their connexion with Newman, Acton, and Simpson; and both short-lived, for they did not suit the views of the dominant

The name of Edward Miall is historic. Along with George Dixon of Birmingham, he led the Parliamentary Dissenting opposition to the Education Act of 1870, and drew from Gladstone the passionate exclamation, 'If he cannot give us his support, in God's name let him take it elsewhere.' The words were remembered: Nonconformist support *was* withdrawn, and the result was the Liberal defeat of 1874. But Miall was no less powerful as a journalist than as a Parliamentarian. Thirty years before this, on April 14, 1841, he brought out the *Nonconformist*, the purpose of which, in his own words, was 'to show that a national establishment of religion was vicious in its constitution, philosophically, politically, and religiously; to bring under public notice the innumerable evils of which it is the parent; to arouse men from the fatal apathy with which they regard it'.

The *Nonconformist*, in fact, though not neglecting denominational news, was mainly a paper of political propaganda: it was an anticipation of that 'Society for the Liberation of Religion from State Patronage and Control' which, under Carvell Williams, exercised such a powerful influence in the seventies and eighties. On general politics it endeavoured to be impartial, 'asking nothing more from the State than protection'; but it was, of course, inevitable that, despite its quarrel with the Erastian Whigs, its tendency should be mainly Liberal.

It is well known that for a long time the Methodists refused to regard themselves as Dissenters. In many places, indeed, till a late date in our period, they took care to hold their services at times which did not interfere with those of the Church, and considered their ministers rather as supplementing the 'defective' work of Church clergymen than as opposing it. Politically, the majority, at least of their leaders, were Tory; and, as Bamford and others tell us, Reformers were exasperated by their indifference to social improvement. Rayner Stephens [1] was expelled for taking part in the Chartist agitation; and, while ex-Presidents appeared without scruple on Tory platforms, ministers were censured for supporting Liberal candidates. A main secret

Ultramontane party. See Ward, *Life of Newman*, and *History of Freedom*, Introduction, p. xiii. A short account of them is given by Dean Inge in *Outspoken Essays*, Series I. At the opposite pole was the *Inquirer*, not unlike the *Prospective*; associated with the name of Bagehot.

[1] Brother of the author of *Runic Monuments*.

of the terrible schisms which rent the denomination from 1820 to 1850 was the quarrel between the growing Radicalism of the rank and file and the Toryism of the chiefs. The *Watchman*, established in 1835, during the full flood of the controversy with Dr. Warren,[1] was the organ of the Tory school; and, when the still more bitter contest of 1849 arose, distinguished itself by the virulence of its attacks on the malcontents. The hatred was reciprocated. When it finally perished (its place being supplied by the *Methodist Recorder* —founded 1861—) a father remarked at breakfast, 'The *Watchman* is dead.' 'Has it gone to heaven?' asked one of his children. 'Certainly not,' replied he. He had been one of its victims. Politically, also, the *Watchman* failed to represent the rapidly growing Radicalism of the pew, a large proportion of which seceded in the early fifties to found the United Methodist Free Church.[2] The one point on which it agreed with these seceders was its opposition to free education for Roman Catholics. On the Ten Hours Bill and the Repeal of the Corn Laws it observed a significant neutrality. It is worth mentioning that the *Nonconformist*, following the lead of John Bright, actually opposed the Ten Hours Bill;[3] and the *Leeds Mercury*, which voiced the Nonconformist politics of the north, was strong on the same side.

Much might be said, did space permit, of other religious periodicals: the *Jewish Chronicle* (founded in 1841), the *Saturday Magazine*, which was started under the aegis of the Society for Promoting Christian Knowledge, and many others. The *Church Times*, the organ of extreme High Anglicanism, did not begin its career till 1863, and had hardly established its position before our period ends. A word may, however, be said about the religious quarterlies, of which the *British* is perhaps the most typical.[4] This, founded in 1845, was edited by Dr. Robert Vaughan,[5] and afterwards by Dr. Allon, the well-known pastor of Islington. In accordance with the tradition of the time, the articles

[1] Father of the author of *Ten Thousand a Year*.

[2] Among the seceders were the father of Lord Justice Cozens-Hardy; the father of H. W. Massingham, the famous editor of the *Daily News* and *The Nation*; and Jonathan Couch, the eminent naturalist, grandfather of 'Q'.

[3] See Hammond, *Age of the Chartists*, 289. 'The Nonconformist clergy befriended the poor against the landowner; the Church clergy befriended the poor against the manufacturer.'

[4] See Albert Peel, *Letters to a Victorian Editor* (Dr. Allon), p. 4 sq.

[5] Assisted by H. R. Reynolds.

were at first lengthy and wearisome—at least to our generation; but they did much to remove from Nonconformity the reproach of want of learning. Among the contributors were —*mirabile dictu*—Mortimer Collins, and, less surprisingly, the great Hebraist Ginsburg, whose review of the *Speaker's Commentary*, though cautiously orthodox, was hardly less severe than some of Driver's later criticisms. The *London Quarterly*, the erudite organ of the Methodists, started a little later (1853), and exhibits similar features—length and learning in the articles, and a marked theological tendency. These reviews, like almost all others, if they have survived, have become, if not less learned, much brighter and briefer: the space of three articles of the fifties is now occupied by ten.

But man cannot live on serious things alone. Even in Paradise our sober first parents demanded mirth, which the elephant clumsily, but cheerfully, provided; and even the most 'serious' Victorian houses had their respectably humorous books and journals. Chambers's publications were often not only instructive, but 'amusing', in the present sense of the word. At about the same time as the *Guardian* was being started for Churchmen and the *Watchman* for Wesleyans, papers intended to be specially humorous were beginning to appear. Within six months five of these papers burst on the world, most of which, for one reason or another, failed quickly. Of these the most important were *Figaro in London*, conducted by Gilbert à Beckett and Henry Mayhew, and *Punch in London*, edited by Douglas Jerrold. The *Figaro*, which contrived to live about a year, was a small quarto of four pages for a penny. Its illustrations, like its jokes, were, judged by modern standards, very poor; but it added some theatrical criticisms, which seem to have raised the average of its articles.

§ 17. *PUNCH*

But all these soon faded out of sight and mind. The one which alone interests the present generation is, of course, *Punch*.[1] This first appeared, under the editorship of Mark Lemon, who had the assistance of Henry Mayhew, on July 17, 1841. Like its predecessors, it had at first great difficulty in surviving, and its earliest real success dates from the appear-

---

[1] On *Punch* see M. H. Spielmann's *History*, G. S. Layard's *Shirley Brooks*, and the various accounts of Mark Lemon, Thackeray, Tenniel, Leech, &c.

ance of a poem which was not comic at all. 'The Song of the Shirt' had been sent in vain to several editors; Hood finally dispatched it to *Punch*, with the injunction that, if not accepted, it should be thrown into the waste-paper basket. After some hesitation, it was received, and came out on December 16, 1843, to take the world by storm and to lift the paper out of the rut. It was, of course, not merely the merits of the poem, great as they were, which explained its popularity. The state of the poor was then occupying the thoughts of all. The Ten Hours Bill was looming on the near horizon;[1] and Mrs. Browning's 'Cry of the Children' had come out a short time before,[2] to create a sensation no less deep and widespread than the Song itself. But whatever the cause of Hood's success, the effect on *Punch* was immediate; and the paper had now been taken into the capable hands of Bradbury and Evans, who put it on a sound business foundation. The change is well illustrated by the fact that Lemon, who started at 30s. a week, was soon receiving £1,500 a year.

Punch was not a paper within the meaning of the Stamp Act, and was able to provide its readers with twelve pages, much more closely printed than to-day, though on worse paper, for threepence. It soon gathered round it a set of writers and artists whose initials or names are to be seen carved on the famous table; but many of whom are still more permanently enrolled in the lists of fame. Tom Taylor, John Leech, John Tenniel, Douglas Jerrold, and, above all, Thackeray, are but a few whose names are thus inscribed. It was, indeed, Thackeray's *Book of Snobs* and Jerrold's *Mrs. Caudle* which maintained, and even increased, the repute secured by Hood; and Leech's pictures, monuments of humour and draughtsmanship, are still unsurpassed in their kind.

But probably the greatest hit made by the paper was the adoption, in 1851, of Shirley Brooks as a regular contributor and, finally, on the death of Mark Lemon in 1870, as editor. Brooks was a practised journalist; he had worked on the *Argus*, on *Ainsworth's Magazine* (the short-lived periodical in which Ainsworth and Cruikshank, having quarrelled with Bentley, collaborated without much success), on the *Era*,

---

[1] Passed, Mar. 1847, after a struggle of several years.
[2] *Blackwood's Magazine*, Aug. 1843; republished in *Poems*, 1844.

Bentley, the *Morning Chronicle*, and the *Illustrated London News*. But it was in the *Man in the Moon* [1] that he made his mark, by a satirical set of verses against *Punch*. When Lemon saw these, he played Henry VII with the Earl of Kildare. 'That young man is formidable. He must be sought as an ally.' Accordingly, he took him on to the staff; and very soon Brooks became the editor's right-hand man. He was, as Layard says, 'suggester-in-chief': nine out of every ten of the proposals for the 'Big Cut'—the central political cartoon, which is still the main feature of the paper—were made by him and accepted—including that for Tenniel's famous 'British Lion's Vengeance on the Bengal Tiger'. Whenever Lemon took a holiday, Brooks carried on his work, and in his spirit.

Of Brooks's own contributions, prose and verse, it is difficult for the present age to judge with fairness. His style of wit is not ours; his incessant puns, his verbal parodies (very different from Sir Owen Seaman's 'criticism by travesty'), and his social satire, are to us wearisome and ineffective. His burlesque of Campbell's *Last Man*:

> Five bottles must at least go round,
> The sixth be nearly dry,
> Before this mortal shall assume
> His inebriety;

his rhyme of 'Phlegethon' with 'eggeth on'; his 'she fetched him a slight refresher with the flat of her wooden spade'; his 'Mr. and Mrs. Naggleton', with its laboured satire of a quarrelsome man and wife, do not satisfy a more critical generation. But they exactly satisfied the generation for which they were written.[2] It was still the age of Theodore Hook and Albert Smith; the age in which that true poet Tom Hood had to make his living by pouring out endless paronomasias. The public, though it would not have Shirley Brooks's novels, liked him as a journalist, and looked for his pieces week by week; nor is it easy to exaggerate the influence he had upon the paper's circulation and popularity.[3]

---

[1] First number, Jan. 1, 1847.

[2] How they satisfied a man of that generation, well above the average, may be seen in Edmund Yates's *Reminiscences*.

[3] The poorness of the humour of the forties may perhaps be partly explained by the narrowness of the range within which humour was permitted to play. So many subjects were taboo that humorists who wished to be 'safe' were almost driven to punning. But this will not account for the want of

Almost from the beginning *Punch* ventured on the perilous paths of politics, not merely in the 'Essence of Parliament' (in which Brooks bore a great part) and in the 'Big Cut', but in the text of the paper. Thus, as is well known, it had its word to say on the Prince Consort's candidature for the Chancellorship of Cambridge University, and, indeed, voiced the Prince's unpopularity at every turn. Brooks, in verse of doubtful merit, supported the cause of the Deceased Wife's Sister; but he was not always on so Liberal a side. Most dangerous of all, however, were the paper's utterances, both verbal and pictorial, on foreign affairs. The most celebrated of all—'General Février turns traitor'—published on the death of Nicholas I, strikes most people now as in very bad taste; and to-day we know too much about the atrocities on both sides in the Indian Mutiny to admire unreservedly even the 'British Lion and the Bengal Tiger'. But worst of all was *Punch's* attitude during the American Civil War. Scorn and hatred were poured out for years on both the contending sides, on Lincoln and on Beauregard, on slave-owners and Abolitionists. Brooks, though a hater of slavery, was one of the chief offenders.

> Rule Slaveownia, Slaveownia rules, and raves,
> Christians ever, ever, ever shall be slaves,

was his doggerel attack on the South, while to the North, in the hour of difficulty, he wrote:

> And having whipped the rebels for a twelvemonth and a day,
> We nearly found them liquoring in Washington in May.

Not even *The Times* did more to embitter relations between England and America than did these stupid, and far from comic, lucubrations. It is pleasing to think that *Punch* repented. When Lincoln died, not only was Britannia pictured as mourning by his death-bed, but Tom Taylor [1] wrote a set of verses of recantation which, it is said, did much

---

finish in the light verse. It is amazing that, with Praed before them, the majority of writers of such verse are rough, clumsy, and usually dull. 'Poet Bunn', rhyming for the opera, was hardly worse than some of the most frequent contributors to *Punch*. Yet *Lyra Elegantiarum* was published in 1867.

[1] The verses were long ascribed to Brooks; but Layard proved their true authorship. Brooks, as a matter of fact, disliked them (as did Leigh and Tenniel). Layard, p. 245.

to avert a war in which South and North might have joined
against us.

> Yes, he had lived to shame me from my sneer,
> To lame my pencil, and confute my pen—
> To make me own this king of princes peer,
> This rail-splitter a true-born king of men.

There can, however, be little doubt that, on the whole,
Punch expressed the political views of its constituency. At
first strongly Radical (Thackeray called himself a Republican, but no Chartist), it gradually tended to give utterance
to the ideas of the middle classes, and by the end of our
period was perhaps, as Justin M'Carthy remarked, moderate
Liberal or Conservative of the Left.

Of other comic papers of the time there is little need
to speak. To the *Comic Times* Edmund Yates and Lewis
Carroll contributed; in 1856 Yates started the *Train*, known
to-day as the vehicle of some more of Carroll's quaintnesses.
Fun, founded in 1861, was later to be made famous by Gilbert's *Bab Ballads*; but in the sixties it was of the second or
third rank. The *Owl*, because only the gods loved it, died
young. It was loftily satirical: written by men of fashion,
who took no payment. The profits were spent on a weekly
dinner of extraordinary excellence; and these profits became a cause of embarrassment, for they very soon were
large enough to have feasted all Mayfair.[1]

§ 18. THE ALBUM

There is another class of publication which, though not
intentionally humorous, has probably given as much
amusement, to later and more frivolous generations, as
Punch itself; and which may therefore appropriately be
touched on here. All whose memory goes back forty or fifty
years will remember the Album, which, reposing in state on
the 'whatnot', was reverentially taken down and presented
to the more eminent friends of the family, that they might
contribute to its variously coloured pages a drawing, a poem,
original or borrowed, a daguerreotype, or, at the very least,
a 'sentiment'. These albums are still preserved in many
families as curiosities, and often throw a vivid light on the
prevailing tastes of the time. Here may be found consolatory

---

[1] See Trevelyan, *Ladies in Parliament*, p. 80. Despite the dinners, the paper
died, apparently of starvation, after a very few years.

texts, favourite verses from Mrs. Hemans, Mrs. Sigourney, Eliza Cook, Charles Mackay, portraits of eminent divines, sketches, decorations, mimicries of Martin or Doré. The custom was old: we know, for example, that Cowper wrote in the album of Patty More, and professed thus to secure the immortality which the *Task* could not give him.[1] It was but a step from the manuscript to the printed volume; and it became, in the early nineteenth century, the fashion for gilded aristocrats to publish their 'effusions' in daintily bound and illustrated annuals, admirably adapted for Christmas presents. The format of these works has sometimes saved them from destruction, and many an old-fashioned library contains a copy of one of them, jostling Gibbon or Hallam in strange propinquity. The *Book of Beauty* is still to be seen on drawing-room tables in out-of-the-way places, and remains a manual of the fashions of 1824. Of them all, the *Keepsake*, which Lady Blessington edited from 1841 to 1849, is the best known: the list of its contributors is like an abridged Debrett. In 1832 two countesses, nine lords, five honourables, two baronets, three M.P.s, and an archdeacon, made up the noble company. High-born as they were, they did not disdain remuneration, which appears to have been liberal.[2]

But *Friendship's Offering* will long be remembered as the incongruous birth-place of Macaulay's *Armada*;[3] and the *Tribute*,[4] to which Tennyson contributed the exquisite verses which were the germ of *Maud*, is still more deserving of fame.

[1]   In vain to live from age to age
      While other bards endeavour,
      I write my name in Patty's page,
      And gain my point for ever.
In one of these old manuscript albums I have seen a choice quotation from Hannah More's *Cœlebs in Search of a Wife*.

[2] See an article in *The Times*, Oct. 6, 1931, where there is an account of the efforts made by Wordsworth to get a place for Maria Jewsbury among the *Keepsake* contributors. 'The *Keepsake* can afford to pay better than any other of these annuals,' says Wordsworth. See also Wingfield Stratford, *Victorian Tragedy*, p. 87. For the 1843 number wrote Lady Blessington herself, Lady Hastings, the Baroness de Calabrella, Monckton Milnes, Lord John Manners, and Bernal Osborne, the society and parliamentary wit.

[3] 1833. See Trevelyan, p. 136, who quotes from the number some 'Lines on a Window that had been Frozen':
      Pellucid pane, this morn on thee
      My fancy shaped both tower and tree.

[4] 1837. The *Tribute* was not an annual. It was an isolated volume, published by Murray for the benefit of Edward Smedley. The contributors were

A superfine sentimentality is the mark of nearly all these performances—no more genuine, perhaps, than the rusticity of Marie Antoinette in the Trianon. Their survival may well have given to many a false idea of the prevailing ideas of the time. Imitators and dilettante versifiers do not always utter their real thoughts.

§ 19. BOOK PRODUCTION

The real value of these annuals, as of many other books which we need not name, lay in their bindings;[1] and it may be desirable at this point to touch briefly on this subject.[2] It was about this time that their bindings began to be textile —silk or satin—and to imitate, after their own style, the fashionable lady's dress. Thus the *Forget-me-Not*, 1823, appeared at first in boards, embossed like Wedgwood pottery; in 1832 it came out in silk. Similarly, the *Literary Souvenir*, in 1824, was bound in pink, green, or violet-patterned boards; in 1832 it donned silk. The *Keepsake*, from 1828 to 1845, was in red watered silk; from 1845 to 1848 it was cloth; and, whereas L.E.L.'s *Drawing-Room Scrap-Book* was either full morocco or else grained cloth gilt, the *Book of Beauty*, after some years of leather, became, in 1839, dark-blue satin. It is clear, as Mr. Sadleir remarks,[3] that the majority of these bindings must have been intended rather for beauty than for durability. Such annuals as have survived, as curiosities in private houses, are usually those that happened to be bound in more lasting materials, and have thus, perhaps, conveyed a deceptive idea of their general character.

It must be borne in mind that until about 1840 the binding of the books was no regular part of the publisher's business.[4]

an illustrious band: Wordsworth, Landor, Aubrey de Vere, Henry Taylor, Southey, Milnes, and others. (Smedley died before the book was published, and the profits went to his family.)

[1] And in their steel engravings.

[2] See Sadleir, *Evolution of Publishers' Binding Styles* (1730–1900), 1930: an admirable work, from which most of the material of this section is derived.

[3] We are apt to forget the ordinary books of the time, in which the covers were often fastened to the spines with caoutchouc or not very good paste. As these rotted or weakened, the books fell to pieces. Again, the cutting of the edges, then almost universal, sometimes spoilt the margins, or even intruded on the text. Especially would this happen when the books were 'repaired'. Thus, while the 'Roger Paynes' have remained, the cheaper-bound books have often either vanished or come down to us in a deceptive condition. A good, brief account of all this is given by Harrison in his little manual, *The Book-Binding Craft and Industry*.

[4] On this see an article in *Times Literary Supplement*, Mar. 10, 1932.

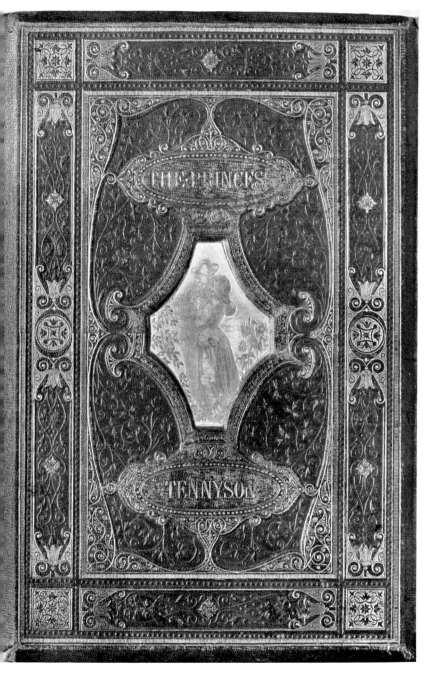

BOOK-BINDING, *c.* 1852

The slow process which, beginning in the eighteenth century, gradually concentrated several businesses in his hands, was not yet concluded. 'The binding phase lagged behind its fellows in the movement to centralized control.'[1] The publisher's care, except in special cases like these annuals, stopped when the book was printed. Books were purchased from him by the wholesale dealers in sheets, not in volumes; of course, at a discount.[2] Thus, in 1834, Longmans purchased 451 copies of the *Last Days of Pompeii*, five days before the official date of publication, at a special sheet-price of 21s. 3d.: of course, undertaking the binding, and selling the bound copies at a profit. The actual publisher might himself bind the presentation-copies; otherwise he left the work to others. In the rush to get a new novel to the libraries, speculative distributors would buy in a hurry, bind in haste, and sometimes repent at leisure. This explains the great variety of material, colours, and labels in which the same book may often be found to-day.

As the publisher took over the binding himself, the speculative purchaser, of course, found his occupation gone. This change happened to coincide with improved methods of binding and lettering which enabled cloth and boards to compete with leather. Hitherto, such bindings had been crude, and the reverse of lasting; but the invention of *graining*, by which smooth fabrics could be roughened or patterned in many styles, brought a complete revolution. Graining allowed the too obvious thread-marks to be concealed, and thus banished an unpopular feature of the old book-cloth. The first forms of graining were, after the usual British conservative manner, advertised as morocco-cloth, or appeared as imitation leather; but very soon they came out undisguised, and the victory over leather, or the textile dress-style, was practically complete.

In 1832, in Murray's complete edition of Byron, begins the custom of gold-printing actually *on the cloth itself*: a recent invention, which speedily put an end to the paper-label;[3] and about this time we find, though rarely, the publisher's name stamped in gold at the bottom of the book's spine. *Our*

---

[1] Sadleir, pp. 33, 34.

[2] Mr. Sadleir mentions a rate of '706 counting as 729': doubtless this might vary according to quantity.

[3] Mr. Sadleir remarks that an Irish paper in 1840 notes with surprise this feature in an edition of Bulwer's novels; it was, therefore, still rare in Ireland.

Village came out in five parts, 1824 to 1832. On the first three parts are paper-labels; part iv is in boards, in labelled cloth, and in half-morocco; part v in cloth and half-morocco. So Mrs. Sherwood's *Henry Milner*'s first two parts are labelled, the last gold-lettered. Harriet Martineau's *Deerbrook*, 1839, is full diapered cloth, gold-lettered. Many books were singularly beautiful, with pictorial gold-blocking on the backs, sometimes even with illustrations taken from the book itself. Thus Saunders and Otley published, in 1837, *Peter Simple* and *Jacob Faithful* in exquisite format.

About 1849 a process of blocking in ink, instead of gold, was discovered. This enabled cheaper books to be published, especially such as aimed at a wide circulation. But, for gift-books and more expensive works generally, the years between 1840 and 1860 show increasing ornamentation: silk or vellum gives way to overlaid cloth, or paper on basic cloth, elaborately designed in gold and black. A slightly cheaper variety was the mottled or marbled cloth, or the canvas overlaid with marbled paper, which is seen in Mrs. Gore's *Castles in the Air*, 1847 (Bentley).[1]

Buckram, so common in the eighties and later, is not seen till 1860, and even then is rare.[2]

So soon as the publishers themselves took up binding, the custom of elaborately covering books for presentation purposes, or to satisfy the tastes of wealthy bibliophiles, developed rapidly. Books like Rogers's *Italy*, those on the *Language of Flowers*, Alaric Watts's *Cabinet of Art*, were very 'elegantly executed'. S. C. Hall's *Book of Gems* 'might also be had in a variety of Elegant Bindings, in which it was kept constantly on sale and for inspection'.[3] Volumes of Mrs. Hemans and Eliza Cook, with Birket Foster's illustrations, were very ornate. Mrs. Trollope's *Manners of the Americans*, a best-seller of the thirties, is in two forms: ordinary cloth with paper label, and a few copies with plates, on India paper, clad in full-tooled leather. Many readers must have seen copies of the *Christian Year* in very elaborate format, obviously meant for Christmas presents or as rewards for 'diligence and good conduct'. Publishers, in fact, knew

---

[1] This has a paper label. Mrs. Gore's *Progress and Prejudice*, 1851, is in black, bright blue, and ochre-marbled cloth, glazed and gold-lettered. Mr. Sadleir thinks this may be an importation from France.

[2] Sadleir, p. 67.   [3] Idem, p. 81.

BOOK-BINDING: QUEEN VICTORIA'S JOURNAL

well how to appeal to Saturnalian liberality. Many of the enormously popular religious biographies of the period may still be picked up, gilt-edged, gold-stamped, in ornamented cloth. Such a work is Catherine Marsh's *Life of Captain Hedley Vicars*, which was probably as often chosen for presentation, during some years, as any book ever written.[1]

There was, of course, a large trade of a second-hand kind. Should a work not succeed in being sold out, a dealer might obtain the remainder sheets at a very low price, bind them cheaply, and possibly secure for it a very considerable sale in this second, less sublime, state. He might combine the three volumes into one or two, or, retaining the conventional number, yet contrive to attract the poorer purchaser. Thus, Ainsworth's *Cardinal Pole* was issued by Chapman & Hall, in 1863, 'in brown grained cloth with a striking scroll-design in gold on the spine', with the publishers' names stamped in gold. Later, it appeared in green cloth, identically grained, but with the spine simplified, and without the publishers' names.[2]

Others were more shrewd. Tegg & Newman would buy from other publishers, but give no indication, even by omission, that the volumes were 'secondary'. A novel by a Mrs. Wallace, called the *King's Cope*, was published by Bentley in 1851, and speedily handed over to Parry & Company, who put on their own cases and printed cancel-titles, but carefully retained Bentley's name. They thus gave the public to understand that the novel had at least been *accepted* by one of the chief publishing firms of the day.[3] This kind of purchase must, it goes·without saying, be carefully distinguished from the sheet-purchasing of wholesalers, such as that of *Pompeii* by Longmans.

[1] A volume might easily be written on the vogue of Evangelical biographies in the first three-quarters of the nineteenth century. In proportion to population, probably, these works had a circulation the like of which has rarely been known. Legh Richmond's *Dairyman's Daughter* (1809) must have sold by the hundred thousand, and have had at least three readers for every copy. The biographies in the *Arminian Magazine* had a sale of 18,000 a month. Half a dozen lives of the Burmese missionary, Adoniram Judson, and his three wives, were published from 1848 onwards, and sold like Dickens's *Christmas Books*. The flood showed no sign of subsiding for many years. In the seventies, Hannah Whitall Smith's *Christian's Secret of a Happy Life* reached its three hundred and thirtieth thousand, and her 'Record' of her son Frank, gilt-edged, ornamented red cloth, admirably printed, cannot have fallen far behind the *Secret*. Books like these were bought, borrowed, lent, and presented in countless numbers.   [2] Sadleir, p. 88.   [3] Idem, p. 94.

To sum up our necessarily brief and inadequate account. Except in one very important point, the Press of 1860 was practically the Press of to-day; it had reached maturity, and was fulfilling its purpose. Its machinery might be a little less advanced; its 'stop-press' took minutes to function instead of seconds; cricket matches or fights were reported after longer intervals; and the circulations, even in proportion to population, were narrower. The art of illustration was then less far advanced; and people of importance or notoriety were not then pictured for the million. But the real power of the Press, within its range, was probably greater than now. No paper wields to-day, or in all likelihood will ever wield, the political influence of *The Times* under Barnes or Delane; and the kaleidoscopic changes of modern times prevent the great 'organs of opinion' from exercising much moral power. A subject is taken up, flaunted, and dropped for another. There is to-day less of the simple faith in the force of publicity than was held by Charles Reade or Jacob Omnium. Some would say that in the sixties the Press had not yet been found out; it had not been discovered that publicity can be purchased by judicious shouting. Be this as it may, the one great and real change which has taken place, and which might have been expected to increase the influence of the Press indefinitely, has, in actual fact, diminished it. There were in 1850 no huge syndicates, controlling armies of papers, and scattering over enormous areas the opinions of two or three great proprietors. For that very reason, it is likely that eighty years ago the papers were more thoroughly trusted. Partly, perhaps, because they were more subject to criticism from other papers, they were supposed, rightly or wrongly, to be more careful; and certainly the views expressed were less frequently discounted by the silent judgement, 'After all, these are only the ideas of Mr. So-and-so, transmitted through a hundred media'. The gradual abandonment of anonymity, also, has to a great extent lowered the prestige of the newspaper. What carried weight as the pronouncement of a great phantasm impresses less when given as the utterance of a single person. It is true that the public *interest* is attracted by seeing a well-known name at the head of an article; but its *convictions* are less likely to be affected. The ghost has put off its grave-clothes, and appears before the footlights as but an actor after all.

Again, the old papers, appealing to an audience passionately, for the most part, interested in politics, found it necessary to report debates with considerable fairness and fullness, and even, in the case of leading men, to reproduce their speeches almost verbatim. The papers took note of the politicians, and the politicians cultivated the papers. Today, the decline of interest in politics is at once a cause and an effect of the neglect of them in the more widely circulated organs. A statesman has them less in mind than formerly, and they, in turn, mark him less. Other species of notoriety are crowding him out—the film-actress, the cricketer, the boxer, and even the author; but as these classes grow more numerous, they occupy less and less proportionate space, flash for a moment on the public eye, and soon find again such bliss as there is in solitude.

Otherwise, however, a few obvious alterations or improvements apart, the Press of the twentieth century is that of the nineteenth. The leading articles are shorter, and less ponderous in style; editors chatter and no longer 'thunder'; more themes are discussed in more ephemeral fashion; but, generally, the papers, being expressions of a human nature that does not greatly change, remain in spirit and temper radically unaltered, unless it be slightly for the worse. Whether they will be able to contend with the radio, or whether they will disappear entirely with the advance of invention, lies in the lap of the most Puckish of the gods.

X

ART

X
ART

By A. PAUL OPPÉ

§ I. THE ARTISTS' WORLD

WITH an annual pilgrimage to the Academy—'the Exhibition' as it was universally called till 1851—the Englishman of the first half of the nineteenth century had done his duty by art. True, the fashionable folk who were invited to the Private View went there less for the pictures than to see, and be seen by, each other, and the middle-class families who paid their shillings were mainly attracted by the portraits, especially the miniatures, of their acquaintances and public characters, but the effort was made in the name of art, and it was a poor year in which no picture furnished some topic for discussion. In the provinces too, where annual exhibitions were still held and local artists still maintained an existence, the consignment of pictures from the Academy formed the principal attraction. Moreover, from 1837 the Royal Academy was housed in a portion of the public building in Trafalgar Square which, since 1869, has been devoted exclusively to the National Gallery. The opportunity of the Exhibition might be taken, say, once in ten years, to extend a visit to the small collection of old pictures which served, if contemporary accounts can be believed, mainly as a refuge for idle adults and infants from the unsavoury locality near which it had been placed.

It was not, however, chiefly in a literal sense that art in England meant the Royal Academy. Such dignity as living art possessed was owed to it. Even its sworn enemy, Haydon, was impressed with the truth of Collins's remark, 'If it were not for the Academy, artists would be treated like journeymen'. The Academy held from the King; its President had direct access to His Majesty; an Academician was created gentleman with the title of Esquire. Occasionally, even, the statesmen and noblemen who were the natural guardians both of the national conscience and of 'Taste' condescended to consult them. In a word the Royal Academy was Art.

Such prerogatives could not be left unchallenged. Since its very inception—and 1769 was, after all, not very long ago—some artists had disputed the predominance of the Academy. As it was the only visible source from which benefits might be hoped to flow, so the disappointed naturally came to identify it with the cause of all their sufferings.[1] In the Reformed Parliament something approaching a public attack reinforced the dissatisfied artists. The mere association with the Throne, the proposed accommodation, at public expense, under the same roof as the National Gallery, and the exclusive management of their own finances were sufficient ground for attack as 'privilege'. Neither the grievances of artists nor a benevolent desire to alleviate the condition of the lower classes by means of art could, by themselves, have moved Commons or public to action. There was, as yet, not enough money in art. There was, however, money in trade, and the deplorable condition into which all manufactures of decorative or 'fancy' character had fallen in the years following the Great War led the Radicals in the House of Commons under William Ewart, M.P., to demand and obtain in 1835 a Select Committee on Arts and Manufactures. To the main subject, 'the means by which a knowledge and taste for art might be extended among the people, especially the manufacturing classes', there was added an inquiry 'into the state of the higher branches of Art and the best mode of advancing them'. The greater part of the evidence taken related to the Royal Academy.

Some of the grievances aired before the Select Committee were vague or childish, others were mutually destructive. While the first witness, Dr. Waagen, was brought from Germany largely in order to denounce the stereotyping effect of the instruction given by all Academies, the ground

---

[1] *Select Committee on Arts and Manufactures, 1835*, ii. 726 and 727.

Mr. Ewart: What is your opinion of the state of the arts in this country?

Mr. Hurlstone: I consider in no nation that has attained so high a degree of prosperity and civilisation, and in which the elegancies of life are generally cultivated as England, are the superior departments of art in so low a state. The works which are produced I consider much below the taste of the higher classes of society, especially since the Continent has been opened, and they have become acquainted with the noble works of the different Italian schools.

Mr. Ewart: To what do you attribute the inferiority of art in England?

Mr. Hurlstone: I consider the Royal Academy the principal if not the sole cause; as at present constituted, it exercises an unbounded and most depressing influence on art.

BURLINGTON HOUSE, 1855

of the attack on the Academy's own school was that so little
instruction was given in it. The Academicians were accused
of usurping all private patronage and at the same time
of employing it solely for commissions for portraits; but,
except for Haydon and Martin, the only instances quoted
of unjustifiable exclusion from Academic rank were Devis,
Harlow, Hayter, Behnes, and Carew, all of whom, except
perhaps the last named, depended just as much as the
Academicians upon the art of fashionable portraiture. Nor,
a generation later when, in changed circumstances, another
Committee inquired into the Academy, was it possible to
add greatly to the list of exclusions. Apart from Watts,
who had never entered his name as a candidate, and Holman
Hunt, who had withdrawn his, the one outstanding name
was that of Linnell. Grave personal defects were the original
reason of his exclusion. As Lord Taunton said in evidence,
the grounds for passing over were, almost invariably,
either known opposition to the Academy's principles or
some great fault of temper. On the other hand, the weak
and useless members whom the Academy inevitably included
did not owe their election to the votes of their like alone.
Constable was among Linnell's most determined opponents,
and it was he who said that the election of Solomon Hart
reflected glory on the Academy. Nor were the weaker
members its chief supporters. Turner's persistent championship is well known, while Constable, whose own election
had been long delayed because of the preference, in accordance with the original charter of the Academy, for figure
painting over landscape, wrote with regard to the Committee of 1835, 'the country, ignorant and ungrateful as it
is in all liberal matters, does not deserve the Academy'.

Apart from election, it was impossible for the Academy
to satisfy every one. With the limited space available at
Trafalgar Square for showing pictures, the only alternatives
open to the Council were wholesale exclusion or overcrowding and bad hanging. The Academy chose the latter,
with the result that flagrant cases of unjustifiable rejection
were remarkably few. Complaints of bad hanging relate
chiefly to very large or very small works which were almost
inevitably debarred from the 'line'[1] to which a somewhat

[1] The 'line' was a ledge running round the galleries at a height of some $7\frac{1}{2}$
feet from the ground. A picture was said to be 'on the line' when the top of its

superstitious importance was attached. No doubt it was
unduly usurped by the R.A.s and A.R.A.s; but *ex hypothesi*
they were the best painters, and occasions were quoted in
which the hangers removed their own pictures in order to
give good places to outsiders' works. In one year (1844)
the experiment was tried of displacing, towards the end
of the exhibition, some of the Academicians' pictures for
works which had proved in the course of the exhibition
to deserve better treatment than had been originally given
to them.

Whatever faults there may have been in English Art at
that date, illiberality on the part of the Academy cannot
be held accountable for them. The R.A. were far too anxious
to secure all available talent to reject anything that seemed
to them to hold promise. It is often represented that the
Pre-Raphaelites of 1849 had to fight their way against
Academic opposition. The charge was not made at the time.
Certainly the press and the public gradually came to attack
them, for reasons which will be examined below, but at most
they were opposed only by 'some of the artists'.[1] Both
in 1849 and in 1850 Millais's and Holman Hunt's large canvasses were hung to their satisfaction; they were even
placed as pendants to each other so that they might absorb

frame reached this ledge. Except in the West Room nothing was allowed to
break it either from below or above. Very large pictures and life-size portraits
even when by R.A.s, were excluded from this position; they were hung tilted
on the ledge. Leslie, *Inner Life of the R.A.*, p. 78, points out that this enabled
them to be seen from the proper distance on a crowded day. According to his
account small pictures sometimes filled spaces left between a larger picture
and the ledge; otherwise they were placed on the floor or near the ceiling
where, as Dicky Doyle, aged fifteen, pointed out in 1840, critics loved to find
them and make them the object of an attack on the R.A. (*Journal*, p. 54).

[1] 'Pre-Raphaelitism in Art and Literature,' *British Quarterly Review*, No. 31
August 1852. This article, which can safely be attributed to Patmore, is the
earliest considered account of the original movement. It has been wholly
ignored, perhaps because it was not sufficiently whole-hearted to satisfy at the
time, or because the appearance at this date of a long and favourable notice in
an important review was inconsistent with the legend of hostility and neglect.
The quotations from Macaulay and Kingsley given by Holman Hunt (*Pre
Raphaelitism*, i. 252) as representing general opinion at this time really date
from 1857. The idea of persecution is largely due to Ruskin, whose absurd
assertion in the Edinburgh Lectures (1853), 'Their fellow students hiss them
whenever they enter the room', may—unless indeed it gave rise to the whole
story—be a garbled reference to the hisses which were said by Holman Hunt
to be evoked by hostile references to the P.R.B. in an Academy lecture and
were interpreted by him in 1886 (*Contemp. Review*, p. 488) as directed against
'us', but later (*Pre-Raphaelitism*, l.c.) as against the lecturer!

EAST ROOME.

Yᴱ EXHYBITYON AT Yᴱ ROYAL ACADEMYᴱ.

the interest of a whole wall.[1] Nor were the R.A.s content to leave the pictures to make their own impression. It was Dyce, R.A., who dragged the reluctant Ruskin to Millais's 'Carpenter's Shop' in 1850, and tried in vain to overcome his horror of its Puseyite ugliness. It was Egg, not even R.A., but an Associate, of thirty-four (not in 'later years' as the legend[2] has it), and therefore all the more likely to be influenced by jealousy, who sold Hunt's 'Rienzi' for him and with Dyce secured him other work and commissions. Nor were they alone. From other sources a long list can be put together of the R.A.s who were friendly to the young painters, Mulready, Maclise, Leslie, Herbert, Ward, Cope, Redgrave and perhaps Creswick. It was not the original Pre-Raphaelite Brotherhood who were ill used by the R.A., but their imitators of the second generation, after 1856, when the manner had become fashionable and a cloak for incompetence. At this time, too, when real novelties were making their appearance, they could meet with the same generous welcome. Whistler's first exhibited picture, the 'At the Piano' of 1860, was not only hung on the line, but was bought, straight off, by a member of the hanging Committee, John Phillip. In rejecting some of his subsequent pictures the Academy shared their obscurantism with the Salon.[3]

The tolerant attitude of the Academy was at least as much responsible for the invariable failure of other periodic exhibitions, except those in water-colour, as the old rule which excluded members of other societies from election

[1] They were just above the line in 1849 (Hunt, *Pre-Raphaelitism*, i. 177) and half on the line (*P.R.B. Diary*, p. 273) in the West Room in 1850. The first complaint concerned Hunt's 'Valentine' of 1851, which, however, was hung in 'much the same position' as his 'Rienzi' of 1849 (*P.R.B. Diary*, p. 297). Hunt himself nullifies his grievance by adding that his picture was unsupported in colour (*Pre-Raphaelitism*, i. 248). The R.A. could not again give him Millais's as pendants since they were smaller and—*hinc illae lacrimae*—already 'on the line'. Its peculiarly virulent colour no doubt also explains the hanging in 1855 of Millais's 'Rescue', which caused such tumult that it was eventually lowered some three feet (*Memoir of T. Seddon*, p. 145 n.).

[2] *Tate Gallery Catalogue, 1929, s.v.* Egg. Previous editions show that these are the incidents to which reference is made.

[3] When, in 1863, Holman Hunt organized at the Cosmopolitan Club, as an object-lesson to the Committee then sitting, a select exhibition of pictures rejected by the Academy, no one seems to have been much impressed. The surprise expressed by Whistler to Henry Holiday (*Reminiscences*, p. 96) that his picture should have been rejected was, perhaps, less complimentary to the artist than to the Council of the R.A.

to their body. Water-colours had never been exhibited to advantage at the R.A. and it was generally believed that an artist in that medium could not be admitted to membership. The two societies for their exhibition, known as the Old Water Colour Society, and the New, were even more strictly limited in constitution than the Academy, and admitted nothing but the works of members and associates; but as they were purely private bodies and their premises were not provided by the Crown, their exclusiveness could not be challenged on the pretext of public interest. Their exhibitions were held at the same time as the Academy's and with similar pomp. Their public, if more limited, was also more select. Thackeray notes the invariable presence of bishops and pretty girls. On the other hand, the two established exhibitions of oil paintings, those of the Society of British Artists in Suffolk Street and of the British Institution in Pall Mall,[1] whatever their original objects, had ceased to possess any characteristic feature except the prevalence of landscape. Various attempts were made to revivify the former, especially under the Presidency of Hurlstone, a capable painter and an ex-gold-medallist of the Academy Schools, but they had no success. Scarcely a good word was ever spoken of it. Lord Northwick advised David Roberts to discontinue exhibiting there; 'insufferably bad' is *Punch*'s short comment on it in 1846, and Thackeray more than once speaks of its rooms as a desert. The exhibition of modern works at the British Institution was held from February when other exhibitions were closed, and existed mainly as an overflow or auxiliary for the Academy.

---

[1] The British Institution, with exhibitions of old and modern pictures and a system of premiums and purchases, was established by a committee of patrons for the encouragement of High Art. On the other hand, the Society of British Artists was founded by the artists themselves under the leadership of Heaphy if not precisely for the purposes of Low Art, at any rate for the exercise of greater realism than was supposed to be favoured by the Academy. Premiums and purchases were discontinued at the B.I. and the noblemen and gentlemen who conducted the exhibition without the aid of artists left all the arrangements to the keeper, one of the brothers Seguier, who was accused of sacrificing the interests of the artists to those of a framemaker (W. B. Scott, *Autobiography*, i. 109). At any rate the hanging was consistently criticized. At Suffolk Street the Committee were accused of hanging outsiders badly in order to force them into the Society, while the fine which was imposed upon any member who attempted to join any other body—designed, of course, to prevent secession to the R.A.—deterred artists of any ambition from becoming or remaining members.

When pictures which had already been shown there were excluded in 1844, the exhibition was said to lose all interest. As, further, the conditions of exhibition at these two galleries were no more acceptable to artists than those of the Academy, a third was established in 1847, with somewhat more liberal intentions. It persisted for some fifteen years, first as the Free Exhibition, and then as the National Institution or Portland Gallery, but it appears merely to have duplicated the Society of British Artists in its character and expired, almost unnoticed, in 1861.[1]

Opportunities for seeing pictures otherwise than at the annual exhibitions of new works increased largely with the century. The Spring Exhibition of Old Masters at the British Institution was an old-established event of the Season, and both public and directors were much more interested in it than in their exhibition of new work. The arrangements made for copying were especially welcome to artists in early days while the National Gallery remained in embryo and every restriction was placed in the way of studying pictures in private or royal collections. In 1848, the year of the formation of the Pre-Raphaelite Brotherhood, a room was devoted to early Flemish and Italian pictures, including the Wilton diptych. In the summer of that year the Prince Consort arranged for the public exhibition at Kensington Palace of the important collection of early paintings belonging to the Prince Ottingen-Wallerstein. In 1851 Lord Ward's collection, also largely of early paintings, which was exhibited free at the Egyptian Hall, was visited by 50,000 persons, at a rate of 500 a day. Comprehensive exhibitions of the work of Mulready and Etty were organized by the Society of Arts in 1848 and 1849, but the public response was said to be insufficient to justify proceeding with a projected third exhibition of Turner next year.[2]

---

[1] This gallery seems to have been the outcome of a movement, noticed by Bell Scott (*Autobiog.*, i. 110), in 1839, for an exhibition controlled by artists with equal rights. The first exhibition, held at the Egyptian Hall in 1847, was a failure. Next year it opened as the Free Exhibition, in premises at Hyde Park Corner. Members and others secured hanging space by paying for it, and elected their Committee. It was also partly 'free' in another sense of the word, for no charge was made for admission during the last six weeks. 'Manufactures' as well as pictures were welcome. The move in 1850 to Regent Street caused a secession, but as the National Institution it lasted there till 1861. Here as in Suffolk Street the prevalence of landscape was noted.

[2] From 1850 there were Winter exhibitions of Sketches in Pall Mall, at first

Occasionally an enterprising artist would make an exhibition of his own work. As a rule, such exhibitions were of a series of paintings, generally water-colours, held by the dealer or publisher who had commissioned them for the illustration of a particular work. So, too, single pictures were publicly shown by dealers or as a speculation by the artist: most often also with the object of securing orders for forthcoming engravings. Subjects of sacred, royal, or sensational interest were most commonly chosen and, as now, after the exhibition in London the pictures were taken on tour in the provinces. Enormous profits are quoted from the days of Haydon's first successful ventures to Holman Hunt's 'Christ in the Temple', which was said to have brought in as much as £4,000 in shillings when it was shown at the German Gallery in 1860. In the same year Frith sold for £750 the exhibiting rights of the 'Railway Station'. Such independent exhibitions were, however, still looked upon with some disfavour. It was regarded as an artist's duty to make the Academy as attractive as possible. In 1865 opposition to the candidature of Madox Brown at the Garrick Club was attributed to the prejudice against men who had held 'one man' shows.

Though even as late as 1863 some optimists still hoped for a chartered republic of artists with free and equal elections to councils and conclaves, it was evident as early as 1835 that the only practicable alternative to the Academy was State control of art, with official exhibitions on the French model. Haydon, though a Tory at heart, was driven to advocate this alternative, but he had few adherents. The nation had been slow to form even a National Gallery and, when forced by benefactors to acquire a nucleus, were slower to house it in the more or less adequate building which was commonly likened to a gin-shop. Even then[1] such additions as were made by purchase, on whatever authority, invariably failed to give satisfaction. In 1831

at private risk, afterwards at a dealer's. Shortly afterwards there was an annual show of French pictures. An exhibiting Society of Sculptors was formed in 1852 and of 'Female Artists' in 1857, while there were Amateur exhibitions, generally for charity, from 1849. For the provinces the Art Treasures Exhibition at Manchester in 1857 was of immense importance.

[1] The history of the National Gallery is conveniently summarized in *The Making of the National Gallery, 1824 to 1924*, by Sir Charles Holmes and C. H. Collins Baker, 1924.

THE VILLAGE CHOIR—*WEBSTER*

Lawrence's unrivalled collection of Old Master drawings was offered to the State at almost a nominal price. 'Si vous n'achetez pas ces choses-là vous êtes des barbares,' said Talleyrand, who happened to be present when a selection was being shown to Lord Brougham. The offer was not accepted. Nor were the Government without support in their barbarity. In the intelligent opinion of the time the State had more serious things to do than to trouble itself about art. Private munificence could be relied upon to fill the National Gallery with the world's best pictures and if it did not, the private owners would lend their pictures (with a liberality unknown in other countries) to the British Institution. The argument of economy was always powerful. Sir Martin Shee pointed out to the Radicals on the 1835 Committee that if the Academy were dispossessed or seriously affected, the State would be obliged to maintain their schools, if they wished instruction to continue at all. Of course, the Academy itself was utterly opposed to State control. When the Government proposed to provide a new site and building for the Academy in order to devote the whole of the premises in Trafalgar Square to the National Gallery, there was opposition from certain Academicians on the ground that such parliamentary aid would involve State control. At the best, the various committees and commissions of taste had shown what blunders could be performed by State nominees however eminent in other walks of life, and with or without artists as assessors; at the worst, as Joseph Hume put it to Haydon, if the State had anything to do with art, the result would be a *job*.[1]

None the less the State was forced to intervene, if in the interests of Trade and not of Art, and their efforts to encourage the one without touching the other led to interminable trouble. Anticipating the Select Committee's report, the Government founded a School of Design in Somerset House, whence the Academy were migrating, and shortly afterwards announced grants to provincial schools with similar aims. The first years of the main institution were very chequered, the battle raging, among other things, around the always vexed question whether instruction in

---

[1] Haydon gives the remark also to Lord Grey. Possibly it was made by both. Lord Melbourne said to him, 'God help the Minister who meddles with art' (*Correspondence*, ii. 344, 359, 388).

design could be divorced from that in art. Originally, students in London and the provinces were compelled to sign a declaration that they did not aim at being artists. The crucial point was the drawing of the figure, for which Haydon had been the protagonist. In the inevitable desire of the State to steer clear of artistic instruction, he divined the jealousy of the portrait-painting clique at the Academy. Equally inevitably art teaching and the figure won. In the provinces the embargo on the intending artist seems always to have been a dead letter; in London the need for teachers in the provincial schools secured the customary compromise when, after the great excitement of the 1851 Exhibition, the Department of Science and Art, both with an industrial purpose, was established at South Kensington.

Disaster compelled the State to intervene in another direction. In 1832 the Houses of Parliament were burnt down, and when plans for the new building were ready the question of its decoration inevitably arose. The 1835 Committee recommended public commissions for important works and instanced this as an obvious opportunity. A Select Committee was accordingly appointed in 1841, and afterwards a Royal Commission, with the newly arrived Prince Consort in the chair. It is clear from Question and Answer alike that both the Committee and the witnesses believed themselves to be assisting at the birth of a spirit of art which would extend far beyond the mere decoration of the walls at Westminster and penetrate into every artistic trade and handicraft in every corner of the land. Their enthusiasm was shared by the artists who had long craved for big public commissions and was reflected even upon the public. Every one had by this time heard of the great works recently executed in Germany. There was, therefore, a national rivalry behind the enterprise. There was also, as later in the Battle of the Styles, a clear issue to determine. People could take sides between 'Fresco' and 'Oil'. By 1842 a writer in *Blackwood's* wrote that there had never been such interest in the arts in England. During the eight weeks of the exhibition of cartoons in Westminster Hall, arranged in 1843 by the Royal Commission, at least half a million persons were admitted.[1]

[1] Lady Eastlake, *Memoir of Sir C. Eastlake*, pp. 173 sqq., says that the attendance was between twenty and thirty thousand a day. A fee of one shilling

The activities of the Commission have been viewed in the distorting light of the disappointment and recrimination that attended its close after the death of its mainstay, the Prince Consort. It has been blamed for not acting at once and for putting off the commissions for competition after competition. It is forgotten that, at the outset, four years were expected to pass before the walls would be ready for decoration; nor could artists be called upon to execute actual designs before they knew the position in which their works would be placed. It was also recognized from the first that a school of designers would have to be trained before a commission for all time was undertaken. However that may be, the work dragged on for years. Some of the frescoes were already faded to invisibility before the work was hurriedly wound up, and the two chief monuments, Maclise's battle pictures, completed, in 1864. Even these were said by great admirers to have aroused little interest and, though the competitions exercised indirectly a very great influence on the art of the country and brought out a number of young and untried men, the effect of the final decorations on the public was little or nothing. The immensely improved market for cabinet pictures during the period when the frescoes were being painted removed all incentive from the majority of painters for undertaking large mural works, while, as London was not a medieval city state nor even a German principality, the walls of a public building did not provide nearly so effective a method of popularization as did engraving.

Royal patronage provided the natural compromise between State encouragement of art and total absence of public support. For the Academy itself this was much more valuable. In 1830, before the attacks by the Radicals had been fully opened, Sir Martin Shee restored the right of direct access to Majesty which had been allowed to lapse during a period of merely internal conflict. Henceforth the Throne afforded protection both against the would-be nationalizers and against the Philistines. In Radical eyes, on the other hand, royal patronage of the arts was a doubtful advantage. The pages of *Punch*, even after 1850, contain frequent charges that the royal acts of condescension

was charged during the first fortnight and on Saturdays; admission was free for the remainder of the time.

to artists amounted to insult. The interest of the Prince Consort in the arts was regarded as more becoming to the ruler of a petty German principality than to the head of an important nation. His painting-room was an object of ridicule, and his appointment to the Chairmanship of the Royal Commission of 1841 was regarded rather as a convenient method for distracting his attention from more essential matters than as a concession to the importance of the arts.[1]

The artists, on the other hand, who came into contact with the Prince appreciated his genuine interest in painting, notwithstanding a habit of indicating possible improvements in their work with some pointed instrument which he carried in his pocket. The decoration in fresco of the Summer House at Buckingham Palace, in 1843, was a move towards the popularization of the new manner.[2] Though he expressed his surprise at the expense of art in this country, he was content after the first years to pay the current price when he made purchases at the Academy and elsewhere. Among other active steps in the interests of the National Gallery, some of which again incurred the displeasure of *Punch*, he prepared and laid before the Select Committee of 1853 on the National Gallery, a scheme for a comprehensive historical collection and had a detailed catalogue drawn up to show at a glance the shortcomings of the collection. In the same year the Royal Speech at the Opening of Parliament contained a reference to schemes for the further encouragement of the arts and sciences which were, no doubt, closer to the heart of Royalty than of the Cabinet. Probably the Crimean War was the reason why nothing came of them.

Royal taste, although, in general, properly conservative, could show signs of unconventionality. At the new Water Colour Society in 1852 the Prince advocated white mounts instead of gold. So far from being shocked at an exhibition

[1] As soon as his Commission set to work there were rumours that he intended to import German artists. On Oct. 4, 1841, Lord Melbourne reported to the Queen Chantrey's strong expression of feeling in the matter, and when in answer to her disclaimers he told her of courteous Sir George Hayter's opposite opinion, it was to administer a sweetmeat after the medicine had acted.

[2] In 1847 he commissioned from Dyce a fresco of Neptune for Osborne, and they hatched out between them the design of illustrating the Arthurian legend as the national saga (*Art Journal*, 1860, p. 296).

THE SUFFERING HUSBAND—*EGG*

of Mulrcady's nude studies in 1853 at an Art School where
the Directors were warned against letting her see them, the
Queen openly admired them and even wished to buy one.
In 1850, when Millais's 'Carpenter's Shop' was denounced
in the press, the Pre-Raphaelite Brotherhood were told
that the Queen, who could not make her customary visit
to the Academy, had it sent to her at Windsor. The cause
of her absence, the birth of the Duke of Connaught, is a sure
sign that her interest was not aroused by abuse in print,
but by private, probably the Prince Consort's, praise of
the picture. Though he was a leader in the growing fashion
for the earlier painters, the Prince could scarcely have out-
raged a section of public opinion by directly patronizing
young men who had given such offence. He had to wait
for the universally applauded 'Cimabue' of Leighton (1855).
It looks, however, as though he attempted to help them
indirectly. In the year after the appearance of the 'Carpenter's Shop' he was for the first and only time a guest at
the Academy Banquet, and as a reporter was present, also
for the first time, he took advantage of the opportunity
to make an impassioned plea for more sympathetic treatment by the press of artistic work offered for exhibition.
Art needed, he said, an atmosphere of encouragement and
appreciation. His reference to artists as tender plants
whose shoots were blasted by merciless and ignorant
criticism must have appeared very sentimental to the hard-
bitten Academicians, while the distinguished guests no doubt
reflected that neither H.R.H. nor the artists had been to
a public school.

The royal example had little power to stimulate the
upper classes to the patronage of art on a large scale;
moreover it came too late. Martin lamented to the Committee of 1835 the death of Lord de Tabley (1827) and
Sir George Beaumont (1829), as the extinction of the old
class of intelligent patron, who had acted on their own
judgement, independently of the Academy. Their number
had never been large, and Haydon perpetually inveighed
against the supineness of the nobility of England in the
cause of High Art. The traditions and accumulations that
they had inherited gave them as a rule neither taste nor
space for modern works; few could determine to sell their
old pictures in order to buy modern, as did the Duke of

1827, despite such unfavourable circumstances for a sale that Lawrence and Turner tried to stop it, English pictures seemed to be a good investment. Without any idea of speculation, the chief reason why men purchased pictures was, as his friend Fisher wrote to Constable, that others coveted them. They hung as trophies rather than for decoration. The walls of the principal collectors were covered with pictures from floor to ceiling in the same manner as the public, or the noblemen's, galleries.[1] When later, from about 1847, the great northern manufacturers appeared as buyers they used their pictures for the adornment of new and empty houses, and might display them better. They were, however, even more shy than the nobles of large decorative schemes. Watts, after painting a fresco in Lincoln's Inn without remuneration and failing to persuade (through Lord Elcho) the London and North-Western Railway to allow him to decorate the Great Hall of Euston Station, was forced to revive the plea that the Academy should initiate, and use its funds for, enterprises of such high character.

The patron of the older generation, nobleman or commoner, bought direct from the gallery or the artist. Picture-dealing was in the hands of somewhat mysterious experts and restorers who negotiated privately the sale of old masters, or of print-sellers who trusted that the success of a print would also lead to the profitable disposal of the original picture. The half amateur go-between persisted and figures largely in the dealings of the first Pre-Raphaelites, but at the same time increased sales and higher prices were converting the print-seller into a true picture-dealer,[2] with a constant stock and occasional or periodic public exhibitions. The dealer was needed both by the patron

[1] Even an artist, Collins, could write to his brother in 1816 not to trouble about the exact tint of his painting-room wall because he would cover it with sketches (*Memoir*, i. 97).

[2] The principal picture-dealers retained throughout the century much of their original print-dealing business. It helped to build their large fortunes. The Belgian Gambart, for example, who was originally an artist, was first employed in London in colouring prints for McLean in the Haymarket, but made enough money by peripatetic print-selling to set up galleries in London and ended, the envy of artists, as the proprietor of palaces in St. John's Wood, his native land, and the Riviera. He bought in 1859 the engraving rights of the 'Derby Day' for £1,500 and in the next year for £5,500 Holman Hunt's 'Christ in the Temple'.

and the artist. The business man from the north knew, for good or ill, what he liked, but where large sums of money were involved he was in the habit of consulting a reliable expert on market value. Naturally prices soared still higher with the entry of the professional dealers. They had enough capital to hold out for their own price, and their interest, both in the sale-room and in private negotiation, was entirely upon the side of a rising market. Competition among them was keen. A pretty picture is given of their clustering in 1859 on the Academy steps before its doors opened on the first day, in their eagerness to have first pick of the treasures within. The higher prices[1] soon benefited the artists, and

[1] Comparison of prices at different dates is difficult because account must be taken of the status of the artist, the size and character of the picture—in early days the ideal was always expensive if it was sold at all—and the inclusion, or otherwise, of engraving, and exhibition, rights. There was, however, certainly a great rise in the upper limit, culminating in 1860 with Frith's £5,250 for the 'Railway Station' and Hunt's £5,500 for the 'Christ in the Temple'. Wilkie's top price seems to have been 1,500 guineas for the immense 'Tippoo Sahib' (1838), but Frith frequently charged 3,000. He received that sum from the Queen in 1863 for the 'Marriage of the Prince of Wales' as against Leslie's 600 guineas in 1840 for his picture of the Coronation. The many statements regarding the increased prices obtained by young men (e.g. Bell Scott, *Autobiog.*, 1892, i. 110, says that they had increased tenfold during the preceding half-century) relate rather to frequency than to individual figures. Millais, aged 20, obtained £350 for the 'Carpenter's Shop' in 1850, but ten years earlier Goodall, aged 21, had sold his 'Marriage Feast' for £400, while ten years later Whistler accepted £30 for the 'At the Piano'. The striking thing is that the P.R.B. were furiously aggrieved when they did not sell at Millais's level, whereas ten or twenty years earlier established men were quite accustomed to remain unsold at even lower figures, and ten years later such prices were quite common. After the Bicknell sale, in 1863, a sensation was caused by the publication in the *Athenaeum* and elsewhere of the prices paid in the thirties and forties for the pictures, together with those realized at the sale. The comparison is the more significant both because Bicknell did not buy at bargain prices, but direct from the painters when they were already established, and because most of the artists were still living. Nine Turners bought from the artist for from 250 to 400 guineas each fetched from 500 to 2,510. On the other hand the 'Palestrina', for which Bicknell gave Turner 1,000 guineas in 1830, only reached 1,900. A picture by Landseer and Callcott, which cost about £450 in 1842, reached 2,950 guineas, and three by the former alone, bought from him in 1850 and 1859 for from 300 to 400 guineas, fetched from 1,800 to 2,300. Stanfield rose from 150 guineas in 1838 to 1,230 and from 700 to 2,550, a pair of Webster's from £161 10s. in 1841 to 1,600 guineas and another from 250 guineas in 1846 to 1,160. Leslie's 'Heiress' commissioned from him for £300 sold for 1,200 guineas, and several by David Roberts, Bicknell's son-in-law, bought from him between 1841 and 1850 for from £40 to 300 guineas reached from 260 to 1,370. Similarly in the water-colours the increase was by no means confined to Turner. Of the famous Swiss drawings of 1842 for which the artist asked the then exorbitant price of 80 guineas, the 'Blue Righi' fetched only 296 guineas, but the 'Lucerne' reached 700. The others (apart

even had the prices been lower, the quicker sales were a clear gain to them. Few could afford, like Turner, rooms in which to exhibit their earlier efforts in the hope of attracting a purchaser; moreover, even without his damp and dust the charms of the standing unsold are always slightly faded. Nor was direct patronage without its troubles. Misunderstandings about prices were constantly arising, even with the blue-blooded. Patrons had, too, an awkward habit of suggesting drastic changes. Sir W. Watkins Wynne would have bought Gibson's group of Hylas between Two Nymphs, Plate 74, if only the sculptor had been prepared to replace the central figure by a clock!

A successful effort to interest a still wider public in painting was made in 1837 with the establishment of the London Art Union. Such an enterprise had been recommended by the Select Committee in 1836, after hearing evidence concerning the success of those which had been established for many years in Germany and more recently in Scotland. In them the Committee chose and bought the prizes which were distributed among the subscribers by ballot. The London Art Union departed from the model in allowing the winners to buy for themselves to the amount of their prizes. This led in due course to charges of illegality serious enough to produce a Royal Commission in 1844, and to constant trouble with the Board of Trade; but the feature contributed largely to the Union's success. Beginning with five hundred or so members in 1837, the subscriptions reached their highest point, £17,871, in 1847, after which they declined and the numbers did not again reach approximately that level for more than ten years. By that time it had greatly lost its importance. The sales at the public

from four early Yorkshire drawings which Bicknell did not buy from the artist and for which Lord Hertford gave 1,970 guineas) bought at 40 guineas each reached from 108 to 200. Prout's rose from 6 and 8 guineas to from 70 to 90, two by David Roberts costing 20 guineas in 1833 and 1838 reached 250 and 410 guineas, while a series of Copley Fielding's for which Bicknell paid from 13 to 50 guineas (the 'Rivaulx' of 1830) brought from 260 to 600 and ended triumphantly with a 'Crowborough' which cost 25 guineas in 1838 and now sold for 760, far outstripping Turner. This and several more of the most highly priced drawings and pictures were bought by Lord Hertford, whose incursion into English art was, doubtless, largely responsible for the level of prices at this sale. (I am indebted to Mr. Peter Bicknell for the loan of the family's annotated copy of the catalogue from which apparently the original prices were obtained for the *Athenaeum* in 1863 and which is now enriched with a mass of press-cuttings and documents.)

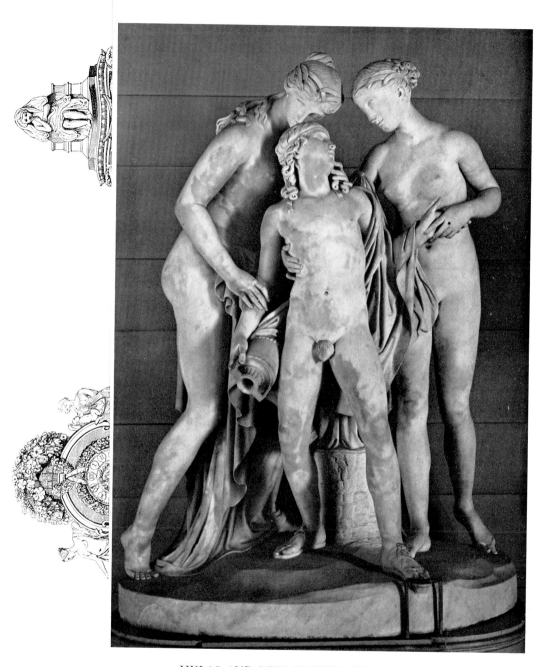

HYLAS AND THE WATER-NYMPHS—*GIBSON*

galleries had become so rapid that everything worth buying
was said to have been sold before the prizes were announced;
while, no doubt, the maintenance of the prizes at the same
low level prevented the winners from securing anything
desirable. Even in early days the more cultivated denounced
the Art Union for fostering the production of, and taste
for, small and bad pictures at low prices, but it was
obviously a real boon to the artists themselves during the
period when sales were few. Linnell's 'Journey to Emmaus'
was engraved and a prize in 1838, while Holman Hunt sold
two of his early pictures to Art Union winners. It also greatly
extended the purchasing public by introducing the possibility of possessing a 'real hand-painted picture' from the
walls of a public exhibition, to thousands of persons who
would otherwise never have dreamt of even asking the
price. Its success, too, bred imitation. Many of the provincial towns set up Art Unions of their own in connexion
with their annual exhibitions; and rivals arose even in the
metropolis.[1]

Another immediate effect of the London Art Union was
the success for the first time of a journal entirely devoted
to the Fine Arts. This was the *Art Union Monthly Journal*
founded by S. C. Hall in 1839. There had been monthly
journals before, but they were always short lived; nor,
according to Hall, did the new paper itself at first pay its
way, in spite of the greatly increasing interest in various
forms of art during its first decade. A rival, the *Probe*, which
also came out in 1839 in precisely the same format, but
in opposition to the Art Union, lasted no more than a year.
Hall himself said that nothing but his own public-spirited
devotion to the arts caused him to continue his journal,
but probably the members of the Art Union always provided
a steady support to the paper, while, even if they were
not directly connected, except in name, its assistance to
the major venture may not have been entirely disinterested.
However that may be, the paper was claimed to have a
subscription list of 15,000 in 1849 when, with no change

---

[1] The sporting spirit joined to free admission gave great interest to the
exhibitions of works purchased by the prize-winners which were held annually
by the London Art Union towards the end of the season. For three weeks these
exhibitions were open to subscribers and their friends, for the fourth to the
public generally. The number of admissions in 1841 was stated to amount to
75,000 and in 1842 to 100,000 (*A.U.J.*, 1842, pp. 109 and 241).

but in name, it became the *Art Journal*, which flourished for the rest of the century.

Certainly the artists needed periodicals of their own for the communication of the news that interested them and their direct public and for the consideration of their work in something of their own spirit. It is true that from 1830 to 1860 the magazines and quarterlies gave far more space to art than they did at the end of the century, and their articles contain the most mature thought of the time on matters of aesthetics, but they reflected the spirit of the enlightened amateur or the scholar, rather than that of the working artist or his immediate public. They were concerned largely with the old masters and tended to disparage the moderns in comparison with the ancients, or, as occasionally with Thackeray, to contrast England unfavourably with France and other foreign countries. On the other hand, the Daily Press had no compunction in treating an artist who dared to exhibit a picture as a malefactor obtruding an outrage upon the public. The tradition dated from the time of Pasquin and it is significant of the position of the arts that in their sphere the savagery of the eighteenth century continued for so long. In 1844 Thackeray notices an improvement, but Gilchrist, Etty's biographer, writing in 1855, is patently ironic in his contrast between the criticism of 1820 and that of his own day. Like the Members of Parliament when anything connected with the arts was debated, the newspaper readers merely wanted some malicious amusement on the few occasions when art was forced into their notice.

The newspaper critics were ill paid, and their employment was very casual. Even after 1860 Hamerton's duties on the *Saturday Review* were so slight and occasional that a couple of short visits to London from his home in France were enough for the performance of the whole year's work. They were generally supposed to be disappointed painters. Often they were casual friends or relations of the editor. Ill pay and hurry, quite apart from the innate difficulties of the task, would alone be some excuse for intemperate, effusive, and, occasionally, unintelligible language.[1] In

---

[1] *Punch* in 1845, i. 247, pillories a notice in the *Morning Post* of Herbert's 'Gregory and the Choristers' which spoke of the 'want of modulative melody in its colours' and the 'ungrammatical development of its general

dealing with the Academy especially, the writers had real ground for irritability. No doubt because of the consistent hostility of the Press towards them, the Academy had always refused to consider the interest of the critics. Though at any rate by 1840 some newspaper editors were invited to the private view, the R.A., unlike other exhibitions, held no proper Press-day. Even if the editor sent him to the private view instead of giving his ticket to his wife and daughters, the critic could have had no real opportunity of judging the pictures in the limited space and among the jostling crowd of society people. Nor had he reproductions upon which to revise his impressions or refresh his memory. His only chance was to gain some acquaintance with the works before their exhibition, and as this depended upon his friendship with the artist it led necessarily to charges of partiality. These might be only too well founded. Palgrave's official description of the Fine Arts at the Exhibition of 1862 had to be withdrawn because of his violent denunciation of Marocchetti in the interest of his friend (and incidentally his debtor), Thomas Woolner. Charges of venality were widely believed even against Tom Taylor, whose notices in *Punch* and *The Times* were outstanding for their liberality and general friendliness to the artists.

Naturally in these circumstances newspaper criticisms were neglected by the comparatively few who really cared for the arts, and ignored by the sensible artist. Constable allowed no newspapers in his house. Gibson found that the constant hostility to his work of the London Press had no influence on his patrons; on the contrary, a bad notice once brought him seven orders. Many artists were, however, so touchy that they regarded any word of criticism, almost any reservation, as an insult. For years Millais saw threats of ruin and evidence of conspiracy in every criticism of his exhibits. In a few weeks the alarm always subsided with the sale of his pictures at huge prices. His excitability on these occasions throws a strong retrospective light on the incidents attending the first attacks on the P.R.B. Even then the astute dealer, Farrer, pasted the hostile notices on the back of the 'Carpenter's Shop' when he bought it as a speculation. Throughout, the Academy, who

effect'. The critics' fondness for using the terms of another art was frequently noted.

were, on the whole, most abused by the newspapers, both as individuals and as a body, remained content that the Press was completely unrepresentative of public opinion.

If public opinion was neither guided nor followed by the Press, the only way in which it could manifest itself, except by occasional demonstrations, was through the purchase of engravings. Indeed, Thackeray in his paper of 1840, *The Artists*, in denouncing as servitude the old dependence on individual patronage, whether princely or private, declared that thanks to engravings, the great public had now become the painter's true patrons. Yet that public was still very limited. Thackeray himself, in his essay on *Caricature and Lithography in Paris*, of the same year, deplored the absence from the English middle-class house[1] of pictures of any sort except an occasional portrait, and contrasted it with the frequency of prints on French walls. In 1843 Cunningham[2] notes that publishers were shy of venturing on large prints of a good class. The publishers who embarked upon them set themselves up, and were flattered (or ridiculed), as benefactors, after the manner of Boydell in the eighteenth century. There were many instances of failure, towards which, it was complained, the large royalties exacted by the most popular artists contributed. No doubt the publisher recouped himself by exploiting the unknown and struggling. For them, apart from the immediate cash, reproduction by engraving, whether for an independent publication or for the adornment of an 'Annual' or a 'Keepsake', provided the only way of keeping their names before the public. It is impossible to over-estimate the effect on the artist, both in choice of subject and in treatment, of catering for a large, uninstructed public through a speculative publisher.

---

[1] Bulwer, *England and the English*, 1833, ii. 206, appears to say the opposite, but he is explicitly speaking of the gentry and the lesser nobles, whose houses were filled at the expense of much the same class on the Continent. Thackeray's contrast is corroborated by Pye, the engraver, who in his evidence before the Committee of 1835 attributes the difference to the excise duty on glass, which made it about eight times dearer than it was in France. The duty was only removed in 1845.

[2] *Wilkie*, iii. 267. The idea that Turner owed his large fortune principally to the sale of engravings is part of the legend that his later pictures were neglected; in fact, as is shown by the lists in Mr. Bell's *Exhibited Works by J. M. W. Turner*, even in the last twenty years of his life he sold considerably more of his exhibited oils than he retained.

The mere processes of reproduction had also a powerful influence on the painters' technique. Many pictures, as for example Martin's and Landseer's, can almost be regarded as a mere stage in the production or publication of a popular print. Steel engraving, rendered, about 1840, cheaper and more lasting by electrotyping, favoured elaborate nicety of execution and helped to turn the painter from broad effects of light and dark to refinements of detail and minute accidents. Wood engraving, too, was used at first for dainty vignettes and pretty detail. Later, perhaps under German influence, it was modified to emphasize line and broad pattern. Prints also formed the painter's taste, especially in early youth, when, unless born in a studio, his opportunities of seeing original pictures or copies would be few. Many strange features in the art of the time become intelligible when it is remembered that in the British Museum and the Academy Library the students met with engravings by, and after, obscure masters which are now scarcely known except to specialists. On the other hand, the old copper-plate renderings of world-famed pictures contributed largely to the aversion with which the originals came to be regarded. Outline engravings, after the manner of Flaxman, were more trustworthy, if scarcely more adequate, guides, but there were German lithographs of the earlier paintings long before the foundation of the Arundel Society in 1849. Photography, invented in 1839, was more influential through its representation of nature. Though its faults of focus (afterwards exploited by the 'artistic' photographer) and warm monochrome caused its influence also to lie in the direction of breadth[1] and not of detail, the word 'daguerreotypic' was used almost from the first to stigmatize the literal minuteness which had become prevalent well before the invention of the process.

§ 2. THE ARTISTS' LIFE

From about the middle of the century, when, thanks in different ways to Thackeray and Ruskin, the arts had become dangerously attractive to young men of education and social position, all the prejudices against them hardened into the conviction that artists led immoral lives, and on that ground parents of every class are represented as refusing

[1] Lady Eastlake's Diary of 1845. *Letters and Journal*, i. 157.

to allow their sons to follow them as a profession. Something of this mentality has been reflected by biographers into the earlier period, but in fact there is little or no indication that in the earlier years of the century any positive idea of immorality was attached to the artist's life. There was no reason why it should have been. As a class the English artists of the eighteenth century were far more respectable than their betters, and there was nothing in the excesses of Morland, the most striking instance to the contrary, that might not very easily be paralleled in every other walk of life. It was not so much that artists were immoral as that the whole nature of art was strange, irregular, un-English, and therefore, on the whole, subversive. More important, the career was very hazardous. Success could not be bought, as in the reputable walks of life, by wealth and connexions; it could not even be guaranteed, as in a trade, to merit and hard work. The more ambitious the form of art chosen, the greater the risk of starvation. London rang with Haydon's financial distresses and eventual suicide, all the more terrifying if his merits were accepted at his own high valuation. Consequently, though there were always some painters who were decently connected—Eastlake, Horsley, Stone, Grant, and Armitage may be quoted as examples—the great majority were either born to the trade or were of very humble origin. The more fortunate art students whom Thackeray describes as being free to flout convention because they had some patrimony at their own command, turned, before it was too late, to more reputable and less exacting professions. The humbler had everything to gain and nothing to lose from the talents with which, *faute de mieux,* nature had endowed them. For them, the prizes were enormous; the discredit and hardships no greater than those attending their natural station in life.

Such instruction as there was in art, while clearly too illiberal for a gentleman, was, at the same time, not entirely suitable as the preparation of an artisan to a craft. The old system of apprentice-assistantship had practically died out, as a result partly of the establishment of the Academy Schools and partly of the want of large works, and, except for Haydon's venture early in the century, established painters did not take pupils. When they did, their charges were deterrent to the poor man; Landseer is said to have asked £500 from

Alfred Stevens. The Academy Schools, indeed, were free, but they were closed from some date in March to August, when the rooms were needed for the Exhibition. If the students were not already driven to premature production by the necessity to maintain themselves during their course, they were encouraged to it by this long period of inactivity. Even at the Antique School, which was open all day and where the student was rigorously confined to drawing, the irregular attendance was explained by the fact that the students were busy painting little pictures of a low order for sale. The much criticized restriction of the Life School to two hours in the evening, though due in part to other reasons,[1] was defended on the same ground. The more advanced students would have attended still more irregularly had it been open during the day or for longer hours. Moreover, admission to the Academy Schools could only be attained by passing a test and undergoing a period of probation. For the preliminary training necessary for this the better-endowed boy could go to Sass's school,[2] meanwhile continuing his general education. Thackeray's description of this school in *The Newcomes* shows that it was not confined to young gentlemen, and Frith, the son of a butler in Yorkshire, was a boarder there with one other pupil; but for such pupils considerable sacrifices were necessary.

[1] Another and perhaps more cogent reason was the lack of a permanent instructor. R.A.s attended in rotation as visitors, and after setting the model for the week might walk round and give hints, or occupy themselves in drawing or reading as they preferred. Clearly they could not give more than the evenings to this. This absence of regular instruction in the Life was much criticized, but it was defended on the grounds, first of the difficulty of finding a sufficiently able teacher who was not already too successful as an artist to undertake the work, and secondly of the greater freedom and originality fostered by the system. The students were said to learn most from each other. Another reason against any extension of the Life School was lack of space for more pupils, and this no doubt led to the rigorous nature of the examination which qualified for admission to it, and to a consequent waste of time in the Antique. The Painting School was even less frequented than the Life Academy. There, originally, nothing was done except copying pictures by the Old Masters borrowed from Dulwich. When other opportunities for copying pictures had become more common, painting from the draped model, in any size, was introduced on three days in the week, but was replaced by studies from the head, life-size, when it was found that the students worked up their exercises into saleable pictures. Lectures on general subjects, anatomy and perspective completed the course.

[2] In Charlotte Street, Bloomsbury (later, from 1842, Cary's). Horsley entered this establishment at the age of twelve, attending it only three days a week. Similarly Eastlake, when he left Charterhouse at the age of fifteen to study under Haydon, continued his classical studies in private.

Those who could not afford to go to Sass's school prepared with difficulty for the Academy test by drawing at the British Museum, or by picking up such instruction and at the same time such livelihood as they could through copying prints and pictures and making cheap portraits which satisfied the circle in which they lived. Others passed into painting from engraving or house- and scene-painting. David Roberts describes how he and some other apprentices to house-painters in Edinburgh, formed a Life academy in a cellar, where they posed alternately to each other for pictures which they actually exhibited and sold. His own effort, produced in this way, was a Battle of Trafalgar. Eventually, at about the age of twenty-four, he secured admission to the Trustees' Academy, but left it after a few days for a scene-painting job at 30s. a week.[1]

The full length of the course at the Academy School was reduced from ten years to seven in 1853, but very few students remained for the whole of it. Long before that time was up the student knew by the acceptance of his pictures at the Academy itself, Suffolk Street or the British Institution, and, with fortune, by their sale, whether he had sufficient chance of making a livelihood. If he had neither funds of his own nor relations from whom to borrow, he would generally be forced to give lessons or paint cheap portraits. It was fortunate for the artists that when photography removed this opportunity of earning money, the picture market had considerably improved. Photography itself provided Madox Brown with a regular income, for he joined Lowes Dickinson in touching up enlargements. Similarly, Frederick Shields, after working at trade tickets, cheap woodcuts for the press, and painting on other men's pictures, embarked on an unsuccessful venture of a huge

[1] From about the middle of the century the Government-aided Schools of Art both in London and in the provinces passed on some of their students to the Academy, while in London private schools increased in number. One which was established in 1848 by Lowes Dickinson in Maddox Street, ostensibly on the Paris model, became famous later as Leigh's, and after it had been transferred to Newman Street, as Heatherley's. Another was maintained from about 1848 to 1851 by the Society of British Artists. Most of these schools were open only, or chiefly, in the evening, and were largely used for painting and study by students who were still confined to the antique at the Academy School and by others whose day was occupied in painting or some other occupation. They, therefore, were nearer to the circles for life-study set up by established artists than to self-contained or preparatory places of instruction.

composite photographic group. To a growing extent, too, illustration, decoration, and design for glass brought more or less remunerative occupation. But, more especially in the early period, the marvel is that the artists managed to survive their early years. Some budgets show the slenderness of their means. In 1816 Collins, though already regarded as popular, could not count on 100 guineas for a twelve-months' work. In 1831 George Richmond, lately married at the age of twenty-one, earned £207 in eleven months by teaching and painting seventy-three portraits. Shields, an extreme example, when living in Manchester, calculated that he had earned £91 8s. 5d. in the year 1859 and overspent his income by 8s. 2½d. Etty, after piling up a debt of some £4,000 to his brother, first reached an income of £500 per annum in 1832, when he was forty-five.

The young artists almost invariably added to their difficulties by marrying at an extremely early age. The practice was officially recognized by the Academy, for their law forbidding students under twenty to work from the female nude model was amended to allow them to do so if they were married. Celibates were few, and there is no need to invoke psycho-analysis to explain why Gibson and Etty, the two artists who were most devoted to the nude, were among their number. Had they been married men their wives would never have allowed them to do anything at once so unremunerative and so improper. A happy family life is an almost inevitable feature in a Victorian biography, but the added responsibilities either produced grave depression or complete surrender to the conventions of the day. Collins when in financial difficulties explicitly registers in his diary his determination to do what the public wants. Inevitably the artist was materially minded, although, compared with others, he might appear unworldly. By 1863 the number of repetitions which were, as they said, 'bred from' a successful picture became a scandal.[1] The Pre-Raphaelites were conspicuous offenders in this respect, but Rossetti, at any rate, was less materially minded than others of the period, if he appears more so because he had not the English reserve in speaking about money matters,

---

[1] *1863 Commission. Evidence of D. R. Blaine.* The practice was, of course, traditional. It only became objectionable with the increase in price and growth of speculative buying.

and his association with continental Bohemians had accustomed him to the notion of the artist flaying the Philistines,
who by this date were crowding to the knife. The high
cost of living, the great prizes to be won by the successful
artist, and above all the fact that a man was judged not by
his art but by the amount that he made out of it, all fostered
a material outlook. It was commonly said, even among
themselves, that artists were ruined by the possession of
means of their own. It was inconceivable that a man could
persevere beyond the stage of mere dilettantism from any
other motive than hard necessity to earn a living.

Like the medical students, whom they resembled also
in their poverty and origin, the artists when young were
allowed to show a certain degree of high spirits and gaiety.
Their costume was conspicuous or untidy and there are
the usual stories of pranks at Sass's and the Academy
Schools. Even Blake's young disciples at Shoreham alternated mysticism and morbid introspection with fits of
boisterousness which were perhaps a natural concomitant.
According to their earliest biographer, Finch's widow, their
midnight excursions were spent at least as much in frolic
as in communing with the stars and nature. If Hunt is to
be believed, the original Pre-Raphaelite Brotherhood was
remarkable for its high-spirited joviality. Rossetti's excesses
are, however, denied for his earlier life. Fault was found
with his young disciples for their casual and disrespectful
attitude towards their elders and their abuse of the word
'jolly'. Burne-Jones even spoke of Venice as the 'jolliest
place imaginable'.

These were the mere exuberances of youth; they were not
allowed to proceed from any more central and pervading
abnormality. Bell Scott, who describes early in his autobiography how he joined with two young men in engaging
privately a model, recurs to the subject at the end of his
second volume in order to make it clear that the model was
a male.[1] Charles Keene was noted for his Bohemianism,
but the incident chosen by his biographer to illustrate his
eccentricity is very mild. Wishing to explain something

[1] On the other hand, the owner of rooms which Rossetti and Deverell wanted
as a studio, stipulated that the models be kept under some gentlemanly
restraint 'as some artists sacrifice the dignity of art to the baseness of passion'
(*P.R.B. Diary*, Dec. 7, 1850).

WAITING FOR THE VERDICT—SOLOMON

by a sketch to a lady sitting next to him at dinner, he brought all the contents from his pocket with his pencil and left them on the table-cloth until the demonstration was completed. Although the established artists and Academicians enjoyed their round games and hunt-the-slipper in their evening reunions with the president and Lady Eastlake, and even the very severe and pietistic George Richmond could be uproarious with his children, the dominant note of their lives is always that of intense respectability. Danby, who had to go abroad for ten years because of some scandal, forfeited his chances of promotion from the rank of Associate, and R. R. Reinagle was expelled for buying a work from a young painter called Yarnold and sending it for exhibition as his own; but these are quite unusual cases. Mulready was separated from his wife, but he gave her his arm when he escorted her to her new home. Remarkably few besides Linton the engraver and J. C. Hook, R.A., made public profession of subversive political doctrine. A suspicion of this may have injured Madox Brown. Kirkup considerately remained in Italy. Only the old and very successful were allowed to be eccentric to the point of notoriety, and, as with George Jones and Herbert, their peculiarities were generally quite external and harmless.[1] Turner in this as in everything else stood apart, and if his life was really coarsely irregular and not merely sordid, his misdeeds were very well hidden from contemporary eyes until his death.

Respectable or not, the artists of the period were almost invariably very pious; indeed piety might easily accompany manners so lowly as to be incompatible even with respectability. Linnell infuriated Constable by the commonness of his behaviour, but though, on principle, he painted on Sunday his devoutness could not be denied. Piety is not marked in the men of the earlier generation. Haydon's flamboyant invocations are those of the gambler who needs a special attachment to the supernatural. But towards the middle of the century the characteristic constantly appears. The gentle Leslie begins each day with a chapter of the Bible. The landscape-painters Cox and De Wint almost set upon each work with prayer. Gibson and Etty were

---

[1] George Jones, R.A., commonly called 'Liquorice Jones' from the rich colour of his sepia drawings, was famous for his pride in his likeness to the Duke of Wellington. J. R. Herbert, R.A., cultivated an absurd French accent.

devout with the childish simplicity of the peasant class to which they belonged. The *exaltés*, whether Blake's pupils, Palmer and his friends, or, later, Rossetti and his first circle, wrapped their ideals of art in the language and thought of religious mysticism. Burne-Jones and Morris gave up the Church for art under Ruskin's and Rossetti's influence as for a kindred and nobler mission. Generally, as became their humble origin, the artists' piety was of a sternly Protestant variety, but Collins became a Puseyite, Redgrave an Irvingite, and after his conversion early in the forties Herbert assumed the mentality of a medieval saint, deprecating even before a Royal Commission the Academy's 'devotion to the revival of pagan art which is as a pall that shuts off the really beautiful and true'.

The day that began with prayer continued with hard work, in the sense of regular and unremitting industry rather than of self-torturing effort after the unattainable. Painting for Haydon was almost a relaxation, and Ruskin's emphatic assertion that all great work is done with ease was not intended, nor was it accepted, as a paradox. To most men, the important matter was the discovery of a suitable subject, the rest was very largely an affair of application and continuous labour. For his subject the figure-painter covered a large amount of reading, making up miraculously for the lack of cultivation with which his, as a rule, humble origin and his illiberal education had handicapped him; and until publications made it easy for him he spent inordinate time in studying for accuracy in historical detail. The landscape-painter underwent strange adventures and real discomforts when travelling abroad in search of novel and interesting scenes. But neither he nor his less adventurous colleagues in Devonshire or Wales found hardship and labour in any way incompatible with enjoyment. On the contrary, blest with their piety their life was unusually happy. The modest Smetham found an image of the pleasures of water-colour painting in Tennyson's poem, *The Brook*, and in retrospect he saw the same roseate contentment pervading the labours of Leslie and Mulready.

Such contentment could not be attained without financial security and some degree of social recognition. About 1840, Thackeray and Dyce[1] gave £500 a year as a high average

[1] Wilkie at the height of his fame fixed his prices on the basis of an income

income for the more respectable artists in England. A few years later the figure had risen. Dyce himself contracted in 1848 to execute his frescoes in the House of Lords for £800 a year for six years, and this would not have occupied his whole time. With an income on such a scale, the artist, like the fashionable physician, whose embryo he had resembled in his student days, could be found at the tables of the great, requiting their condescension with the flattery which genius (or its still more agreeable imitation) owed to superior rank. If he possessed personal attraction and a comparatively rare degree of culture, he was more genuinely welcome in the semi-Bohemian world of literary men which was on the fringe of real society. But for either circle success was essential, and since, except in rare instances, success meant membership of the R.A. or one of the water-colour societies, social consideration was almost confined to these. Landseer indeed might be reputed to be marrying a Dowager Duchess, but, as Thackeray put it, in contrasting England with France, where the mere profession of art gave a man a position above his merits, a grocer would not allow his daughter to marry an ordinary painter.[1] With all men who lived on their talents, the artist was suspect because he had no capital nor stake in the country; membership of one of the societies, if it did not give him this, could at any rate give him the respectability of a more or less assured income.

of £1,000 per annum (*Life*, iii. 496). Dyce (*1841 Committee*, 500) acknowledged that the prospect of an income of £500 a year would not tempt portrait-painters, but they were obliged, as Uwins wrote in 1827 (*Memoir*, ii. 47), to live in style, with an establishment in the most expensive part of the town and a man-servant. Their prizes were correspondingly large, though probably no one at any time could rival Lawrence, who sold to Hurst and Robinson in 1822 the engraving rights in his portraits for £3,000 per annum (Pye, *Patronage*, p. 244). George Richmond's income reached about £3,500 in 1868 (*Richmond Papers*, p. 69). Other successful artists also amassed large fortunes. Turner's £100,000 was at least equalled by Chantrey and Landseer. After 1850 large incomes became still commoner. Linnell's fortune was estimated by his biographer at £200,000 as against the £300,000 with which he was popularly credited (*Life*, ii. 234), while the list appended to the life of David Roberts shows that in many years his income, from the sale of principal pictures alone, must have exceeded £2,000. Before he was forty Rossetti's annual income was approaching £3,000 (*Memoir*, i. 249). In 1862 Holman Hunt astonished his friends by telling them that Millais had spent £6,000 in furnishing his new house in Cromwell Road (*Ruskin, Rossetti and Pre-Raphaelitism*, p. 311).

[1] The reader will remember the disguise in which Tennyson's Lord of Burleigh won his love. ' He was *but* a landscape-painter, and a village maiden she.'

The Academy and the established water-colour societies had, moreover, almost a monopoly of such artistic society as existed. Apart from their business meetings and periodic convivialities the former had until 1852 their envied week of varnishing days, which actually brought them together in the presence of their works. Even among Academicians, however, intimacy was admittedly difficult and occasional in London. The obvious explanation given was that the distances between their homes were too great. From the neighbourhood of Fitzroy Square, where the artist had continued to set up his plate from the eighteenth century, the successful painter moved out to suburbs where air was purer, noises less, and houses more comfortable. It was not possible for busy men to come together from Hampstead, Bayswater, Kensington, or Blackheath even if they had wished to seek each other's company. Residence in the country meant complete isolation. But there were more fundamental reasons. The 'originality' upon which the English artists prided themselves flowered best in solitude. Moreover, the whole tendency of the Englishman was to be reticent about his professional ideas and work. Very young men could meet together and talk about their mediums and their megilps, rejoice in their esoteric slang of 'woolliness' or 'pulpiness' or 'slosh', and declare their admiration for the ancients or their preference for the idol of the moment among the moderns, but the established painter, like any other professional, would prefer to talk of anything but 'shop'. Admission to more reputable society would give him a distaste for that of his colleagues, and the humbler his origin the more anxious would he be to prove that he had risen above the condition implied by a brass plate and to impress by just those among his qualities which were least connected with the arts.

The absence of congenial artistic companionship in England was freely contrasted with the very different conditions which the painter or sculptor found on the Continent, not only among the natives but also among such Englishmen as were settled abroad. Those who went to Italy were reluctant to return, and some, like Gibson, Wyatt, and Kirkup, remained away for ever. Over and above the climate, the abundance of models and picturesque material, and the familiarity with works of ancient art, Gibson extols the habit among the artists at Rome of visiting each other's studios and of freely criticizing each other's work in a manner unknown in his time in England. The patrons, too, appear in the artists' letters from Italy to have become more genial when on holiday and under the southern sun. In a land where art had always been held in honour, they developed something approaching a real interest in it, and they laid aside when in the company of the artists some of their habitual preoccupations and condescension. Not entirely indeed. Artists were explicitly excluded from the English Club at Rome. As late as 1856, the *Morning Post* correspondent tells of a serious controversy about the eligibility for membership of a diplomat who had once been a painter. But in Rome the artist did not care. He was content to grow a beard, to look like a bandit or a revolutionary, to be accused by Hazlitt of lounging and loafing and by Haydon of acquiring dirty habits. Something essential to artistic development was acquired through the loafing under the southern sun, if not through the beard and the dirt, and to professional independence by working whole-heartedly among his fellows. The full danger of such independence was not recognized, and the criticisms levelled against residence abroad were merely those brought against the possession of a patrimony; it did away with the incentive of making a living. Nor did the English artist in Italy lose himself, as did his continental brother and sister, in ecstasies of unhallowed love and romantic exaltation. When he was not enjoying, with the simplicity of unspoilt youth, the freedom of travel and the unconventional life, he was more attracted by the solemn pretensions of the German *Nazarener* and their return to earlier truths and primitive devotion. Paris, though far more influential in all matters of art than could be acknowledged, was always suspect on moral grounds, but many artists went to Munich, where, as in Italy, they found an environment of respect and sympathy entirely unknown in England.

Efforts were made publicly and privately to overcome the isolation of artists in London and, at the same time, to create, or rather re-establish on a wider basis, an appreciative public. Both together were necessary if art was to attain any measure of independence, and, inevitably, the Academy must either assume the direction or in the end suffer its predominance to decline. The Academicians, however, were of all artists the least in need of such support, while opposition to them, if it provided the first ground of cohesion, proved almost immediately a source of weakness.[1] Bell Scott, an acute if rather bitter observer, says explicitly that the young men among whom he found himself when he first came to London about 1840, Kennedy, Dadd, O'Neil, Frith, Egg, and Scott Lauder, while they regarded themselves as rebels and in opposition, were far too intent upon election to associateship to form a really intimate society. The Institute of Fine Arts, which was established in 1843, seems to have started with an anti-Academic bias, since its Committee included several noted opponents of the Academy and none of its members, except the outcast Danby, while its leading spirit was T. Wyse, M.P., who had been very active in his criticism of the Academy both on the Committee of 1835, and before it was set up. It had a club-room and library in Marlborough Street, and regular meetings were held for the discussion of professional topics. Its membership, however, never rose above three hundred, and despite a desperate effort to attract fresh blood by offering works of art to subscribers, it came to a complete dissolution at the end of 1849.[2] The various Artists' and Amateurs' Conversaziones, which from about 1830 held monthly meetings during the winter in public rooms in London and the suburbs, provided some intercourse between the artists and the middle-class amateur and patron and an opportunity of enjoying each other's works or possessions, ancient or modern. Such societies served a very useful missionary purpose in the provinces where they were connected with the annual local exhibitions, but they were too modest to produce much result in London, and even they were said to tend to be sectarian. The Graphic Society, which lasted from 1833 till towards the end of the century,

[1] There was also a suspicion that the old law of the R.A. forbidding election to any member of another Society of Artists in London might apply to any such institution, whether exhibiting or not.

[2] The Réunion des Arts, a somewhat similar institution, but of a more social nature and with the inclusion of music, was established in 1851. In spite of its 'splendid suite of apartments in Harley Street' it had failed by 1859, in which year a Society for the Encouragement of Fine Arts was established under the presidency of Lord Carlisle with an ambitious programme of prizes, meetings, exhibitions, and even a provincial organization (*Art Journal*, 1851, p. 202; 1855, p. 94; 1859, p. 30, &c.).

was successful either because it was confined to 'the *élite* of the artistic professions' or because ladies were not admitted to its meetings.

Of the exclusively professional groups, the evening circles for the study of the Life were a mere convenience and a means of economy to a heterogeneous body of subscribers. One of them, however, the Artists' Society, with nude and draped models, lectures and conversaziones, library and lending wardrobe of historical costumes, was of the greatest service, and after its removal in 1854 from Clipstone Street to Langham Place became a vigorous, if somewhat casual and promiscuous, centre of artistic life in London.[1]

The bond that painting by itself was unable to supply was provided by poetry. At a time when public support was notoriously lacking for art of an 'elevated' character, the painters needed all the encouragement that they could give each other in the exercise of their imagination. From the days of Girtin's Club, 'The Brothers', at the beginning of the century, several groups of painters, generally limited, as was their model, to seven members at the outset, held monthly meetings in each other's rooms for the illustration of a passage of poetry chosen for the evening and some mild conviviality afterwards. The most celebrated were Chalon's Sketching Society and the Etching Society, the members of which had mostly reached Academic rank by 1840, while the former secured the notice of Royalty.[2] Independently of these, but clearly in the same tradition, Blake's disciples, Richmond, Palmer, Calvert, Finch, and others, held regular monthly meetings at which, though design to a set quotation was not practised, each member produced a painting for discussion under the watchword 'Poetry and Sentiment'. Calling themselves or nicknamed the 'Ancients', they became so well known that their first historian refers to them as needing no description. Of other groups which had similar aspirations and were perhaps even more intimate because less formal, the most memorable is a circle, recorded by Bell Scott, which met in the studio of Patric Park, a Scottish sculptor. Its most interesting member was Theodor von

[1] A note of its history is given in the *Studio*, xxxii. 138 (Sept. 1904), p. 279.
[2] Their leading feature was adopted in 1838 by the Artists' Society, whose Sketching Meetings on Friday evening became later a great element in its popularity, and by several other coteries. By this time exercise in composition, rather than in poetic inspiration, probably provided the main attraction.

Holst, who painted in 1842 a portrait on a yellow background imitating the gilt of a primitive picture, and was notorious both for the macabre character of his pictures (commissioned among others by Bulwer Lytton) and for the irregularity of his domestic life. He died in 1844 when only thirty-three. Through Rossetti's early and lasting admiration for his work the Pre-Raphaelite Brotherhood is linked with this group just as his keen interest in Blake connects it with the Ancients, and its emergence from a drawing club called the 'Cyclographic', apart from other features, places it in the succession of the Sketching Societies.

Regarded simply as a group, the Pre-Raphaelite Brotherhood is differentiated from its predecessors not only by the outstanding personalities of at least three of its seven members, but also by its self-assertiveness. Coming into existence at a moment of reviving prosperity for painters, its members had no intention of remaining in any wilderness for the sake of their principles. They were quite childishly determined that in expressing themselves—the one clear motive of their community, however little it distinguished them from others—they should at the same time command the attention of the world. For this they, or at any rate Rossetti, saw the value of team-work and publicity. When in 1850, the second year of their activity, their name brought them too much notoriety because it emphasized characteristics in their pictures which offended Protestant feeling at a time of violent hostility to Rome, they debated whether it should not be discontinued, and afterwards they tried to explain away the more offensive part of it. Almost the earliest and certainly the best-informed notice of them[1] says that they had originally called themselves the 'Pre-Raphaelite Clique' and had merely adopted 'Brotherhood' as a more agreeable synonym. 'Brotherhood' was, however, the most colourless word that could cover their vague notion of a community based on an artistic ideal of primitive purity instead of revealed religion, and extending even to a common household and reformed clothing after the model of the Germans at Rome.[2] Nor, though they later

---

[1] *British Quarterly Review*, No. 31, Aug. 1852. Cf. *supra*, p. 104, n. 1.

[2] In the same year, 1848, the young Gothic enthusiasts around G. E. Street projected a novitiate of religion and architecture on even more monastic lines (*Life*, p. 57).

THE CROSSING-SWEEPER—*FRITH*

accused one of their friends of a breach of confidence in divulging their name, had they any real ground of complaint. They had affixed the initials P.R.B. to their names in the addresses of their letters and had placed them on their pictures. All their friends seem to have been told of their society. They had, moreover, brought out a slender Monthly, the *Germ*, as the expression of their principles, and if, at the last moment, 'a big P.R.B.' was removed from the head of its prospectus[1] and its somewhat affected title was changed after the second number to *Art and Poetry*, they paraded posters advertising its fourth (and, as it proved, final) number in front of the Academy in Trafalgar Square during the Exhibition.

An effort to restore the Brotherhood on a regular basis and to secure a declaration of faith from each of its members seems to have brought it practically to an end in 1851. Its dissolution may be dated from 1853, when it attained orthodox success in the shape of the election of Millais to Associateship, as soon as he had attained the qualifying age of twenty-four. The name, however, largely through its use by Ruskin, obtained the currency of fashion and antagonism. By 1857 the circle had increased sufficiently in numbers and prestige to allow Ford Madox Brown to organize an exhibition of his and their works on a semi-private footing, in rooms in Russell Place. Next year the Hogarth Club was founded, partly as a social centre for the artists of this group and their clients, but also as a permanent place for exhibition and sale. It lasted only three years, the violence of the quarrels which it engendered straining friendships to the utmost. In 1861, the year of its extinction, Rossetti and Madox Brown, with their young half-amateur disciples, found a more enduring bond than that of any club or brotherhood in the typically British form of a Joint Stock Company. The necessary capital was furnished by one of their number, William Morris. For the first time, thanks to the Great Exhibition

[1] *P.R.B. Diary*, Nov. 19, 1849: 'To this Hunt now most strenuously objects.' The passage that followed was destroyed by Rossetti. Hunt, who was no doubt a cautious and restraining influence throughout, came to believe later that the whole society was secret. So far as I am aware the only contemporary suggestion of secrecy is the retrospective note in the *P.R.B. Diary*, July 1, 1850: 'The designation is now so notorious that all concealment is at an end', a piece of wistful wisdom after the event. The offending note by Reach in the *Illustrated London News* of May 4, 1850, refers to the initials as being already familiar to readers of art-criticisms.

of 1851, that of Art Treasures in Manchester in 1857, and the prospect of a still greater in London in 1862, the chances of profit in art were sufficient to justify one of Thackeray's young enthusiasts with a patrimony in risking his fortune while indulging his tastes.

At the same time other coteries and associations were gathering. The most important, because of its social influence, was the circle which formed round Watts and the Prinsep family at Little Holland House, with Hunt and Rossetti, Leighton and Burne-Jones as visitors, if the first two only came on different days. Largely through the influence of Ruskin, a narrow but powerful interest in art was reviving among aristocrats and intellectuals, with earlier Italian painting as the standard instead of the later, and with seriousness of import and moral edification as its mission instead of dignity and cultivated enjoyment as in the early days of the century. The St. John's Wood or 'Gridiron' Clique consisted like the P.R.B. of seven members who were sworn to help each other. Some of its members had been ardent Pre-Raphaelites in their earliest days and all had some continental experience. With the 'Paris Gang' which appears at the same time but had a less formal constitution, they had brought from abroad a conception of the independence and natural superiority of the artist which, although it no doubt influenced the half-foreign Rossetti, could not have maintained itself for a moment in a London atmosphere in earlier days. Outside these groups the artists gathered at Leigh's, Heatherley's, and Langham Place, and in 1863, two years after the Hogarth Club had expired, through its sectarian limitations and jealousies, the Arts Club was founded in Hanover Square and flourishes to this day.

The Pre-Raphaelite exhibitions in Russell Place and the Hogarth Club were kept on a semi-private footing lest the exhibitors should be disqualified from election to the Academy. They were, however, now regarded as definitely in opposition. Madox Brown was openly hostile, Rossetti had never sent a picture to Trafalgar Square,[1] and Hunt, no doubt piqued by the slowness of his success there in

[1] It is sometimes said that the 'Annunciation' was rejected by the R.A. Apart from W. M. Rossetti's explicit statement to the contrary (*D. G. Rossetti, Letters and Memoir*, i. 160), the Private View of the National Institution, where it was exhibited, was on April 12, and the R.A.'s sending in days April 8 and 9 (*Art Journal*, 1850, pp. 128 and 138).

comparison with Millais's, was learning that even greater prestige and wealth could be attained by exhibition outside. The Academy had also shown some impatience with the medieval affectations in the subject pictures of their followers, and had either rejected their landscapes or hung them where their microscopic detail could not be appreciated. To the aristocrats of the Little Holland House circle and the Cosmopolitan Club, as to their predecessors of the British Institution, the Royal Academy was a mere body of vulgar professionals lacking in all the higher qualities of art. At the same time the increased prosperity of the artists generally, the recovery of a national self-esteem since the success of the British section of the Paris Exhibition of 1855, and the influx of continental ideas had increased the self-confidence, and strengthened the always present discontent, of the Associates and the outsiders, and had caused several of the Academicians themselves to question the adequacy of their constitution and the value of the instruction in their schools.

The necessity for the removal of either the Academy or the National Gallery from Trafalgar Square, in order to provide more space for the latter, gave the opportunity for a fresh inquiry into the position of the Academy. On the motion of Watts's friend, Lord Elcho, a Royal Commission was appointed in 1863. Its recommendations that the Government should obtain control over the institution in return for the provision of site and buildings and that a lay element should be added to the Academicians proclaimed a revival of cultured interest, but necessarily were without effect. Apart from improvements in the position of the Associates and other internal reforms which already had considerable support in the Academy itself, the most important consequence of their report was the cancellation of the rule which required artists to put their names down on a list if they wished to be candidates for election. It is very significant of the change in the position of the artist during the period, that this practice appears to have caused little or no resentment in 1835 but had become the principal grievance by 1863. When this obstacle had been removed, the Academy elected Watts and Armitage, and a new era of unity appeared to be dawning for the move to Burlington House in 1869. The spirit of artistic independence had, however, gone too far. In the social and literary circles of Watts and Rossetti, later reinforced by

Burne-Jones and Whistler, the beginnings had been laid down of a movement which was to culminate in 1875 with the establishment of the Grosvenor Gallery and to lead to the aesthetic outburst of the eighties.

§ 3. THE ART

If one clear feature emerges in the period of confusion and transition through which English art passed between 1830 and 1865, it is the complete predominance of subject over treatment, and of the intellectual and moral elements over the sensory and aesthetic. The British public, as Lady East-lake wrote as late as 1863, 'had scarcely advanced beyond the lowest step of the aesthetic ladder, the estimate of a subject'. Where all pleasure was in itself suspect and even natural beauty was regarded as a temptation from the serious business of life, any special delight which belonged to the arts became a still more dangerous delusion and snare. Art and artists alike, if they were not to be condemned as profligate and mere panderers to sensuality, had to justify themselves both to the more serious minds and to the puritan public, not by their selection and arrangement on aesthetic grounds, but by the moral or intellectual tendency of their interpretation or imagination. The more independent the artist, whether through success, force of character, or the accident of birth, the greater his ambition to manifest his qualities of soul, either by the nobility of his conceptions and interpretations or by his humble and thorough representation of divinely created forms. Turner, who might be regarded as an outstanding exception persisting from the previous generation, himself introduced his almost pure manifestations of delight in form and colour by rhapsodies of incoherent and mystical verse, and it was his fate to find a prophet who extolled him as the embodiment of precisely those qualities of mind and purpose with which he was least concerned. This was no wilful paradox. The powerful emotions aroused in Ruskin by the purely aesthetic qualities in Turner were in themselves suspect; they could only be justified, whether in self-delusion or in a frantic effort of self-persuasion, by attributing them to a source which had the universal sanction of respectability.

Not that either the artists or the more mature, if less sensational, of the writers were by any means neglectful of artistic qualities. On the contrary, the artists of the commoner sort were constantly upbraided for their preoccupation with the merely technical, and there was a perpetual clamour for more literary and general culture in their training as the only salvation for English art. They in their turn demanded that some knowledge of the artistic point of view and understanding of a work of art should form a necessary part of every liberal education. When the new philosophy of the beautiful with the unfamiliar name of Aesthetics was introduced from the Continent about 1840, the establishment of a chair at King's College was hailed as the beginning of a new era.[1] No doubt the philosophers were more concerned with natural and literary beauty than with the specifically plastic or decorative; but the existence of an antithesis between the two was recognized. Reviewers in *Blackwood's* and the *Quarterly*, Eagles and Lady Eastlake, philosophic artists such as Dyce, Rippingille, and Leslie, were quite aware that a picture or statue was a thing in itself which called for appreciation to some extent apart from the objects represented or imagined. Theories of the fundamental qualities of decoration abounded; they were even expounded by David Hay and Reinagle, in their evidence before the Committee of 1835. Much as he might denounce the systems of others, Ruskin's own attempt to deduce as a law from the natural world the superiority of pointed to rounded curves was merely a counter-attack with the same weapons. There were, also, theories of pure or abstract art. Eagles[2] in the thirties wrote of tone and colour as the true subject of a picture and hesitatingly foreshadowed an art of music in colour. The establishment of the principles of such an art became from about 1844 the dominant interest of Calvert's life. Already in 1839 Thackeray had included line with colour in a possible pictorial music, and in 1856 Leslie is recorded by Storey as expounding, in the privacy of his garden, the musical qualities of finely drawn lines. A year later, Kingsley in *Two Years Ago*, busied his amateur painter, Claude Mellot, before he gave up painting for photography, with a treatise on the

[1] T. Wyse, M.P., at the Freemasons' Tavern, Dec. 12, 1842 (Pye, *Patronage*, p. 180). Dyce was appointed in 1840, but according to Hearnshaw (*Centenary History of King's College*, p. 158) nothing came of the appointment.
[2] *The Sketcher*, pp. 43 and 53. The musical qualities of Venetian art, always regarded as inferior to the 'intellectual' Florentine, were a commonplace long before Ruskin wrote the often-quoted passage in the *Stones of Venice*.

'Principles of Beauty' which wandered into the abyss of conic sections and curves of double curvature.

Such ideas could not gain credit either with the artists or with the public. Calvert kept his notions entirely secret, Eagles was pilloried by Ruskin, and Leslie's Academy Lectures, in which he modestly attempted to stick to his last, were characterized by Madox Brown as 'twaddle' and publicly vilified by Ruskin. Art in itself was something for which the artist must apologize. Thackeray in a letter of 1849 to Mrs. Brookfield begins to ask before the Venus of Milo why certain waves of line, like the colours of Titian's pictures, fill the senses with such pleasure, but he breaks off suddenly because 'These feasts are too earthly for you'. All that was the specific property of painting was contemptuously dismissed, in the phrases employed by Ruskin, as the mere language, or sheer upholstery, of art; the visual attractions of a picture were likened in the superficiality of their appeal to the binding of a book, and the public were conjured to demand from a picture not enjoyment but a sermon. What budding artists may have been eternally stifled by this atmosphere no one can ever know, but inevitably they became so careful to subordinate their art to thought and accumulation of detail and association that any primarily artistic instincts that they may have possessed were all but atrophied. The paradox is that, notwithstanding everything, art constantly manifested itself and in many directions ultimately became paramount; that under Ruskin's denunciations and moral explanations, a real enthusiasm for pure art somehow conveyed itself to sections of the public and eventually turned to his undoing; or, to take a concrete instance, that after Alfred Stevens's model for the Wellington monument in St. Paul's had gained only the sixth prize, partly, perhaps, because it was primarily decorative in character and, therefore, lacking in obvious and appropriate symbols, it was dragged forth for apparently inconsistent reasons, and ultimately was actually carried into execution.

To some extent an exception to this general depreciation of all the purely sensory features of art was made in favour of colour. In the eighteenth century gaiety and variety of colour had been regarded as a mark of the tawdriness and frippery of French taste, but from the reopening of the Continent after the Great Wars the English artists boasted

'OPEN YOUR MOUTH!'—*MULREADY*

of their predominance in colour, while yielding to the French in drawing and other 'technical' virtues and to the Germans at Rome for the inspired simplicity of their approach to Nature. The older school of critics may be said to have died out with Sir George Beaumont in 1827, but for at least another decade there was a tendency to denounce the Academy for the prevalence of 'effects' which were regarded as illegitimate because they were in violent colours, whereas even more melodramatic contrasts were readily accepted when they were confined to more or less monochromatic light and shade. As in the eighteenth century, the conditions of the exhibition were held responsible for the progressive brilliance of the canvases; some attributing it to the frosted glass of the Galleries, while others, whose senses had been rendered more delicate by foreign travel, blamed the foggy climate of London which on most days of the year prevented subtleties of tone and colour from being appreciated. Certainly exhibitors were compelled to signalize themselves by their colour since the smallness of the rooms prevented large pictures from being properly shown; and while there were no public commissions, as in Paris, to reward feats of drawing or composition, the private purchaser might be tempted to carry some brightness into his drab interior or, later, to match the gaudiness of his new furniture and his wife's tartans and floral tapestries. Many of the public must have remained shy of colour as tending to the carnal; even at a later period a R.A. forbade his family to use chalk or paint on Sunday though, with unusual liberality, he allowed drawing with pencil or the 'Etching pen'. But the mass of the public and the artists found their mouthpiece in Ruskin, who, though he at first accepted the traditional relegation of colour to a position of secondary importance, came to glorify it as the painter's first duty. At the lowest, colour gave painting its most obvious advantage over photography, indeed constituted its sole distinguishing feature if, as he sometimes seemed to maintain, painting was only the humble and unselecting representation of nature. More important, brilliant colour meant sunshine and implied cheerfulness of heart, a virtue all the more valuable because so little justified by the circumstance of life. In the end, in his extreme distress of mind, Ruskin came to look upon all shadow in a picture as the lurking place of Satan himself. Constable's devotion to chiaroscuro contributed to his damnation; the use of black in Japanese prints placed them beyond the pale. A true Victorian, Ruskin could always identify the object of his dislike with sin, but, in reality, colour, with rhetoric, was his, and his contemporaries', form of intoxication. Art being, throughout the period, something apart from life and not a direct outcome of its activities, excess and abuse of violent colours served as an outlet for passions which current morality forced men to subjugate and painting was forbidden otherwise to express.

The change in the appearance of the picture had already been effected when Ruskin wrote the first volume of *Modern Painters* in 1843. He justified popular taste and the actual practice of painters against the criticism of conservative connoisseurs. As early as the twenties the correspondence of artists is full of dispute about the merits of the white or silvery picture and the golden or brown. In 1829 Eastlake wrote that the silvery picture kills the golden at Somerset House. Moreover, just as Ruskin's conclusions were founded on the precepts of landscape in water-colour, so the technical methods which underlay the change were largely influenced by that medium. Sir George Beaumont, according to Wilkie, already characterized the Exhibition as tainted by water-colour. By 1842, *Blackwood's Magazine* criticized the oil-painters for 'endeavouring to make their pictures like drawings, and those the drawings which show most white paper', and the water-colour men for again attempting to outdo the oil-painters in precisely this respect. The pace of the movement was accelerated by the use of body-colour by the one and of the white ground and direct painting by the other. Apart from Turner and his innumerable following among the landscape-painters, both Etty and Mulready painted on a white ground, the latter beginning with the top note of colour and painting up to it in the manner which the Pre-Raphaelite, F. G. Stephens, expressly attributes to the early Germans and his own Brethren.[1] Except for conventional portraits and the Scotch followers of Wilkie, the dark and shadowed manner scarcely survived in the Academy. The competitions for the decoration of the Houses of Parliament gave it a death-blow even in its stronghold of heroic painting. The battle which raged between oil and fresco was really a contest

[1] *Mulready*, 1890, p. 5.

THE SONNET—*MULREADY*

between the white picture and the dark. The published conditions of the competition all but forbade the use of chiaroscuro. When Haydon adopted the new method and attempted to carry out in it conceptions which belonged to the old order, his works stood out at once as hopelessly old-fashioned. His suicide was the end of an epoch, Ruskin's denunciations of the dark picture scarcely more than an epitaph.

These changes in the colour of the picture involved a revolution in all the qualities which go by the name of 'Composition'. Insistence on local colours need not in itself conflict with the artificial representation of objects in space, but it was necessarily difficult to reconcile with the traditional methods, which were based upon the building up of mono-chromatic material.

In landscape, where observation, experiment, and feeling had engrafted themselves gradually upon convention and where there was a greater variety of models, the new colour-ing was more readily absorbed. Even so, the principal charge brought against Turner was that in his freer and, as they put it, more mannered pictures, dignity of composition and the character and structure of objects were sacrificed to a whirl of colour. The article in *Blackwood's* of 1836 which roused the anger of Ruskin as a boy because of its criticism of Turner, asked how 'in these days of extravagant excitement could the quiescent art of landscape arise?' Yet Eagles, the writer of it, demanded green trees and the variety of spring colouring as well as Poussinesque composition or the broad simplicity of landscape earlier in the century. Constable strove hard to combine the two, but he alienated, by the flickering white lights with which he tried to reproduce atmo-spheric effect, both the critics who should best have appreci-ated his aims and the ordinary public who could not value his efforts for composition. They preferred his sketches to his finished pictures and the superficial brilliance of Boning-ton and his imitators to either. With these, composition in the ordinary sense was not an aim, while in the hands of the crowd 'who lived off the crumbs from Turner's table' the effort to combine brilliant colour with heroic composition produced an effect of such artificiality that it fell before the first blow.

On the other hand, the art of massing figures in space had

never attained any excellence in England. In illustration and small groups where spatial treatment was not called for, effective and imaginative disposition of figures and rhythm of line and movement never died out. The decorative instincts of the eighteenth century survived, through Stothard, Fuseli, and Blake, in the work of the 'Ancients' and helped to produce in such works of Mulready's second manner as 'Bob Cherry', 'Brother and Sister', and the 'Sonnet' (Plates 76 and 77) design that sprang freshly from the inspiration of the subject. Elsewhere, all the more because there was no inspiration or real interest in the subject, as, for example, in Maclise's 'Kitely' at the Victoria and Albert Museum, and in his and Etty's Diploma pictures, the artist was thrown back on a very pronounced linear pattern. But for works of a more ambitious character the English artists, though they were generally over-conscious of their deficiencies in drawing, were scarcely even familiar enough with the conception of group composition to be aware that in it they were still more wanting.[1]

At the Royal Academy nothing was seriously taught but the drawing of the human figure in isolation. It is characteristic that the first and only visitors who dared to pose the model in some sort of relation to surrounding objects were Constable and Turner, and their innovation was ridiculed by the figure-painters as an instance of the absurdity of entrusting instruction in drawing to landscape-painters. In this respect more than any other the artists suffered from their long isolation from the Continent. Haydon in his national self-complacency maintained that the Great Wars had saved the country from the contagion of Brick Dust as from Gothic, the other branch of the same Upas tree. By brick-dust he meant the hard colourless classicalism of David and his school. Repelled by their lack of colour, dry treatment, and to some extent also by the violence of subject which is an aid both to effective grouping and to the display of feats of drawing, the English did not realize that through their very avoidance of colour and effects, the French artists had been compelled to rely upon, and carry farther, the architectonic

---

[1] J. M. Leigh, who had found fault with the English School for its weakness in design in his evidence before the 1835 Committee (ii. 1915), gave special attention to composition at his school in Newman Street (*Art Journal*, 1860, p. 200). That may be why Ruskin advised a beginner not to go there but to the R.A. (*Letters*, Library edition, vol. xxxvi, p. 223).

CARTOONS FOR THE HOUSES OF PARLIAMENT
COPE AND *SEVERN*

grouping and spatial massing that they had inherited from the eighteenth-century academicians.

For the traditional figure-painter the one method of obtaining emphasis in space was by means of spots of light in fields of blackness simulating shadow. It had served for Opie's 'Murder of Rizzio' and for Fuseli,[1] and persisted to some extent in Haydon, Howard, Hilton, and 'Liquorice' Jones, the Keeper of the Royal Academy, and no doubt some traditional hints or 'tips' that were based upon its practice were still repeated. But by 1830 the method had become so nearly obsolete in practice that when Wilkie, the one painter of the period who was regarded as excelling in composition—and he composed with so little facility that he was obliged to construct models for his groups and lighting—returned from the Continent with his enlarged and more ambitious manner, he alienated his contempories by his adherence to large fat shadow. Except for his friend Burnet, engraver and theorist, he had little following. Without the aid of shadow, Haydon's 'Punch' at the Tate Gallery, adroit as it is in the manipulation of paint, and Mulready's 'Seven Ages' at South Kensington, though successful in single groups, show how little power there was to give the figures and groups relation to each other and weld them into a consistent whole.

In despite of Haydon, the fresco competitions in Westminster Hall sent the artists flocking to the Continent, especially to Rome and Munich. French influence is discernible in the cartoon of Armitage which gained a first prize in 1843, while Maclise in Paris in 1844 hunted up every remnant of old fresco in the churches and went nearly every day—it is said, for three weeks—to study Delaroche's famous Hemicycle at the *Beaux-Arts*.[2] But for the majority, composition naturally reverted to more primitive methods and became primarily the mere intellectual collocation of appropriate actions and accessories. In default of spatial composition, the claims of decoration which were also necessarily inherent

---

[1] But Fuseli ridiculed the new Guercino style of Wilkie even before he went abroad (Leslie, *Constable*, p. 109).

[2] Letter from Maclise to Forster of 1844 in O'Driscoll, *Memoir of D. Maclise*, p. 88, and Lowes Dickinson, *Letters from Italy*, p. 6. Of Paris generally Maclise says: 'My belief is that we in London are the smallest and most wretched set of snivellers that ever took pencil in hand; and I feel that I could not mention a single name with full confidence, were I called upon to name one of our artists in comparison with one of theirs.'

in fresco could only be met by rhythm of line and two-dimensional patterning. Something of this lesson which was learnt in Italy can be traced in the prize cartoons of Cope and Severn in 1843, while Alfred Stevens's design in 1844 was criticized as Giottesque, and formal architectural balance was one of the features in Madox Brown's designs of this type which Holman Hunt subsequently denounced. While he adhered to Raphaelesque forms, Watts explicitly described his fresco at Lincoln's Inn as an attempt in flat, monumental painting, and when he was urging before the Commission of 1863 that the Academy should subsidize young students to decorate public buildings, in order to give them practice in monumental design, he recommended that they should make for this purpose coloured enlargements of Flaxman's outlines which are purely two-dimensional and owe all their decorative character to their flow of line.

The hope that practice in fresco would enlarge the English manner while strengthening the drawing, was expressed to the Fine Arts Committee of 1841 by Dyce, and was so widely spread that it could be echoed by the future Pre-Raphaelite Rossetti, then a boy of fifteen. But the hard dry manner and the niggling touch to obtain fullness which were denounced by Wilkie on his return from abroad grew still more prevalent. In water- and body-colour they belonged to the enlarged miniature style of W. Hunt and Lewis. In oil, excessive detail was chiefly noted in Maclise, Redgrave, and Herbert. Though the upholders of broad handling and dashing touch, which still survived, especially in landscape sketches and portraits, denounced it as daguerreotypic and unpainterlike, it was the obvious substitute for good drawing and was encouraged by the restricted space of the exhibition rooms, the needs of steel engraving, and the constant demand of an uninstructed public for elaboration and the appearance of finish.

Moreover, insistence on detail like heightened colour and absence of construction and design or, as they would have put it, disregard of mere pictorial treatment, were all marks of that striving after Reality or Truth to Nature which was the dominant note of the Victorian attitude to art. Admiration of the ancients, whether the Elgin Marbles or Graeco-Roman copies, of the earlier Italians, or the Dutch was expressed in terms of truth; denunciations of the eighteenth century, of the dark masters, of the classic landscape were

ENGLISH AUTUMN AFTERNOON—*FORD MADOX BROWN*

By permission of the Museum and Art Gallery Committee of the Corporation of Birmingham

all based upon their mannerism, affectation, and insincerity. The doctrine was preached by sculptors, subject-, portrait-, and landscape-painters alike; but landscape was the leader. In natural scenery the good, the true, and the beautiful presented themselves in perfect combination, and mere contemplation of reality led straight to God. If the Divine Voice was more easily recognizable by the richness of its tones and the elegance of its diction, it could also be heard and appreciated in simpler language. Northcote's demand for art that it should reveal something new out of nature was universally accepted in its most obvious sense, as the discovery and representation of new scenes or of more features in the familiar. The great observation and infinite skill inherited from the naturalistic movement of the first quarter of the century turned from effects of light and atmosphere on broad masses to accurate notation of detail. Broad effects were regarded, even when not melodramatic, as mere superficial accidents; precise study of detail seemed to imply penetration into deeper and more enduring realities, the steady light of day to reveal more of truth than twilight or broken gleams of sun. When Constable had alienated sympathy from himself by the excessive breadth of his effects and treatment, his detractors found consolation in the detailed works of Creswick, Lee, Stanfield, Linnell, or Anthony, 'like Constable' according to Ford Madox Brown, 'only better by far'. In the end, insistence on detail, while producing such a masterpiece as Madox Brown's 'English Autumn Afternoon' (Plate 79), all but killed landscape-painting. In 1857 when an exhibition of English pictures was held in New York, complaint was made that landscape was almost entirely absent, and during the previous decade the lack of landscapes at the Academy was frequently noted. None the less its influence was dominant. Even the *Germ* in 1849 quotes English success in landscape as the authority for a new and simpler outlook on nature, while the first volume of *Modern Painters* is entirely concerned with landscape, and all the effective doctrines contained in it are based on the precepts which the youthful amateur imbibed from leading water-colour draughtsmen.

Interest in landscape was not so much lost as transferred to the figures placed in it. To the earlier landscape-painters, whether intent on composition or on representation of nature, the figures were little more than useful accidents, in no way objects in themselves. The landscape-painter was not ex-pected to draw with any facility or correctness; Linnell's ability in both spheres was even held to be an obstacle against his classification and consequently his success. With Collins, Mulready, Hunt, Heaphy, and Lewis, whether in oil or water-colour, the personages placed in the landscape became the principal subject, and the fidelity to nature which had been demanded from the scenery became extended to the actors in it. The appropriateness of the figures in Cox's later drawings is a constant element in their praise, while Ruskin tried to convert even Turner's personages into a principal element in his purpose and performance. For Collins, especially, both in his earlier English subjects and later when, in Bonington's footsteps, he found more colour on the French coast, the avowed aim and the chief merit in contemporary eyes was a break-away from the studio atmosphere. This meant less that the figures were represented in their surround-ings as visual units in light and air, than that they were care-fully studied from the life and not fancifully concocted in the manner of, say, Wheatley in the previous generation. His journeys to Hastings for the purpose of studying fisher life for his pictures are spoken of by his biographer, though they only lasted for a few weeks, as being a new departure, almost as were, in the next generation, Holman Hunt's expeditions to the East. Long before Holman Hunt, Wilkie had made the same venture and for the same purpose, to collect appro-priate material for illustrating subjects from the Bible; just as, in a similar desire for realism, Etty anticipated Madox Brown by studying decaying corpses in a charnel house for his 'Sirens' of 1837. At home, antiquarian books were studied, and Knole, Ightham, and Haddon had their swarms of pain-ters seeking accurate detail for the favourite Tudor subjects, whether incidents from history or fiction or larger composi-tions of picturesque manners such as Frith's 'Old English Merry-making'; while Lewis, Phillip, and Hurlstone travelled to Spain and a host to Italy, in their search for picturesque and multicoloured figure and *genre* subjects.

A letter from Cotman,[1] written in a moment of great excite-ment in 1834, throws a vivid illumination upon the change

[1] Letters of Nov. 25, 1828, and Feb. 25, 1834. I am indebted to Mr. Sydney Kitson for my acquaintance with Cotman's unpublished letters.

BORROWDALE—*W. COLLINS*

of taste from landscape to figure and towards even brighter
colouring. Five years before, he had declared the age to be
one of splendour and imagination, bottomed, though they
needed to be, on truth, and he had held up as models Danby,
Turner, Martin, and Prout. Now, after seeing a number of
Lewis's drawings of Spain at the Artists' Conversazione, he
ordered his sons to discontinue landscape and to turn to
figure, piling on the colour. 'My poor Reds, Blues and Yel-
lows for which I have in Norwich been so much abused and
broken-hearted about are *faded fades* to what I saw there.
Yes and Aye, FADED FADES and trash, nonsense and stuff.'
And for practice in his new style and for painting, 'with
God's help', in Red, Blue, and Yellow he determined—with
another significant impulse—to begin by copying Dawson
Turner's 'Jan Bellini'.

Truth to the details of nature, though essential, was not
in itself sufficient. In landscape, sentiment or association was
required; in the actors, expression and character. Owing
partly, however, to the very growth of precision in representation and partly to a general softening of manners,[1]
demonstrativeness of expression and violence of action became unpalatable. Few were willing to be harrowed in their
homes, and as Bell Scott says, the English School had no place
for morbid and macabre imaginations. The melodrama of
Maclise's Macbeth subjects gave place to the subdued tension
of his 'Play Scene in Hamlet' and the polite drollery of his
'Malvolio', while Leslie pleased the whole world with the
apt delineation of his drawing-room charades. The artists
were criticized by literary malcontents for perpetually choosing the same characters and trite and vapid incidents from
Gil Blas, Don Quixote, and the *Vicar of Wakefield*; but they
had to reckon upon considerable familiarity with their subject-matter if their points were to be made without exaggeration, and it was by constant repetition of the same legends
that they refined and perfected their types. Something of
the same gentility was extended even to the lower orders, at
home and abroad, but a gentlemanly reserve was not essential
in peasants, while children might actually be demonstrative.

---

[1] This is very marked in political caricature, where H. B. replaced Rowland-
son, and Cruikshank was largely confined to the lower orders. In the fifties it
was counted by the old-fashioned bad form in the Pre-Raphaelites that the
eyes of their characters were made to stare out of the pictures.

Naturally, therefore, realism began in the farm-yard, the cottage, or the playground. Following Wilkie, but always with more detail and precision, and with greater clarity and less of studied shadow, the painters in water-colour and oil alike, William Hunt and Heaphy, Mulready, Collins and Webster, found scope for their psychology in the expressions and attitudes of rustics and children. The huge success of Barraud's 'We Praise Thee, O God', with its rapt choir-boys, was the object of emulation to the young Pre-Raphaelites. Animals were even more capable of expressing their emotions without reserve, of being human without vulgarity. With them Landseer became probably the most popular and typical painter of the period.

Of course, in all these pictures the dominant interest for the painter might lie in the forms, colours, or movements of the objects represented, just as in the landscapes the artist was concerned[1] with visual qualities of emphasis, contrast, or balance which, though they are not colour nor decoration in the ordinary sense, and are inherent in the object as well as in the picture, must, in default of further analysis, be classed as aesthetic. The historical- and costume-painter was not concerned solely with the antiquarian associations of his properties; he delighted in their curious forms and mellow colours and, like Rembrandt before him, in the glint of light upon an old breastplate. Landseer was not attracted to paint animals merely as a vehicle for their humour or sentiment, but primarily because he delighted in the grace or strength of their bodies. When Gibson's Graeco-Roman statue of Huskisson was denounced by Liverpool because the toga left the shoulder bare, the widow herself protested against the idea of covering 'the beautiful arm'. But all such plastic and visual sensitiveness was regarded as merely technical, almost to the same extent as was the professional joy in handling or 'paint'. It might suffice for a sketch or give value to an accessory, but it could not constitute a picture. For that, a subject with moral or intellectual content was essential. Even in portraits, where critics constantly asked for simple representations of simple people, and where, most obviously, the artist can reach beyond the individual by happy observation and apt representation of some detail of poise or arrangement

---

[1] Samuel Palmer's *Life and Letters*, ed. A. H. Palmer, 1892, shows how fully conscious the artist could be in his selective processes.

'WE PRAISE THEE, O GOD'—*BARRAUD*

of drapery, the human body in ordinary clothes was scarcely worthy of serious attention; an attitude was only fit for representation as an indication of some desirable characteristic.

It is one of the most illuminating paradoxes of the period that while every one complained of the predominance of portraits, there were no outstanding portrait-painters (except in Scotland). One reason is that the portrait-painters were tied to conventions which were utterly out of keeping with contemporary life. Portraits of aristocratic clients had to fit with those of their ancestors beside which they were to hang; other people had to be made to look like the aristocrats. A second reason was the low repute in which 'face and hand' painting was held. A painter of any ambition passed to 'higher' things as soon as he could afford it; the rest had to make money in order to maintain their connexion and deteriorated as soon as they had obtained a vogue and had learned that nothing was required of them but a likeness and some flattery. It would not, indeed, be difficult to make a considerable list of good portraits either by young men or by painters whose habitual output lay in other directions, such as Wilkie, Herbert, Brigstock, Alfred Stevens, and the early Watts. But these are mainly heads only and of an occasional nature. No one saw in assiduous study of the casual clothed model an opportunity for perfecting almost every quality of the painter's art. All the difference between the art of the two countries lies in the contrast between the series of early portrait studies by Degas in the late fifties and their nearest English analogue, the charming but amateurish chalk or pen studies of Elizabeth Siddal, by Rossetti, of about the same date. The small water-colour portrait which had given scope for something of this talent in Chalon, Linnell, and Richmond was displaced by photography, if the miniature revived for a moment in the Pre-Raphaelite heads of Mrs. Wells and Millais. The professional portrait-painters kept alive the tradition of bold handling and lively touch, but their short-sighted fear of coming to look obsolete with the next change of fashion in dress kept them even more than the subject painters from finding artistic material in what lay before their eyes. Their works have, therefore, not even 'period-interest' for later ages. Partly because he came with the fashions from abroad, it was left to a foreigner,

II   X

Winterhalter, with his combination of 'keepsake' sentiment, metallic finish, and piquant, angular elegance to represent the character of the period for posterity.

In these circumstances contemporary life could scarcely give subjects to painting except when scenes such as events in the life of Royalty were ordered to be commemorated for purely historic purposes. The pretty girl with a 'keepsake' face was more acceptable in Albanian or rustic costume; 'Hunt the Slipper' had to be decked out by Chalon in 1831 in Watteau dress and placed by Goodall in 1849 in the uncomfortable surroundings of a village green. When modern subjects did enter, slowly and invariably in the wake of costume illustration, they were judged by their possession of pronounced sentiment or a positive moral. Redgrave was held to have introduced a new type of picture, 'the elegant familiar', in 1843 when he followed his popular 'Reduced Gentlewoman', which illustrated an incident from the *Vicar of Wakefield*, by a contemporary 'Poor Teacher'. This picture, the 'Sempstress' of 1844, 'Fashion's Slaves' of 1847, and other works, were all devised, as he himself wrote, to 'help them to right that suffer wrong'. These works were accepted for their moral purpose, though they invited the ridicule of Thackeray because of the commonplace sentimentality which made misery manifest by an untouched plate of bread and butter beside an empty tea-cup. But without their moral, such undistinguished characters would have been almost as objectionable as the girl lighting a cigarette, whose memory haunted Frith throughout his life with a sense of frustration because public opinion forbade him to attempt a subject so completely suitable to his talents. A decade later when, thanks largely to Frank Stone's 'Duet' of 1849, modern subjects had fully established themselves, and were even said to be ousting the costume pieces from the market, fault was found with Frith's 'Ramsgate Sands' because it contained no grateful mother nursing a convalescent child; and it was solely because of the vulgarity of its subject and not on any aesthetic grounds that the Pre-Raphaelites denounced Frith's 'Derby Day', which, with its sparkle, lively curiosity, and naïve disposition, has much more of the spirit of Raphael's predecessors than their own work.

Fundamentally, the age was obsessed by the ambition for High Art. Mere realism, whether in landscape, portrait, or

genre, was Dutch a
of incidents from
Bulwer, in 1833, d
art; lacking the 's
thing to 'raise, ele
and always, the '
But popular as M
frenzy could not r
it long exercised i
himself fell foul c
marrying the fant

In the human f
God's works, turl
able. Here sculptl
Roman copies and
Canova and Thor
canon of all that '
art. Gibson at R
devoted single-hea
gentleman, school
serenity, control,
while the puritan
which seemed to t
without the superf
or curious detail.
the antique mode
tion and balance,
they may not hav
inherent and tech
even more truly t
teristics that were
decoration with '
luxuriance of the
restore to the tra
sun, and the antiq
and inhuman. In
casts became mer
drawing-school of
to be adequately

THE DUET—*FRANK STONE*

[1] Andrew Robertson
papers were written l
Sass's pupils at the F

Elgin Marbles, and ineffectual, because there was no force of passion to justify the control, the classical ideal came to be looked upon as the stock-in-trade of the drawing-master or, refreshing itself with timid touches of naturalism, which culminated in the tinting of Gibson's famous 'Venus', laid itself open to denunciation as mere pagan sensuality. More searching realism found no place in England, while Protestantism forbade religious sculpture and the Renaissance, when it made its appearance with Alfred Stevens, was denounced even more vigorously than the classic. Ruskin, who admitted that he did not care for sculpture except when in association with architecture, was blind even to this aspect of Alfred Stevens's art.

The effect on the painters of their training in the antique was incalculably great in reinforcing their native sobriety and good sense and restraining them from their youthful tendencies towards pettiness[1] or extravagance; but this was largely a negative benefit. The influence of the superficial characteristics of the classic is much more obvious. Freed from the material restrictions of marble and encouraged by the Raphaelesque tradition which was no less imperfectly understood than the antique, dignity became heaviness and pomposity, sugariness replaced suavity of form and rhythm, and grace developed an elegant and genteel anaemia. The puritan effort to emphasize chastity by engrafting upon painting the polished hardness of marble entirely defeated its object. The charges of excessive nudity constantly brought against Etty, the analogue of Gibson in painting (and the only artist of the period, according to Beckford, who worked for posterity) were not due solely to moral qualms. A writer in *Blackwood's* in 1843 actually asks for a softer and more luxurious roundness and criticizes his Graces for looking as though they had worn stays. The latter criticism no doubt became, if it was not already, a commonplace, and in its more obvious sense of too close adherence to an unselect model it was repeated by the Pre-Raphaelites, who did not realize that they were denouncing as a fault in Etty a feature which they regarded as a virtue in themselves. But in its

invocation to the Antique in his evidence in 1835 reads like the parody of his manner, under the name of Gandish, in *The Newcomes*.

[1] Cf. the boy Samuel Palmer's 'Sedulous efforts to render the marbles exactly, even to their granulation' which led him 'too much aside from the study of organization and structure' (*Life*, by A. H. Palmer, p. 14).

context the criticism bears another meaning. Had Etty in his finished pictures treated his forms with the freedom of his backgrounds and given them the glow and amplitude of flesh in light and air, with which he invested them in his sketches, they would not, however casual and unselect they might have been, have looked so naked and so startling.

In a sense, sculpture also provided the transition from classic to 'Gothic' art.[1] It was the 'statuine' quality of Giotto that Fuseli learnt to admire in Italy, and it was through the relief-like designs of Flaxman—always recognized with Ottley as leading the movement—and his German imitators, that something of the simplicity of form and the intensity of spirit which were admired in early Italian art were conveyed to those who knew nothing of the original works themselves. There was real kinship between the two spirits; a puritanism which in both alike showed itself in a repudiation of the flesh and an ascetic revulsion from all the truly picturesque elements of painting. The movement was general throughout Europe, but whereas in France there was a logical division between the schools of paint and contour, English restraint and good sense rejected for long the clear-cut austerity of the French archaizers of the school of Ingres as it did the more violent romanticism of Delacroix and his followers. As with the Germans, the romantic element clothed itself in a classic exterior and the two spirits showed themselves in mutually destructive compromise in the same canvas. The hunger for romance was not, as Burne-Jones said, born about 1850, nor was it first satisfied by Rossetti's drawings. While the semi-classic pastoral of the poets inspired the 'Ancients', Shelley learned to appreciate Goethe's *Faust* through Retzsch's outlines, and these and their myriad followers, German and English, for long contented Englishmen with their fantastic primness and restricted frenzy.

The letters of English artists from Italy show that immediately from the opening of the Continent after the Great Wars, they were affected by the prevalent revulsion of taste towards the art of the so-called Primitives. They were immensely impressed by the purity and inspired simplicity[2] of

[1] The debt of 'modern' art to Pompeian painting was also recognized, cf. Wilkie's letter to T. Phillips, July 3, 1826 (*Life*, ii. 336).

[2] It was too much for Wilkie, who wrote: 'Simplicity . . . by itself, and always by itself, a tiresome and dubious virtue' (*Life*, iii. 215).

the Germans at Rome. Either from their accounts, or more probably through personal acquaintance with earlier pictures which had found their way in increasing numbers into the possession largely of artists, Constable in 1822 maintained that art before Raphael was affecting and sublime because in those days the artist went to nature directly and not through pictures. Admiration for the earlier Italian frescoes found full official expression in Thomas Phillips's Academy Lectures of 1827, and in 1841 Eastlake could say in evidence that artists were now much more interested in the earlier schools of painting than in the later. It was through an artist, George Richmond, and two dons of philistine Oxford that in 1844 Ruskin awoke from his dogmatic slumbers to a belated appreciation of early Italian masters.[1] Such, despite Haydon, was the growth of this branch of the Upas tree that Leslie in his *Life of Constable* of 1845 speaks, with alarm, of the mimicry of primitive art which had entirely changed the appearance of British painting since foreign travel had begun. Possibly, since the note was not in the first edition of 1843, the fresco competitions had opened Leslie's eyes to the development. Importations from Munich were inevitable since the Germans were the chief masters in the revival of fresco, and ignorance of their actual works only added to the glamour of their example. The desire to produce in a Gothic building an English art in commemoration of scenes from English history or English poets necessarily threw back the English artists, as it had the Germans, upon what was regarded as a northern, and still more as a Christian, art as against the pagan Greek and Renaissance. The association was sealed by the employment in the frescoes and in the School of Design of Herbert, neo-catholic and painter of a Holbeinesque portrait of Pugin, and of Dyce, famous in Rome and Germany for his Umbrian Madonna. Both were denounced as German by Haydon. Wedge-shaped heads, staring eyes, shocks of hair, tense expressions, and angular frozen attitudes marked the invasion of the Gothic notions. They engrafted themselves easily upon the excesses of Blake, who was much influenced by the earlier forms of art, and of Haydon himself. The frequent caricatures in *Punch* were

---

[1] Ruskin to Liddell, Oct. 12, 1844. 'That pure old art which I have at last learnt (thanks to you, Acland and Richmond) to love' (*Works*, Library ed., iii. 668).

perhaps more influential in spreading the extravagances of the style than the originals themselves.

Frescoes and cartoons were not alone in throwing the artists back upon the Middle Ages. The interest of the painters in historical subjects and details necessarily imported something of the style of the works from which their material was collected. The age of the Eglinton tournament appeared to itself to be antiquarian. Public shyness of the nude and the artists' inability to handle it assisted. Still more, the most fundamental and persistent characteristic of English art, its anecdotal quality, reasserted itself and fastened upon precisely those features of later medieval art, especially German and Flemish painting and illuminated manuscripts, which the earlier generation had rejected as childish. If their Reminiscences are to be trusted, the 'Chaucerian' quality of the Campo Santo frescoes enchanted both Leigh Hunt,[1] when he was in Pisa in 1822, and Holman Hunt, when he saw engravings from them thirty years later; but while the earlier writer found it somewhat confusedly in the whole range of the paintings, the latter associates it explicitly with the quaint charm and sweet humour of Benozzo Gozzoli. Further, their fond imitation of detail, human, animal, or vegetable, flattered the almost equally primitive love on the part of the English painter for the easily assimilated. As early as 1841, Thackeray could give this development a philosophic explanation. In writing of the French mystical painters at the Salon, he pointed out that in their works, as in medieval illuminations, extreme accuracy of detail in flowers, birds, and branches gave an air of truth and simplicity, and, with the force of scent or song, seemed to make nature an accomplice and actor in the scene.

§ 4. THE PRE-RAPHAELITES

The spark of genius that was needed to fuse the characteristics of a decade into works of art was supplied, not by one man, but by the momentary convergence of an exceptional group. Because they were individuals and in a measure sincere, the paintings of the Pre-Raphaelite Brethren were

[1] Leigh Hunt, *Autobiography*, 1850, c. xix; W. H. Hunt, *Pre-Raphaelitism*, i. 133. Phillips (*Lectures*, p. 39) couples Donne with Chaucer as illustrating Giotto. Reynolds, when in Flanders in 1781, had already compared Pieter Brueghel to the former for his weight of thought (*Works*, ed. Malone, 3rd ed., ii. 408).

necessarily original and different from those of other men;
but originality was always the boast of the English school
and, despite Ruskin, they had no monopoly of sincerity.
Their confusion of aim and admitted inconsistency were
characteristic of their age. They were not even consistent
in the idea of rebellion. As much as any of their predecessors
they aimed, quite simply, at distinction in the Academy. In
a list of Immortals which they drew up at an early date in
their association they included Haydon, Hilton, and Wilkie,
besides contemporaries whose names Holman Hunt was
ashamed to reproduce. In 1851 they were in ecstasies over
Cope's triptych of 'Clerk Saunders'. If they were in opposition against anything it was against precisely the triviality of
sentiment and sameness of subject-matter which were most
constantly criticized by the Press. Their hostility on these
grounds was mainly directed against their immediate predecessors, Frith and Stone, but they were in accord with these
painters in aspiring to depict actual life and in hoping to substitute a more realistic treatment of nature for classical conventions of form and composition. Indeed, their revolt from
the antique teaching in junior days at the Academy was but
the commonplace attitude of young students who saw their
instructors daily ignoring their precepts in practice, and it
came with a specially bad grace from students to whom the
Keeper himself, old 'Liquorice' Jones, had expounded, if he
had not introduced, the 'Baptistery' doors in which they
found the counter-influence to the antique. In the seriousness and elevation of their approach they not only had the
direct example of Dyce, Herbert, and Redgrave, but they
also inherited the spirit of the Westminster Hall competitions. No impulse of revolution, but mere acceptance of
economic fact, led them to transfer their energies from large
designs to cabinet works at a time when the former had
ceased to promise a reward and the market for the latter was
soaring. Moreover, by discarding their ambition to paint
compositions of many figures, they evaded the principal consequences of adopting the conventions to which they owed
their name and by means of which they were enabled to dis-
pense with the last remains of both the Graeco-Roman and
the 'picturesque' traditions and to unify their pictures by
bringing background, accessories, and figures into the same
pictorial plane. In this also they had the example of the

fresco-painters before them, while in their insistence upon detail they were following an almost universal tendency. Their white ground, which in Madox Brown's phrase killed everything else in the exhibition, was but a further stage in a movement which Eastlake had noted in 1829 in almost the same words; the technical method by which their effects of violent colour were obtained being admittedly a development from Mulready's practice.

It is not, therefore, surprising that the exhibition in 1849 of their first works was greeted with an acclamation which should have satisfied even their youthful determination to take the world by storm. With the Wallerstein pictures still at Kensington Palace, the special exhibition of 'Primitives' at the British Institution fresh in memory, and the Arundel Society actively in course of formation, even their archaism was at first accepted or only gently challenged by the critics. Their first exhibited picture, Rossetti's 'Girlhood of Mary Virgin' at the Hyde Park Gallery was found by the *Art Journal* to be 'the most successful as a pure imitation of Florentine early art yet seen in this country'. When Millais's 'Isabella' and Hunt's 'Rienzi' appeared at the Academy, the same paper wrote, without trace of hostility, that 'we have this year seen more essays in the manner of early Art than we have ever before remarked within so short a period', and while Hunt was characterized as a man of genius, though austere in his denials, Millais was said to arrive 'with apparent ease at a result which others with old reputations have been vainly labouring for half a life-time to acquire'. His picture was perhaps 'on the whole the most remarkable of the whole collection'. *Punch's* praise was more important because it was contained in Percival Leigh's note to Dicky Doyle's drawing of the Royal Academy which became classic in the series of 'Manners and Customs of the English'. It clearly referred to the pictures of the Brotherhood—his 'dear young friends' of subsequent years—as the best historical pictures of the year, though somewhat 'lacking in fancy and imagination and seeming original through a certain quaintness that do smack of Church window Saints and Illuminated Missals'.

Next year Millais's 'Carpenter's Shop' all but brought about a complete disaster. The picture was intended as presentation of a sacred subject, in the 'Early Christian' or German manner, with the appeal of homely detail and familiar characterization.[1] With his customary sound sense, Millais kept out of the painting much of the extreme attenuation and angularity which marked his preparatory drawings, but partly because he had chosen his models badly and adhered too closely to their peculiarities, and partly because something of their rigorous asceticism formed a necessary part of his conception and of his design, the detailed realism with which he treated the nude portions of his figures and, it seems, their rawness of colour created violent offence. It was not merely that he refrained from the suavities and rotundities to which people were accustomed in the representations of heroic or religious subjects; he seemed actually to have chosen to mark the sacred personages with dirt and disease. Within a week *Punch* printed a note, apparently by a doctor, who diagnosed them in strictly medical terminology as displaying every symptom of 'scrofular or strumous diathesis'. Even the *Illustrated London News*, in a highly laudatory notice in which 'what is called, somewhat slightingly, the Pre-Raphaelism of the picture' was said to be its leading excellence, deprecated 'its intentional deformities such as the frostbitten toes of Joseph and the sore heel of the Virgin'. The woodcut illustration with which it meant to honour the picture (Plate 83), as one of the best of the year can only have horrified thousands who had not seen the original. The suggestion of ascetic mortification aroused the cry of Puseyism, and that of dirt and disease in the Holy Family seemed positively blasphemous, while the powerful sentiment which seemed to some evidence of real sincerity struck others as repulsive ugliness. Six years later Ruskin denounced this picture for restraining the advance of Pre-Raphaelitism because of its insistence 'upon the harshest lines of form and most painful conditions of expression, both in human feature and natural objects'.

To a section of the artists and most of the newspaper critics, this popular outcry was welcome enough. Aroused by the *Germ*'s admittedly childish aspirations for the moral purification of art and by personal attacks in word and

---

[1] Was Millais inspired by the fresco in Carpenter's Hall which, discovered in 1845, earned fresh notoriety by escaping from the conflagration in 1849? The same fresco contains Mary spinning with the distaff and may also have suggested Rossetti's first picture.

a

b

THE CARPENTER'S SHOP—*MILLAIS*

writing,[1] some of them had already, on the appearance of Rossetti's 'Annunciation' (in a form very different from the present[2]), strengthened their mild warnings against archaism of the year before. They now denounced it as a stale and pernicious artistic heresy masquerading as a novelty. They found further justification for this attitude in Millais's second picture, 'Ferdinand and Ariel'. Hunt's 'Druids' and Collins's 'Berengaria' came into the same category, though the latter, which is so feeble an example of the method as to be almost a parody, was regarded, because it contained no nudities, as comparatively unobjectionable.

The newspaper clamour was repeated in 1851, although both Millais and Hunt refrained from religious subjects and pronouncedly archaic treatment. The chief offence was caused by Collins's 'Convent Thoughts', which joined to the minute detail and staring colour of the school an obviously medieval ecclesiasticism of subject. Millais lacked neither admirers nor buyers, but since the papers appeared, as Hunt wrote at the time, to be 'endeavouring to ruin their interest with the Academy and the patrons' the Brotherhood secured, through Patmore, the assistance of Ruskin, to whose teaching they already owed more than they afterwards cared to acknowledge.[3] If his two letters to *The Times* were as effective as is commonly stated it must have been through the mere fact of their appearance, for he admitted the Brother-

[1] The hostile notice of the 'Annunciation' in the *Athenaeum* appeared on April 20, 1850. It was generally attributed to Frank Stone. Six weeks before, on Feb. 15, D. G. Rossetti, to whom his brother had entrusted the notice in the *Critic* of that painter's pictures at the British Institution (*P.R.B. Diary*, Feb. 5, 1850), wrote of his 'Sympathy': 'All we can know for certain from the picture is, that on some occasion or other, somewhere, a mild young lady threw her arms (with as much abandon as a lay-figure may permit itself) round another sorrowful but very mild young lady; that the faces of these young ladies were made of wax, their hair of Berlin wool, and their hands of scented soap.' The whole notice is interesting as showing the attitude of the young P.R.B. towards their predecessors in a type of picture—the problem subject in modern dress—which they shortly afterwards claimed to have invented themselves.

[2] It was described by the *Art Journal*, 1850, p. 140, as having 'every portion stippled with the utmost nicety', and by W. M. Rossetti in the *Critic* in similar terms. Rossetti worked upon it heavily in 1850 and 1853.

[3] Hunt, in 1905, *Pre-Raphaelitism*, p. 73, says that he borrowed *Modern Painters*, and read it in one night. But in 1886, *Contemporary Review*, xlix. 478, he says that it was lent to him for a few days and he sat up 'most of the night more than once' to read it. In any case the doctrines of the first volume were known to Stephens and Patmore, and by 1849 had become available to all through the public Press.

hood's morbidity and lack of any sense of beauty,[1] and in praising somewhat superciliously their accuracy of detail he was only repeating a point which had been universally conceded. But in his second letter he rather grudgingly withdrew the charge of Romanism, which was certainly deserved by Collins's picture and substantiated by the associations of the Brotherhood at Oxford, and since he had been abroad during the exhibition of their first pictures in 1849,[2] and knew nothing either of their drawings or Rossetti's pictures, he could deny the charge of archaism and uphold their perspective against almost all the other pictures in the Academy. Later in the year, after coming into personal contact with Millais and Hunt, he issued a pamphlet under the name that they had adopted, and attributed to them principles which not only coupled them with Lewis and William Hunt who were accepted by all, but also somehow served to identify them with Turner, whose work they hated and who seemed to the public the very antithesis of all their pretensions.

Ruskin's championship in this pamphlet, and still more in the *Edinburgh Lectures* of 1853 and his popular *Notes on the Academy* which began in 1855, encouraged the painters while it modified their practice and it consolidated the strong opinion that Millais at any rate had secured in his favour. But Ruskin exasperated the older artists and critics by the irreconcilability of his theories and by his arrogant employment of his favourites for the denunciation of all other work. He thus served to keep alive an antagonism which was as confused as his own praises or as the principles exhibited in the works themselves. In a few years the leaders of the movement had come to differ more from each other than the group as a whole from the rest of the Academy. The public asked in vain what was this thing to which the name Pre-Raphaelitism was attached. By 1856 Ruskin himself found the whole Exhibition Pre-Raphaelite. No doubt their example had already bred imitation among their contemporaries and had encouraged some among their elders, such as Dyce, to give rein to proclivities which they had previously been somewhat shy of indulging,[3] but the essential truth was that

[1] Meaning the faces, of course. As a result of this criticism the head of Sylvia in Hunt's 'Two Gentlemen of Verona' was repainted.

[2] He might have seen the 'Isabella' in B. G. Windus's collection if the owner ever showed him anything but the Turners.

[3] That this should first appear in 1856 affords a strange commentary upon

their emergence—and probably some deaths among the older men—opened the eyes of Ruskin and the public generally to the real character of the movements in painting that they had been witnessing for most of their lives. The praise that the Pre-Raphaelites received at the Paris Exhibition of 1855, in words which have often been quoted, and, as usual, without their context, was shared with Leslie and other painters of the day. They struck the French merely as outstanding examples of general English qualities. At home the tradition of classic treatment and of broad paint and lively touch, the 'loose, vague, careless, off-hand, bold, free and dexterous execution—taken together the bane, reproach and excellence of the English school' as Rippingille put it, persisted only as an ideal with which to combat what remained of Pre-Raphaelite 'quaintness of conception, cold, dry, hard and meagre manner, equalised distribution of parts and laborious and superabundant detail of particulars'. In oil there was no living master who could be quoted in opposition to them. To stage a debate in 1856 between the contrasted schools, *Punch* had to go to the Water Colour Society and pit Cox against Lewis. Three years before this, Millais had lightheartedly expressed his view of the distinction: 'When the sun burst out ...the distant mountains changed suddenly from David Cox to the Pre-Raphaelites!'

For this momentary consummation, Millais was primarily responsible. The most completely a painter among the Brethren, he readily forswore, when he was singled out by Ruskin for his favours, every trace of medieval angularity and, doubly fortunate in his models and in a power, surpassing even Leslie's, of presenting their most attractive features and of placing them in restrained but dramatic action, he gained instant and almost universal success with his 'Ophelia' and 'Huguenots' of 1852. The latter was held to be his masterpiece even by Rossetti (in 1855). Next year the 'Order of Release', with its conventional black background, brought him still greater popularity. Insecure on his pedestal and always capricious and excitable, he varied his subjects and his manner from picture to picture, at one moment alienating Ruskin, who ignored the 'Blind Girl' (1856), in his *Annual Notes*, and fulminated against 'Sir Isumbras' and 'The

the belief of the Brotherhood in the previous year, that there was a determined effort to keep them out of the Academy.

Heretic' (1857), at another moving him to ecstasy with 'The Rescue' (1855). Similarly he puzzled the public and the generality of critics with 'Autumn Leaves' (1856), where, because its poetry was inherent in the things seen and felt, and not explained by purposive action, they suspected the 'transcendentalism' which they connected with other works of the school, but he delighted them with such works as the 'Random Shot' (1854) and 'Peace Concluded' (1856) in which the story was as plainly written as in his historical anecdotes, and the subjects had the added attraction of contemporary life. By mischance the work of this type which succeeded in combining the sting of actual observation and experience with a clear story and complete fidelity of detail, Madox Brown's 'Last of England' (1855), was withheld from the general public until 1862,[1] when it is said to have been with Martineau's 'Last Day in the Old Home' the most popular picture in the great exhibition.

In Millais's more Pre-Raphaelite pictures vividness of colour and precision of detail, for which he had extraordinary facility, arose purely from the instinct of emotional selection and emphasis. He pieced together his figures and his background, whether studio or outdoor work, with the utmost disregard for visual integrity or atmospheric truth. Where, as in 'Sir Isumbras' and 'The Woodman's Daughter', the result was gross and tangible disproportion, the pictures had to be repainted after the exhibition was over. But in the 'Ophelia', when a rat had been removed because it was as large as a rabbit,[2] the disparity between the rose-bush, the

[1] Brown's Diary, March 2, and April 3, 1855 (*P.R.B. Diary and Letters*, 168 and 174), shows that he intended it for the R.A. of that year, but could not complete it in time, thus invalidating the statement (F. M. Hueffer, *F. M. Brown, a record*, &c., p. 84) that the decision never again to exhibit at the R.A. dated from the skying in 1852 of 'Christ and Peter' and 'Pretty Baa-Lambs'. He also exhibited 'Waiting' at the R.A. of 1853. The 'Last of England' was sold as soon as it was finished. When exhibited at the semi-private exhibition in Russell Place, p. 137, in 1857 it was given by the *Athenaeum* in a friendly notice to Holman Hunt (*Ruskin, Rossetti and Pre-Raphaelitism*, p. 173). 'Pretty Baa-Lambs', which, to judge from the sketch at Oxford, was still more instinctive and unconventional than Millais's 'Autumn Leaves', is said (Hueffer, op. cit., p. 85) to have found little favour anywhere. Millais, however, noted his admiration for it in his diary, Oct. 25, 1851 (J. G. Millais, *Life and Letters of Sir J. E. Millais*, i. 128). 'Christ and Peter' was so much rehandled after its exhibition at the R.A. of 1852 that it is impossible to draw any conclusions from its treatment there.

[2] Although, as Hunt naïvely remarks (*Pre-Raphaelitism*, i. 304), 'perfectly correct in perspective'. Millais himself in his diary (*Life and Letters*, c. iv)

WAITING—*MILLAIS*

*By permission of the Museum and Art Gallery
Committee of the Corporation of Birmingham*

river and the willow, and the lack of atmosphere went almost unnoticed. In the convention in which the picture was painted, visual consistency and coherence were as little needed as in a miniature or a fresco. Only some among the old-fashioned artists, in their clamour against medieval flatness and lack of perspective, were confusedly aware of the fulfilment in the Pre-Raphaelites of Constable's old prophecy. In thirty years, as he had foretold in 1822, painting as he understood it was no more, and—though the models were not those that he had in mind—for the very reason that he had anticipated, the imitation of ancient pictures.

With Holman Hunt, on the other hand, the quality of 'Intensity' which supplied one of the equivocal catchwords for the Pre-Raphaelites declared itself at once as intensity of vision, intensity of light and colour, and intensity of moral purpose. With this equipment he essayed in turn every subject of the current artistic repertory. In the 'Hireling Shepherd' of 1852, painted side by side with Millais under the renewed influence of Ruskin, the ground idea is a pastoral idyll after the manner of Mulready, and the landscape is still elected, as with Millais, solely for its intrinsic 'delectability', but where the earlier artist was content to leave his subject vaguely evocative, Hunt elaborated his beer-fed shepherd and hoydenish maiden, his sheep and his accessories, with a fierce exactitude of detail, and sought to express by a crowd of intellectual symbols the moralizing intention which had supplanted his original lyrical idea. Here, also, although Hunt does not appear, any more than Millais, to have painted figures and background together in the open air—that was left to the foreign trained Madox Brown, who tortured himself and his wife in the attempt—a deliberate theory of representing objects in strong sunlight accompanied the exact rendering of detail. The notion of an art progressing, like the sciences, through thorough investigation of detail somehow joined itself in Hunt to the Pre-Raphaelite conception of primitive simplicity, and because he adhered to it in practice long after all the other members of the Brotherhood had drifted completely away from their earlier manners, he

describes his troubles with the beast, which obviously split the picture into its diverse components even before the figure was added in the studio. At this date Millais and Collins respectively painted the backgrounds of 'The Huguenots' and of a picture which was never completed before they had even settled what subjects to place in front of them (op. cit., pp. 133–6).

almost succeeded in persuading the world that it had been from the first their leading principle. In the 'Hireling Shepherd' and in the landscape exhibited in the following year, the careful painting of the sheep was a rebuke to all 'insincere' and superficial artists, not least, perhaps, to Millais, who had flattered himself on his Pre-Raphaelite fidelity to nature when he procured a real sheep's head from a butcher and constructed out of it the whole flock in the 'Carpenter's Shop'. Four years later Hunt returned with his 'Scapegoat' from the East, whither he had gone partly, like Wilkie before him, to secure convincing local colour for the illustration of Bible story and partly, perhaps, in the unfulfilled hope of finding models who would stand as long as he needed them in a strong outdoor light.[1] In it, with a minuteness of detail and a fierceness of colour surpassing even that of the 'Hireling Shepherd', he showed to what depths of human expression animal painting might attain in the hands not of a Landseer but of the painter whom the Lord had chosen for full and faithful representation of His works. The public, whose laughter at the 'Hireling Shepherd' was the instinctive expression of surprise and pain, were puzzled and awed by the 'Scapegoat', and Ruskin, who hated its agony and its starkness of design, characteristically found fault with the painting of the wool.

Hunt secured his first real success in London and became in Rossetti's words, 'the world's great man at last', with the 'Claudio and Isabella' of 1853. It was said to be more popular than the Landseer. But this was an earlier picture in which the Pre-Raphaelite intensity expressed itself in the familiar Gothic features of fancy dress, a wedge-shaped head, a shock of hair, and staring eyes. Hunt had already passed beyond such medievalism and perhaps had from the first regarded it as a mere practising ground for his psychological and dramatic power before employing them on the modern and religious subjects which had always been included in the all-embracing Pre-Raphaelite ambition. His first attempts in these directions, the 'Awakened Conscience' and the 'Light of the World' of 1854, seem to have met with

[1] T. Seddon wrote to F. Madox Brown from Egypt in 1854 (*Life of F. M. Brown*, p. 99): 'Poor Hunt is half-bothered out of his life here in painting figures but, between ourselves, I think he is rather *exigeant* in expecting Arabs and Turks in this climate to sit still (standing) for six or eight hours. Don't tell any one this, not even Rossetti.'

reception little better than that of the 'Hireling Shepherd', until Ruskin again came to the rescue with two letters to *The Times*. Certainly both pictures needed a commentary. The original effect of the 'Awakened Conscience' is lost to posterity because, as so often with pictures of the school, the face of the lady was repainted, but Ruskin's letter explained to the public that the familiar air carelessly strummed on the piano by the 'fast young man' who had enmeshed her in his toils had aroused thoughts of pristine innocence in her mind and moved her to repentance and remorse. He led them to admire the eloquence of the accessories, the painfully new furniture, the books whose uncut leaves show them to be unread, the cat torturing a bird. This is precisely the type of symbolism that Thackeray had ridiculed ten years before in Redgrave's 'Poor Governess', but Hunt's still more elevated moral pupose and his choice of a complicated and indirectly scabrous subject, as in the 'Claudio and Isabella', raised him to a higher plane. The rigorous realization of intellectually significant detail and exclusion of everything that was pleasurable in subject, design, or handling, reconciled the simple-minded desire for pictorial representation with the Puritan distrust of the senses. At last art proved that it need be neither 'picturesque' nor 'profligate'.

Its possession of an ulterior meaning, perhaps, too, the grim intensity of the face and the signboard character of its design, have caused some to regard the 'Light of the World' as a typically Pre-Raphaelite picture. But even its technique departed so far from the principles of the school, that Ruskin was forced to invent for it still another definition of Pre-Raphaelitism which, if followed out, would have covered all that he had previously denounced as mere 'imitation', and included what came later to be known as impressionism. Further, both the conception and the execution of the ideal figure lay outside the bounds of Hunt's theoretic realism. Similarly, in the large picture, the 'Christ in the Temple', painted after a second journey to the East, Hunt's passion for accuracy (which had forced him, as his panegyrist[1] said, to paint even the *maison damnée* of the 'Awakened Conscience' in 'an appropriate habitation') could enable him to elaborate the accessory figures with all John Lewis's fidelity, and to heap up a glittering mass of erudite detail, but it could not

[1] [F. G. Stephens], *Holman Hunt and His Works*, 1860, pp. 32 and 36.

supply an Oriental atmosphere. Still less could it inspire the central figures of Christ and the Mother. Painted, as usual, in the London studio and from London models, they both belong, with their deliberately idealized limbs and faces and their nondescript drapery, to precisely that semi-classical convention which the Pre-Raphaelite Brotherhood had originally set out to replace. They might have been conceived by Goodall or Horsley. Hunt's tortuous and almost suppurating mind was ready with a justification which was in effect a criticism of the early Christian affectations displayed by Millais in the 'Carpenter's Shop' and, still more, the growing eccentricities of Rossetti. It was not needed by the public; they flocked in thousands to see the picture which was certainly England's masterpiece and perhaps the world's, not only because it had taken longest to paint and had fetched the longest price, but also because it contained the greatest mass of detail and the brightest colours, with no novelty of conception to puzzle the mind and no disconcerting visual feature of atmosphere or design.

While Hunt and Millais were thus reverting to, and, each in his own way, perfecting, the common type, Rossetti, the original motive force of the Pre-Raphaelites, was becoming the centre of an ever-widening group, his vast potentiality being all the more influential because largely withdrawn from criticism and untested by performance. It was always towards him that the new men gravitated, and the fascination of his personality, coupled with the generosity of genius towards talent in other men, secured the revival and persistence of a concrete Pre-Raphaelitism in something approaching the form to which it owed its origin and its name. Had it not been for his pietistic upbringing, his taste for the exotic and sensational in French caricature, German print, and such paintings as those of Holst or David Scott would have led him into the dead end of morbid and continental romanticism. As it was, he had found in medievalizing poetry and art, the 'Art-Catholic' as he called it, the expression of his youthful and very mixed passions, searching for antique words in the manuscripts of the British Museum and saturating himself in archaic forms and attitudes in the illuminated missals for which, as early as 1851, his passion had become notorious. He was the master, conceivably the inventor, of the archaic and angular method of pen drawing which was the first and most adequate vehicle for the 'intense' feeling of the Brotherhood. Like Millais and Hunt, he had largely repressed this feature in his two exhibited pictures. In them he had invested themes from sacred story with even more of the homely symbolism of a German folk-tale than Millais had given to the 'Carpenter's Shop' and without that picture's offence. Eager for a time to paint ambitious pictures with the others, he almost broke his heart in a fruitless attempt to present with microscopic detail a modern subject of sentimentalized prostitution, and took years to complete a commission for an altar-piece for Llandaff Cathedral. Actually repelled by close study of nature, and with a very imperfect command of technique, he was all the more thrown back upon his natural bent for medievalized emotion and the astonishing power that he possessed, in design as in poetry, for extemporization. Unlike the others he seized with extraordinary vividness the intellectually insignificant but visually valuable accident of form or attitude, and his immediate, child-like, representation of it was the more effective because it was embodied in an imperfectly realized figure. His marionettes could only suffer from being elaborated into life-like dolls; and while (except in his pen-and-ink sketches), they could not pretend to represent any external world, they served as evocations of a distant and highly emotional past. Working with enjoyment only in what he called the 'Drowsing Style', he allowed his figures to fall automatically and dreamily into colour and rhythm as the natural expression of an overwhelming sentiment, almost a medieval ecstasy, which could only have been dispelled by any effort to represent it accurately in terms of observed nature. In this he arrived at something of the same end as the Ancients before him, and he shared with them an admiration of Blake, and a mystic and profound belief in the power of painting to express the greatest and deepest truths.

More fortunate than the Ancients, Rossetti early acquired through these drawings a reputation that surprised him. From 1854 he found a market for them to, and through, Ruskin, who sought him out partly, no doubt, because of the need to replace Millais, who at that very moment was absconding with his wife, but also in genuine admiration of a drawing in which, with astonishing infidelity to Turner and his own

published principles, he found 'the most perfect piece of
Italy, in the accessory parts, I have ever seen in my life—nor
of Italy only, but of marvellous landscape painting'.[1] In
1856 he was confidently invited by Lewis, the President, to
stand for membership of the Old Water Colour Society. He
did not comply because membership would have interfered
with his ambition to paint in oils, and after the Winter Exhibition in Pall Mall in 1853 he appeared only occasionally and
at the semi-private exhibitions of his friends. He recognized
no doubt that his work looked better alone. Its choiceness of
subject and sentiment demanded intimacy with the observer,
its unreality and weakness in representation would have
been startling in the company of normal pictures, while its
decorative character demanded isolation from works of con-
flicting tendency.

Book illustration, which had always in one way or another
allowed more scope for decoration, provided Rossetti with
another outlet for his talents and brought him before a wider
public. In the comparative privacy of the book the stimulus
of lust (as in his 'St. Cecilia') or savagery (as in Madox
Brown's 'Prisoner of Chillon') could express itself in design,
or at any rate shelter behind a decorative embroidery, in
ways that were scarcely tolerable in a completed picture. The
comparative severity of a new form of woodcut, fashioned
apparently under German influence, restrained Rossetti from
too sudden a relapse into his congenital floridity, which under
the name of 'Slosh' was at the outset anathema to the whole
Brotherhood, and there was enough superficial resemblance
between his minute tracery of detail and their precise naturalism to give him the necessary support of contact with the
original members of the group. For their first common
undertaking of this kind, Moxon's Tennyson, which was
begun in 1854, but not issued till 1857, Hunt worked up an
old drawing, the 'Lady of Shalott', which was as full of their

---

[1] Ruskin to D. G. Rossetti, April 10, 1854. This letter, described as 'in-
credible' by D. G. Rossetti himself when writing on April 14 to Madox Brown
(W. M. Rossetti, *D. G. Rossetti, Letters and Memoir*, i. 179), has not, so far as I
am aware, been printed. It appeared in an imperfectly described volume of
Rossetti's correspondence at Sotheby's, July 26, 1932, Lot 495, and Nov. 15,
1932, Lot 455. Millais's behaviour with regard to Mrs. Ruskin, of which the
Brotherhood were well aware (Letter from A. Munro, Jan. 28, 1854, *apud* W. B.
Scott, *Autobiog.*, i. 320), no doubt confirmed Ruskin's belief that the taint of
morbidity in the Pre-Raphaelites was due to him (*supra*, p. 162) and thus helped
to blind him to that aspect in Rossetti.

original common spirit as his other designs of merely formal quality, while Millais, besides diverting into this more appropriate medium the highly charged and sentimental illustration of modern problems that had given Hunt his 'Awakened Conscience', foreshadowed in some plates after Rossetti's manner his 'Parables' of 1864, which in other days and with other opportunities would have seemed entirely conceived for monumental mural decoration.

It was largely through a book illustration that Rossetti found the most influential of his new disciples. His 'Maids of Elfenmere' for Allingham's *Day and Night Songs* (1855) came as a revelation to Burne-Jones at Oxford, and entirely altered the whole bent of his talent. The feature that most impressed him was the musical quality of the design. Naturally he was not conscious of the unfamiliar force in these abstract terms; the maidens are playing musical instruments and, just as at much the same time and in much the same way Courbet's 'Burial at Ornans' could appear to be an especially successful rendering of the music of the ceremony, so this plate merely struck Burne-Jones as a superlatively good illustration of its subject. Other attractions were not wanting; indeed, there was a more immediate appeal in the poetic medievalism of the subject and in the new type of physical beauty, which seemed Christian and spiritual, even English, in its unclassical irregularity.

Through Burne-Jones and a band of his young friends at Oxford, Rossetti found an opportunity of indulging his decorative ambition on a larger scale. With their assistance and under the influence, no doubt, of Watts, he set out to paint vast enlargements of medieval miniatures on the ceiling of the Oxford Union. The effect of water-colour on whitewashed brick, though described as beautiful for the moment, lasted little longer than a firework display. None the less, when the group, aided by Ford Madox Brown, set themselves up in business as complete artistic furnishers under the name of Morris & Co., the supply of pictures 'properly so called' and mural decoration was placed in the forefront of their prospectus.

The firm's public was, however, perhaps the least disposed to buy easel pictures and decorate walls by contract and on an estimate. Apart from painting on panels of furniture, the painter members found their chief employment in stained glass, which was already, through the Gothic revival, a flourishing artistic industry. It, in its turn, exercised a powerful influence on their pictures by giving them a spiritual and hieratic justification for the decorative distortion of the figure and thus encouraging them to emphasize rhythm of contour line, flat pattern, and glowing or transparent colour. One step only remained to be taken. The flatness, angularity, exaggeration of detail, disproportion, brightness of colour, and absence of spatial effect of medieval European work had always been likened by traditional critics to the Chinese. With or without Pre-Raphaelite influence, English painting at about this date seemed to continental observers to have a Chinese air. Not unnaturally, therefore, Rossetti passed about 1860 from his passion for missals to enthusiasm for Chinese and Japanese art.

Although Rossetti and his group offer the most convenient field in which to watch this development towards design, they were still too obscure to effect by themselves even the beginning of a revolution. More especially in view of the inclusion of pictures in the sphere of Morris & Co., it would be nearer the truth to regard this aspect of their activity as a part of the widespread movement for reintroducing visual beauty into daily life which manifested itself in the two great Exhibitions of 1851 and 1862 by a confused orgy of archaistic revival, naturalistic travesty, and exercise in associative fitness, and in which the main line was the return of Alfred Stevens and South Kensington to the Renaissance. Nor was design a conspicuous feature in the work of the other Pre-Raphaelites with whom Rossetti was still associated. On the other hand, the charge of excessively decorative treatment was explicitly brought against Leighton. Watts, too, combining the Renaissance with the Elgin Marbles, was again raising the cry for monumental opportunities, while after the Paris Exhibition of 1855 and the *rapprochement* with France which accompanied the Crimean War, more and more young men went to Paris to study, and returned with a more frankly naturalistic and picturesque outlook which even when it was not decorative was at least akin, in its recognition of the purely visual value of the thing as seen and represented without reference to moral or associative qualities.

The broad naturalism in landscape which came to England from France was clearly but a return of the tradition of

Constable which had always been kept alive even under the fiercest denunciations of Ruskin, though it had shown itself chiefly in minor works at the lesser galleries and in the repression by the Academy of the Pre-Raphaelite landscape. Similarly, Leighton's classicism and Stevens's revival of the Renaissance were not fresh births but revivals of tendencies which had only been obscured for a moment. New ideas expressed themselves in new rhythms, but Watts's demand for large fields of heroic decoration was an echo from Haydon, which had reverberated throughout the period of the frescoes and only became again insistent through the disappointments of Westminster Hall. The kaleidoscopic changes of Ruskin's theories epitomize the turmoil of the period with their conflict between the ideal of a serene central art, whose expression he could not admire, and the attractions of the curious, troubled, quaint, realistic, provincial performances of the day which in principle he deplored. Although in the background, Blake and the Ancients, with their combination of inspiration and design, had always remained a real force.[1] Even Rossetti in his enthusiasm for Chinese Art was picking up a forgotten thread. As a boy at King's College he learned from Cotman, whose later water-colours, especially those of medieval figure subjects which date from his appointment at that school, not only have the hot colour and rich texture of Rossetti's work in that medium, but also revived the deliberate patterning of his early exercises in flat transparent wash, which, although no doubt independent of any direct Oriental influence, strike every observer with their affinity to Chinese or Japanese art.

It was explicitly as the outcome of these influences, native and foreign, that about 1860 the critics, W. M. Rossetti and Hamerton, who had been the prophets of the narrowest Pre-Raphaelitism, began to uphold the virtues of style and the doctrine of the picture in itself. The cry of 'Art for Art' was beginning to be heard.[2] But the pendulum did not swing

[1] When the importance of form was again reasserted, Blake provided authority with his pregnant note, 'Invention depends altogether upon execution or organization', quoted by W. M. Rossetti in *Fraser's Magazine*, 1863; *Fine Art*, p. 28. His brother's nearest approaches to a doctrine of 'pure art' were contributed to Gilchrist's *Life of Blake* of that year.

[2] Hamerton, 'The Artistic Spirit', 1865, in *Thoughts about Art*, p. 203. He refers to Whistler's 'Woman in White' (*sic*). The phrase 'Aesthetic Art' occurs as early as 1855, *Art Journal*, 1855, p. 169: 'We remember the good old days of

either rapidly or completely. Both artists and public still regarded the eye, in the phrase of the time, primarily as the channel to the head and the heart. The revolt against the Academy, so far as it was not merely a personal and professional matter, was founded on demands not for more pictorial treatment, but for greater moral elevation and more profundity of soul, and when their new building gave them more space for exhibition and larger canvasses in which to dissipate their hardly won achievements, the Painter was again forgotten in the old opposition between the commonplace, the elevating, and the eccentric, the Public, the Preacher, and the Poet.

Somerset House, when the rule was freedom of handling and what was called a "spirited touch"; anything approaching to "aesthetic Art" (we thank thee, Jew, for teaching us that word) was regarded as the essence of imbecility.' Though the writer here seems to stigmatize 'microscopic manipulation' as 'aesthetic', he was probably thinking more of the Pre-Raphaelite fondness for red hair and ugly faces for which even the early Millais was abused. In this respect the antithesis is a revival in a new form of the old contrast between 'natural' and 'picturesque' beauty.

PHOTOGRAPHIC COMPOSITION, *c.* 1855

XI

ARCHITECTURE

XI

ARCHITECTURE

By A. E. RICHARDSON

§ I. THE CLASSIC TRADITION

THE characteristics of Victorian architecture were in the main the expressions of two distinct traditions, or to be more accurate two mannerisms. It was the recollection of great things that inspired the will to produce new works which in spirit should compete with the masterpieces of the past. For more than two centuries architecture had been influenced by literature dealing especially with the subject and by illustrations of buildings. This process of revitalizing secondary forms and of recomposing recognized pictorial effects in architecture now entered upon its culminating mood.

The duality of the movement with its twin streams of literature is perhaps the most striking feature. By the end of the eighteenth century the classical manner was changing to Greek. This was due to the dilettantism which led architects to become studious of the antiquities of Athens. On the Classical side, the turning-point betwixt old and new was reached when the Elgin Marbles were acquired for the British Museum. The Gothic revival proceeded at first with less rapidity of action, although the time was to come when its exponents could claim nearly all the advantages. In this branch, as in the Greek revival, literary architecture was conspicuous.

Judgements as to the origin of the Gothic revival are mostly wide, one school believing that no real break with Gothic took place, and another seeing in romanticism the beginnings of an entirely new form of pointed architecture. From the time of Wren experiments in Gothic had been made; there are such evidences as the model for a Gothic church in Worcester by Thomas White, 1734. On the whole 'Georgian Gothic' was largely 'the five orders Gothicized'. When the Gothic revival developed towards maturity architects became less content to copy, and a few of the leaders proceeded to investigate structural truths. At first the revival was governed by the Antiquary, later under architectural direction there was the inevitable compromise between old and new, followed by ineffectual attempts to recapture the quality of the old work according as more authoritative books on medieval architecture were published.

It is not surprising, therefore, to find that continental travel broadened the outlook, or that the historic medieval buildings of Belgium, France, and Italy were laid under contribution by Victorian artists, architects, and amateurs. In this regard the name of the Reverend J. L. Petit is prominent. He was the leader of a movement which led subsequently to the magnificent sketches and drawings by Norman Shaw, and the voluminous sketch-books of Street. But it was the earlier writers, Augustus Welby Pugin and Rickman, who completely changed architectural and ecclesiastical opinion. The increasing influence of architectural draughtsmanship and topographical drawing offers an explanation of the Victorian grasp of the picturesque in grouping.

But at the beginning of the nineteenth century there were no sharp contrasts in architectural expression; the general theme was classical, and as the classical school at first preponderated and eventually outlived the revived Gothic, precedence will be given to its facts and exemplars.

The difficulty of imposing time limits to the beginnings and mergings of art during historical periods is well known, and in this regard the Victorian is no exception. The early period established the new Greek for public buildings and encouraged the revival of Gothic for colleges and churches. But the movement towards the new in both branches had begun in the eighteenth century; the spirit of research and discovery that followed also left its traces on public and domestic buildings. Thus while the Hellenic movement effected a compromise with Palladianism, the slender pointed style was more rarely employed, and then only for exceptional buildings.

The lessons of the early period are many; the impracticability of rules and formulae in art was continually shown, as well as the need for structural congruity. The exponents of both schools, Greek and Gothic, aimed at clearly pictorial values in their buildings; in so doing they touched upon one of the essentials of civics. As time went on the logic of handicraft was demonstrated and this resulted in improved

THE NEW VICTUALLING OFFICE, DEVIL'S POINT, PLYMOUTH

technique in the use and working of material. But alas! the old intrinsic qualities evaded even those who were most zealous for their re-establishment.

The new spirit of scholarship on the classical side was stimulated by Sir John Soane, whose position as a great teacher has, hitherto, not been sufficiently appreciated. Soane has been described as 'the most original British Architect since Vanbrugh'. Born in 1753, he died a few months before the accession of Queen Victoria. His was the distinction of continuing the traditions of the late eighteenth century, which he combined with his own abstract inventions. During the first part of Soane's professional career his work had much in common with that of the Adam Brothers; at a later stage he became more individualistic, and at the last touched on the Italian manner initiated by Barry. The remodelling of the entire Bank of England was his principal work, and in this vast building he showed his ingenuity as a thoughtful constructive architect. Soane's chief inspiration was derived from the etchings of Piranesi and the works of the great French engineers. Soane's attachment to classical architecture was sincere. This accounts for the fact that the Gothic revival offered him no great attraction. Beyond a slight echo of Strawberry Hill, in the Monk's Parlour at Lincoln's Inn, he left Gothic severely alone. His work differs from that of his contemporaries in the importance given to structure; by comparison the works of Nash are superficial and monotonous. It was this vital if singular quality of originality that caused his designs to be received with derision. As an architect he practised between two schools, neither of which he influenced directly by his own buildings.

Viewed disinterestedly his life's work forms a brilliant contribution to architectural development. For over thirty years he was Professor of Architecture to the Royal Academy, and it was through the medium of his pupils and assistants that his teaching was extended to the art of the Victorian period. Soane's methods as a designer were too specialized to be generally imitated, but his teachings were accepted without reserve. In his professional career he touched on most things, ranging from the design of furniture to steam apparatus for warming buildings. As a pioneer of architectural education he was pre-eminent. It is, therefore, in the founding of the Soane Museum, and the instruction he gave to the younger generation of architects, that the value of his example is best seen. The list of his pupils who subsequently became famous is a lengthy one. George Basevi was in his office for six years, David Laing was a pupil, and the names of Mocatta, C. J. Richardson, Sir Robert Smirke, George Wightwick, John Sanders, Thomas Chawner, Joseph Gandy, and Henry Parke, are identified with many Victorian buildings. Five years before Soane's death Gilbert Scott entered as an assistant into the office of Sir Robert Smirke's former assistant, Henry Roberts, architect of the new Fishmongers' Hall. Scott says that Smirke's tastes, habits, and modes of construction, and drawing, had been thoroughly imbibed by his new master. The fact that Scott at this time attended a course of lectures given by Sir John Soane to the students of the Royal Academy reveals another link between the old and the new régime. Soane aimed at combining classical scholarship with individualism, but he experienced the opposition of the classical purists who looked upon his works with dismay, while the Gothic school could see nothing in common with their ideas. Yet Soane in his way was as original as Blake, and his structural inventiveness is now recognized to be logical. When Soane was in active practice the architectural background was mainly Georgian, interspersed with new buildings of Greek character. True, the support given to Greek architecture in the twenties and late thirties became stronger although it remained incomprehensible to the Gothic school.

The scope of this essay does not permit of the exact biographical method in dealing with the architects and their works. In that vast sea of facts the surface has to be trawled again and again for relevant material. There's magic in the net, might be said, but there is also the embarrassment of an over-yield. Among Sir John Soane's contemporaries John Nash held a unique position at the time of the Regency and as Court architect to George the Fourth. As an architect his education was deficient, but to-day he ranks as the originator of town planning on the grand scale. Most of his brother architects admitted his courage but damned his buildings with faint praise. The massing of groups of buildings and the treatment of landscape gardening were his strongest points. His architectural opinions were mainly classical; his feeling was towards grandeur of effect.

Yet it is evident from a comparison of his works that he lacked Soane's scholarship and power of invention. Professor Cockerell remarked that an air of superficiality is seldom absent from his elevations. At the time no other architect existed with such terrific energy. Nash borrowed and adapted types of classic buildings from every conceivable source, and he did not scruple to imitate certain features of Soane's work. He astonished the rest of the architectural world by rearranging the orders out of sequence; he reproduced the Greek Doric order from Paestum in cast iron, and he committed many other improprieties. In the eyes of the old school his reputation was far from high, but he enriched London with palatial blocks of symmetrical architecture and showed the greatest skill in variety of composition. To be brief, the formalism of the 'Regency' was his. Whether the credit is due to his control or to the skill of his assistants is still in doubt. His conception of Regent Street with its colonnaded quadrant was grandiose, and its interpretation into terms of brick and stucco was Herculean. The contribution of this architect was truly remarkable. It includes the lay-out of Regent's Park with its fine terraces, Buckingham Palace and the Marble Arch, churches, schools, and mansions. He lived at a time of princely patronage and he was not backward in taking every advantage of the opportunities which were showered upon him.

Nash's schemes resulted in a mania for architectural improvements not only in London but at Plymouth, and later at Newcastle-upon-Tyne and many other cities and towns in the United Kingdom. The building of London Bridge had directed attention to the need for further civic improvements. The inferior appearance of many parts of London was looked upon with dismay. People acquainted with Paris and other continental cities were frankly disgusted with the aspect of the narrow and tortuous London streets. Cockspur Street, for instance, was then scarcely twenty feet wide; the Royal Mews stood on the site of Trafalgar Square; the Haymarket, crowded with country wagons, resembled the market-place of a provincial town. Near Waterloo Bridge, Cross's Menagerie and Exeter Change choked the Strand, while a congeries of slums marred the connexion between Oxford Street and Holborn. Nearer the City the Fleet Market with its booths and hovels filled Farringdon Street. Tallis's *Views of the*

London Streets illustrates the hasty refronting of shops and other premises that took place between the years 1825 and 1840.

The problem of rebuilding the heart of London was a difficult one, but it was tackled with astonishing expedition by the appointment of the 'Committee of Taste' for such improvements as were immediately needed. The first work of the committee, of which Lord Farnborough, John Wilson Croker, Sir John Soane, Sir Robert Smirke, and John Nash were members, was to supervise the remodelling of the neighbourhood of Charing Cross, the Strand, Holborn, and Oxford Street. Nearly all the undertakings then advised were carried out with the exception of a new street from Waterloo Bridge to Oxford Street, which was allowed to meander along existing thoroughfares instead of being formed in a straight line of ample width. The scheme projected by Sir F. Trench for constructing quays along the banks of the Thames from Whitehall to Blackfriars Bridge received support from the younger Rennie, but this fine idea was not revived till much later.

Meanwhile the Greek ideal was being pursued with vigour, and this introduces William Wilkins, a formidable scholar. A master of Greek detail, he contributed University College with the remarkable portico in Gower Street. His design for the National Gallery, on the site reclaimed by the Committee of Taste, was hampered by the condition of utilizing the Corinthian Columns of the demolished Carlton House. Wilkins was a fastidious designer and for a time he was associated in practice with Gandy-Deering. On the death of Sir John Soane, Wilkins was appointed Professor of Architecture at the Royal Academy, but apparently he did not lecture. Wilkins was responsible for three of the largest works then built in London, i.e. University College, the National Gallery, and St. George's Hospital. At Cambridge he had already carried out two sides of Downing College, and at York he had built the Museum. Among his lesser works the monument to Nelson at Yarmouth is the most original. Wilkins's architecture is distinctive for its academic precision. As events proved he became known as a college architect. In spite of the impressive character of his elevations it is surprising that they did not constitute a style which other architects could follow. The nearest approach to

DESTRUCTION OF NASH'S COLONNADE, REGENT STREET, 1848

his manner is shown in the façades of the British Museum, designed at a later date by Sir Robert Smirke.

Although Greek architecture found favour in London it fared better in Scotland, the cities of Edinburgh and Glasgow proving even more amenable to the works of Greek enthusiasts than the Metropolis. The Greek manner remained fashionable for many years; most architects brooding over Hellenism till 'Greek Thomson' alone held the field. The leader of the Greek revival, Thomas Hamilton, 1785–1858, became famous as the designer of the High School at Edinburgh. Critics could quote no building that stood more handsomely or was more perfectly executed than this Theseion of modern Athens. The site was unique; there was scope for pictorial massing. Hamilton, who had never travelled to Greece, took his motives from authentic literary sources, and he recomposed them in his façades. But, however tenacious the architect was in his application of Greek detail, it was obvious that the process could not be continued indefinitely. Changes were already foreshadowed, and in the design of the Royal College of Physicians in Queen Street, 1845, also by Hamilton, there is evidence of Barry's new Italian manner.

The advances made in classical scholarship, and the accumulation of literary knowledge, became apparent in a diversity of small buildings of the Greek revival. For some years prior to 1837, nearly every important English town was in the throes of improvement, a particular architect being identified with each of the projects, for example, John Foulston at Plymouth, who later was associated with Wightwick, a pupil of Soane's. The other instances are those of Dobson at Newcastle, Decimus Burton at Hastings, Brighton, and Tunbridge Wells, and John Buonarotti Papworth at Cheltenham. In all these places there is evidence of remarkable variety in the design of buildings, and a variation of the manner of Soane and Nash, therefore, is not a matter for surprise. One of the ablest of the group was Papworth, whose attainments secured him commissions from every quarter; but it is his work at Cheltenham that is best known. In the design of the Rotunda and Montpellier Terrace he followed the tenets of Soane; for the Police Station his elevation resembles the work of Nash. Papworth's name is likewise associated with designs for the buildings facing the

II   B b

Promenade and Lansdown Place, and in the treatment of small houses he evolved the very genesis of early Victorian design. No other architect so far had succeeded in attaching external verandahs to the façades of terrace houses, and few could design shop fronts with greater delicacy. Among other buildings at Cheltenham it is probable that Papworth designed the Queen's Hotel. Chronologically this building is the first classical building of the Victorian period, and certainly the first in which medallions bearing the Queen's profile form part of the design. It was fortunate for Cheltenham that the services of John Papworth were available to endow the incomparable surroundings with such graceful architecture. John Papworth's younger brother, George, went over to Ireland, where it was said

' he was the first to introduce into Dublin and Ireland exterior decoration in architectural design, combined with a light and elegant appearance, particularly in private dwellings; in fact, he was the father of a new school; in which Turner, a builder of Dublin, took pattern from him in various places, and other persons copied his ideas. His cast iron bridge across the Liffey was, at the time he designed it, a novelty in bridge building.'

The career of Sir Robert Smirke, 1781–1867, covers the whole of the early and middle Victorian period. The various tendencies of Soane's teaching were assimilated by this distinguished pupil, who in addition had the advantage of foreign travel and study in Greece. His chief work was the rebuilding of the British Museum, which he completed in 1847; the domed reading-room was added by his brother Sidney Smirke in 1855. He designed the façades for the buildings forming the north and south approaches of London Bridge, but those to King William Street and Moorgate Street are not generally known. His other works were the alterations to the Royal Mint and buildings in the Temple. As an architect of the Greek revival his favourite motive was the Priene Ionic order which he first introduced in the elevation of the old General Post Office. The eastern portion of Somerset House, which he completed in accordance with the lines of the original building, provided accommodation for King's College. The Council House at Bristol is perhaps the most ornate of his works. When the foundations of Laing's Customs' House failed, Smirke was called upon to remedy the defects. The centre portion of the river front now standing

DEMOLITION OF OLD LONDON BRIDGE, 1824

is from his design, but it does not equal the dignity of Laing's façade which it replaced. Up to this period Soane's teachings were still a strong influence, but in no single case were his pupils controlled by the mannerisms of his buildings.

In the work of George Basevi (1799–1845) there is evidence of greater power and more dashing effect than Soane ever attempted. Basevi was in Soane's office for five years, and after this term of pupilage he left for an extended tour through Italy and Greece, returning to England in 1819. At first he was engaged on the lay-out of Belgrave Square and the surrounding streets, a scheme recommended by Thomas Cundy, then surveyor to the Westminster Estate, and financed by Messrs. Cubitt. Basevi designed all the houses in the Square, with the exception of those at the angles, a work which occupied him for some years. This important commission hardly belongs to the early Victorian period, for both the design of the terraces and the lay-out of the Square are Regency in character. The chief reason for the development of Belgravia as a first-class residential area can be attributed to the rebuilding of Buckingham House as a Royal Palace. The above-mentioned works were considered a great success and led to Basevi being engaged to plan Pelham Crescent and Thurlow Square. Eaton Square, by comparison with Belgrave Square, is inordinately dull, a fact attributable to the design being supplied by the builders. Basevi did not grow wanton with success but steadily pursued the classical manner in which he had been trained, but with fresh experience he turned with more regard to the Italian. His superiority to his predecessors is shown in the design of the Conservative Club, St. James's Street, in which he was associated with Sidney Smirke. This building shows considerable variations from the usual classic façade then in fashion, an especial feature being the balance of the club 'bow window' with the main entrance.

Soon after, both architects were nominated to design the new Carlton Club, Pall Mall; Basevi, however, met his death at Ely Cathedral, and Sidney Smirke carried out the building alone. Prior to this Basevi was proceeding with the Fitzwilliam Museum at Cambridge, a building so justly classical in scale and so novel in composition as to rank with the vigorous examples of the previous century. Although the characteristics are early Victorian the academical qualities

are outstanding. To contemporary opinion the Fitzwilliam
Museum presented no mean travesty of a Greek or Roman
temple; the giant portico introduced as the central feature
in a composition of balanced masses combined the imagination of Soane with a more relevant selection of classical
detail. The interior of the Museum was incomplete at the
time of Basevi's death, and it was left to Professor Cockerell
to make some alterations in the plan of the main staircase
and to supervise the finishings. As it stands to-day the
original building, both externally and with its sumptuous
decorations, is recognized to be one of the finest works of
the early Victorian period.

Lingering traces of Soane's influence are to be seen in the
buildings designed by his pupils in London, and further
afield, down to the mid-Victorian period. This is more
essentially the case in the works of George Wightwick, who
for a time was in Soane's office. Wightwick eventually
became a partner of John Foulston and practised at Plymouth, where he refronted the Proprietary Library, and after
1850 built many of the terraces in the 'Three Towns'.

So far the nineteenth century had a fine record of classical
buildings evidencing the new fashions in architecture and
forming the basis of Victorian scholarship. It has often been
said that early Victorian architects solved their problems out
of hand by copying historical motives. This may be true of
the lesser men but it cannot apply in any sense to Sir Charles
Barry, whose classical works are an entire contrast to those
of his predecessors, his contemporaries, and his successors.
He was primarily a classical architect; that 'he had an
artist's eye for the picturesque' sums up his viewpoint to a
nicety. Three years of foreign travel gave him unique
opportunities to develop his sensitive reaction to architecture. And it was during this period that Greek, Egyptian,
and Italian buildings came under his review; but he returned
to England with an open mind. Barry was a consummate
draughtsman. There can be no doubt that if his energies had
led him to devote his time exclusively to pictorial art he
would have rivalled David Roberts. As an architect he
favoured the perfection of proportion and unity of composition, two factors which led to the official character of
his buildings. This is not the place for a catalogue of the
whole of Barry's classic buildings, nor for a discussion of his

LANSDOWN TERRACE, CHELTENHAM

success as Architect to the Houses of Parliament, which forms part of the story of the Gothic revival. His reputation as a classicist stands upon the design of the Travellers' Club in Pall Mall in which the new 'Barry Italian' first appeared as a protest against 'Old-fashioned Palladian'. At the time the completed building was both praised and censured, it was described as a copy of the Pandolfini at Florence, and it was subjected to other wayward criticism. Barry himself deplored the lack of balance in the façade due to the placing of the entrance on one side. But there were few among his contemporaries who did not praise the beauty of the proportions and the delicacy of detail. The truth that the work was original, in the sense that it recast a time-honoured theme, apparently escaped notice; there was likewise little or no appreciation of its asymmetrical values. The story of the widening of the social circle in Victorian England is in more than partial evidence in the design of the Pall Mall Clubs; and no survey of the time would be complete without reference to these unique institutions.

Barry's energy for work was unwearied. He completed the Travellers' Club in 1831, and six years later he won the competition for the Reform Club. In this second design the model of the Palazzo Farnesi was in his mind. While it is true that both plan and elevation are reminiscent of the spirit of the famous prototype, the comparison ceases in the adaptation. This building, like its neighbour the 'Travellers', has a stately character and courtly proportions. The newer order of club life was summarized in the spaciousness of the internal arrangements. Flushed with success, Barry carried his adapted Italian manner to the design of other buildings such as the Manchester Athenaeum, Bridgewater House, Cleveland Row, and the new wing of the mansion at Trentham. If the plan of Bridgewater House is studied it will be seen to recall the plan of the Reform Club; in elevation alone is it dissimilar. By this time the architect had advanced into his third version of neo-Italian. In this case the problem demanded the style of a private palace. As a classicist, Barry was never fantastical; he was perhaps unusual in his treatment of detail, but he was not cast in the mould of contemporary opinion. There is no mistaking his classical buildings for those of any other style or country; they are eminently Victorian, but at the same time they retain the impress of individuality. The shade of difference that marks his Italian essays from those of his fellow architects is to be found in the interest of the silhouette, for he was invariably a good profiler. The skyline of Bridgewater House, especially when the ensemble is viewed from the Green Park, shows this marked tendency. Barry, however, was to depart from his early classical methods, perhaps as a concession to popular views which demanded that a building should appear interesting. The real cause appears to have been of his own making, i.e. the rivalry of crockets, pinnacles, and buttresses which feature in the vertical lines of the Houses of Parliament. In his remodelling of Soane's Treasury Buildings, broken entablatures appear, and in the design of Halifax Town Hall, completed by E. M. Barry, the silhouette went far towards the realization of medieval verticality rather than classic horizontality. The front of the College of Surgeons in Lincoln's Inn Fields, a very successful remodelling of Lewis's design in which the earlier Greek portico is preserved, avoids such peculiarities.

In 1837 Barry was commissioned to convert Highclere in Hampshire, and he had recourse to what he called 'Anglo-Italian'. In reality he was experimenting with the Elizabethan style. Except for historical purposes it would be kinder not to mention this extravagant and bizarre example. Yet the high regard in which he held this work is curious. On the domestic side he was associated with the building of new mansions, the lay-out of gardens, and the remodelling of old houses. His first essay in this regard was Mr. Attree's house in Brighton Park. His latest work at Trentham for the Duke of Sutherland was in the nature of remodelling the existing house and entirely replanning the entourage. Loudon was not sparing of encomiums; after seeing the plans he wrote:

'We could not help doubting whether even Mr. Barry could make anything of this great dull flat place, with its immense mansion, as tame and spiritless as the ground on which it stands; we have seen the plans, however, for the additions and alterations. Let no man henceforth ever despair of a dead flat.'

Duncombe Park was another conversion, and between the years 1843 and 1850 Barry was engaged by the Earl of Harewood to alter the mansion built by Carr of York in 1759. Barry was the foremost among Victorian architects to appreciate the pictorial value of the Italian garden as part of

HIGHCLERE HOUSE, BEFORE AND AFTER RECONSTRUCTION

the architectural ensemble of a country mansion. His work at Shrubland Park is as distinguished as Trentham, but it is at Cliefden in Berkshire that his Italian theories are seen in the most varied and delightful form. There is a reflection of his treatment of levels in the Italian manner in the lay-out of Trafalgar Square, 1840, the least successful of his works. But the details of the parapets and steps are good, and the design of the angle lamps and supports is superb. In his scheme for 'General Metropolitan Improvements' exhibited in 1857, he wished to embody all the designs then current for the betterment of London. The scheme was brought forward in the names of his sons, Charles and Edward, and it was left for the consideration of those who should come after him.

Barry was a versatile architect and an individualist; whether he is considered as a master of classic or as a participant in the Tudor version of revived Gothic, his reputation stands the test of time. The attraction of novelty, the desire to be pictorial, to excel in the public estimation and to overcome opposition, prove him to have been neither eccentric nor hasty in his judgements. His associations with Pugin, which extended over many years, were of undoubted benefit to him in the design of the Houses of Parliament, and the share both had in this national work is now clearly understood.

This is perhaps the appropriate place to discuss the most perfect building of the Victorian Classic school, i.e. St. George's Hall, Liverpool. The architect, Harvey Lonsdale Elmes, must be considered as one of those brilliant artists who appear without warning and whose talent defies explanation. Elmes was born in 1814, his father being an architect as well as the author of various works and essays on architecture, including a life of Sir Christopher Wren. In due course Elmes entered his father's office, and in 1835 found employment with the elder Goodridge, a classical architect practising at Bath. About this time Elmes came into contact with Beckford, for whom Goodridge was building Lansdowne Tower. Beyond ordinary office routine his training does not seem to have been profound, but he found inspiration in Goodridge's copy of Piranesi's etchings, which he studied on every occasion. In 1839 he decided in secret to enter for the competition for St. George's Hall, which was then advertised, and to his own surprise from among eighty-six competitors he was awarded the first premium. A short interval followed, during which he studied various classical works in London, and finally he visited Germany to examine the new buildings designed by Schinkel and Leo von Klenze. At this juncture the counter-influence of German classic on the Victorian school was strong. In April 1840 Elmes succeeded in obtaining the first premium for the new Assize Courts at Liverpool. This led to the production of a new design showing the combination of St. George's Hall and the Assize Courts in one vast building. The scheme met with universal approval; the revised plan, based on a study of the Thermae of Caracalla, was acknowledged to be masterly. Elmes as an architect had extraordinary gifts, he could sketch out his ideas with great rapidity, and he prepared his own scale drawings and full-sized details. When the task of building St. George's Hall was in hand the strain of incessant work proved to be too great for his strength. He was advised to leave for Jamaica in the spring of 1847, and he died there a month after his arrival.

In the design of St. George's Hall, Victorian classic reached its zenith. In matter and form the building was academic, but the composition was new, the power of expression more profound. The youthful architect had succeeded at one great stroke of plan and mass, not by trifling with details, eking out ornament, or regrouping columns and porticoes. There was no other disguise in his methods but great force united to extreme simplicity. Elmes's success was that he got rid of the trammels of indecision and sentimentality. He had the gift of vision and the perception to benefit by the purpose and example of other great architects. At this juncture, with Gothic in the ascendant, it was a wholesome relief to the classical school to welcome such a champion. One other circumstance should be taken into account, and this concerns the growing regard for classicality inspired by the Munich school. Fergusson's denunciation of the classic revival, as distinct from the Renaissance, was too sweeping. He was living too near to the period to appreciate the conditions which determined architectural expression. Hitherto, Barry had reverted to the Italian manner for club houses and mansions, and had created a vogue; Elmes, on the other hand, had gathered all known classical principles into one grandiose conception.

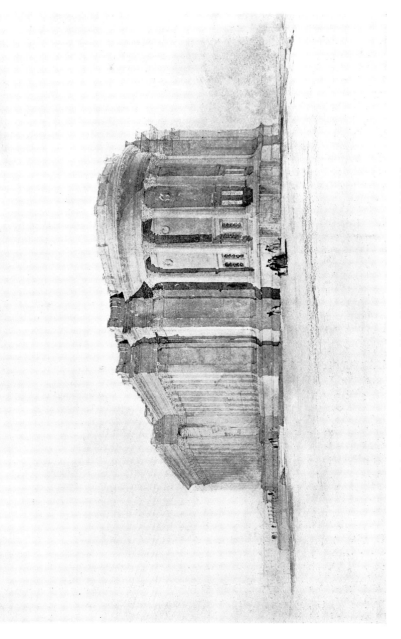

ST. GEORGE'S HALL, LIVERPOOL—*ELMES*

In contradistinction the genius of Professor C. R. Cockerell was reserved to impart Greek refinement to the classical school. Cockerell's position in the annals of Victorian architecture is that of the savant. His early adventures and researches in Greece are too well known to be recounted here, therefore it will be sufficient to recall that his training began in his father's office, where he remained for four or five years, and that afterwards he entered Robert Smirke's office as an assistant. After seven years' absence abroad, four of which he spent in Greece, Cockerell returned to England and became an acknowledged authority on Greek archaeology. From the outset his taste was only slightly influenced by the Gothic revival. True, at Harrow he had tried his hand at Gothic in the Schools and Chapel, and at Lampeter College he produced an example of early nineteenth-century Tudor. Somewhat late in life, bowing to the inevitable, he included an account of Gothic in his lectures to the Royal Academy students. The story is told of how Clarkson Stansfield introduced Cockerell and Pugin and left them to chat together. Afterwards he asked each of them what he thought of the other. Cockerell said: 'Pugin is the most earnest and enthusiastic man in his profession and has the greatest belief in it of any one I have ever met.' Pugin remarked of Cockerell: 'The man is a great artist, though I don't believe in the style he works in.' Cockerell's first classical work of importance, the Literary and Philosophical Institution, now the Freemasons' Hall, at Bristol, is marked with great purity of detail. Then followed the commission to build Hanover Chapel in Regent Street, a design based upon Hittorf's church of St. Vincent de Paul, Paris. It is clear that at this period Cockerell, apart from his own ability as a classical scholar, was not unaware of the merits of the neo-Grec school in France; later he showed preference for the works of the German classicists, especially favouring Schinkel.

His fame as an authority on Greek architecture next brought association with Playfair for the Scottish National Memorial on the Calton Hill at Edinburgh. And although the joint project of these architects was not carried out there exists that fragment of a Greek portico which is a landmark in 'Modern Athens'. When Cockerell's practice increased, he entered for several competitions, amongst others the Cambridge University Library and Museum, a fragment of the latter design being carried out in 1834. Trinity Church, Hotwells, Bristol, another of his works, was completed in 1833. In the previous year he had been engaged to design the Westminster Insurance Office in the Strand. This building is important, for it formed the basis of the design for the three branches of the Bank of England, at Liverpool, Manchester, and Bristol. Of the series the Liverpool bank building is the finest, and as a contribution to Victorian architecture it is unique in composition. Cockerell's appointment as Architect to the Bank of England dates from 1832; sixteen years later he remodelled Soane's ineffective skyline over the Threadneedle Street front. Another of Cockerell's buildings, the Sun Assurance Office, also in Threadneedle Street, was begun in 1841. The appearance of this building has been considerably altered by the addition of another story. In the design of the London County and Westminster Bank, Lothbury, in 1837, he was associated with Mr., afterwards Sir William, Tite. His design submitted in the Competition for the Royal Exchange was too startling in its baroque tendencies to please the pedants; had it been built it would indubitably have exercised an influence upon contemporary classical design. The largest but not the most successful of his works, the Taylor and Randolph Buildings at Oxford, was completed in 1845. To Cockerell fell the task of completing two of the great buildings already described, i.e. St. George's Hall, Liverpool, and the Fitzwilliam Museum, Cambridge. The meticulous respect he bestowed to the purposes of the original architects in no small measure contributed to the success of both buildings. He not only subordinated his own inclinations to the known wishes of those he succeeded, but his charity to those whom Elmes had left dependent is not widely known.

Great as Cockerell was as an architect and scholar, he was unequalled as a draughtsman; the slightest sketches from his pencil are admirable; he revelled in draughtsmanship, using the backs of envelopes, old letters, accounts, and invitation cards, all of which abound with delicate jottings. His note-books likewise are filled with careful drawings of architecture and sculpture. But his energies did not stop at buildings, for he had an artist's love of scenery, and he drew with the precision of Edward Lear. As Professor of Architecture to the Royal Academy he continued the series of lectures

THE ROYAL EXCHANGE—*COCKERELL*

which had been in abeyance since Soanc's death. These
lectures, remarkable for their erudition, are totally unlike
those given by his predecessor Soane; they are not dull statements but are pregnant with deductions and comparisons.
They read as the compilations of a scholar who disliked
writing, but who nevertheless had garnered up too much to
remain silent. Cockerell advocated the study of precedent in
all his lectures, and in this there is a resemblance to the
famous Discourses of Sir Joshua Reynolds. It is, however, to
the first six lectures that the architectural student should
turn for inspiration. But of all his productions the brilliant
restorations of Rome, now in the Royal Academy, and the
famous tribute to Sir Christopher Wren, are outstanding.
Cockerell was the first of the Victorians to direct the attention of other architects to the qualities of Sir Christopher
Wren's buildings. As Surveyor to St. Paul's, the charge of the
fabric revealed to him the underlying mastery of structure
which was Wren's by right of genius. Cockerell could see
beneath the surface; he cherished no illusions regarding
Wren's detail nor did he admire the selection of ornament
characteristic of the seventeenth century, but he saw that
Wren's work had the crown of immortality and that no
imitation could have the same quality attached to it.

In the design of the Liverpool and London Insurance
Buildings at Liverpool, the last work of his life, the Professor
was assisted by his son, F. P. Cockerell, who will be best
remembered for the design of the Freemasons' Hall in Great
Queen Street. For many years Cockerell's chief assistant,
Goodchild, prepared the working drawings from sketches for
the buildings already mentioned. Apart from considerations
of style and the blending of Greek detail with Italian
motives which latterly became part of Cockerell's method,
he was a proved master in the treatment of masonry in the
grand manner. The size and proportions of the stones form
part of the subtle harmony of all his structures, an attribute
due to his study of the construction of the Greek Temples.
The completion of St. George's Hall was described by Sir
James Picton in the following terms: 'With all its defects
St. George's Hall constitutes not only the architectural glory
of Liverpool, but is one of the greatest triumphs of art in
modern times.' Fergusson wrote of it as producing 'an
effect of grandeur unequalled by any other modern building

known' and as 'the culminating and by far the most successful specimen of this style of art in England and perhaps in Europe'. The versatility of Cockerell's genius is apparent in all his works; he was many-sided, as a professor should be, a brilliant draughtsman, a learned archaeologist, and one who understood sculpture. In his lectures he made clear to the students not only the underlying principles of design but the purpose of the buildings of classical antiquity.

In a manner, similar to the works and influence of many of the architects already described, the life of Professor Cockerell links the classical traditions of the late eighteenth century to the classicalities of the mid-Victorian period. After his death in 1863, his theories remained a subtle force on the minds of those who at this time represented the classical school, and in consequence many buildings erected in the City between the sixties and the seventies bear the impress of Cockerell's teachings. It was, however, in the works of his son that familiar touches were revealed. One outstanding example of the Cockerell-Elmes manner exists in the design of the Harris Library at Preston, which was completed in 1896.

Among other Victorian architects Decimus Burton, 1800–81, is identified with the active side of the classical movement. He was deservedly popular at the beginning of his career, and then, for no apparent reason, suffered obscurity. It was Burton's lot to design 'Greek architecture' in the days of George the Fourth, and to survive to the time when Norman Shaw was building Lowther Lodge at Kensington. The tenth son of James Burton, a speculative builder, he first studied architecture under George Maddox, the designer of early Victorian shop fronts. When only twenty-one he began to practise, designing several private houses in Regent's Park, including The Holme; St. Dunstan's Lodge came later. Clarence Terrace and Cornwall Terrace with some authority are also attributed to him.

His first large work was the Colosseum in Regent's Park, a building intended for panoramic displays. In 1831 he designed Charing Cross Hospital, and a club in Lower Regent Street. His reputation rests chiefly on the Athenaeum Club, Pall Mall, which was projected soon after Barry's success with the 'Travellers'. This building is Greek in conception, but there is a strong Italianate feeling in the

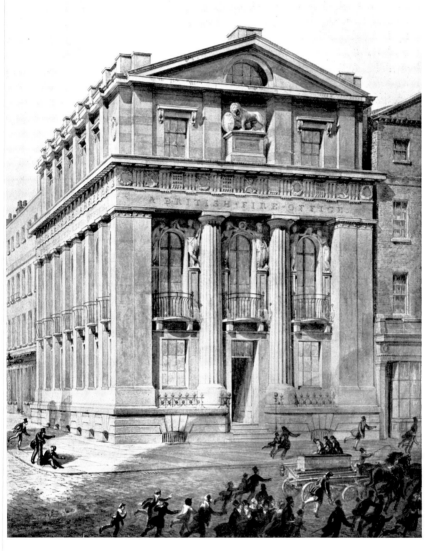

AN ASSURANCE OFFICE—*COCKERELL*

Market House, and Calverley Place formed the main part of the development, and in addition there were numerous four- and six-roomed cottages 'for the humbler classes of society'. The whole of the buildings were faced with stone from a quarry on the estate. The only departure from classic was Baston Cottage 'in the Gothic style', which the architect built for his own use. The design of the semi-detached villas of Grove Hill, as well as the development of Nevill Park, Mount Ephraim, and Mount Sion, were all controlled by the architect.

By virtue of his design for the Royal Exchange, the third to be built on the site, Sir William Tite may be considered among the leaders of the classical school. This was his principal architectural work and resulted from a competition in which four leading architects took part. While the plan is good and the frontispiece distinctive, the detail is bookish and over-conscious. The chief fault is that the side elevations do not blend happily with the portico, a lesser defect being the restless skyline. The trapezoidal site demanded considerable ingenuity in planning, and from this point of view the design is admittedly a success. In addition there is a quality of scale combined with richness of detail which is conspicuous in the interior of the building. The architect, however, had set himself the difficult task of combining a Roman portico with an Italian building, and as a result was only partially successful.

Tite's first work, the rebuilding of the Golden Cross Inn at Charing Cross, was connected with the Metropolitan Improvements that came after the Regency; it was neither an accomplished piece of composition nor did it show any feature out of the ordinary. But when Tite was associated with Professor Cockerell to design the London and Westminster Bank in Lothbury, his work improved in interest and quality, although the division of labour was such that Tite was employed solely for the interior. He was next engaged to design the first railway stations on the London and South-Western line, as well as to prepare plans for stations in France between Havre and Paris. This period of railway construction continued to be lucrative for architects as well as for engineers, and in view of his reputation it is not surprising to find that the designs for the stations and termini on the Caledonian and Scottish Central Railways were entrusted to him. Tite was a capable architect and his theories of scale were well founded, but by comparison his work lacks the refinement of Cockerell's, although largeness of handling conceals minor deficiencies.

The next architect, Sir James Pennethorne, maintained his reputation as a classicist over a much longer period. Born in 1801, he eventually entered the office of his uncle, John Nash, whom he assisted in the design of Buckingham Palace. Like most young architects of the day he travelled in France and Italy, and after 1826 again assisted Nash, this time completing the western block of Carlton House Terrace. Six years later he was commissioned by the Crown Authorities to prepare plans for many street improvements. Among these were New Oxford Street, New Coventry Street, Endell Street, Buckingham Gate, and other parts. His designs for Christ Church, Albany Street, 1836, and Trinity Church, Gray's Inn Road, 1837, follow the rigid manner of Nash. Then, as now, fashion played no unimportant part in the work of architects; this explains why Pennethorne followed the manner of Barry for the Jermyn Street front of the Geological Museum. This building was in course of erection for eleven years and the construction of the main gallery was much admired. Pennethorne's undoubted artistry was shown in the masterly treatment of the projecting balcony and the remodelling of the shops to the Quadrant, Regent Street, in 1848; but it was the completion of the western group of buildings to Somerset House that earned him the greatest praise. In this addition to Chambers's group of buildings he captured the spirit of the earlier work and he evolved one of the noblest pavilion groups in the Metropolis. It was not only an accomplished piece of classicality but it demonstrated the value of complementing an existing masterpiece by following the same details. His other works include the Ball Room at Buckingham Palace, the Offices of the Duchy of Cornwall, 1854, and the New Stationery Office at Westminster. The London University Buildings in Burlington Gardens, also a fine pictorial group, were practically his last work in the classical manner. As a contrast the Public Record Office in Chancery Lane shows that the Gothic revival did not affect his work till late in life.

Another classical exponent, Philip Hardwick, is identified with several important public buildings including Euston

Station, which he built for the London and Birmingham Railway. The son of Thomas Hardwick, a pupil of Chambers, he was trained in sympathy with the best classical traditions of the previous century. His first work, the warehouses and offices for the St. Katherine's Dock Company, was begun in 1825. In this design he followed the prevalent taste for Greek, as is evidenced in the façade to Tower Hill. Eleven years after this he was appointed to design the Hall of the Goldsmiths' Company in Foster Lane, the façade of which has the repose of a sixteenth-century Italian palace, with vigorous detail and trophies. The interior of this building is especially noble, the chief feature being the staircase and the lantern. Hardwick shared Barry's gift of imparting an interesting silhouette to buildings in which horizontal lines predominated; he was conscious of the excellence of antique art, and he sought to bring back the quality of scale which was so conspicuous a feature of the works of Chambers. As a classicist he was less ambitious than Barry; in consequence the elevation of Goldsmiths' Hall shows no deterioration from the best manner of the eighteenth century. There was also a departure from immediate precedent in that the built-in-order had nothing in common with the portico method of Wilkins or Smirke. Another improvement is to be observed in the structural quality of the masonry, which deviates entirely from the stuccoed manner of the Regency. The leading architects of the classic school were now, almost without exception, firm believers in the principle of structural building, and, even if they did not admit a larger conception of architecture than the historical, they were at least consistent.

Hardwick's drawing of the gateway to Euston Station, shown in the Diploma Gallery at the Royal Academy, is a free adaptation of the entrance to the Athenian Agora. At the time of its erection it was not so entirely purposeless as it has since become, for in 1836 the surrounding districts to the north-west had not been built up. The architect's intention was that the northern heights should be viewed from within the frame of the Doric columns, and this affords another instance of the Victorian grasp of pictorial effect. The gateway, moreover, was intended to be a monument to railway engineering. But to Londoners Hardwick is best known by his design for the Great Hall at Euston, which he

a

b

RAILWAY STATIONS

(*a*) FUNCTIONAL, BY MOCATTA

(*b*) ROMANTIC (SHREWSBURY)

completed in 1847. This magnificent interior was inspired by the interior of the Palazzo Vecchia at Florence and the details of the Palazzo Massimi at Rome. A complete list of Hardwick's buildings is too extensive to be given in these pages; mention of a few of the more important must suffice; these include the City Club in Broad Street, the Victoria Hotel, the Great Western Hotel, Paddington, and the huge blocks which form the Railway Clearing House in Seymour Street. After 1838 P. C. Hardwick was associated with his father in many works, including those buildings which will be described as part of the Gothic revival.

During the first half of the nineteenth century an increasing number of architects had ranged themselves on the classic side, either by virtue of their training as pupils or assistants of classical architects, or because they preferred classic to the caprices of Gothic. They actually succeeded in maintaining an academic standard within their somewhat exclusive circle. The mass of building, not excepting the vast speculations on the Pimlico estates which were undertaken by Cubitts, who employed their own architectural staff, was pronouncedly classical. True, this volume of housing lacked the charm of the vernacular of the eighteenth century, but it had the merits of conspicuous uniformity and precision. Outside these circles the lapses into drab mediocrity were more palpable; then as now there was no controlling the grasping speculative builder; no guidance for the perplexed mechanic. Any attempt to understand the art of the period must make allowances for the ease in which the speculator was then allowed to work. But for the intervention of the District Surveyors, but for the general desire of the middle class to be respectably housed, the vernacular might have been much worse.

Previously it has been shown that the change to Italian was due to Barry, who for many years led the Italian school, and influenced the design of the Queen's Palace at Osborne and the Orphan Working School at Haverstock Hill, besides many other works. The last contribution to the success of this particular mode was made by Lewis Vulliamy. Beginning as an exponent of Greek, Vulliamy built the offices of the Law Institution in Chancery Lane, and in 1838 he refronted the Royal Institution in Albemarle Street. His brother, George Vulliamy, was a pupil of Barry's, but this fact provides no clue to any connexion between the works of Barry or Vulliamy, for the latter would have gravitated towards Italian in response to the general tendencies of the classical school to which he belonged. His earlier works had inclined to both Greek and Roman prototypes; the commission to build Dorchester House, Park Lane, afforded him a unique opportunity not only to compete with Barry's individual style but to show his skill in the treatment of a difficult site. The model chosen by the architect was that of the Palazzo Farnesina at Rome, and he proceeded with more than ordinary ingenuity to adapt this theme until the design ceased to represent the original. The process of transposing an Italian model resembled the methods initiated by Barry for the Travellers' Club, but in this case the result was even more successful, for the plan suited the requirements and the entourage enhanced the picturesque grouping. From every point of view the mansion composed well; the side elevation presented twin masses, each three stories high; these were linked by the central portion of the house, which was only two stories high. The critics were not slow to detect the similarity of the details to those of Peruzzi. On the whole this attempt to recast an historical model was reasonable, and few cared to disparage the external grandeur of the building or its admirable placing. In 1857 the work was sufficiently advanced for Alfred Stevens to prepare his schemes for the internal decoration, which, as already described, proved to be lively, various, and instructive.

No modern architectural movement, whether it is directed by coteries or inspired by fashion, has any claim to unqualified success. A similar verdict of the Victorian revivals is apposite, even the 'Battle of the Styles' was kept going by the champions of both camps, until Ruskin, and pursuit of the brick architecture of northern Italy, caused further idealism. What is most striking is the common sense of the classical group who, after the death of Sir Charles Barry, attempted to enlist Government interest in his project for combining the public offices. A competition was held, and eventually Sir Gilbert Scott was commissioned to prepare plans for the Home, Colonial, Foreign, and India Offices, which he did, choosing Gothic for the elevations. At this juncture, unfortunately for the architect, the Government changed and Lord Palmerston, who hated Gothic, became

COFFEE ROOM, PADDINGTON—*HARDWICK*

Premier. Scott was staggered when his scheme was turned down with the remark that the new Government buildings should be something better than a 'Jesuit College'. Scott then purchased Letarouilly's three volumes on Italian buildings, and proceeded to recast his elevations; as might have been expected the result was spiritless, the exception being the courtyard to the India Office, which was designed later by Sir Digby Wyatt. This rebuff dealt a staggering blow to the universal adoption of Gothic for public buildings, but the end of pseudo-medievalism was no more in sight than the end of revived classicism. By this time classical architecture had entered upon an intensive literary phase; photography had been perfected, and copyism was made easier. To the fine scholarship of Cockerell and the striking genius of Elmes there now succeeded a mixed company of architects who viewed Italian art through Victorian glasses and lost all perspective of architecture as a living and vital art.

The ablest of this new group, E. M. Barry, is best known by his design of Covent Garden Theatre, the interior of which is neither singular nor insipidly bizarre, as was so frequently the case in contemporary theatre design. Another of his buildings, the Art Union in the Strand, is pleasantly innocuous in its Italian statement. Charing Cross Station, on the contrary, presents a bewildering repetition of monotonous windows, and repeats with less certainty some of the excitements shown in his father's drawings for the unification of the public offices. There are signs too that the classicists were wavering and were seeking for a new old style which would effect a compromise between the formal and the free classic of the early French Renaissance. In this regard there is the evidence of E. M. Barry's own predilections, for the buildings facing Temple Gardens attempt the style of Chambord.

His brother, Charles Barry, remodelled Dulwich College, and later in 1866, with his partner Banks, rebuilt Burlington House, Piccadilly. This design, which incorporates the old building, more nearly reflects the designs of the father. The classical features are there in correct sequence, the detail is exact, and the proportions are sound. Yet, notwithstanding such academic qualities, the design is uninspired. It is evident that the classical architects were already at a loss for ideas; their work had become dull by repetition and no amount of scholarship could redeem it.

In order to estimate the development of the classic school in its lesser workings it is necessary to include a brief summary of the architects who followed rather than led contemporary opinion. Among these men Charles Fowler was probably the most skilful. He first became known for his work at Exeter, where he built the two markets. In 1830 he designed Covent Garden Market, and in the following year was commissioned to design Hungerford Market, which is distinguished by construction and planning more than imaginative design. In Glasgow, Clarke and Bell erected the Merchants' House and Courts in the Greek style in 1844, and at Paisley they designed and built the County Buildings. A far more versatile architect was Sidney Smirke, who with his brother, Sir Robert Smirke, designed the Oxford and Cambridge Club in Pall Mall in 1837; and later associated with Basevi on the design of the Conservative Club, as already stated. Sidney Smirke seems to have shared some of his brother's reputation, for he was engaged to rebuild the Carlton Club, between the years 1847 and 1854, basing the design on the style of Sansovino. In view of his brother's connexion with the British Museum, the design of the circular reading-room was entrusted to him.

Apart from the public buildings, the relatively high standard which attended the development of first-class residential centres in the early and middle periods must be stated. It is clear that such results could only have been gained by skilled direction. It is known, for example, that the majority of the buildings carried out on the Westminster estates by Cubitt were designed or controlled by the estate surveyor, Thomas Cundy. Cundy was a talented architect and, as far as can be ascertained, in addition to the ordinary nature of estate supervision he designed the staircase at Northumberland House, the screen to Grosvenor House, in which he followed the manner of Henry Holland at Carlton House, and the picture gallery in Park Lane. Meanwhile the influence of the leaders had found many imitators. For instance, David Bryce, the architect of the British Linen Company's Bank, St. Andrew's Square, Edinburgh, was influenced by Sir Charles Barry's later work. On the other hand David Rhind, also of Edinburgh, followed the manner of Playfair. In the provinces the name of John Dobson of Newcastle, 1787–1865, is identified with most of the Victorian buildings in that

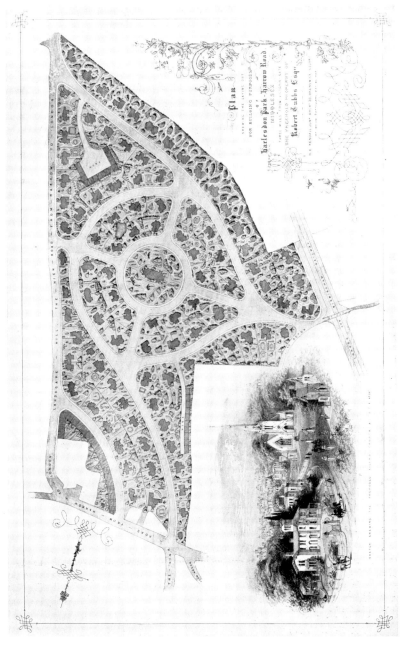

Plan

SHEWING THE LAYING OUT

FOR BUILDING PURPOSES

OF

Harlesden Park, Harrow Road

MIDDLESEX

BEING PART OF THE FREEHOLD ESTATE

THE FREEHOLD PROPERTY OF

Robert Cubbs Esqr.

SKETCH SHEWING THE PROPOSED VILLAS UPON A.A.A. PLAN

TOWN-PLANNING, c. 1850

city; his greatest achievement, the Central Station, was opened by the Queen and the Prince Consort. Dobson was primarily a classicist, and, as can be imagined, his early lapses into Gothic were almost as startling as Barry's first experiments in that style. In Dublin the names of J. F. Mulvany and Sancton Wood are identified with railway stations; whereas the Broadstone Station, Dublin, which Mulvany built in 1850, belongs to the Greek school; the Kingsbridge terminus designed by Sancton Wood is neo-Italian. Sancton Wood also had an extensive railway practice in England; he designed the Eastern Counties Stations at Cambridge, and he associated with Mr. Bruff, the Company's engineer, to design the station at Ipswich. His activities, however, did not end with railway practice, for between the years 1856 and 1858 he designed Leinster Square, Leinster Terrace, and Upper Hyde Park Gardens, all of which show classical features, but as works of art do not lend themselves to analytical description.

The career of Professor Thomas Leverton Donaldson comes within an entirely different category. In addition to being a distinguished archaeologist and a scholar he was a recognized authority on architectural history and construction. As an architect his chief works, those at University College, London, include the central Library, alterations to the Flaxman Gallery (in which he was associated with Professor Cockerell) and the Church, now the Great Hall of the College, in Gordon Square. Donaldson favoured the Italian manner, and on the domestic side the mansion at Shobrooke in Devonshire is perhaps his most important work. Misrepresentation of Victorian architecture has led to misleading generalizations about the types of buildings. It is therefore only fair to state that the standard of taste where architects were concerned was consciously high. Among the City buildings of the period the Atlas Fire Office in Cheapside by Thomas Hopper shows evidence of thoughtful study. When these lesser buildings are examined the influence of Barry is seen to be general. This characteristic is perhaps more marked in the case of buildings erected in the provinces, and is particularly the case of Leeds Town Hall, designed by Cuthbert Brodrick, although the main idea is based on the design of St. George's Hall at Liverpool. Brodrick's most successful work is without exception Leeds Corn Exchange. Further evidence of the influence of Barry's

Italian Classic is afforded by Free Trade Hall, Manchester, by Edward Walters, and in the work of John Gibson, Barry's pupil and assistant, who designed the head offices of the National Provincial Bank of England, and nearly all the important branch banks of that institution. Gibson's last work, the Town Hall at Todmorden, was built in 1870. Even towards the mid-Victorian period the classicists were tenacious of their beliefs and became more suspicious of innovations, hence the disapproval which greeted the highly original designs of Alexander Thomson, which show such a wide divergence of character from those of the Greek or the Italian schools. Alexander Thomson was more ambitious than his contemporaries; he attempted with some degree of force to combine Hellenic, Egyptian, and Hindoo motives, and the Church of St. Vincent, Glasgow, which shows the working of his mind, is an outstanding example. A master of abstract form, he outdistanced Soane in the higher flights of originality; never condescending to trivialities, he thought of details as integral to grandiose design. His buildings show direct purpose; he neither bowed to current opinion nor allowed criticism to interfere with the explicit statement he desired to convey. His work vindicated the purpose of the earlier classic school, and at the eleventh hour, when classicality seemed finally doomed, he revived it in the streets and high places of Glasgow. A man of artistic courage, he was appalled at the confusion around him, and he sought for a way out of the maze by inventing a new classical style, never dreaming it to be an accomplishment beyond the power of a single artist. It was only reasonable that with so many inborn resources and with such resolution that he gained a number of followers, especially among the younger men. Towards the end of his career he designed and built the fine group of Glasgow houses known as Great Western Terrace. Here he showed the greatest restraint and it is no exaggeration to say that a finer example of Victorian architecture of similar character does not exist.

Within the short space of fifty years the classical architecture of the nineteenth century had passed from the severe Greek of the Wilkins school to the dramatic Greek compositions of Alexander Thomson. There had been many interludes but the enigma of a perfect style had not been solved. The truth is there can be no finality to the judge-

ment of the art of any period. Not only must the achievements of the artists of one's own country be known, but those
of neighbouring countries as well. The inner workings of art
dexterity may be guessed at, but the intimacies of a period
almost defy speculation, and a really satisfactory analysis
of historical architecture is next to impossible.

The prominent feature of Victorian architecture on the
classic side is the intensity and force of the pictorial element.
This goes to prove that the Victorians studied their buildings
as complete entities and not merely as elevations. This
observance of the pictorial constitutes the Victorian style;
the variations of the classic manner which have been noted
are those of fevered inner movements which ran their course
and returned to the main theme. The object of the classical
architects of this prolific period was to invent anew, to
stimulate public interest in architecture, and to placate the
moods that demanded artistic excitement. Thus the procedure that advanced from pure Greek to Italian with
Elizabethan and French by-play, and ultimately under the
direction of Alexander Thomson returned to Greek. As will
be subsequently described, a somewhat similar process
accompanied the Gothic revival. Clearly the architectural
camps of Victorian times were not divided on the subject of
revival, *qua* revival, of antique art. The main contention
was Medieval versus Pagan. Victorian art at its best was
never dull; it was not created out of nothing; if it was
exciting in its perversity it at least rested on a solid substratum of historical precedent. The attempts made by
both classic and Gothic factions to reinstate historical
motives amounted to scene painting on the great scale—
a process only partly true of the Italian Renaissance.

The Victorian leaders of art as well as the amateurs and
the critics were, had they known it, merely extending the
dilettantism of the preceding century into an age of more
intensively literary architecture. But they did not know,
and even if they had realized the enormity of their procedure
they could not have emancipated themselves from the mesh
of time and circumstance. Architecture in the last century
became entirely professional; the art of building developed
into a highly specialized business, in which the trade workers
were mere ciphers. Victorian architecture, therefore, must be
viewed as the outcome of style exploitation and directional

tactics, rather than a national development, such as medieval art or the *ad hoc* principles of the English Renaissance. On this assumption the nature of Victorian classic at its best was academic design; in other words, the reassembling of the components of old styles within the scale of revivals which could be predetermined and defined. With this idea in mind it has been the purpose of this essay to differentiate between the finer aspects of nineteenth-century building and the mass of work which represents the Victorian vernacular. But, conversely, it is the popular art which provides the real key to the temper of an age; by this it is judged and its welfare assessed. In the eighteenth century some measure of control existed in art matters; in the nineteenth century control *en masse* became impossible. Hence the piteous appeals for architectural betterment, and the withering scorn of Ruskin, who saw clearly but could not put his theories into action, and only succeeded in adding to the confusion of both architects and public.

The great merit of the Victorian period was that it left the countryside comparatively unspoiled. The railways canalized transport, the country towns remained secluded and prosperous, the great estates flourished, and time-honoured traditions lingered outside the towns longer than is commonly supposed. It was indeed blessed that mid-Victorian expansion and commercial prosperity was in the main confined to the towns, and in these centres Victorian Architecture, good and indifferent, flourished.

§2. THE GOTHIC REVIVAL

The restudy of medieval architecture and the application of Gothic forms and ornament to modern buildings is one of the strangest episodes in the history of art. No change from old methods to new is presented, but rather a reversal of the process. Even this is not a strict definition, for the Gothic revival began by ignoring structure and imitating the external effect of the pointed arch. If we would study the architecture of the nineteenth century with profit we must accept the axiom that neither its art movements nor its traditions of literary architecture were planned or premeditated by groups of interested persons. Apparently all such movements are brought about by a concurrence of opinion which for a time favours change. In every art experiment the

THE BALL-ROOM, BUCKINGHAM PALACE—*PENNETHORNE*

tendency is to advance as rapidly as possible towards higher cultural perfection.

The Gothic revival, which so completely records one aspect of Victorian thought, proved to be no exception to this general rule. But considering the mechanical progress of the time the reversion to pseudo-medievalism is all the more striking. From comparatively slight antiquarian beginnings the revived Gothic style eventually became more popular than Greek, public interest in the subject being maintained by illustrations of designs for semi-Gothic buildings and furniture in the *Architectural Magazine* and elsewhere.

The purely Victorian development of the revival which took place after 1840, that is to say the change to academic Gothic, was due to the scholarship of certain architects and to the extraordinary ability of a group of writers who believed in their ability to impose a Gothic formula on the scientific art of building. At the beginning of the nineteenth century James Wyatt was regarded by the public to be the recognized authority on Gothic. He had achieved this reputation by building the mock abbey at Fonthill, and by his ruthless alterations to Salisbury and other Cathedrals. That strange pseudo-fortress, Belvoir Castle, was his; the traceried façades with the turrets and pinnacles at Ashridge as well as the more delicate lines of Cassiobury came from his pencil. For a time Wyatt was pre-eminent, especially in clerical and academic circles, but the only really creditable instance of his work as a restorer of a medieval building is the refacing of Henry VII's Chapel at Westminster, which he completed in 1809.

The progress of the change of taste on the part of the aristocracy can nowhere be more clearly seen than in the princely mansions which were built at the time of the Napoleonic Wars. The number of these is remarkable and affords proof of the confidence of the ruling classes. In the political situation once again we encounter the versatile John Nash, who appears to have been first attracted to Gothic by attempting 'the Grand Old Castle style' at Luscombe near Dawlish in 1804. Like many others of his works it had the fault of insincerity; it was undistinguished and repellent in the crudity of its statement. In greater contrast to the mock fortalice, which for a time was considered by architects and clients to be the ideal motive for country seats, Porden's remodelling of Eaton Hall in the Gothic taste, for example, bordered on the fantastical.

> You well might ask me why I praise
> What bears the shape of other days,
> Or rather why we do not see
> Palladian art and symmetry.
>
> (Dr. Syntax's *Tours*.)

Thus at the very beginning the Gothic movement divided into two branches and during the first decade of the last century the Castle style became an obsession, especially in Scotland, where Smirke vied with Gillespie in adorning magnificent natural sites with fortress-like buildings. To quote another instance, Blairquhan in Ayrshire was described by William Burn, with some satisfaction, to be 'a correct specimen of the architecture of Henry VIIth's time'. The most forbidding example of 'Castle Gothic', however, is Eastnor in Hereford, by Robert Smirke, who in 1811 designed the 'Council buildings' at Carlisle on similar lines. Going back a little, into the late eighteenth century, 'the Grand Old Castle' manner seems to have received support from such an accomplished classicist as Henry Holland, but the claim to the title of 'Castle Builders' beyond doubt belongs to Smirke, Gillespie, and Nash. The remodelling of Windsor Castle by Sir Jeffrey Wyattville is perhaps the strangest essay of all.

It is almost equally strange that William Wilkins, who professed to be an exponent of the Greek style, should have chosen 'Collegiate Tudor' for the mansion at Dalmeny. The truth was that Wilkins at an early stage in his career at Cambridge had succumbed to the spell of Gothic. The beauty of Ely Cathedral, the delicacy of the mouldings and tabernacle work of Prior Crauden's time as well as the majestic proportions of King's College Chapel, appealed to his refined taste. Such evidence as the foregoing shows that the Gothic revival was slowly but surely passing from the Antiquarian to the professional stage, and that authoritative works describing medieval buildings in greater detail were now required before the desired perfection could be reached. From this period the whole character of architectural scholarship was to undergo a complete change and literary influence became more pronounced. The earliest of the new series of architectural books, *Specimens of Gothic Architecture*, vols i and ii, were undertaken by the elder Pugin, who acted on suggestions made by John Nash. In the text the editor remarks:

'Indeed, it is to the tastelessness of persons, who occasionally impose, or rather build, such edifices without well planned and well digested designs that "Modern Gothic" has been treated with sneers and contempt, and has been sarcastically termed Egyptianized, Grecianized, Romanized, Gothicized, Castleized, Abbeyized, building". Whether a design be for a mansion, a cottage, or a church, does not appear to have entered into the calculation of many builders. They blunder on with some confused notions of pointed arches, slender columns, and embattled parapets: and at length produce a nondescript building, which cannot degrade them because they have no reputation to lose.'

The numerous buildings of Gothic character erected during the first quarter of the nineteenth century must at least receive cursory mention, but, almost without exception, they are of relative unimportance. We are mainly concerned with the change towards the first phase of academic Gothic. This was evidenced by the building of the Hall[1] to Christ's Hospital in Newgate Street, by John Shaw in 1825. This design was not only an important advance on previous essays, but, paradoxical as it may seem, it revealed a closer adherence to precedent. The main façade was rigidly symmetrical, but the selection of detail appears to have been well studied. The new influence came from Cambridge, where William Wilkins had already employed Tudor detail for the Screen and Lodge at King's. It is also significant that at this period Perpendicular was the style chosen by architects not only for collegiate buildings but for churches. Later on it will be suggested that these preliminary events affected the Government decision that Tudor should be the style of the new Houses of Parliament. The church tower of St. Dunstan's in the West, Fleet Street, also by John Shaw, was another attempt to recapture the spirit of Perpendicular architecture. In this case Boston Stump was the model.

Another contemporary building, St. Katherine's Hospital, Regent's Park, built by Ambrose Poynter in 1826, shows not only regard for a more literal transcription of Tudor Gothic, but the interior of the church as well as the proportions are

[1] Since destroyed.

good; in addition the wood carving is more tolerable than was hitherto the case. The interior gains especially from the inclusion of an ancient canopied tomb removed from the old church by the Tower of London. This indicates a newer respect for conserving historical features. It was not only by such means, but with each experiment in Gothic, that architects determined upon greater accuracy. The next stage is marked by St. Luke's Church, Chelsea, built in 1824 by James Savage; this building was received at the time with a chorus of approval. Britton in writing it up remarked on 'the modern characteristics of Christian or ecclesiastical architecture, as employed in the imitation of Gothic edifices'. This is one of the first instances of the Gothic revival being so described, and it is not surprising that Britton was eloquent upon its merits; one of his many encomiums was, 'The architect has treated his subject in the spirit of a true artist'.

Little is known of James Savage beyond the fact that he had been a pupil with Daniel Alexander, the architect of the War Prison and the Gothic church at Princetown on Dartmoor. Savage gained from his master the flair for construction, which is revealed in the structural lines of St. Luke's. Critics were agreed that the stone vault over the nave was a distinct improvement on the sham plaster groinings which featured in many contemporary churches. Architectural literature now formed part of the nutriment of the Gothic manner ruminated by the profession, and in this regard the model upon which St. Luke's was based appears to have been Bath Abbey. Flushed with this initial success, Savage subsequently specialized in churches and schools; his other important works include Plowden Buildings, Middle Temple Lane, and the first repairs to the Temple Church.[1]

In view of the redistribution of Society then in process it is not surprising to find that the majority of the churches of the early revival were almost invariably built in towns. Later on there were slight departures from this rule, but in the twenties and the thirties of the last century the new conditions of housing called for new places of worship in growing districts. In London 'Commissioners Churches', as they were described, led to a better grasp of the problem of church building; in Edinburgh there is the example of St. John's Chapel, which William Burn designed in 1819. This

[1] The later alterations were made by Robert Smirke.

THE MEDIAEVAL COURT, GREAT EXHIBITION, 1851

is a rigid building reflecting rather faintly a Perpendicular type. In Liverpool, St. George's Church, Everton, 1814, and the tower of St. Nicholas' Church, Chapel Street, were built by Harrison of Chester, St. Luke's Church by John Foster, a Liverpool architect; each and several are representative of the early stages of the revival in the provinces. In the treatment of existing Gothic buildings there was also an improvement upon the methods of Wyatt and more attention was given to accuracy of detail. For example, the restoration of Lambeth Palace by Edward Blore must be considered to be one of the best works of the time.

If it were to be believed that Gothic was adopted merely as a change from classic, there would be no need to dwell on the intimate workings of the revival, but it was something more than that and it eventually became the name for a widespread purpose. With the exception of the younger Pugin, who combined art with religious propaganda, the most able exponents of the revival were often at a loss to know what to do next. Thus with each fresh impulse of research there ensued a change of front in design, and the search for the secrets of the medieval style eventually resulted in the rediscovery of the principles of structural planning, which none of the pioneers really understood. Even Charles Barry's early contributions to the revival were crude and can be conveniently ignored; it was the timely arrival of the younger Pugin in the professional arena that brought new expositions of fact and fresh arguments to spur Gothic zeal. The celebrated *Contrasts*, a most telling satire, appeared in 1836, and the illustrations more than the text made the greatest hit. Most contemporary architects agreed with the author, but instinctively disliked his froward ability; it was beyond expectation that such a high-principled genius should be helped entirely by his professional brethren even though he drew and wrote for their especial benefit. In his case patronage was absolutely necessary and this was forthcoming from the Earl of Shrewsbury. Pugin was already crowding three lives into one; the stream of literary works and drawings dealing with the ecclesiastical side of medieval art that flowed so easily from his brain now attracted the notice of the ecclesiologists. There seemed to be no limit to Pugin's energy, and under his management Gothic was presented with new force and singular directness. By this time

most architects and the leaders of the trades were alert to
the business possibilities of Gothic, but it was not until
Pugin's connexion with the Exhibition of 1851 that his influence on such firms as Hardman, and Minton, was realized
in full.

As an architect Pugin presents an appearance not only
unusual to the period in which he lived and worked, but one
that is not likely to occur again.   While comparatively
young he rose to the highest reputation as an authority on
medieval art.   Such was the force of his arguments, so great
was his facility as a draughtsman, that he manipulated both
ecclesiastical and professional opinion.   But he alienated
public sympathy by his conversion to Rome.

Pugin's association with Barry is said to have begun with
the Birmingham Grammar School, but this may not mean
that he assisted with the drawings for that building.   Alfred
Barry writes, 'The first aid which he (Sir Charles) received
from Mr. Pugin was under the pressure of shortness of time
in making the original competition design,' i.e. for the Houses
of Parliament.   When Barry was appointed architect for this
work his association with Pugin became firmer, and eventually Pugin was formally appointed superintendent of the
wood carving.   The truth was the controlling architect found
himself in an invidious position.   Pugin had ascended so
rapidly in the estimation of the profession that Barry's prestige as a Gothicist was in danger of being overshadowed.
Such rises as Pugin's are comparatively rare and almost
unexampled, but the Victorian period in its vast scope was
to prove that no one man could lead in architecture; that
many were essential to revive a former style, and that, notwithstanding the opportunities, in the end the honours would
be divided.   The relationship between Barry and Pugin has
been well described in Alfred Barry's *Memoir*, from which the
following has been extracted:

' It was no ordinary amount or quality of work which satisfied Mr.
Barry.   But with no tools but a rule and rough pencil, amidst a continuous rattle of marvellous stories, slashing criticism, and shouts of
laughter, Mr. Pugin would get through an amount of good work
which astonished his friends. . . . Whenever Mr. Barry's fire of enthusiasm began to pale, a visit from his Comet sufficed to brighten it.'

The controversy as to the authorship of the Houses of
Parliament is no longer in doubt.   It is clear that the plan

was Barry's, as well as the composition; but the detail shows the touch of one who was a consummate Gothicist, and that man was Pugin. 'I could not have made the plan,' said Pugin. 'It was Barry's own. He was good at such work—excellent; the various requirements conveyed by the plan, and above all the Fine Arts Commission, would have been too much for me.'

The apotheosis of the revived Tudor manner coincided with the erection of the Houses of Parliament. After 1850 the Gothic revival became a highly professional movement demanding exceptional powers of design and selective skill. Ruskin and others might make pronouncements but the architects finally decided. In the interim experiments in First, Second, and Third Pointed had resulted from Rickman's classification of the styles. Architects in force now proceeded to study insular Gothic buildings of all periods, as well as continental Gothic, but for a time Ruskin and Street diverted young students to northern Italy.

Whatever may be thought of Pugin's own work to-day, a proper view of it in relation to the period is essential. Eastlake says:

'The man whose name was for at least a quarter of a century a household word in every house where ancient art was loved and appreciated—who fanned into a flame the smouldering fire of ecclesiastical sentiment which had been slowly kindled in this country—whose very faith was pledged to Medieval tradition—such a writer and such an architect will not be easily forgotten, so long as the aesthetic principles which he advocated are recognized and maintained.'

A mere list of Pugin's work conveys more perhaps than a detailed description of any one building. In 1833 he built for his own use St. Mary's Grange near Salisbury, a curious house that cost upwards of £2,000 to build and when sold fetched only £500. His principal churches include St. Giles at Cheadle, St. Mary at Uttoxeter, and St. Alban, Macclesfield. The most important London example of his work, the pro-cathedral in St. George's Fields, Southwark, was completed in 1843. This building, although refined in line, lacks structural vitality; the walls are thin, and the ornament and the mouldings, although orthodox, are uninspired. But despite these faults there is the hall-mark of genius in the treatment of the chancel; the double screen with its graceful arches and light tracery is delightful. A much more important work was the Church of St. Chad, Birmingham, but in this building, with the exception of the design of the chancel, the rood screen, and the furniture, the effect of the interior is depressing. These and other of Pugin's early churches are, no doubt, singular enough, but they go to show how very human he was as an architect, and how his strength of purpose was accompanied with weakness. The early work of Pugin undoubtedly presents the problem of immaturity which he himself proceeded to answer in the Church of St. Augustine at Ramsgate. In the design of this building, to use his own language, he was 'paymaster, architect, and builder'. It was in this design that he made a real advance towards structural solidity; there was improvement in the handling of the woodwork, the scantlings of the timbers were increased, the detail full-sized with greater surety. The plan of St. Augustine's in its general arrangement also shows that Pugin was trying to conform to local Kentish traditions; he had come to understand that true Gothic depended on the observance of structural principles and that masonry and roofs were of equal importance to altars and rood screens.

Pugin's house with its private chapel stands close to the west end of St. Augustine's; in fact it was intended to form part of the ensemble. The furniture recalled the designs shown in many of his etched plates; true it was Gothic in character, but by no amount of skill could the author endow the moveables with the grace of the antique.

To give all due weight to the contribution Pugin made to ecclesiastical architecture a short list must be included. The principal churches are those at Derby, Kenilworth, Cambridge, Stockton-on-Tees, Newcastle-on-Tyne, Preston, Rugby, Northampton, Pontefract, Nottingham, and Woolwich. There are many others besides alterations and additions to old buildings. His domestic works include Bilton Grange, Adare (Ireland), Scarisbrick Hall, St. John's Hospital, Alton, and the restoration of Chirk Castle, Denbigh.

Viewed retrospectively, Pugin's fame is well deserved. His influence on architecture and on the revival of symbolism in Christian worship was undoubtedly great. His task was that of the missioner rather than that of the prophet, for others had already begun the work he so passionately furthered. But his influence as a designer was of great benefit at the time he lived, especially to that section of trade which specialized in ecclesiastical furnishings, and, although the impress of that influence has been stamped so thoroughly in every catalogue dear to the clerical mind with effects that are still sometimes painful, we recognize the enthusiasm of the Victorians. In Pugin we view a great artist, a man who, his doctor said, had done a hundred years' work. His short life as an architect represents the strivings and the emotions of one who laboured while other men slept. He was a man of deep endowment and gifted insight, one who offered no resemblance to any other Victorian architect, one moreover whose influence permeates the works of his contemporaries as well as those of his more fortunate successors. He was a man who struggled bravely as a writer, a thinker, a designer, and an executant; he never faltered in his quest of excellence. We feel that he would have liked to have been a bishop and to have invented a new creed.

By virtue of Pugin's association with Sir Charles Barry a brief account of the Houses of Parliament will be opportune. It is needless to say how dexterously the two architects worked to achieve such a magnificent result. In all probability, but for the decision of the Government that the style of the new Palace of Westminster was to be Gothic, Barry would have remained a classicist. It has already been explained that he first became famous through the invention of the 'Italian Clubhouse'; further, the Italianate ideal for English buildings, which eventually produced many imitators, resulted from his extensive travels as a young man. It appears, therefore, all the more strange that he should have interested himself in Gothic at a time when its idioms were almost unknown to him. The truth was that Barry combined the business instinct with professional dilettantism. At the outset he was in the position of any ordinary Victorian practitioner, but later he found it expedient to become interested in Gothic. His first churches at Prestwick and Campfield were fearsome; a much larger church, St. Peter's, Brighton, was in the Rickman manner; the three churches he designed for the rector of Islington were Gothic in name, and nothing more need be said of them. A more successful essay in revived 'Tudor', i.e. the Grammar School at Birmingham, owed its success to the architect's aptitude as a classical planner; the Gothic features were borrowed from *Specimens*

steep roofs and picturesque skylines; he carried in his mind impressions of the great tower at Malines, but while so engaged he found little which could be of service as auxiliary motives. There were many diversities between Barry and Pugin, yet throughout the duration of the works the vital enthusiasm of Pugin was necessary to a man of Barry's logical views, and the association of the two in the details of the exterior was beneficial. It is, however, next to impossible to ignore Pugin's continental studies in the treatment of the tourelles, and the nicety of balance of the minor features. This is especially noticeable in the design of the features to New Palace Yard.

As a whole the building suffers from the monotonous repetition of minute and elaborate detail, but this is a trivial defect by comparison with the grandeur of conception. The chief faults are those revealed in the design of the two towers. For example, the Victoria Tower does not diminish in general outline, a principle almost always observed by medieval builders. The clock tower, on the other hand, presents the absurdity of a gigantic long case clock. The genius of Barry, however, is not to be disputed; he was a wise designer, a man of excellent taste and extraordinary organizing ability. His reputation increases with the years and his masterpiece is now well established in architectural history. For a long period the nation which led the world in industrial progress could boast of a triumph which, although isolated, had effected a revolution in foreign opinion of English architecture.

In the design of the interior of the Houses of Parliament the hand of Pugin is everywhere to be seen. His mind was well fashioned by constant application for the purpose in hand; and the number of his working drawings must have been prodigious. Because there was no precedent for this type of public building everything had to be detailed and a new body of craftsmen trained. As a result Hardman's productions became famous, Thomas, the Birmingham sculptor, reaped a rich harvest, and Minton's encaustic tiles started a new fashion. It was by reason of his work at Westminster under Pugin that Crace rose in popularity as a decorator. All the artists connected with the building were united in a common purpose; no men observed more diligently the spirit of the period. In view of the ramifications of this great building and the length of time it took to build it is not surprising that the architect did not escape official meddling. His case became somewhat analogous to that of Wren during the building of St. Paul's Cathedral, but Barry triumphed in the end. The appointment of the 'Fine Arts Commission' to control the interior decoration was soon found to have been a mistake; the architect was not included in this body and this he considered to be a slight. The Commission learnt that the architect had undertaken on his own responsibility the whole of the decorative works, except the stained glass, and they deemed it right to abstain from all interference, and disclaim all responsibility in the matter. The Commission accordingly confined their attention to 'Works of Art', and decided that (generally speaking) the painting and sculpture should be historical, and that their subjects should be chosen from English history and literature. Barry very justly looked upon the design of the Houses of Parliament as his own especial province. He was, however, seldom free from petty annoyances; the co-operation of Dr. Reid for the heating and ventilation was irksome to him, and the designer of the great clock proved to be petulant.

The service rendered by Sir Charles Barry to Victorian taste may not mean much to the general reader, but the visual effect of his work at Westminster ranks as one of the twin peaks of nineteenth-century architecture. Viewed in retrospect the success of the building can be attributed to two causes, first the masterly conception of the plan and the dignity of the elevations, secondly to the meticulous beauty of Pugin's detail. The decision of the Government in favour of Gothic can be set down to circumstances which were largely accidental. It is, therefore, to a combination of multitudinous factors that we owe the Houses of Parliament in their singular completeness. Not only does the design embody the essentials of antique Perpendicular but it marks a definite change towards the broader outlook which accompanied the Gothic revival in its later stages.

Before dealing with these changes, mention must be made of Lincoln's Inn Hall, the work of Philip Hardwick, R.A., and his son, P. C. Hardwick. By comparison with the Houses of Parliament this is indeed a simple group, consisting as it does of only two main blocks. The principal feature, the Great Hall, is parallel with the east side of Lincoln's Inn

Fields, with the Library at right angles. Built in 1843, additions were made to the Library thirty years later. The design in general is reminiscent of the Hall at Hampton Court, the material of which it is built being similar, i.e. brick with stone dressings. The advent of Hardwick and his son into the sphere of Gothic is difficult to explain, but it can be observed that they spared no pains to be correct with their version of Tudor proportions; they aimed at competing with ancient methods of construction, and came within an ace of success. But, advanced as their scholarship was at that day, they could not encompass perfection in the handling of material; the most unpleasing feature being the red brick-work, which despite the chequering with black headers, is too precise in bond and pointing. The interiors, however, are surprisingly exact, especially the carving and the generous scantlings of the timbers. The roof of the Great Hall is excellently framed, and the roof of the Library recalls that of Eltham Palace. There can be no doubt that these buildings deeply impressed the public, but the temper of Victorian architecture is to be gauged neither by the selection of styles nor the richness and profusion of ornament. The pomposity and the gigantic scale of many of the undertakings conveys nothing of the secret ambitions of the architects. Yet, apart from such merits, or demerits, the gamut of the revival shows regard for artistry of grouping and placing, most architects having the gift of perspective and a grasp of the picturesque; in all such matters they excelled. The Houses of Parliament in relation to the Thames is splendidly significant; the Hall and Library of Lincoln's Inn in relation to the green spaces and the older buildings belongs to a picture hidden from ordinary eyes. With unerring instinct for conventional scenery the architects in both cases achieved superb structures, and all they did entitles them to our esteem.

The next transition of the revival was towards church building on freer and more modern lines. The Tower of St. Dunstan's in the West has already been mentioned, also the Hospital of St. Katherine in Regent's Park. In 1844 Ambrose Poynter, departing from Tudor, designed Christ Church, Westminster, the nave of which recalls French models of the thirteenth century, the detail being early English. Another architect, Hadfield of Sheffield, for a time divided with Pugin the share of Roman Catholic churches; J. L. Pearson assisted

Philip Hardwick, and Sharpe furthered the progress of the new Gothic by his writings and his work. In all this, as in every art movement, there was something of insincerity which became more pronounced as the revival became increasingly fashionable and cultured. But the great work of raising Gothic to an academic platform went on and there was no exponent more able than Benjamin Ferrey to succeed Pugin and to prepare the way for others. To mention only one of this architect's works, St. Mary's Church, Chetwynde, Shropshire, is to call attention to a building novel in composition and remarkable for purity of line. Architectural taste was now advancing towards fourteenth-century English exemplars, as well as towards continental Gothic. In the meantime R. C. Carpenter had built the Church of St. Stephen at Birmingham, and St. Andrew's in the same city. Architects in the interim became more literary in their works and the stone spires of the Nene Valley and the Somerset towers were now studied as models. The nature of the change can be ascertained by comparing Vulliamy's anaemic Gothic at Christ Church, Woburn Square, with Carpenter's fine Church of St. Paul at Brighton. A newer and freer spirit of scholarship was abroad compounded of enterprise and restraint. In 1854 Carpenter began the group of buildings comprising Lancing College, one of the earliest instances of the new system of planning in which the stereotyped lay-out was avoided. And at this time the building of St. Augustine's College, Canterbury, was entrusted to Butterfield, then a young man at the threshold of his career.

Butterfield's work is in a category of its own; it belongs neither to the pedantry which inspired the large cathedral churches designed by Hadfield and Weightman, nor to the academic manner of the Brandons. There is, for example, a marked difference between the Catholic Apostolic Church in Gordon Square built by Raphael Brandon in 1855, in the early English style, and All Saints', Margaret Street. In the one there was the strictest observance of antique detail, in the other a freedom of planning and structural adventure which is stimulating; it appears extraordinary that both churches were designed about the same time. After his success with All Saints', Butterfield commanded a large practice; he designed churches at Leeds, Huddersfield, Eton,

Sheen, Wykeham, Milton, near Adderbury, and Braisfield in Hampshire. He had a strong persuasion that the whole secret of modern church design was within his power, and he proceeded to eliminate accepted details with a contempt that seems fiendish. St. Alban's, Holborn, built in 1858, is perhaps more characteristic of his real purpose than the peculiarities evidenced in the design of All Saints'. Here again, as in the case of Margaret Street, the site was an awkward one. Yet the architect contrived to scheme a church with an extremely wide nave, and a proportionately high roof. The saddle-back treatment of the tower, despite the odd shape of the gable, and the thin coping stones, was a novel contribution. It was, however, in his treatment of brickwork that he differed from most of his rivals. The question whether he was inspired by Ruskin's *Seven Lamps* is uncertain, but his work does suggest the influence of Venetian Gothic. Two other works of importance, Yealmpton Church in Devonshire and the Anglican Conventual Establishment of Abbey Mere, overlooking Stonehouse Lake, Devonport, are among his important works in the provinces.

Butterfield produced some excellent mouldings and his treatment of ironwork was original; he avoided sculpture of the naturalistic type and aimed at the permanent decoration of wall surfaces by introducing coloured brick. The strength of his individual manner is to be seen in Balliol College Chapel and the powerful composition of Keble College. Apparently it was the architect's intention to invent a new form of surface decoration, to make plain walls interesting, and to contrast strong architectural lines by fainter horizontal ones formed in the material. He believed in colour that would remain permanent and he even introduced grey and purple tiles in the roof of Balliol Chapel.

There is in all his works a certain defiance of beauty which is not atoned for by the excellence of geometry. His designs reveal a striking personality, a mind that could envisage all the details of a building *ab initio*, and one able to carry them to a successful conclusion. The intense force of his work is its strong point, but there is invariably a lack of graciousness and his buildings appear forbidding. That he was opposed to the average thought of the Gothic revival, namely the outpourings from sketch-books and the complexity of crockets and pinnacles, is equally apparent. His zeal to achieve novelty was greater than his power, and he sought by example to persuade others to his way of thinking. For a brief space architectural opinion wavered between Ruskin and Butterfield, until the imitators of the latter became legion and their imitative works were scattered about the country-side. It is safe to say that nearly all the village schools, parsonage houses, and parish rooms which were built between the years 1850 and 1865 show traces of Butterfield's manner. Nothing is more characteristic of the revival at this stage than the care with which each departure was watched and emulated. The work of John Norton, particularly the International College, Spring Grove, Isleworth, as well as Emmanuel Church, Bristol, on this account can be classed between the manner of Brandon and Butterfield. There was, however, nothing servile in Norton's work; he paid homage it is true, but he had a supremacy of his own. Good architects were now numerous enough, the grammar of Gothic had been mastered, and opportunities to build were probably greater than at any time.

Yet the older men were about to give way to a younger and more vigorous rival, Gilbert Scott, whose name is blazoned in mid-Victorian highways and by-paths. Scott is perhaps best remembered by the volume of his works; he was the trophy hunter of the revival, the winner of great competitions, the popular champion of the pointed arch. Scott has been represented setting out on his architectural career as an enthusiast for new churches, but he did not despise the chances offered to become a specialist in work-house design. Once awakened from humdrum routine by the writings of Pugin he was no longer uncertain of his way; the mists were quietly dispelled, the possibilities of architectural leadership inspired him, and in time he achieved his ambition. His version of Gothic was his own, he made it as he went and literally nothing came amiss to his power of organization nor escaped his keen eye to business. Almost any example of his architecture shows the manner in which his style formed, for it was indubitably a style, and one intrinsically peculiar to his personality. As the years passed his popularity grew and was shown off to full advantage by contrast; it was seen that the major portions of his designs were forceful and precise, moreover they were exempt from careful imitation. During his subsequent career as a church architect he trained up a host of competent assistants, built hundreds of new buildings, and he altered old ones almost beyond recognition. On the whole his work was neither admirable nor thoughtful; it lacked genuine grace; its feeling was brittle and hard. Yet it is not to be denied that his opportunities to inspire the public were probably greater than those of any other architect of his day. He preached against the 'hindrances to the perfect success of our Revival, and the great object which we must set before us in all our future efforts'. Yet when he encountered the opposition of Lord Palmerston to his scheme for the new Government Offices, he forswore martyrdom for the more lucrative choice of immediate business. Gilbert Scott professed to be the humble pupil and follower of Pugin, but he gained an ascendancy which at one time threatened to be universal in England.

Scott's rise to fame began after 1844 when he won the competition for St. Nicholas' Church, Hamburg. This had the immediate effect of bringing him to the notice of the church authorities in every diocese. Commissions to restore cathedrals now began to accumulate, such for example as the alterations to the lantern at Ely, and the design of the screen to the choir, both of which are typical of his limitations. With regard to historical buildings Scott's principal aim was 'restoration'; but his system of reconditioning was almost as drastic as that pursued sixty years previously by James Wyatt. Scott's system in effect was more reprehensible, for knowledge of the principles of Gothic architecture had by this time become profound. At Oxford he pulled down the east end of the cathedral and rebuilt it in the Norman style; his doctoring up of the little church at Clifton Hampden, near Abingdon, obliterated many interesting medieval features. On one occasion it is said he pulled down some Saxon work with his own hands. The main purpose of Scott was to recreate Gothic; but he only succeeded in producing a cold modern version of it, devoid of sublimity of expression. Still it is impossible not to be interested in his amazing energy; from beginning to end he neglected nothing to achieve his ultimate purpose, and he unfortunately carried the bulk of ecclesiastical opinion with him. The age was undoubtedly productive of architects to whom scholarship was the means to an end, but such men were not always suitably employed. Scott, on the other hand, was an architect of demoniac power; he found time to lecture, to write books, to attend committees, and to sketch. A considerable part of his life was spent in the seclusion of first-class railway carriages, accompanied by books and materials for study. Of all the Victorian architects he was the most practical and the most persuasive; on occasion he exercised great restraint, as for example when he rebuilt the tower of St. Mary's, Taunton, almost exactly on the old lines. No one ever expressed the superficialities of Gothic art so well, no other architect so completely deceived himself and his patrons. In the cleaning up and clearing out process of 'Restoration', whether of great cathedrals or of humble churches, it was the reputation of the architect that came first, not the conservation of history. Perhaps the time will come when expedience will decree the writing up of the full list of his destructions, but the tale will be long in the telling, and it will point its own moral. The melancholy feature of the whole matter was Scott's influence on the rank and file of the profession, the curious sameness of his style which was repeated in a score of second-rate churches; even the Wesleyans commissioned their architects to build churches with spires on the Scott model. The *Builder* and other journals praised his zeal from time to time, and by the subtle process of emulation Scott's 'mid-Victorian Gothic' became familiar not only in provincial towns but in the Colonies. That he was an architect of more than average ability cannot be denied, but he was not a great artist. His design for the offices in Broad Sanctuary, Westminster, proves that he could not escape the tendency to make his façades interesting at all costs. This office façade at Westminster is crowded with features, and it exhibits interesting mouldings and carvings arranged with industry; the interpenetrations are confusing in their intricacy, the skyline is unconvincing, but at the time of its erection this building received considerable praise. In 1858 Scott rebuilt Exeter College Chapel at Oxford and here is to be seen the influence of his studies of continental Gothic. He had already observed the value of lofty proportions, of massive buttresses and convenient splays. He now concentrated on bolder mouldings and vigorous well-selected ornament, but he had not mastered the secret of medieval sculpture, nor did he understand the treatment of canopies.

His singular design for the Martyrs' Memorial at Oxford belongs to the earlier stages of his work and he was proud to compare it with anything that Pugin could have produced. Scott's works are almost endless, they appear to multiply as they are encountered; they are the standard works of mid-Victorian optimism, the products of a strange fertility which seemed to defy opposition.

Scott's larger churches include St. Mary Abbott's, Kensington, and others at Nottingham, Cirencester, Doncaster, and Halifax. In London he was engaged on extensive restorations at Westminster Abbey; there was not a diocese in the country that he failed to advise. His secular works include the Town Hall, Preston, Lancashire, built in 1862, in which he introduced columns of polished granite. The Infirmary at Leeds, built in 1863, is an enormous building showing the influence of Ruskin; here the style inclines to Venetian Gothic, and Beckett's Bank at Leeds was designed under the same general influence. Far more successful in mass were the buildings for University College, Glasgow, which were begun in 1866 and finished in 1872. Here the scale is generous, for the site demanded a bold silhouette. As a group of buildings Glasgow University ranks as one of the best of his works; the main fronts are over 600 feet in length, and the use of Griffrock and Bannockburn stone was wise. But the work Scott set most store upon was the design of the terminus and hotel buildings at St. Pancras, surely one of the strangest medleys of steep roofs, gables, and chimney stacks that the mind could possibly conceive. There is something akin to Harz mountain-top scenery in the silhouette, while the main elevations show a confusion of continental motives scarcely expressive of the purpose. The design is said to have included the principal features of the rejected perspective of the new Government Offices in Whitehall. In fairness to the architect there was a considerable adaptation, for a complete re-use of the design was not possible. Scott's own remarks illustrate the high regard in which he held St. Pancras:

'It is often spoken of to me as the finest building in London. My own belief is that it is possibly (*too good*) for its purpose, but having been disappointed through Lord Palmerston of my ardent hope of carrying out my style in the Government Offices, I was glad to be able to erect one building in that style in London.'

At the time of its erection St. Pancras was described as being a capacious and elaborately detailed structure of brick, stone and iron, the first instance of the adaptation of medieval design for such a purpose in London. To modern eyes the best part of this huge caravanserai is not the hotel but the mighty vault of iron and glass which the genius of Barlow the engineer devised before Scott was called in. In the planning, however, there is everything to show Scott's astonishing power as an organizer; not only are the ramped approaches from Euston Road admirable, but the study of traffic circulation for cabs and other vehicles is sound. While the architect wavered between Venetian Gothic for the porch and medieval detail for the timber-framed roof over the booking hall, he touched the two extremes of contemporary theories. On the whole the details of St. Pancras show the influence of Ruskin, but the architect was also under the spell of continental Gothic, which he attempted to anglicize in the Scott manner. The façade includes the inevitable Victorian clock tower at the eastern extremity, and the steep roofs are liberally checked with high-pitched gables at convenient points. The fusion of such diverse elements was Scott's extreme difficulty, and of all the forced inventions of the revival the design of St. Pancras is most typical. But the architect remained oblivious of the fact that Pugin's *Contrasts* had come to a strange reality in the Euston Road, or that his reputation was in danger by the proximity of King's Cross Station and the assemblage of third-rate Regency-houses. Strange as these contrasts were in the seventies they are even more dubious with the added untidiness of to-day.

Scott's favourite design, the Albert Memorial, has been the subject of criticism from the time of its completion, and these adverse criticisms have been studiously fomented. One of Professor Cockerell's young grandchildren, when asked for an opinion after a visit to the Memorial, repeated the remark of her Cockney nurse, 'Mamma, it is a hornament'. But that which distinguished its inception from similar works was the austere morality which is said to have accompanied its erection. It is acknowledged by the most zealous writers that no truer symbol of mid-Victorian sentiment exists, for it was erected by national subscription, and it had perforce to be rich and costly looking. The architect felt that some sort of canopy was needed for the colossal statue of the Prince Consort and that the whole design should express the grief of the bereaved Sovereign and the sympathy of the nation. Scott was just the architect needed; 'the realization in an actual edifice of the architectural designs furnished by the metal work-shrines of the Middle Ages' seemed the right motive. He determined upon an effect of intricate interest arising from the use of precious material. He proceeded accordingly to introduce Sicilian marble, granite, mosaic work, enamelled stones, and gun-metal, and to employ gilding wherever possible. The sculptured base, by far the best feature, included the portraits of leading Victorian statesmen and artists. In the realization of this monument the architect had subconsciously created a symbol of the approaching end of revived medievalism.

In consequence of the constant changes which accompanied the Gothic revival it was perhaps inevitable that a critic should arrive who at first approved its purpose. This was John Ruskin, whose life coincides almost exactly with that of Queen Victoria; he was born in 1819 and died in 1900. During sixty years of activity Ruskin became universally famous as author, artist, and social reformer. His first published writings were in the *Architectural Magazine* and Loudon's *Magazine of Natural History*. He began by encouraging the revivalists when he published *Seven Lamps of Architecture* in 1849; he lived to see a change of feeling which negatived his own teachings. Ruskin did not begin to draw until middle life, but in the capacity of social reformer he had taken charge of drawing-classes at the Working Men's College, Great Ormond Street, as early as 1854, and he had continued to teach for four years. His industrial experiments included the revival of the hand-made linen industry at Langdale, and the establishment of a weaving industry at Laxey, Isle of Man. He became the first Slade Professor of Art at Oxford in 1870. Endowed from early youth with the instinct to describe and criticize works of art, he eventually became the acknowledged art critic of the later period. But his theories were not entirely original; while he was apt in gathering up current ideas and re-expressing them he very wisely remained aloof from professional controversy. In his role of art regulator he found that little or nothing had been done to re-establish craftsmanship. He thought the one way to help was by exposing shams and advocating a return to English and French Gothic of the thirteenth century. But how was this theory of approaching the subject of architecture from the artist's standpoint to be carried into effect? To Ruskin's way of thinking the realization of beauty meant uniform picturesqueness, the significance of a population enslaved to commercialism being apparently disregarded. The middle-class architects were not disposed to surrender everything, and the middle-class intellectuals to whom Ruskin appealed in his writings merely smiled their approval.

It is commonly believed that Ruskin made a New Era in Architecture; this, however, is erroneous, for many of his ideas were current long before his contradictory aphorisms were made public. Pugin was not only a greater force than Ruskin; he was a trained architect. Ruskin could excite middle-class interest, but he failed to control it. In later life when he suffered disillusionment, he wrote:

'I would rather for my own part that no architects had ever condescended to adopt one of the views suggested in this book.[1]

'I have had indirect influence on nearly every cheap villa builder between this and Bromley, and there is scarcely a public-house near the Crystal Palace but sells its gin and bitters under pseudo-Victorian capitals copied from the Church of the Madonna of Health or of the Miracles. And one of my principal motives for leaving my present house is that it is surrounded everywhere by the accursed Frankenstein monsters of indirectly my own making.'

It is extremely doubtful whether Ruskin was entirely sincere in his praise of All Saints', Margaret Street, or Waterhouse's Assize Courts, Manchester. These buildings, although built at different periods, pay a left-handed compliment to his teachings. He was not slow to recognize this and in return dealt faint praise to both. The one really interesting building, designed on the principles advocated by Ruskin, was the new library of Trinity College, Dublin, by Deane and Woodward. The competition for the New Oxford Museum resulted in the selection of the scheme entered by this firm of architects, and during the progress of the works Ruskin himself took a hand in designing a few features, probably the only instance of his work in this connexion. For a time Woodward's work was the fashion; he built the Union Library at Oxford, and the Kildare Club at

[1] *The Stones of Venice.*

Dublin; in praising the latter Ruskin spoke of it as the finest modern building in Europe. Here can be seen the naturalistic carvings, the monkeys, and other animals which the brothers O'Shea delighted to introduce. If Ruskin's direct influence on architectural design was bad, his indirect influence was beyond question good. He was uneasy and in direct opposition to the Scott method of restoration; in fact any form of substitution appalled him; to his sensitive mind, restoration meant 'the most total destruction which a building can suffer'. It was through his teachings that the Society for Protection of Ancient Buildings came into existence; and in the works of William Morris and Lethaby can be seen the fulfilment of the best of Ruskin's doctrines.

The last phase of Gothicism from 1860 to 1870 produced many diversions which spread widely and were swayed by a return to the style of North Italy and later on by the publication of James Fergusson's *History of Architecture*. The younger architects of the mid-Victorian period were now in the ascendant; they were beginning to think and act for themselves; the attractions of French Gothic became stronger; the publication of Viollet-le-duc's *Dictionnaire Raisonné de l'Architecture Française du XIe au XVIe Siècle*, now encouraged a more thoughtful study of structure. The Baptistery of St. Francis's Church, Notting Hill, by J. F. Bentley is the first example of the change, but the chief exponent of the new manner of handling Gothic was a born artist. The inclinations of George E. Street were scholarly; he had travelled abroad, and he wrote extremely well. His earliest work, the Church of St. Philip and St. James, Oxford, had pleased the critics, the building was said to be fine in tone, and definite in its silhouette. Its style was acclaimed as being neither pedantically English nor a slavish copy of French thirteenth-century Gothic. No architect opposed pedantry with greater virulence, and it will be seen later that Street was eminent among men of talent. From now onwards, the aim of the younger men was structural devisement and original planning. In this regard the early works of J. L. Pearson, and of Teulon, in London, show an extraordinary sense for graceful and original structural composition. Burges, on the other hand, developed a tendency towards an early type of French Gothic; he was among the first to recognize the merits of the naturalistic school, but as a trained architect he avoided Ruskinism and evolved his own manner of carving and ornament. The sketch-book of Wilars de Honecourt may have inspired him to produce his own remarkable sketch-books, but he certainly understood figure drawing and decoration. His model lodging-house in Soho, and the warehouse in Upper Thames Street, are examples of his simpler work. The mansion of Knights Hayes, Tiverton, and his own house in Melbury Road, S. Kensington, indicate his extraordinary versatility; but these buildings are too special to be considered as part of the great volume of Victorian Gothic. The new cathedral of St. Finbar at Cork is beyond question his masterpiece. By this time the revival had already lost force as a collective movement, but it had gained in the number of individualists who reacted the one on the other. In this regard the work of Alfred Waterhouse in some measure recalls the later manner of Sir Gilbert Scott. Waterhouse as an architect was gifted; like his senior contemporary he also was an organizer, and he had a similar genius for winning competitions. Moved by such considerations, the whole body of architects entered for each new competition and the era of huge coloured perspective drawings had set in. Nothing could be more typical of Victorian architectural prosperity than these tremendously respectable drawings, so expensively produced and framed and so totally uninspired by any sense of artistic decency. The huge perspective drawings shown in the Architectural Room of the Royal Academy in modern times represent the unenviable legacy of this period.

Among the older men who had lived through so many years of disturbing changes in architecture there were many who were content to practise in quietude; hence the number of Gothic churches of the Victorian period which need little comment.

The most thoughtful architect of this later period, however, was Street, and it fell to his lot to produce the last great Gothic building. In the design of the Law Courts there is a picturesque informality which is not unpleasant; the grouping of the façades, particularly the Strand front, is ambitious, the skyline is interesting, and the flèche over the central hall is really beautiful. It was, however, in the arrangement of the fenestration and the treatment of sub-motives that Street distinguished himself. The theme of the

Law Courts is French Gothic, and this style is maintained in every part of the building. The plan was marred by the interference of the lawyers themselves, but notwithstanding almost insuperable difficulties Street succeeded in producing a group of buildings worthy to take their place as part of the impressive scenery of London.

At the present time, sated as we are with the pitiful relics of the Gothic revival in almost every town in England, it is difficult to estimate the intrinsic qualities of the best work of the period. The landmarks are conspicuous enough, i.e. the Houses of Parliament, Lincoln's Inn Hall, the Catholic Apostolic Church, Gordon Square, and Street's Law Courts. These and many lesser buildings connote the boundless interest of the leading Victorian architects. Towards the end of the nineteenth century, when Gothic had ceased to be a creed, some of the finest work was done. But we are mainly concerned with events up to 1865, a time when Gothic was still the chief medium of stylistic expression, a time when architects believed in it, and the public accepted Gothic as inevitable. There was one sphere, that of the Established Church and particularly the High Church party, where Gothic was encouraged by every means, thus the real success of the revival was to re-establish church building. It also partly revived the creative instinct in the crafts, and it led surely to the greater perception of the meaning of structure which is now common to Europe, and is so well understood in Sweden. No style other than Gothic could oppose such sharp contrasts to the horizontality of the eighteenth-century streets, nothing was more out of sympathy with modern life than a Gothic railway station, nothing more repellent than the abuse of the pointed arch which at one time appeared as a feature in almost every detached villa. The Gothic style was thought by the Victorians to be more right and Christian than the classical. For similar reasons Gothic art and religion were discovered to be one and the same thing. Yet curiously enough the Italian Renaissance was also accepted. Unstinted praise, therefore, is due to Ruskin, who saw everything commendable in the quest for artistic beauty. As an amateur, before he became disillusioned, Ruskin hoped for some miracle to happen which would restore a sense of beauty, such as he enjoyed, to all men. In an opposite direction Pugin had aimed at a revival of medieval art combined with the Catholic faith. The industry of Sir Gilbert Scott as a church designer and restorer shows the magnanimity of the Middle Church party in surrendering to a compromise, which under the circumstances left them no option. That the movement was supported by men of religious eminence and artistic talent is obvious to the most superficial observation, but nevertheless it presents an inexplicable phenomenon which is best described as a rebellion against classicality. Early Victorian Society found itself hurled into a maelstrom of pseudo-medievalism and imposed sentimentalism; all that was religious, poetic, artistic, and commercial began to lose a measure of independence. It can hardly be doubted that towards the end of the sixties the barometer pointed to change, for the Gothic enthusiasts had made little allowance for the tastes of those to whom the eighteenth century with its diabolical cleverness and originality appeared remote, and therefore attractive. The truth that in art 'there is no advance, only return', was again to be demonstrated. The persistence of classicality for the design of public buildings as well as houses led to the revival of the so-called Queen Anne Style, and this new movement caused the break up of the Gothic party. Thus by degrees the Gothic revival languished and finally joined the shades of tradition.

§3. DECORATION AND FURNITURE

In addition to architecture the nineteenth century has provided an amazing legacy of decoration and furniture. The mass is so overwhelming as to prohibit chronological arrangement, neither is it possible to state the names of even the leading artists and executants in any sequence.

Put briefly, Victorian decoration, in its tenacity, resembles the smother of ivy on ancient walls. The analogy can be carried still farther; it climbed by its roots, bore two forms of leaves, and in season showed small flowers. Because of its partial divorcement from architecture, decoration became more easily commercialized and in consequence its popularity increased. The basis of Victorian art knowledge is suggested by the remarkable collection of furniture and objects of art made by Sir John Soane in the early part of the nineteenth century. The illustrations of interiors in Ackermann's *Repository of Art* also evidence the inventive fecundity of the designers who were the pioneers of subsequent developments. The alternating over-richness and frigid spikiness which appears in art forms can be attributed to hesitation between classic and Gothic. To return to the analogy of *Hedera Helix*, the small flowers of which secrete a great deal of honey, the flowerings of early Victorian art were pollinated. The growth spread, and deceived by its parasitic luxuriance.

At a first glance what a confused picture is presented, a mingling of every human achievement, a medley of objects embellished to captivate fleeting fancy. We encounter ideas taken from primitive art and joined to products of Birmingham; in the quest for novelty the whole world was then laid under contribution. There is to be seen an extraordinary combining of the austere with the bizarre, startling colours, sharp contrasts, hard profiles, voluptuous curves, monotonous repetitions; painful stampings predominate. The debasement of classical and the imitation of Tudor architecture were conjointly producing strange effects in household decoration. To modern eyes the whole entourage forms a glass sea of inventions. The shapes of furniture, the surface treatments, the unnecessary articles, and the over-rich interiors at the time of the Exhibition of 1851 were profound fiascos. The Victorians had launched into the immensities of art exploitation, and to their view the art treasures of the world constituted a dazzling fantasy.

But art was not to be courted in this middle-class fashion; time has brought its revenges, the household gods once venerated now rest in strange Valhallas. No blame, however, is to be attached to our great-grandparents, nor must their artistic advisers be blamed for the productions which we are pleased to think amusing. The aim of the Victorians was to reconcile art and industry, in other words to apply art to ordinary objects and uses.

The Great Exhibition of 1851, heralded by the noise of cannon and the blare of trumpets, showed the futility of industrial and international art to the clear-minded; but middle-class opinion refused to be shaken. Thirty years later the choicest specimens of 'Exhibition Art' had passed to the auction rooms and the fashion of spindled elegance and blue china was the rage of the 'artistic eighties'. During the Victorian period, very few writers dared to describe the ordinary furniture and decoration which changed each

VASE IN ELECTRO PLATE, GREAT EXHIBITION, 1851

season. Even then the task would have been an impossible one, for decoration had passed into the hands of specialist firms who catered for those whose incomes ranged from £1,000 to £10,000 a year. For the rest, the lower middle-class, it was the cheaper emporium, the catalogue, and the directional views of the wall-paper manufacturer. In early Victorian times decoration was graded; it was either one of three things, i.e. distinctive, mediocre, or shoddy. In opposition to the modernists the antique dealers flourished in Wardour Street, and the Rows at Chester; the demand was for carved oak and furniture of the Stuart period. The Georgian era was too recent for its treasures of mahogany and satinwood to be appreciated. The revival of interest in Georgian art came later, and this change was encouraged by Thackeray's novels. There was, however, a genuine appreciation for the works of Hogarth and for pictures of the Dutch school, a real regard for large seascapes as elements of decoration as well as for copies of Italian paintings. The oleographs which found their way into England by the thousand did not appear until the late sixties. The early Victorian public favoured small articles, such as Tunbridge Wells ware, papier mâché trays and work-boxes, as well as pseudo-Chinese tea-poys inlaid with mother-of-pearl, and fans with brightly painted nosegays. These were the days when McCullum and Hodgson of Birmingham were renowned for their papier-mâché products. Only rarely did such things repose in mansions; they were the expensive toys of middle-class families and could be found in almost every parlour and small drawing-room in town and country. But no class of society despised guidance, and thanks to the stupendous labours of Mr. J. C. Loudon, with his *Encyclopaedia*, illustrated by more than 2,000 engravings, this was forthcoming, or our great grandparents would have fared much worse than was actually the case. Loudon tried to act Mr. Turveydrop in a world demoralized by commerce. His book became immeasurably popular, copies were sent to every quarter of the British Empire and to the United States. After his death a new edition was issued by Mrs. Loudon, and this was in circulation as late as the eighties. It is, therefore, to J. C. Loudon that some attention is due, as will be seen from this extract from his preface:

'Among the important uses of this work will be that of pointing out the various capacities for improvement in comfort and beauty, of which each class of building, and each kind of furniture, is susceptible. Now, so far from this having a tendency to injure Architects, it will not only enable those who wish either to build or to furnish, to express more clearly to the Architect or upholsterer those wants which they already have; but it will elicit new ones, of which they had previously no idea, and which the Architect, the builder, and the upholsterer will be called upon to supply.'

This curious desire to direct taste on the part of one individual was genuine enough; it suited the mental atmosphere of the time; it was at one with the social consciousness of respectability, but it was fatal to art. Mr. Loudon's method of encouraging deportment was liable to be misinterpreted by others less disciplined than those for whom the book was compiled. In early Victorian times, as now, there was a difference between schemes of decoration designed by competent architects, and schemes emanating from the studios of commercial specialists. In the main the best Victorian decoration took its tone from the designs of the leading architects. It can be assumed, therefore, that the designs of James Pennethorne for the new Ball-room and other State apartments at Buckingham Palace were not without effect on the minds of the nobility. Pennethorne's treatment of the Library and Royal suite within the Duchy of Cornwall offices in Buckingham Gate is consistent in its classicality down to the chairs and fire-irons, but it was not possible for the general public to view the effect. Sir Robert Smirke's design for the King's Library in the British Museum on the contrary could be seen and admired by the public. The interiors of the London Clubs were designed by architects and so were the theatres; while decoration became the subject of general conversation no mere upholsterer could expect to compete with such masters as Professor Cockerell, Pugin and Barry, or Alfred Stevens. Neither could the middle-class as a whole hope to engage the services of such artists. The majority of the architects were likewise engaged on the routine work of the period, namely banks, insurance offices, railway stations, workhouses, warehouses, and shops. The architects who were church specialists were working at high pressure; the great building firms such as Cubitt employed their own draughtsmen, and the lesser speculative builders could obtain plans from young architects struggling for a place. The Royal Institute of British Archi-tects, then recently founded, was a lofty institution mainly concerned with professional etiquette, and the Royal Academy had no control over national ideals of household taste. True, the aristocratic aspects of art were influenced by men who believed in scholarship and tradition, and this to some extent accounts for the great differences that exist between the best secular and ecclesiastical work of the Victorian period, and the massed contributions accepted without question by middle-class society. Once this truth is realized the present state of the arts will be apprehended, for the public are but the heirs of the ages.

In studying attentively the art then in favour we learn this lesson: first, the decorations of the furniture designers were respectful to current architectural opinion; if they fall short of the virtues we require of them it was due to the limits in which the designers worked. Secondly, decorative designs were required to be showy and at the same time economical. The common idea that the interiors of the best Victorian houses were akin to junk shops is erroneous. The seaside lodging, and the popular conception of nineteenth-century taste, is not fair to the solid comfort which was characteristic of Victorian home life. It must be conceded that by comparison with the Georgian period Victorian art in every connexion was inferior; we have, therefore, to view things as our grandparents saw them. It is to the credit of the leaders that after the Great Exhibition of 1851 they awakened to the fact that improvement in furniture and decoration was more than desirable; but the majority among the middle-class remained apathetic for a much longer period. To-day typical Victorian interiors are difficult to describe, for so many changes have ensued and so many representa-tive schemes have been altered, but from such examples as do exist accurate facts have been obtained.

The Great Library at Cassiobury, as drawn by the elder Pugin, can be taken as representative of the transition from Georgian to Victorian. The apartment measured 54 feet by 23. The room itself was early Georgian but the furniture was typical of the first quarter of the nineteenth century. The main theme of the furnishing centred around the bookcases, the carpet, and the curtains. The latter were crimson in colour and were festooned over each window after the Empire manner. Between the end windows were large pier-glasses with square commodes supporting Empire candelabra. The fire-place was of the flat panelled type of 1825 then in fashion. The carpet was grey, divided into small squares; the border consisted of circles between a double frame; black was sparingly introduced as a contrasting colour. The minor features of the furnishing of this room consisted of two L-shaped settees arranged on either side of the fire-place. The room was lit at night by Argand oil-burners from within a lantern suspended from the centre of the room. This type of formal furnishing has been maintained in many country-house libraries to the present day. The Great Library at Southill, completed in 1806, can be cited as another model. At Ampthill House, built in 1829 by Cubitt and furnished by a London decorator, the original festooned curtains are retained in the drawing-room. Here the permanent decorations and cornices are Greek and recall the manner of Papworth. At Trensham in Worcestershire, built in 1830, the whole of the interior decoration is severe Greek. The walls are panelled in stucco and painted, the ceilings framed by stuccoed margins running clear of the cornice, the doors are of mahogany, and the gilt mirrors are placed between the French casement windows.

At this period 'Grecian' drawing-rooms were the speciality of an architect named Lamb, who appears to have followed the precepts of Thomas Hope. His designs were highly Corinthian, but the furniture he favoured has a sinuosity quite foreign to the Greek spirit. Mr. Lamb, Mr. Mallet, and Mr. Vardon were promising young architects, who, as Loudon observes, 'could draw with equal ease whatever comes before them'. There was at least something consistent in the Greek manner of the early Victorian decorators; the exponents were attempting to follow prevalent architectural tastes. But when they essayed Elizabethan and Gothic they floundered; the lesser architects and decorators in those happy times, however, contrived to pick up many rich plums. The Tudor design of the Anchor Inn at Tempsford, with its strange Gothic chairs and tables, no doubt gave great pleasure to both architect and client, as well as to stage-coach travellers on the Great North Road. John Shaw, already mentioned as the architect of Christ's Hospital, was famous for his designs for 'Elizabethan furniture'. In the late thirties

FIRE-PLACE AND COAL VASES

the English, French, and Dutch Renaissance was racked for
specimens of decoration and furniture. On the other hand,
Nixon & Son of Great Portland Street specialized in furnishing according to the style of Louis XIV. Antique Elizabethan and Dutch furniture, as well as copies and fakes, could
be bought from Wilkinson of Oxford Street and Hanson of
John Street, as well as from Kensett of Mortimer Street, the
latter being one of the earliest reproducers of antiques. The
more celebrated Victorian house-painter and decorator, Mr.
Fair, began his business in Mortimer Street, before moving
to Hanover Street. He made his reputation by fitting up
a room with Elizabethan fragments. This passion for the
Elizabethan style seems to have been an undercurrent in
both architectural and decorative circles. In 1840 the
guiding principles of decoration were the following. Halls
were to be of two stories, stuccoed with a marble cement
to receive a polish; on the walls 'basso-relievos' of appropriate subjects. The mouldings of the doorways were to be
of stone or marble cement. The doors could be either of
mahogany or wainscot, but were not to be painted. The
halls of smaller houses followed the same general recipe, but
in such cases marbled paper took the place of stucco; even
the smallest passages were called halls. In dining-rooms the
ceilings were coffered or panelled with wood; the walls were
either painted or finished in scagliola and the sideboard
recess formed the principal feature. In large reception
rooms two roses were introduced from which glass chandeliers were suspended. The margins of the windows were
frequently decorated with ornamental coloured glass. Plate
glass now began to displace the quarried sashes of the earlier
period. Broad masses of light and shade, continuous lines
and square openings were deemed equally necessary in
schemes of decoration.

The early Victorian drawing-room was always well pro-
portioned. In London houses 'the first-floor pair' was ideal
for receptions; the comedy was that so many of these rooms
were alike. The proportions were $30 \times 20 \times 14$ feet in height
if possible. A white marble chimney piece was essential,
and this could either be cut in the Louis Quinze style or
'copied from one of the most magnificent designs common
in old English houses'. At Hawnes in Bedfordshire there
is a typical example. The numerous marble merchants of

Westminster were relied upon to import fire-places from France and Belgium. One type of Belgian design for fourth-rate houses was advertised at the low price of from £1 to £2 according to size. Generally speaking, there was usually a large chimney-glass over the fire-place and the garniture consisted of a French clock with candelabra, or in the best houses a clock by Vulliamy. In drawing-rooms apple-green satin was favoured for the upholstery, the walls were hung with watered rose-coloured silk, and the ground colour of the carpet was dark mulberry with floral decorations. French carpets were very usual. Between the side windows were two pier-glasses with console tables. The drawing-room was lit by wax candles in the sconces of an Osler chandelier. Glass chandeliers for gas lighting were seldom introduced into the best rooms. Sometimes buff was the colour chosen for the walls, or as an alternative watered buff silk having satin and watered stripes alternately. Flock papers were frequently used and were considered handsome. Curtains have already been mentioned, but not the inner curtains of figured muslin edged with blue silk ball fringe, which were deemed indispensable. The arrangement of the multitudinous furniture was left to the lady of the house, and here the decline of good taste was most apparent, for the early Victorian designers knew that crowding should be avoided, their lady clients did not. The treatment of the fire-place as the domestic centre was not considered complete without a steel grate with brass and ormolu ornaments with a bright steel fender and fire irons; above all things a japanned purdonium was required.

From observation of actual examples the attributes of first-class decoration appear to have been constant throughout the Victorian period from 1837 till 1870; in other words there was no departure from the basis of Georgian tradition. The decoration of Grosvenor House by Thomas Cundy after 1842 was really excellent for its period. Nothing, however, could compare with the beauty of Alfred Stevens' work, as for example, the Red Drawing Room and the Dining Room at Dorchester House. Alas! this masterpiece is no more, the famous mantelpiece of Bardiglia marble has been torn from its setting, and the whole of the decorative scheme representing the work of the greatest Victorian decorator has vanished. For some time the decorators had been playing amongst themselves a most complicated game of mixed styles. Lack of co-operation was so apparent that in 1843 Mr. Hansom, the inventor of the hansom cab, advertised his plan for the instruction of 'architectural decorators and furnishers which shall combine the advantages of the school, the office, and the workshop; so that general education, professional training, and handicraft skill may be acquired and perfected together.' Whether this proposed Academy ever matured cannot be ascertained. Hansom's idea seems to have been an extension of Sir John Soane's pupilage system. Lack of co-operation and want of co-ordination spelt disaster alike for British decorators and the public. The former were too independent and the latter were helpless. In France the decorative arts had declined from the standard of the *grand siècle,* but there was still a certain unity of design in French work, an avoidance of absurdities, and a graceful dignity which the ordinary English decorator failed to approach. The leading English manufacturers realized this and they did their best to remedy matters. They either imported French goods and set their workpeople to make copies, or they engaged young designers fresh from the Government school of design to work in the styles demanded by fashion. The amateurs also were not inactive. They ranged from Earl de Grey, the first President of the Royal Institute of British Architects, to the Duchess of Sutherland. The chief amateur, however, was the Prince Consort, whose influence spread to the nobility. The spending classes demanded exceptional novelties, and the manufacturers were out to meet the demand. The choice of show-rooms was wide: Broadwood and Collard & Collard for pianos, grands and uprights; Jackson & Graham, Howard, Morant, Gillow, Trollope, Howell & James for furniture and decoration. There was also the saloon of the ubiquitous decorator, Mr. Fair, whose clients could be numbered by scores.[1] The best steel and brass fire-places designed by Alfred Stevens came from Hoole's of Sheffield. Blews and Potts of Birmingham supplied candlesticks and lamps; Faradays, and Oslers, the glass chandeliers for wax candles and gas which were the glory of Victorian nights. The delightful china and porcelain door furniture was made by Copelands, and Mintons and Wedgwood supplied masses of pottery. The show-rooms of

[1] His house still stands in Hanover Street.

Apsley Pellatts were also frequented by customers in search of chandeliers and glass. From Bennet, Dent & Vulliamy came the clocks with protecting glass shades; and from Garrards the best of the Victorian silver and the Brassey testimonial. This remarkable example of Victorian craftsmanship, known as the 'Great Railway Salver', exhibited portraits of the chief railway engineers and their chief works in enamel.

By 1851 the Victorian method of decorating became a byword among the thoughtful; it is now a traditional jest. The model of State apartments in town and country mansions was taken, according to income, on a descending scale, to every pretentious villa and semi-detached house in the United Kingdom. The drawing-room became sacrosanct with its white and gold ornaments, white marble mantelpiece, console tables, pier-glasses, chairs of rosewood, circular album table, glass chandelier, ottoman, chiffonier, whatnot, grand piano, fire screen, purdonium, and musical box. Add one or two papier-mâché chairs and a set of coffee tables, one or two trifles under glass shades, a set of Indian chess-men, and a model of a Swiss châlet to the previous list and the perfect Castlenau drawing-room results. Deduct 20 per cent. of the cost of the above-mentioned articles and allow for inferior finish and a fair idea of a drawing-room in Milner Square, Islington, or Highbury Crescent can be gained. All familiar with the furnishings of seaside lodgings forty years ago will recall the harsh contours of heavy mahogany, the black shining horsehair, the mirrors that reflected the coffee-coloured lace curtains, and the parody of a French clock that refused to go. This section of Victorian produce was comic; no designer could have been responsible for its depressing vulgarity. The tragedy of the period was that the great Victorian public remained estranged from the simplicity of art; the middle-class mind abhorred handicraft which it did not understand and looked down on the older school of workmen who used their hands. The decorative arts, therefore, are a frank mockery of middle-class independence. The workers are shown to have been slaves, the masters careless, and the public fools; it becomes clear that the criticisms of Professor Cockerell and Pugin were singularly apposite.

The greater part of the art writings of the nineteenth century are associated with these expressions of solid com-

TABLE, designed by the Duchess of Sutherland

BUFFET

fort which meant so much to the average Victorian family. There were excitements when escape was temporarily possible, excursions to the Rhine and to Italy, walking tours in England's green and pleasant places, expeditions and extended journeys by gig and private carriage from the drab monotony of suburban London. Small wonder that Ruskin encouraged the drawings by Prout which he thought most suited to the middle-class home.

It is a characteristic of every period for some persons to stretch their hands to the receding past. The mid-nineteenth century proved no exception, and it is not surprising that the opening of the Great Exhibition was celebrated by a State Ball at Buckingham Palace at which all the guests wore Stuart costume. This was significant of a new dilettantism. A little later Thackeray led cultured opinion towards the days of Queen Anne and the Georges; in the meantime painters were fabricating supposititious views of eighteenth-century life. The lead given by the Government in choosing Tudor for the Houses of Parliament in 1834 had already been ignored, but the efforts of Pugin helped the artistic aspect of the Oxford Movement. Apart from the specialist decorators the leading architects had shown their devotion to one or the other of the two styles, i.e. Gothic and classic, which the public understood in a vague way. By the time of the Great Exhibition the average Victorian had been led by his artistic advisers to mistake the unreal for the real, to place the picturesque higher than the formal. Ruskin, the champion of newer thought, was now the avowed admirer of Prout and the advocate of Venetian truths. For a time art opinion was hurried off after the chimera of nature, but greater than the power of Ruskin's silver tongue was the intuition of the public for the works of the previous age.

A writer in 1860 expressed his desire for an ideal house in the following terms. The stipulation that it should not be earlier than 1650 nor later than 1750 fits in with emotions then current.

'This house and this neighbourhood should not be far from London —from the centre of the old town.

'What luxury would there be, about equal to anything we read of in the Arabian Nights, in turning on one side from the busy crowd, unlocking a tiny door that promised to lead to nothing but a miserable court, and passing, at once, into a secret secluded garden.'

'What pleasures would be equal to those of hearing the splash of cool fountains; the sighing of the wind through lofty elms and broad beeches; of standing amongst the scent and colours of a hundred growing flowers; of sitting in an oaken room with a tiled fireplace, surrounded by old china in cabinets, old folios upon carved tables, old portraits of men and women in the costumes of a bygone time, and looking out over a lawn of grass with a winding vista of trees, so contrived as to shut out all signs of City life, while the mellow hum of traffic came in at the open window, or through the blinds, and you felt that you were within a stone's throw of Temple Bar.'

As a contrast the following shows dissatisfaction with events as they were:

'I detest a modern, well-advertised building estate—I should feel that when I retired to rest, perhaps eight hundred masters of households were slumbering in eight hundred bedchambers exactly the same size and the same shape as my own. When I took a bath, or lingered over the breakfast table, I should be haunted by the knowledge that eight hundred people might probably be taking similar baths, and similar breakfasts, in precisely similar apartments. . . . If I gazed from a window, or stood in a doorway, I should see hundreds of other windows and hundreds of other doorways that matched mine in relative position and design. My dreams at night would probably be a mixture of the past and the present, of my old tastes and my new sufferings. . . . My old books, my old prints, my old china, my old furniture, my old servants would pine away in such a habitation. Finally, I should die of a surfeit of stucco, and be the first lodger entered in the records of the adjoining bleak, unfinished cemetery.'

The luxury of middle-class life during the late fifties and the sixties can be best understood by a study of the streets of London. A tour on foot through Bayswater, Paddington, and Pimlico might be continued to Camberwell and Dulwich. The districts have changed, the houses have gone down, but the evidence of former ostentation remains. Who would undertake the responsibility of these huge residences to-day? And but for the indomitable courage of Victorian parents and the lure of large families few would have dared the risk in those days. The difference in the value of money, then and now, should not be forgotten. The head of a middle-class family might have had an income ranging from £500 to £1,500. A perfect warren of a house could be rented at £80 per annum. £50 was more usually paid for rent, which the Victorian placed at one-tenth of his income.

Every large town can show similar houses to those in

London, whose original occupants have passed without record, except for their names in the rating books. Through these houses runs the same soulless scheme of decoration, the same plan, the same pretence and unrighteousness of purpose. They have no true place in the story of Victorian art; they contributed little to the craft of building or decoration; they came to be repositories for the products of Birmingham and Sheffield and the meaningless impedimenta that poured from the Cornucopia of Free Trade. The finer thoughts of Victorian architects and artists could not penetrate these inaccessible fastnesses, so different in style and comeliness to the 'bricklayer's packing cases' of the eighteenth century, so entirely a product of immense pride. Reflection will show that even these dull habitations have the merit of spaciousness, a certain dignity, a drab uniformity and aloofness. They were the cradling places of our parents and grandparents, and apart from art considerations these houses are entitled to some respect. Inspired by Barry's Italianate manner, built often in feeble imitation of Gog and Magog, the twin monsters of Princes Gate, claiming no true architectural ancestry, they are pre-eminently middle class and on that account are worthy of a saga.

With the succession of Democracy the inner suburbs of London began to change. The railway carried the middle-class families out of town; houses were built in the suburbs to smaller dimensions and the Gothic revival as well as Ruskinism found ultimate triumph in the building speculations of the eighties. Thirty years after the closing of the Great Exhibition of 1851 the same anomalies of furniture and decoration which had previously horrified thoughtful artists now found a new stimulus among a lower level of society. Except in isolated cases, or where the strictest discipline was maintained, art could not hope to rise to a status of uniform excellence. The great comedy of Victorian art, which had created such a stir at the beginning, at last revealed the tyranny of universal freedom. The spectacle of its dry and discouraging scenery stretched back over the years depicting the struggles of society and the turmoil of its happenings. More than this cannot be written of the callousness of the Victorian ideal, that immensity of purpose which neither statesmanship could control nor artistry adequately express.

XII

EARLY VICTORIAN MUSIC

XII

EARLY VICTORIAN MUSIC

By EDWARD J. DENT

IF we consider the history of music as a whole, there are few periods so interesting—so exciting, one might almost say—as the years between 1830 and 1860. The Romantic movement had received its first impulse from Weber, who died in 1826; the whole musical style of the nineteenth century had been given its fundamental character by Rossini, whose career as a composer came to an unexpected end in 1829. The decades which followed saw that astonishing outburst of Romantic music which is associated with the names of Berlioz, Liszt, Chopin, Schumann, and Mendelssohn, as well as the first rise to fame or notoriety of the youthful Verdi and Wagner. To that galaxy of genius England contributed only the comparatively modest names of John Field and William Sterndale Bennett. They were the only British composers of the time who achieved more than a merely domestic reputation, and even in their own country they had little chance of either fame or fortune. Field left England as a young man, and when he returned to London was so much a stranger that he was known as Field of St. Petersburg, or 'Russian' Field; Bennett spent practically his whole life in England, and found himself forced to sacrifice his career as a composer in order to support his wife and children by the more lucrative profession of teaching the pianoforte.

As composers, it must be admitted that neither of them are much remembered nowadays. Field was overshadowed by Chopin, as Bennett was by Mendelssohn. Yet Chopin's Nocturnes, and much more of his music besides those, could never have come into being without the example of the Nocturnes of Field, and Field's Nocturnes, when we strip them of their decorative passages and reduce their melodies to their simplest terms, can be clearly seen to owe their inspiration to the tunes of the English ballad operas. And Bennett owes no less to Field than he does to Mendelssohn; it is from Field, rather than from the German composer, that he derives that singular elegance and refinement of style which seems so appropriate a reflection of the social graces of his epoch.

It was a period when England was regarded abroad as a definitely unmusical country, but one in which all foreign musicians might be certain of making their fortunes. It was true enough that England was musically unproductive, and English musicians were curiously indifferent to the new movements that were being developed in other countries. The English attitude towards music may well have been determined by English social conditions. The eighteenth century had liberally patronized the arts, music no less than the others, and the tradition had not altogether died out during the days of the Regency; but by 1830 the magnificence of the aristocracy had become more restrained, while the middle classes, whose rise to power was perhaps the most significant factor in Victoria's reign, had not yet attained general artistic culture, far less the courage to enjoy it with the freedom that only comes of long experience of possession. The social change is reflected in the musical life of England, and in the course of these thirty years, 1830–60, we shall see the foundations laid of that musical renaissance which began in 1880.

The English, even in 1830, were not an unmusical nation, but a very large proportion of the nation was musically uneducated, and the class which had the fullest opportunities for the enjoyment of music regarded the art more as an entertainment than as a religion. It was inevitable that music of the highest type should have been practically limited to the uppermost classes of society, partly on the ground of its cost, and mainly because both literature and all the arts, no less than music, were patronized only by the uppermost classes. English society was at least willing to spend a good deal of money on music. Foreign performers could earn larger fees in London than anywhere else, and resident teachers of music were also paid at a liberal rate. Operas—Italian operas, that is—and concerts of chamber or orchestral music depended on the upper classes for their audiences and the rates of subscription were proportionately high. It was a time when English people demanded, in every branch of life, goods of the best quality and were willing to pay a suitable price for them. Pianofortes were expensive, but not unreasonably so, and English pianofortes were generally considered superior to those of continental make. Sheet music, too, was expensive, but English music printing was incomparably better than that of any other country.

Professional musicians, whose living depended on the support given them by the amateurs, regretted the fact that their audiences and pupils were drawn almost exclusively from the female sex and from the clergy. There still remained a few noblemen who were enthusiastic amateurs of music, but their number was diminishing. Just as in Vienna it was a body of noble amateurs who founded the Conservatoire of Music in 1818, so it was a committee of noblemen and gentlemen, headed by Lord Burghersh (afterwards Earl of Westmorland), himself an amateur composer of some skill, who founded the Royal Academy of Music in 1823. But in the succeeding generation music came to be looked upon more and more as an accomplishment for ladies; if the clergy practised it, it was not for professional purposes as a rule, but simply because the Church was then regarded as the natural and obvious profession for young men of good family whose tastes were artistic and intellectual rather than political and sporting. That a gentleman should become a real professional musician remained utterly unthinkable until almost the end of the Queen's reign. The life of leisure, and the absence of many distractions now available, led to the achievement of a distinctly high standard of accomplishment among many amateurs of those days. London was the permanent home of several famous pianists, such as Clementi, Cramer, Moscheles, and Sterndale Bennett, so that pianoforte-playing was cultivated and appreciated; the immense admiration enjoyed by Thalberg in London no doubt contributed to the fact that innumerable young ladies rose at early hours to practise *morceaux de salon* which the modern musical young woman would altogether refuse to waste her time upon. Elderly readers of this book will probably remember among their acquaintance many old ladies of late Victorian days who were thoroughly well-trained and skilful pianists. And as Sterndale Bennett was in great request as a teacher of young ladies there were many whose musical taste was firmly grounded on the works of Mozart, Beethoven, and Mendelssohn.

It is characteristic of English musical people that when

they develop a devotion for any particular musician, be he composer or performer, it is a devotion arising more from affection than from critical admiration. This probably accounts for the long-continued devotion to the music of Handel, which even now is not entirely extinct, and has, indeed, been overlapped by a revival of interest in Handel on the part of those whose natural instinct it is to revolt against traditional devotions. It certainly accounts for the almost equally intense, but shorter-lived, devotion to Mendelssohn, which was peculiarly characteristic of the Victorians, just as Haydn's long personal sojourns in this country may well have contributed a good deal to the popularity of his music. The general taste of English musical people about 1830, as far as it is possible to make an estimate of it, was conservative, as it is still to a large extent, although music in those days did not suffer as severely as it does now from the tyranny of 'the classics'. England still preserved a certain native tradition in music derived from Purcell and Arne; Elizabethan madrigals were still being regularly sung in certain circles, and the glees of the previous century were still popular—so popular, indeed, that the composition of glees had not yet been abandoned. The music of J. S. Bach was practically unknown, though the modern cult of him may be traced to the missionary efforts of Victorian musicians, notably T. A. Walmisley, Professor of Music at Cambridge, and still more his successor in that office, Sterndale Bennett. But, until the advent of Mendelssohn, Handel was the acknowledged greatest master of all. Haydn was universally accepted for his symphonies and quartets; Mozart's operas were gradually becoming popular. The more advanced musicians proclaimed the greatness of Beethoven, but even the advanced were unable to follow him into the mysterious region of his third period. The general musical tradition of England was partly English and partly Italian, owing to the general domination of almost all music by the Italians in the eighteenth century. It was a long time before this Italian influence was obliged to yield to a German one, and even to-day there still exists in England a subterranean Italian tradition in music of which many professional musicians and critics are hardly aware, as it manifests itself in circles with which they have little contact.

From a social point of view the most important musical

activity of London was naturally the Italian Opera, the home of which was Her Majesty's Opera House in the Haymarket, although H. F. Chorley, looking back (about 1860) over a period of thirty years, deplored the fact that the Opera had lost much of the social exclusiveness and distinction which characterized it in the reign of George IV. But in 1830 the Opera still depended on regular subscribers living in London. It gave performances only on Tuesdays and Saturdays; on Thursdays there was the 'long night', attracting a different public with a mixed programme of enormous length. The development of railway travelling made it gradually possible for the visiting public to attend the Opera more freely, so that by 1860 the management depended almost more on casual visitors than on regular subscribers, and the number of nights on which the Opera was open was gradually increased. At the same time the length of the season diminished; in 1830 it sometimes began as early as February, although the best singers did not make their appearance until after Easter.

The standards of performance in 1830 are drastically described by Chorley. 'The orchestra was meagre and ill disciplined; the chorus was an ear-torment rather than an ear-pleasure; the scenery and appointments were shabby to penury.' The gradual improvement which took place later was due mainly to the appointment (in 1832) of a young man from Naples, Michele Costa, who, in the course of the next generation, became the most dominating personality in the world of orchestral and choral music. In 1830 the lower ranks of the musical profession were disreputable and ill mannered; by 1860 they were not only much better educated in music itself, but had acquired a new sense of dignity and self-respect. This change was due partly to the general change of social standards among the middle classes, but largely to the artistic and moral influence of Costa.

The repertory of the Italian Opera was based chiefly on Rossini, Bellini, and Donizetti. Cimarosa appeared in earlier days, and Mozart was always popular. Meyerbeer's *Robert le Diable* was first given in 1832; in 1845 Verdi's *Ernani* was received 'with curiosity rather than with sympathy'. There were occasional performances in French at the Opera, and at other theatres we hear of seasons of Italian Comic Opera and some notable seasons of German Opera. The most remarkable of the German seasons was that of 1832, during which Wilhelmine Schröder-Devrient made Beethoven's *Fidelio* an astonishing popular success. It would be superfluous to enumerate the great singers of the Italian seasons. Grisi, Mario, Tamburini, and Lablache were the four favourites; Malibran had enthralled London, both in Italian and in English Opera, in the days of William IV, but her short life came to its tragic end in 1836. It was in 1847 that Jenny Lind made her first appearance in London, singing the part of Alice in *Robert le Diable*. Her arrival had been heralded by an extraordinary amount of publicity, and a lawsuit between two rival operatic managers had provided her with an excellent advertisement. Further, she enjoyed the enthusiastic admiration of Mendelssohn, then at the height of his popularity in England. Gifted as she was with a voice of singular beauty and a reputation for blameless purity of domestic life, she naturally met with a welcome in England such as few singers have ever obtained before or since. Her operatic career did not last long; in 1852 she married Otto Goldschmidt, and after settling down in England in 1856 she appeared only in oratorio and at concerts.

English Opera (under which heading we include all Opera performed in English) appealed to a different class of audience. The production of *The Beggar's Opera* in 1728 had led to a long series of English 'Ballad operas', which continued into the following century. Satire gradually gave way to sentimentality, and towards the end of the eighteenth century the influence of the romantic movement gradually made itself felt. The English operas of Bishop were for the most part *pasticcios* made up from the music of various composers, both English and foreign, to suit popular English taste. Foreign comic and romantic operas, such as Mozart's *Figaro* and Weber's *Freischütz*, were ruthlessly 'adapted'; but the success of *Der Freischütz* in this form in 1824 was so enthusiastic that Weber was invited to compose a new opera for Covent Garden. This was *Oberon* (1826), written to an English libretto by Planché modelled more or less on the tradition which had come down from Purcell's *King Arthur*. There was a good season of English Opera in 1833, at which Malibran almost eclipsed Schröder-Devrient by her impersonation of Leonora in *Fidelio*.

A more serious attempt at English Opera began with J. F.

AFTER THE OPERA

Barnett's *The Mountain Sylph* (1834). Barnett's name was originally Beer, and he was a cousin of Meyerbeer. This work was followed by a number of Romantic English operas by various composers, hardly any of which are now remembered. The general style of English Opera at this period is derived partly from traditional English Ballad Opera, partly from the current Italian Opera, with a certain admixture of German Romanticism derived from Weber and Marschner. The only survivors at the present day are Balfe's *Bohemian Girl* (1843) and Wallace's *Maritana* (1845). Benedict's *Lily of Killarney*, still popular and often associated with these two operas, was not composed until 1865. Balfe in his day was an extraordinarily successful composer of operas, both English and Italian; his works were performed all over Europe. It is, however, hardly conceivable that any of them should ever be revived again, and *Satanella*, *The Siege of Rochelle*, and *The Rose of Castile* must probably remain in oblivion along with Loder's *Nourjahad* and *The Night Dancers*, and the innumerable operas of G. A. Macfarren.

English Opera, like Italian Opera, was never a financial success, in spite of momentary popularity. The memoirs of the period reveal a chronic state of chaos and ruin as regards the business side of these undertakings. From 1856 onwards some success was achieved by an English opera company directed by William Harrison and Louisa Pyne. It enjoyed the encouragement of the Prince Consort, always a keen supporter of musical interests, and he even went so far as to promise that influence should be brought to bear to secure them a subsidy from Parliament. Unfortunately, the Prince died in the very year that this promise was held out, and the company very soon met with the usual fate of all English operatic enterprises.

The most important concert organizations of the period were the Ancient Concerts (founded in 1776) and the Philharmonic Society (founded 1813). Both societies depended upon a subscription audience drawn from the upper classes. The Ancient Concerts, as their name implied, represented a conservative taste. It was a rule of the society that no music should be performed that was less than twenty years old. The programmes were drawn up in rotation by the directors, who were often royal dukes or archbishops, and by 1830 the repertory hardly extended beyond Haydn and Mozart.

From 1834 onwards the name of Beethoven gradually became more familiar; it is noteworthy that in 1847, at a concert chosen by the Prince Consort, Mendelssohn played a prelude and fugue of Bach on the organ. The Ancient Concerts came to an end in 1848.

The Philharmonic Society differed fundamentally from the Ancient Concerts in that it was started by professional musicians and not by aristocratic amateurs. The impulse came, no doubt, from the success of the Salomon concerts, for which Haydn had composed his most celebrated symphonies during the last ten years of the previous century. The Philharmonic Society stood for contemporary music, and showed its courage in introducing to England the works of Beethoven while the composer was still alive. The Ninth Symphony was originally written for the Philharmonic Society. In 1813 London had no permanent orchestra capable of interpreting music of the classical symphony type. Such orchestras as existed, or were got together for special occasions, had been required merely as accompaniments to operas or to vocal and instrumental soloists. Chorley's criticism of the Italian Opera band has already been quoted; Hogarth confirms it, and tells us that the English Opera band and the orchestras employed at the theatres for the Lent Oratorios were still worse.

The Philharmonic Society's programmes for many years included not only symphonies and other purely orchestral works, but also much music which we should now class as chamber music—string quartets and works for larger combinations of solo instruments. Concerted vocal music was also encouraged, provided it had orchestral accompaniment; but all solos, duets, and concertos for a solo instrument were rigorously excluded. The Philharmonic Society aimed at what for its time were the highest artistic standards, and it did not intend to encourage the appearance of 'stars'. At first the old custom was kept up by which the orchestra was 'led' by the principal first violin, the composer, or some other responsible musician, sitting at the pianoforte and keeping the band together as best he could; this had, indeed, been the practice in Haydn's day, but Spohr, on his visit to London in 1820, insisted on conducting with a baton in the manner now universal.

From 1813 to 1830 the concerts were given in the Argyll

Rooms at the corner of Regent Street and Oxford Circus; after the destruction of these by fire in 1830 the Society met at first in the concert-room of the Italian Opera House, and from 1833 onwards in the Hanover Square Rooms, which, until the building of St. James's Hall in 1858, remained the principal concert-room of London.

Mendelssohn paid his first visit to England in 1829, and from that date onwards his music was in constant demand at the Philharmonic concerts. The *Italian Symphony* was composed for the season of 1833. Spohr was another frequent visitor. The Philharmonic made a great point of commissioning composers to provide new works, and in those days concert programmes were happily free from the everlasting burden of the classics. The rule against solos and concertos was abolished within a few years of the Society's foundation, and the Philharmonic provided occasion for the appearance of all the most distinguished performers of the period. Liszt played there in 1840, Mendelssohn on many occasions. Of the English pianists, the most eminent were Sterndale Bennett, Mrs. Anderson, and Cipriani Potter. Joachim, at the age of thirteen, played Beethoven's Concerto in 1844, and some amusement was caused by the simultaneous advertisements of *The Hungarian Boy* and *The Bohemian Girl*. After 1845 programmes assumed a more conservative character. The directors seem to have fought shy of novelties, and preferred to keep on the safe side with works by the composers whom we now regard as classics. Berlioz was invited to conduct in 1853 and Richard Wagner in the following year, but their own works were coldly received; London remained faithful to Mendelssohn. Costa had been engaged as conductor in 1846, the chief previous conductor having been Sir George Smart. Costa had hitherto been known only as a conductor of operas, but he soon proved himself an efficient conductor for symphony concerts too. He was succeeded in 1855 by Sterndale Bennett.

During the earlier years of the Philharmonic Society its programmes had included chamber music as well as music for full orchestra. This system, strange as it may seem to the modern concert-goer, had its justification in days when orchestras were much smaller than they are now, and when there were no opportunities elsewhere for hearing chamber music except in private. In 1845 John Ella, a violinist who had for many years directed the private concerts given by Lord Saltoun, Sir George Warrender, and other musical enthusiasts in aristocratic circles, founded the 'Musical Union' for the performance of chamber music. Three classical works were played at each concert, and leaflets were circulated to the subscribers before the concerts, giving analytical notes on the music; the performers were musicians of the highest obtainable eminence. Ella was perpetually laughed at by the journalists for his aristocratic connexions, and it was alleged that the innermost ring of listeners (the performers were placed in the middle of the room) consisted exclusively of duchesses, while the rest of the audience were accommodated in order of precedence. But the concerts (as the writer has often been told by one who was a regular subscriber to them) maintained a high artistic standard, and the analytical programmes were genuinely instructive. The Monday Popular Concerts at St. James's Hall, which began in 1859, eventually took the place of the Musical Union in a period when the taste for chamber music had become more widely spread; but it must be remembered that these latter originated not with string quartets but with popular songs sung by Sims Reeves and popular pianoforte solos played by Arabella Goddard.

The occasional concerts organized by individual artists were often of very mixed character. Pianoforte recitals were unknown; if a pianist gave a concert for his own benefit, he was expected to engage an orchestra and the services of singers as well. Both singers and players seem to have been very generous in giving their services to assist their colleagues, but in such cases they could not be asked to rehearse, and concerted music, as well as the orchestral accompaniments, was often very raggedly performed. Programmes were of enormous length, as indeed they were at all concerts except those of the Musical Union. The unfortunate organizer generally had to go round in person to beg his friends to buy tickets, and the parents of his pupils usually felt it their duty to support him. They did not, however, always attend the concert themselves, and Ella tells us that on such occasions 'a peeress has been brought into social contact in the reserved stalls with her neighbour's waiting-maid, both enjoying the banquet set before them'.

Choral music was occasionally performed by the Phil-

ERARD'S PIANOFORTE: GREAT EXHIBITION, 1851

harmonic, but the Hanover Square Rooms were too small for large choruses, and the Society did not often repeat the experiment. The Ancient Concerts gave more space to choral works, especially to those of Handel, and oratorios were now and then organized by the theatres. The singers were drawn partly from the theatres, partly from the cathedrals and churches; at some concerts the treble parts were sung by boys, at others by women. For the better class of oratorio concerts women singers were imported from Lancashire, where choral singing was more generally practised; these ladies were popularly known as the 'Lancashire witches', in allusion to Shadwell's well-known play. Complete oratorios, as a matter of fact, were very seldom performed before about 1830; the oratorio concerts at the theatres in Lent were of a very mixed character, including secular vocal music as well as sacred. In 1832 the Sacred Harmonic Society was founded for the practice of choral music by amateurs. It met at first in various chapels, but from 1834 to 1880 its home was at Exeter Hall. Its first conductor was Joseph Surman. After 1836 it adopted the principle of giving complete oratorios instead of selections, and after Costa became its conductor in 1848 its performances reached a very high level.

Choral singing received a great stimulus in 1844 by the institution of popular singing classes directed first by Joseph Mainzer and afterwards by John Hullah. J. Alfred Novello, the music publisher, began the issue of cheap editions of oratorios and other choral music; in the same year he began the publication of *The Musical Times and Singing-Class Circular*, with each number of which (costing $1\frac{1}{2}d$.) a part-song or anthem was included. Hitherto, choral bodies all over the country had been dependent mainly on vocal parts copied by hand, as sheet music was costly, and the complete vocal score of an oratorio was generally priced at a guinea or more. (Mendelssohn's *St. Paul* cost 32s., and the single voice parts 5s. each.)

The oldest of the provincial choral festivals was that of the 'Three Choirs' of Gloucester, Worcester, and Hereford, records of which go back to 1724. Most of the provincial festivals originated in cathedral cities; the Birmingham festival, dating from 1768, was also associated with a church. By 1830 several festival centres had become regularly established, and musical performances were organized on a very large scale, solo singers and leading instrumentalists being procured from London. The chief supporters of the festivals were always the nobility and gentry, and even down to our own times these events have always been regarded locally as important social functions. These triennial orgies of music were reasonable enough in days when travelling was difficult and few people in the country had opportunities of visiting London. The development of railways, as well as the spread of popular education, soon enlarged the scope of the provincial festivals. The Birmingham festival was carried on triennially from 1796; Norwich started triennial festivals in 1824, Leeds in 1858. York organized annual festivals from 1791 to 1803, as well as four festivals between 1823 and 1835; at Manchester there were important festivals in 1828 and 1836.

The oratorios of Haydn, Spohr, and Mendelssohn supplied a welcome change from eternal Handel. Church music by Haydn, Mozart, and Beethoven, as well as works of Cherubini, Hummel, and others, also came to a hearing after they had been provided with English words not offensive to Protestant consciences. Oratorio made a peculiarly fervent appeal to English audiences, especially in the provinces; there was a long-established tradition of choral singing, especially in the north, and it satisfied to some extent the dramatic instincts of both singers and listeners of a class that still regarded the theatre as morally dangerous.

Another new movement which contributed to the musical education of the masses, especially in the north of England, was the formation of brass bands, which began about 1855. The invention of valves for brass instruments, which had been developed since 1824, made these much easier to play, as well as extending their range. In military music England lagged behind France and Germany, although at the end of the previous century English military bands were quite as good as continental ones, and English military music even influenced that of other countries through the introduction of the quick-step march in 6/8 time, which is derived from the English country dances of the seventeenth century or earlier. A decisive step was taken by the military authorities in England when the Duke of Cambridge founded the Royal Military School of Music at Kneller Hall in 1856.

Fenimore Cooper, describing England in 1828, speaks with

COTTAGE PIANO: GREAT EXHIBITION, 1851

The publication of *Hymns Ancient and Modern* in 1861 set the official seal of the Church on the practice of hymn-singing, which in earlier generations had been confined mainly to the Nonconformists. Metrical versions of the Psalms had been sung in churches since the Reformation, but hymns written as original poems were considered suitable only to private devotions. The early Tractarians disapproved even of those of Isaac Watts being sung in church services. Hymn-singing, however, proved too strong an attraction to be resisted, and the popularity of Victorian hymn-tunes became in fact so overwhelming that in our own day they seem almost to have become folk-songs. It was characteristic of the British soldier in the European War that he did not sing the traditional folk-songs of his ancestors but the later Victorian hymn-melodies, to which he set words of his own which might have considerably surprised the original composers.

The chronicle of early Victorian music is of necessity somewhat dull. But it was none the less a period of steady and careful preparation. It produced nothing exciting, nothing even outstanding, but it was the necessary development of a musical environment that in the later years of the Queen's reign was to bring forth the new re-birth of English music.

XIII
THE THEATRE

XIII

THE THEATRE

By ALLARDYCE NICOLL

THE first decade of Queen Victoria's reign witnessed a revolution in the world of the theatre, the effects of which can be described only as epoch-making. Up to the year 1843 there had been continued a convention which dated back to the period of the Restoration, nearly two centuries previous; after 1843 the theatres, instead of always looking back, turned their attention to the future. It is, indeed, not too much to say that the basis of the present-day drama is to be found in the results of the Theatres Act, introduced into Parliament and passed in that year. By this Act the monopoly in 'legitimate' drama (five-act tragedy and comedy without the introduction of music), hitherto held by Drury Lane, Covent Garden, and the Haymarket, was revoked, all theatres were placed equally under the jurisdiction of the Lord Chamberlain, and the necessity of obeying the convention of the 'burletta'[1] disappeared. At first glance, we might be inclined to say that, although in theory the new Act wrought a great change, in practice there were no serious innovations. Drury Lane for many years, owing to the rivalry of the 'minor' theatres, had been producing melodrama and burlesque; for their part, the 'minors' had succeeded, by introducing a few songs and the ghost of a musical accompaniment, in performing any plays they desired. Even *Hamlet* with a song or two for Ophelia and a lugubrious ditty for the melancholy prince, could pass unchallenged as a 'burletta'. The terms 'legitimate' and 'illegitimate', 'major' and 'minor', still endured long after the year 1843, and theatrical repertoires exhibited no immediate and startling innovations in the kind of entertainment provided for their patrons.

This hasty judgement, however, is one which cannot be substantiated by a more detailed analysis of the available

---

[1] The term 'burletta' is difficult to define exactly. It was applied to the plays with music (serious and comic) which alone were permitted to be performed in the 'minor' theatres.

evidence. Indeed, we require to go no further than the activities of two theatres to see how the provisions of the Act
were opening up fresh paths for those currently interested
in dramatic entertainment. These two theatres are *The
Princess's* and *Sadler's Wells*. The former, situated in Oxford
Street, had been opened as a theatre in 1830, but before 1850
its career was undistinguished. One might have witnessed
there variety entertainments and occasionally performances
of operas in English, but nothing more. In 1850, however,
all that was changed. Charles Kean, son of the unhappy
Edmund, seeking for a house in which he might realize his
dreams of Shakespearian production, decided to lease it, and
for seven years drew London to its doors. The acting of
Kean and his wife was competent but in general uninspired;
that which really attracted attention was the elaborate
nature of the theatrical display and the attempt made by
the manager to present as accurate a picture as possible
of the times in which the action of any particular play was
set. Kean himself was an enthusiastic student, and, adding
to his own knowledge the information which he borrowed
from many archaeological experts, he endeavoured both to
please the eye by the colour of his shows and to entertain the
mind by presenting historical 'truth'. In him the movement towards 'realism' in stage setting reached its culmination. He banished Shakespeare's Bohemia because that
conflicted with the references to the Delphic oracle, putting
in its stead a Bithynia which permitted him to display bar-
barian garments alongside classical Greek costumes; and
when he came to *Macbeth*, recognizing the difficulty of discovering authentic information regarding Scots dress in the
eleventh century, he boldly 'borrowed material from those
nations to whom Scotland was constantly opposed in war',
the Norsemen, and thus clad his actors in 'the tunic, mantle,
cross-gartering, and ringed byrne of the Danes and the Anglo-
Saxons', retaining, however, 'the striped and chequered
garb' peculiar to the Celts. As he learnedly observes in his
programme:

'Diodorus Siculus and Pliny allude to this peculiarity in their
account of the dress of the Belgic Gauls; Strabo, Pliny, and Xiphilin
record the dress of Boadicea, Queen of the Iceni, as being woven
chequer-wise, of many colours, comprising purple, light and dark red,
violet and blue.'

Mrs. Warner as Lady Macbeth

Mr. Phelps as Macbeth

N° 6.

Mr. H. Marston as Macduff

Mr. Phelps as Macbeth 3rd dress

STAGE ATTITUDES, c. 1830

From the Gabrielle Enthoven Collection: Victoria and Albert Museum.

The architect George Godwin provided him with the information necessary for the accurate depiction of domestic architecture in these far-off times. Controversy raged over these productions, some seeing in them an innovation of the utmost importance for the stage, others sneering at the pedantry and the splendour, declaring that Shakespeare was buried under a wealth of learning and a voluptuousness of scenic appeal. Especial discussion was called forth by *The Winter's Tale* (in which Ellen Terry made her first appearance as Mamillius), a play where Kean could let his imagination run free riot.

Before the passing of the Theatres Act Kean could not thus have experimented in the production of Shakespeare; nor could Samuel Phelps have dreamed of presenting other of that dramatist's plays at Sadler's Wells theatre. Up to 1843 Sadler's Wells had been only one of a number of outlying melodrama houses, frequented by local audiences. It had been more successful than most, perhaps because of its aquatic spectacles, water having been introduced into a large tank from the New River. Thus as early as 1804 a great drama called 'Ὠκεανία, or, *The Siege of Gibraltar* afforded there

'a grand Naval Spectacle, presenting that monument of British Glory, the Siege of Gibraltar; with an exact representation of the armament both by Land and Sea, of the combined forces of France and Spain, with real Men of War and Floating Batteries, built and rigged by professional men from His Majesty's Dock Yards, and which float in a receptacle containing nearly 8,000 cubic feet of real water.'

In 1844, immediately after the freeing of the 'minor' theatres, Samuel Phelps leased it for the production of legitimate dramas, and, although every one smiled at the folly of his attempt, succeeded in drawing conservative West End spectators to Islington. Phelps himself was a great actor of the 'physical' school, but he could not afford to engage a strong company or to compete with Kean in numbers of supernumeraries and in lavishness of scenic display. Henry Marston and Miss Cooper ably stood by him throughout the period of his management (1844–62), but they were but mediocre performers at the best. Phelps, however, succeeded in exciting interest, apart from the manifestation of his own histrionic genius, by exhibiting a care in the presentation of the dramatist's text and by tasteful methods in production. His scenery was not so rich as

Kean's or so scrupulously accurate, but many competent judges professed themselves better satisfied with the Sadler's Wells performances than with those at the Princess's.

The importance of the Theatres Act is thus immediately apparent. Neither Kean nor Phelps could have hoped to do a tithe of what was actually accomplished if he had been confined to one of the 'major' theatres. These major playhouses had indeed proved that their very greatness was a cause of failure. *Covent Garden*, rebuilt after the disastrous fire of 1808, had had for a few years a notable career. The opening, certainly, had been attended by the notorious O.P. Riots occasioned by the attempt of the management to raise the prices from 3s. 6d. to 4s. for the pit and from 6s. to 7s. for the boxes; but, immediately after this had been quietened (it took a whole month to do so), the work of the directors was, if erratic, capable and at times brilliant; in particular Charles Kemble and Edmund Kean raised its standard of excellence during the twenties of the century. The following decade, however, witnessed a rapid decline. Alfred Bunn assumed control and failed to make ends meet, and he was succeeded by others only a trifle less unsuccessful than himself. For a brief period (1837–9) Macready seemed to have recovered its waning fortunes, but gradually the theatre sank lower and lower until in 1847 it had to be abandoned as a home of drama and was officially renamed *The Royal Italian Opera House*. As such it continued until another disastrous fire in 1856 destroyed it utterly. Here, under the direction of F. Gye and to the conducting of Costa one might listen to the music of Berlioz, Donizetti, and Verdi—provided that one was willing to don the costume alone permitted at the opera, long-tailed coat with ruffles at the wrist, severely white cravat and white kid gloves. Going to the Italian opera was a fashionable duty rather than a popular entertainment.

Drury Lane's fate had been not dissimilar, although it still succeeded in carrying on as a playhouse. The old theatre had been destroyed by fire in 1809, but a new theatre was opened three years later under the management of a committee including in its number Lord Byron. Here too it had been found difficult to make ends meet. At Covent Garden attempts to raise prices had been met by stern opposition, and later endeavours to reduce prices in order to entice the public had met with disaster. Stephen Kemble's

PHELPS AS FALSTAFF, 1846

From the Gabrielle Enthoven Collection: Victoria and Albert Museum.

decision (1818) to lower prices at Drury Lane from 3s. to 2s. proved no whit better a scheme. Famous actors, however, continued to make an appeal here—Edmund Kean, Liston, and Macready are the chief—but soon the house was being controlled, like Covent Garden, by Alfred Bunn, who was at best but a showman. On his departure still another showman took command—the genial, versatile, and moderately capable E. T. Smith. Smith was the son of an admiral and in the course of his life had been midshipman, policeman, auctioneer, company promoter, and restaurant keeper. Perhaps because of the variety in his own life, he liked to mix the matter of his entertainments and engaged artists of all kinds from tragedians to acrobats. The current *bon mot* said that he was quite capable of putting the famous Madame Rachel on the stage with, or after, a pantomimic clown. In his hands Drury Lane came nearer in spirit to the old despised 'minors' than to some at least of the new 'minor' houses.

Alone among the former major theatres, the *Haymarket* continued a moderately 'legitimate' policy, perhaps because it was a much smaller building and was not encumbered by such enormous overhead expenses as the others. The tradition of the Haymarket went back to the eighteenth century. Starting as the Little Theatre and as such being associated with the theatrical activities of Henry Fielding, it entered on a new phase of its existence when, rebuilt by Samuel Foote in 1766, it opened under a special licence for the performance of legitimate plays during the summer months. In 1820 it had been taken over by George Colman the Younger, and in 1837 Benjamin Webster assumed the management. Under his direction (1837–53) it had a distinguished career. The policy of the Haymarket was to present a good repertoire of old and new plays, without making any special experiments in scenic methods or in general production, the only important exception being in 1844 when Webster got *The Taming of the Shrew* performed without scenery in the spirit of the Elizabethan stage. During Webster's period of management many of the best plays of the time appeared first on the boards of this theatre, among them Lord Lytton's *Money* and *Masks and Faces* by Charles Reade and Tom Taylor. In 1853 the house was leased by the versatile actor and prolific author, J. B. Buckstone, who opened it with a revival of *The Rivals*. Throughout the period it held its own, partly because it always gave excellent value for money expended. Performances started at 6.30 and ended at midnight.

This Haymarket Theatre was usually called *The Theatre Royal* to distinguish it from *The Opera House* in the Haymarket, now named *Her Majesty*'s. Her Majesty's flourished (so far as any Italian opera house has ever flourished in London) until 1852, when it was found necessary to close the theatre. All the properties and effects were disposed of in April 1853 for the sum of £11,000.

The Princess's and Sadler's Wells unquestionably stand out above all the other contemporary playhouses, but there were several other of the old 'minors' which presented interesting programmes, quite apart from those which carried on, almost unaltered, the earlier illegitimate traditions. These may now be put rapidly under review. Chief of all were *The Olympic* Theatre and *The Lyceum*, both associated with the names of Madame Vestris and Charles Mathews. The former, built in Wych Street, Strand, had been opened by Philip Astley in 1806. For a couple of decades it was merely one among other insignificant minors, but in 1831 Madame Vestris, becoming manageress, gave to its productions a singular grace and tone. Vestris was undoubtedly among the most gifted actresses of her day, adding to her inimitable powers of mimicry a skill in dancing and in singing. Her songs—notably 'Buy a broom!'—were on every one's lips. Gossip chattered, and not without reason, of her immoralities, coupling her name with scores of persons from royalty downwards, but peccadilloes of this kind seemed not to disturb her happy artistic co-operation with her husband, Charles Mathews, or to interfere with the tastefulness of her productions. Partly inspired by the theories of J. R. Planché, Somerset Herald, archaeologist and wit, she brought a refinement and a delicacy to the performance and setting of the popular extravaganza which had an enormous influence on all subsequent theatrical endeavour. Her reign at the Olympic from 1831 to 1839 was the most notable management of that decade. After her departure, however, the fame of this theatre gradually declined. Lessee after lessee abandoned it in despair. In 1849 the old theatre was burned; the new house, opened in December of that year, left its manager, Watts, bankrupt in three months. Later, the elder Farren

MIDSUMMER NIGHT'S DREAM, ACT V (*KEAN*, 1856)

took it over, but, with his nondescript repertoire, failed to bring back prosperity. Typical is the bill for February 10, 1853, which announces a dramatized version of *The Vicar of Wakefield*, a pantomime, and some entertainments by Signor Nicolo and his two children. Greater success came later when Alfred Wigan and his wife engaged the 'great little Robson', the most accomplished comic actor of his time.

The other playhouse mentioned above, The Lyceum, had been opened in 1834 'for the representation of English operas and the encouragement of indigenous musical talent', but this worthy venture did not meet with much success, and the theatre had been taken over by Mr. and Mrs. Keeley, who, in 1847, abandoned it in favour of Mathews and Vestris. Here the latter endeavoured to continue the style of performance which, a few years before, had made The Olympic so famous a theatrical resort. They still had Planché as author, vigorous and witty as ever after having penned over three hundred plays, but time was having its revenges. Both Mathews and Vestris were incurably extravagant. She, for example, was reputed on good authority to have cut up an Indian shawl valued at £300 because she fancied its pattern for a turban in an Eastern extravaganza. Bankruptcy soon descended upon them. Some six years after they had leased The Lyceum a considerable storm arose over the question of the privilege of the Press, a subject which thereafter occupied much attention. On January 1, 1853, some one signing himself 'Philo-Dramaticus' had written a severe attack on The Lyceum performances, declaring 'that the pieces produced here during the Keeley management were far superior to those of a later date'. To this Mathews took exception, openly accused Angus B. Reach as the pseudonymous author, an implication which the latter indignantly denied, and sought to abolish the system by which the Press had the right of issuing almost unlimited 'orders' for the playhouses. When a number of newspapers commented on this affair and pleaded their privileges, Mathews replied by announcing that 'the free list' was 'entirely suspended'—the first time a management had dared thus to oppose the Press. After Mathews left the theatre two years subsequently, The Lyceum had a varied career. Charles Dillon and Marie Wilton attracted attention to it in 1856 and Fechter made a great stir later, both because of his own skill in the interpretation of Shakespeare, and because he introduced many novelties of a mechanical nature on its stage. For most, however, the name of The Lyceum will inevitably be linked with that of Henry Irving, who, first appearing here in 1871, eventually undertook the complete management of the theatre seven years later.

While, between 1847 and 1855, Vestris was the presiding genius of The Lyceum, another manageress and star, Madame Céleste, ruled over the nearby *Adelphi* Theatre, situate in the Strand. The Adelphi originally started as *The Sans Pareil* Theatre in 1806, being renamed in 1819. It had had a not undistinguished career among the minors and lost none of its glory when it came into the hands of Benjamin Webster, with whom Céleste was associated. Madame Vestris' name alone was foreign; but Céleste was truly French, having started her career as a child in Paris with the great Talma. Outside of France she had first shown herself in non-speaking parts at The Bowery Theatre, New York, and assumed a small spoken role originally at The Surrey. She was known mainly as a danseuse, mimic, and vocalist; as an actress she sprang into fame in a melodrama, *The Child of the Wreck*, specially written for her by Planché. Her policy at The Adelphi was not unlike that of Vestris at The Lyceum. Divertissements of a colourful nature, extravaganzas, and burlesques were the regular fare, spiced by a certain amount of thrilling melodrama.

In alluding to Madame Céleste, reference may here be made to *The St. James's* Theatre, situated in King Street, St. James's, famous as the home of the French drama in London. It too had begun, in 1835, as a house devoted to English opera, but, failing in that, it had gradually become identified with foreign companies. The building was a pleasant one, designed by the architect, Samuel Beazley, who was responsible for so much early Victorian theatre building. Here French drama, new and old, might be seen almost every season, and from 1852 dates the appearance of German companies, that of Herr Emil Devrient and Fraülein Fuhr appearing on several successive visits.

The Strand Theatre has not such special importance. Its early career is interesting (1832–5) because of its frantic and skilful endeavours to evade the old theatrical monopoly. Under Douglas Jerrold in 1840 it was noted for 'its tiny

RICHARD II (*KEAN*, 1857)

spectacle, humorous burlesques, and spirited actors', and became even more popular eight years later when William Farren took control. Shortly after 1850, however, it, too, fell for a time on evil days. In 1853 it was housing pieces like H. Russell's 'entertainment', *The Emigrant's Progress*, and only recovered its old prestige when it witnessed, during the sixties, the triumphs of H. J. Byron's burlesques as interpreted by Marie Wilton.

The Soho Theatre never had any distinguished name. Its repertoire of old and new plays, embracing everything from *Hamlet* and *Othello* to *Oh dear! what can the matter be?*, presented nothing beyond mediocrity. It was a house of which public opinion had not much good to say, and, although situated in the West End, it was, except when utilized by amateur groups, always nearer in spirit to the various out-lying minor theatres, the activities of which must now be surveyed.

Of these, most important perhaps is *The Surrey* Theatre, in Blackfriars Road. Commencing as *The Royal Circus*, it became The Surrey first in 1810 and had a successful career under T. J. Dibdin and R. W. Elliston with a programme of spectacle and melodrama. With the passing of the Theatres Act sporadic attempts were made to introduce specimens of the legitimate drama, but the clientele of this house, like the clientele of most of the minor houses, persisted in displaying a marked preference for the old melodramatic fare. Here one might find an essentially popular audience and rudely popular manners. Attendants moved round with thick sandwiches of boiled bacon, pieces of fried fish wrapped in newspaper, and hot saveloys; others bore mugs of ale and more potent glasses of gin and brandy. Chattering and noise abounded, but when the exciting moments of the melodrama arrived, gossip ceased and munching jaws were still. No heartier laughter could be heard at comic scenes in any London theatre, and the expressions of sentiment, if crude, tasteless, and rough, were sincere and heartfelt. Perhaps we shall not be far wrong in likening these minors to the cinemas of to-day, where seats might be had at half-a-crown or a shilling, and where demand was made for a long and varied entertainment.

Akin to The Surrey was the neighbouring *Victoria* Theatre, in Waterloo Road. The Victoria had been so named since 1833, but had opened first fifteen years previously as *The*

Royal Coburg Theatre, under the patronage of H.R.H. Prince Leopold of Saxe-Coburg. Its career had been no inglorious one, even although it almost always provided performances of a distinctly 'illegitimate' kind. Here *Uncle Tom's Cabin* or *The Gold Regions of Australia* or *The Slave Hunt* or *The Wandering Tribe* or *The Mystery of the Abbey* or *The Gipsy King* was always sure of making its appeal.

Northwards, similar tastes were catered for by *The Marylebone* Theatre in Church Street, Edgware Road, a house that had started originally as *The New Royal Sussex* Theatre, changing its name in 1837. During the fifties it provided another venture for E. T. Smith, who directed its fortunes while he managed Drury Lane. The repertoire was as mixed as that provided at the larger house. Deani, the contortionist, J. Doughty and his dog, Joe and the Aztec Children appeared together with classical dramas such as *Macbeth* or *Othello* and with modern melodramas such as *The Old Man's Curse, The Turn of the Tide,* or *The Blood Red Knight.*

In the same district was *The Queen's* Theatre, in Fitzroy Square, Tottenham Court Road, originally opened in 1831. Until this was taken over by the Bancrofts and rechristened *The Prince of Wales's* Theatre in 1865 its career was of a mediocre kind. The usual melodramas of the *Uncle Tom's Cabin* type alternated here with material from the 'legitimate' repertoire.

Out at Norton Folgate was *The City of London* Theatre, opened in 1837 and closed, after a somewhat disreputable life, in 1868. Its best period was about 1853, when it was managed by Nelson Lee. Nelson Lee was another E. T. Smith. His christian name he derived from the great Nelson himself, for his father (a colonel) had been on duty at the hero's funeral at the very time when his son was born. Intended for a military or naval career, he had early shown a love of vagabond life, taught himself conjuring and appeared thus at several of the old minors. At last, after many adventures, he settled down as manager of a theatre and as prolific author of Christmas pantomimes. He, too, loved variety in his shows.

Slightly farther off, *The National Standard* Theatre provided similar entertainment for Shoreditch. Although 'National' in the fifties, this playhouse had been 'Royal' when it was opened in 1835 and merely 'New' after being

THEATRE ROYAL,

..adler'. .. 'ells.

Lessees, — Messrs. GREENWOOD and PHELPS

THIS THEATRE,
THOROUGHLY REPAIRED & RE-DECORATED
WILL BE
OPENED FOR THE SEASON,
UNDER THE MANAGEMENT OF
Mr. PHELPS,
On SATURDAY, July 25th, 1846,

With, (for the **First Time here**) the **FIRST PART** of SHAKSPERE's

HENRY IV.

The Scenery by Mr F. FENTON.   *The Costumes by Mr COOMBES and Miss BAILEY.*
The Decorations and Properties by Mr. HARVEY.

King Henry IV, — — — —		Mr. G. BENNETT.
Henry, Prince of Wales, } *Sons to the King* {	Mr. HENRY MARSTON,	
Prince John of Lancaster, }	Mr. G. MASKELL,	
Earl of Westmorland, } *Friends to the King* {	Mr. MONTAGUE.	
Sir Walter Blunt, }	Mr. STILT.	
Thomas Percy, Earl of Worcester, — — —		Mr. H. MELLON,
Henry Percy, Earl of Northumberland, — —		Mr HOLLINGSWORTH.
Henry Percy, *surnamed* Hotspur, *(his Son)* Mr. CRESWICK,	his First Appearance in London.	
Archibald, Earl of Douglas, Mr. MORTON,	Sir Richard Vernon, Mr. GRAHAM,	
Sir John Falstaff, — —	Mr. PHELPS,	
Poins, Mr. HOSKINS, Gadshill, Mr. C. FENTON,	Peto, Mr. FRANKS	
Bardolph, Mr. KNIGHT, Francis, Mr. SCHARF,	Chamberlain, Mr WILKINS,	
Travellers, Messrs SCHOLEY & MASON. 1st Carrier, Mr. A. YOUNGE, 2nd Carrier, Mr. WILLIAMS,		
Lady Percy, *(Wife to Hotspur, and Sister to Mortimer)* Mrs. BROUGHAM,		
Mrs. Quickly, - *(Hostess of a Tavern in East Chepe)* - Mrs. HENRY MARSTON.		

Lords, Officers, Sheriffs, Vintners, Chamberlains, Drawers, Travellers, and Attendants.

To conclude with the Petite Comedy, by C. DANCE, Esq. of

NAVAL
ENGAGEMENTS!

Admiral Kingston, Mr A. YOUNGE,	Lieutenant Kingston, R.N., Mr HOSKINS,
Short, *(Landlord of* The Fountain, *at Portsmouth)* Mr WILLIAMS,	
Dennis, *(his Waiter)* Mr H. MELLON,	
Mrs Pontifex, Mrs H MARSTON,	Miss Mortimer, Miss COOPER.

Stage Manager, Mr PHELPS, Acting Manager, Mr T. L. GREENWOOD,
The Decorations and Properties by Mr HARVEY.
Scene Painters, Messrs F. FENTON and FINLAY Machinist, Mr CAWDERY
The Costumes by Mr COOMBES and Miss BAILEY.
Musical Director, Mr. W MONTGOMERY.

Boxes, First Circle (to which a Private Entrance has been secured) 3s. **Second do.** 2s. **Pit** 1s. **Gal.** 6d.
The Box Office Open from Eleven till Three, under the Direction of Mr. AUSTIN. Bill Inspector, Mr. PHILLIPS.
Private Boxes £1 1s. and £1. 11s. 6d, to be obtained on Application to Mr. AUSTIN, at the Box-Office, at Mr. SAMS' Library,
St. James's Street, and of Mr. MITCHELL, Royal Library, New Bond Street.
Children under Three Years of Age, cannot be admitted, and all Children entering the PIT, must pay the Full Price of Admission.
Doors open at Half-past Six o'Clock, and the Performances commence at Seven,
All applications relative to the Bills of the Theatre to be made to Mr. GREENWOOD, at the Box-Office.
S. G. Fairbrother, Printer, 31, Bow Street, Covent Garden.

partly rebuilt in 1845. Melodrama, farce, and operetta ruled here as well. John Douglass was its best-known manager.

Eastwards still we find, in Whitechapel Road, *The Pavilion*, a house which had been flourishing (though with grievous set-backs at times) since 1828. Its greatest speciality was drama of the Newgate stamp, but it both aspired upwards towards *Othello, Hamlet*, and *A New Way to Pay Old Debts* and descended downwards to Francati's Soirées Magiques, Alfred Smith's 'Vocal Entertainment', which included a 'Moving Panorama of the Gold Regions of Australia', performing dogs, southern minstrels, and dissolving views.

A peculiar and distinctive kind of spectacle belonged to *Astley's Theatre* in Westminster Bridge Road. Commencing as a mere circus ring, it soon won popular esteem under Ducrow (1830–41) for its equestrian drama. Those who sought for the combined amusements of the circus, the music-hall, and the melodrama house could find them here in plenty. 'Les Jeux Cybistique on the four trapez', prancing horses and trained monkeys, 'Mr. Cooke's trained elephants' and the like were mixed with dramas of a thrilling nature, of which H. H. Milner's *Mazeppa* proved most famous. Mazeppa followed Mazeppa at Astley's until, in the sixties, Adah Isaacs Menken assumed the role under E. T. Smith's management and engraved her image in the hearts of all true Astleyites. Menken was one of the most talked of actresses of her day. Starting as a danseuse at New Orleans and Mexico City, she turned to the drama and made a considerable hit in New York some years before she came to London. Her acting powers were not outstanding, but she was reputed to have a perfect figure and, besides her physical attractions, had plenty of gossip surrounding her to create good advertisement.

Astley's was a house which, because of the special nature of its shows, even the great (Prince Frederick of Holstein, for example, and Lord Wellington) could publicly patronize; but alongside of this theatre and the rest of the minors existed a number of other houses, half theatres, half popular cabarets, which provided characteristically early Victorian amusement for the masses alone. The best known of these was *The Grecian Saloon*, situated in Shepherdess Walk, Britannia Fields, Hoxton, sometimes called *The Eagle*

Saloon, and as such familiarly referred to in that touching and never-to-be-forgotten ditty:

> Up and down the City Road,
> In and out the Eagle,
> That's the way the money goes—
> Pop goes the weasel!

Here, under Benjamin Conquest, amid an atmosphere thick with tobacco smoke and the smell of porter, lurid melodramas might be viewed amid interludes of contortionists and vocalists. Dickens has given a vivid description of its early character in *Sketches by Boz.*

Mrs. S. Lane, one of the best beloved manageresses of her time and a kind of fairy godmother to the district, ran a companion house—*The Britannia Saloon,* in High Street, Hoxton. 'The Old Brit', as it was familiarly styled, held a place in many hearts similar to that now held, albeit with different theatrical associations, by The Old Vic. Melodramas, burlesques, and pantomimes here, too, followed one another in rapid succession. The other saloons merit less attention—*The Albert,* also in Hoxton, *The Bower,* in Lambeth, which became later *The Royal Stangate Theatre,* and *The Effingham,* in Whitechapel.

A seeker for entertainment in the fifties of the last century might, however, have found some other buildings where entertainment of a slightly different kind might be had at the cost of a shilling or two. One of these was *The Egyptian Hall,* where were presented moving panoramas and conjuring displays; another was *The Myriographic Hall,* where W. S. Woodin gave his 'Soirées Comiques'. Slightly more dramatic was *The Royal Living Marionette* Theatre in Leicester Square, with its miscellaneous repertoire of old and new pieces performed by infant geniuses. 'Young Garrick' was billed here strongly in 1853, along with an 'Infant Marionette Rope Dancer' and 'Young Bradbury on the Trapeze'. Kindred shows were presented at *The Marionette Theatre* in Adelaide Street, Strand. Here, at various times, one might watch Wellington Young's 'Ethiopian Marionettes' in *Uncle Tom's Cabin,* the 'Aztec Lilliputians', and a Hungarian Band conducted by Kalozdy—for a round price of 1s. or reserved seats half-a-crown.

These minor houses—from The Olympic down through the Saloons to the lilliputian shows—were vastly popular during the whole of this period, and there, as has been indicated, one might meet with noisy, malodorous, and sometimes indecorous audiences reminiscent of those spectators at the beginning of the century who were so heartily condemned by Sir Walter Scott. Yet, in spite of this, any constant playgoer of the years 1835 to 1860 must have been impressed by a gradual, yet none the less definite, alteration in theatrical audiences. In 1820 it was difficult for a self-respecting, moral, London middle-class citizen to take his family to the theatre. Quite apart from the physical inconveniences attendant on the unruly manners of the crowd, he would find the playhouse filled almost entirely by the young bloods and the riff-raff of lower-class society. Prostitutes walked the lobbies and spectators were liable to insult or abuse from uncontrolled drunkards. As a result, the more sober members of London's population looked upon the theatre with aversion and considered the acting profession as sordid and degraded.

A change was wrought about 1850, and that change was probably due more to the action of the Queen than to any general movements in social life. The Theatres Act had, it is true, given a more stable and logical foundation for metropolitan amusements, but that in itself would not have wrought any great alteration in the character of the audience. When, however, Victoria, in 1848, revived a long-disused habit and commanded some of the principal performers to appear at her Christmas 'theatricals' at Windsor Castle and continued to order similar entertainments in ensuing years, she inevitably induced a revised opinion in society generally of the theatre and its players. Add to this the fact that the Queen herself and members of the royal family frequently attended the London theatres, and we realize that, first the less riotous members of the aristocracy, and, after them, the great body of the upper middle class, would be bound to follow her example. As a result the theatres became more comfortable, the more rowdy spectators confined themselves to their own special haunts, experiments were made in the way of reserving seats, the stalls increased in number and, being filled now with a solid mass of serious persons instead of the noisy 'Corinthians' and their lady friends, led to more refined and subtle methods of acting.

The growth of realism reflected in Kean's ventures at

The Princess's may be referred back, too, to this changed audience. These middle-class spectators believed in realism —practical minded as they were—and perhaps found in their hearts excuse for a theatre which aimed, as Kean's did, not only at amusement but at instruction as well. *King John* at The Princess's was really as good as a history lesson. On the other hand, it must be borne in mind that this movement towards realism had been already developing in the minor theatres, where, before the passing of the Licensing Act, all true theatric vitality resided. It was at the minor theatres that real properties were introduced in domestic melodrama; it was at the minors that Edward Fitzball experimented with a setting which showed four rooms of an inn at once; it was at the minors they devised vampire-traps and other new *trucs* of the stage. What happened after 1850 was that these experiments which had been undertaken merely to create momentary surprise and were displayed in a rudely popular, tasteless manner, became the material whereby a new theory of stage representation was realized.

Those more refined and subtle methods of acting to which allusion has been made may be also directly referred back to the changing tastes of the audience. Spectators during the earlier part of the century had welcomed the solemn and artificial declamatory 'classic' style of J. P. Kemble and Mrs. Siddons, watching eagerly to see whether these performers made all the requisite 'points' in the traditionally high passages of the Shakespearian repertoire; they applauded, too, the equally artificial Edmund Kean for his wild outbursts of uncontrolled passion. Gradually, however, a demand came for something more refined and life-like. Macready's colloquial style, although it still retained elements of the older conventionalism, marked one step forwards, just as did that of Charles Kean in the performance of 'gentlemanly melodrama' during the fifties. Similarly, the exaggerated and eccentric low comedy and light comedy acting of the twenties—acting which bore no relation to comic types in real life—was transformed in the burlesque and farcical methods of Vestris and Charles Mathews. Spectators, instead of demanding always the familiar type, sought now rather for individualized expression. Just as they transferred their applause from the easily recognized

'points' of the Siddons school to the frankly new interpretations, first of a Macready and then of a Fechter, so in comedy
they abandoned their love of the stock characters, arti-
ficially conceived and recognizable in hundreds of farces and
comedies, turning to welcome instead figures which had been
newly observed by the dramatists, and thus departed from
the traditional standards.

In every respect, therefore, the period between 1843 and
1860 was a period of theatrical change. Maybe we shall find
it difficult to fix on any tremendous innovations; the movement may appear at times to be but slow and tentative, and
the record of alterations from the past may have to deal
rather with minute details than with major principles. The
providing of carpets for the stalls, the more careful printing
of theatrical programmes, the provision of ceilings for
indoor 'box' sets, the tendency of actors to move behind the
proscenium arch, and the consequent diminution of the
'apron'—these may all seem trifling and unimportant; yet
the carpet tells of an audience demanding more comfort, the
better prepared programmes indicate an increase of taste
and care, the ceilings are due to the prevailing naturalistic
tendency, and the disappearance of the apron marks the
arrival of the 'picture frame' stage.

With the work of Tom Robertson in the sixties all these
movements reach artistic expression. Sentimental as *Ours*
and *Caste* and *School* may be for us, they were, in comparison with the prevailing comic fare of their own day,
naturalistically conceived, and were so planned, moreover, as
to harmonize with the younger school of acting. Robertson,
invited by the Bancrofts to direct his own plays, is not only
the first important author thus permitted to control the
interpretation of his work; he is in reality the first modern
producer. The ideal behind all his activities is not the providing of material through which an individual actor or
actress may display his or her virtuosity; it is the building
up of an impression of truth. Realism, towards which the
stage under the influence of romanticism had been fumblingly
groping, now becomes an accomplished fact. At The
Britannia and The Surrey the din may be unabated; there
the old melodramatic horrors, and thrills, and jests may
continue to make their popular appeal; but out of a despised
old minor house, 'The Dust-Hole' as it was irreverently

styled instead of The Queen's, the Bancrofts and Robertson, free to carry out their ideas because of the liberation of the theatres and profiting from twenty years of tentative experimentation, succeeded in establishing what we must regard as the first of our modern English theatres.

XIV

TRAVEL AND HOLIDAYS

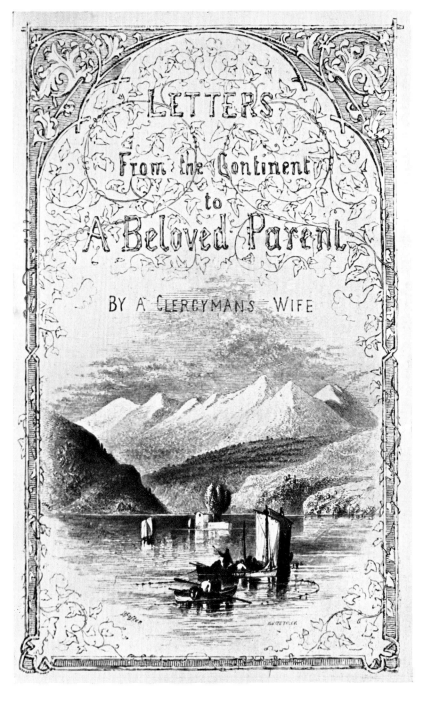

LETTERS

From the Continent

to

A Beloved Parent

BY A CLERGYMAN'S WIFE

XIV

TRAVEL AND HOLIDAYS

By MONA WILSON

In the olden days of travelling, now to return no more, in which distance could not be vanquished without toil, but in which that toil was rewarded, partly by the power of deliberate survey of the countries through which the journey lay, and partly by the happiness of the evening hours, when from the top of the last hill he had surmounted, the traveller beheld the quiet village where he was to rest, scattered among the meadow beside its valley stream; or, from the long-hoped-for turn in the dusty perspective of the causeway, saw, for the first time, the towers of some famed city, faint in the rays of sunset-hours of peaceful and thoughtful pleasure, for which the rush of the arrival in the railway station is perhaps not always, or to all men, an equivalent,—in those days, I say, when there was something more to be anticipated and remembered in the first aspect of each successive halting-place, than a new arrangement of glass roofing and iron girder.

THIS passage from *The Stones of Venice* brings into contrast two types of travel, the one coming to an end and the other opening out in the early years of our period, the contrast between travel as a deliberate and enjoyable adventure and the conventional mobility of modern times. The prelude to a journey in 1830 was a visit to Long Acre to select a coach, and the purchase of a travelling library, but before 1860 this was transformed into a call at Mr. Cook's office and the acquisition of Mr. Murray's appropriate Handbook. The rapid increase and development of mobility (in Arnold's Sixth form at Rugby there were boys who had never seen the sea) was the product less of restlessness than of a growing curiosity about the world. Napoleon's campaigns had made the map of Europe, with the field of Waterloo for focus, intensely interesting. Artists, poets, and novelists had stimulated a desire to enjoy the romance not only of Italy but of the British Isles. Turner's *Liber Studiorum*, with its alluring sub-titles, the *Pastoral*, the *Marine*, the *Historical* and so forth, his *England and Wales*, his illustrations, with those of Prout, Stodhart and the rest, to Byron and Scott and Rogers, the Landscape Annuals by the Findens and others, had given a new zest for travel at home and abroad. 'Why should we not go and see some of these places in reality?' said Mrs. Ruskin while her husband and son were feasting their eyes on a book of Prout's foreign sketches.

In a time of renewed prosperity many other families were asking the same question, and the increased facilities for transport made it easier every year to gratify their wish.

§ I. HOME TRAVEL

Home travel required no courage. Our period opens in the classical age of the road, the bridge, and the canal: Telford and Macadam had already transformed the face of England, and, like Buonaparte, Captain Macheath was a vanquished bogy. Travellers could choose their mode of transit according to their means. The Arnolds possessed their own roomy olive-green coach for their annual visit to the Lakes. The Ruskins borrowed a chariot large enough to accommodate two grown-up persons and a child.

'The one in question was hung high, so that we could see well over stone dykes and average hedges out of it; such elevation being attained by the old-fashioned folding steps, with a lovely padded cushion fitting into the recess of the door,—steps which it was one of my chief delights to see the hostlers fold up and down; though my delight was painfully alloyed by envious ambition to be allowed to do it myself:— but I never was,—lest I should pinch my fingers.

'The "dickey",—(to think that I should never till this moment have asked myself the derivation of that word, and now be unable to get at it!)—being, typically, that commanding seat in her Majesty's mail, occupied by the Guard; and classical, even in modern literature, as the scene of Mr. Bob Sawyer's arrangements with Sam,—was thrown far back in Mr. Telford's chariot, so as to give perfectly comfortable room for the legs (if one chose to travel outside on fine days), and to afford beneath it spacious area to the boot, a storehouse of rearward miscellaneous rubbish.'

George and Harriet Grote made their delightful expeditions to the West Country in their own postchaise, with an extra horse that Mr. Grote might vary carriage exercise by riding. For travellers, single or less wealthy, there was the public coach. This vehicle does not seem always to have run strictly to schedule: sometimes the passengers took charge of the excursion, appointing a chairman, and choosing their stopping places by vote, perhaps electing to spend an extra day of leisure on the journey from London to York. It is recorded that, at any rate in Scotland, the driver was sometimes in conspiracy with the inn-keeper, and travellers had to combine against his attempt to hurry them away from an untasted breakfast, tardily produced when the bill

A THAMES STEAMER

By courtesy of Thomas H. Parker, Ltd.

had been paid and the coach was at the door. Ten miles an hour was the proper pace for a coach with four horses. It is not altogether surprising that a writer in the *Quarterly Review* should comment on the proposed railway line from London to Woolwich with a speed of eighteen miles an hour: 'We should as soon expect the people of Woolwich to be fired off upon one of Congreve's *ricochet* rockets, as trust themselves to the mercy of such a machine, going at such a rate.' 'Your pulse is going at sixteen miles an hour,' a doctor of the eighteen-thirties would say to his patient, indicating a breakneck speed.

An annual holiday was becoming an indispensable part of the routine of family life for all who could afford it. To humbler Londoners the Thames steam-boat to Gravesend or Margate offered a simple and cheap alternative to the road. The run to Margate was six or nine hours according to the tide. The brilliance of Bath and Weymouth was on the wane, but Brighton still maintained its distinction, and sea-coast resorts and inland spas were adding yearly to their amenities. With the growing self-consciousness of the middle-class, social considerations were an important factor in the choice: it was better to be elegantly dull at Folkestone than to join in the indiscriminate gaieties of Margate or Ramsgate. After Brighton, Eastbourne, Bognor, and Cowes were the most fashionable resorts for Londoners; after Margate, Yarmouth, Hastings, and Southend the liveliest. Those who sought retirement chose Broadstairs or the West Country places, Lyme Regis and Sidmouth. Cromer, Southwold, and Worthing were coming up fast. The Midlanders made for Tenby and Aberystwyth. Scarborough was the fashionable resort for Yorkshire families, and Blackpool, with the advertised modesty of its bathing arrangement, was rising into fame: 'The time of bathing is generally at flood, a bell then rings for the ladies to assemble, and no gentleman must afterwards be seen on the parade, under the penalty of a bottle of wine; when the former retire, the bell sounds a summons for the latter to enjoy the same invigorating amusement.' Bathing machines were an eighteenth-century invention, but the nigger minstrel arrived from America after the close of our period. The standard equipment of a rising watering-place was copied from Bath—an assembly room, a parade, a band, a circulating library, a theatre, and a place of worship. Then followed, in imitation of Brighton, the esplanade and the pier. Those who preferred to drink the waters inland must weigh the claims of Cheltenham and Malvern, Leamington and Tunbridge Wells. The fame of Cheltenham was spread from Java to Jamaica, wherever gentlemen suffered from liver-trouble. Tunbridge Wells was by tradition evangelical; and Decimus Burton's laying out of the Calverley estate is the best surviving embodiment of Early Victorian seriousness and refinement.

Holidays were not always a family affair. The development of University examinations had led to a new institution, the reading-party, whose members preferred some out-of-the-way retreat in the Lakes, Scotland, or Wales. Already in 1821, the inhabitants of Llanrwst, subjected to such an invasion, had presented Macaulay and his friends with a testimonial, confirmed by twenty-five signatures, to their good conduct, demeanour, and public spirit: the scenery and sentiments of a later reading-party are commemorated in *The Bothie of Tober-na-Vuolich*.

Travellers with private conveyances could linger by the way, and turn the journey to their ultimate destination into a tour: some, like the Ruskins, converted a business tour into a leisurely holiday.

'We went from forty to fifty miles a day, starting always early enough in the morning to arrive comfortably to four o'clock dinner. Generally, therefore, getting off at six o'clock, a stage or two were done before breakfast, with the dew on the grass, and first scent from the hawthorns; if in the course of the midday drive there were any gentleman's house to be seen—or, better still, a lord's—or, best of all, a duke's—my father baited the horses, and took my mother and me reverently through the state rooms; always speaking a little under our breath to the housekeeper, major domo, or other authority in charge; and gleaning worshipfully what fragmentary illustrations of the history and domestic ways of the family might fall from their lips.'

'What went they forth for to see?' Ruskin's father has already answered this question in part. The Great House was a subject of never-failing interest. That indispensable companion for a tour, Paterson's *Roads*, indicates the gentlemen's seats on every route: the Gardiners would have visited Pemberley as a matter of course even if Mr. Darcy had been unknown to all the party. The galleries with their pictures and statues were studied the more eagerly when foreign

BONCHURCH IN 1837

travel was still comparatively rare. Gilpin had standardized
the picturesque: the ladies knew which trees to admire and
what to sketch. The Picturesque Guides indicated the exact
point from which the view should be taken. It was important
to get the 'station' right or one might admire the wrong thing,
and the refined traveller still carried his landscape mirror,
a convex looking-glass which softened the colour of Nature
and improved her composition. Scott's devotees would go
out of their way to see Kenilworth and Woodstock and
Cumnor. Architecture, thanks to Rickman's *Attempt to
discriminate the Styles of Architecture in England from the
Conquest to the Reformation* and Parker's *Glossary of Terms*,
was becoming a popular study: churches and castles were
visited for the architectural as well as their historical
significance. Botany was a favourite pastime, nor was the
youthful Ruskin the only traveller with a passion for geology.
William Smith's *Strata identified by Organised Fossils* had
awakened interest as early as 1816, and the three volumes
of Lyell's *Principles of Geology*, which appeared between
1830 and 1833, had a wide sale. In short, the early Victorians sought and used their mobility to satisfy the intellectual curiosity which marked their era. Nothing came
amiss.

> O brave new world,
> That has such factories in it!

They wanted to know how a pin was made and a bottle
blown. The early Railway Guides assume that travellers
will wish to inspect the breweries and foundries on the route.

During the first fifteen years of our period the great
transformation took place, the substitution of the railway
for the coach. Locomotives had been used in mines from
1802 onwards. In 1814 John Rennie, watching one drawing
a weight of twenty tons at the rate of seven miles an hour,
said to himself, 'Something more will come out of this hereafter,' and a year later James, a land agent and surveyor,
made the audacious suggestion in a letter to the Prince
Regent that locomotives could be used for the conveyance
of passengers. For years to come the proposal seemed
preposterous to the general public. 'How', it was asked,
'would the carriages ever get up hill? How would they ever
be able to stop, when going down hill? What would happen
if a cow were to come in the way?' It was absurd to suppose

that passengers could be carried with any degree of comfort or safety. A passenger coach, named 'The Experiment', was drawn by horses along the Stockton and Darlington line, but locomotives were considered as out of the question for passengers. In 1829 Wellington was satisfied that there was no ground for supposing that the steam-carriage would 'force itself into extensive use'. Yet in 1823 the prescient Sir Walter Scott had written to Joanna Baillie:

'The increasing powers of steam, which, like you, I look on half-proud, half-sad, half-angry, and half-pleased, in doing so much for the commercial world, promise something also for the sociable; and, like Prince Houssein's tapestry, will, I think waft friends in the course of a few hours, and for aught we may be able to tell, bring Hampstead and Abbotsford within the distance of—"Will you dine with us quietly tomorrow?"'

And the engineers persisted. By 1828 the line between Manchester and Liverpool was sufficiently advanced to make the choice of locomotives a practical question. A competition took place at Rainhill, when a speed of eight to ten miles an hour was expected by the makers, but the prodigies performed by the engines took even their breath away—twenty-eight to twenty-nine miles an hour! George Stephenson's 'Rocket' was proclaimed winner, and he gave Fanny Kemble a thrilling trip on it.

'You can't imagine how strange it seemed to be journeying on thus, without any visible cause of progress other than the magical machine, with the flying white breath and rhythmical unvarying pace, between these rocky walls, which are already clothed with moss, and ferns, and grasses; and, when I reflected that these great masses of stone had been cut asunder to allow our passage thus far below the surface of the earth, I felt as if no fairy tale was ever half so wonderful as what I saw. Bridges were thrown from side to side across the top of these cliffs, and the people looking down upon us from them seemed like pigmies standing in the sky. . . . You cannot conceive what that sensation of cutting the air was; the motion is as smooth as possible too. I could either have read or written; and, as it was, I stood up and with my bonnet off "drank the air before me". . . . When I closed my eyes this sensation of flying was quite delightful, and strange beyond description; yet, strange as it was, I had a perfect sense of security and not the slightest fear.'

The railway was duly opened in the presence of the Duke of Wellington in 1830, but the death of Huskisson, who stepped in front of the engine not yet provided with a brake, cast

TRAVELLING

BY THE

Liverpool and Manchester

RAILWAY.

THE DIRECTORS beg leave to inform the Public that on and after TUESDAY, the 1st of March, the several Trains of Carriages will start from the Station in Crown-street, Liverpool, and from the Station in Liverpool-road, Manchester, in the following order :—

HOURS OF DEPARTURE.

FIRST CLASS TRAIN .... Seven o'clock,	SECOND CLASS TRAIN	½ past 7 o'clock,
———————— .... Ten o'clock,	————————	One o'clock,
———————— .... Two o'clock,	————————	½ past 5 o'clock,
———————— .... Five o'clock.		

N. B. This last Train, on the Manchester Market Days, (Tuesdays and Saturdays,) will leave Manchester at Six o'clock instead of Half-past Five.

SUNDAY.

FIRST CLASS TRAIN .... Eight o'clock, | SECOND CLASS TRAIN .. Seven o'clock,
———————— .... Five o'clock. | ———————— .. Six o'clock.

FARES.

By First Class Train, Coaches, Four Inside 6s. | By Second Class Train, Glass Coaches 5s. 0d.
,,   Ditto,   Ditto,   Six Inside 5s. | ,,   Ditto,   Open Carriages 3s. 6d.

The want of a superior description of Carriage, at a higher fare, having been frequently represented to the Directors, they have caused one Four-inside Coach, in each First Class Train, to be fitted up in a superior style, for which an extra charge of 1s. is made.

SHORT FARES.

From Manchester.

	1st. Class.		2nd. Class.	
	s.	d.	s.	d.
Cross Lane	1	6	1	0
Eccles	1	6	1	0
Patricroft and Reid's Farm......	1	6	1	0
Bury Lane	2	0	1	6
Kenyon Junction	2	6	2	0
Park Side	3	0	2	0
Newton Bridge	3	0	2	6
Viaduct	3	6	2	6
Collins Green	3	6	2	6
Bottom of Sutton Incline	3	6	2	6
Top of Ditto	4	0	2	6
Kendrick's Cross Gate	4	0	3	0
Huyton Lane Gate	4	6	3	0
Roby Lane Gate	4	6	3	6
Broad Green	5	0	3	6
Wavertree Lane	5	0	3	6

From Liverpool.

	1st. Class.		2nd. Class.	
	s.	d.	s.	d.
Wavertree Lane	1	6	1	0
Broad Green	1	6	1	0
Roby Lane Gate	1	6	1	0
Huyton Lane Gate	1	6	1	0
Kendrick's Cross Gate	2	0	1	6
Top of Sutton Incline....	2	6	2	0
Bottom of Ditto	2	6	2	0
Collins Green	2	6	2	0
Viaduct	3	0	2	6
Newton Bridge	3	0	2	6
Park Side	3	0	2	6
Kenyon Junction	3	6	2	6
Bury Lane and Reid's Farm	4	0	2	6
Patricroft	4	6	3	0
Eccles	5	0	3	6
Cross Lane Bridge	5	0	3	6

BOOKING.

In order to insure punctuality in the times of starting which has frequently been prevented by Persons claiming to be booked, even after the appointed time of departure, no Passenger, *unless previously booked*, will be admitted into the outer Door of the Railway Stations after the Clock has struck the hour of departure ; and Passengers too late to take their Seats, or otherwise prevented going, may receive back half the fare paid, if claimed not later than the day after that for which the places were booked.

(Turn over)

STOPPING PLACES.

With a view to obviate, in some measure, the inconvenience occasioned by the frequent stoppages to take up and set down Passengers on the Road, all short Fares, excepting those to Newton Bridge, will in future be taken only by the *Second Class Trains*, namely, at Half-past Seven o'clock, One o'clock, and Half-past Five o'clock, to which will be attached one or more Glass Coaches, by which, Passengers may also book through to Liverpool. The First Class Trains are intended to make one stoppage only on the journey, viz. at Newton Bridge, for the purpose of oiling and examining the machinery; as the stoppage will be very short, and as the Directors are determined, by every means in their power, to prevent the practice of supplying liquor, &c. on the Road, Passengers are particularly requested not to alight.—The Second Class Trains will stop at any of the places named in the list of Short Fares, but, to avoid delay, Passengers are requested to have the money ready to pay to the Guard.

OMNIBUSES.

Omnibuses, free of charge to all Passengers, by the First Class Trains, at the Manchester end, leave the Company's Office, Market-street, Manchester, twenty minutes before the time appointed for the departure of the Trains from Liverpool Road. And Omnibuses, free of charge to all Passengers, at the Liverpool End, leave the Company's Office in Dale-street, Liverpool, half an hour before the departure of the Trains from Crown-street. The Routes, which will be strictly adhered to, are, at the

MANCHESTER END.—FIRST ROUTE, *Auxilium*, No. 1.—From Market-street Office, through St. Mary's Gate, Deansgate, Quay-street, Water-street, to Liverpool-road Station.

—————— ——————SECOND ROUTE, *Auxilium*, No. 4.—From Market-street Office, through Pall Mall, King-street, Deansgate, Bridge-street, Water-street, to Liverpool-road Station.

—————— ——————THIRD ROUTE, *Auxilium*, No. 3.—From Market-street Office, through Mosley-street, Bridgewater-street, to Liverpool-road Station.

LIVERPOOL END—FIRST ROUTE.—Dale-street, Sir Thomas's Buildings, Williamson-square, Clayton-square, Ranelagh-street, Mount Pleasant, Oxford-street.

—————— ——————SECOND ROUTE.—Dale-street, North John-street, Lord-street, Church-street, Bold-street, Leece-street, Hope-street, Falkner-street.

—————— ——————THIRD ROUTE.—Dale-street, Manchester-street, Lime-street, London-road, Seymour-street, Russel-street, Clarence-street, Mount Pleasant, Oxford-street.

The Omnibuses will take up or set down at any point in the above-mentioned Routes, but in offering this accommodation, the Company cannot engage to *call* for any Passenger at any particular place in the Route, nor to *secure* room in the Omnibus, after it has once set out from the Coach Office.

LUGGAGE.

The Weight allowed for each Passenger is 60lb. beyond which a charge will be made at the rate of 3s. per cwt.

PORTERS.

The Company engages to load and unload Passengers' Luggage, upon and from the Railway Carriages and Omnibuses, and to deposit it in any of the Coach-offices free of charge; for any service in addition to this the Porters are allowed to make a reasonable charge.

GUARDS.

No gratuity is allowed to be taken by any Guard, Engine-man, Porter, Omnibus Driver, or other servant of the Company.

SMOKING.

No smoking will be allowed in any of the First Class Carriages, even with the general consent of the Passengers present, as the annoyance would be experienced in a still greater degree by those who may occupy the same coach on the succeeding journey.

PARCELS.

*** Parcels must be delivered at the Company's Offices, HALF AN HOUR before the departure of the respective Trains.

1st March, 1831.

[J. BROAD, PRINTER, MANCHESTER.

a shadow over the proceedings. From that day the road was doomed, but the change was gradual, and at first not altogether welcome. The Eton masters petitioned Parliament for a wall ten feet high at Slough, that the boys might not be distracted from their studies, and actually secured a promise that there should be no station, which the company evaded by hiring two rooms in a public-house as office, and stopping trains there. Lady Hastings complained that a proposed line would be visible from her windows. One noble lord asked a railway witness what possible difference it could make whether a journey took one hour or eleven. Prince Albert himself was alarmed by the speed at first, sometimes saying when he alighted, 'Not quite so fast next time, Mr. Conductor, if you please'. Queen Adelaide seems to have been the most sporting member of the royal family: she was a frequent passenger, and in 1842 did the seventy-eight miles from Southampton to Vauxhall in 1 hour 59 minutes. It was not till 1842 that Queen Victoria made her first journey from Windsor to London 'in half an hour, free from dust and crowd and heat, and I am quite charmed with it'. Lord Palmerston's mare, Iliona, accomplished the unheard-of feat of running at Newcastle on Wednesday and at Winchester on Friday. The Duke hesitated for long— he had suffered the shock of Huskisson's unfortunate accident—but in 1843 his duty obliged him to accompany the Queen to Southampton. The Dover line complimented him by painting their carriages Wellington brown. Mr. Grote, who had ventured two years earlier, expressed disgust at 'this age of steam and cant', but Dr. Arnold was pleased with the new views of the countryside, and still more with the moral effect of increased mobility. He remarked, watching a train on the Rugby line, 'I rejoice to see it, and think that feudality is gone for ever. It is so great a blessing to think that any one evil is really extinct.'

The question of public amenities seems to have troubled John Stuart Mill: in 1836 he protested that the beauty of the Mickleham valley would be spoiled by a railroad. But already by a remarkable and unexpected feat of anticipation Wordsworth had divined that the new civilization might breed its own beauty. The Sonnet of 1833,

> Motions and Means, on land and sea at war
> With old prophetic feeling,

with its noble close—

> In spite of all that beauty may disown
> In your harsh features, Nature doth embrace
> Her lawful offspring in Man's art, and Time,
> Pleased with your triumphs o'er his brother Space,
> Accepts from your bold hands the proffered crown
> Of hope, and smiles on you with cheer sublime.—

gave the aged poet the right to protest against the violation of Windermere, Ambleside, and Grasmere by the projected Kendal Railway in 1844. His two letters to the *Morning Post* in that year are compact of good sense and feeling. Th innocent vandalism of projectors—the fine West Gate of Canterbury was very nearly pulled down by the City Fathers to let a circus through—evoked a conscious interest in the preservation of ancient monuments. Furness Abbey was saved by a detour which the engineer had not thought of: the Roman amphitheatre at Dorchester was rescued by the poet William Barnes when the railway company were preparing to cut through it. Times change; and few of those who grieved over the desecration of the countryside would have guessed—though Wordsworth and Turner might have been among them—that of all material records of the Victorian age the things on which later eyes would rest with most satisfaction, even as works of art, would be the austere magnificence of its railway embankments and the Roman directness of its viaducts.

In their experimental stage railways were uncomfortable and none too safe. Passengers themselves were reckless in boarding a train when it was going at full speed, or jumping off to pick up their hats, or sitting, contrary to regulations, on the tops of the carriages. An important personage who missed his train would chase it in a special, or on an engine which might collide with the tail carriage and break the legs of one or two passengers. The guards sat on the outside of the carriages, the head guard on the last carriage facing forwards, and the under-guard on the front carriage looking backward in order to make sure that the train was following, a necessary precaution as it was apt to break loose and get left behind. As the passengers suffered from the same tendency the guards checked them from a 'way-bill' on which their places of departure and proposed arrival were filled in by the 'station-clerks'. They were then locked in, with the prospect of being roasted alive if the train caught fire, a practice against which Sydney Smith discharged a volley of humorous invective. There were three classes of 'department', the first imitative of the coach, the second of the wagon with a tilt, the third of the truck. Passengers could, if they preferred, ride in their own carriages, hoisted on to a lorry attached to the train. Some of the coaches were also hoisted on to trucks: the 'Beaufort Hunt', a Bath and London coach, made use of the Maidenhead line, soon after it was finished. Smoking was strictly prohibited, and could only be compassed by discreet bribery, or, if we may believe *Punch*, by throwing the blame for a suspicious odour on a bishop, who had just alighted, except that one company provided a first-class carriage named 'the divan'. The second-class passengers complained loudly of draughts, but their lot was happy compared with that of the third-class. These unfortunates, originally charged $1\frac{1}{2}d.$ per mile for their privileges, could only travel by cattle trains, so prolonging their tortures: the run—crawl would be a more appropriate word—from London to Taunton took sixteen hours, and passengers from London to Liverpool or Manchester had to wait at Birmingham from 3 p.m. to 6 a.m. The 'departments' did not always contain seats, and the sides were so low, two or three feet, that the occupants frequently tumbled overboard. The provision of this accommodation was regarded by the companies as a charitable enterprise; those, supposed able to afford greater luxury, who availed themselves of it were treated as meanly electing to travel *in forma pauperis*.

Emergencies were not always adequately dealt with. The South-Western, for instance, a few days after it was opened in 1838, advertised eight trains to Kingston on Derby Day. A crowd 5,000 strong assembled at Nine Elms early in the morning: several trains were dispatched, but more intending passengers arrived, and finally the mob broke into the station, and took possession of a special, which had been chartered by a private party. After that the police were sent for, and a notice posted that no more trains would run that day.

The foundations of the present railway system were securely laid by 1843; the great companies, with the exception of the Great Northern and the Chatham and Dover, were already in existence, 1,800 miles of rail were open for traffic, nine-tenths of it in England. George Bradshaw had first published a railway time-table in 1839: two years later his *Monthly Railway Guide* made its first appearance, bearing, as it still does, the signature of its quakerly origin (1st month, 2nd month, &c.). The average speed exclusive of stoppages on the faster lines was as follows:

Northern and Eastern (London to Bishop's Stortford)	36 miles per hour.
Great Western . . .	33 ,, ,,
Newcastle and North Shields	30 ,, ,,
North Midland (Leeds to Derby)	29 ,, ,,
Birmingham and Derby .	29 ,, ,,

During 1842 and 1843 famous coaches, the Sleepy Leeds, the Peak Ranger, the Red Rover, and many others, ceased running: travellers without carriages of their own had no longer a choice of conveyance. Coach-bodies were bought up 'for the vulgar purpose of summer-houses'. The expense of travelling by road had increased just before railways came in: Scott notes in 1828 that his journey from London to Edinburgh in a post-chaise had cost £50 instead of £30. But now, where coaches still existed their fares were reduced by railroad competition; for example, although there was no line nearer than Southampton, the outside fare from Salisbury to London dropped from £1 to 13s. At first there was some reluctance to entrust the railway with mails, but by May 1843 the number of mail coaches leaving the General Post Office daily had been reduced from some eighty to eleven. In 1844 Parliament obliged the companies to run cheap trains daily: third class tickets must not be charged at more than a penny per mile, or first class more than three-pence. Some observers thought that any further developments, an east coast railway, for example, would be superfluous and absurd: what object could it serve save that 'the passengers by the railway, if any, might have the amusement of looking at the steamers on the sea, and reciprocally the passengers by sea might see the railway carriages'? None the less by 1846 the railway boom was at its height. George Eliot wrote:

'Our midland plains have never lost their familiar expression and conservative spirit for me; yet at every other mile, since I first looked on them, some sign of world-wide change, some new direction of human labour, has wrought itself into what one may call the speech of the landscape. . . . There comes a crowd of burly navvies with pickaxes and barrows, and while hardly a wrinkle is made in the fading mother's face or a new curve of health in the blooming girl's, the hills are cut through, or the breaches between them spanned, we choose our level, and the white steam-pennon flies along it.'

Lawyers' clerks, surgeons' apprentices, merchants, tradesmen, officers in the army and navy, gentlemen with private means, left their professions to become engineers without any previous training. The result was reckless expenditure upon impracticable proposals. The committee rooms of both Houses of Parliament were crowded with engineers, lawyers, and witnesses. The lawyers and parliamentary agents, and those engineers lucky enough to be paid, made their pile. M. Jeames de la Pluche and the general public speculated wildly, and most of them lost their money. But the boom had one advantage: it was a great labour-absorber. The navvy became a national type: transported abroad by Brassey, his working powers were an object of admiration to foreigners and of pride to English travellers.

There was considerable speeding up in 1848: the 'Great Britain' did the fifty-three miles from Didcot to London in forty-seven minutes, and expresses (1st class only) ran between London and Edinburgh and Glasgow in thirteen hours. Some other companies were less successful: 'even a journey on the Eastern Counties must have an end at last', said Thackeray. And of this line the story was told that a strapping lad of sixteen, detected travelling half-price, explained that he had been under twelve when the train started. By 1850 the Railway Joke, like the Refreshment Room with its boiling soup and leathery bun, was an established institution.

The success of the railway entailed complete alteration of the conditions of travel. A speedy and uninterrupted journey to the destined spot replaced the picturesque tour with its leisurely pauses. The inn, one of our national glories, deteriorated into the hotel, a national disgrace. 'A coffee-room ingeniously designed on the principle of an oven, the windows not made to open; a dinner on yesterday's pease-soup, and the day before yesterday's cutlets; not an ounce of ice; and all beverages, wine, water, and beer—in exactly the state of the Church of Laodicea.' Such is Macaulay's description of the New Steyne Hotel at Brighton in 1843. Mine host gave way to that less estimable national type, the landlady of a lodging-house. Villages, which had been in touch with the great world, and thrived as halting-places for the coach and the post-chaise, declined again into isolation. The Dover Road no longer greeted returning exiles with its almost continuous flower gardens. Shop-keepers in the smaller towns suffered: Lancashire housewives, for example, formed the habit of going by rail to shop in Manchester. But contrary to all prognostications, there was more demand than ever for horses, for carts and station flies.

§ 2. FOREIGN TRAVEL: THE ROAD TO ROME

The development of travel on the Continent came rather later but followed the same lines. During the eighteenth century Paris had been the Englishman's ideal of a gay and fashionable holiday. Every one who could afford it must see Paris once at least. Intercourse had been interrupted by the Napoleonic Wars, but there was a rush of travellers after the Peace of Amiens, and many plans were thwarted by its short duration. William Blake, for instance, was dreaming that at last he would see the art treasures of Paris. Now, at the beginning of our period, crowds were flocking over: Paris itself was as attractive as ever, and the main starting-point for an Italian tour. A passport was still essential, and held good for a year. It could be had from the English Foreign Office for a fee of two guineas. But a French passport was preferable: it cost nothing and was more readily understood on the Continent. A peer or M.P. presenting himself at the French Passport Office would be immediately supplied with one, but less distinguished persons were required to leave their name and address the day before. Passports were then given out in order of application, but it was observed that in the case of ladies the gallant French clerks were apt to waive this regulation. Or, if the traveller were pressed for time, the French consul would supply a passport on the spot for the sum of ten shillings. Passport in pocket, his next concern would be to obtain one of Messrs. Herries' circular letters: by this means he could ensure a supply of ready money at convenient points on the journey,

TO BRIGHTON AND BACK FOR 3s. 6d.—ROSSITER

By permission of the Museum and Art Gallery Committee of the Corporation of Birmingham

his letters could be safely forwarded, and courteous agents would spring up to extract him from any difficulties into which he might fall through ignorance of foreign tongues or customs. If he were contemplating a long sojourn abroad he must also arrange with the Custom House agent to forward his heavy baggage. Travellers settling for a time in France in order to economize, or for some less honourable reason, often went no farther than the fishing village of Boulogne, which was fast becoming a haven for all sorts and conditions of English.

A bad sailor would have no hesitation about his route: the three-hour passage from Dover to Calais would be all too long. Before the railway came the posting to Dover with the smartest of postilions was famous. By day the road was lovely; a renowned inn, the 'Ship', offered repose before the crossing. For those who did not fear the sea there was the alternative of a gay start from the Tower pier, thronged with envious lookers-on. The expense was rather less than the other route to Calais and rather more to Boulogne. Other possible routes were Brighton to Dieppe and Southampton to Havre. Travellers to Paris via Havre could vary their journey by taking the steamboat, an earlier rival of the road than the train, as far as Rouen.

The wealthy, especially if they were going beyond Paris, would take their own or a hired carriage rather than rely on the chance of finding a suitable one at Calais or Boulogne. The visit to Long Acre, in the eyes of the Ruskin family at least, was one of the excitements and pleasures of travel.

'The poor modern slaves and simpletons who let themselves be dragged like cattle, or felled timber, through the countries they imagine themselves visiting, can have no conception whatever of the complex joys, and ingenious hopes, connected with the choice and arrangement of the travelling carriage in old times. The mechanical questions first, of strength—easy rolling—steady and safe poise of persons and luggage; the general stateliness of effect to be obtained for the abashing of plebeian beholders; the cunning design and distribution of store-cellars under the seats, secret drawers under front windows, invisible pockets under padded lining, safe from dust, and accessible only by insidious slits, or necromantic valves like Aladdin's trap-door; the fitting of cushions where they would not slip, the rounding of corners for more delicate repose; the prudent attachments and springs of blinds; the perfect fitting of windows, on which one half the comfort of a travelling carriage really depends;

and the adaptation of all these concentrated luxuries to the probabilities of who would sit where, in the little apartment which was to be virtually one's home for five or six months ;—all this was an imaginary journey in itself, with every pleasure, and none of the discomfort, of practical travelling.'

This commodious vehicle required four horses. The French *Tarif de la Poste aux Chevaux* regulated the number of horses according to the type of carriage and the number of its occupants. The cost of travelling post was 9*d*. per mile for two persons, and increased to 1*s*. 8*d*. for six, and the best road was via Boulogne, Abbeville, and Beauvais, 32½ posts.

Humbler travellers, who intended to go by diligence, might book their seats in London, but a better choice could be secured by attending to the matter personally on arrival at Calais. An outside seat in the banquette, beside that agreeable companion the driver, although the cheapest, was the most desirable since Frenchmen had already acquired the national habit of shutting all the windows. The expense of the journey from London to Paris, including the passage, which cost 10*s*. 6*d*., would be about three guineas, and considerably less for the outside passenger. The *malle-poste* offered a quicker, but less comfortable, alternative to the diligence. Arrived in Paris the sightseer must supply himself with Galignani's excellent guide, and Galignani's rooms would take the place of the fashionable bookseller's library in an English watering-place: he could see newspapers and books, and obtain information about lodgings and amusements. His meals were in themselves a new form of entertainment. The restaurant in its modern shape had come into being as a result of the Revolution, when the cooks of the noblesse had been obliged to turn their hands to feeding the democracy. Another attraction was the café, where he could sip his coffee, liqueur or sorbette, see the newspapers, and get a game of billiards.

One vital question had to be decided by the tourist who was going on from Paris to Italy in his own carriage. Should he take a courier? If he had not already engaged one from the Italian Couriers' Club in Golden Square should he pick one up in Paris? A courier was almost indispensable, if, as frequently, the traveller's knowledge of foreign languages was limited to *mangez* and *changez*, supported by dumb show, and a good courier an inestimable treasure. He would select the inns on the road, engage rooms, order meals, shop with the ladies, discover from his fellow couriers the names of other guests—without a courier you might rub shoulders with a duke and never know it. He would take his party to see the right sights, filling the role of Murray's Handbooks, before Mr. Murray had dreamt of their existence. But an honest courier was a rare bird: a dishonest one might be in unholy alliance with the worst inns and the most exorbitant shops: his opportunities for cheating his employer were endless, and he was probably insolent into the bargain. The courier secured, another problem arose: should he ride ahead to make the arrangements? This was the smart thing, but middle-class Mr. Ruskin thought it ostentatious and extravagant: he saved the extra horse by seating his courier in the dickey with the maid. Then the traveller must attend again to his passports before leaving Paris: for some of the Italian States the signature of the Austrian ambassdor was essential, unless he had already obtained that of Mr. Rothschild, Austrian consul in London, before leaving home. Next came the choice of route to Lyons: should he go via Auxerre and Châlon-sur-Saône, or Nevers and Roanne, or take the longer road to Châlon through Troyes, Dijon, and the Côte d'Or? The second was the favourite: the Forest of Fontainebleau seemed a paradise of the Picturesque to Mr. Gilpin's disciples—it reproduced his own sketches on a grander scale —and visitors were permitted to see the room in which Napoleon had signed his abdication, and buy, again and again, the instrumental pen; later on came the valley of the Loire with its celebrated châteaux. If he were not hurried— and foreign travel was a leisurely pastime in those days— the traveller might indulge his passion for scenery by taking Auvergne *en route* for Lyons. Once at Lyons a few days would be well spent in the museum, the factories, and the gardens.

He had now a further choice of route. If he decided on Genoa via the Corniche road, completed in 1827, and a boon to invalids who could now winter in Italy without braving an Alpine pass, he might proceed to Avignon either by road or by *coche d'eau*. These huge barges were popular with the English. Although they were not over-clean, and there was always the risk of sticking on a sand-bank, or of a smash in shooting the arches of the Pont d'Esprit, it was an amusing way of seeing life, and a refreshing change to be towed along after the jolting diligence: the owner of a private carriage could sit comfortably on board in that retreat. The weary pedestrian—and it must be remembered that, though Wordsworth and Jones had had few companions of the road, the foreign walking-tour, like the reading-party, was now coming into fashion—would welcome a stage or so of the *coche d'eau*. Laurence Oliphant, who spent eight days and five nights in the diligence between Boulogne and Marseilles, when journeying to the East in 1841 may well have sighed for it.

If the traveller preferred to cross the Alps, he would enter Savoy, then a duchy of the State of Sardinia, at Beauvoisin, where his passport, trunks, and person were subjected to examination by the custom-house officers: it was a reproach against the English that they were too apt to lose their tempers on these occasions. He would then enjoy the gorgeous scenery of the road, remembering that Rousseau on his way to visit Mme de Warens at Les Charmettes had amused himself by rolling stones into the roaring torrent below, watching them bound from ledge to ledge, or, if innocent of any acquaintance with the *Confessions*, instinctively imitating him. The old route to Chambéry had been superseded by one of Napoleon's fine roads, and the Grande Chartreuse might be visited on the way. From Chambéry the traveller would proceed to Turin by the Mont Cenis, again giving thanks to Napoleon for the excellent road, and faring lusciously on the monks' trout at the hospice, and fresh fruit from Piedmont. But the favourite crossing for those who could afford the time was from Martigny to Aosta; the arrival at the Hospice of St. Bernard in *Little Dorrit* is one of the famous pieces of Victorian prose; and pictures, stories, and poems made the faithful hound with his little barrel of brandy and the half-buried traveller, whether grasping the banner or not, familiar to every English child. At Turin he might rest for a day or two, visiting the University museum, the King of Sardinia's Egyptian collection, then the finest in existence, and the picture gallery in the Palazzo del Re, and climbing up to the Superga for the magnificent view, or his interest in his fellow Protestants of the Vaudois might lead him farther afield. There is no better way to recapture the early Victorian travelling spirit, and its blend

PEGWELL BAY—*DYCE*

BY THE SEA: A PHOTOGRAPH

of romance and sentiment, nature worship, and safe adventure, than to turn over Beattie's *Waldenses* with its seventy-two shimmering landscapes engraved on steel.

When ready to leave Turin, he must determine on his route to Florence: that by Genoa, Lucca, and Pisa, some three posts longer than by Parma and Bologna, would be the most attractive. If he is going post he must obtain a *bolletone* from the police for the use of post-horses, and, unless he can leave such details to a trustworthy courier, he must also grasp the fact that posts vary in length in all the Italian States, and master the tariff for horses, varying with the class of carriage, number of persons, weight of luggage, and sometimes with the nature of the road. English fervour for a United Italy was doubtless influenced by the sufferings of indignant travellers at the hands of the officials of the Italian States. During the first few years of our period, if dependent on diligence, he would have to miss seeing Florence on his way to Rome, as it was not yet on a diligence route. But he might hire a carriage, and the vetturino would act as courier, making all arrangements on the road, and charging a fixed sum for bed and board. The drawback was the difficulty of securing an honest vetturino: a detailed agreement on stamped paper was an essential safeguard, but even so the postmaster was apt to be cheated of his dues. One unfortunate traveller writes: 'The postmaster's wife at Turin said, the Virgin Mary had told her, as she was going to chapel, that a vetturino had left, with four horses, without paying: she turned back, and he sent a man after us. I think the V.M. might attend to her own affairs.'

However he arranged matters, he would clatter down that glory of Turin, the Street of the Po, and cross the river by a fine new bridge. At Asti he would visit Alfieri's house, and drink a glass of the celebrated wine to the poet's memory. Passing through Alessandria, he might pause at Marengo in honour of Napoleon, so on to Novi, and thence by an admirable new road to Genoa. After admiring the city and its palaces he follows the road along the Eastern Riviera, crosses the Bracco pass, and so to Spezia and Carrara. At Pietra Santa he enters the State of Tuscany, and must have his passport ready, but a search can be avoided by judicious bribery. Thence he proceeds to Lucca, and up the beautiful valley of the Serchio to the Bagni di Lucca, a favourite retreat in the summer of English families living in Florence or Rome, and so on to Pisa. There he will admire the famous group of buildings and the Campo Santo, and either make an excursion by road or canal to Leghorn, visiting Smollett's grave in the Protestant burial-ground, or take it on his way to Florence. But if he is in a hurry to reach Rome he will go from Pisa to Sienna by the new road through Volterra. Should he go to Florence he will be well advised to offer another bribe to the custom-house officers, and he must at once buy a local guide-book, that he may realize what the sights are and the hours at which they can be seen. In the pre-Murray and Baedeker days he would be dependent everywhere on these guides, which, designed, especially in the smaller towns, to decoy visitors into a prolonged stay, exaggerated the importance of local attractions. Like Rome and Lausanne, Florence had had its substantial English colony before continental intercourse was interrupted by the Napoleonic Wars. Now the English were living abroad in large numbers for at least a part of the year: a foreign domicile was a pleasing addition to the amenities of the prosperous rich, and increased mobility made it an economy for poor gentlefolk. Our traveller might have friends in Florence, an additional reason for breaking his journey, or an introduction to Landor, the Brownings, or the Trollopes.

Before leaving Florence he would do well to ask his banker at Rome to forward a *Lascia passare* to the frontier by which he is about to enter the Papal States and another to the Porta del Populo, in order to save fresh delay and examination of luggage. Again he had a choice of routes, that by Sienna, $4\frac{3}{4}$ posts shorter but less interesting, and the attractive road through Perugia, which allowed him to visit Vallombrosa, murmuring Milton. Macaulay, who did not linger long on the way, took about a month to reach Rome. The record journey is Peel's, when he was sent for to become Prime Minister, twelve days, about Hadrian's pace as a contemporary remarked. Rome was only too English for the taste of some travellers. Macaulay complains that it was difficult to escape the usual Mayfair tattle. 'We could furnish exceedingly respectable Houses of Lords and Commons. There are at present twice as many coroneted carriages in the Piazza di Spagna as in St. James's parish.'[1]

[1] 'Le fond de la société à Rome est composé d'une foule d'Anglais qui

in the evening across th
magna comitante caterva-
Surely earth feels like
men! Honour and glor
twenty shillings each, ai
board by the side of De
Alfred Wills, who pu
Alps, with illustratic
in 1856, could clain
proper.

The development (
as might be expected,
jealousies. Up to 185
Zürich and Baden, a
Department of Publ
largely by English er

Cologne, still notori
manufacture, was tl
After an excursion tc
travellers boarded tl
eight hours to Cobler
to Frankfort. The sc
were using the river i
Hills the thrills began
declaim 'The castle
greeted as the place
shivered at Ehrenbr
for ten years, and ac
shadow which Prussi
the West. At Coble
might be acquired fr
self. After this the
great rafts swirling b
said to be the secret
patient warden of the
a bugle or let off a p
the company might
fifteen echoes. At I
could impart to his n
men taught their littl
farers in order to ext
accommodation, poe

The time spent in travelling was gradually shortened by the development of railways in France and Italy, in which British engineers and British workmen were largely instrumental. In 1843 the line was opened between Paris and Rouen, and the traveller was confronted by a choice of eight different methods of reaching Paris from London, varying from $20\frac{3}{4}$ hours to 39 hours in length, and from 59s. 6d. to 76s. in cost. The shortest and cheapest route was as follows: London Bridge to Brighton (railway), Brighton to Shoreham Harbour (railway), Shoreham Harbour to Dieppe (steamer), Dieppe to Paris (diligence and railway from Rouen). When Fanny Kemble joined her sister in Rome in the winter of 1845, the body of the diligence was lifted off its wheels at Rouen by a crane, set on wheels to fit the railroad, and hooked on behind a roofless second-class car: at Paris it was taken off the rail, and fitted with fresh wheels. Fanny, in spite of her courageous trip with Stephenson, found the experience uncomfortable and somewhat alarming. She then pursued her journey to Marseilles by road, varied by a steamboat between Lyons and Avignon, thence by boat to Civita Vecchia, and diligence to Rome.

In the early fifties Italy followed suit. Her first railroad was that from Turin to Novara, a distance of sixty miles. The success of this undertaking, which greatly exceeded expectation, gave an immediate impetus to railway construction. By the end of our period a traveller by the Mont Cenis route could reach Turin from London in 33 hours; Venice or Florence took 12 hours more, and Rome 26. By the Simplon he was at Milan in $56\frac{1}{2}$ hours, by the Brenner at Venice in 56 hours, and via Marseilles and Civita Vecchia at Rome in 60 hours. The reduction in expense was proportionately even greater. The corresponding fares to Turin were £7 8s. first class, £5 8s. second class, to Milan £7 3s. and £5 9s., to Rome first class £12 9s. Italy was open to the tourist without either wealth or enterprise, but the tour as an object in itself had disappeared.

§ 3. SWITZERLAND; THE RHINE; NORWAY

If the grand bus route lay through France to Italy, and the little bus route along the Rhine, tourists could combine passent lentement d'un salon dans un autre, traînant à leur suite l'ennui et la nullité' (Countess Anna Potocka, 1826).

II

the two by
via Schaffha
of the two ro
land. Durin
summer onl
there was st
hardy pedes
a family affa
tion of 2,42
and the innk
to regard t
to their mai
continental
carriages frc
borders of S
the pace did
and the hors
By 1858 the
facilities for
pedestrians.
act as courie
the more d
governed by
strictly in
insisted on.
among the §
secure the n
guide was re
guess that l
1858 editior
the more diff
hire of a ho
tional six fr
varied accor
required; fo
with four gu
to £12. In t
had not bee
till the latt
talked of for
and prayers
'Great is th

tour the most sympathetic, as it was one of the cheapest, of all the Victorian jaunts.

Beyond these two bus routes lay a middle zone, which might be defined as the borders of Germany and Austria and France. To pass beyond it, to get as far as St. Petersburg, Budapest, or Madrid, ceased to be a holiday and became a journey. The chief attractions of this middle zone were the German watering-place and the Norwegian salmon river. The former was cheap, and exhibited real live Princes, some of them related to Queen Victoria or her Consort. Life at these bads—Wiesbaden, Baden Baden, and so forth—had a mellowing effect on the aggressive manners of English tourists: they admired and imitated the cheerful sociability of the well-conducted Germans.

Travel in Norway, on the other hand, was a happy pseudo-adventure into the wilderness: the traveller encountered his thrills and his hardships with a clean background of homely Protestant virtues. The angler was advised to set aside the comfortable sum of £150 to £200 for the trip exclusive of tackle. The cost of the journey from London to Christiania, via Hamburg, Kiel, and Copenhagen was about £9, and the English consul at Hamburg would supply a 'land-pass' which obviated all those delays and examinations by which the traveller was pestered in southern Europe. Posting *en carriole* cost about 1s. 1½d. for every seven miles, and a carriole with harness and bottle case complete could be purchased at Christiania for £8 or £9, to which might be added for a further £2 or £3 a cart for the transport of luggage, food, and drink, particularly the last. A trustworthy servant might be engaged on the recommendation of the English consul, and a Bachelor's Kitchen, the compact invention of Mr. Tozer of Soho, could be relied on to cook a dinner with incredible speed.

Russia and Spain were a genuine adventure, the former rarely undertaken except for some specific purpose. Borrow's account of his travels for the Bible Society, attractive enough to read, did not commend Spain to the ordinary traveller as a holiday resort, but a daring spirit here and there might be stimulated by Ford's voluminous details with the alluring pages on 'Robbers, and precautions against them'. He must not take his own carriage as the duty was prohibitive, and rather than post was advised to travel by mail or diligence, a mode far from luxurious but patronized by the grandees themselves. The inns, he was warned, could only be classified as bad, worse, and worst.

§ 4. GUIDE BOOKS

Our earlier travellers were, as has been said, dependent on local guide-books, which often led them astray to visit objects and places unworthy of their attention. Of travel books they had good store, since there was a flood of these after the Napoleonic Wars, some, like Lady Morgan's entertaining travels in France and Italy, or Mrs. Trollope's impressions of Paris, controversial in character. Eustace's *Classical Tour through Italy* was the cultured traveller's *vade mecum*: first published in 1813 it ran into eight editions, the latest in 1841. The *Tour* is written in the form of a diary, describing scenery and objects of interest, historical and artistic, with suitable references to Horace, Virgil, and Cicero: the author's politics are anti-Napoleonic, his religion Roman Catholic, of a conciliatory, if not latitudinarian type. Eustace died in 1815, and four years later Sir Richard Colt Hoare published the supplementary *Classical Tour through Italy and Sicily, tending to illustrate some districts which have not been described by Mr. Eustace.* But no one dreamt of going to Italy without reading *Childe Harold*: many hundreds went solely because they had read it. Hobhouse's *Historical Illustrations of the Fourth Canto* added to its value as a traveller's companion, and Hobhouse wrote cruelly of 'Mr. Eustace, who appears never to have seen anything as it is'. In 1817 Hobhouse wrote to Murray from Italy:

'If any one writes a book of travels without telling the truth about the masters and the subjects in this most unfortunate country, he deserves more than damnation and a dull sale, and I trust you will take care he has a niche in your temple of infamy, the *Quarterly*. If any but a gentleman, and a scholar, and an accomplished man in every way presumes to hazard such an undertaking, "be ready", Mr. Murray, "with all your thunderbolts to dash him to pieces".

'There is a wide field of glory open for any and for all answering the above description: but it would perhaps be almost impossible to find the requisite variety of acquirement and talent in one individual. The work should be done like a cyclopede dictionary, by departments.'

The modern guide-book may be described as out of the local guide by the travel book. The forerunner was produced the villas that *have* been, than those that now exist. Look at Horace Walpole's "Song on Strawberry Hill". How many places are there mentioned which have historical recollections connected with them, which would be worth preserving? There must be always great interest about localities in the neighbourhood of the Metropolis. In that Song alone are mentioned Gunnersbury, Sion, Chiswick, Strawberry Hill, Greenwich, Marble Hill, Oatlands, Claremont, Southcote. You might add Wanstead, Wimbledon, Holland House, and a hundred others—many with very curious anecdotes of local and personal history connected with them. Perhaps I overrate the interest with which such a book would be read. I certainly do not, if it would equal that (with) which I myself read the account of places in the neighbourhood of Paris, remarkable in history, but the traces of many of which are fast fading away; such as Maisons, Meudon, Sceaux, Chantilly, &c. Hampton Court, the ancient palace at Richmond, Kew and others, might enter into the work. The County Histories would furnish a substratum, but everything would depend upon the liveliness and accuracy of the details.'

Peel's suggestion led to Peter Cunningham's *Handbook of London*. The County Guides began to appear in the fifties.

§ 5. COOK'S EXCURSIONS

After the construction of railways in Great Britain another important development in travelling facilities took place. It occurred to Thomas Cook, a Baptist missionary and one of Father Mathew's temperance converts, that the success of a temperance meeting in Loughborough Park in 1841 might be promoted by arranging with the Midland Railway for a special train from Leicester to Loughborough, the first advertised excursion train. This led to other temperance and Sunday School trips, and in 1845 Cook began to organize excursions for the Midland Railway Company, receiving a percentage on tickets sold. That year he arranged for a pleasure trip from Leicester to Liverpool, issuing hotel coupons to his tourists. This was followed by a guinea excursion from Leicester to Glasgow, by rail to Fleetwood and steamer to Ardrossan. By the time of the Great Exhibition the excursion habit had been fully formed: five shilling tickets were issued from Bradford and Leeds, and pawnbrokers were receiving silver watches by the bushel. In 1855 Cook arranged a thirty-one shilling trip from Leicester to Calais and back for the benefit of visitors to the Paris

RAMSGATE SANDS—*FRITH*

By Gracious Permission of H.M. the King

Exhibition, and next year he advertised 'a grand circular tour on the Continent'—Harwich to Antwerp and back by Havre and Southampton—visiting Brussels, Waterloo, Cologne, the Rhine, Mayence, Frankfort, Heidelberg, Baden-Baden, Strassburg, and Paris. His efforts gave a strong stimulus to working-class mobility, and to the habit of taking an annual holiday, however short. He arranged 'moonlight trips' on moonlight nights during the summer months from the chief towns in the Midlands to Scarborough and other seaside places: both journeys were made by night in order to secure a full day by the sea. Educational possibilities were not neglected: in 1856 two thousand children were taken from Newcastle to Edinburgh, and conducted to places of historic interest. In 1861 a committee under the presidency of Sir Joseph Paxton organized a working men's demonstration in Paris for which Cook issued 1,673 tickets. Next year he began to extend operations beyond Paris, and by 1864, when he personally conducted two tours to Switzerland, complaints were ripe that Cook's tourists were desecrating the Continent. Dickens commissioned Edmund Yates to investigate the matter for *All the Year Round*. In 'My Excursion Agent' Yates gives an admirable analysis of the various types of tourist, and his blessing to Cook.

'The trip to Edinburgh, and the shorter excursions in England, attract tradesmen and their wives, merchants, clerks away for a week's holiday, roughing it with a knapsack, and getting over an immense number of miles before they return; swart mechanics, who seem never to be able entirely to free themselves from the traces of their life-long labour, but who, my Agent tells me, are by no means the worse informed, and are generally the most interested about the places they visit. In the return trips from Scotland to England come many students of the schools and universities—raw-boned, hard-worked youths, who, in defiance of the popular belief, actually do return to their native country for a time, probably to make a future raid into and settlement in the land whose nakedness they had spied into in early youth. As to Swiss excursions, the company is of a very different order; the Whitsuntide trip has a good deal of the Cockney element in it, and is mostly composed of very high-spirited people, whose greatest delight in life is "having a fling", and who do Paris, and rush through France, and through Switzerland to Chamounix, compare every place they are taken to with the views which formed part of the exhibition at the Egyptian Hall, carry London everywhere about them in dress, habits, and conversation, and rush back, convinced that they are great travellers. From these roysterers the July and September excursionists differ greatly: ushers and governesses, practical people from the provinces, and representatives of the better style of the London mercantile community, who form their component parts, all travel as if impressed with the notion that they are engaged in fulfilling the wishes of a life-time, in a pleasant duty never to be repeated. They stop at all the principal towns, visiting all the curiosities to be seen in them, and are full of discussion among themselves, proving that they are all thoroughly well up in the subject. Many of them carry books of reference with them, and nearly all take notes.'

Charles Lever, on the other hand, then Vice-Consul at Spezia, was a formidable opponent. Writing unofficially in *Blackwood's Magazine* under the pseudonym of Cornelius O'Dowd, he speaks of 'the cities of Italy deluged with droves of these creatures. I have already met three flocks, and anything so uncouth I never saw before, the men, mostly elderly, dreary, sad-looking; the women, somewhat younger, travel-tossed and crumpled, but intensely lively, wide-awake, and facetious.' Worse still, he told his credulous Italian friends that the tourists were convicts rejected by the Australian colonies, and that Cook had arranged with the English Government to dump a few in every city in Italy. The Italians took it seriously and Cook appealed in vain to the Foreign Office for redress.

Foreign travel changed in our period from a social experience for the few into a holiday for the many, and, with the help of Cook's tickets, into a scamper for the multitude. The internationalism of culture perished with the ascendancy of the class that maintained it: increasing mobility served rather to intensify the insularity of the islanders. The new travellers were no longer prepared to enter into the lives of the people whom they visited: they were apt to encounter no one but the douanier, the hotelkeeper, the guide, and the beggar. This attitude to the foreigner varied from a condescending patronage of the Swiss, the Norwegians, and the Tyrolese to an increased aversion from Frenchmen who habitually violated the Sabbath and Italians who ignored the canons of veracity and hygiene. Even the educated traveller was liable to have his reactions determined for him, to see only what Mr. Ruskin thought it was good for him to see, and to return only with memories—and photographs—

of what Mr. Ruskin admired. Of the peasant life of France, as of the intellectual life of Germany, perhaps the most solid and most progressive elements in Europe, he knew very little, and he could not help being unduly conscious of his wealth. In this as in so many ways the recent American is the Victorian Englishman enlarged.

XV
CHARITY

XV

CHARITY

By E. C. P. LASCELLES

'There is a substantial tho' unnoticed charm in the visit of a superior. There is a felt compliment in his attentions, which raises an emotion in the breast, the very opposite of that disdainful sentiment towards the higher orders of society, that is now of such alarming prevalence amongst our operative population.'
CHALMERS on *Christian and Civic Economy.*

TRADITION, helped by the caricaturist, portrays the early Victorian as a prosperously comfortable bourgeois strong in his confidence that nothing should or could disturb that social order on which his solid opulence depended. But the comfortable classes of the eighteen-thirties were by no means conscious of that feeling of impregnable security which is so often attributed to them. The outlook of Mr. Podsnap was the product of a later age, and does not at all represent the mind of the eighteen-thirties. That mind might more fairly be described as alarmed, indignant, and puzzled.

They had some cause for alarm. The thunderous demand for Reform, 'the Bill, the whole Bill, and nothing but the Bill', was disquieting to nerves already quivering from the rick-burnings of Captain Swing and the machine-wrecking of the Luddites. There was, of course, nothing new in a riotous England. An earlier generation fifty years ago had accepted riots almost as a matter of course, and had endured them with a composure bordering upon indifference. For Londoners of that generation were accustomed to the spectacle of Wilkites besieging the mansions of noble Lords, silk weavers of Spitalfields assembling in force, and menacing processions of seamen, tailors, or coal-porters on strike. But Horace Walpole, describing the scene to his friend, does not seem excited.

'We have', he wrote, 'independent mobs that have nothing to do with Wilkes, and who only take advantage of so favourable a season. The dearness of provisions incites, the hope of increase of wages allures, and drink puts them in motion. The coal-heavers began, and it is well it is not a hard frost, for they have stopped all coals coming to town. The sawyers rose too, and at last the sailors, who have committed great outrages on merchant ships, and prevented them from sailing.'

Even in the Gordon riots, when on successive nights the rioters broke open prisons and treated London almost as they pleased, the panic was only temporary; and it was a common experience for legislators to find threatening crowds blocking the approaches to their House and to hear their debates punctuated by the crash of broken glass. But the French Revolution had shown that riots, and the discontent which causes riots, may lead to something more serious than broken windows; and Pitt and Dundas had taught their countrymen to treat the smallest tendency to sedition with a gravity which might have surprised their fathers. The new generation after Waterloo was even more apprehensive of revolution than Pitt and Dundas; and, when 1830 brought new convulsions of unrest to the countries whose destinies had so recently been settled by the statesmen of Vienna, few Englishmen could contemplate the future with any feeling of security.

The causes of their indignation were obvious. They felt that they were unfairly treated. They had weathered the storm; they had saved Europe; they had destroyed the Corsican Ogre. They had earned the repose and dignity of victors. Was it right that after subduing the Tyrant they themselves should be accused of tyranny? Was it fair that they should be called 'tax-eaters' and threatened with the fate of the French aristocrats? They believed, not without reason, that they were the backbone of Britain, and if proof of their benevolent humanity were needed, it would be amply forthcoming in the list of British Charities, which had increased so remarkably during the last hundred years. In the face of that record of hospitals and dispensaries, loan funds and doles, endowed schools, pensions and annuities, private penitentiaries and reformatories, all founded and supported by private benevolence, should it be said—could it be said—that they were oppressors of the poor?

They had good reason also to be puzzled, for they were anxious to remove the causes of discontent, and greatly oppressed by the difficulty of doing it. Unwilling students of the French Revolution and the hand-to-mouth devices by which Government is conducted during a great war, they had no enthusiasm for changes in the structure of society.

And yet experiments in 'tiding over' a crisis had not been encouraging. There had been, for instance, the attempt to do something for agricultural labourers when prices were rising, but to avoid increasing their wages, because, as was rightly apprehended, it would be 'difficult to reduce them when the cause of it had ceased'. The result had not been at all what was intended. It had brought all the economic disasters of Speenhamland and the 'rate in aid of wages'.

'A stripling', wrote Nicholls in his criticism of that experiment, 'marries a girl as ignorant and youthful as himself. They immediately apply to the overseers to provide them a house, and for something also towards getting them a bed and a little furniture. The birth of a child approaches and the overseer is again applied to for a midwife, and for money to help them in the wife's downlying. Perhaps the child dies, and the parish then of course has to bury it; and if it lives the parish must surely help to maintain it. And so it was throughout the whole range of their existence—in youth and in age, in sickness and in health, in seasons favourable and unfavourable, with low prices or with high prices—the parish was looked to and relied upon as an unfailing source from which every man considered he had a right to obtain the supply of every want, even though it were caused by his own indolence, vice, or improvidence.'

This was, of course, disastrous, but it was not easy to discover an alternative which would not cause Sir Leicester Dedlock and his friends to complain that 'upon my reputation and principles, the floodgates of society are burst open, and the waters have obliterated the landmarks of the framework of the cohesion by which things are held together'. When every way was difficult, one way seemed on the whole to offer fewer difficulties than the others. It was the way of private charity and private endowment, and they turned to it with enthusiasm. Their motives, as we shall see on examining their actions, were mixed; but, among the motives which brought about the remarkable increase in charities during the first half of the nineteenth century, fear of the rising discontent and genuine desire to improve the condition of the poor were prominent. Of the two the second probably was the stronger, for private benevolence persisted long after the fear of revolution was removed, and continued to find its scope when many of the services formerly undertaken by charity had become the care of the State.

Mr. Sampson Low's summary of the London Charities in 1862 shows the course of development:

Number in existence in 1860.	Founded between 1850 and 1860.	Founded 1800 to 1850.	Founded during 18th century.	Founded before 18th century.	Annual income from voluntary contributions (1860). £	Annual income from property or trade (1860). £
14 General Medical Hospitals	2	5	5	2	58,049	126,809
66 Hospitals, Infirmaries, or other Institutions for special medical purposes.	15	39	11	1	73,950	81,075
39 Dispensaries	8	21	10	—	23,377	2,500
12 For Preservation of Life, Health, and Public Morals	2	8	2	—	34,674	11,815
1 Institution for Foundlings	18	16	4	1	42,387	51,594
22 Hospitals and Penitentiary Institutions for Females						
16 Relief to Prisoners, Reformatory, and Refuge Institutions						
29 Institutions for the Relief of Street Destitution and specific claims	5	20	3	1	54,551	10,213
21 Homes for Needle Women and Servants, &c., and otherwise aiding the Industrious	14	7	—	—	6,250	2,005
9 Benevolent Pensions or Annuity Funds	8	—	—	1	15,314	4,300
14 Societies and Funds for the Benefit of Poor Clergy of the Church	4	8	6	2	18,873	30,735
6 For Protestant Dissenting Ministers						
72 Professional and Trade Provident and Benevolent Funds	14	43	15	—	55,513	117,058
21 Funds arising from City Company and Parochial Trusts	—	—	—	—	—	38,000
1 Indian Famine Fund	1	—	—	—	114,807	—

4 Indian Famine Funds (closed but producing income) .	3	—	—	1	—	53,000
124 Colleges, Hospitals, Almshouses and other Asylums for the Aged .	4	29	27	64	9,734	85,587
16 Charities for Blind, Deaf and Dumb, and Poor Cripples .	5	5	4	2	14,274	29,247
31 Societies and Funds Promoting and aiding Schools, including 9 Associations for Adult instruction .	8	17	5	1	73,443	14,934
14 Asylums for 1,986 Orphan children	1	9	4	—	48,017	16,930
20 Asylums maintaining 2,894 children	5	4	9	2	48,747	63,791
56 Bible and Home Missionary Societies and Funds .	20	31	4	1	332,679	35,780
25 Foreign Missionary Societies and Funds .	7	13	5	—	570,440	66,000
4 Miscellaneous Societies .	—	4	—	—	5,515	—
640 Institutions	144	279	114	103	1,600,594	841,373
						1,600,594
						Aggregate Income 2,441,967

II

T t

The acceleration of benevolence during the first half of the nineteenth century is obvious. Out of 640 institutions 279 were founded between 1800 and 1850, and 144 between 1850 and 1860.

The full income derived from charitable gifts in London was much larger than the figure shown by Mr. Low; for private charity in the form of individual gifts and special subscriptions for deserving objects was common. No estimate of the amount of such gifts is possible, but we have a glimpse of their nature in the systematic benevolence of the Brothers Cheeryble, when Mr. Trimmers called with his subscription list 'for the widow and family of a man who was killed in the East India Docks this morning, Sir. Smashed, sir, by a cask of sugar.' These visits were expected. 'Trimmers', said Mr. Cheeryble, 'is one of the best friends we have. He makes a thousand cases known to us that we should never discover of ourselves. I am *very* much obliged to Trimmers.' Such applications were, of course, not invariably successful. Did not Mr. Jorrocks reply to an appeal for the redemption of Margaret Lucas's patent mangle that 'the M.F.H. having laid it down as a rule never to subscribe to redeem patent mangles can't depart from it in her case'?

But, even without allowing for the benevolent activities of Trimmers and his like, the income of charities in London exceeded the provision made from public money for the relief of distress. According to Mr. Low's survey the poor rates expended in the Metropolitan district in 1857, which he considered an average year, amounted to £1,425,063, and this included the cost of Lunatics in Asylums, salaries and rations of officers, and various charges which were only partly connected with the relief of the poor. Of course, the expenditure from the poor rates is not strictly comparable with the income of the charities, because the charities included missionary and educational organizations which were not the concern of the poor rates. But, allowing for that difference, there can be no doubt that the poor had to rely more on charity than on public funds.

'There are distinctly two classes of poor in the Metropolis,' said a witness before a Parliamentary Committee in 1861: 'one coming under the notice of the ministers of religion of all descriptions, and district visitors, and very frequently medical men; the others apply to the Poor-Law authorities, the Boards of Guardians. Those who come under the notice of the ministers of religion, that is to say, the more respectable portion of the poor, as well as a considerable addition from women who cannot wait the amount of time required to get at the relieving officer, are equal to or more numerous than those applying to the Poor-Law authorities.'

Since charities were responsible for so much in the national life it is worth while to consider the sort of people who came to them; what help, for instance, Oliver Twist might have expected from them if he had not met the Artful Dodger, or what they might have offered Jo of Tom-all-Alone's instead of his precarious existence on door-steps. Neither Oliver nor Jo could have hoped to become one of the 450 inmates of the Foundling Hospital, because it provided only for 'poor illegitimate children, whose mothers are known', and it would receive foundlings only if 'the reception of the child will in all probability be the means of replacing the mother in the course of virtue, and the way of an honest livelihood'. But the number of orphan asylums and orphan schools was steadily increasing in London, and a boy who could secure enough subscribers and patrons to vote for his election had a good chance of admission. Of course, it was improbable that a homeless child in London would have any wide acquaintance among subscribers to orphanages who could give him letters of admission or vote for his election, and the chances of Oliver and Jo without friends or influence would have been remote. Influence and friends indeed seemed a necessary condition of help from most of the charitable societies. With such influence a poor boy might be apprenticed to a trade by one of the Provident Societies or by one of the City companies, and might even 'receive entire suits of clothes from its funds', and when once he had become a beneficiary from such funds in his youth he might hope for other advantages as he grew up. But Jo was probably not an exaggerated picture of the homeless child without friends.

Probably Oliver's associates, the Dodger and Charley Bates, would have found more chance of assistance from London charities than Oliver himself, for Reformatories for Juvenile offenders, Refuges and Industrial Schools, maintained by charitable funds and subsidized by Government grants, were gradually being set up. Most of them were founded after 1850, but a few existed in the thirties. There was Bridewell Hospital, which was 'not merely a prison, but what its royal founder intended it to be, a charitable institution for affording aid to the poor and destitute, as well as for correcting the idle and dissolute'; there was the Philanthropic Society's Farm School for the Reformation of Criminal Boys which received the destitute sons of felons, and boys who have themselves been criminals, 'with the purpose of training them for a useful life'; there was the Operative and Training Institution for Boys 'to provide a refuge to which the fallen and those who may be exposed to temptation may flee for shelter' and be trained for the Navy; and, as the system of giving special treatment to young offenders developed, refuges and schools for 'abandoned, degraded, and outcast boys', for boys 'on the verge of a criminal course', for 'the depraved and the destitute', and other categories of unhappy children appeared in many parts of London. No doubt Bates and the Dodger could have found places in some of them; but while they could count on the more stirring pleasures of Mr. Fagin's kitchen, it was unlikely that they would be attracted by schemes, however laudably conceived, of 'training them for an industrious life'.

For young women, on the other hand, and above all for young women who were 'desirous of returning to the paths of virtue' the Charities offered a wider range of opportunities. There were orphanages where they would be trained for domestic service or taught needlework, the reformatories and refuges for those who had been convicted, and a remarkably large number of institutions for the 'reformation of fallen women'. These agencies had greatly increased since Horace Walpole recorded his entertaining impressions of a visit to the Home for Penitents, and they provided for those who were 'desirous of abandoning a course of sin', and for those who were 'on the brink of sin' or 'exposed to peculiar temptations'. Many of them would gladly have opened their doors to Sikes's Nancy and her friend Bet, but here again it is doubtful whether the invitation would have been accepted until other means of living had failed, for the references to 'much wholesome discipline', 'productive industry of the inmates in washing and needlework', and 'inmates trained to habits of industry, laundry work forming their principal occupation' must have sounded ominous to the prospective penitents. Young women also had their share of training and apprenticeship from the Provident Societies 'for aiding the resources of the industrious'. There was, for instance, the Association for the aid and benefit of Dress Makers and Milliners, established in 1843, 'to induce the principals of houses to shorten the hours of work, and abolish Sunday labour, and for providing qualified assistants to meet sudden demands or pressure of work', and various homes where young women could be trained for needlework and domestic service. Indeed, if all the philanthropic bodies which offered training or encouragement to future domestic servants were successful in their objects, the supply and quality of domestic servants in London must have reached their highest point during the nineteenth century.

The arrangements for the adult and able-bodied poor were less definite. There were shelters for the Homeless, but these offered only temporary hospitality 'during inclement winter seasons', and there were the Baths and Wash-houses for the Labouring Classes 'supplied with tepid water continually flowing'. There were various funds administered by the City Companies from which an unemployed workman might possibly get help, and the 'poor-box' at the police courts would sometimes relieve 'cases of urgent destitution or great misfortune', although the magistrates at Marylebone, where £306 was distributed during a winter among 2,000 applicants for relief, besides a large quantity of coals, soup, and bread, placed at the disposal of the court, found how 'utterly incompetent they were, from their position, to act as public almoners to so large an extent'. But the main hope of the able-bodied in adversity lay in a number of societies whose purpose was to visit and relieve the deserving poor in their homes. The Benevolent or Stranger's Friend Society, founded in 1785, employed 400 visitors attached to districts of London, and gave relief in nearly 7,000 cases, while the Society for the Relief of Distress, organized in 1860, gave relief in over 23,000 cases, and the Association for the Relief of the Poor of the City of London supplied fuel at 4d. a cwt. 'to thousands of families during severe weather'. This method of relief through district visitors was an essential feature of Victorian charity, and embodied one of the principles on which Chalmers and the supporters of the charitable system based their views.

The aged and infirm could scrutinize a long list of almshouses and pension funds, not with a view to taking their choice among competing institutions, but in order to see whether the constitution and rules of any of them offered any hope of success, for charitable arrangements for the aged were often of a specialized nature which restricted their benefits to those who fulfilled the peculiar conditions of the original benefactor. Many of the almshouses, such as the Fishmongers' Almshouses at Wandsworth, the Haberdashers' at Hoxton, and the Free Watermen's and Lightermen's Almshouses at Penge, were reserved for members of the City Company which controlled them. Others required special qualifications of residence, occupation, or character. Thus candidates for the St. Pancras Almshouses 'must have paid poor rates in the parish for not less than ten years, have sustained a good character, have not received parochial relief, be upwards of sixty years of age, and in indigent circumstances'; Whittington's Almshouses at Highgate had only the general condition that the inmate must be 'meek of spirit, destitute of temporal goods in other places by which he might comfortably live, chaste, and of good conversation', but those almshouses were managed by the Mercers' Company and were 'of course available more especially to livery and freemen of the Company'. The Institution of London Almshouses at Brixton, founded in 1832 'in lieu of an Illumination to commemorate Reform in Parliament', was for 'aged and decayed freemen and householders of London, and their wives or widows, of good character and repute, in reduced circumstances through casualties of fortune or visitation of Providence', and Morden College at Blackheath was for 'poor, honest, sober, and discreet merchants, of the age of 50 at the least, who may have lost their estates by accidents, ways or means, in their honest endeavour to get their living by way of merchandise'. The restriction to residents of the district was common, and the applicant in many cases must have been a householder or ratepayer. Although almshouses were many, vacancies were few and the approach was far from easy.

It was the same with pensions. The list of funds was long but the conditions were difficult. Some of them attempted to define the social standing of their beneficiaries. The National Benevolent Institution, established in 1812, gave pensions of £20 to £30 a year to 'indigent gentry, merchants, tutors, governesses, and persons who have been engaged in professional pursuits, or in the higher departments of trade'; the Royal General Annuity Society allowed permanent annuities to 'decayed merchants, bankers, professional men, tradesmen, clerks, and the widows and daughters of persons belonging to the same classes'; and the British Beneficent Institution refused all applicants who were not 'widows and unmarried daughters of persons who have moved in superior stations in society'. Many others were for members of a particular profession or trade, and were sometimes in the nature of insurance in that pensions were granted only to former subscribers. These included several funds for the clergy and their families, and funds for architects, schoolmasters, artists, governesses, doctors, master mariners, booksellers, printers, butchers, hairdressers, and tallow chandlers. It is an imposing list but not encouraging to the aged applicant who did not happen to possess the qualifications or influence which would make him eligible. Mrs. Squeers might possibly have qualified for a pension if her husband had contributed to one of the Schoolmasters' Funds before he went to jail, and Charity Pecksniff would no doubt have applied to the Architects' Institution; but old Riah, Mr. Chuffey, and the unfortunate grandfather of Little Nell would have experienced considerable difficulty.

The history of hospitals and the provision for the sick is well known. Voluntary Hospitals were among the oldest forms of charity since Rahere founded St. Bartholomew's in 1123. There was a development of hospitals during the first years in the eighteenth century, when Guy's was founded on a lucky speculation in South Sea Stock, but progress became slower from the middle of the century when attacks of typhus, known as 'Hospital fever', raised a passing doubt in the efficacy of hospital treatment. But development was renewed in the nineteenth century, and the zeal of founders and subscribers was no doubt encouraged by a severe epidemic of cholera in 1831. Mr. Low's table shows the rapid increase. Many of them offered and still offer examples of that form of patronage known as the letter system, which was not unusual in Victorian charities. Admission was through hospital letters, which could be obtained from subscribers. No doubt the efficiency of the treatment was as good as could be hoped from the standards of the time, but early Victorian nursing brings an echo of Mrs. Gamp and Mrs. Prig 'of Bardlemy's' which is far from reassuring.

Education is too big a subject to be treated as one of the aspects of London Charities. Its history during the period is one of transition from private to public enterprise, as will be found by a study of the successive Education Acts. For our present purpose only a few schools need be mentioned. Many of the City Companies controlled schools provided by the gifts of charitable members. Two examples are enough. The Mercers' Company controlled the property given by Dean Colet in the reign of Henry VIII for the foundation of St. Paul's school. This is an example of a successful foundation, although in 1826 the school was criticized for the 'absurdity and profusion' of its management. At the other end of the scale comes Trotman's school, founded by bequest of £80 a year by Throckmorton Trotman in 1663 to the Haberdashers' Company. But the Haberdashers were less successful in their venture than the Mercers, for a visitor in 1826 found the school in disrepair and a 'Great Boy' deputizing for the master who was seldom in attendance. It was no doubt to some such establishment that Mr. Dombey sent the engine-driver's son 'Biler—christened Robin—him as you was so good as to make a Charitable Grinder on', with unfortunate results for Rob the Grinder.

'"A son of this man's whom I caused to be educated, major," said Mr. Dombey, giving him his arm. "The usual return!"

'"Take advice from plain old Joe and never educate that sort of people, sir," returned the major. "Damme, sir, it never does! It always fails!"'

It is significant that one of the unendowed charities for primary education should have been named the Ragged School Union. It was established in 1844, and in 1861 Mr. Low found that the objects of its care were 'to be numbered by tens of thousands'.

Home Missions were closely allied to education. At the beginning of the century they consisted largely of organizations for the distribution of tracts, and until the fifties there was little sign of those tendencies which lead to the modern Settlements and Public School Missions.

Londoners had many opportunities of subscribing to foreign missions. The list on the whole is not unlike that of the present day, and it contains nothing so romantic as the project of Mrs. Jellyby to 'have 150 or 200 healthy families cultivating coffee and educating the natives of Borrioboola-Gha, on the left bank of the Niger'. But it is a little staggering to read an announcement by the Foreign Aid Society in 1861 that 'the issue of the Italian war has given the promise of religious liberty in countries which hitherto have been inaccessible to the Gospel, and opened the Gates of Florence and the ports of Tuscany for the word of God to enter'.

The charities controlled by the City Companies were so important in London that they need special attention. A few examples will show their responsibilities and powers.

The Drapers' Company were trustees of many bequests which included the gift of Howell for marriage portions for maidens next of kin to the donor, that of Pennoyer for apprenticing, and that of Grainger for giving pensions of £10 to the blind and for apprenticing. They were also the controllers of funds for the release of prisoners, for pensions to released prisoners, and for providing bread in various prisons. They were trustees of Queen Elizabeth's College in which were maintained twenty poor persons. In all they were said to pay out over £4,000 a year to the poor.

The Mercers' Company, whom we have already met as ruling the destinies of St. Paul's school, controlled a remarkably wide range of charitable funds. Besides St. Paul's they were responsible for the Mercers' School, where in the early part of the century thirty-four boys were being educated, and a free school at Horsham, where a simpler curriculum was offered to the children of the poor. As directors of education for the young they seem to have been successful, although a critic suggested that the expenditure of £229 9s. for an Apposition dinner at St. Paul's involved a rather free construction of the founder's statute that on the day appointed for the audit of accounts there should be 'an assembly and a littell dinner ordeyned by the surveyors, not exceeding the pryce of fower nobles'. They were, at the beginning of the century, less successful perhaps in their administration of the Gresham Trusts, which provided for occasional lectures on divinity, astronomy, music, and geometry; for, although the lectures were duly advertised, a visitor in 1826 had the utmost difficulty in discovering the lecture-room, and when at last he obtained admission, he found that the lecture, advertised as treating of geometry, dealt in fact with the nature and properties of Fire, which, as the seeker after geometry observed, 'was not the sort of science understood by that term at the present day'.

The Mercers were also Trustees of Whittington's Alms-houses in the City, Lady Mico's almshouses in Stepney, Dauntsey's almshouses at West Lavington in Wiltshire, and the Trinity Hospital for poor men at Greenwich. We shall see more of the Trinity Hospital when we accompany the Senior Wardens and visitors of the company to their annual dinner at Greenwich on the Monday next after Trinity Monday.

But the Mercers were chiefly remarkable for the number and diversity of the funds which they were called upon to administer. There were funds to provide coal for the poor of certain parishes; to give three poor widows of freemen of the Company 7d. a week each; to relieve poor prisoners; to appoint preachers; to provide for 'clothing with hose, shoes and shirts and such like, poor and naked men, women, and children wandering in the streets of London, and that have no dwelling'; to lend money gratis to young men; to make gifts of 'good sweet bread'; and to 'bind out' poor appren-tices. To carry out all their duties as the charitable bene-factors intended, the Mercers would have needed many remarkable qualities, and it is not surprising to find them delegating their responsibility by handing over to the Society for the Suppression of Mendicity money intended for 'poor distressed objects in the streets of London'.

The value of their Trust estates had, of course, greatly increased since the gifts were made, and in 1826 the known revenue from land was said to be £14,581, without any estimate of the value of endowments which were not examined by the Charity Commissioners, and the capital value of the bequests was over £12,000. Hostile critics in the early part of the century were suggesting that too much of the increased income found its way into the general fund of the company, and they acidly expressed the hope that it had not been 'wasted in sumptuous Pitt dinners, in ostentatious entertainments to the members of the Holy Alliance, nor in magnificent embellishments of their hall, making them more like palaces than buildings appropriate to the occasional meetings of industrious tradesmen'.

Outside London charitable foundations were unequally

distributed. In the new industrial towns there were, of course, few endowments, and the state of those towns was sometimes favourably compared with that of places which had the benefit of funds for schools, doles, and pensions. Many of the older towns had their endowed charities, and the town of Lichfield may be taken as an example of them. Lichfield had a free grammar school of high reputation as the school of Addison and Johnson. It had also an English School where thirty children of the poor were to be 'taught gratis, English reading until they could well read chapters in the Bible'.

By way of almshouses there were a Women's Hospital for poor women, 'from among the most respectable of the lower classes, weight being generally given to the circumstance of their not having received parochial relief', and St. John's Hospital for men with a constitution and rules which carry a faint suggestion of Barsetshire and the immortal foundation of John Hiram. The constitution provided that the hospital was to be governed by a Warden with the assistance of a Master of grammar who was to instruct 'the poor, who have not the opportunity of learning by reason of the indigence of their parents', an usher, who was to be 'fully contented' with a stipend of £10, and a chaplain of 'honoured and approved conversation'. The inmates were to be present at prayers every day, to take an oath of obedience to the bishop and the master, and to receive 7d. a week every Friday after dinner, 'with which 7d. thus weekly paid the poor men are to remain content; nor must they presume to beg on pain of expulsion from the house, after a third admonition'. When the Commissioners made their survey in 1821 there were thirteen almsmen and their dole of 7d. had been raised to 4s. 6d. Lichfield had also an almshouse for six 'ancient and impotent widows'.

The remaining charities of Lichfield offered a strangely mixed assortment of bread, garments, and doles. Under the bread charities penny loaves, threepenny loaves, and sixpenny loaves were distributed every Sunday after morning prayer and on other suitable occasions. Doles of varying amounts were offered to poor men reputed honest, to poor men and poor widows of Lichfield, to honest poor widows, to poor householders, chiefly widows, and to many other classes of beneficiaries. The clothes were of a rather miscellaneous nature. There were new caps and new coats for twelve men, new cloth gowns for four women, six waistcoats for poor widows, cloth gowns with W.F. on the sleeve in honour of Mr. William Finney the donor, and caps for poor men and poor widows. Indeed provision for widows appears so frequently as almost to suggest that widowhood might have been a lucrative occupation in Lichfield.

The charities of Lichfield had been carefully preserved, for the Commissioners found little to criticize, and the commentator, who had spoken so severely of City Companies in London, said that 'eleemosynary administration of this place has been more exemplary than that of any other which has yet come under our notice', with congratulations to the civil and ecclesiastical authorities of Lichfield that the surplus revenues of their charities had not 'been carried to the guttling fund of the trustees, or consumed in wasteful salaries to their dependants, as is too frequently observed in corporate bodies'. After such a testimonial it is disappointing to read the report of an inspector forty years later. He found that from the endowed charities upwards of £800 a year was distributed in Lichfield in doles, and the results were not encouraging.

'The charities', he reported, 'have turned half the inhabitants of Lichfield into beggars; hence idleness, drunkenness, poaching and thieving. It is impossible to exaggerate the evils they produce. . . . I have received testimony from some of the most intelligent inhabitants, who take the greatest interest in the welfare of the poor, that the charities produce a vast amount of beggary, idleness, lying, and profligacy, and destroy the feelings of self-respect and independence, and thus are great instruments of demoralisation in Lichfield.'

It is melancholy to find that even with careful administration charities may do harm, and that a town of the size of Lichfield could be debauched for the trifling sum of £800 a year.

A survey of the objects and methods of early Victorian charities suggests certain general characteristics which are worth considering. To take first the less attractive features, it is difficult to avoid in many cases an impression of acquiescence, and almost complacent acquiescence, in the existence of extreme poverty and distress. The establishment of children's schools under the name of 'Ragged' schools, and the many charities designed to relieve a few of the many destitute, give some support to Blake's attack:

> They compel the poor to live upon a crust of bread by soft mild arts,
> They reduce man to want, then give with pomp and ceremony.

And in some of the reports one almost hears the echo of Mr. Podsnap when the meek man ventured to remind him of the people who had lately died in the streets of starvation.

'"There is not," said Mr. Podsnap, flushing angrily, "there is not a country in the world, Sir, where so noble a provision is made for the poor as in this country."

'The meek man was quite willing to concede that, but perhaps it rendered the matter even worse as showing that there must be something appallingly wrong somewhere.

'"Where?" said Mr. Podsnap.

'The meek man hinted, wouldn't it be well to try, very seriously, to find out where?

'"Ah!" said Mr. Podsnap. "Easy to say somewhere; not so easy to say where! But I see what you are driving at. I knew it from the first. Centralization. No. Never with my consent. Not English."'

And he ended the conversation with his usual repudiation.

'"I must decline to pursue this painful discussion. It is not pleasant to my feelings. I have said that I do not admit these things. I have also said that if they do exist (not that I admit it) the fault lies with the sufferers themselves. It is not for *me* . . . to impugn the workings of Providence. I know better than that, I trust, and I have mentioned what the intentions of Providence are. Besides . . . the subject is a very disagreeable one. I will go so far as to say it is an odious one. It is not one to be introduced among our wives and young persons, and I——" He finished with that flourish of his arm which added more expressively than any words, "and I remove it from the face of the Earth."'

Podsnap was no doubt a caricature, but he was a not unfair caricature of the attitude of prosperous Englishmen of the early nineteenth century, who set the example of generous contributions to charities, but were opposed in principle to the extension of national responsibility. But that attitude was by no means universal. The champions of *laissez-faire* lived as contemporaries with a body of ardent reformers. Oastler and Lord Shaftesbury were securing the early factory acts; Trade Unions were legalizing their position; and the pressure for a national system of education was becoming strong.

Another unattractive feature of the charities was the system of patronage which was, and often still remains, attached to them. Beneficiaries were chosen not for merit, but by a form of competition for the interest of subscribers. Admission to hospitals was obtained by nomination or 'letter' from a subscriber, and for many of the charities the applicant had to obtain votes from patrons who knew very little of competing claims. When charity was relied upon to provide much of what is now provided by state services the disadvantages of such a system are obvious, and its existence implies a belief that funds could be raised only if the subscribers were offered some right of patronage in return for their money.

Still less attractive was the waste of money which was so often involved in administration. The day of the trained secretary, who, to do him justice, is seldom paid at his commercial value, was only beginning, and in many cases the control of charities involved Courts of Governors, formal audits, and reception of visitors, which were often a heavy expense. The charity dinner was far too common a method of using surplus income, and there was no excuse for it. Dinners like the Apposition dinner at St. Paul's for £229, or the Quarterly dinners for the governors of St. Olave's free grammar school at a cost of £100 a year were not unusual, and gave rise to the sarcastic comment that 'the opprobrium of gluttony which attaches to the national character has chiefly arisen from foreigners observing the periodical feasting which takes place through the country, out of the funds left for pious and charitable uses'.

In a speech in the House of Lords on May 18, 1846, on the introduction of a Charitable Trusts Bill, Lord Lyndhurst described a charity dinner at its worst. His description has its value not only for the light which it throws on the administration of charities, but as illustrating the dining capacity of our ancestors. *Fortes vixerunt.* Such achievements deserve commemoration.

'There was,' said Lord Lyndhurst, 'a charity established, I think, in the reign of James the First, by the Earl of Northampton. It was established at Greenwich; and it was to consist of a warden and 20 objects of the charity; and the whole was put under the Government of the Mercers' Company, who were to be visitors and on every Trinity Monday in each year were to proceed to Greenwich, for the purpose of examining the accounts, inquiring into the manner in which the charity was administered, and seeing that everything was proceeding upon a safe and regular principle. The founder of the charity, Lord Northampton, stated in the charter, that it would not be convenient that a great number of persons should attend on the occasion of the visit; he therefore limited the number to 12, and he allowed the small sum of £5 a year to defray the expenses of the boat hire, and of the dinner that should be given on the occasion. Now, my Lords, this visitation has been going on for a great number of years. I hold in my hand a document which also appears in the Report of the Commissioners on charity; and I give this as a sample, for the purpose of seeing whether you can safely and implicitly rely upon the manner in which persons in this situation perform their duty with respect to charitable trusts. I call your Lordships' attention to it as one of several cases; there are very many of the same description and character. Here is an account of the items of expenditure on June 3rd, 1833: "to breakfast, 18 gentlemen at 3s., £2 14s." I do not mean to say that before they proceeded upon their expedition to Greenwich it was not proper that they should assemble for breakfast; and I do not mean to say that the charge for breakfast was extravagant (*laughter*). Well, here is the account:

1833, June 3rd.

	£	s.	d.
To breakfast, 18 gentlemen at 3s.	2	14	0
Two tongues, eggs, bacon, and Bath chap . .	1	8	0
Waiters		10	0
	4	12	0

Then come the expenses of the journey to Greenwich:

	£	s.	d.
To 6 carriages & pair, 1 day town and Greenwich .	7	12	0
Coachman	1	16	0
Hostler		3	0
Gates		13	6
	10	8	6
Three dozen of flowers for the hall	1	1	0

'I do not find this last item in Lord Northampton's list. Then, my Lords, comes the luncheon. I do not find fault with this luncheon. These gentlemen having obtained a great deal of experience in this kind of business, would not much like an extravagant luncheon in point of quantity, because it might operate in that case very unfavourably in regard to what was to follow. The luncheon, therefore, was moderate: "Sixteen sandwiches, twelve lemonades, six punch, one and a half pints of cherry brandy, two and a half dozen soda, lemon, sugar." That was the luncheon—moderate I admit. No great fault can be found with it—I come now, my Lords, to the substantial part of the feast; and your Lordships will recollect that this is the

Mercers' Company, which claim to be exempted from the operation of the bill on account of the strict and faithful manner in which they have hitherto discharged their duties, and are likely to discharge them again—here is the dinner:

'"Dinner,—four dishes flounders, two ditto turbots, three ditto stewed eels, two ditto mullet, three ditto water smilie, three ditto eels, tomatoes, two ditto salmon, one ditto spiced eels, two collops of turbot, one ditto sturgeon, whitebait, potatoes and cucumbers, and sauces."

'That is the first course. . . . Having gone over the fish I now come to something more substantial:

'"Two dishes boiled pullets and white sauce, two ditto ducklings, two ditto raised pies, two ditto hams, one dish of roast turkey poult, one ditto pigeon pie, two ditto geese, one ditto tongue, one ditto quarter of lamb, one ditto roast fowls, one capon."

'All this, my Lords, is tolerably and sufficiently solid, but there is a *pièce de résistance,* as it is sometimes called—"One baron of beef". Then we have:

'"One baron of beef, two dishes of lamb cutlets, curry with rice, asparagus, peas, ditto stewed, Italian salad, prawns, rice, new potatoes, French beans, cauliflowers, lobster, cucumber, mushrooms, collar, garden beans, sauces, gravies, jellies, baskets, tarts, blancmange, custards, tourts, lemon pudding, plum puddings, officers' dinners."

'That was the dinner. Lord Northampton having allowed £5 for the whole expense. . . . I now come to the dessert:

'"Six quarts ice cream, two almond cakes, six pound hot-house grapes, ten plates strawberries, six ditto oranges, six ditto almonds and raisins, five ditto preserved ginger, four ditto ditto nutmegs, four ditto biscuits, seven ditto olives, two dishes apples, ice for wine—Cooks and charcoal, hire for china and glass, allowance on forty-one bottles of wine, shilling each, waiters."

'The explanation with regard to the wine at a shilling a bottle I must mention to your Lordships. These gentlemen are prudent. They supply their own wine, Mr. Lovegrove furnishing the dinner; but, as he does not furnish the wine, he puts a charge of a shilling upon every bottle they drink. I may mention that by the charity accounts, it appears that no less than £70 was paid at one period for wine, and £40 at another, it being placed in the cellars belonging to the hospital, and brought out on the recurrence of these visits. It appeared that on this particular occasion forty-one bottles were consumed by the eighteen persons present. We now come to the tea:

'"1½ pounds hyson tea at 12s.; 1½ pounds souchong tea, at 10s.; 2½ pounds mocha coffee, at 3s.; 8 pounds refined sugar at 11d.; 4 pounds Bengal ditto at 8d.; ½ pound Crown chocolate at 4s.; 13 nutmegs; 1 pound canister sugar."

'And now for the summary of expenses:

	£	s.	d.
Breakfasts	4	12	0
Coaches	10	8	6
Flowers	1	1	0
Dinner	63	6	6
Baker		16	6
Cheesemonger . . .	1	13	2
Brewer . . .	1	16	0
Men's beer, etc. . . .		19	4
Grocer	3	0	11
Butler	1	10	10
Laundress		10	5
	89	12	5'''

But the most important feature of Victorian methods of administration was their system of district visiting. The beneficiaries were visited in their homes by members or agents of the charitable body, and it was the duty of the visitor to satisfy himself that alms were really needed, to make sure that they were properly used, and to give any advice and help that might be suitable. This was not a matter of mere administrative convenience; it was a matter of principle. The advocates of district visiting believed with good reason that the main influence for civilization in country districts was the parish priest with his regular visits to his parishioners, and they thought that an extension of the visiting system to the towns might produce the same results.

The most convinced exponent of this view was Dr. Chalmers, who anxiously strove to develop visiting in the manufacturing towns.

'In a provincial capital,' he says in his treatise on Voluntary Assistance, 'the great mass of the population are retained in kindly and immediate dependence on the wealthy residenters of the place. . . . This brings the two extreme orders of society into the sort of relationship which is highly favourable to the general blandness and tranquillity of the whole population. In a manufacturing town, on the other hand, the poor and the wealthy stand more disjoined from each other. It is true they often meet, but they meet more in the arena of contest than in a field where the patronage and custom of one party are met by the gratitude and goodwill of the other.'

But Dr. Chalmers aimed at something more than blandness and tranquillity. He believed that charitable gifts from the hands of district visitors could and should take the place of the Poor Law. Fortified by his convictions that 'the new doctrine of the possibility of a general glut is altogether a chimera', and that 'reason will make anything palatable to the lower orders', he boldly affirmed that 'the virtue of humanity ought never to have been legalized, but left to the spontaneous working of man's own willing and compassionate nature', arguing that 'the first great blunder of the legislator was to ordain a law of compulsory relief at all; and when, to save the ruinous consequences of the law, the relief was made as degrading as possible, this was attempting to correct one evil by another, or to bring about a right result by what mathematicians would call a compensation of errors'. A little illogically he excepted Health and Education from his scheme of voluntary provision, but he was careful to add that his exception did not include Old Age.

His theory is interesting, because it is in extreme form a common theory of the time. Although few of his contemporaries agreed with his view that the Poor Law could be abolished, many of them hoped that, by developing charities, the scope for state services of relief would be limited.

As to the efficacy of district visiting, much depended on the visitors. At the worst they recall the visit of the formidable Mrs. Pardiggle to the brickmaker, who tried in his despair to discount her questions by answering them in advance.

'Have I read the little book wot you left. No, I an't read the little book wot you left. There an't nobody here as knows how to read it; and if there was, it wouldn't be suitable to me. It's a book fit for a babby, and I'm not a babby. If you was to leave me a doll, I shouldn't nuss it. How have I been conducting of myself? Why I've been drunk for three days; and I'd a been drunk for four, if I'd a had the money. Don't I never mean for to go to church? No, I don't never mean for to go to church. I shouldn't be expected there, if I did; the beadle's too genteel for me. And how did my wife get that black eye? Why, I give it her and if she says I didn't she's a Lie.'

But Mrs. Pardiggle obviously did not know her business. Good visitors knew how to make themselves pleasant, and although they might not possess the almost magic properties which Dr. Chalmers was inclined to attribute to them, their work confirmed the judgement of those theorists who believed that the parish with its resident and visiting parson was a civilizing agency of importance.

The Victorians showed considerable courage in extending

so widely their charities at the beginning of the century, for charities were under suspicion before Brougham appointed his Inquiry Commissioners in 1818, and his remarks on their appointment showed that he knew what to expect.

'They must', he said, 'be persons not only of incorruptible integrity, but of stern disposition and inaccessible to the cajolery which oftentimes shuts the eyes of those whom the grosser arts would assail in vain. They must be easy of approach to all accusers, never closing their ears to suggestions or even information because it may proceed from spiteful or malicious motives, or may denounce abuses too enormous to be creditable, or accuse parties too exalted to be suspected. . . . In a word, their propensity must be to suspect abuses, and lean towards tracing them; their principle must be that no man who complains of an evil is to be disregarded, be his apparent motives what they may.'

If we may accept the scene in Crotchet Castle as an accurate description of their activities, the Commissioners must have possessed some of the qualities which their originator considered essential. The Reverend Dr. Folliott found himself in the presence of three 'well-dressed and bulky gentlemen' who announced that they had been appointed 'to inquire into the state of the public charities of this village'. Dr. Folliott knows of no public charities, but the Commissioners have been informed that the manorial farm of Hautbois is charged with an annual rent for the endowment and repair of an almshouse. Mr. Bluenose, a churchwarden, knows nothing of it, and appeals to Mr. Appletwig, the parish clerk.

'*Mr. Appletwig.* I do remember, gentlemen, to have been informed, that there did stand at the end of the village a ruined cottage which had once been an almshouse, which was endowed and maintained by an annual revenue of a mark and a half, or one pound sterling, charged some centuries ago on the farm of Hautbois; but the means, by the progress of time, having become inadequate to the end, the almshouse tumbled to pieces.

The First Commissioner. But this is a right which cannot be abrogated by desuetude, and the sum of £1 per annum is still chargeable for charitable purposes on the manorial farm of Hautbois.

The Rev. Dr. Folliott. Very well, sir.

Mr. Appletwig. But sir, the sum of £1 per annum is still received by the parish, but was long ago by an unanimous vote in open vestry given to the minister.

The Three Commissioners (*unâ voce*). The Minister!

First Commissioner. This is an unjustifiable proceeding.

Second Commissioner. A misappropriation of a public fund.

Third Commissioner. A flagrant perversion of a charitable donation.

The Rev. Dr. Folliott. God bless my soul, gentlemen. I know nothing of this matter. How is this, Mr. Bluenose? Do I receive this £1 per annum?

First Churchwarden. Really, sir, I know no more about it than you do.

Mr. Appletwig. You certainly receive it, sir. It was voted to one of your predecessors. Farmer Seedling lumps it in with his tithes.

First Commissioner. Lumps it in, sir! Lumps in a charitable donation!

Second and Third Commissioners. Oh-oh-oh-oh-h-h!

First Commissioner. Reverend Sir, and gentlemen, officers of this parish, we are under the necessity of admonishing you that this is a most improper proceeding; and you are hereby admonished accordingly. Make a record, Mr. Milky. . . .

The Rev. Dr. Folliott. Is that all, gentlemen?

The Commissioners. That is all, sir, and we wish you a good morning.

The Rev. Dr. Folliott. A very good morning to you, gentlemen.

'What in the name of all that is wonderful, Mr. Bluenose,' said the Rev. Dr. Folliott as he walked out of the inn, 'what in the name of all that is wonderful, can those fellows mean? They have come here in a chaise and four, to make a fuss about a pound per annum, which, after all, they leave as it was. I wonder who pays them for their trouble and how much.'

Mr. Appletwig. The public pay for it, sir. It is a job of the learned friend whom you admire so much. It makes away with public money in salaries, and private money in lawsuits, and does no particle of good to any living soul.'

The Commissioners pursued their inquiries from 1818 to 1837 and produced thirty-eight volumes of reports, which contained stories of abuses far more serious than the annual pound lumped in with Dr. Folliott's tithes. There were many cases of lost funds; surplus incomes of charities appropriated by Corporations for their own purposes, funds misapplied, and visitors entirely neglecting their duties. Only a few examples of what was happening in many parts of the country need be quoted. In one of the Bristol parishes it was found that part of a bread fund had been misapplied for several years, and the amount owing to the Charity was £3,891. A charitable fund at Preston had disappeared, and it was doubtful whether any part of it could be recovered.

A school in Westmorland had been turned into a carpet factory by one of the trustees; it had afterwards been used as a farm; and a successor of the trustee had sold part of the estate as his own property. In Ripon, and in other places, the free grammar schools were being misused. In Ripon the master was found to be making unauthorized charges and depriving the boys of their playground. In other schools he was accused of encouraging the paying boarders at the expense of the day boys who brought him no profit. Although it was found that charitable trusts had on the whole been strictly, sometimes too strictly, administered, the cases of misappropriation were enough to call for interference, and for many years successive governments struggled to obtain the necessary powers to supervise the administration of charities. The opposition to government interference was extraordinary. When the establishment of permanent charity commissioners was proposed, the City companies made violent protests. This was to be expected, and it was also to be expected that the legal profession would oppose a measure which would destroy a mass of litigation. But it was surprising to find the Bishop of London protesting on the grounds that even when Bishops were not appointed to be visitors of educational charities, it was their duty to act as such, and 'no provision ought to be agreed to which would interfere with the influence which the Church had over Charities established for educational or church purposes'. Ten bills were introduced before the Charity Commission was at last appointed in 1853, and a further Act was necessary in 1860 to enlarge its powers. The long controversy with its repeated stories of fraud and lack of trust was bad for the reputation of endowed charities.

Loss and misappropriation, serious as they appeared, were not the gravest charges which were being made against charities. Loss can be made good and fraud punished, and the work of the charity goes on; but it is less easy to survive the general charge that, while many of the charities did excellent work, whole sections of them were of doubtful value, some were positively useless, and some were even mischievous. This view is suggested in the reports of Brougham's Commissioners, which frequently call attention to the survival of foundations whose purposes and methods were of little use, and it gained ground as charitable foundations were displaced by public services during the nineteenth century.

The educational charities were among the first to be attacked as a national system of education was developed. Witnesses giving evidence on elementary education declared that 'in general unendowed schools are better administered than others', that it was 'a fact which admits of no controversy, that, as a whole, schools with small endowments are worse than any others', that investigators have found 'a general dullness and want of life to be the general characteristics of endowed schools', and that 'endowments in connexion with schools of the working classes are, generally speaking, unmitigated evils—in most cases the evils of endowments are so great that parishes would be far better without any such schools at all'. These expert opinions were supported by an array of deplorable examples—endowed schools with no pupils, a school with two masters and one boy, schools with boys and only a deputy or an understudy to do the teaching, and schools where the curriculum and teaching were altogether insufficient for modern standards. This was not surprising, for in many cases the charitable founder provided an income for the schoolmaster but no direct incentive to him or any one else to maintain the efficiency of the school or to try experiments in new methods. The commission on popular education in 1860 found that 'a large proportion of them are not turned to good account at present. . . . It is not so much abuse that now calls for a remedy, as inefficiency, languor, and inadequacy of the results to the pecuniary means of the foundations. . . . Our general evidence as to the present state of these endowments and their present influence on education, we find almost without exception unfavourable and decidedly pointing to the necessity of remedial measures.' And a few years later a Commission on secondary schools reported that 'it is clear from the information which we have ourselves received that there are few endowments applicable to secondary education which are put to the best use, and very many which are working, to little or to bad use'. Popular education was no longer to depend on charity, and pious founders must in future look elsewhere for objects of their benevolence.

The attack on dole charities was even more damaging. As modern theories of relief, with their implications of less eligibility, adequacy, and deterrence were studied, it became clear that the dole charities departed sadly from accepted principles. A charity was founded in Bedford in the reign of Edward VI and endowed with £40 a year. It increased enormously in value, and in 1833 a clergyman of Bedford gave evidence that 'there are very few labouring men in my parish who save anything. The great Bedford Charity has a bad effect on the minds of all the working classes. I have heard an engineer resident in this town say that he dare not employ a Bedford hand, they are so idle.' In Canterbury an Inspector found a population of 18,000 and a dole income of £2,000. He reported that the candidates 'could earn the money over and over again while canvassing for it. . . . A wine merchant said that on the day of the distribution of the 10s. gifts he received seventy sums of 10s. over the counter.' Even worse was the effect of gifts accompanied by the condition that the recipient should attend service in church or perform an act of worship, such as a gift to forty-one poor persons in Leicester who were to receive 4d. each in church on St. Bartholomew's Day 'and to depart glorifying God', while the minister was to receive 4d. for exhorting them after the second lesson 'to praise God for His mercy in providing for the poor', or a gift in another parish for 'such poor women as are most regular in their attendance during divine service'. A curate of a parish where several bread charities were distributed in the church reported that there was not a dissenter in the district, but the gift had a bad moral tendency. The Commissioners in 1833 had no doubts on the subject. 'As to the administration and effect of those charities which are also receivers of the poor's rates,' says the report, '. . . such charities are often wasted and often mischievous. . . . The majority of them are distributed among the poor inhabitants of particular parishes or towns. The places intended to be favoured by large charities attract, therefore, an undue proportion of the poorer classes, who, in the hope of trifling benefits to be obtained without labour, often linger on in spots most unfavourable to the exercise of their industry. Poverty is thus not only collected, but incited, in the very neighbourhood whence the benevolent founders manifestly expected to make it disappear.' And one of the Commissioners, writing in the less restrained pages of the *Edinburgh Review*, went so far as to say that 'any trustee of a public charity for the distribution of Doles who, instead of distributing the substance as intended; consumed it in good cheer for himself and his friends . . . really produced less immorality . . . and was *pro tanto* a benefactor to the public'.

These views gained ground until we find in 1863 members of Parliament speaking of dole charities 'representing an income of £200,000 a year which is frittered away for purposes almost always useless and generally mischievous'.

There were also doubts as to the use of the apprenticeship and loan charities. In 1860 an inspector reported that £50,000 a year of charity revenues was spent on premiums for apprenticeship. He pointed out, a little prematurely perhaps, that apprenticeship 'has almost ceased to exist in our greatest seats of industry' owing to mechanization and subdivision of labour, and, where it still existed, a premium was not as a rule necessary. As for the loan charities the difficulty was to find any use for them at all. There was plenty of money waiting to be lent, but industrious young men were strangely reluctant to borrow it. They preferred, it was said, to obtain private credit, rather than undergo the scrutiny of a Board of Trustees. And it was suggested that loan charities could be used by unscrupulous beneficiaries who could borrow money from the charity at a low rate of interest and immediately lend it out at the current rate.

There was one remarkable exception to the general criticism of charitable foundations. While services of sanitation and public health were being developed, accelerated no doubt by the cholera epidemics of 1831 and 1848, no suggestion was made that hospital treatment was no longer a suitable subject for charity, and, on the whole, the same view prevails to-day, notwithstanding the increasing provision of public institutions offering hospital treatment. This unquestioning acceptance of the voluntary principle was, perhaps, due partly to the known superiority of voluntary hospitals over public infirmaries in the early nineteenth century, and partly to the influence of the leading doctors who gave their services without payment to the hospitals and were not at all attracted by the prospect of control by public authorities.

It is not surprising that, when charitable foundations were being superseded and charitable administration was being criticized, the motives of the charitable should also be called in question. The case against endowers of charities was elaborately set out by Lord Hobhouse in 1868 in a paper on the Characteristics of Charitable Foundations, in which he analysed the motives of pious founders. The leading motives, in his opinion, were 'love of power, ostentation, and vanity'.

'The soul of the dying Testator', he said, 'beats against the barriers of the law which appear to him to confine within such narrow limits the power which he thinks ought to be his, over the property which he fondly believes to be his; . . . he thinks himself ill-used when he finds that he cannot regulate the affairs of two or three unborn generations. It is needless to say how warmly a man of this mental attitude may embrace the notion of extending his dominion by giving his property to public uses for ever. The passions akin to love of power are ostentatiousness, which is gratified by the perpetuation of one's name and money, and vanity, which induces a man to think that he can judge better what Society is likely to want, than Society itself can.'

Next comes superstition, which 'actuates those who believe either that the donor of their estates can promote their advantage after death or that the gift to Charity is in itself a good action atoning for misdeeds'. Spite was also a factor to be noticed. 'Here is credit to be gained, and at the same time the pleasurable sensation of knowing that the faces of the heirs expectant will look very blank when the will is read.' To Patriotism and Public Spirit he awarded only 'a minor place'.

The unkindest blow was struck by Mr. Gladstone, who proposed in 1863 to tax the incomes of endowed charities. In his Budget speech he showed the tendency of Liberal opinion.

'Charitable gifts', he said, 'may be attended in some cases with much benefit, in others with very little; but which very generally tend to gain credit and notoriety for the individual himself, which he would probably not otherwise have enjoyed. As for example, sometimes by his name posted in enormous letters, sometimes by appointing bodies of governors who may meet together at sumptuous banquets from year to year in the name of charity, and thus periodically glorify some pious and immortal memory of a founder.'

Mr. Gladstone and Lord Hobhouse could quote cases to support their views. In many cases the terms of the endowment make it clear that the founder was largely, if not mainly, interested in the perpetuation of his own name. As we have seen, the fortunate beneficiaries from one of the Lichfield charities received cloth gowns with the letters W.F. embroidered on the sleeves in honour of Mr. William Finney the founder. There were also the gift of Henry Greene to supply four poor women with four green waistcoats trimmed with green galloon lace; the gift of Thomas Gray to provide poor men and women with coats and waistcoats of grey cloth; the gift of Edward Rose, which was conditional upon the upkeep of rose-trees on his grave; and the gift of Elizabeth Townsend, conditional upon the singing at morning and evening service on the Sunday before mid-summer day 'the anthem composed by my late husband's grandfather, from the 150th psalm'. And there were charities for the benefit of persons bearing the donor's name, 'the charity', as a Member of Parliament put it, 'of the immortal Jarvis; and the Smith charity, which is devoted to pauperizing the Smiths, and the Guy charity, which is devoted to pauperizing the Guys'. There is pathos in the report of an inspector who found an almshouse bearing an inscription with the name of the founder 'whose glorious memory as well as illustrious favours ought not to be forgotten, but kept, as 'tis to be hoped they will, in everlasting remembrance'. The inspector reported that the almshouse was a nest of disease and a permanent nuisance.

Most of those eccentric trusts, which were freely quoted in Parliament, were created long before the nineteenth century. But there were in the early Victorian charities enough indications of patronage and enough of the practice of commemorating the name of the donor to make it impossible to deny that 'love of power, ostentation, and vanity' were in many respects connected with them.

But if we admit that these motives were often not absent from the minds of Victorian benefactors, we need by no means admit that they were the leading motives. We have an advantage over Lord Hobhouse and Mr. Gladstone, who were perhaps too closely involved in the history of their time to take that detached view which becomes possible to a later generation. An examination of Victorian history makes it clear that one of the great qualities of charitable Victorians was persistence. The great increase in charitable subscriptions in the early nineteenth century may have been due in part to fear of revolution. But if they began to give in fear they went on giving long after fear had given place to complete security; they continued to give when public services were displacing the institutions which their gifts had supported; and they gave no less freely when the possibilities of ostentation and self-glorification were replaced by the modern method, which tends to limit publicity to an entry in the annual report. Their motives were no doubt mixed, but the persistence of their contributions through changing circumstances shows that their ruling motives were genuine philanthropy and a steadfast determination to perform what they believed to be their duty.

XVI

EXPANSION AND EMIGRATION

EXPANSION AND EMIGRATION

By DOUGLAS WOODRUFF

§ I. COLONIAL POLICY AND EMIGRATION

THE overseas possessions of the English Crown at the time when Victoria came to the throne, though geographically very much what they are at present, were hardly settled at all, and their small populations aroused little interest at home. The East India Company held most of what is British India to-day and in addition trading settlements farther east, at Penang and Singapore, which were both to be centres from which in the later Victorian decades British influence was to spread over the Malay Peninsula. The port of Hong Kong was acquired and created for the China trade, and a vague and general protection was accorded to the King of the Sandwich Islands, but otherwise the Pacific islands had not been collected by the various powers. Although the whole island of Australia had been taken for the Crown and the fear of French settlements led both in Australia and New Zealand to hasty British settlement, the parts of the continent in actual occupation were no more than the coast round Sydney harbour, Van Diemen's Land, not yet rechristened Tasmania, small new settlements destined to be Victoria and South Australia, and the first beginnings of the Swan River Settlement, which was after much travail to become Western Australia. A group of colonists at the Cape of Good Hope had already begun to force the Home Government to attend to South African politics and to watch their interests in relation to Boer and Hottentot and Zulu. Farther up the African coast, trading forts on the Slave and Guinea Coasts languished since the suppression of the slave-trade. There were no settlements on the east coast and the interior was still a dark mystery. The West Indies, just facing the problem of how to produce and trade after the emancipation of the negroes, had such old and strong commercial ties with Great Britain that the fortunes of the sugar interest could never be a matter of indifference. In the north of the new world the Canadas meant two uncomfortable settlements of

French and English agriculturists, few in number and failing to get on either with each other or with the governors sent out from England. The various islands, of which Malta was perhaps the chief and St. Helena among the least, which had been retained from the era of the Great War, had governors and garrisons and were involved in the widespread general dislike of anything military. Disraeli, as yet far from the Imperial dawn of the seventies, made them the objects of his youthful scorn in the *Voyage of Captain Popanilla* (in 1828), and while the Army and Navy found the governorships of these places useful for disposing of half-pay officers with claims, and the Duke besprinkled them with garrisons as a way of hiding the Army and concealing its size from civilian jealousy, radicals and humanitarians alike felt a strong distaste for a colonial system which seemed an appanage of the warlike services.

Harriet Martineau, writing in the late forties her extremely popular *History of the Thirty Years' Peace*, declared roundly 'the government of our Colonies has long been so intolerable, that we cannot expect to retain them, unless some speedy and comprehensive reform is carried out'. She selected for special denunciation 'Taxes trebled at a stroke, favouritism towards public officers, or ill-usage of them, quarrels between governors and their coadjutors, tricks with the currency, executive extravagance', and she represented a generation profoundly aware that the United States had succeeded in breaking away and prospering, and equally convinced that despotic control, whether by the Colonial Office or naval and army officers made into governors, was rightly bound to fail. People who had cheered themselves hoarse over the Reform Bill of 1832 could not but believe that Parliaments were good everywhere and for everybody, and if you had sympathy with the Chartists you would at once side with the first colonist with a grievance against his governor.

The Tories had little enthusiasm for remote places, especially after Parliament agreed to the free admission of Canadian corn in 1843. Behind the small Canadian crop they saw the large American one, and they were unconvinced that duties in Canada itself against American corn would give the necessary protection. They had no time to become convinced, because free Canadian corn proved the forerunner of general free trade in a few short years. Free trade made the

THE LAST OF ENGLAND—*FORD MADOX BROWN*

By permission of the Museum and Art Gallery
Committee of the Corporation of Birmingham

whole idea of Colonies look as if it belonged to a bygone age, but in a few years the Radicals had the chagrin of witnessing the freely elected assemblies which they had supported for the Colonies, mark their appearance on the political scene by tariffs against Great Britain.

The countries which are now the Dominions received from Great Britain in these, their critical early days, the men and the money by which they grew. But they received them unofficially and erratically at a time when the current political feeling at home was often hostile and generally indifferent. The very people who shouted most dogmatically that the colonists must enjoy complete freedom were the most determined, as lovers of peace and retrenchment and free trade, that Great Britain must spend as little as possible. But most public men specialized in other questions. Mr. Gladstone, after a long speech in 1851 in favour of increasing the legislative independence of Australian colonies, comments on the apathetic House—'spoke $1\frac{1}{2}$ hours on the Australian Colonies Bill to an indifferent inattentive House. But it is necessary to speak these truths of Colonial policy even to unwilling ears.' The spirit of Adam Smith, the principal tutor of the nineteenth century, ruled the majority, and Adam Smith had declared that 'under the present system of management Great Britain derived nothing but loss from the dominion over her Colonies'. Through the thirties and the forties and the fifties, the general attitude of responsible public men was that the Colonies should be encouraged to become as independent as possible. Utilitarians like James Mill, Grote, and Warburton, Radicals like Cobden and Joseph Hume, evangelicals with missionary interests like Sir James Stephen, the permanent head of the Colonial Office, Parliamentarians like Roebuck, all looked on the Colonies as problems which in time would solve themselves by walking away.

Gladstone represented a school of thought which made it a matter of high and painful duty to continue to administer the Colonies until they had developed not only representative institutions but the capacity to use them. He asked his contemporaries a disturbing question when he asked why the Colonies, with all the ready talk there was in England of conferring freedom upon them, were failing to produce citizens at all comparable in elevation of understanding and character with the men who made the United States and signed the Declaration of Independence. Disraeli modified his earlier petulant expressions about the wretched Colonies being millstones round our necks, and by the early fifties was pointing out that every emigrant became an English colonist and every colonist a customer who stimulated trade at home. After the long honeymoon of Free Trade was over and the first doubts about Great Britain's permanent ability to under-sell the rest of the world began to be felt, more voices were heard suggesting that the Empire might be an asset after all, but that was not the point of view of early Victorian days.

There was, indeed, a group of men who differed from the prevailing view that Colonies were offences against the laws of economics and progressive politics, and this group, though small, had some influential members and was able to force many of its ideas upon ministers who had no particular ideas of their own. The name of Lord Durham, who, as one of the lieutenants of the Lord Grey of the Reform Bill, served an apprenticeship in Liberal doctrine, stands affixed to the report on Canada which is the classic statement of the doctrine of self-government. The Colonial Reformers were an active group some years before the Queen's accession. They derived their impetus from a remarkable character, Edward Gibbon Wakefield, a man of Quaker stock, related to the Frys. He was not over-scrupulous and his sojourn in Newgate for abducting an heiress (his second abduction) disqualified him for the public positions to which he might have aspired. But his restless energy and wide ideas enabled him to work through other men, and he influenced notably Lord Durham and Charles Buller and Sir William Molesworth. These men all died young and left no school. Their heyday was the thirties, when they were the only people with constructive proposals, and the only people less interested in the West Indies and Emancipation than in the new countries. But they worked against inertia, and a general ignorance which saw the Colonies, if it saw them at all, only as a further field for applying one or other of the ruling political philosophies, not as something new and unique. In the absence of active public opinion, the Colonial Office enjoyed almost unfettered power, and the colonial reformers, when they could not convert officialdom to their plans, indulged in bitter attacks on the Office, on Mr. Mother Country, and on Mr. Over-Secretary Stephen.

In the first half of Queen Victoria's reign the Colonial Office stood at the top of Downing Street, where the steps to-day go down to St. James's Park. It consisted of old houses of the kind of which numbers 10 and 11 are now the sole survivors, houses which had been built for private occupation in the reign of Charles the Second and which were recognized from the very beginning of the Queen's reign to be quite unfitted to house the ever-growing accumulation of papers and the constantly extending staff both of the Colonial Office and of the Foreign Office which adjoined it. In 1839 the Parliamentary Commission which considered these buildings described them as wholly unsuitable, and put forward the first plans for the buildings which twenty to thirty years later were actually to arise, and which stand to this day. In the evidence before that Commission, the librarian and architect to the Office stated that the quantity of correspondence had doubled in the last twelve years and had risen to ten or twelve thousand letters a year. But the Office was a minor one, and if the Colonial Secretary sat in the Cabinet it was primarily because he was Secretary for War at the same time. Between the Napoleonic Wars and the Crimean War the Colonies were the charge of the War Minister, and it has been well said that it needed one war to take the plantations away from the Home Secretary and another war (the Crimean) to take them from the Minister of War.

There was a rapid succession of Colonial Secretaries—over twenty in the first thirty years of the Queen's reign—the longest tenures being those of Stanley, afterwards Prime Minister as Lord Derby (1841–5), the third Earl Grey (1846–52), and the fifth Duke of Newcastle (1859–64). Except Newcastle, who accompanied the Prince of Wales to the Chicago Exhibition via Canada in 1860, none visited any part of the Empire or showed any real comprehension of the new communities. Stanley disliked the whole idea of responsible government and only yielded to it from necessity and because he was equally averse to any full assumption of responsibility and expense by Great Britain. His defects as a Colonial Secretary come out very clearly in *The Statesman*, published by one of the ablest men in the Colonial Office, Sir Henry Taylor, in 1836. Taylor was then only thirty-six, and it is obvious that the chief on whose conduct his apophthegms are based was Stanley. He writes much about the disadvantage it is to an Office when its head is more intent on general parliamentary business and upon cutting a figure in Debate than upon the actual subjects with which the Office is concerned. Stanley had some sympathy with migration, but otherwise he made no positive contributions to the future. Earl Grey developed much greater enthusiasm for the Colonies, and the long vindication for his actions which he published, a year after leaving office in 1852, is one of the best handbooks remaining to us in which to follow the workings of the early Victorian mind in Colonial matters. Accepting to the full the dogma of Free Trade, Grey accepted less readily the doctrine of Free Government. Sir Charles Adderley (Lord Norton), himself Colonial Secretary in 1866, published on leaving office an exhaustive review of Earl Grey's work, definitely charging him with failure to appreciate feeling in the Colonies or the possibilities of the new communities. Adderley's book, at the end of the sixties (in sharp contrast to the works which enjoyed so much interest in the forties, like George Cornwall Lewis's *Treatise on Colonies*, proving that they had no advantages whatever), may be taken with Charles Dilke's *Greater Britain* in 1867 as the beginning of the new Imperialism which was to grow and flourish in the seventies and eighties.

But the most important figure from the point of view of the Empire was not one of the politicians, but Sir James Stephen, the permanent head of the Colonial Office from 1836 to 1847. Stephen, the nephew by marriage of Wilberforce, came from the heart of the Clapham abolitionists and was as ardently devoted to the cause of the abolition of slavery as any of those who worked for it inside or outside Parliament. His father, a barrister in the West Indies, had become the ally and brother-in-law of Wilberforce, and from inherited devotion to the cause of abolition Stephen himself soon forsook his good prospects at the Chancery Bar to become first standing counsel to the Colonial Office and then first permanent Under-Secretary. He was a man of enormous capacity, who drafted the Act of Abolition during a week-end, but he damaged even his powers by the wide range of the labours which he conducted single-handed.

Government posts were elastically filled, and Stephen, after ceasing to be permanent Under-Secretary, left to become Professor of History at Cambridge, while his successor was Herman Merivale, who had already been Professor of Political Economy at Oxford. Sir Henry Taylor, who was only second in importance to Stephen himself and who was offered and who refused, through delicacy of feeling, the succession to the Under-Secretaryship, was also a man whose interests were very much wider than his work. His auto-biography makes it plain that he thought of himself first and foremost as a poet who would be remembered by *Philip van Artevelde*. He was appointed to the office as a young man mainly on the strength of literary articles he had contributed to the *Quarterly Review*. He was a man, like Stephen, of great intellectual ability, who in Gladstone's judgement only lacked ambition to become one of the great public men of his time. He specialized in the West Indian business and the reputation he assumed in the minds of planters contrasted ludicrously with his youthful appearance and the literary predilections which made him anything but the crabbed dictator of planters' imaginations. James Spedding was marked out for high place in the office, but academic interests soon gained complete ascendancy and he left to devote himself to pro-ducing the standard edition of Bacon.

In 1846 the defence of the Colonies was costing Great Britain £4,000,000 a year, while the total value of the export trade of the Colonies was only £8,000,000. For every £1 worth of goods sold the country was finding 10s. for defence, and this had much to do with the general lack of enthusiasm with which the whole Colonial question was regarded. The successive Acts conferring political freedom upon overseas communities met with no strong opposition because every-body hoped that, by these Acts, the burden of the defence would be transferred to the Colonies themselves. About native peoples opinion had become less sanguine. Merivale in 1861 could not descry any real missionary progress in the twenty years since he had pointed to religious instruction as the chief means of raising native races, and he had begun to talk of extinction as the melancholy termination of the pros-pects before them. At the time when his Oxford lectures on the Colonies were first given in 1837–40 he, like everybody else, was largely influenced in his picture of the natives by the accounts of the North American Indians and the romances of Fenimore Cooper. It was natural to assume a degree of progress which did not in fact take place anywhere, and successive tales of

Kaffir wars, of Maori wars, and of trouble in Australia, changed
the general attitude into one which was the forerunner of the
later Imperialism and supported the Strong White Ruler in
whatever measures he might take. This attitude was greatly
strengthened by any outbreaks in Colonies where there was
no frontier, and the rising in Ceylon in 1848, the great Indian
Mutiny, the Jamaican rebellion of 1865 all supplied arguments for the view of which Carlyle had made himself the
great exponent in his Occasional Discourse on the Nigger
Question (1849), soundly rating Exeter Hall philanthropy
and crying out beware lest the Universal Abolition-of-Pain
Association should become a Universal Sluggard and Scoun-
drel Protection Society, and reiterating that the lower races
must be firmly ruled and made to work.

Merivale is the permanent official whose views have come
down to us in most systematic form. But the letters and
diaries of his immediate predecessor and successor, and of the
copious Taylor, make their attitudes not less plain. All were,
with greater or smaller intensity of conviction, separatists.
It was in the prevailing intellectual atmosphere that Colonies
belonged to an old and vanishing order of affairs, to the days
of the old French and Spanish monarchies and not to the new
age. It was the North American settlements in particular
that people in England were prepared to lose, and the fear
of becoming embroiled with the United States, whose general
attitude was unfriendly while their power was growing, gave
edge to the ordinary economic and political arguments in
favour of separation. The argument from prestige, that it
became the greatness of England to have Colonies, was one
that riled alike the severely practical and prosaic men like
Sir George Lewis and the deeply religious men like Stephen
and Rogers. Frederick Rogers, later Lord Blachford, the
third of the distinguished men who were the real rulers of the
Colonial Office, succeeded Merivale in 1859 and retired in
1870. He was as devout a Tractarian as Stephen was an
Evangelical, a fellow of Oriel who in the thirties and down
to 1845 had been the closest of Newman's friends. His other
intimates were men belonging to the same Oxford school, like
Hope Scott, and it was through Gladstone that he became, in
his middle thirties, a Commissioner for Emigration in 1846
and so entered the Colonial Office.

Roebuck was not alone in arguing that even if the other

Colonies remained, Canada ought to be vigorously and promptly emancipated to clear away the danger of a war with the States. So far from there being an eager acquisition of oversea territory, such cupidity had no responsible advocates; English statesmen had just taken a leading part in destroying the Empire of the French and in freeing, for purposes of international lending and trade, the great colonies of Spain and Portugal in the new world, and the gilt on the Imperial idea was very dull. It was as though Colonies were somehow not quite correct, an embarrassment inherited from a wilder youth, to be schooled and set up in respectable trades as soon as possible, and not to be talked about too much. The few who saw the possibilities, given the right policy in the first stages, of the wonderful new lands, achieved much because there was no clear will opposed to them, but they could not prevent the continuance of the half-hearted policy which let the new countries pass suddenly into a complete independence, at first political and then deeper, jumping from minute control by the Colonial Office to the ownership of whole continents with protective tariffs against the mother country.

There was, however, one point at which the Colonies always aroused a wide measure of interest. Through the distress of the thirties and the hungry forties, when unemployment relative to population was as bad as anything we have known since, the remedy of emigration was widely discussed. There were plenty of Free Traders before Free Trade was achieved who belittled the possibilities of emigration because they thought it was being introduced as a red herring to lead discussion away from the primary necessity of cheap food for the mass of the poor. They feared the argument that emigration could relieve distress and that the population, thus judiciously pruned, could be supported from the land at home. But, this apart, the Radicals had to approve a movement which was so clear an illustration of the mobility of labour.

As soon as Lord John Russell became responsible for the Colonies in Melbourne's administration he created a Government body, an offshoot of the Colonial Office, to exercise a measure of control over emigration in accordance with Wakefield's ideas. This body was the Colonial Land and Emigration Commission. It consisted of two men and a secretary of long experience in emigration matters. Its duties were wide on paper but small in practice. It established emigration offices at the ports and supervised the Passenger Acts regulating the conditions under which emigrants travelled. It collected and disseminated accurate information about conditions overseas and on the journey. But its most important duty was to pay the passage of emigrants, in particular, and indeed mainly, to Australia, from money received from the sale of crown lands in the Colonies. During the forties, when it was busiest, the Commission did not attract any parliamentary attention. During the fifties, when its work had begun to lessen because the Colonies could make their own arrangements, while there was no longer the same measure of poverty in Great Britain, Parliament debated its Vote every year. By the sixties it was ripe for abolition, but it lasted down to 1878, when its information side was carried on by another Board.

This body, which boasted when challenged that it received and answered on an average a hundred letters a day, deserves its niche in any record of the Victorian attitude to the Empire. But its political chiefs were always emphatic that it did not exist to promote emigration, to increase the flow, but only to control it. Nevertheless the fact that the fare to Australia—a matter then of £17 at the least—could be paid for the emigrant was an obviously important inducement. This money was found as a gift after various unsuccessful trials at advancing it with an understanding, cheerfully ignored by emigrants, that it was to be repaid. It was advanced in the interests of the Australian Colonies, in accordance with Wakefield's insistence upon a supply of labourers, who would be unable to set up straightaway as farmers on their own because land had to be paid for, and it was not, like the money which parish authorities were allowed after 1834 to use for emigration, intended primarily to relieve destitution in the United Kingdom. Of this Parochial Emigration there was at no time very much. The overwhelming majority of emigrants paid their way with their own savings or with the help of those who have always been the chief emigration agents, relatives and friends already overseas.

The few keen advocates of systematic emigration carried on their work amid general indifference and apathy. Thomas

Carlyle in *Latter-Day Pamphlets* (1850), Charles Kingsley in *Alton Locke,* could speak enthusiastically on the importance of emigration for the working classes. But actual plans came from a very small group. In 1848 the newly formed Society for the Promotion of Colonization laid down that its aim was rather 'to regulate the course of emigration than to swell its content, to afford correct information, and (so far as its funds permit) direct assistance to those whose emigration may seem desirable, not only on their own account but on that of the Colonies or of this country'. The Society avowed that it aimed at 'making emigration what it ought to be, a premium on good conduct'. It had begun as the 'Labourers' Relief Emigration Society', and it was praised in the press and held successful public meetings. It devised a scheme for assisting emigrants who were healthy and able-bodied, and laid down careful rules for the amount and kind of provisions and clothing they must take. A number of trade unions had emigration funds, to buy lands which they then sold to their members. Thus the Potters' Joint Stock and Emigration Company in 1844 set out to purchase 12,000 acres in the Western States, to which many of its members, paying six-pence weekly, eventually emigrated. The Potters' Union, like other unions, was trying to find a way of affording per-manent relief to its unemployed members and the practice was fairly common for some twenty years. It has never altogether ceased, but as a general rule unions found all emigration money swallowed up immediately by an endless number of applicants.

There was an annual Government Vote available for emigration throughout the years with which this chapter deals. It was not large and never exceeded £25,000, and it went to maintain emigration agents (half-pay Lieutenants) at the chief ports. Special grants were made in times of special difficulty, as in 1847, and parish authorities had power, after 1834, to raise money on the rates for the pur-pose of freeing themselves for good and all of poor people who were settled in their parish. This power was transferred in 1844 to Guardians from churchwardens and overseers. At a time when some 18,000 people on an average were emigrating every year, this parochial relief only accounted for some 1,400, and parish assistance gradually fell off even from that low standard. The people who became chargeable on the rates were, as a class, aged or infirm, or else their need for help was very temporary, and a parish did not see why it should make the large outlay of several pounds which emigration involved.

In general, the mass of emigrants had to make their own way, and if they received help it was from relatives already established on the other side. The Government, which noted the beginnings of voluntary enterprises, was afraid to smother them by doing a great deal itself. The side of emigration about which it took most trouble was the actual journey, which was the subject of unresting regulation, and, as we shall see, such regulation was plainly called for.

Victorian fiction takes, on the whole, very slight notice of the Colonies, but Victorian novels with black sheep in them could hardly fail to use emigration as a remedy. Judged on their literary remains the Early Victorians found Australia the most useful part of the Empire, and there is a majority among the writing men in favour of the Antipodes as a solution, permanent or temporary, of the difficulties in which they involve their characters. Those most famous emigrants, the Micawbers, and Abel Magwitch, are matched by the central figure of Charles Reade's enormously popular *It's Never too Late to Mend*, where much of the action is boldly placed in Australia, although the author had never seen the country, by Henry Kingsley's *Geoffry Hamlyn*, and by many a minor Trollope character, as e.g. in the *Three Clerks* or *Dr. Thorne*. Trollope, alone of major Victorian writers of fiction, had a keen interest in the colonies and made a number of journeys from 1858 onwards, giving conclusions based on first-hand observation. If he was in favour of separation, it was from the point of view of the Colonies themselves, and he wrote the soundest of sense against the people who objected both to seeing the Colonies independent and to paying for their defence, an attitude which reminded him of 'an ancient pater-familias who insists on having his children and grandchildren under the old parental roof, and then grumbles because the butcher's bill is high'. He could write in the strain of exaltation later to become commoner about England's 'noble mission', but it was a mission to beget nations, and civilize countries, not to maintain them in subjection to the Queen.

Trollope was much more interested in the White Empire, the countries which even while he wrote were beginning with

Canada to find the blessed word Dominion for themselves. But as the later half of the Queen's reign began, the backward peoples, slow to be taught, and full of hidden fires, had come only too plainly into the consciousness of people at home. Little wars in South Africa and New Zealand, sudden outbreaks in Ceylon and the West Indies, the descriptions of Livingstone and other African travellers, above all the great Indian Mutiny, these events provided the basis for a new Imperialism, for the view that the dominant white race must not abdicate before barbarians but must rule, and as news also came home which showed how in the least settled parts of Africa or the Pacific the unofficial white man, trading without conscience for his immediate profit, was the actual alternative to the flag and the official, the early Victorian enthusiasm for standing aside and keeping out of fresh commitments gave place to a recognition, on which later Imperialists built their large structure, that it was better to settle down to the interesting business of governing than to tolerate the evils of unregulated intercourse or to yield the work to foreign powers.

§ 2. CANADA: THE ATLANTIC PASSAGE

In the first thirty years of Queen Victoria's reign, over three-quarters of a million people left Great Britain and Ireland to settle in British North America. Nearly another million went to Australia or New Zealand. But over three and a half million went to the United States. Well over five million people emigrated, of whom about two million were Irish. In the five years following the potato famine of 1847 a million and a half of these Irish were driven overseas to be the ancestors of the Irish Americans of to-day. They have little place in a story of Victorian England, and their exodus from the statistical tables, and a further deduction which must be made for the foreign emigrants, especially in the sixties, who sailed from U.K. ports, leaves a still high figure in proof of the steady streams of English people who were driven by poverty or adventure or reasoned hopes of betterment to take their chance in the new world.

The English and Scotch divided themselves between the States and Canada. The United States was already a country of ten million people—what Canada is to-day—when the Queen came to the throne. These were the great days of the

America of the Mississippi and the Western democracy. They begin when Andrew Jackson has just installed himself in the White House as the representative of the common man from the West, the man who had been held under in the careful plans of Hamilton and the Fathers of the Constitution, who had made his way to the great river and who was making the new states year by year. They close, a generation later, when Lincoln, another common man from the West, has preserved the Union and settled the future development of the country as a dangerously large political unit. What the growing States were like in those years, many travellers have put on record, and the pages of *American Notes* and *Martin Chuzzlewit*, of Miss Martineau's *Society in America* and Mrs. Trollope's *Domestic Manners of the Americans*, describing her courageous attempt to keep shop in Cincinnati, revealed to early Victorian England a clear view of the strange new society beyond the Atlantic, highly repugnant and reciprocating the dislike it inspired, but singularly open, and free for the acquisition of fortune.

The American Chamber of Commerce had opened an office in Liverpool in 1823 in order to persuade men to emigrate. In 1831 His Majesty's Commissioners followed the example and began to distribute information about Canada. But the great tides of emigration were moved by the success of those who had gone before. The United States were an old country compared with Canada. They had manufactures and had for a generation been enticing skilled workmen from England to help them to become independent of English goods, so that in the first decade of Victoria's reign exports from Great Britain in many articles declined, and many an artisan short of work heard from an older relative, now prospering in the States, of the land where there was a growing market for whatever he could do. The States were the place for the urban pioneer, the man with a trade. They were a magnet, as they remained till very recently, drawing away from the Canadian settlements a heavy toll of skilled men, because they were able to reward them well.

Nevertheless, a steady stream of settlers went out to Canada. In the forties it was commonly over 30,000 each year. The year of the Queen's accession was the year of rebellion in Canada, which sharply checked emigration for the moment, but which led in a year to greater interest in and official care for the Canadas, with the publication of Lord Durham's report.

The passage to North America in sailing vessels took on an average six to eight weeks, but might often last longer, perhaps eleven weeks. The large numbers of emigrants prevented any effective competition to provide good conditions on the ships, which did, after all, take emigrants very cheaply. Three pounds, without food, was a common price. Every few years since the beginning of the century, Parliament had issued regulations. In 1835 all former laws were repealed and a comprehensive Statute was issued. Ships had to be surveyed and declared seaworthy. If they carried more than a hundred people, there must be a surgeon on board. The quantity of spirits sold was limited. If the ship did not sail on the appointed day, the emigrants had to be fed. And so on. What the conditions were like is on record in Lord Durham's report, telling how emigrant ships could be known by their smell alone at gunshot range, how typhus and other diseases spread rapidly among a congested company of ill-nourished people, and how infectious disease was repeatedly carried to Quebec. Lord Durham declared that two actions of the Provincial Government, a head tax on passengers landing, whose proceeds supplied health services, and the establishment of a quarantine station, had done more to remedy matters than the Act of 1835. Effective control at the English end only came in 1840, following the Durham report. Then the Colonial Land and Emigration Commissioners were appointed to supervise emigrant ships. A new Act, in 1842, regulated the amount of space each emigrant must have, and the Commissioners eventually took the important decision that food must be included in the cost of the ticket. The food which the emigrants had had to provide for themselves and to cook gave Mark Tapley an excellent chance of being cheerful, because it was a source of much suffering. Passengers only too often under-estimated the length of the voyage, and were encouraged to do so by captains who came to their rescue when supplies were exhausted by selling them food at extortionate prices. The well-advised took food for ten weeks. Potatoes were liable to rot, and the best provisions were oatmeal, beef, eggs in salt, ship's biscuit, and hard-baked loaf bread. But the new rule whereby ships had to feed their passengers commonly resulted in the provision of very miserable fare. A philanthropist who travelled steerage in 1850 and published his experiences describes the extreme brutality of the crew of the ship. The passenger who wrote a letter of complaint to the captain was felled by the first mate and the whole of the passengers were punished by receiving half rations next day. What food was given was raw, and to get near the fires it was necessary to bribe the sailors. Some serious injuries were wantonly inflicted on the passengers by the mates and 'twelve children died of dysentery, or, more truthfully, from want of nourishing food'.

The rules which were laid down after experience of the Acts of 1835 and 1842, by the Emigration Commissioners, are set out in the Colonial Land and Emigration Commission Annual for 1848.

(1) Every passenger to rise at 7 a.m. unless otherwise permitted by the surgeon.

(2) Breakfast from 8–9 a.m., dinner at 1 p.m., supper at 6 p.m.

(3) Passengers to be in their beds by 10 p.m.

(4) Fires to be lighted by passengers' cook at 7 a.m. and kept alight by him till 7 p.m., then to be extinguished.

(5) Three safety-lamps to be lit at dusk; one to be kept burning all night in main hatchway; two others may be extinguished at 10 p.m.

(6) No naked light to be allowed at any time or on any account.

(7) The passengers when dressed, to roll up their beds, to sweep the decks, including the space under the bottom of berths, and to throw the dirt overboard.

(8) Breakfast not to commence till this is done.

(9) The sweepers for each day to be taken in rotation from the males above 14, in the proportion of 5 for every 100 passengers.

(10) Duties of the sweepers to be to clean the ladders, hospitals, and roundhouses, to sweep the decks after every meal and to dry, holystone, and scrape them after breakfast.

(11) The occupant of every berth to see that his own berth is well brushed out.

(12) The beds to be well shaken and aired on the decks and the bottom boards, if not fixtures, to be removed and dry scrubbed and taken on deck at least twice a week.

(13) Two days in the week to be applied by the master as washing days, but no clothes to be washed or dried between decks.

(14) The coppers and cooking vessels to be cleaned every day.

(15) The scuttles and sternposts, if any, to be kept open (W.P.) from 7 a.m. to 7 p.m., and the hatches at all hours.

(16) Hospitals to be established with an area, in ships carrying 100

MARCO POLO

JAMES BAINES

EMIGRANT SHIPS

By courtesy of Thomas H. Parker, Ltd.

passengers, of not less than 48 superficial feet with two or four bed berths.

(17) On Sundays the passengers to be mustered at 10 a.m., when they will be expected to appear in clean and decent apparel. The day to be observed as religiously as circumstances admit.

(18) No spirits or gunpowder to be taken on board by any passenger.

(19) No smoking allowed between decks.

(20) All fighting, gambling, riotous behaviour, swearing, or violent language to be at once put a stop to. Swords and other offensive weapons, as soon as passengers embark, to be placed in the custody of the Master.

(21) No sailor to remain on the passenger deck among the passengers except when on duty.

(22) No passenger to go to the ship's cook-house without special permission of the Master.

But the old traditions died hard, and the plan of making of the passengers model prisoners could not always succeed in making of the ship a model jail. Nor could any regulations at sea remove the sufferings at the port of embarkation. Emigrants were a simple class. Arriving with bundles containing all their possessions, they became the ready prey of rogues at the ports who exploited them to the full. They were not allowed on board ship till just before sailing time and had to hang about for days among people who sold them rubbish for the voyage and changed their money at exorbitant rates.

The Government was ashamed of the class of people who emigrated, and Lord Grey, in the Apologia which he published in 1852, on leaving the Colonial Office after six years as Colonial Secretary, frankly declared that one of the leading considerations against Government emigration was that it deprived the Government of its best answer to the complaints from North America—the plea that there were no powers of selection or prohibition and that anybody who chose could leave Great Britain.

How bad things could still be, after years of remedial legislation, is told in an account of the voyage of the *Mary Bradford* to New York as late as 1865. On this ship, all the clean counterpanes and mattresses were removed as soon as the emigration officer had left the ship: the overcrowding and poor food, especially when storms had thrown out the calculation of direction, were as bad as twenty years before. The real salvation of the emigrant came from the steamship.

The Cunard Company had four liners by 1840, and by 1850 steamships were rapidly capturing the traffic. There were fewer small owners in the business, and with regular sailings in shorter time the death-rate began to fall. The horrors of shipwreck, which had been far too frequent among the sailing ships, faded into memory, and by 1860 the voyage had been robbed of its worst hardships. By that year six out of every seven emigrants were going under steam.

National societies existed in Canada, St. George (founded in 1835), St. Andrew, and St. Patrick, to look after the poor emigrants on arrival. Emigrants who had been sent out by a parish and who found themselves stranded, perhaps with a wife and young children, were rescued by these Societies, and their wants relieved. The tax which the Colonial Legislatures placed on emigrants aroused some irritation in England, and Lord Stanley, speaking in the House in 1849, said that he would have to advise his tenants to choose the United States. Earl Grey in reply said that the tax was used in services to the emigrants, such as transporting them to localities where there was work for them.

The emigrant landing in Canada found himself amid primitive conditions. The text-book which, in the words of one pioneer settler, 'first awakened among tens of thousands of British readers a keen interest in the backwoods of what is now the Province of Ontario' was Martin Boyle's *Hints on Emigration to Upper Canada*. This popular little work appeared first in 1831. It argued in favour of Canada against the United States, claiming for Canada a better climate and better prices for produce, as well as the advantage of life among one's own people. It inspired confidence by its honest tone and avowed that any one in a good position in England should remain content and said, frankly and admirably, that North America was not suited to ladies and gentlemen of very small means, who were unused to doing anything for themselves. What it did offer was vicissitude of climate, and the chance to work hard, and it was the best possible place for those without a shilling in their pockets.

The author of another popular work, *The Emigrant's Handbook of Facts*, published in Glasgow in 1843, hailed Canada as 'the poor man's home'. He uttered a strong warning against going to the United States, quoting a statement that more than a third of the European emigrants died within three years of arrival. The great danger was being set upon by harpies in the American ports, and inveigled into lodging there and looking for town employment. Savings dribbled away and poverty led to crime and misery. The country was the salvation of the emigrant, and in Canada there was little else. Much, the author warned would-be emigrants, must be cheerfully forgone. The refinements of life as lived in England would not be possible, and country labourers made the best emigrants. But all with the strength for outdoor labour, especially if they were married with the asset of children, should do well. The handbook thought it necessary to destroy a widespread impression that poor emigrants were supported by the Government on arrival, and were forwarded free to whatever place they wished to reach.

The information in these and similar books was accurate enough. English emigrants at this time went to Ontario, and particularly along the Ottawa river: they found good land, a climate that became extremely cold in winter, the roads rough and few. The Red Indians were already, by the beginning of the reign, 'disappointingly respectable'. The towns were few and small, Toronto, Hamilton, London, Newcastle, Woodstock, and were crowded with the poorest of the Irish emigrants. The forest roads of Ontario are vividly described by a traveller of the time,[1] driving in the coach between Hamilton and Woodstock.

'The seemingly interminable line of trees before you; the boundless wilderness around; the mysterious depths amid the multitudinous foliage, where foot of man hath never penetrated, which partial gleams of the noontide sun, now seen, now lost, lit up with a changeful, magical beauty; the wondrous splendour and novelty of the flowers; the silence, unbroken but by the low cry of a bird, or hum of an insect, or the splash and croak of some huge bull-frog; and the solitude in which we proceeded, no human being, no human dwelling, within sight, are all exciting to the fancy, or oppressive to the spirits according to the mood one may be in.'

And the mood was often a dispirited one, due to the strain of travelling in primitive Canadian coaches over primitive Canadian roads.

'We often sank', says this same traveller, 'into mud-holes above the axle tree; then over trunks of trees laid across swamps, called here

[1] *Winter Studies and Summer Rambles*, by Mrs. Jameson, p. 113.

first alarmed at the finding of gold, and tried to suppress the news, until it was pointed out that there could be no better way of securing free immigrants, and of attracting people who were going to California. Government rewards were offered for gold, and the Ballarat diggings, enormously successful, were begun. Although licences, costing 30s., were necessary, no such slight restriction could impede the rush, and Ballarat, from being a place of peaceful repose, of wattles and cattle, and an almost painful solitude, became a second San Francisco, with men sitting up all night with pistols to guard their heaps.

Governor Latrobe wrote to Earl Grey that within three weeks Melbourne and Geelong and their suburbs were practically emptied, men in good positions going off into the crowd, very often because they had no alternative when their assistants all forsook them. 'Cottages are deserted, houses to let, business is at a standstill, and even schools are closed. In some of the suburbs not a man is left.' Thousands of newcomers flocked into Australia, and the profits made by buyers were enormous until the Sydney Mint was established, with a fixed price for gold, in 1855. The pastoral industry, which found a sudden new demand for food and clothing, was greatly strengthened by the gold rushes, but there entered into the political life of the colonies a new and violent radical element.

Episodes like that of the Eureka Camp Stockade, in 1859, when miners resisted the Government by force to prevent the collection of licences, spread in Great Britain a lively sense of the roughness and perils of Australian life, but, in fact, the gold-mining business was passing rapidly into the hands of companies. Ousted in the economic field, the free diggers placed more and more reliance on political action. In the fifties manhood suffrage became the law in South Australia, Victoria, and New South Wales, and a population which had risen from under half a million in 1851 to over a million ten years later, was launched on the full experiment of Parliamentary democracy.

§ 4. NEW ZEALAND

Although Captain Cook's *Voyages* had dealt so largely with New Zealand, New Zealand was the last of the present Dominions to arouse interest in Great Britain. Two Maori chiefs had been brought to England in 1820, to help produce a Maori grammar at Cambridge, but this was the doing of the missionaries, notably of the Church Missionary Society, and Samuel Marsden, who had his base in New South Wales. The stories of Maori fierceness made the islands seem most formidable and uninviting. When private schemes for colonization began to be mooted, they received no countenance from the Government, which was doubtful of the economic benefits to the settlers and quite clear about the moral wrong that would be done to the natives by occupation. Private schemes were put forward in the twenties and thirties, culminating in the formation, in the year of the Queen's accession, of the New Zealand Association by Gibbon Wakefield, Lord Durham, Sir William Molesworth, and other men of public influence. Both the Colonial Secretary, Lord Glenelg, and the permanent head of the Office, Sir James Stephen, represented the school of thought which held that the missionaries must be left without the handicap of white settlers. But the same principles which made them refuse any Government support to the Company prevented them from attempting to stop private adventurers from going to lands over which the Queen claimed no control. The Government stood aside and the company went ahead. It was the initiative of the company which prevented New Zealand from being annexed by the French. The same history which was to be repeated all over the Pacific, and notably in the acquisition of the Fiji Islands in 1874, rendered untenable the first instinctive attitude of the British Government. Private traders and settlers began visiting New Zealand and acquiring land. Many of the worst characters in New South Wales and Van Diemen's Land made the journey of 1,200 miles to islands where they were free from any control. The French colonization plans included convict labour, and that news converted the missionary element which had been most opposed to official action by Great Britain.

Lord Glenelg, before his resignation in 1838, had become increasingly aware that the anarchy of free intercourse between rival camps and uncontrolled private traders cried out for regulation and had himself prepared a compromise whereby the New Zealand Association should become a chartered company under Government. That actual scheme came to nothing, but the Association led to the creation of a company, with many of the original directors, and active steps were taken to find settlers, to sell them land and to arrange for them to sail. The hand of the Government was forced and it sent out a warship to obtain a cession of sovereignty from the Maoris. The warship, and the company's expedition, reached New Zealand in time to anticipate French occupation of the islands, and with 1840 the English rule in New Zealand begins. The company was a commercial rather than a patriotic undertaking, and it began advertising in German newspapers for German settlers, and appointed a representative at Bremen. It even planned to make completely German settlements in the Chatham Islands near by, and in New Zealand itself. Although the company made many bad mistakes in the early colonization of the North Island—the plans for Wellington were drawn in London on the assumption that its site was flat—the publicity was well managed in England and popular opinion was interested and favourable from 1841. Dr. Arnold was representative of many aspiring Englishmen when he played with the idea of devoting his days to this new field.

'I have actually got' (he wrote to Sir Thomas Pasley in 1840) '200 acres in New Zealand, and I confess my thoughts often turn thitherwards; but that vile population of runaway convicts and others who infest the country deters me more than anything else, as the days of Roman Proconsuls are over, who knew so well how to clear a country of such murderers. Now they will, I suppose, as they find it convenient come in and settle quietly amongst the colonists as Morgan did at Kingston: and the ruffian and outlaw of yesterday becomes to-day, according to our Jacobin notions of citizenship, a citizen and perhaps a magistrate and a legislator.'

And in the same year (in a letter to H. Fox):

'Every good man going to New Zealand or to Van Diemen's Land not for the sake of making money, is an invaluable element in those societies, and remember that they, after all, must be by and by the great missionaries to the heathen world, either for God or for the devil.'

There was from the first a special affection for New Zealand among Englishmen whose imaginations were kindled by thoughts of settlement overseas. There was really virgin land, not marred by any political experiments of earlier generations. A west-country squire like Molesworth could feel to the full the call to settle in the new country, and in the South Island were made the original and on the whole success-

Cape Colony and the adjacent territory of Kaffraria has of late excited an unusual degree of interest in England'. The special reasons for this were the refusal of the colonists to let Cape Colony be used in the place of Van Diemen's Land for a convict settlement, and the exciting tales which came home from Natal of the constant fighting with the Kaffirs. When the 1820 settlers were sent out, to the number of some 3,500, by the Government to relieve want at home and to increase British strength at this key-point on the route to India, and onwards during the twenties and thirties, when the settlement on the south-east coast was started by enterprising individuals, Kaffirs and Zulus were underrated in England. The abolitionist sentiment made all black men appear helpless and oppressed, and the Hottentots were in fact not at all formidable. English missionaries, the chief source of information, were mainly concerned in protecting the lower races against the Boers. The cheapness of good land—from £5 down to 2s. an acre in Natal in the forties—and the presence of black labour made South Africa look a promising place for the enterprising settler. The skilled labourer from England could earn £5 or £6 a month and his keep, and could and did very quickly become his own master and himself the employer of Kaffirs.

In the fifties the population of Natal rose to over 8,000. The Colonial Government paid the passage of emigrants, if some resident in the Colony guaranteed that £10 would be refunded, and under this impetus the slow and shabby little ships followed each other across the mysterious ocean, in the retrospective language of a well-known South African, looking back on 1850 'each with its company of helpless, ignorant, trustful people, wandering to a wild and unknown country on the shores of savage Africa, in quest of a new home and a new life, amid scenes and surroundings utterly alien to their past experiences, and absolutely without any personal knowledge of the conditions they had to encounter. Had any of them been questioned as to their expectations in setting forth, the answer would probably have been largely tinged by recollections of *Swiss Family Robinson* or *Masterman Ready* or by the romantic stories of imaginative travellers and adventurous missionaries.'[1] The voyage took 80–90 days, although mail steamers did the journey between England and the Cape

[1] Sir J. Robinson, *A Lifetime in South Africa.*

in 35 days, and after a day or two of delay at the Cape the Natal mail did the last portion of the journey in 10 days more. Letters which left England on the sixth day of one month used to arrive at Durban on the 28th or 29th of the month following. The fare was 60 guineas by these mail steamers, while the 'slow shabby boats' took steerage passengers for from £10 to £20.

The steerage passenger who had perhaps learned of an opening by consulting the Natal newspapers at Lloyd's Coffee House or the Jerusalem Coffee House in London, where they were displayed, found himself expected to provide himself on the ship with tin or enamel eating and cooking utensils, canvas bags, and a large jar for his day's supply of water, and his journey was held out to him as an excellent training in that self-help upon which he was so soon and so completely to depend. The books of guidance and advice warned him that Kaffir servants, though cheap, were very likely to prove more trouble than they were worth, and that while a working wife or daughter would prove an invaluable aid, Natal was no place for a delicately nurtured lady. Others than the delicately nurtured only too often found that the hardships of this part of the world had not been minimized. The Kaffirs became increasingly dangerous as they obtained firearms. A prominent exhibit at the Great Exhibition was an elephant's tusk from the Cape. It weighed 163 lb. These trophies were gained not only by hunting but by trading, and one famous hunter, Mr. Gordon Cumming, described how he cleared a profit of 3,000 per cent. by exchanging muskets, for which he had paid less than a sovereign apiece, for ivory. These stories produced the reflection at home that while the chiefs who parted with the ivory oppressed the bushmen and killed the elephants they deserved little sympathy, and that civilized consciences in England had an obvious duty to introduce some measure of civilization into such barbaric parts.

The problem which journalists could thus easily indicate was a standing though minor preoccupation in Whitehall. The lectures on the Great Boer Trek which Cloete himself, fresh from signal service as a peacemaker, delivered in London between 1852 and 1855, did much to spread a wider recognition of the tangled situation which the home government had to face. There were great difficulties, but it is plain to-day that official policy was singularly vacillating and feeble. The necessity for doing something was continually at war with the desire not to become deeply involved. The idea of fighting either Boers or blacks was highly repugnant, yet hostilities were not avoided and a firmer policy from the beginning might well have diminished their extent. The magistrate, the missionary, the schoolmaster, the trader, all were in their way promoters of civilization, but also of discord. Policy which, at the beginning of the reign, was avowedly not to extend British sovereignty or commitments, had to be modified in the forties and still more in the fifties as the results of administrative *laisser-faire* showed themselves in raids and private wars. Just as fear of the French precipitated the decision to occupy New Zealand, so the calls for help to secure the recognition of their independence which the Boer settlers made to Holland, in ignorance of Holland's feebleness, made the English authorities more resolute not to abandon their claims to overlordship. With the idea of minimizing trouble, the British Government did in the early fifties formally renounce all claims to sovereignty over the Boers who had crossed the Vaal river, and even over those in the Orange River Colony. The protests of the English colonists who resented this abandonment, though they were clearly made in the House of Commons, had no effect. It was the appointment of Sir George Grey, whose success in New Zealand and prestige with the home government enabled him to have a free hand, which led to the crystallization of British policy as the maintenance of such conditions of civilized order as should enable individuals to improve their property and so build up the wealth of the country. The Government had to be dragged every yard of the way towards a full policy; powerful as were the reasons for doing as little as possible, the argument that Government could not stop where it pleased gained force as the facts became known.

The main burden of the parliamentary report on Aborigines which came out at the beginning of the reign had been that Great Britain had at length cleared herself of the stigma of slavery and was paying compensation to make amends for having sanctioned the institution for so long. But slavery was an old thing, which could plead prescription in its favour; if Great Britain sinned, she sinned with the rest of the world in an age-old way. Such considerations did not excuse slavery. But they made the duty of the nation more obvious in the presence of new evils which white men were inflicting on black. The evidence given to the Commission had been in the main the evidence of missionaries, bearing detailed witness to the devastation wrought by white traders bringing firearms and strong drink to primitive peoples. Such evils were new and could claim no toleration, and the Government were called upon to make it British policy to nip them in the bud. The Commission had surveyed the whole overseas field, the condition of the Red Indians equally with that of the South Sea Islanders, but it was in Africa that the problem was to be encountered in its largest dimensions.

Before any policy had crystallized for South Africa, statesmen were being asked to think about the west coast, and to realize that the Slave Trade could only be extinguished if the west coast was itself civilized, and made into a possible field for legitimate trade. The efforts to suppress slave-trading were real, and in the long run successful, and such measures as the sending of three ironclads up the Niger in the early forties, while it aroused some feeling—which *The Times* supported—that Government was disposed to meddle in traders' business, encouraged those who asked for the presence of the flag as the prelude to trade. The palm oil trade, already established in the slavery days, grew, to the advantage of Liverpool, and men began to talk of raw cotton. At the time of the Great Exhibition of 1851 there was much speculation as to what West Africa would send and rumours were current about the wonderful skill of native manufactures. It must be Great Britain's task, said the idealists, to teach the African that he had more valuable commodities to sell than human beings. The actual exhibits did not disappoint and the *Illustrated London News* exclaimed (May 1851), 'West Africa offers articles so various in kind, so abundant and so valuable in commerce, that when compared with the barbarism of the people, they irresistibly compel the admission that trade alone does not solve the problem how men are to become civilized'. Cotton, both raw and manufactured, pottery, dyes, medicines, even poisons, all suggested a vast new field for enterprise. Palm oil and cotton-growing held the first places, and when McGregor Laird introduced trading steamers to the Niger, to fetch cotton grown by liberated Africans and other natives, their cotton cargoes rose in three years (in 1859) to £9,000. Manchester, which had taken no more than 1,810 lb.

of African cotton in 1852, was taking nearly half a million lb. by 1859.

But to many anxious watchers the Slave Trade seemed an unconscionable time in dying. Very soon after the abolition of slavery voices began to be heard, chief among them those of Lord Brougham, speaking in 1838, and Sir Thomas Buxton in his book on *The African Slave Trade and the Remedy* (1840), pointing out that the trade still continued. Lord Brougham attacked the system of indentures and apprenticeships by which natives were brought from Africa and Asia to South America and the West Indies for a term of years. Buxton laid special emphasis on the need for civilizing Africa itself, and believed that an era of free trade would soon demonstrate the superior economic worth of free labour. Brougham made his point, that millions of pounds were still being spent on the business of slave trading between Africa and Brazil and Cuba, and urged that the British market should be closed against Brazilian sugar. The Duke of Wellington expressed, as usual, the general sentiment when he promised Brougham, in 1842, to carry the Government with him in any measures likely to remedy the state of affairs. After 1846, when the complaints of West Indian planters at their plight began to be heard, less was heard of the earlier idea that after the first reaction against compulsory toil, negroes would show the same readiness to work as Europeans in temperate climates. People who were wedded to the idea of free trade and who would not meet the planters by special tariffs, began to blame the negro character. There was reaction, fed by the reports from Natal and from Australasia, towards a fatalistic idea that inferior races must perish at the approach of the superior races. From all sides less began to be expected from experiments of the Sierra Leone type, and opinion veered towards the view that civilization must take its course and that natives must have it administered to them, with all gentleness, but quite firmly.

The British public had thus done a good deal of thinking and feeling about Livingstone's life interests when he himself appeared in England and made his great lecture tours in 1856. His public revered the missionary calling, and had formed most of its ideas from missionaries, but it was also a public becoming increasingly interested in applied science. Livingstone's own evolution from an exploring missionary to an explorer who was also an active Christian was an epitome of a generation. Without abandoning his calling, he shifted his emphasis and in the end he stood first and foremost for the discovery of unknown land and the intrepid conquest of natural obstacles, and it was only secondarily that he was thought of as a missionary. The consular cap which he always wore after he left the London Missionary Society in 1856 and became the leader of expeditions was a far-reaching symbol. No one would call the *Missionary Travels* a well-written book. Greater smoothness of diction and a saving of time, the author aptly confessed in his preface, might have been secured by the employment of a person accustomed to compilation. But it had the grand merit in a travel book of vivid detail: the smallest matters had been noted and nothing was spared. It was a completely convincing picture, and it was a great and instantaneous success. In the year in which it appeared Dr. Livingstone visited Oxford and Cambridge and appealed to the Church of England to enter the missionary field in Central Africa. The result was the Universities Mission to Central Africa, which began its work three years later, with much cheerful underrating of the difficulty of life by the banks of the Shire; the dangers of the climate were made light of, and the natives were depicted in glowing terms. The Universities Mission did a good deal to change the spirit in which missionaries spoke of natives. In the thirties and forties the tradition was one of gross sentimentalism to arouse Mr. Jellyby's feelings for distant blacks. The *African Cry*, published in 1842 and soon established as a popular gift book, has good examples of this vein. 'Our hearts expand with sensations of delight when we think how the Hottentot has abandoned a filthy caross for clean and comfortable clothing, a miserable hut for a neat white cottage, a scanty supply of raw roots and disgusting entrails for a well-cultivated field and garden, beside a wholesome supply of milk and animal food.' (In fact, milk was the chief food of wild Hottentots.) The London Missionary Society had the reputation of being the most uncritically pro-native, more than the Church Missionary Society or the Wesleyans, who took the side of the European settlers on the frontier against the Kaffirs.

But missionary influence was declining all the time. At first the only people who were educated and articulate and interested in Africa had been missionaries or their friends, and they had dominated the Commission on Aboriginal races of which Thomas Fowell Buxton (a brewer who was, like Wakefield, a relation of the Quaker Frys) was chairman. The impulse which brought about abolition and kept England ready to spend further millions to make abolition a reality and to lead foreign nations into effectual co-operation, was a religious impulse. But it gained increasing commercial support as the argument was spread that slavery could only be finally destroyed by legitimate commerce. African rulers must be given another outlet and taught to deal in other commodities than men. This was the constructive side of Buxton's thesis in *The African Slave Trade*, and Lord Melbourne's government, in which the Colonial Secretary was Lord Glenelg, like Stephen, a child of the Clapham sect, co-operated in fitting out an expedition of three ships, *Albert*, *Wilberforce*, and *Soudan*, to sail up the Niger and prepare the way for peaceful trading. But when fever had turned the expedition to fiasco it was not repeated, and Government activity was confined to naval operations against the Slave Trade. In thus underrating the dangers to health the promoters of the Expedition put back the movement for opening up West Africa, but the direction of their thought was sound enough, though it needed many more decades before it became an accepted policy of Government to provide a commercial alternative for the excitements and profits of slave-raiding. In early Victorian days the more usual idea was to get rid of the costly and unhealthy garrisons as soon as possible and then to take no further official interest in the ill-fated coast.

§ 6. THE WEST INDIES

In the middle of the reign, in 1859, Trollope was moved to protest against the ignorant idealization in England of the emancipated negro in the West Indies. 'A man and a brother and shall we not regard him? Certainly, my philanthropic friend, let us regard him well. He *is* a man, and, if you will, a brother; but he is the very idlest brother with which a hardworking workman was ever cursed, intent only on getting his mess of pottage without giving anything in return.' There was, in truth, plenty of substance in Trollope's contention that the negro's idea of emancipation was not emancipation from slavery but emancipation from work. But it is not surprising if that was not easily recognized at home, where a generation of propaganda on the iniquities of the slave system had established a conventional view which resulted in the huge sales of *Uncle Tom's Cabin* from its first English edition in 1852, and the authoress's popular success on her visit. The West India Land Investment Company, which began operations soon after emancipation, was founded with the avowed purpose of protecting negroes who might suffer unfair economic pressure from their former owners. Although it set out to raise £100,000, it had actually to begin operations with £10,000, and *The Times* reflected balanced opinion when it deplored, in April 1839, the mistake of economic interference on so trifling a scale and advised the promoters to use their small funds elsewhere. The small sum was symbolic of the whole position. There was much easy sympathy and indignation, but with so many calls upon their charity and such small ideas about charitable gifts, the Victorians could not be expected to go beyond the large sum voted in Parliament to achieve emancipation. The negroes had either to continue in the paid employment of their reluctant emancipators or they had to live a hand-to-mouth existence if they wanted freedom from severe discipline. The negroes in the United States had a powerful and victorious political party vowed to look after them and to prove emancipation a success, and lived in a country advancing rapidly in wealth. The West Indies, further injured by the anti-tariff legislation of the forties, fell more deeply into depression. The Government had to hedge the employment of negroes with conditions, if their freedom was to amount to anything real, at a time when the planters whom such conditions burdened were finding market prices steadily worse. The labour question became acute and what discussion took place in Great Britain on the possible fresh sources of supply dwelt much more on the humanitarian risks of depressing the labourer's position by competition than on the economic gains. Between 1848 and 1858 some 200,000 immigrants did in fact enter the West Indies, nearly all of them from East India.

The West Indies continued to go down hill, but they also continued to be a source of income to a great many English families. They had from the first been so regarded, and when economic difficulties came to a head they were ill equipped because for generations their profits had been spent in England instead of being reinvested in capital improvements. Even the money paid in compensation to emancipation did not find its way to the West Indies, because ownership was so largely concentrated in Great Britain. Not only this, but the actual planters had always been very much at the mercy of the West Indian merchants who financed their crops under a system whereby the merchant also acted as the planter's buying agent in England, taking a commission both on what he bought and what he sold. A single Bank had a monopoly which it used, in the manner of Banks, to maintain a dividend of 10 per cent. throughout the century, refusing advances on land or crops and only making them on abundant personal security.

The absence of Government facilities for land development and in particular of a Land Bank, the long decline in the price of sugar, and the preoccupation of business people with more paying regions, led to a great decline in the relative importance of the West Indies. At the beginning of the Queen's reign, Herman Merivale in his lectures could describe the West Indies as far ahead in wealth and numbers of all other Colonies except the Canadas. They had a million people and imports worth £3,339,441. The next Colony was the Cape, with 150,000 people and imports of £623,323. Half a century later, the West Indies had a population but little larger and was importing nearly £8 million, and had been completely outstripped by the future Dominions.

Free trade was a much graver blow than emancipation, and the decision not to give a preference to sugar grown by free men over sugar grown by slaves, in the South American States, was as harsh as it was unreasonable. The price of sugar fell. The quantity coming from the West Indies did not fall after 1846. It rose in the next decade from 14 million cwt. to 18 million cwt. But the 18 millions fetched £7 million less than the 14 millions, and this fall of the price by a third (from 37s. 3d. per cwt. to 24s.) alarmed the merchants who made advances on crops. Capital took fright and could not be obtained. It was the tragedy of the sugar planter that he did not obtain a greater share of the English market after 1846, when consumption of his product doubled as its price dropped a third. This was particularly unfortunate because one of the effects of emancipation was to ruin the subsidiary coffee

industry. Where 20 million lb. of West Indian coffee came
to Great Britain in 1831, under 3 million were coming by
1858.

The fortunes of the islands as the result of home policy
were uneven. Trinidad and even British Guiana made slight
progress all the time. Jamaica suffered worst, and it was not
accidental that when in the eighteen-sixties the West Indies
flared into prominence at home it was because of Jamaica
and a riot there. In Colonies like Antigua and Barbados,
where there was not much unoccupied land, the negroes had
found themselves compelled to go on working from lack of
lands to squat on. But Jamaica had a high proportion of
unoccupied land. Its output of sugar had been diminishing
long before emancipation. The size of the island meant that
there was plenty of unexhausted and fertile land, had capital
been forthcoming to enable sugar to adapt itself. But the old
glory of Jamaica life had vanished. The class that played
host to Trollope and Froude, that insisted on dressing for
dinner, because black clothing was the thing in England, that
kept splendid tables with every delicacy of their own part of
the world and of England, gradually dwindled and gained no
new recruits. 'Sore and vituperative and unconvinced' Trollope found the planters, in proportion as they carried vivid
memories of their fathers' homes, with the full country-house
life—even to hunting—and the constant arrivals of younger
sons looking for fortune or mellow security and English girls
looking for eligible men. They resented the way they were
forgotten in their leaner days by people in England, and felt
their diminished status in the substitution for noblemen, with
large incomes of their own to spend, of professional governors,
using Jamaica as a stepping-stone to one of the newer but
more coveted colonial posts in Africa or North America.

Sir Charles Metcalfe, after being Governor of Agra and
provisional Governor-General of India, accepted the gover-
norship of Jamaica in 1839, and went four years later to be
Governor-General of Canada. His time in Jamaica had been
the early years of emancipation, but he conciliated everybody
except the Baptist missionaries, who were the source, in his
opinion, from which negroes derived excessive ideas of their
own importance. Metcalfe's career, it may be noted, was a
good instance of the great flexibility conferred by the loose
organization of colonial government and the freedom of

ministers at home from the need to remember the effect on a regular colonial service of repeated appointments from outside. After Metcalfe Jamaica had Elgin, destined later to govern Canada and India and to leave an abiding reputation. These men and others little less eminent came to Jamaica not as autocrats but as constitutional rulers, for the resident white population enjoyed large powers of self-government dating from Charles II.

But gradually and inevitably the position changed and Jamaica lost its glory. After free trade the planters were felt to have a moral claim to assistance, and Lord Grey, while he would not and could not consider protection, found money for advances and for the cost of emigrating free labour from Africa. The planters continued to place their hopes in the Tories and protection, in George Bentinck and Stanley and Disraeli, and there was sufficient recognition of their case in England to maintain differential duties on sugar and rum. Disappointment at what could be obtained in London, and a recognition that the strongest champions of free trade were also advocates of self-government, made the planters press for more self-government than they already enjoyed. Although Sir Henry Taylor had nearly achieved the abolition of the Assembly in Jamaica, Lord Grey, true to his general philosophy, was ready to consider full representative government. It took the rebellion of 1865 to bring about the abandonment of partial self-government and to set up Crown Colony rule. When Grey left office in 1852 Jamaica was in visible decline and he painted a poor picture of its prospects. The other West Indian possessions were reviving under indentured immigration, mainly from India, and Trinidad and British Guiana could look ahead with confidence. Psychologically Jamaica was the worst place to be hardest hit, just because of its vivid past memories. Violent as the dislocation caused by free trade was, it was in no sense a fatal blow, and even Jamaica found an eventual solution by growing fruit. But the recovery was slow and to the generation which faced the difficulties of the forties and fifties impatience with the policy and talk of people at home was natural and constant.

Things came to a head in 1865, over the case of the unfortunate and indefensible Governor Eyre. He was a man who had distinguished himself in Australia and had been appointed to Jamaica simply on his merits. He failed to prevent and had

J to suppress a negro rising. The rising was not a colour rebel-
t lion or war of servile revenge, but an agricultural demonstra-
e tion which had had many parallels in English and European
w history. It was a demonstration of peasants concerned with
n land grievances. But it was fraught with more peril than its
fi instigators knew, and might easily have led to a general
w massacre of Europeans. The Governor not only suppressed
n it with extreme severity, and hundreds of summary execu-
t tions, but he even kidnapped a leading coloured Baptist,
v Gordon by name, carried him into the martial law area, and
g hanged him out of hand. Local opinion in Jamaica, vividly
remembering how all the French in Haiti had been massacred
a generation before, acclaimed the Governor as a man whose
severity was a blessed thing. But in England there was immediate outcry and a deputation the size of a public meeting, led
by the Aborigines Protection Society and the Anti-Slavery
Society, waited on the Colonial Secretary. Eyre was suspended while a Commission of Inquiry visited Jamaica. The
I Governor did not lack defenders at home, notably Carlyle
c and Kingsley. Carlyle saw in him one of his strong men, and
l Carlyle had already expressed his views on negroes and their
t reluctance to put their free noses to grindstones. Kingsley
i was on his mother's side of West Indian planter stock.
As in the matter of Rajah Brooke ten years before, so here
x he hastened to express his sympathy with Eyre. That sym-
j pathy was more widespread than it would have been before
x the Indian Mutiny. Thus *The Times* wrote of the negroes as
l a bloodthirsty race, filled with hatred of the white man. On
c a close knowledge of the case, Sir Henry Taylor, who was no
t partisan of the planters, could defend even the execution of
t Gordon as 'just in itself and needful for the purpose of avert-
x ing great dangers'. But the Commission of Inquiry, while
l praising the Governor's promptitude and vigour, gave judgement against his severity and after his recall he was prosecuted by a private Jamaica Committee in England. It was
this private Committee, supported by Mill and Herbert
Spencer and Huxley and Goldwin Smith, which caused a
counter mobilization in support of Eyre. Tennyson and
Ruskin and, less openly, Dickens were on the side of the
Governor, as was Disraeli. Grand Juries always threw out
the bills brought by the Jamaica Committee against Eyre,
and in the end, in 1872, a Liberal Government indemnified

the nineties, he could not see that there was in fact much difference in the health of the English population.

And if Englishmen could prosper, the opportunities were numerous. Cotton had been proved suitable. Why should not India take the place of America as our cotton field? The import into Great Britain had risen to 77 million lb. by 1840 when it had been 4 million in 1808. The sale of Indian manufactured cotton goods fell away before Lancashire competition, but the raw product remained an important crop. A new commodity appeared in 1838 with the arrival in London of the first consignment of Assam tea. Rum, silk, sugar, tea, indigo, all were growing industries at the time of the Queen's accession. The tendency which became more pronounced was for India to become an exporter less of luxuries than of raw materials, cotton, grain, jute, and to begin to take a place as a manufacturing nation.

Although the number of commercial posts for Englishmen was increasing, there was reluctance among people in England to contemplate settling in India and the attempts to encourage soldiers to remain with their wives and to bring up their children in the hill stations made little headway. The Mutiny, among its other vast results, effectually put an end to the chances of a successful propaganda in favour of permanent European settlement. It is difficult to exaggerate the psychological importance of the Indian Mutiny, not only as it affected the Englishman's view of India, but his view of coloured races and of Imperialism. Before the Mutiny, India had never been the centre of great popular interest. Justin MacCarthy well describes it as associated in the minds of some with tiger hunting, and in the minds of others with Bishop Heber and missions to the heathen. In the House of Commons, he well says, a debate on any question connected with India was as strictly an affair of experts as the discussion of some local gas bill.

The Indian Mutiny startled the people of England out of their indifferent placidity. Macaulay notes in his diary for June 1857, when the first terrible news of Sepoy atrocities, sometimes garnished with stories subsequently found to be without foundation, arrived in England:

'The cruelties of the Sepoy natives have inflamed the Nation to a degree unprecedented within my memory. Peace Societies, Aborigines Protection Societies, and societies for the reformation of criminals are silent. There is one terrible cry for revenge. The account of that dreadful military execution at Peshawar, forty men blown at once from the mouths of cannon, heads, legs, arms, flying in all directions, was read with delight by people who, three weeks ago, were against all capital punishment. Bright himself declared for the vigorous suppression of the Mutiny. The almost universal feeling is that not a single Sepoy within the walls of Delhi should be spared, and I own that is a feeling with which I cannot help sympathizing.'

So general was the rage that *The Times* felt it necessary to justify itself against the charge that it was not doing enough to make the horrors widely known. Undoubtedly *The Times*, like many other people, underrated the Mutiny at first and took for granted its very speedy suppression. The first moral drawn was that the Sepoys had too little to do, frontiers being quiet, and that it was not sufficient to have conquered India, it was also necessary to civilize it. These first generalities gave way to a closer study of existing evils as India remained in the news, month after month. It was gradually borne in upon the public that British rule had concentrated too much upon protecting commerce, that local administration was bad, that the native police were exceedingly corrupt, that the material position of the country was still wretched. There were some, like Richard Cobden, who had always disliked British adventures in the East and seized the occasion to point out the moral. Cobden had consistently spoken against the whole idea of an Indian Empire. When the Indian Mutiny came, he used it as a text to prove the hopelessness of attempting to lead to a higher level of civilization people capable of such crimes as the Indians had committed.

'Now,' he said, 'now that the trade of Hindustan is thrown open to all the world on equal terms, what exclusive advantage can we derive to compensate for all the trouble and risk of ruling over such people, a people which has shown itself, after a century of contact with us, to be capable of crimes which would revolt any savage tribe of whom we read in Dr. Livingstone's narrative which had never seen a Christian or European till he penetrated among them. The religious people who now tell us we must hold India and convert it, ought, I should think, to be convinced by what has passed that sending Red coats as well as black to Christianize the people is not the most likely way to ensure the blessing of God on our missionary efforts.'

He added on this occasion that 'Indians will prefer to be ruled badly according to our notions, by their own coloured kith and kin, than to submit to the humiliation of being better governed by a succession of transient intruders from the Antipodes'.

It was perhaps not surprising that Cobden held a low opinion of his fellow countrymen who lived and worked out East. In the same year, in a letter to John Bright, he says:

'I have lately been in the society of some ladies who had lately returned from India where they were accustomed to barrack life, their husbands being officers in a native regiment. I find the common epithet applied to our fellow subjects in Hindustan is "nigger". One of these ladies took some credit for her condescension in allowing a native officer answering to the rank of subaltern to sit down in her presence when he came for orders to her husband. All this might have been borne, though with difficulty, if the English with whom the natives came in contact displayed exalted virtues and high intellectual powers, but I hear the traits most conspicuous in our countrymen have been of a very different character.'

Lord Elgin was recording the same thing in his diary at the time. 'It is a terrible business this living among inferior race. . . . Detestation, contempt, and vengeance, whether Chinaman or Indian be the object.'

The Mutiny became the occasion for a general airing of grievances, and planters and retired officials vied with each other in contributing diagnoses and complaints. The general conclusion emerged from the official inquiries following the Mutiny that Government must be much more wholehearted and efficient, and drastic reorganization set in. The new officials found themselves under much closer control than had been the servants of the Company. The supervision from London became more detailed. Sir William Hunter summed up (in *The India of the Queen*) by saying that whereas the servants of the Company used to write back for approval of what they had done, the new officials had to write back for sanction for what they intended to do. The class of official was already high and the days of eighteenth-century fortunes were long past. In Bengal, Bombay, and Madras, the Regulation Provinces, only civilians were employed, but in the newly acquired territories, like Sind and the Punjab, the practice of appointing officers from the army to administrative posts had been established since the days of Lord Cornwallis. The principles for successful work among the Indians had been clearly formulated by men like Henry and John Lawrence before the Mutiny, and the success of their practice was shown in the way the Punjab stood the crisis. Haileybury, the Company's school and the nursery of so many of its leading officials, was in its prime in the forties, with a staff of unusual distinction. Although the system of nomination by Directors meant that many considerations besides merit came into play, the successful cadets were a good crop year after year, and, after paternal admonishment in Leadenhall Street, when they were told to think kindly of the native and to respect his intelligence, they went out fortified by a very strong *esprit de corps*, and filled with pride in the service they had succeeded in entering. At Haileybury a smattering of basic Oriental languages was picked up, but the main education was in political economy and law, and 'we left' (said Sir George Campbell in his Memoirs) 'with a few priggish economical statements (which dropped off after a year or two) and a very sound belief in the greatest happiness of the greatest number'. The India Act of 1858, introducing open competition, abolished Haileybury and made the Indian Civil Service an appanage of the Universities.

To the south of India, in the island of Ceylon, the attractions of the Civil Service were much smaller. In 1833 drastic reforms had been introduced at the instance of the Treasury, and the position of civil servants had been made in all respects much less favourable. The doctrinaire had been allowed to wield his unintelligent axe and after some years Sir James Stephen frankly regretted that the Colonial Office had accepted changes which, he said, had been made by 'unskilful and unsparing hands, changes more distinguished by parsimony than economy'. The Ceylon civil service was a small affair, less than forty permanent civil servants, so that promotion was very slow, and as pensions were also abolished there was much ground for disgruntlement. It was an unwritten law that promotion should only be by strict seniority. When Sir Colin Campbell was Governor in 1841, he reported so alarmingly that Lord Stanley had to take action. It was not only that civil servants had taken to coffee-growing and were more inclined to be interested in their private business than in public affairs; more seriously, they felt no incentive to master the vernacular. Ceylon had in its centre the ancient kingdom of Kandy and the changes and improvements in the service which were introduced in the forties came too late to anticipate and prevent the rebellion of 1848. The Kandyan rebellion came as a complete surprise to the Government, which was not well served, but it was trouble which, even when investigated, admitted of no simple solution. It was in a sense the result of the economic depression, which sharpened the reluctance of the British Government to provide full and adequate funds for the Buddhist priesthood. The Kandyans had never really been absorbed into the British system. There had been outbreaks in 1817 and 1823, and outbreaks which were nipped in the bud in 1820. In 1848 martial law had to be proclaimed and remained in force for ten weeks before the rebellion was crushed. A number of ringleaders were executed, and in due course an outcry began in England against the Governor, Lord Torrington. The first attempts of the Colonial Office under Lord Grey to block the inquiry were overcome and the proposal for a commission was carried. Gladstone, in a speech three years later, took a balanced view, representative of general feeling, that it was unnatural to expect the Kandyans not to feel exasperated at the failure to make any provision for their religion. The rebellion and the complete ventilation of the Government of Ceylon in all its shortcomings cleared the air, but there was no real need for Ceylon to have continued for three years as the centre of bitter controversy. Peel, in the last month of his life, interested himself in supporting Gladstone in criticism of the Government. Lord Grey, in his defence of his colonial policy published in the aftermath of the events, was very vigorous in championing the Governor and claimed that the most sustained attempt to incriminate and condemn him had had to fail after two and a half years. 'I am aware', he said, 'that the Governors of distant colonies in times of rebellion are placed in situations of so much difficulty and responsibility that any generous mind will be disposed to put the best construction on their conduct, and believe, till the contrary is clearly proved, that they have acted to the best of their judgement.' Grey complained that these attacks and the appointment of a committee in the House of Commons had done great injury in Ceylon, in particular since Ceylon newspapers had been furnished with evidence taken before the report was completed.

In the ten years following the rebellion, Ceylon made such economic progress that the financial stringency which had been the underlying cause of the trouble passed. By 1864 Mr. Cardwell was able to call upon Ceylon to pay once again, little by little, the full cost of the troops stationed on the island. The unofficial members of the local legislature at once resigned, but their protest did not succeed in saving Ceylon from becoming the only Colony which paid the full cost of its defence. With that controversy there began agitations on the part of the unofficial element in Ceylon which led gradually and steadily to the later successive introduction of representative institutions. The coffee-planters had a terrible lesson from the economic depression in 1847 which was one cause of the revolt. They saw plantations become almost unsaleable; one bought in 1843 for £15,000 was sold by auction in 1847 for £440. The industry made a temporary recovery, only to perish altogether through the attacks of fungus and the depression of 1876–80, and Ceylon found its salvation in the tea which had been no more than an experimental crop nursed by the enthusiastic and far-seeing Dr. Thwaites in the forties and fifties, and had only begun to make its mark in the later sixties.

The Ceylon outbreak occurred in 1848, and two years later the same question of exceptional severity arose in connexion with the picturesque figure of Sir James Brooke, Rajah of Sarawak. Brooke is one of the most significant figures in early Victorian history. After lively schooldays at Norwich, where George Borrow was his schoolfellow, he had gone out East in the service of the East India Company and then had drifted down to the Malay peninsula. He had established himself with a grant from the Sultan of Brunei as Rajah of Sarawak and had at the same time a commission as consul from the British Government. When news came home of his vigorous operations against the Dyak pirates in 1849, operations in which hundreds of lives were lost on each side, agitation began in England that his position was anomalous, that his deeds were discreditable, and that Government should at least dissociate themselves from him. In both cases of Ceylon and the pirates, the chief agitator in Parliament was old Joseph Hume. Hume is interesting, and in some respects representative of a perennial school of thought. Of humble origin, he had accumulated as a very young man, and before his thirtieth birthday, a fortune of £40,000 in the old India before Wellesley, where he became,

> In something less than sixty days,
> By industry and honest ways
> Inordinately rich.

Having secured his independent income, he began to practise virtue and was prominent through a long career of parliamentary service, an unresting, often vindictive and ardently doctrinaire Radical. In the cases of Ceylon and Borneo he had powerful missionary support. The *Spectator* and the *Daily News* joined the hunt, which was conducted with loud exaggerations by the Peace Society and the Aborigines Protection Society. Cobden and Sidney Herbert were prominent in support of Hume, who kept demanding a Commission of Inquiry, describing the pirates as harmless and timid people, the victims of atrocious massacre. For two years in succession these motions were lost in the House by huge majorities, by 145 to 20, by 164 to 24, and then by 230 to 19. But his pertinacity made its impression. Gladstone was not alone in thinking that an inquiry was called for, because it was called for so loudly. But Brooke was strongly supported. In 1852 a dinner was given him by over two hundred supporters, including many leading men in politics and the City. But the Aberdeen coalition granted the Commission, which sat in Singapore in the later half of 1854. It exonerated Brooke on the charges of massacre and unjust attack, but the presence of such a commission at Singapore was a blow to his peculiar authority, and the navy was not again made available to assist him, because of the danger of mutiny at home. Brooke felt keenly both the lack of appreciation and the damage done. When Kingsley in 1855 dedicated *Westward Ho!* to him he showed how much he valued such moral support. But his exoneration had no effect upon the hostile forces at home, and over twenty years later Mr. Gladstone, who had not been a bitter partisan at the time, showed that a legend had established itself when he said, apropos of Bulgarian atrocities, that he could remember no more shameful proceeding on the part of any country than the slaughter of the Dyaks by Her Majesty's forces and by Sir James Brooke.

XVII

PORTRAIT OF AN AGE

XVII

PORTRAIT OF AN AGE

BY G. M. YOUNG.

I

A MAN born in 1810, in time to have seen the rejoicings
after Waterloo and the canal boats carrying the wounded
to hospital, to remember the crowds cheering for Queen
Caroline, and to have felt that the light had gone out of the
world when Byron died, entered manhood with the ground
rocking under his feet as it had rocked in 1789. Paris had
risen against the Bourbons; Bologna against the Pope;
Poland against Russia; the Belgians against the Dutch. Even
in well-drilled Germany little dynasts were shaking on their
thrones, and Niebuhr, who had seen one world revolution,
sickened and died from fear of another. At home forty years
of Tory domination were ending in panic and dismay;
Ireland, unappeased by Catholic Emancipation, was smouldering with rebellion; from Kent to Dorset the skies were
alight with burning ricks. A young man looking for some
creed to steer by at such a time might, with the Utilitarians,
hold by the laws of political economy and the greatest
happiness of the greatest number; he might simply believe
in the Whigs, the Middle Classes, and the Reform Bill; or
he might, with difficulty, still be a Tory. But atmosphere
is more than creed and, whichever way his temperament led
him, he found himself at every turn controlled, and animated,
by the imponderable pressure of the Evangelical discipline
and the almost universal faith in progress.

Evangelical theology rests on a profound apprehension
of the contrary states: of Nature and of Grace; one meriting
eternal wrath, the other intended for eternal happiness.
Naked and helpless, the soul acknowledges its worthlessness
before God and the justice of God's infinite displeasure, and
then, taking hold of salvation in Christ, passes from darkness
into a light which makes more fearful the destiny of those
unhappy beings who remain without. This is Vital Religion. But the power of Evangelicalism as a directing force
lay less in the hopes and terrors it inspired than in its

rigorous logic, 'the eternal microscope' with which it pursued its argument into the recesses of the heart, and the details of daily life, giving to every action its individual value in this life, and its infinite consequence in the next. Nor could it escape the notice of a converted man, whose calling brought him into frequent contact with the world, that the virtues of a Christian after the Evangelical model were easily exchangeable with the virtues of a successful merchant or a rising manufacturer, and that a more than casual analogy could be established between Grace and Corruption and the Respectable and the Low. To be serious, to redeem the time, to abstain from gambling, to remember the Sabbath day to keep it holy, to limit the gratification of the senses to the pleasures of a table lawfully earned and the embraces of a wife lawfully wedded, are virtues for which the reward is not laid up in Heaven only. The world is very evil. An unguarded look, a word, a gesture, a picture, or a novel, might plant a seed of corruption in the most innocent heart and the same word or gesture might betray a lingering affinity with the class below.

The discipline of children was becoming milder because it was touched with that tenderness for all helpless things which we see increasing throughout the eighteenth century, and with that novel interest in the spectacle of the opening mind which was a characteristic product of the Revolutionary years. But it was, perhaps for the same reason, more vigilant; and moral, or social, anxiety made it for girls at least more oppressive.[1] Yet if, with Rosalind and Beatrice in our eye, we recall Dryden's remark about 'the old Elizabeth way for maids to be seen and not heard', we shall realize how easy it is to misunderstand our grandmothers. Diana Vernon, Argemone Lavington, and Rose Jocelyn might stand for three generations of one house, and each of them we know had a living original. The outstanding Victorian woman is a blend of the great lady and the intellectual woman, not yet professional, and we can graduate the proportions until, at the opposite ends of the scale, we encounter the limiting instances of the Queen herself and Harriet Martineau. In Mrs. Grote, who would have been a far more effective Mem-

[1] But any one who supposes that there was such a thing as a 'Victorian' family or 'Victorian' father should meditate Norris of Bemerton's *Spiritual Counsel*, 1694, or *The Ladies' Calling* (Oxford University Press, 1673).

ber of Parliament than her husband, who sat with her red stockings higher than her head, discomfited a dinner-party by saying 'disembowelled' quite bold and plain, and knew when a hoop was off a pail in the back kitchen, the great lady is formidably ascendant; in Mrs. Austin the intellectual woman. In Mrs. Austin's daughter, Lady Duff Gordon, in Lady Eastlake—another product of the high secluded culture of the provinces—and, with the emphasis of genius, in Miss Nightingale, the kind achieves its balance. But for working use the eighteenth century had conceived a standard type of womanhood, sensitive and enduring, at once frailer and finer than the man,[1]—in a word, Amelia—and this type, repeated and articulated in a thousand novels, had blended insensibly with the more positive type evolved, in a humanitarian age, by the persuasive working of a religion of duty. Laura Pendennis in fiction, Mrs. Tennyson in life, might serve as examples; Miss Nightingale's caustic allusion to 'woman's particular worth and general missionariness' as a corrective. In making up the account of English morals in the nineteenth century it is necessary to bear in mind that the most influential women were reared in an atmosphere which made them instinctively Custodians of the Standard. The two who had most aptitude and most capacity for rebellion were fanatics, Charlotte Brontë for the moral, Harriet Martineau for the economic law. Mary Wollstonecraft had, unhappily, no equal successor, and George Sand could never have grown in English soil. Thus it came about that the pagan ethic which, in the decline of Christian beliefs and sanctions, carried into the next, the agnostic, age the evangelical canons of duty and renunciation, was a woman's ethic. George Eliot's rank in literature has, perhaps, not yet been determined: in the history of ideas her place is fixed. She is the moralist of the Victorian revolution.

That the ethic could be so transposed from a Christian to a Stoic key shows how native the discipline was. It had its roots deep down in the habits of a northern race,[2] vigorous

---

[1]   God! she is like a milk-white lamb that bleats
    For man's protection.

God! indeed. But this is Keats (1817), and is Rousseau's Sophie rather than Fielding's Sophia. One does not easily picture Emma Woodhouse (1816) bleating for Keats.

[2] I may refer to Hazlitt's contrast of Northern and Southern manners in *Hot and Cold* (Plain Speaker).

and self-controlled, not sensitive but not unkindly, in country rectories and manor houses, in the congregations of City churches, in the meeting houses of Yorkshire clothing towns. It rose and spread with the advance of the class which principally sustained it: Wesley and his followers carried it into regions which the old churches had hardly touched; Wilberforce and Hannah More brought wit and fashion to its support; Cowper brought poetry. By the beginning of the nineteenth century virtue was advancing on a broad invincible front. The French wars made England insular, and conscious of its insularity, as it had not been since the Conquest. The Evangelicals gave to the island a creed which was at once the basis of its morality and the justification of its wealth and power, and, with the creed, that sense of being an Elect People which, set to a more blatant tune, became a principal element in Late Victorian Imperialism. By about 1830 their work was done. They had driven the grosser kinds of cruelty, extravagance, and profligacy underground. They had established a certain level of behaviour for all who wished to stand well with their fellows. In moralizing society they had made social disapproval a force which the boldest sinner might fear.

By the beginning of the Victorian age the faith was already hardening into a code. Evangelicalism at war with habit and indifference with vice and brutality, with slavery, duelling, and bull-baiting, was a very different thing from Evangelicalism grown complacent, fashionable, superior. Even its charity had acquired what a Yorkshire manufacturer grimly styled a 'diffusive, itinerant quality'. The impulses it had quickened showed at their best in the upper ranks of society, where they had been absorbed into an older tradition of humour, culture, and public duty; or at the Universities, where they blended with new currents of intellectual eagerness and delight. The piety of a fine scholar like Peel or a haughty Border lord like Graham, of Gladstone or Sidney Herbert, had not much in common with the soul-saving theology of the money-making witness-bearers, those serious people whose indifference to national affairs Bright was one day to deplore. But, morally, their way of life was the same. Evangelicalism had imposed on society, even on classes which were indifferent to its religious basis and unaffected by its economic appeal, its code of Sabbath observance, responsibility and philanthropy; of discipline in the home, regularity in affairs; it had created a most effective technique of agitation, of private persuasion and social persecution. On one of its sides, Victorian history is the story of the English mind employing the energy imparted by Evangelical conviction to rid itself of the restraints which Evangelicalism had laid on the senses[1] and the intellect; on amusement, enjoyment, art; on curiosity, on criticism, on science.

II

The Evangelical discipline, secularized as respectability, was the strongest binding force in a nation which without it might have broken up, as it had already broken loose. For a generation and more the static conception of society[2] had been dissolving because society itself was dissolving. 'A nobleman, a gentleman, a yeoman,' Cromwell told one of his Parliaments, 'that is a good interest.' But the good interest was splitting into a hundred aristocracies and a hundred democracies, button-makers and gentlemen button-makers,[3] all heels and elbows, jostling, pushing, snubbing, presuming. On the whole, the articulate classes, whose writings and conversation make opinion, were gainers by the change—it has been estimated, for example, that between 1815 and 1830 the purchasing capacity of the classes above the wage-earning level was all but doubled—and the Victorian belief in progress was bottomed on the complacency which comes of steadily rising incomes and steadily improving security. Mixed with this, no doubt, was the vulgar pride in mere quantity, the thoughtless exultation of a crowd in motion. But no one can read for long in the literature of the thirties and forties without touching a finer and deeper pride, portentously draped in tables of trade and revenue, and the publications of the Useful Knowledge Society, but glowing

---

[1] Kingsley (who described Shelley as a lewd vegetarian) acutely diagnosed Byron as an Evangelical gone wrong. Byron's objection to mixed bathing, even when the parties are married, as 'very indelicate' comes from his Venetian period.

[2] As explained, for example, by an Irish judge in 1798. 'Society consists of noblemen, baronets, knights, esquires, gentlemen, yeomen, tradesmen and artificers.' The jury found that, as the subject had ceased to be a breeches maker without becoming a gentleman, he must be a yeoman.

[3] For whom there were separate doors in the Birmingham taverns.

with the authentic sense of war and victory, man against nature, and reason against the traditions of the elders.

Great things are done when men and mountains meet.

To travellers descending from the moorlands the smoke and roar of Lancashire seemed like the smoke and roar of a battle-field and the discipline of the factories like the discipline of a great army. It is hardly an accident that the first history of the Renaissance came from Liverpool[1] and that the most conspicuous memorial of the Utilitarians is a History of Greece. Across the ages, the modern Englishman recognized his peers.

We must be careful, also, if we are to keep the picture true, not to view the early Victorian age of production through that distorting medium, the late Victorian age of finance. Science touched the imagination by its tangible results. It was immersed in matter, and it conformed directly to the Augustan canon of historic progress by its immediate contribution to the 'order, regularity, and refinement of life'. Romance and the Revolution bred ideas of human purpose which only slowly permeated the English mind. Even in 1830 —far more powerfully in 1840—they were beginning to work. But the common intelligence was still dominated by the solid humanism of the Augustans to which the Eighteenth Proposition of Oxford Liberalism would have seemed a self-evident truth:

Virtue is the child of Knowledge: Vice of Ignorance: therefore education, periodical literature, railroad travelling, ventilation, and the art of life, when fully carried out, serve to make a population moral and happy.[2]

'The objects of this Society', so ran the prospectus of the Rochdale Pioneers, 'are the moral and intellectual advancement of its members. It provides them with groceries, butcher's meat, drapery goods, clothes and clogs.' Gas-lighting of the streets was hardly an improvement so much as a revolution in public security;[3] cheap cotton goods in

---

[1] 'The historian of the Age of Leo (Roscoe) has brought into cultivation the extensive tract of Chatmoss.' (Mrs. Barbauld, 1811.)

[2] Newman: *Apologia Note A*. But what does *serve* mean? The almost magical effect of ventilation on the moral habits (temper and sobriety) of a poor quarter was demonstrated again and again.

[3] 'Without presuming to play on words,' said the Lambeth magistrate, 'I regard gas as essential to an enlightened police.' It was once proposed to

personal cleanliness, paraffin lamps in domestic comfort.
Finance, the manipulation of wealth and credit as things by
themselves, three or four degrees removed from the visible
crop or ore, was an adjunct. Production was the thing itself, and the great producers—the three most famous names
in Victorian industry, Armstrong, Brassey, and Whitworth
may serve for examples—were as much craftsmen in their
trade as were the agricultural reformers, Blamire in Cumberland, Philip Pusey in Berkshire.

A generation which has come to take invention for granted
and is, perhaps, more sensitive to its mischief than its benefits,
cannot easily recover the glory of an age when knowledge,
and with it power, seemed to have been released for an
illimitable destiny.[1] The Englishman might reluctantly allow
that in social amenity the French, in care for the well-
being of the people, the Prussians, went beyond him. He
might at moments be chilled by the aesthetic failure of his
time, so profuse and yet so mean: alienated by its ethical
assurance, at once so pretentious and so narrow. In a
petulant mood, he would talk, like Grote, of the Age of
Steam and Cant, but all the while he knew that in the
essential business of humanity, the mastery of brute nature
by intelligence, he had outstripped the world, and the Machine
was the emblem and the instrument of his triumph. The
patriotism of early Victorian England, not yet blooded by
the Crimean War and the Indian Mutiny, irritated by
Napoleon III, or exalted by the vision of empire, was at
heart a pride in human capacity, which time had led to
fruition in England, and in the great humanist, who brought
all history to glorify the age of which he was the most
honoured child, it heard its own voice speaking.[2]

To articulate the creed of progress, to state its evidences

illuminate thieves' quarters with lamps of a special construction so that law-
abiding pedestrians should pass by on the other side.

[1] The admiration of Bacon, almost amounting to a rediscovery, is very
characteristic of the period. So is the Utilitarian preference for the more
scholastic, less imaginative Hobbes. When his editor, Molesworth, stood for
Southwark the populace paraded the streets shouting NO OBBS.

[2] *Il a son orgueil d'homme.* Taine's fine saying of Macaulay is true of his
whole age. 'That wicked XVIII century' died hard: under his Romantic ornament Macaulay is through and through Augustan; and contemporary critics
(Brougham and Harriet Martineau are examples) reproduce against him the
charges which the early Romantics had laid against Gibbon—materialism and
want of philosophy.

and draw out its implications, was the mission of that remarkable group of men variously known as the Utilitarians, or the Philosophic Radicals. In discipleship or reaction no young mind of the thirties could escape their influence. Bentham's alliance with James Mill, Mill's friendship with Malthus and Ricardo, had created a party, almost a sect, with formularies as compact as the Evangelical theology and conclusions not less inexorable. However far the Benthamite disciple went, he would find the old sage had been there before him; every trail was blazed, every pitfall marked, and in every path stood a lion, the Sinister Interest of privilege. Between rulers and ruled there exists an inherent antagonism[1] which can only be resolved if rulers and ruled are identified by means of universal suffrage and the ballot-box, and the identity is preserved by publicity and a cheap press.[2] The sovereignty thus created is to be exercised through a carefully balanced system: of Parliament to legislate, central organs to direct, local organs to execute. On the question of Women's Suffrage, the Utilitarians were somewhat inconsistently divided; Bentham, a flirtatious old bachelor, being more logical than James Mill, who, in spite of Malthus, had begotten more children than he could afford on a female whom he despised. On all other matters, above all on the sovereign authority of Economic Law, they spoke with one voice.

Reduced from an aspiration to a schedule, progress might seem a gloomy business for the mass of mankind. It rests on competition, and always and everywhere competition is reducing the profits of the employer, and the wages of the workman, to the level of bare subsistence. Only the landowner, the common enemy of all, continually profits by the growing demand for sites, and for food, because, always and everywhere, population is pressing on the means to live. Such is the law. But Nature has not left her children without

---

[1] Translate this into economic terms, substitute for the antagonism of rulers and ruled, the antagonism of employers and employed, and some curious consequences will follow.

[2] 'The principle of human nature, upon which the necessity of government is founded, the propensity of one man to possess himself of the objects of desire at the cost of another, leads on, by infallible sequence, not only to that degree of plunder which leaves the members (except the instruments and recipients) the bare means of subsistence, but to that degree of cruelty which is necessary to keep in existence the most intense terrors.'—James Mill on Government. Of James Mill as an historian Maine said that his inaccuracy was only equalled by his bad faith.

all hope of escaping the fate to which her mathematics seem to have consigned them. By industry, and abstinence, the employer may enlarge the market for his goods; by industry, and continence, the workman may increase the purchasing power, and limit the numbers, of his class: progress, like salvation, is the reward of virtue; of diligence and self-education; of providence and self-control; and all the evolutionary speculation of the next age has for background Malthus's Stoic vision of that remote, austere, divinity 'whose purpose is ever to bring a mind out of the clod'.

In the early thirties the Philosophic Radicals were a portent, men whose meetings were watched, the spear-head of a revolution beginning with the ballot and going on, Heaven knew how far, to compulsory education and a federated Empire. Then, frigid and scholastic, as a party they fade from the view. The popular Radicals made more noise; the people preferred the Tories. Their place was not in Parliament, but in the administration which did not exist and which it was their mission to create. Grote lived to decline a peerage; when the ballot was at last conceded in 1872 John Mill had decided that he did not want it and had moved on to proportional representation instead; Leader vanished into an aesthetic Italian exile; Molesworth's features are more familiar at Ottawa than his name at Westminster. The case for Free Trade was taken out of their hands by men who had learnt their economics in the counting-house, their logic on the platform, and their rhetoric in the pulpit.[1] But they had done inestimable service. They came down into a world where medieval prejudice, Tudor law, Stuart economics, and Hanoverian patronage still luxuriated in wild confusion, and by the straight and narrow paths they cut we are walking still. The Gladstonian Liberals have gone where the Peelites followed the Canningites; the Evangelical creed long ago foundered on the Impregnable Rock of Holy Scripture, and the great Whig name has not been heard for fifty years. But it would be hard to find any corner of our public life where the spirit of Bentham is not working to-day.

It is dangerous to force historic movements into exaggerated symmetry. But the parallel operation of Evangelicalism

[1] The supersession of Charles Villiers by Cobden, Bright, and W. J. Fox is typical.

and Utilitarianism cannot be ignored. Their classics, Malthus on Population and Wilberforce's *Practical View*, appeared almost simultaneously, one in 1797, the other in 1798. Their greatest victories in public affairs, the Abolition of Slavery and the Reform of the Poor Law, were won in 1833 and 1834. When a distracted Government threw the Old Poor Law at a Royal Commission, the Benthamites rose to the height of their opportunity. The Secretary of the Commission was Edwin Chadwick, whom the Patriarch had selected to be his apostle to the new age, and in his hands there was no fear lest the faith should grow cold. Born in 1801, in a Lancashire farm-house where the children were washed all over, every day, the mainspring of Chadwick's career seems to have been a desire to wash the people of England all over, every day, by administrative order. In practical capacity Chadwick was the greatest, in the character of his mind, in the inhuman simplicity of his ideas and the inexhaustible fertility of his applications, the most typical of the Benthamites. Napoleon III once asked him what he thought of his improvements in Paris. 'Sir,' he answered, 'it was said of Augustus that he found Rome brick and left it marble. May it be said of you that you found Paris stinking and left it sweet.' It might stand for Chadwick's epitaph. He found England stinking. If he did not leave it sweet, it was certainly no fault of his. Through the Poor Law Commission, the Benthamite formula—inquiry, legislation, execution, inspection, and report—was incorporated in our working constitution. It was rounded off by the invention of the Public Audit and the Grant-in-aid to tighten central control and stimulate local activity. But the corresponding formula for unofficial effort—information, agitation, the parent society, the local branch, the picture, and the handbill—had been discovered by the Evangelicals and humanitarians in their warfare against slavery, and by them it was imparted to the Chartists and the Free Trade League.

The Evangelical and Utilitarian movements both rested on a body of doctrine which to question was impious or irrational; in both cases the doctrine was the reflection of an exceptional experience, the religious experience of a nation undergoing a moral revival, its social experience during a revolution in the methods of production; and in both cases a larger view was certain to show that neither was a more than provisional synthesis. In the meantime they furnished England with a code and a great company of interpreters: with their almost Genevan rigour, and almost Latin clarity, they imposed themselves like foreign task-masters on the large, ironic English mind, and their great doctrines were all too readily snipped into texts for the guidance of those who did not wish to think at all, and the repression of those who wished to think for themselves, into Cant for Practical Men and Cant for Serious Men. Finally, they were alike in this, that each imparted its peculiar virtue: the Evangelicals their zeal for holiness, the Utilitarians their faith in reason, to the movements, even to the reactions which sprang out of them, to Tractarians and Agnostics who denied their introspective ethic, to Conservatives and Socialists who challenged their conception of the competitive State.

III

Much of accident goes to the making of history, even to the history of thought, which might seem to be most exempt from contingencies. The Victorian record might have been very different if Canning had lived to the years of Palmerston, if the new writers had grown up under the shadow of Byron, Keats, and Shelley. But the old men lived and the young men died. Blake, we may remember, outlasted them all. A strange pause followed their departure, and the great Victorian lights rose into a sky which, but for the rapid blaze of Bulwer Lytton, was vacant. Tennyson and Macaulay, Carlyle and Newman, Gladstone and Disraeli, Arnold and Dickens appear above the horizon together. In Sydney Smith's stately compliments to the Graduate of Oxford,[1] the eighteenth century bows itself off the stage and introduces its successor. With the appearance of *Vanity Fair* in 1847, the constellation is complete and the stars are named. It was part of the felicity of the fifties to possess a literature which was at once topical, contemporary, and classic; to meet the Immortals in the streets, and to read them with added zest for the encounter.

Anchored to its twofold faith in goodness and progress, the early Victorian mind swung wide to the alternating

---

[1] 'He said [*Modern Painters, I*] was a work of transcendent talent, presented the most original views in the most elegant language, and would work a complete revolution in the world of taste.' (*Praeterita*: Chapter ix.)

currents of sentiment and party spite, but the virulence of the Press,[1] and the gush of the popular novel were play on the surface of a deep assurance. There are whimperings, sometimes bellowings, of self-pity, but defiance was no longer the mode. The greater and better part of English society accepted the social structure and moral objective of the nation, as a community of families, all rising, or to be raised, to a higher respectability. To these postulates their criticism of life was not directed: they were satisfied, not indeed with the world as it was, for they were all, in their way, reformers, but as it would become by the application of those reasoned and tested principles which made up the scheme of progress and salvation.

Poised and convinced, they could indulge, too, in a licence of feeling impossible to a generation bred in doubt, and they could take their ease in an innocent vulgarity which to a later age would have been a hard-worked and calculated Bohemianism. They could swagger and they could be maudlin. In public they could be reserved, for they were a slow and wary race, and reserve is at once the defence of the wise and the refuge of the stupid. But cynicism and superciliousness, the stigmata of a beaten age and a waning class, were alien to the hopeful, if anxious, generation which had taken the future into its hands. In their exuberance and facility, the earlier Victorians, with their flowing and scented hair, gleaming jewellery and resplendent waistcoats, were nearer to the later Elizabethans; they were not ashamed; and, like the Elizabethans, their sense of the worth-whileness of everything—themselves, their age, and their country: what the Evangelicals called seriousness; the Arnoldians, earnestness; Bagehot, most happily, eagerness—overflowed in sentiment and invective, loud laughter, and sudden reproof. Once at Bowood, when Tom Moore was singing, one by one the audience slipped away in sobs; finally, the poet himself broke down and bolted, and the old Marquis was left alone. We are in an age when, if brides sometimes swooned at the altar, Ministers sometimes wept at the Table; when the sight of an infant school could reduce a civil servant to a passion of tears; and one undergraduate has to prepare another

---

[1] It was a Cambridge joke that

> The abysmal deeps of personality

meant *The Times*.

undergraduate for the news that a third undergraduate has doubts about the Blessed Trinity—an age of flashing eyes and curling lips, more easily touched, more easily shocked, more ready to spurn, to flaunt, to admire, and, above all, to preach.

A young man brought up in a careful home might have heard, whether delivered or read aloud, a thousand sermons; an active clergyman was a social asset to a rising neighbour-hood, his popularity a source of spiritual danger to himself. The form of preachers was canvassed like the form of public entertainers, and the circulation of some Victorian sermons is a thing to fill a modern writer with despair. If we consider the effect, beginning in childhood, of all the preachers on all the congregations, of men loud or unctuous, authoritative or persuasive, speaking out of a body of acknowledged truth to the respectful audience below them, we shall see why the homiletic cadence, more briefly Cant, is so persistent in Vic-torian oratory and literature. It sufficed to persuade the lower middle classes that Tupper was a poet and the upper middle classes that Emerson was a philosopher. Mr. Gladstone formed his style by reading sermons aloud and his diaries are full of self-delivered homilies. Old Sir Robert Peel trained his son to repeat every Sunday the discourse he had just heard: a practice to which he owed his astonishing recollec-tion of his opponents' arguments and something, perhaps, of the unction of his own replies. The sermon was the standard vehicle of serious truth, and to the expositions and injunctions of their writers and statesmen the Victorian public brought the same hopeful determination to be in-structed, and to be elevated, which held them attentive to the pleadings, the denunciations, and the commonplaces of their preachers.

The body of acknowledged truth, out of which this early Victorian literature speaks, appears, at first sight, to consist of little more than all those dogmas which a victorious middle class had imposed on the nation. There is not much in it which the Compleat English Tradesman could not understand, and still less that he would not approve; as he could not understand Browning, Browning had to wait outside. But to take the height of the Victorian classics we must view them from the waste land of dreary goodness, useful information, and tired humour, stretching all about them, and no one who has survived the exploration will underrate the genius which could raise such a fabric on such foundations. The world desired to be instructed: it was given Grote and Thirlwall, Milman and Macaulay, Lyell's *Principles of Geology*, Mill's *Logic*, Mill's *Political Economy*; to be elevated: it had *Past and Present, Modern Painters*, and *In Memoriam*; it asked for theology and got Newman, for education and got Arnold. Out of the Minerva Press came Disraeli, out of the horseplay of sentimental Cockneys, Dickens.

It is only necessary to set these names down in order to realize what potent agencies of dissolution were working in the early Victorian years. English society was poised on a double paradox which its critics, within and without, called hypocrisy. Its practical ideals were at odds with its religious professions, and its religious belief was at issue with its intelligence. We, for example, should probably count an employer who kept children of nine working nine hours a day in a temperature of 98 degrees as, at least, a very stupid man. If he went farther and insisted that, when they wished to lift up their hearts in song, it must not be in carnal ditties like 'A Frog He Would A'Wooing Go', but in hymns—

> By cool Siloam's glassy rill
> How sweet the lily grows,
> How sweet the scent upon the hill
> Of Sharon's dewy rose—

we might credit him with a touch of diabolical humour. We should be wrong in a matter where it is both important and difficult to go right. He may have been a low hypocrite who slept with pretty mill girls on the sly. He may have been a kindly and intelligent man who had convinced himself that only by production, kept down to the lowest cost, could the country be fed, and that the sufferings of the poor in this present time were not worthy to be compared with the glory which should be revealed in them hereafter. Or, like most of us, he may have been something in between: borne along partly by conviction, partly by example, and neither disposed nor able to analyse ideas which proved themselves by their material results. Cheap labour meant high profits; respectable work-people meant good work.[1]

[1] In the eighteenth century the mill often furnished the millowner's harem: in our period rarely. I cannot resist the conclusion that the current religion did sometimes act as a provocative to sadism. Any one who looks at Sewell's

It could not last. It was impossible to maintain for ever the position that Christian responsibility was a duty everywhere except in economic life, and that strength and vigour, the control of nature by science, of events by prudence, are good things everywhere except in the hands of the State: not less impossible to suppose that the criticism which was unravelling the constitution of the rocks and the legends of antiquity, would always consent to stand in respectful submission before the conventions, or the documents, of contemporary Protestantism. So long as the fear of subversion persisted, criticism could not act with freedom: clerisy[1] and *bourgeoisie* stood together, and where they differed the clerisy, on the whole, preserved a loyal silence. Indeed, in State affairs they did not differ greatly. When, in his tract on Chartism, Carlyle essayed to translate the verities into practice, he had nothing to suggest that half the parsons in the land did not know already: that everybody should be sent to school and the odd man to the colonies. In religion they were coming to differ deeply, as the strong surviving vein of Augustan rationalism was reinforced by the conclusions of Victorian science. But the sanctions of orthodoxy were still formidable and in a world where *Prometheus Unbound* might be judicially held to be a blasphemous libel, a certain economy in the communication of unbelief was evidently advisable.

The sense of being under a Code accompanies us through the early Victorian decades. To the age of revolt which runs from Rousseau to Shelley succeeds the age of acquiescence: the Titans are dead, or they have been tamed. It seems as if speculation had ceased: there is an answer to every question and usually the answer is no. Milman is ostracized for calling Abraham a sheik: Miss Mitford is publicly reproved for calling a pudding a roly-poly: old lords have to guard their words for fear of shocking young lords, and a Member of Parliament wishing to say contracted pelvis must put it in the decent obscurity of a learned language.

Radley Sermons will know what I mean. A ghastly story came out in the Courts of a private tutor who prayed with a backward pupil, beat him to a jelly, kissed him and left him to die. The connexion between religious professions and fraudulent dealing started many criminals on the downward path—or so they assured the prison chaplains. But, again, this is an old story. In *Areopagitica* the City Man and his Religion almost twists a smile from Milton.

[1] Coleridge's useful word for the educated classes acting as a body.

A Parliamentary Committee, who asked a factory woman if she had ever miscarried, brought on themselves the anger of *The Times* for violating the principles which should preside over such inquiries, 'a dread of ridicule and an anxious avoidance of indecency', and *The Economist*, a paper of exceptional intelligence, declined to go into the details of the Public Health Bill of 1847 and fill its columns with a number of unpleasant words. A guilty conscience has never betrayed itself by a more superior sniff. Absurdity and impropriety, like domesticated dragons, guard the stability of society and the peace of the home, and absurdity seems to mean any way of thinking, impropriety any way of behaving, which may impair the comfort, impeach the dignity, and weaken the defence of the middle class. We remember with surprise that we are dealing with a race which had once, and not so long ago, been famous in its island for an independence and even eccentricity which it now only displayed abroad, and we ask what has happened to make it submit its behaviour, its language, and its ideas to this drastic and vigilant censorship.

IV

Every period of history may be interpreted in various ways, and the richer it is in event or thought the more numerous will be the interpretations. Early Victorian history might be read as the formation in the thirties of a Marxian *bourgeoisie* which never came into existence, the re-emergence in the forties of a more ancient tradition, a sense of the past and a sense of social coherence, which never fulfilled its promise, and a compromise between the two which possessed no ultimate principle of stability.[1] But we must all the time remember that the Victorian age is only the island counterpart of a secular movement, as significant as the turn from the Greek middle ages in the fifth century or the Latin middle ages in the fifteenth. Twice the European mind had been carried to the verge, and twice it had been baffled. In the nineteenth century it won the top and saw stretching before it that endless new world which Bacon had sighted, or imagined, where nothing need remain unknown, and for everything that is known there is something that can be done; the world of organized thought where even modern

[1] The three phases are conveniently marked by Miss Martineau's *Illustrations of Political Economy*, *Coningsby*, and Bagehot's *English Constitution*.

scientific man was only the rudiments of what man might be. But European currents have a way of changing their direction when they touch our shores: it was so with the Renaissance, it was so with the Reformation. We borrowed our Party names from France and Spain; only Radical is all our own.[1] But the Conservative Party is a much more vital element in the State than a Parti Conservateur, and Continental Liberalism had little to teach a people who counted their freedom not by revolutions but by dynasties. 'You see,' said Mackintosh, when the latest French pamphlet on Liberty was exhibited for his admiration, 'in England we take all that for granted.' Of Continental Socialism we may say we gave as good as we took, and the Nationalism, which was to glorify the heroisms and to poison the conflicts of a century, made little appeal to a race which had no memories of foreign oppression to brood over, and is always more disposed to grudge the cost of its victories than to spend fresh money in avenging its defeats. On the other hand, the special and domestic preoccupations which give the European movement its English colour, being of a kind which our peculiar and isolated history had engendered, the call of the sea, the constant embarrassment of English policy by Irish agitation, the persistence of the religious interest into a secularist age, aristocracy into a commercial age, and monarchy into a radical age, cannot be expounded in European terms.

To all these themes, the ground-tone was given by the growth of population, the result of many combining tendencies, humanitarian and scientific, which since the middle of the eighteenth century had operated with ever-increasing force. In 1730 it seems that of every four children born in London three failed to reach their fifth birthday.[2] A hundred years of improvement had almost reversed the proportion.[3] Life was safer and longer, and every census was swelled by the numbers of babies who now grew up, young people who

---

[1] Possibly Communism, which is claimed, as a colloquial inspiration, for Mr. Barmby of Hanwell. He must be distinguished from Mr. Baume, who planned a Communist University at Colney Hatch.

[2] It was a European phenomenon. The French death-rate seems to have fallen from 39 to 29 between 1780 and 1820.

[3] This in London over all. The infantile mortality about 1840 was—upper classes 1/10; middle classes 1/6; lower classes 1/4. In Manchester and Leeds the mortality under 5 was about 57/100.

now lived into manhood, old people who lingered on the earth which a hundred years before they would have quitted in middle life. But if the process was a just ground for pride, the results could not be contemplated without deep apprehension, and the gravity of the problem was at once demonstrated and accentuated by the state of Ireland, from which, crossing St. George's Channel at deck cargo rates, the starving Papists swarmed by thousands to gather the harvest in English fields or fill the slums of English towns. Those who traced them home, in books, or by the new tourist route to Killarney, and heard or saw for themselves the worse-than-animal wretchedness of a people withal so intelligent and so chaste, might well ask themselves what relief was in prospect unless Nature intervened and ordained depopulation on a scale from which Cromwell might have shrunk, and whether the misery of Ireland was not a foreshadowing of the doom of England herself.[1]

The only visible relief was by way of emigration, and already some minds had been fired by the thought of the great spaces waiting to be peopled or, with an even larger sweep of the imagination, by the picture of a vast Eastern Empire ruled from Australia. But the English of 1830, with six generations of the Law of Settlement behind them, were not easily up-rooted, and, publicly, the only restraint that could be recommended was late marriage and the abolition of those provisions of the Poor Law which set a premium on reckless unions. There was much active, if furtive, discussion of birth-control in Radical circles: John Mill was once in trouble for poking pamphlets down area railings; and one writer proposed that instruction in the subject should be included in the rules of all Trade Unions.[2] But contraception

[1] Down to the French wars England had been on balance a wheat-exporting country. After Waterloo it was plain that the balance had been reversed and that foreign wheat, though there were still years when the import only amounted to a few days' consumption, was normally required to make good the English harvest. The sliding scale of 1828 was contrived to steady home prices, and therefore rents, while admitting foreign supplies as they were needed: in theory the Radicals preferred Free Trade, in theory the Whigs were for a fixed duty; but in the early thirties the issue was not raised, the schism between the commercial and landed interests was latent and speculative.

[2] Wade in his *History of the Middle Classes* (if indeed I have correctly interpreted his mysterious hintings). Place gave instruction at Charing Cross: Mrs. Grote, I suspect, more than instruction to her village neighbours. Croker's attack on Miss Martineau was quite unpardonable, but it is fairly clear that Miss Martineau did not know what she was talking about.

did not seriously affect the birth-rate until, after the end of our period, it returned from America, to which it had been carried by the younger Owen. Malthus had raised a spectre which could be neither ignored nor laid.

More immediately significant than the growth of population was its aggregation in great towns. Down to the French Wars the moral habit of society was definitely patrician and rural and had still much of the ease, the tolerance, and the humour which belongs to a life lived in security and not divorced from nature. What differences existed in the lives and outlook of a gentleman, a yeoman, and a cottager were mitigated by their common subjection to the ebb and flow of the world, the seasons, and the hours. In correspondence with its traditional structure, the traditional culture and morality of England were based on the patriarchal village family of all degrees: the father worked, the mother saw to the house, the food, and the clothes; from the parents the children learnt the crafts and industries necessary for their livelihood, and on Sundays they went together, great and small, to worship in the village church. To this picture English sentiment clung, as Roman sentiment saw in the Sabine farm the home of virtue and national greatness. It inspired our poetry; it controlled our art; for long it obstructed, perhaps it still obstructs, the formation of a true philosophy of urban life.

But all the while Industrialism had been coming over England like a climatic change; the French wars masked the consequences till they became almost unmanageable. It is possible to imagine, with Robert Owen, an orderly evolution of the rural village into the industrial township, given the conditions which he enjoyed at New Lanark, a limited size and a resident, paternal employer. Belper under the Strutts, Bolton under the Ashworths, the cosy houses and flourishing gardens of South Hetton, to which foreign visitors were carried with special pride, the playing fields of Price's Candle Works, the Lancashire village where Coningsby met Edith, all have some affinity with the Owenite Utopia, bold peasants, rosy children, smoking joints, games on the green; Merrie England, in a word, engaged in a flourishing export trade in coal and cotton.[1] But any possibility of a general development

---

[1] I have read an Owenite fancy of the thirties in which the world is organized as a federation of Garden Cities. One episode is the return of a delegation, clad

along these lines had already been lost in the change-over
from water to steam power, in the consequent growth of the
great urban aggregates, and the visible splitting of society,
for which the Enclosures had created a rural precedent, into
possessors and proletariat. The employers were moving into
the country; their officials followed them into the suburbs;
the better workmen lived in the better streets; the mixed
multitude of labour, native or Irish, was huddled in slums
and cellars, sometimes newly run up by speculative builders,
sometimes, like the labyrinth round Soho and Seven Dials,
deserted tenements of the upper classes. In a well-managed
village with a responsible landlord and active parson, with
allotments for the men and a school for the children, the
old institutions and restraints might still hold good; in a
neglected village, and in that increasing part of the population which now lived in great towns, they were perishing.
Off work, the men could only lounge and drink; the girls
learnt neither to cook nor to sew. Lying outside the orbit
of the old ruling class, neglected by their natural leaders,
the industrial territories were growing up as best they might
undrained, unpoliced, ungoverned, and unschooled.

Yet the physical separation was not so complete that the
world beyond the pale could be ignored, and the Evangelical
ascesis was imposed on a generation to which the spectacle
of bodily existence was at once obtrusive and abhorrent.
Physically, the national type was changing; the ruddy, careless Englishman of the eighteenth century, turbulent but
placable, as ready with his friendship as his fists, seemed to
be making way for a pallid, sullen stock, twisted in mind
and body. And if the eye which ranged with such complacency over the palaces of Regent's Park, the thronging
masts of wide-wayed Liverpool, the roaring looms of hundred-
gated Leeds, descended to a closer view, of Finsbury, say, or
Ancoats, it would have observed that the breeding ground
of the new race was such that in truth it could breed nothing
else. The life within the factory or the mine was doubtless
rigorous, and to children often cruel, but the human frame
is immensely resilient, and with such care as many good
employers took, the working hours of a labourer's life were
probably his happiest. But the imagination can hardly

in chitons, from Bavaria, where, if I remember right, they have been showing
their German brethren how to lay a drain.

apprehend the horror in which thousands of families a hundred years ago were born, dragged out their ghastly lives, and died: the drinking water brown with faecal particles, the corpses kept unburied for a fortnight in a festering London August; mortified limbs quivering with maggots; courts where not a weed would grow, and sleeping-dens afloat with sewage.[1]

And while the new proletariat was falling below the median line of improving decency on one side, the middle classes were rising above it on the other, becoming progressively more regular, more sober, more clean in body, more delicate in speech. But not only were the middle classes drawing apart from the poor, each stratum, in a steady competition, was drawing away from the stratum next below, accentuating its newly acquired refinements, and enforcing them with censorious vigilance. The capriciousness, and over-emphasis, of Victorian propriety betrays its source. When we have set aside all that England shared with New England, all that nineteenth-century England had in common with nineteenth-century France[2] and Germany, and all that the England of Victoria had in common with the England of George III and George V, there remains this peculiar element, what Clough called 'an almost animal sensibility of conscience', this super-morality of the nerves and the senses, of bodily repulsion and social alarm.

Cleanliness is next to godliness. The Victorian insistence, whenever the poor are the topic, on neatness, tidiness, the well-brushed frock and the well-swept room, is significant. 'The English', Treitschke once told a class at Berlin, 'think

---

[1] The following figures tell their own tale:

Expectation of Life at Birth

	Bath	Rutland	Wilts	Derby	Truro	Leeds	Manchester	Liverpool
Gentlefolk . . .	55	52	50	49	40	45	38	35
Traders & Farmers	37	41	48	38	33	27	20	22
Labourers . .	25	38	33	21	28	19	17	15

In London the mortality was twice as great in the East End as in the West. In adjacent streets it varied from 38 to 12.

[2] Much nonsense about 'the Victorians' is dissipated by the reflection that it was the French Government that prosecuted *Madame Bovary*.

Soap is Civilization.' Neatness is the outward sign of a conscious Respectability, and Respectability is the name of that
common level of behaviour which all families ought to reach
and on which they can meet without disgust. The Respectable man in every class is one whose ways bear looking
into, who need not slink or hide or keep his door barred
against visitors, the parson or the dun, who lives in the eye
of his neighbours and can count on the approval of the
great and the obedience of the humble. 'The middle classes
know', Lord Shaftesbury once said, 'that the safety of their
lives and property depend upon their having round them a
peaceful, happy, and moral population.' To induce, therefore, some modicum of cleanliness and foresight, to find some
substitute for savage sport and savage drinking, to attract
the children to school and the parents to church, to awaken
some slight interest in books and the world beyond the end
of the street, on such limited, necessary ends as these was
bent that enormous apparatus of early Victorian philanthropy: of individual effort by squires and parsons and their
wives and daughters,[1] of organized effort by Hospital Committees, City Missions, Savings Banks, Mechanics' Institutes,
and Dispensaries, by institutions of every creed and size
and object, from the Coal Club, the Blanket Club, and the
Ladies' Child Bed Linen Club up to the great societies for
the diffusion of useful knowledge, religious knowledge, education, and temperance, and the provision of additional Curates.
Respectability was at once a select status and a universal
motive. Like Roman citizenship, it could be indefinitely
extended, and every extension fortified the State.

V

In 1830 one aspect, and not the least formidable, of the
new civilization, was suddenly forced on every mind. For
half a generation, the cholera had been wandering at large
across Asia and eastern Europe. It spread, in spite of the
most active precautions, into Germany; from Hamburg it

---

[1] As early as the twenties, the young lady in the country was expected to do
her district-visiting seriously, with a register and account book. It is, I think,
true to say that the pruriency which we find so offensive in Victorian morals
(the Blush-to-the-Cheek-of-the-Young-Person business) is mainly an urban,
and therefore middle-class, characteristic. There could not have been much
about the 'facts of life' that a country girl who taught in school and visited
in cottages did not know.

crossed to Sunderland; in a few weeks it was in London. Measures were hastily improvised to meet a visitation which might, for all that science could tell, be as destructive as the Great Plague. A Central Board of Health was established in London; local boards in the provinces; a day of fasting and humiliation was proclaimed. Of the local boards the most active was in Manchester, and the report of their secretary—it is only thirty pages long—is one of the cardinal documents of Victorian history. For the first time the actual condition of a great urban population was exposed to view. There was no reason to suppose that Manchester was any worse than other towns, and the inevitable conclusion was that an increasing portion of the population of England was living under conditions which were not only a negation of civilized existence, but a menace to civilized society.

Nor, it seemed, was the countryside in better condition. The Labourers' Rising of 1830 served, like the cholera, to call attention to a problem which without it might have been neglected till it was too late. The land was breaking under the burden of the poor rate, and the administration of the Poor Law was degrading the labourer whom it was designed to support. But the rural problem was simplicity itself compared with the problem of the towns. Let the able-bodied man be given the choice of earning his own living or going into the workhouse, and then, if he still cannot find work on the land, send him to the factory or the colonies. So long as the Poor Law Commissioners were at work in the south, pauperism disappeared as by magic. But, as they moved northwards, unexpected difficulties appeared. 'We grasped the nettle all right,' one of them ruefully acknowledged, 'but it was the wrong nettle.' Machinery had so reduced the value of labour that at any moment the workman might find himself starving in the midst of a plenty which his own hands had helped to create. But the urban problem could not be solved by marching the unemployed in and out of the workhouse as times were bad or good. That rural England was over-populated, the slow increase, in some counties a decline, through the years of prosperity proved. Industrial England was neither over-populated nor under-populated, but periodically over- and under-employed.

Unemployment was beyond the scope of any ideas which Victorian reformers had at their command, largely because they had no word for it.[1] Their language and their minds were dominated by the Malthusian conception of over-population. Sanitation and education were within their reach. But these are remedies which need time to do their work, and in the interim the catastrophe might have happened. A fermentation unknown to an earlier England was stirring in the commons. Eighteenth-century society was stable, and felt itself to be stable. From the Revolution to the fall of the Bastille, the thought of subversion, of any social crisis more serious than an election riot or a no-popery riot, never entered the mind of Governments. From Waterloo to 1848 it was hardly ever absent. Looking back from the serene and splendid noon of mid-Victorian prosperity, Kingsley wrote of the years when 'young lads believed (and not so wrongly) that the masses were their natural enemies and that they might have to fight, any year or any day, for the safety of their property and the honour of their sisters'. Young lads will believe anything. But men old enough to remember the French Revolution, or the Committees of Secrecy and the Six Acts of 1819, had their fears, too, when they reflected that as the country became more and more dependent on machines, its stability turned more and more on the subordination and goodwill of the savage masses which tended them.

To fortify the State against these and all other perils by admitting the respectable class as a body to the franchise was the purpose of the Reform Bill. For two years, beginning with the Paris Revolution of July 1830, England lived in a sustained intensity of excitement unknown since 1641. But when the dust had settled down Tories might have asked themselves what they had been afraid of, Radicals what they had been fighting for. Never was a revolution effected with more economy in change. The right of the magnate to appoint the representatives of the lesser boroughs had gone: his influence, if he chose to exercise it with discretion and decorum, was hardly impaired, and it soon appeared that if there was less fighting and less bribery at an election, there was still much bribery, and more intimidation, and election day was still a carnival which usually ended in a fight. Open voting kept the tenant under his

---

[1] I have not observed it earlier than the sixties. Thornton's (very able) Treatise on Overpopulation (1845) is really an analysis of unemployment.

landlord's eye; the tradesman under his customer's; and in every county the fifty-pound tenants at will, prudently enfranchised by a Tory amendment, made a solid block of dependable voters. The country was satisfied: even the Radicals accepted the Reform Bill as a fair instalment of their demands without pressing to know when the other instalments—the ballot, one man one vote, one vote one value—would be paid.[1]

The reforming impulse of the Whigs was exhausted with the passing of the Municipal Reform Act of 1835. The reorganization of the Judicature which Brougham ought to have effected in 1833 was left for Selborne in 1873. Graham, their best administrator, Stanley their best debater, left them. Lord Grey gave up; Lord Melbourne lounged along. The genial Althorp, who kept the Commons in good temper, was taken from them to the Lords. Harried by the Irish, baited by the Radicals, blocked by the Peers, divided among themselves, equally unable to pass their bills or balance their budgets, the Whigs sank in public esteem and dragged Parliament with them. Their one admitted success did them as much harm as their numerous failures. They kept Ireland quiet, but their pacts with O'Connell seemed to English opinion a disgraceful subservience to a rebel. They accepted Penny Postage, but on a falling revenue it sent their finance to pieces. Palmerston, marching steadily and buoyantly on a line of his own, brightened their last days with a diplomatic triumph over France and a naval victory over Mehemet Ali, of which, perhaps, in the long run, the most that can be said is that it gave England something to think of beside the misery of 1840. All through the thirties we are aware of a growing disaffection, of which Carlyle and Dickens are mouthpieces, with the delays and irrelevancies[2] of parlia-

[1] The figures of the first registration show how oligarchical the new Constitution was:

Counties, England	345,000	Scotland	33,000.
Boroughs	,, 275,000	Scotland	31,000.

The £10 householder in town was in effect a man with £150 a year and upward. Boroughs of 200 and 300 voters were still common: Thetford had 146. In very general terms one might say that from 1832 to 1867 one man in six had a vote, after 1867 one in three. In the same period over fifty returns were set aside for malpractices. *Electorate* is a L.V. word: *constituency* which appeared (colloquially) for the first time in 1830/1 originally meant *the whole body of electors*: then, *a particular body.*

[2] And mysteries. The procedural history of Parliament is a struggle between an old principle (freedom of debate) and a new one (to make a programme and get through it). In the thirties freedom, exercised through (*a*) a multitude of

mentary government, which, as the years went on, seemed to be degenerating more and more into an unseemly scuffle between Ins and Outs. The political satire of Dickens is tedious and ignorant. But it registers, what *Past and Present* conveys more passionately, the disillusionment which followed on the hopes of 1830.

Socially, the first reformed Parliaments were hardly distinguishable from their predecessors. The days of extravagant expenditure, when the poll was open for three weeks and a candidate might spend, as the virtuous and religious Acland did in Devon, £80,000 on four contests, were over and done with. But an election might easily cost a candidate £5,000. The just influence of landed property was preserved, and the old humanity of the South was still politically ascendant over the new industry of the North. The Whigs had introduced a self-adjusting device into the constitution, but it worked slowly. So late as 1845 three notes of exclamation were required to convey Prince Albert's amazement at the thought of Cobden in the Cabinet. The Tories had learnt by experience to adopt capacity from whatever quarter it appeared: they admitted Peel, the son of a cotton-spinner; Canning, whose mother was an actress; and Huskisson, whose origin, if possibly more respectable, was even more obscure. The Whigs in exile had drawn closer together and farther from the main stream of English life; they came from the eighteenth century when privilege was taken for granted and they brought the eighteenth century with them; and one result of the Reform was to give England, growing more and more resentful of privilege, the most aristocratic Government that any one could remember, and to set the Lords almost in equipoise with the Commons. And all the while, with a suspicious, but obedient, party behind him—150 in '32, 250 in '34, 300 in '37—Peel was biding his time. With the return of the Conservatives in 1841 and the impending grapple of Land and Industry, Parliament recovered its standing as the debating-place of public issues, and, what to the new electorate was even more important, as the guardian of the public purse. The country preferred an Income Tax from Peel to one deficit more from Baring.

formal stages, (b) irrelevant amendments on going into Committee or adjourning, was in the ascendant. The public, intensely interested in Parliament, was in consequence often baffled to know what Parliament was doing or why.

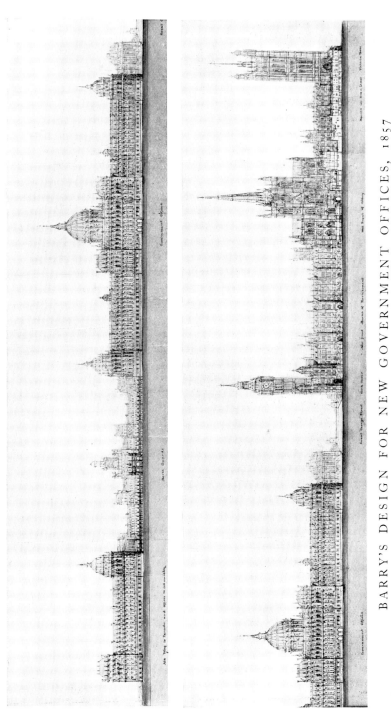

BARRY'S DESIGN FOR NEW GOVERNMENT OFFICES, 1857

Until 1834 the traveller approaching London over West-minster Bridge saw on his left a foreshore where watermen lounged among their boats: behind it a walled garden front-ing a low range of red-brick Tudor houses. At the far left the Chapel of St. Stephen projected almost to the water's edge, and high above all stretched the grey roof of the Hall. The towers of the Abbey were just visible behind. After the fire of 1834 the Commons found room in the old House of Lords, the Peers sat in the Painted Chamber, while the palace of Barry and Pugin was rising to overshadow both Abbey and Hall: the Lords entered their new house in 1847: the Commons in 1852. Business commonly began at four, mornings being kept for Committees, with questions, few, but often involving voluminous reply, and followed by some desultory conversation, and the presentation of petitions. These opportunities for demagogic eloquence, which at one time threatened to overwhelm the House, were cautiously restricted, and finally abolished in 1843. Two nights were reserved for Government business. Lord John Russell tried to get a third and was refused. Party allegiance was loose, party management dexterous and sharp. Private members had more freedom and opportunity than in a modern Parliament, and much legislation was drafted, introduced, and carried from the back benches.[1] After the first few speeches the audience scattered to dinner and left the bores in possession. From nine the attendance and the excitement increased. There was no eleven o'clock rule, and often the sun was up before the Commons, with parched throats and throbbing heads, escaped to enjoy, if they could, the majestic spectacle of London from the bridges, before the smoke had risen to make every street dark and every face dirty.

The manners of Parliament in the thirties seem to have been the worst on record, and they were not improved when, in 1835, the Whigs, in their brief interval of Opposition, chose to put out a strong Speaker, Manners Sutton, and put in a very weak one, Abercromby.[2] Under his amiable governance, with the windows shut—and the stench of the

---

[1] The career of Ewart (son of Mr. Gladstone's godfather) is typical. He was in Parliament thirty-four years. He carried three important bills (capital punish-ment, defence of felons, public libraries) besides being very active on free trade, schools of design, and competitive examinations. But he was never in office.

[2] Lord John Russell urged the view, which fortunately did not become canonical, that the Speaker should always be in sympathy with the majority.

Thames made it impossible to keep them open—the mooings, cat-calls, and cock-crows, what O'Connell once called the 'beastly bellowings', of the faithful Commons could be heard fifty yards away. The eloquence which could master such an audience was of a new kind. The great rhetorical tradition which begins with Halifax and runs through Pitt to Canning, sent up an expiring flash in Macaulay. The modern manner was less declamatory and more closely reasoned: we might call it more conversational if we remember that conversation still kept some of the amplitude of an earlier day.[1] Speeches were very long, but the contentions over the currency and the fiscal system had created a new style, of which Huskisson was the first exponent, Peel the most specious master, and which Mr. Gladstone wielded like a Tenth Muse: knowledge of the facts and an apt handling of figures was now the surest proof of capacity, and among the most memorable feats of Victorian oratory are speeches on finance.

In this development Parliament reflected a movement in the national mind. It was the business of the thirties to transfer the treatment of affairs from a polemical to a statistical basis, from Humbug to Humdrum.[2] In 1830 there were hardly any figures to work on. Even the Census was still far from perfect: in that of 1831 the acreage of England is given twice over, with a discrepancy as large as Berkshire. Imports were still reckoned by Official Values based on the prices of 1690. But statistical inquiry, fostered very largely by the development of the Insurance business, was a passion of the times. The Statistical department of the Board of Trade was founded in 1832; the department of the Registrar-General in 1838; the Royal Statistical Society sprang out of the Cambridge meeting of the British Association in 1833. Two private compilations of the thirties, McCulloch's *Statistical Account of the British Empire*[3] and Porter's *Progress of the Nation,* are

---

[1] The Brookfields in the fifties claimed to have introduced the new style of conversation, brisk and allusive. Mrs. Carlyle used to torture London parties with the elaboration of her anecdotes.

[2] As a symbol of the age, one might cite the Lords' Report on 'the expediency of Discontinuing the present Mode of Engrossing Acts of Parliament in Black Letter and substituting a Plain Round Hand'. But until Lord Thring took it in hand, the actual drafting of statutes came far short of these good intentions.

[3] Which gives more space to Oxford than to Canada. *Empire* in E. V. English is stylistic for *realm, kingdom,* and imports no overseas reference. 'Dog's Hole Lane has been widened! Main drainage has been installed! Soon X will

still the best approach to Victorian history. Then come the great inquiries, by Parliamentary Committees or Royal Commissions, following the Poor Law Commission of 1832. To Sydney Smith it seemed that the world had been saved from the flood to be handed over to barristers of six years' standing, and a Prussian visitor apprehended that the object of the Whigs was to Germanize England by means of Royal Commissions. In a few years the public mind had been flooded with facts and figures bearing on every branch of the national life, except agriculture: the collection of agricultural statistics was resisted till after the end of our period. No community in history had ever been submitted to so searching an examination.[1] Copied or summarized in the Press the Blue Books created a new attitude to affairs: they provided fresh topics for novelists and fresh themes for poets. *Sybil* is a Blue Book in fiction; *The Cry of the Children* a Blue Book in verse. With the parliamentary inquiries must be ranged the local investigations made by individuals, societies, and municipalities. I have spoken of Kay-Shuttleworth's Report on Manchester. In a few years a score of great towns, Bristol, Westminster, Southwark, Hull, Liverpool, Leeds, had all been put through the same mill and with much the same results.[2] Douglas Jerrold, who had once produced an unsuccessful play called *The Factory Girl*, complained that in 1833 no one was thinking about the poor and in 1839 no one was thinking about anything else. But in 1839 the depths had not been sounded.

VI

The years following the Reform Act were for the towns a time of quiet prosperity, which culminated in the golden harvest of 1835. Towards the end of 1836 a warning shiver ran through the commercial world: over-production and speculation were producing their natural consequences. There was a parallel depression in America, and the European States were raising their tariffs. Lancashire went on half-

take her rightful place among the Cities of the Empire!' I quote from memory from the history of some 'glad aspiring little burg'.

[1] The Parliamentary papers were first put on sale in 1835; division lists first published in 1836.

[2] The impulse came from the Statistical Society of Manchester, which, as a control experiment, also investigated Rutland. Leeds was, I believe, the first municipality to investigate itself.

time; the harvest of 1838 failed; gold was exported to buy food and the Bank of England was barely saved from default by credits in Paris and Hamburg. That a bad period was approaching was evident. But few could have guessed through what misery the country would have to pass before the clouds lifted again. In Stockport nearly a fourth of the houses were empty. Thousands of families were living on relief administered at the rate of a shilling a head. Out of 15,000 persons visited, not one in ten was fully employed. Wages had fallen from a pound and more to 7s. 6d.; the average weekly income was less than 1s. 6d. Manchester and Bolton were in like case: the Potteries, the Black Country, the cloth towns of the west, all told the same tale. It was the background of Chartism and the Free Trade League.

The Chartists wished to make a revolution: the Leaguers asserted that the revolution had happened, and drew out the consequences. Lancashire, the home of the movement, was the most typical product of the new civilization, and it needed little argument to prove that Lancashire could not live without imported cotton, could not maintain her increasing population without expanding markets, could not expand her markets unless the foreigner was kept in funds by the sale of food to England. Did the workshop of the world need a hobby farm, with a subsidized gentry to manage it, especially a gentry which was beginning to show an inconvenient interest in factory children and the tendency of the fourteen-hour day, *minuere et contrahere pelvem*?[1] The League was founded in January 1839. For the first years of its existence it was fighting on two fronts, against the Protectionists and against the Chartists. Free Trade lecturers ran the double risk whenever they stood up in a marketplace of being fined by the magistrate and ducked by the mob. To hungry men the prospect of relief by Free Trade was more remote than the prospect of relief by direct action, and it was as easy to represent the League as a coalition of mill-owners bent on reducing their wages bill, as a coalition of democrats bent on destroying the landed interest. 'You are a Chartist, Sir; you are a leveller,' the Home Secretary shouted at the respectable Mr. Ashworth, manufacturer,

---

[1] Lord John Manners let the cat out of the bag when he talked, apropos a Factory Bill, of 'putting a curb on the manufacturing interest and making it know its rider'.

when he came on a Free Trade deputation. The self-protec-
tive instincts of the aristocracy felt in the League its most
dangerous enemy. But the instinct of society as a whole
was more sensitive to the growing menace of Chartism.

The political creed of the Chartists was an amplification
of the Radical formula, one man one vote, one vote one
value. How they were going to get the vote was not so
clear, and what they were going to do with it remained even
to themselves unknown. Judged by what they did, they
might be considered a body of decent, hardly used, and not
particularly intelligent men, whose allegiance, given with
equal readiness to high-minded leaders like Lovett and
Hetherington and to pitiful demagogues like Feargus
O'Connor, would probably be at the service of the first
Conservative or Liberal who showed that he deserved it.
Judged by what they said, or by what O'Connor, 'false,
malignant, and cowardly', said for them, both their objects
and their methods seemed to involve a bloody progress from
confiscation, through anarchy, to famine and a dictatorship.
The Socialism of Robert Owen, the doctrine that industrialism
was not an impersonal force to be adored or bewailed, but
a way of life to be controlled by co-operation, had gone
underground. The young Queen was gracious to him for her
father's sake, who had been his friend in the days when
Napoleon had studied his projects in Elba and Castlereagh
had laid them before Congresses. But his mind was failing,
and to most people Owenism meant a crazy multiplication
of Trade Unions with long names and the combination of
economic heresy with irreligion and sexual depravity. 'You
tell us', a Parliamentary Committee once said to a clergyman, 'that the railway navvies are mostly infidels. Would
you say that they are also socialists?' 'In practice, yes;
because though most of them appear to have wives, few of
them are really married.' The more intelligent workmen
professed a belated rationalism, nourished on the writings
of Tom Paine, with which often went, for philosophy, a
wondrous addiction to the phrenology of George Combe.[1]

[1] Which was shared by Cobden. Phrenology was regularly taught in
Mechanics' Institutes, and did, I think, help to keep the idea of personality alive
under the steam-roller of respectability. Otherwise, science (for want of apparatus) did not much affect the workman. The culture of the self-educated man
was still literary. He began with the Bible and its commentators and worked
up through Milton to the economists, philosophers, and historians. This was

The older sects meant little to the working classes. The Wesleyans, whose services in humanizing the masses were handsomely recognized by authority, on principle held aloof from political contests; and Chartism, which disgusted fair-minded men by the violence of its invective, terrified a still larger class by its supposed designs, not only on movable property, but on religion and the family. Yet there was much silent sympathy with the Chartists as men: if the new rich had been their only enemies, many young gentlemen would have been glad to strike a blow for the old poor. Young England was a sincere if boyish gesture of goodwill, and to play King Richard to somebody else's Wat Tyler has always been a Tory fancy.

How far the mass of the work-people were at any time seriously engaged is a question not easy to answer. The Londoners, who were most closely allied with the Parliamentary Radicals, stood for caution and constitutional methods. The admixture of cheap Irish labour and cheap Irish rhetoric alienated the Englishman, and the party of physical force were unlucky in their choice of military advisers. In no age are Count Chopski and Colonel Macerone names to conjure with in English working circles. The Convention summoned to London withdrew to the less frigid air of Birmingham: it was known that Lancashire was arming; regiments were recalled from Ireland, the army was increased by 7,000 men, a White Guard instituted, and Sir Charles Napier, a wise and sympathetic choice, was sent to take command of the Northern Division. In 1839 the Charter was presented and rejected: the Convention considered a general strike and a march on London. There was no strike; no one marched, and the insurgents had to be content with a wild riot in Birmingham. In a few weeks 400 Chartists were in prison, and the revolution ended in a splutter of musketry and a dozen men killed outside the Queen's Hotel, Newport. Chartism, though there was some brief, fierce rioting in 1842, when the Charter was again presented and rejected, was effectively dead.

It is impossible to gauge the danger of a revolution which refused to happen. But in estimating the alarm we must

of some importance politically. If any speech of Bright, Gladstone, or Disraeli *ad Quirites* is examined, it will be found to imply a large body of literary culture common to the speaker and at least a great part of his audience.

allow for the melodramatic streak in the early Victorian temperament. When Wellington said on the morrow of the riots that no town sacked in war presented such a spectacle as Birmingham, he did not mean that he had gone to see it for himself, any more than when Lord Shaftesbury said that *Ecce Homo* was the foulest book ever vomited from the jaws of hell, he meant that he had read all the others. Events, like books, still came widely spaced, with time between to set the imagination working; and that generation was still overshadowed by the revolutionary years and read itself in their volcanic light. In 1840 there were many men living who could recall the flight of the French nobility. The sacking of Bristol was still fresh in all memories, and England had hardly the elements of a civil force capable of stopping disorder before it reaches the point where factories are burnt and the troops must shoot. London was provided for by the Peelers and the mounted patrol who kept order within five miles of Charing Cross. The parish had its constable, and the police of the boroughs were reinforced in emergencies by specials: on election days and other occasions of riot the specials might be numbered by hundreds. There were five hundred private associations for the prosecution of felons; but there was no county police;[1] and the mainstay of the public peace was not the constable but the yeoman, and behind the yeoman, though cautiously and reluctantly employed, the soldier.

Lord John Russell, accounting to the Queen for the progress of the Tories at the elections of 1838, added that the Military had in all cases conducted themselves with great temper and judgement. They were employed on even humbler duties: once, at least, troops were called out to enforce the Act of 1823 and save a poor ox from being baited on his way to market. England as a whole, and the country gentlemen in particular, were highly suspicious of anything in the nature of a national police, and the Act of 1839 went no further than to permit the Justices of a County to appoint a Chief Constable and form a police force if they so desired. The boroughs already had the power. But in that alarming year it was discovered that neither Birmingham nor

---

[1] This is not without its bearing on Victorian psychology. With 25,000 vagrants on the pad, and all the village idiots at large, the unprotected female really had something to be afraid of.

Manchester could maintain a paid force, and an emergency detachment had to be sent from London. So sensitive was the feeling of sound constitutionalists in the matter of police, that Lord John, having sent London constables to Bradford to help with a Poor Law riot, decided on reflection to withdraw them and enjoined the magistrates to use dragoons instead. The Permissive Act of 1839 was generalized by the Compulsory Act of 1856. The interval had been well employed. Essex selected as Chief Constable a retired Naval Officer. He very soon made it appear that a paid constabulary was not only more efficient but actually cheaper than the gratuitous service of Dogberry and Verges. One by one the counties adopted the model he had devised, and all that was necessary in '56 was to bring the laggards into line. There are many famous men to whom England owes less than she owes to Admiral M'Hardy, Chief Constable of Essex.

But his career, and his achievement, are typical of a general rule. The English administration was made by administrators throwing out their lines until they met and formed a system. In the fustian phrase which exasperated clear-headed Radicals, it was not made, it grew. In 1830, except for the collection and management of the revenue, for defence, and the transmission of letters, there was hardly anything which a Frenchman or a Prussian would have recognized as an administration. The national expenditure was £50,000,000, of which the debt absorbed £29,000,000, defence £15,000,000, leaving £6,000,000 only for collection, for the Crown and the whole civil administration. The total and the proportions did not vary greatly till the Crimean War. But by 1860 the cost of defence was £26,000,000, the balance for civil purposes £15,000,000. These figures, which illustrate the growth of the armed administrative State, show also with what a light equipment early Victorian government operated. Local revenue was about a quarter of Imperial, and on an average one-half went in the relief of the poor. The rest was spent on Police, Bridges, and Highways; on Lunatics; on the upkeep of Parish Churches. The Church rate, an inconsiderable sum, but the occasion of much agitation and some painless martyrdom, was persistently evaded, made voluntary in 1853 and abolished in 1868.

The Civil Servants who ran this light machinery were of

two sorts: clerks, infallible in accounts, writing a fair hand, the repository of precedent; gentlemen, or the protégés of gentlemen, of the political class, whose position when young might be anything from a copying clerk to a private secretary, and who when old were rather assistants and advisers to an executive chief than executants themselves. There was much routine, so much that by the time the juniors were seniors they were usually unfit for anything else and the higher posts had to be filled from outside, but in the civilian branches almost everything that rose above routine was, except at the Treasury, policy requiring the personal attention of the Minister: the intermediate sphere of administration did not exist, because there were hardly any laws to administer. Readers of Disraeli's novels must sometimes have been puzzled by the importance of the Under-Secretaries as a class. When the Cabinet was open only to birth, to exceptional genius or exceptional influence, men of excellent gifts had to be content, and were content, with Under-Secretaryships, and the unbroken Tory régime had given some of them a very long innings. Croker was of this class, so was 'gray-headed, financial' Herries; and the Whigs of 1827 could not master their wrath when they were asked to accept as a Cabinet colleague a fellow whom they had always looked upon as a Treasury clerk. A Treasury official in Early Victorian English means a Junior Lord.

Well on into our period the line between politics and administration could be crossed and recrossed as it was by Endymion. Cornewall Lewis was a Civil Servant for fourteen years before he entered Parliament, where he reached Cabinet rank in eight. Benjamin Hawes from Parliamentary Secretary became Permanent Secretary to the War Office. William Blamire made his mark in Parliament with a speech on tithes and was given a post which made him, in effect, for twenty years a non-parliamentary Minister of Agriculture. But the dismissal of the Under-Secretaries with their chiefs in 1830, the inexperience of the new Whig Ministers, and the reform of the Poor Law, made a fresh departure. The Benthamite conception of a trained staff dealing with specific problems entered the Civil Service at the very point where the Civil Service impinged most forcibly on the public. The Poor Law filled the whole horizon in 1834. And here, there, and everywhere were Chadwick's young crusaders, the

Assistant Commissioners, scouring the country in stage-coaches or post-chaises, or beating up against the storm on ponies in the Weald, returning to London, their wallets stuffed with the Tabular Data so dear to philosophic Radicals, to draft their sovereign's decrees declaring the Union and stating his austere principles of administration, and then back to see that they were carried out. It was an exciting life. Once they had to be protected with cavalry. When they appeared at Todmorden, Fielden rang his factory bells and beat them out of town. In so splendid and imperial a manner did the English Civil Servant first take his place in the national life.[1]

The Radicals had conceived the possibility of applying disinterested intelligence to social problems. Chadwick realized the idea and created the organ of application. The administrative temper was in being before there was an administration to give it effect. The Poor Law schools at Norwood were taken as a model by the new Education Department. The Poor Law framework was adopted in 1838 for the registration of births, marriages, deaths, and the causes of death. In the same year a London vestry, baffled by an outbreak of fever, turned to the Poor Law Board for help, a step from which descends by regular stages the Health Board of 1848, the Local Government Board of 1870, the existing Ministry of Health. What was growing up, in fact, in the thirties, under the vigorous impulsion of Chadwick and Kay and the bewildered gaze of Ministers, was a Public Welfare Service, which was bound sooner or later to demand compulsory powers, and to receive them as soon as the public mind was sufficiently moved, enlightened, or alarmed.

But the rapid growth of our administrative services is on the whole due less to head-quarters than to the Inspectorate. Inspection was in the air: the Factory Inspectors of 1834 were followed by the Prison Inspectors, and these by the School Inspectors, the Railway Inspectors and the Mines Inspectors. The Inspectors, like the higher officials, were often

---

[1] The distinction of administrative and clerical duties which lies at the root of the Arbuthnot-Trevelyan reforms in '53 was carried out at the Poor Law Commission from the first. James Mill had already introduced it at the India House. The confusion of functions reached its height at Dublin Castle, where the duties of the Under-Secretary were, *inter alia*, to deputize for the Lord-Lieutenant, to docket incoming letters in red ink, to advise on all criminal business, and to see that the stationery was not wasted.

The decision of the Cabinet is no longer a secret. Parliament, it is confidently reported, is to be summoned for the first week in January ; and the Royal Speech will, it is added, recommend an immediate consideration of the Corn Laws, preparatory to their total repeal. Sir ROBERT PEEL in one house, and the Duke of WELLINGTON in the other, will, we are told, be prepared to give immediate effect to the recommendation thus conveyed.

An announcement of such immeasurable importance, and to the larger portion of the community so unspeakably gratifying, almost precludes the possibility of comment. No pen can keep pace with the reflections which must spontaneously crowd upon every thoughtful and sensitive mind. They who have long desired this change, and have long traced its manifold bearings on the welfare and happiness of the world, will in one moment see the realization of that fair prospect, and will hardly endure to be informed of what they already behold. The approaching event, therefore, which we this day communicate to our readers, must be left to speak for itself.

From The Times, 4 *December* 1845

men of mature experience who came to their duties with ideas already formed. Leonard Horner, whose reports underlie so much of our industrial legislation, was nearing fifty when he entered the factory department, and was already a name of note in education and science. Hugh Tremenheere, entering the education department at thirty-five, had fourteen Acts of Parliament to his credit when he retired. With them must be ranked the specialists in public health; above all, Southwood Smith and John Simon. Smith, a Unitarian minister, whose devotional writings must have had some singular quality to be admired both by Wordsworth and Byron, came late to the profession of medicine, but he found his place at once with an Essay on Fever. Cholera was a visitor: typhus a resident whom Southwood Smith believed could be expelled. Joining forces with Chadwick he became, in effect, Medical Adviser to the Poor Law Commission. His junior, Simon, a cultivated surgeon of French descent, a connoisseur and the friend of Ruskin, covered in his official life the development of the Board of Health into the Local Government Board, of which he was the first secretary. In the careers of men like these, or of Arthur Hassall, who took the adulteration of food for his province, we see the impact of the educated intelligence on the amorphous, greedy fabric of the new civilization, and I know nothing which brings the epic quality of the early Victorian warfare against barbarism into such vivid relief as the reports, eloquent, impassioned, and precise, which from 1848 onwards Simon addressed to the Corporation of the City of London.

VII

The thirty years from Waterloo have the unity and, at times, the intensity of a great drama. Castlereagh and Canning adjusted our insular relations to the Old World and the New. The Reform Act and the Municipal Reform Act gave the islands a rational political framework; steam unified their economic structure. Of all these processes, the Repeal of the Corn Laws in 1846 was the logical and historical culmination. The operations of the League, which had gone with a swing all through the bad years, flagged with the return of prosperity in 1843 and the absorption of the unemployed by the railway boom; by 1845 manufacturers did not know where to turn for hands. Peel himself was slowly moving towards Free Trade in corn, but he was restrained, not by a political, but by an economic scruple: the belief that cheap food meant low wages and that the loss of rents to the land-owner would be followed with no compensating advantage to the working classes. When this doubt was resolved his way grew clear. The great Budget of 1842, in which he had swept away the accumulated muddles of the Whigs and raised an income tax to lower the customs, marks the opening stage of classical Victorian finance. Incidentally, the sliding scale of 1828, which had refused to slide, was re-adjusted. In 1845 he repeated his stroke, and circumstances were gradually imposing a larger policy on his mind. All his young men—Gladstone, Lincoln, Canning, Herbert—were Free Traders, and Peel, behind the repellent front which he turned to the world, and which, indeed, cost him his life, was exceptionally sensitive to the ideas, and the sufferings of others.[1] The prosperity of the mid-forties had not spread to the villages; whatever the cause, the consequences were plain enough: 'I be protected and I be starving.' One good harvest more, to keep the League quiet, and he would go to the country as a Free Trader, with the compensating offer of a credit for the re-conditioning of the land and the absorption of the next wave of unemployment, and return with the middle-class Conservatism he had created, solidly based on the gratitude of the towns and the regeneration of the farming interest. The disaster which depopulated Ireland shattered the Conservative party on the threshold of a generation of power.[1]

The Irish difficulty went deeper than the philosophy of the age could reach. The twin cell of English life, the squire administering what everybody recognizes as law and the parson preaching what everybody acknowledges to be religion had no meaning in a country where the squire was usually an invader and the parson always a heretic. England had staked the good government of Ireland on a double specula-

---

[1] Peel's long-distance programme will be found in a memorandum by Prince Albert, Christmas 1845. His character is not easy to read, because his mastery of Parliamentary methods masked an intense dislike of the party system, while his frigid efficiency covered an almost passionate concern for the welfare of the people. On his last ride an acquaintance, who recognized his horse as a bolter, was afraid to warn him, but in a begging letter-writer's list of people most likely to be touched for a fiver, Peel's name was found with good Queen Adelaide and Dickens.

tion, that the Irish would conform to the Protestant establishment and that they would accept the English use of landlord, farmer, and labourer. The Irishry preferred to misgovern themselves as Catholics and small-holders, and the Englishry, after a few generations, were all too ready to take up the part of tribal chiefs. To analyse the Irish trouble into racial, religious, and agrarian is impossible because in Irish history these three are one, and when England had conceded Catholic emancipation against her own Protestants, and insisted on agrarian reform against the Irish landlords, and both in vain, the logic of history left her no alternative but to concede all the rest, never quite understanding what it was the Irish wanted or why they wanted it.

Thus throughout the nineteenth century Ireland was an uneasy place in the body politic which could be neither forgotten nor assuaged. In the thirties it is tithes and crime. The establishment was a grievance which an English government might alleviate if it could not remove. Disorder was a pestilence which it was bound to stamp out. Hence the history of Lord Grey's Government is taken up very largely with Irish Church bills and Irish coercion bills. On the whole the Whigs were successful, mainly because they sent two honest gentlemen, Drummond and Ebrington, to the Castle and left them alone, and in '41 they handed over to their successors an Ireland neither prosperous nor contented, but at least reasonably quiet. The nationalist agitation which sprang up suddenly in the following years was unexpected. Had it fallen a little earlier so as to coincide with the Chartist movement in England, the results might have been memorable. But in 1839 Ireland was so peaceful that soldiers could be spared for England, and in 1843 England was in such good humour that they could be safely sent to Ireland. On October 5 a great demonstration was to assemble at Clontarf; it was proclaimed and O'Connell arrested. Convicted, almost of course, by a Protestant Dublin jury, he was set at liberty by the House of Lords. The incident added a phrase to the language—Lord Denman saying that trial by jury as practised in this case was 'a delusion, a mockery, and a snare', and the Nationalist movement died down. Peel's Government used their victory not unwisely. They issued a Royal Commission of Enquiry into Irish land tenure and, in the teeth of a frantic Protestant opposition, they carried their proposal to increase the grant for training Irish priests at Maynooth. On the report of the Commission, a classic document for the history of the Irish question, they introduced a Bill to secure compensation for improving tenants. The Lords objected and the Bill was withdrawn for further consideration. The occasion had passed and it did not return.

Early in August 1845, at the end of a successful session, with a thriving country and a full exchequer, Peel received a letter from a potato-dealer, warning him that the crop was diseased and the disease spreading. Half the population of Ireland lived on potatoes, and by the beginning of October it was doubtful whether half the crop would be saved. England had been accustomed to take on an average 2,000,000 quarters of wheat from Ireland. It looked as if she would have to send 2,000,000 quarters to keep the Irish alive and the English harvest was short. It was out of the question to ask the English to pay duty both on the corn they ate themselves, and on the corn they bought for the Irish: equally impossible to suppose that the Corn Laws once suspended could ever be reimposed or that the Conservative party as it stood would ever consent to repeal them. Peel, with the support of the Whigs and with a fragment of his own party, undertook to admit foreign corn at a nominal fixed duty.[1] Supported by imminent famine, the arguments of the League could not be answered: they could only be opposed. It seemed as if nature, which was solving the Irish problem in the sense of the economists by killing off the surplus population, would solve an English problem in the sense of the Radicals by killing off the superfluous landlords. In fact, it did no harm to the English gentry, and it made the Irish problem insoluble. The Encumbered Estates thrown on the market were bought up by investors who proceeded to reorganize them economically by wholesale evictions, and for years hardly a ship sailed to the west without its freight of exiles carrying to America an unappeasable passion for vengeance on the dispossessor.

Yet there was never an Irish tragedy without its satyric afterpiece. In 1848, Smith O'Brien, a respectable and humourless Member of Parliament who seems to have been drawn

---

[1] It is characteristic of Early Victorian manners that in the Cabinet paper announcing his conversion, Peel can hardly bring himself to call That Root by its proper name. It was observed that in all prayers offered up for our Irish brethren, potatoes were never mentioned.

MANNERS AND CVSTOMS OF Yᵉ ENGLYSHE IN 1849. Nº 38.

A BANQVET SHOWINGE Yᵉ FARMERS FRIEND IMPRESSYNGE ON Yᵉ AGRYCVLTVRAL INTEREST THAT IT IS RVINED.

to Repeal by simple despair of the Union, was caught levying war on the Queen's Majesty in the widow McCormack's cabbage garden. The campaign was brief, as O'Brien had forgotten to provide his army with anything to eat. He was sentenced to the usual penalty, which was at once commuted to transportation. With the maddening logic which Irishmen have at command he argued that as he had not been convicted of anything deserving transportation, he must be pardoned or he must be hanged. The Law Officers admitted his contention, and a short Act had to be passed providing that, in spite of the earnest expectation of the creatures, O'Brien and others in like case might lawfully be required to remain alive.

VIII

Later Victorians, to whom Free Trade had become a habit of mind, tended almost instinctively to divide the century into the years before and after 1846. But twenty years later one social observer laid his finger not on the Repeal of the Corn Laws in '46, but on the Factory Act of '47, as the turning-point of the age and, with our longer perspective, we can hardly doubt that he was right. Of facts which, in Gibbon's phrase, are dominant in the general system, by far the most significant in this period is the emergence of a new State philosophy, of which the overt tokens are the Factory Act, the Public Health Acts,[1] and the Education Minute of 1846. The great inquiries of the thirties and forties were the Nemesis of the middle-class victory of 1830; an unreformed Parliament would never have persisted in them, and they led, silently and inevitably, to a conception of the State and its relations to its subjects which the electors of the first Reformed Parliaments would almost unanimously have repudiated. The cataclysm of 1830 proved to have been the beginning of a slow evolution, by which, while an aristocratic fabric was quietly permeated with Radical ideas, an individualist society was unobtrusively schooled in the ways of State control. Engels' *Condition of the Working Class*, which projected the image of the exploiting capitalist on the mind of the European proletariat, appeared in 1845: it was based on the English Blue Books. So was the

[1] The principal are: Baths and Washhouses Act '46 and '47; Town Improvements Clauses '47; Public Health '48; Lodging Houses '51; Burials '52.

legislation of 1847. History, which sometimes condescends to be ironic, had chosen her dates with meaning.

From 1832 to 1847 the student of Victorian history finds himself the bewildered spectator of a warfare between Radicals who upheld Factories and Workhouses, Tories and Chartists who abhorred them both, infidel Benthamites leagued with Conservative Anglicans against dissenting manufacturers, landowners denouncing the oppressions of Lancashire, and cotton masters yearning over the sorrows of Dorset. The movement for Factory Reform and against the New Poor Law, against Protection and for the Charter, are mixed in an inextricable confusion of agitation, of which, nevertheless, the main pattern is clear. The Factory Act of 1833 introduced, in all textile factories, the ten-hour day for young persons under eighteen and a forty-eight-hour week for children under thirteen, with the obligation to attend for two hours every day at a school which often did not exist. In this last provision, and in the four inspectors appointed to observe the operation of the law, we see the Radical hand. Otherwise the Act is a watering down of the demands made by the Evangelical Tories, Oastler, Sadler, and Lord Ashley, on the basis of the Ten Hour movement in the West Riding. To the work-people it was a disappointment, and their resentment went to animate the growing body of Popular Radicalism. Thrown on themselves, they turned towards Direct Action, Trade Unions, and the Charter. To the employers it was a warning, since the reduction of children's hours of necessity brought with it a rearrangement of all working hours, which ultimately the State might generalize. Outside the factories, indeed, the seventy-two-hour week was becoming common in many trades.

But for the next few years the focus of agitation was not Factory reform, but the New Poor Law. The resources of the Poor Law Commissioners were limited; the Benthamite watchword—aggregate to segregate—remained a watchword only; and their comprehensive scheme for dealing separately with the young, the sick, the aged, the vagrant, and the destitute was never put into effect. In its place nothing was visible but the New Bastilles, and the proposal which the workhouse system seemed to involve of applying factory discipline—if not prison discipline—to the pauper, lashed the working classes to fury. It was at this time that The

House acquired its sinister meaning and the Poor Law first inspired that repulsion which has hobbled our administration ever since. The Forty-third of Elizabeth, which declared the Right to Work, had degenerated into the Right to Relief without working. But it was the Charter of the Poor. The New Poor Law was the charter of the ratepayer, and it was failing of its purpose. The formula which had worked in the rural south failed when it was applied to the industrial midlands and the north. Reluctantly the Commissioners surrendered their principles and set the people to task work, or road-making, as if they had been Tudor magistrates faced with a short harvest. And the poor rate rose again.

The failure of the New Poor Law to fulfil its promise, the inevitable harshness of a new administration suddenly applied to a people with no idea of administration at all, the brutality that went on in some workhouses and the gorging in others,[1] the petty tyranny of officials and the petty corruption of Guardians, discredited the scientific Radicals and brought the sentimental Radicals to the front. *The Pickwick Papers* is not a Victorian document: it belongs to a sunnier time, which perhaps had never existed. The group of novels that follow, *Oliver Twist, Nicholas Nickleby, The Old Curiosity Shop*, are charged with the atmosphere of the thirties. They have the Radical faith in progress, the Radical dislike of obstruction and privilege, the Radical indifference to the historic appeal. But they part from the Radicalism of the Benthamites in their equal indifference to the scientific appeal. Dickens's ideal England was not very far from Robert Owen's. But it was to be built by some magic of goodwill overriding the egoism of progress; not by law, and most emphatically not by logic.

The economists and the reformers had drawn the bow too tight: it almost snapped in their hands. But so, too, had the Evangelicals, and even goodwill was suspected if it came arrayed in religious guise. At the sight of Wilberforce, Cobbett put his head down and charged. Young Anglicans were prepared to defend black slavery only because the

---

[1] Against the oft-repeated tale of the Andover gristle set the dietary discovered in one workhouse: bread 72 oz., gruel 7½ pints, meat 15 oz., potatoes 1½ lb., soup 4½ pints, pudding 14 oz., cheese 8 oz., broth 4½ pints, and compare it with the tables, in Mrs. Peel's chapter, of ordinary working-class food.

Evangelicals were against it. Sir Andrew Agnew's Sunday Observance Bill, the most rigorous piece of moral—and, indeed, class—legislation since the Long Parliament, supported by 128 members of the Commons, with Lord Ashley at their head, brought the two humorists of the age into the field together. Dickens riddled it in words; Cruikshank in pictures. But in all Dickens's work there is a confusion of mind which reflects the perplexity of his time; equally ready to denounce on the grounds of humanity all who left things alone, and on the grounds of liberty all who tried to make them better. England was shifting uneasily and convulsively from an old to a new discipline, and the early stages were painful. To be numbered, to be visited, to be inspected, to be preached at, whether the visitors were furnished with a Poor Law Order or a religious mission, whether they came to feed the children or to save their souls, frayed tempers already on edge with mechanical toil, and hurt—often unreasonably, but still it hurt—that very sense of personal dignity on which the scientific reformers, as strongly as the sentimentalists, relied for the humanization of the poor.

The one field in which they might have co-operated without reserve was the care of children. The Factory Act of 1833 was incidentally an Education Act as well, though a very imperfect one, since for the purposes of the Act any cellar might be entered as a school and any decayed pedlar as a schoolmaster. The year 1840 saw the chimney-sweeping children brought under public protection. The next advance was inspired by the revelations of the Employment of Children Enquiry of 1840 and registered in the Mines Act of 1842. In the following year Peel's Government tried to carry the Act of 1833 one step farther. They were beaten by a union of manufacturers and dissenters: 'worthy and conscientious men', Brougham wrote, 'who hate the Established Church more than they love education.' In 1844 Graham reintroduced his Bill, omitting the educational clauses which had given so much offence, but reducing the hours of children's labour to six and a half, of men's to twelve. Lord Ashley stood out for ten: the Government resisted. Peel pointed out that the Bill dealt only with textile factories and that notoriously the conditions in other workshops were worse. 'Will you legislate for all?' he asked. It was a rhetorical question. But it was answered with a solid shout of 'Yes'. Without meaning it, the House of Commons had undertaken to regulate the factory system throughout the land, and a few nights later they recalled their decision. But the tide was running fast and the conversion of Macaulay is symptomatic. As a young man he had dealt his blows impartially between paternal Toryism and deductive Radicalism, between Southey, Owen, and James Mill. His economics, like those of most Englishmen, were in descent not from Ricardo, but from Adam Smith and Burke.

'It is one of the finest problems in legislation, and what has often engaged my thoughts whilst I followed that profession, "what the State ought to take upon itself to direct by the public wisdom, and what it ought to leave, with as little interference as possible, to individual discretion." Nothing, certainly, can be laid down on the subject that will not admit of exceptions, many permanent, some occasional. But the clearest line of distinction which I could draw, while I had any chalk to draw it, was this: that the State ought to confine itself to what regards the State, or the creatures of the State, namely, the exterior establishment of its religion; its magistracy; its revenue; its military force by sea and land; the corporations that owe their existence to its fiat; in a word, to everything that is *truly and properly* public, to the public peace, to the public safety, to the public order, to the public prosperity. In its preventive police it ought to be sparing of its efforts, and to employ means, rather few, unfrequent, and strong, than many, and frequent, and, of course, as they multiply their puny politic race, and dwindle, small and feeble. Statesmen who know themselves will, with the dignity which belongs to wisdom, proceed only in this the superior orb, and first mover of their duty steadily, vigilantly, severely, courageously: whatever remains will, in a manner provide for itself. But as they descend from the State to a province, from a province to a parish, and from a parish to a private house, they go on accelerated in their fall. They *cannot* do the lower duty; and, in proportion as they try it, they will certainly fail in the higher. They ought to know the different departments of things; what belongs to laws, and what manners alone can regulate. To these, great politicians may give a leaning, but they cannot give a law.'[1]

A great body of principle, self-interest, and sentiment had to be shifted, before the public mind could pass this point. Of principle, because State intervention was still commonly pictured as that system of State-regulation of industry

[1] *Thoughts on Scarcity*, 1795.

which Adam Smith had confuted. Of self-interest, because it does undoubtedly mean a restriction of a man's right to do what he will with his own. Of sentiment, because the intense dislike of interference and domiciliary visits which history has bred in us, took into its field the work-people and the factory; and the religious, the economic, and the social codes all combined to emphasize the vital importance of individual effort, whether the prize was domestic comfort or heavenly joy. But experience tells, and by 1845 it was becoming evident that the line between what the State may do and what it must leave alone had been drawn in the wrong place, and that there was a whole world of things where the individual simply could not help himself at all. He could not build his own house, or even choose his own street. He could not dispose of his own sewage or educate his own children. In Macaulay's mind the sphere of State interest now includes not only public order and defence, but public health, education, and the hours of labour. It includes, what is most remarkable of all, that triumph of private enterprise— the railways.

'Trade considered merely as trade, considered merely with regard to the pecuniary interest of the contracting parties, can hardly be too free. But there is a great deal of trade which cannot be considered merely as trade, and which affects higher than pecuniary interests. Fifteen years ago it became evident that railroads would soon, in every part of the kingdom, supersede to a great extent the old highways. The tracing of the new routes which were to join all the chief cities, ports and naval arsenals of the island was a matter of the highest national importance. But unfortunately those who should have acted refused to interfere. That the whole society was interested in having a good system of internal communications seemed to be forgotten. The speculator who wanted a large dividend on his shares, the landowner who wanted a large price for his acres, obtained a full hearing. But nobody applied to be heard on behalf of the community.'[1]

Was Hudson listening that night? For Hudson, 'Mammon and Belial in one', was nearing his apogee and his fall. The Midland and North-Eastern systems were under his control: he had carried the Sunderland election against Bright and Cobden in 1845, when *The Times* chartered a special train to bring the news of his return; his financial triumphs, his

---

[1] Speech on Fielden's Factory Bill: May 22, 1846.

country houses, his parties in Albert Gate, his friendship with Prince Albert, gave him an almost legendary prestige. Mrs. Hudson hardly kept pace with her husband's elevation; once, on a visit to Grosvenor House, she was shown a bust of Marcus Aurelius: 'It ain't the present Markis, is it?' she inquired. But Hudson was one of those not uncommon characters who persuade themselves that an aptitude for business carries with it a genius for fraud. He kept one block of shares in demand by paying the dividends out of capital: with even greater simplicity he helped himself to others which did not appear in the books and sold them at a profit. Naturally he was the strenuous, and, no doubt, the sincere, opponent of Government supervision; and naturally when the bubble burst, with a loss to the investor, it was reckoned, of nearly £80,000,000, the public attitude to Government supervision underwent some change.

In this atmosphere Fielden's Bill was finally carried. Those who have read the debates will probably agree that the opponents had the best of the argument. The 58-hour week (which, in effect, was what the Bill established) was a plunge, and an opposition supported by Peel, Graham, and Herbert for the Conservatives, by Brougham,[1] Roebuck, and old Jo Hume for the economists, and backed by the warnings of the most experienced officials, is not to be ignored. But the debates mark at once the waning of the economics of pure calculation and the growth of that preoccupation with the quality of life which is dominant in the next decade. There is a remarkable passage in Peel's speech, in which he refers to the criticism of the Italian economists that their English colleagues concentrated on wealth and overlooked welfare. But he need not have gone to Italy for it. He could have heard it from Sadler and Southey: he could have read it as far back as 1832 in the *Quarterly Review*. This alternative economic was not thought out: it remained instinctive, sentimental, feudal, and the natural alliance of the scientific Benthamite administrator and the authoritative Tory gentleman was never fully achieved. But it was creeping in and on. 'Of course, all legislative interference is an evil—but' runs like an apologetic refrain through the

---

[1] Brougham was particularly puckish. It was known that the Bishops meant to vote for the Bill and he trusted that, 'with Divine assistance', he might persuade them to change their minds.

speeches of those who supported the Bill. And the 'but' grew larger as the conviction of evil grew less assured.

Note. I may here refer to Mrs. Tonna's *Perils of the Nation*, hurriedly compiled for the Christian Influence Society in the alarm following the Chartist Riots of 1842. It undoubtedly represents a great body of educated opinion of, broadly speaking, a Tory Evangelical cast and furnishes a link between the Sadler-Ashley thought of the thirties and *Unto this Last* of 1860. Her analysis of the social trouble is (*a*) defective conceptions of national wealth; (*b*) exorbitant power of the employing class; (*c*) unwillingness to legislate between employer and workman; (*d*) competition, which had (i) destroyed the notion of fair wage, fair price, and fair profit, (ii) lowered the quality of goods. It will be seen how near all this comes to the Ruskin of twenty years later. Mrs. Tonna's remedies are naturally somewhat vague: specifically, education, housing, and direct industrial legislation; generally, the organization of a better opinion among the upper and professional classes. Incidentally she believes the beautiful doctrine that when God sends mouths he sends meat, and regards contraception (and Harriet Martineau) as the 'most horrifying abomination of Socialism'. The book had a wide circulation, but I refer to it, not as an agent, but as a symptom in the struggle to get away from the impersonality of Capital and Labour to the idea of a fair deal and a decent population. Directly, Carlyle contributed little: but the atmospheric effect of his insistence on personality, immaterial values, and leadership was immense.

IX

'Railway companies may smash their passengers into mummy and the State may not interfere![1] Pestilence may sweep our streets and the State may not compel the municipalities to put their own powers in operation to check it! We have heard of the Curiosities of Literature and some day this book will be numbered among them.' So did *Eliza Cook's Journal* dispose of the already antiquated individualism of Herbert Spencer's *Social Statics* in 1851. Eliza Cook knew what the lower middle classes were thinking about. 'There have been at work among us', a Nonconformist preacher told his people, 'three great social agencies: the London City Mission; the novels of Mr. Dickens; the cholera.' It had never been forgotten: it was always due to return. It came in 48/49 and again in 54.

[1] Railway travelling was much more dangerous in England than on the Continent. Fatal accidents were more than fifteen times as frequent as in Germany.

The Health Legislation of the Victorian age is a blended product of Poor Law and Municipal Reform. By 1830 the old boroughs were falling into imbecility; they had for the most part ceased to perform any useful service; improvements in lighting, draining, gas, water, markets, streets, even in police, were carried out under special Acts by special commissioners, and the corporations were little more than corrupt electoral colleges. When the franchise was bestowed on the ten-pound householders at large, the corporations had lost their reason for existing unless some one could find something for them to do, and make them fit to do it. One article in the Benthamite code prescribed representative local bodies for all purposes—miniatures of Parliament and Cabinet, with trained officials selected by open competition. The Municipal Reform Act did not go so far as this: it created 178 elected corporations, but with limited powers and little supervision from above. London was reserved for separate treatment: even a Benthamite quailed before the magnitude of the metropolis, which was misgoverned by four counties, innumerable vestries and commissions, the Bailiff of Westminster, and the Corporation of the City of London. The field of the new municipalities was the police and good government of the towns. They were allowed, though not compelled, to take over the duties of the Special Commissioners, and it was by the gradual assumption of these activities that the great municipalities mastered the problems of town life.

That of all these problems health, in the widest sense, was the most important, had been realized at the time of the cholera visitation, and the lesson was constantly hammered home by Chadwick from the Poor Law Commission. All that the science of the day could discover or suggest—and the discoveries were as awful as the suggestions were drastic[1]—was embodied in his Report of 1842. In 1848—another Report and two abortive Bills had intervened—the results were brought together. In the early Poor Law administration, the Commissioners had no representative in Parliament, so that the Tyrants of Somerset House were without a Minister either to control or to defend their masterful proceedings: they really were bureaucrats, as Palmerston

---

[1] The principal were: municipal water supply, scientific drainage (land and town), an independent health service (with large summary powers for dealing with nuisances), and a national interment service.

explained the new word to Queen Victoria, from *bureau* an office and *kratos* power. The defect was made good in 1847, and the Commission was provided with a Parliamentary President. The Act of 1848 created a parallel Board of Health in Whitehall with power to create Local Boards and compel them to discharge a great variety of duties, from the regulation of slaughter-houses, to the supply of water and the management of cemeteries. It was a patchy and cumbrous piece of legislation: one municipality might adopt the Act and its neighbour not, and cholera might bear down on a district, while the average mortality of the last seven years had been too low to give the Board a ground for intervention. And when they were allowed to intervene, they must first inquire and then report, and then make a provisional order and then get the order confirmed, and then, most difficult of all, see that it was not evaded by local jobbers, backed by the Private Enterprise Society.[1] There was not enough staff to go round: the local doctors could not be got to report their wealthy patients for maintaining nuisances: it is not supposed that municipal affairs as a rule engage either the most intelligent or the most disinterested of mankind, and the impact of the irresistible Chadwick on the immovable incuriousness of the small municipal mind could only end in explosions.[2] There have been few more useful Acts than that of 1848, but its virtue lay less in its immediate results than in the large opportunities it gave for local initiative and scientific intelligence to work together. Gradually, over the country as a whole, rapidly in some aspiring boroughs, the filth and horror which had crawled over the early Victorian towns was penned back in its proper lairs, and perhaps the first step towards dealing effectively with slums was to recognize them as slums and not as normal phenomena of urban existence. In the mid-fifties returning exiles were greeted by a novel sight. The black wreath over London was thinning; the Thames was fringed with smokeless chimneys. The Home Office had begun to harry offenders under the Smoke Nuisance (Metropolis) Act of 1853.

[1] Founded in 1849 to resist the operation of the Act. There is a good account of the working of the Act in *Two Years Ago*, which is drawn from the Megavissey outbreak of '54.

[2] He was dismissed in '53. One of his last feats was a circular enjoining Local Authorities to consider 'insolvency, bankruptcy, and failure in previous pursuits as presumptive evidence of unfitness'.

But the great development of municipal administration belongs to a later age. John Bright's call to the boroughs to be 'more expensive' comes from the very end of our period.

'I only hope that Corporations generally will become much more expensive than they have been—not expensive in the sense of wasting money, but that there will be such nobleness and liberality amongst the people of our towns and cities as will lead them to give their Corporations power to expend more money on those things which, as public opinion advances, are found to be essential to the health and comfort and improvement of our people.'[1]

John Bright, whose glory it was to have opposed every smoke abatement bill introduced into the House, preaching Municipal Socialism in the diction of Ruskin, symbolizes the evolution of thirty years.

The advance of education was much more rapid. In fact, by 1846 it had already passed out of its first phase of mass production by monitors and private initiative into the phase of trained teachers and public control. Under the monitorial system, the more forward children imparted the elements to the juniors in groups. As a device for getting simple ideas into simple heads as fast as possible it was successful. Up to a certain point the Bell and Lancaster children made astonishing progress; most children like playing at school; and the system was not intended to carry them further than the Three R's. The British and Foreign School Society backed Lancaster and simple Bible reading; the National Society for Promoting the Education of the Poor in the Principles of the Established Church stood for Bell and the Catechism. A fine class-distinction tended to keep them apart through the Victorian age; the British day scholar was not, as a rule, of the poorest class. The success of the two societies in diffusing elementary instruction was admitted, and the first intervention of the State in the education of the people took the shape of a grant in aid, in 1833, for school-building; of £11,000 to the National Society and £9,000 to the British and Foreign. Six years later the distribution was entrusted to a Committee of Council, nominally: effectively, to their Secretary, Kay-Shuttleworth of the Manchester Report.

A survey of elementary education in the thirties revealed to thoughtful contemporaries a profoundly disquieting picture.

[1] Birmingham, January 29, 1864.

School-buildings were rarely good, often indifferent, sometimes thoroughly bad. The same might be said of the teachers. The average school-life was perhaps two years, perhaps eighteen months. The Society Schools, which represented the best practice of the time, were helped out by Sunday Schools which also gave a little instruction in reading and writing, sometimes in arithmetic, and by a mob of private ventures, of which the one kept by Mr. Wopsle's great aunt and attended by Pip was, if anything, a favourable specimen. At Salford it was found that of 1,800 children nominally at school, less than half were taught to read or write. In Liverpool less than half the child population under fifteen went to school at all, and the other half did not miss much. The fees were 6*d*. for readers, 9*d*. for writers, 1*s*. for counters. Masters made 17*s*. a week, Dames 6*s*. A curious difficulty occurred in the collection of these statistics. 'Catch me counting the brats,' one Dame replied. 'I mind what happened to David.' At Newcastle half the children escaped from schools which are briefly described as horrible. Bristol was rather better; more than half the children were at school, paying a penny or twopence a week. Leeds was worse, for there 15,000 went untaught altogether; Sunday schools provided for 11,000, and less than 7,000 were in such rudimentary secular establishments as existed. In Hull a close investigation revealed that of 5,000 children who had been to school, 800 could not read, 1,800 could not write, and just half could not do a sum. It was much if the victims could write their names. From the marriage registers it would appear that in the thirties about one-third of the men and two-thirds of the women could not. Nor was there much evidence of improvement in the past thirty years. In Manchester, about 1810, the Signers were 52, the Markers 48; by 1838 the proportion had only moved to 55 and 45.

Clearly no society could be left to rest on a substratum of ignorance so dense as these figures show, especially after the Reform Bill had divulged the arcanum of party government, that the franchise might be extended. Of what use were cheap papers to a population which could not read them? The passion for an educated people, which united all reformers and gives a lasting nobility to the tortuous career of Brougham, was frustrated by the absence of any foundation on which to build, and the Mechanics' Institutes from which so much was hoped sank into play-centres for serious clerks. The Philosophical Radicals had their solution. As usual, it was entirely right, and, as usual, it was entirely impracticable. In dealing with the difficulties of Victorian administration it is necessary to remember that hardly any one had yet thought of the county as an administrative unit, except for its ancient functions of justice and highways. Twice in the thirties a Radical Bill for the creation of elected County Boards fluttered for an evening in the unfriendly air and died. There was the Imperial Government: there were the boroughs. But between Whitehall and the people at large there were, except for the Poor Law Unions, no administrative links or gradations. Chadwick, who thought of everything, had meditated a system of local authorities for all purposes based on the Poor Law Unions, but he was darkly suspected of a design for abolishing the counties to begin with and cutting up the immemorial map of England into Benthamite rectangles. The Radicals proposed to divide the country into School Districts, levying an education rate, maintaining infant schools, elementary schools with a vocational bias, continuation classes, and training colleges. In process of time the schools would be wholly staffed by trained teachers; education should be compulsory from six to twelve, and it should include instruction, by means of Government text-books, in political economy. The Radicals had substituted the inspiration of Ricardo for the inspiration of Scripture. Otherwise, this project has a very modern air. Radical projects always have, after their origin has been forgotten.

It was far too modern for 1833. Parliamentary Government can only operate with the equipment and feelings of the current age. The Voluntary Schools were there. And any attempt at educational reform had to reckon with the most intense of Victorian emotions, sectarian animosity. It must be allowed for everywhere, and a few years later it flamed up with a vehemence which consumed the most promising experiment yet projected. Immediately on his appointment Kay-Shuttleworth produced, and the Committee of Council accepted, a plan for a Training College, complete with model school and practising school. It broke down on the question of religious instruction. The Dissenters would not stand the parson in a State school. The Establishment would not stand any one else. Even the Church of Scotland, which might have minded its own business, took a hand in the game. The plan was withdrawn. With an energy typical of himself and his age its author opened the College himself and for some years lived a double existence, as an official at Whitehall and the Principal of a Training College at Battersea. The example was decisive. Voluntary training colleges sprang up in quick succession and the foundations of a teaching profession were laid. The system was consolidated by the Minute of 1846—apprenticeship to a master, a course in a Training College, the Certificate, additional pay for the Trained Teacher, and the unkept promise of a pension at the end. Charley Hexam—surely the most detestable boy on record—was apprenticed to Bradley Headstone. Sue Bridehead was a Queen's scholar at Salisbury Training College when she made her disastrous expedition to Wardour with Jude. They are products, perhaps unusual products, of the Minute of 1846.

But the new grant system which the Minute established —£1 from the Treasury, in augmentation of salaries, for every £2 raised locally—brought up the whole issue of State intervention or State abstention. The Dissenters, who had wrecked Graham's Bill of 1843 for educating factory children in Church schools, with a conscience clause, took the field against the Committee of Council. As of all the churches the Church of England was the richest and, in fairness it must be added, the most generous, it was foreseeable that the two pounds would be more readily forthcoming for Church schools than for any other. In effect, therefore, and in the circumstances inevitably, the Government grant would be a subsidy in aid of the education of little Churchmen, or the conversion of little Dissenters. That the bulk of the child population might better have been described as little heathen seems to have escaped the notice of the reverend opponents of the measure. But the onslaught of the Voluntarists was encountered with a conviction equal and an eloquence superior to their own, and probably the only speech on Education which has ever been read with pleasure by any one except the author is Macaulay's defence of the new grants against Mr. Duncombe, Mr. Baines, the Congregational Union, and John Bright. Henceforth the education of the people was admitted to be a primary function of the State. From this admission it is not far to the Radical position—education universal, compulsory, and secular—and the only question remaining was how slowly and by what devious routes and compromises it would be reached, and how much energy would be squandered by the way on the interminable rancours of Church and Dissent.

X

The Tory ascendancy under George III had modified the political colour of the Anglican body. In the earlier Hanoverian decades, the hierarchy, nominated by the Government, was, on the whole, Whig; the clergy, appointed by lay patrons, Tory. Then, gradually, the Sees came to be filled with men in closer sympathy with the mass of the clergy, men, too, for the most part, of a type superior in piety and learning to the bishops of the first two Georges, while, with the improvement of the land, Holy Orders became a more and more attractive profession for the sons of gentlemen. Thus the Church of England after its long lethargy was reconsolidated, with a distinctly aristocratic colouring, about the time when the Evangelical example was raising the moral level of its ministers. The result was that phase which Froude declared to be the golden age of the Church, when her princes were still princes, and her pastors enforced the simple morality and administered the simple consolations, of village life, with the authority due rather to personal character, birth, and learning than to any pretensions as priests.

There was another side to the picture. The ministers of the Church were at once too rich and too poor. The Archbishopric of Canterbury and the Bishopric of Durham were each worth £19,000 a year; Rochester, £14,000; Llandaff less than £1,000. Of 10,000 benefices, the average value was £285. Less than 200 were worth £1,000 and upward, but among them were livings of £2,000, £5,000, and one of over £7,000 a year. The poor parson was therefore very poor; the curate poorer still, best off in Rochester on £109 a year, worst off in St. David's on £55. The mischief was aggravated by pluralism, non-residence, and nepotism. A great Church family, taking sons, nephews, and sons-in-law together, might easily collect £10,000 a year among them and leave the greater part of their duties to be discharged by curates at £80. The best of parsons could not help being a little too much of a magistrate and landowner, and not enough of a pastor.[1] Into the gaps left in his spiritual ministrations crept dissent, with its opportunities for personal distinction,[2] close converse, and mutual inspection. At the beginning of our period it was estimated that the Church, the Dissenters, and the Romans were in the ratio of 120, 80, and 4. The figures of Church attendance taken in 1851 show the Establishment decidedly preponderating in the south and south-west, except in Cornwall; and holding its own, with varying majorities, everywhere, except in the old Puritan strongholds of Bedford, Huntingdon, and the West Riding, and in Northumberland. An absolute figure of effective membership is impossible to give. Out of a population of 2,000,000 in the diocese of London it was reckoned that there were 70,000 communicants.[3] But a distinction must be drawn between the country and the old towns on one side and the new agglomerations on the other. In the one, everybody, except the free-thinking cobbler, would at least have called himself one thing or the other, and there were few families which were not at least sometimes represented at the Sunday service. In the other, great multitudes were as indifferent to the distinction as the inhabitants of Borrioboola-Gha. It was to these masses that the Churches, often in unfriendly rivalry, had next to address themselves.

In dogma there was little to choose between a worthy clergyman of an evangelical cast and a worthy dissenting minister. Socially, by their University education, and their relations with the gentry, the clergy as a body stood in a class apart and, with the preachers who collected little congregations about them in hamlets and the back streets of

[1] Whateley of Cookham is the best example. 'A Whateley in every parish' was a catchword of Poor Law reformers. Froude was thinking of his own father, the Archdeacon of Totnes.

[2] In 1860 H. F. Tozer wrote of Norway, 'The priest's residence is usually the nicest house in the neighbourhood, and the priest's daughters are the most eligible young ladies. It is surprising in these circumstances that dissent does not spring up.' The implication is as illuminating as P. G. Hamerton's remark that few educated people had ever seen a dissenter eat.

[3] Lord Robert Montagu's statistics in 1860 are at least amusing. He reckoned: Baptists, Congregationalists, Jews, Mormons, &c., 16½ per cent.; Wesleyans (seven sorts) and Roman Catholics, 16½ per cent.; Church of England, 42 per cent.; Irreligious Poor, 25 per cent. I fancy they are pretty near the mark. Of the great underworld, Lord Shaftesbury said that only 2 per cent. went anywhere. The figures of 1851 are not very trustworthy, but it would appear that of 100 possibles 58 went somewhere.

towns, who ministered in Zoar and Bethel and Mizpah and Shebaniah, they had little in common. But the ministers of the older bodies were often as learned as the clergy, and their congregations more exclusive than the mixed multitudes who, from habit as much as conviction, were gathered in the parish church. The Unitarians were, on the whole, the most intellectual of the dissenting bodies: they went to the theatre. The Independents represented traditional middle-class Puritanism: the more fervent, and more rhetorical, Baptists struck lower in society, among the tradesmen in small streets. With them and with the dissident Wesleyans we approach that brand of unattached Nonconformity with which Dickens was so familiar, and which is represented for us by Mr. Stiggins and Mr. Chadband. The 4,000 Quaker families were a body, almost a race, apart.

But between them all there was, at the beginning of the nineteenth century, a state of stable equilibrium which the political advance of the middle classes, the Oxford Movement, and the growth of the Wesleyans destroyed. As it left the hands of its founder, the Wesleyan body was a society, autonomous in government and independent in action, but essentially supplementary to the Established Church. Under his successors, especially Jabez Bunting, it developed into a church itself. Active, zealous, and resourceful, it gave a personality to the somewhat formless individualism of earlier Dissent, and it satisfied, and steadied, thousands of men and women who, but for the Wesleyan church, would, in the break-up of the old society, have drifted without direction or restraint, into vice, or crime, or revolution. By providing a far larger sphere of action for the laity than the Church or the older denominations furnished, it brought romance and ambition into a class which, under the pressure of the new civilization, was losing both purpose and aspiration; and the Wesleyan organization—the class meeting, the circuit, the conference, the Legal Hundred—has powerfully affected the constitution of political parties and Trade Unions. The activity of the Wesleyans radiated through the older denominations and was not without effect on the Church itself. By 1840 it was supposed that they numbered half a million members in England and Wales, and their attitude on any political question was anxiously calculated by the managers of both political parties. They were as a body not unfriendly to the Church: they were zealous upholders of the Constitution. 'Wesleyanism', Bunting said, 'is as much opposed to Democracy as it is to Sin'; and among the causes which led to the defeat of Chartism and the great pacification of the fifties must be numbered the resolute opposition which the Wesleyans offered to subversion in society or the State.[1]

In the eighteenth century the ancient opposition of Rome and Oxford had died down; courteous gestures were exchanged across the frontiers; in the French wars the Pope became an almost sympathetic figure. Yet the growth of a new anti-Roman feeling was inevitable. Evangelicalism emphasized the points of difference and gave them alarming value for the individual soul; travellers reported the shocking condition of the Papal States. And there was always Ireland. To be misgoverned in this world and damned in the next seemed to many thousands of sober English families the necessary consequence of submission to Rome. Nor could it be comfortably pretended that the claims or activity of Rome were abating, and no Englishman could read the contemporary history of France without a running commentary in which Louis XVIII played the part of Charles II and Charles X stood for the fanatical James. If the Bishops had seen their way to vote for Reform in 1831, they would have made themselves as popular as the Blessed Seven in the Tower. It was the misfortune of the Church that her politics were officially branded as illiberal just when her theology was about to come under suspicion of Romanism. The combination, coinciding with the Radical drive against privilege, produced that Political Protestantism which waxed with the growth of the middle-class electorate and waned in our time with the spread of religious indifference

[1] The writings of Mark Rutherford show E. V. Nonconformity at its self-righteous worst. Of its other side, as a civilizing agency, credulous, conceited, but of heroic tenacity, one of the most sympathetic records I know is *Warminster Common* by W. Daniell. Daniell (who had gifts of healing, the nature of which he did not recognize) must have been very like an early Christian bishop up country. Incidentally, this little work enables me to determine one important question of social history—the origin of the chapel tea-fight. It was invented by Daniell, and the first was held on December 13, 1815. Tea was an expensive and select drink, and the tea-drinkings at Warminster were, as the following extract shows, almost Eleusinian in their rapture:

'Christmas 1829. Drank tea at Chapel with the Christian friends (a purely religious meeting). A holy unction attended and great was the joy. We could all say (we trust experimentally) "Unto us a child is born".'

and with the dilution of the middle-class vote by universal suffrage.

In its origins the Oxford Movement was as practical a response to a practical necessity as the Corn Law agitation, the immediate occasion being the suppression of ten Irish bishoprics by the Whig Government. The danger was exaggerated, but in 1833 much seemed possible that time proved imaginary. It was believed that Government emissaries had directed the attack on the Bishop of Bristol's palace in 1831. It was known that James Mill, an official man in the confidence of the ruling powers, had prepared a plan for the conversion of the Church into a Benthamite institution of public utility. Sunday services, without, of course, any form of prayer or worship, were to be preserved: the parish would attend, in their best clothes, to hear a lecture on botany or economics and receive prizes for virtuous behaviour. The day of rest and gladness would end with dances expressive of the social and fraternal emotions, but avoiding any approach to lasciviousness, and an agape at which, naturally, only soft drinks would be served. In principle there is no difference between amalgamating the see of Ossory with the see of Ferns, and applying the revenues of the Church to magic lanterns and muffins. In their alarm, certain divines, their imagination outstripping the practical difficulties in the way (and, in fact, the Whig Government having rearranged the revenues of the Irish Church split on the question what to do with the surplus) decided to act before it was too late. Seven thousand clergy assured the Archbishop of their attachment to the Church: a lay address, signed by 230,000 heads of families, followed. Eminent Nonconformists allowed it to be known that they could countenance no aggression against the Establishment, which was still the national bulwark against infidelity; and the storm blew over. In the peace that followed, the rulers of the Church showed that they had taken their lesson.[1] The vexatious question of tithes was equitably settled by the Commutation Act of 1836. Pluralities were regulated, the grosser inequalities of church livings levelled out. There the movement, having demonstrated, and stimulated, the vitality of the Church, might have been re-absorbed into the main

---

[1] The guiding hand was Blomfield of London, who also edited Aeschylus, and was a principal originator of the Sanitary Enquiry of 1839.

stream of invigorated Churchmanship. But feelings had been too deeply stirred. In any case, it was inevitable that in a generation which had been enchanted by Scott and bemused by Coleridge,[1] the corporate and sacramental aspect of the Church should re-emerge, and that religion would have to find a place for feelings of beauty, antiquity, and mystery, which the ruling theology had dismissed or ignored as worldly or unprofitable or profane. Now, too, the question had been raised, on what foundation could the Church of England, disendowed and disestablished, take her stand, and it had to be answered even though the danger had passed. Hitherto, Churchmen had taken their Church for granted as the mode of Protestantism established by law. The Oxford Movement created an Anglican self-consciousness, parallel to the self-consciousness of the Protestant denominations, based on the assurance of apostolic descent, and inevitably, therefore, tending to sympathy, at least, with the one Church whose apostolic origin could not be denied.

Apart from these two processes, the crystallization of Anglicanism round the Tractarians and of Nonconformity round the Wesleyans, a larger and more fluid conception of the Church was gathering strength. The Oxford divines took little note of Nonconformity. Their object was to brace and fortify the Church against the coming onslaught of Liberalism and infidelity, and in the thirties, after the Oxford leaders, Newman and Pusey themselves, perhaps the most conspicuous, certainly the most influential, figure in the English Church was one who by his own profession was a Liberal and in the belief of his critics was not much better than an infidel.[2] But neither Anglicans nor Protestants had any real conception of the forces which were gathering against that stronghold of their common faith, the inerrancy of Holy Scripture; they were only beginning to learn, when they went out of the University or the seminary, how little religion meant to the half-barbarized population of the great towns. The diffusion of scientific knowledge among the educated, the spread of old-fashioned rationalism downwards through the masses, had created a new problem for the religious teacher.

[1] One critic divided the rising generation into fluent Benthamites and muddled Coleridgians. S.T.C. once said to Miss Martineau: 'You seem to regard society as an aggregate of individuals.' 'Of course I do,' she replied. There is much history implicit in that encounter, and by 1850 Coleridge had won.
[2] 'But is Dr. Arnold a Christian?' Newman once asked.

Milman, walking through the City early one morning, was held up by a group of porters and made to deliver his opinion: did God really command the Israelites to massacre the people of Canaan? It was the test question. Macaulay, putting himself on Butler, wrote that in the Old Testament we read of actions performed by Divine command which without such authority would be atrocious crimes. Lyell—who could sometimes be led on, in a small company after dinner, to admit that the world was probably 50,000 years old—called on him and asked him to speak out. He refused. At the height of such a reputation as no other English man of letters has enjoyed, he could not face the storm that would have broken on the head of the infidel who questioned the humanity of Joshua or the veracity of Moses.

Here, not in schism or disendowment, in the rabbling of bishops for their votes, or the burning of their palaces in a riot, lay the danger which only Arnold clearly apprehended. The union of the Churches was an incidental stage in his programme. The foundation was a new conception, in which, no doubt, we can detect something of Lessing, something of Coleridge, something of Carlyle, but which in purpose and direction was Arnold's own, of the significance of history as the revelation of God. The world, as he conceived it, needed new rulers, and the rulers needed a new faith, which was to be found in the historic record, in the Bible, doubtless, most of all, but in the Bible—and here he broke definitely with Oxford and current Protestantism alike—interpreted not by tradition, but by science, scholarship, and, above all, political insight. 'He made us think', a pupil wrote, 'of the politics of Israel, Greece and Rome.' In this sentence we come as near as we can hope to get to the secret of Arnold's power. He took the self-consciousness of the English gentry, benevolently authoritative, but uneasily aware that its authority was waning and gave it religious and historic justification.[1]

XI

Of these three schools, united in their emphasis on personal conduct, the Protestant, on the whole, accepted the social philosophy of the age, the Anglican ignored it, the Arnoldian challenged it. The Nonconformist business man, like Bright,

---

[1] On the whole, William Arnold's *Oakfield* seems to me to convey most completely the effect that Arnold made on those who came under his influence.

severe with himself and others, within reason generous and
within reason honest, is one of the central Victorian types.
So, and of the same ancestry, is the preaching politician,
like the Corn Law rhetorician, Fox. Another, of which
Mr. Gladstone may serve as the representative, is the new
High Churchman, instructed in his faith but submissive to
his teachers, touched by the art and poetry of old religion,
inclining to regard the Church as the one immovable thing
in a changing and shifting world, and therefore less concerned
with its future than with its past, less with the application
of his faith to the circumstances of the world than with its
integrity as transmitted from the fathers. As individuals,
the High Churchmen worked as manfully as any: Walter
Hook in Leeds created a new standard of duty for every
parish priest who came after him. But as a school, they
shook off with well-bred impatience the humanitarian professions which had become associated with the Evangelical
creed, and few Tractarian names will be found connected
with the reforms which are the glory of the Early Victorian
Age. This rather was to be the sphere of action of the third
school. In the forties we are aware of a new type issuing
from the Universities and public schools, somewhat arrogant
and somewhat shy, very conscious of their standing as
gentlemen but very conscious of their duties, too, men in
tweeds who smoke in the streets, disciples of Maurice,
willing hearers of Carlyle, passionate for drains and co-
operative societies, disposed to bring everything in the state
of England to the test of Isaiah and Thucydides, and to find
the source of all its defects in what, with youthful violence,
they would call the disgusting vice of shopkeeping. These
are the Arnoldians.

In the meantime the Oxford Movement had gone into
liquidation. Through the thirties it advanced, in the face of
authority, with irresistible force. But the farther it went,
the more certain appeared its ultimate objective, and with
the publication of Tract XC it seemed to have unmasked
itself. The purpose of the Tract was to clear away the popular
interpretations which had grown up round the formularies
of the Church, to prove that the Articles rigidly construed
were more susceptible of a Catholic than a Protestant
meaning, or, as Macaulay put it, that a man might hold the
worst doctrines of the Church of Rome and the best benefice

in the Church of England. In this sense, at least, the Tract was received and condemned by the University, and the Tractarians stigmatized as Romanists without the courage of their convictions. And by 1843, when Newman left St. Mary's, Protestantism was beginning to work almost hysterically even on sober English opinion, which, having accepted Catholic emancipation as the completion of the Union, was now challenged by O'Connell to regard it as the basis of disruption to be achieved, if need be, at the price of civil war. Deviations of doctrine, like novelties of observance, were watched by ten thousand critical eyes; the Hampden controversy and the Gorham controversy were followed as attentively as any debate in Parliament, and, far away in Borneo, Rajah Brooke wrote home to his mother that he had not had much time for theology, but he had composed an answer to Tract XC. The decision of Pope Pius IX to revive the Roman Hierarchy in England was answered with an outburst of frenzy of which the Tractarian clergy were almost as much the objects as the Papists themselves.

But to the new Englishman of the late forties and fifties, a travelled man bred up on Carlyle and Tennyson and the romantic classics, the world was a far more interesting place than it had been to those late Augustans, imprisoned in their island, among whom Evangelicalism struck root, and his religion conformed to the awakening of his senses. The theology of Oxford he still viewed with distrust: at sisterhoods and processions he frowned with dark suspicion. Insensibly, however, the Tractarian influence was affecting his notions of public worship. The Hanoverian vulgarity of a Royal christening, with a sham altar loaded with the family plate and an opera singer warbling in the next room, shocked a taste which was insensibly forming for simplicity and reverence and the beauty of the sanctuary. Churches were swept; churchyards tidied; church windows cleaned. High pews behind which generations of the comfortable had dozed the sermon out, red velvet cushions on which the preacher had pounded the divisions of his text, the village band in the gallery, the clerk under the pulpit, gradually disappeared: very cautiously, crosses were introduced, and flowers and lights. Liturgical science became a passion with the younger clergy. The wave of restoration and church building brought with it a keen, sometimes a ludicrous preoccupation with symbolism, and Dickens with much truth observed that the High Churchman of 1850 was the dandy of 1820 in another form.[1]

The great ritualist controversy belongs to later years: its originating issue was the fashion of the preacher's garment.[2] The custom at the end of the morning prayers had been for the minister to retire and reissue from the vestry in the black gown of a learned man. As the practice spread of reading the Ante-Communion service after the sermon, the double change from white to black and back into white again was felt to be unseemly. But preaching in his whites—his vestments as a minister—the parson might be thought to claim for his utterances an authority more than his own, the authority of a priest, and so surplice riots became a popular diversion of the forties. In 1850 the ritual of St. Barnabas, Pimlico, was holding up the Sunday traffic, and we have a glimpse of Thackeray testifying in the crowd: 'O my friends of the nineteenth century, has it come to this?' Ten years later blaspheming mobs stormed St. George's in the East in defence of the Reformation Settlement. Protestant vigilance was easily alarmed, but even an Ulsterman could hardly suspect the hand of the Pope was at work when the Communion Table ceased to be a depository for hats, the font a receptacle for umbrellas, and new standards of dignity, reverence, and solemnity gradually assimilated the worship in the ancient meeting place of the village, the portentous assembly room of a London parish, and the Gothic churches which were rising by hundreds in the populous suburbs and industrial towns.

Like the Utilitarians, the Tractarians vanish as a party to work in widening circles out of sight, and when, years afterwards, their memory was recalled by Kingsley's tempestuous challenge and the genius wasted on Rome was at last recognized by England, it was in an age less concerned to know whether Newman's faith or some other faith was the right one, than whether in the modern world there was any

---

[1] Newman, in *Loss and Gain*, has put the same point with more dexterous satire.

[2] And the material, wood or stone, of the Holy Table. In the ruling case (Holy Sepulchre, Cambridge) a document was tendered under the title *Restoration of Churches the Restoration of Popery*. Which, after all, was what Pugin wanted.

room for faith at all. For all this vehemence of surface agitation, it had been growing every year plainer, on a deeper view, that neither Pauline nor Patristic Christianity, neither the justification theology nor the infallibility of the Church, could be maintained as a barrier against the 'wild, living intellect of man'. Religion had, somewhat hastily, perhaps, made terms with the astronomers. The heavens declare the glory of God, and the better the telescope the greater the glory. The geologists, attacking one of the prime documents of the faith, the Mosaic cosmogony, were more difficult to assimilate or evade. One of the earliest of them had taken the precaution of inviting his theological colleague to sit through his lectures, as censor and chaperone in one; and, on the whole, the religious world seems, in the forties, to have been divided into those who did not know what the geologists were saying and those who did not mind. A far more serious onslaught was preparing from two quarters, abroad and at home. English divinity was not equipped to meet—for its comfort, it was hardly capable of understanding—the new critical methods of the Germans: it is a singular fact that England could in our period not show one scholar in the field of Biblical learning able and willing to match the scholars of Germany. Thirlwall, whom good judges declared to be the ablest living Englishman, was silent, and what was passing in that marmoreal intellect remained a secret. The flock was left undefended against the ravages of David Strauss. On the other side, the English mind was particularly well equipped to grasp the arguments of the biologists. The natural sciences in all their branches—rocks, fossils, birds, beasts, fish, and flowers—were a national hobby; the *Vestiges of Creation*, issued with elaborate secrecy and attributed by a wild surmise to Prince Albert, was a national sensation; translated into golden verses by Tennyson, evolution almost became a national creed. *In Memoriam*, which is nine years older than the *Origin of Species*,[1] gathered up all the doubts of Christianity, of providence, of immortality, which the advance of science had implanted in anxious minds, and answered them, or seemed to answer them, with

---

[1] Some of the evolutionist parts of *In Memoriam* are actually older than *Vestiges*. Tennyson really understood the workings of the new scientific mind, as of the upper class political mind. He was the natural laureate of an age morally conservative and intellectually progressive.

the assurance of a pantheistic and yet personal faith in progress.

In Memoriam is one of the cardinal documents of the mid-Victorian mind, its ardent curiosity, its exquisite sensitiveness to nature, and, not less, perhaps, its unwillingness to quit, and its incapacity to follow, any chain of reasoning which seems likely to result in an unpleasant conclusion. In his highest mood, Tennyson sometimes speaks like an archangel assuring the universe that it will muddle through. The age was learning, but it had not mastered, the lesson that truth lies not in the statement but in the process: it had a childlike craving for certitude, as if the natural end of every refuted dogma was to be replaced by another dogma. Raised in the dark and narrow framework of Evangelical and economic truth, it wilted in the sunlight and waved for support to something vaguely hopeful like the theology of Maurice, or loudly reassuring like the hero worship of Carlyle. New freedom is a painful thing, most painful to the finest minds, who are most sensitive to the breaking-up of faiths and traditions and most apprehensive of the outcome. The stress of the age is incarnate in Arthur Clough. Deeply influenced by Arnold in his boyhood, he had stayed long enough in Oxford to feel all the exhaustion and disillusionment which succeeded the excitement of the Tractarian movement. In the Church was no satisfaction. He had lost, as most educated men were losing, his hold on what had been the middle strand of all Christian creeds, faith in the divine person of Christ. The natural way of escape was into the open mockery to which Clough's temperament inclined him, or into such a pagan equanimity in face of the unknown as the agnostics of the next age practised and proclaimed. But to his generation, so powerful still was the appeal of lost faith, so intricate the associations of right belief and right conduct, that that way was closed. Ruskin's final assurance, that it does not matter much to the universe what sort of person you are, was impossible to a generation impressed by its teachers with the infinite importance—and therefore self-importance—of the individual soul. The Tractarians by pointing to the Church, the Arnoldian school by their vivid realization of history, had relieved the intense introversion of Evangelicalism.[1] But

[1] For Newman, see the profound diagnosis of Evangelicalism at the end of

lacking faith, the individual was released from his own prison only to find himself alone in an indifferent universe. Kingsley was relieving many souls of their burden by communicating his own delight in the body, in the ardours of exploration, sport, and sex. Unluckily the world is not entirely peopled by young country gentlemen, newly married to chastely passionate brides. Nevertheless, the name of Kingsley, naturalist, health reformer, poet and preacher, on the one hand silenced as an advocate of socialism, on the other, denounced as a propagator of impurity, may stand for the meeting place of all the forces at work on the younger imagination of the years when, as it seemed to those who recalled the sordid and sullen past, England was renewing her youth, at Lucknow and Inkerman, with Livingstone in the African desert, with Burton on the road to Mecca, and speaking to the oppressors of Europe in the accents of Cromwell and Pitt. Of all decades in our history, a wise man would choose the eighteen-fifties to be young in.

XII

Mr. Gladstone, dwelling on the responsiveness of the people to good government, once said that every call from Parliament had been answered by a corresponding self-improvement of the masses. The years through which we have been passing afford some confirmation of this sanguine philosophy. The labouring Englishman in the fifties was much better governed than the labouring Englishman of 1830, and he was, taken in the mass, a much more respectable man. He was better governed, inasmuch as the State had definitely resolved to concern itself with the conditions of his life and labour and the education of his children. He was more respectable because, with rising wages and cheaper food, with some leisure at home and the grosser kinds of insanitation put down, he was recovering his self-respect. More strictly, it might be said that the proletariat, which in the thirties seemed to be sinking into a dull uniformity of wretchedness, had been stratified. In this light the contradictions which we encounter whenever we turn our eye to the

the Lectures on Justification, which, translated out of the technical terms of theology, is applicable to the whole age. Introspection within a closed circle of experience was the trouble. I cannot doubt that if Arnold had not been a schoolmaster he would have been a very good historian. *Introverted* is, somewhat surprisingly, a word of the forties: Wilberforce used it of Peel.

condition of the people in mid-Victorian England are resolved. There was a vast, untouchable underworld. But the great industries were manned with families, often much better off than the neighbouring curate or schoolmaster, and not burdened by the middle class necessity of keeping up a position. This right wing, hopeful, comfortable, within sight of the franchise, the Respectable Poor, the Conservative working man, drew away. Crime, poverty, and drunkenness, which had reached their peak about 1842, were dropping year by year. The maypole had gone: the village feast and the club-walk were going; but the zoo, the panorama, the free-library, the fête, and the excursion ticket were bringing hundreds of thousands within the reach of orderly and good-humoured pleasure. It is a curious observation of the early fifties that the workmen were wearing the same clothes as the gentlemen. Still more oddly, the French artist, Delacroix, noticed that the gentlemen were wearing the same clothes as the workmen.

One grey patch remained, growing drearier as the life ebbed out of the villages; but the brooding apprehension of thirty years had lifted. The testing time had come in 1848. The last Chartist demonstration was a demonstration only; for the artillery men who lined the Thames from Waterloo Bridge to Millbank, the shopkeepers who patrolled the streets, the Government clerks who laid in muskets and barricaded the windows with official files,[1] and the coal whippers who marched from Wapping with a general idea of standing by the Duke and a particular intention of breaking every Irishman's head, it was a demonstration and a festival. The storm which swept away half the Governments of Europe passed harmlessly over the islands, and the words which Macaulay wrote at the beginning of his history, that his checkered narrative would excite thankfulness in all religious minds and hope in the breast of all patriots, had a deep significance for his first readers, watching the nations of Europe sink one by one from convulsive anarchy back into despotism, and seeing, in the recovered unity, as much as in the prosperity of England, a triumphant vindication of the historic English way. The Great Exhibition was the pageant of domestic peace. Not for sixty years had the throne appeared so solidly based on

---

[1] The Foreign Office consented to receive reinforcements from the Colonial Office 'if we lose any men'.

Sir ROBERT PEEL is no more. After three days of excessive suffering, at a few minutes past eleven last night, the greatest statesman of his time quitted the scene in which he had performed so conspicuous a part. Even the anxiety and the rumours which have penetrated every household since the first alarming intelligence will have failed to prepare the country for the deplorable result. Except, indeed, in the field of battle, never was the transition from life to death so marked and so touching. On Friday the House of Commons, which for more than forty years has witnessed the triumphs and reverses of the great Conservative chief, was filled with an extraordinary assemblage anxious for the result of a great political crisis. Sir ROBERT addressed them with an ability and a spirit which recalled his more youthful efforts, and more powerful days. It was the first occasion for four years that elicited any serious or direct opposition to the policy of HER MAJESTY's present advisers, and, not to reopen a debate full of mistakes and crosspurposes, it must be allowed that the speech was at least an admirable defence of the principles on which Sir ROBERT and his colleagues had ever proceeded. He sat down, as our report says, amid " loud and long-" continued cheering." Within a few hours the statesman who had commanded the applause of that listening senate was a wreck of life and strength, shattered, feeble, restless, and agonized. The feverish interval is past. That heart has ceased to beat ; that tongue is ever still. That ardent spirit and capacious intellect are now in another and an unknown world.

From The Times, 3 *July* 1850

the national goodwill as in that summer of hope and pride and reconciliation. After all the alarms and agitations of thirty years the State had swung back to its natural centre.[1]
Victoria was not in her girlhood a popular Sovereign. She was tactless: she was partisan: the tragic story of Lady Flora Hastings showed her heartless as well. The figure that made its way into the hearts of the middle classes was not the gay, self-willed little Whig of 1837, but the young matron, tireless, submissive, dutiful. Her Court was dull, but the Royal nursery was irresistible. Prince Albert had seized the key positions behind which the Monarchy was safe—morality and industry.[2] A revolt of the special constables would have been formidable: a virtuous and domestic Sovereign, interested in docks and railways, hospitals and tenements, self-help, and mutual improvement was impregnable. Such a Sovereign, and much more beside, Prince Albert would have been, and in this mild, beneficent light he displayed his Consort's crown to the world. As its power pursued its inevitable downward curve, its influence rose in equipoise.

In 1834 King William had strained the prerogative to the breaking point by putting the Tories into office before the country was quite ready for them. In 1839 the Queen had kept the Whigs in office when the country was heartily tired of them. But ten years later the Crown was called upon to exercise that power of helping the country to find the Government it wants, which makes monarchy so precious an adjunct to the party system. After repealing the Corn Laws, Sir Robert Peel was defeated by a combination between his late allies, the Whigs, and his own rebels, the Protectionists. Lord John Russell came in, with Palmerston at the Foreign Office, Disraeli leading the Opposition. In 1850 Peel died, the only English statesman for whose death the poor have cried in the streets, and it soon appeared whose hand had kept the Whigs in power. In 1851 they were defeated; Stanley tried to form a Tory Government, failed, and the Whigs came back. Palmerston was dismissed for impertinence to

---

[1] In 1848 Thackeray declared himself 'a Republican but not a Chartist'. In 1851 he was writing odes to the Crystal Palace. But *Punch* was still Radical enough to resent the sight of Goldsticks walking backwards.
[2] Again, like most things in Victorian England, this was a European episode. The English Court struck a mean between the pietism of Berlin and the bourgeois decorum of Louis-Philippe.

his Queen, and Lord John groped about for a coalition. He was unsuccessful, and in 1852 Palmerston had the gratification of turning him out. Derby and Disraeli formed a Government, struggled through a few months against united Whigs, Peelites, and Radicals, and resigned. Old Lord Lansdowne was sent for and dear Lord Aberdeen was commissioned to form one coalition more. He succeeded, and went to war with Russia. Went is hardly the word. But the mismanagement of the opening campaign in '54 broke up the Cabinet, and with universal applause, superb assurance, and the recovered confidence of his Sovereign, Palmerston bounded into the vacant place. A brief eclipse in '58 hardly impaired his ascendancy, and till his death at eighty-one, with a half-finished dispatch on his table, in the eyes of the world and his country Palmerston was England and England was Palmerston. The political comedy has never been more brilliantly staged, and at every turn the Crown was in its proper place, selecting, reconciling, and listening, its dignity unimpaired by party conflicts and its impartiality surmounting individual distastes. 'I object to Lord Palmerston on personal grounds,' the Queen said. 'The Queen means', Prince Albert explained, 'that she does not object to Lord Palmerston on account of his person.' In place of a definite but brittle prerogative it had acquired an indefinable but potent influence. The events of 1846 to 1854 affirmed for some generations to come the character of the new monarchy, just at the time when events abroad—Australian gold discoveries, India, and the Crimea—were giving the nation an aggressive, imperial self-consciousness.

From 1815 to the Revolution of '48 foreign affairs had engaged but a small share of the public attention. First came the depression after Waterloo and the slow recovery, with a terrible set-back in 1825. Then Ireland and Catholic emancipation take the stage, then Reform and the Poor Law, and Ireland again with O'Connell; then come the Oxford, the Chartist, and the Free Trade movements, the depression of the first years of Victoria, Ireland once more, and the Repeal of the Corn Laws. But from 1850 onwards the focus of interest is overseas; the soldier, the emigrant, and the explorer, the plots of Napoleon III and the red shirt of Garibaldi, take and fill the imagination. Domestic politics are languid. Once, if not twice, in twenty years, the franchise had brought

England in sight of civil war: in the fifties a Franchise Bill was four times introduced

Quater ipso in limine portae
substitit, atque utero sonitum quater arma dedere,[1]

and was forgotten; the annual motion on the ballot became an annual joke. Ireland was prostrate, old Chartists were lecturing on Christian evidences, or, more usefully, working quietly in the new trade unions; old republicans were shouting for war; old pacifists declaiming to empty halls. Nothing is so bloody-minded as a Radical turned patriot. Roebuck was all for bombarding Naples. Bentham's old secretary, Bowring, crowned his astonishingly various career by actually bombarding Canton. Only those whose memories went back fifteen years could understand what a change of sentiment made the arming of the volunteers in '59 possible, or how completely the confidence which inspired that gesture was vindicated by the patience of Lancashire in the cotton famine.

Adventurous and secure, the ruling class in the years of Palmerston was excellently qualified to found a commonwealth or re-conquer an empire abroad, and, within the range of its ideas, to legislate wisely at home. After the fierce contentions of the past it is strange to observe with what ease and confidence the changes of the mid-Victorian time are effected. University reform, divorce reform, the government of the metropolis, the re-settlement of India, colonial self-government, the creation of the Public Accounts Committee, the Post Office Savings Bank, the Atlantic cable, that generation took in its stride, and the conversion of the vast and shapeless city which Dickens knew—fogbound and fever-haunted, brooding over its dark, mysterious river—into the imperial capital, of Whitehall, the Thames Embankment and South Kensington, is the still visible symbol of the mid-Victorian transition.

Parties were changing; the strong and steady currents of Whig and Tory opinion were splitting into eddies. The friends of the late Sir Robert Peel, as they move to and fro

---

[1] Robert Lowe, of course. I put this second among Virgilian quotations, the best being Gladstone's, when the Spanish Government unexpectedly met some bills and so stopped a hole in the budget.

'via prima salutis
Quod minime reris, Graia pandetur ab urbe.'

Pitt's 'Nos ubi primus equis' is not quotation, but inspiration.

across the stage, make Conservatism a little less Tory, and Liberalism a little less Whig. A new and popular Liberalism is forming of definite grievance and redress, Church rates and University tests, Army Purchase and Irish Disestablishment, and a humane and frugal distrust of Empire, aristocracy, adventure, and war. The re-education of the Conservatives, paralysed by the Free Trade schism, has begun, and the field is setting for the encounter of Gladstone and Disraeli when once Palmerston has departed. But the virulence of party conflicts is abating in a humorous, sporting tussle, where Palmerston keeps the ring against all comers, while Gladstone's budgets swing majestically down the tideway of an unexampled prosperity. In twelve years our trade was doubled and the trade returns, indeed, of those years are a part of English literature because they furnished footnotes to Macaulay's third chapter. In four years from 1853 the profits of agriculture increased by a fifth. The whole debt left by the Russian war was less than one-half of a year's revenue and the revenue no more than a third, perhaps not more than a fifth, of the annual savings of the nation. But age and crabbed youth cannot live together; age is full of pleasure, youth is full of care; and the unfriendly and mistrustful union of Palmerston and Gladstone, a union almost breaking into open hostility over the French panic and the fortification of Portsmouth, and again over the Paper Duties, is typical of the poise of the age, looking back to the proud, exciting days of Canning and Pitt and another Bonaparte, and forward to a peaceful prosperity of which no end was in sight; an ignorant pride which forgot that Prussia had an army, a thoughtless prosperity which did not reckon with American wheat.

Parliament was changing, too. Till 1832 it was in effect and almost in form a single-chamber assembly, since a large part of the Commons were appointed by the Lords, and a man might easily have one vote—or one proxy—in the Upper House and half a dozen in the Lower. Separation implies the possibility at least of conflict. That it was avoided, that, for all the hostility of the Radicals to the Peers, neither reform nor abolition of the Lords was seriously mooted, followed from the fact that socially the landed interest ascendant in the Commons had no hostility towards its chiefs in the Lords, and that politically the Duke

LATEST INTELLIGENCE.

THE FALL
OF
SEBASTOPOL.

WAR DEPARTMENT, SEPT. 10.

Lord Panmure has received the following telegraphic despatch from General Simpson, dated
"CRIMEA, SEPT. 9.

"Sebastopol is in the possession of the allies.

"The enemy, during the night and this morning, have evacuated the south side, after exploding their magazines and setting fire to the whole of the town.

"All the men-of-war were burnt during the night, with the exception of three steamers, which are plying about the harbour.

"The bridge communicating with the north side is broken."

Sir Charles Wood has received the following despatch from Sir E. Lyons :—

"During the night the Russians have sunk all the remainder of the line-of-battle ships in Sebastopol harbour."

WAR DEPARTMENT, SEPT. 10.

Lord Panmure has received the following telegraphic despatch from General Simpson, dated
"CRIMEA, SEPT. 10.

"The casualties, I regret to say, are somewhat heavy.

"No General officer killed.

"Names shall be sent as soon as possible."

From The Times, 11 *September* 1855

could always induce the Tory Lords, in a crisis, to give way to the Whig Commons. They yielded in 1832; they yielded in 1846; and by neither surrender did the Lords as a house, or the aristocracy as a class, lose any particle of real power. After the first shock of dismay they had rallied to the land, and the upward tilt of prices gave them the confidence they needed. Rents did not fall; they even began to rise; between '53 and '57, helped by the war, they rose by more than a tenth. The basis of mid-Victorian prosperity—and, indeed, of society—was a balance of land and industry, an ever enlarging market for English manufactures and a still restricted market for foreign produce. The home harvest was dominant: a short crop meant high prices, low prices meant an abundant crop. If all other grounds were absent, the obstinate survival of aristocracy in Victorian England is capable of economic explanation. An eminent authority has pronounced the opinion that production has never passed the level of the fifties, has doubted whether, with all the resources of science, it ever can. For another generation the gentry stood firm on their broad lands, the capitalists and directors of the chief English industry: 3,500,000 acres under wheat, crops from 30 bushels upwards to the acre:[1] encircled by a prosperous and respectful tenantry, as proud in their own way as themselves, and a landless peasantry at the feet of both.

But their ascendancy rested hardly less on immaterials. If they had the one thing the plutocracy most respected in themselves, they had all the other things which the people missed in the plutocracy. In morals and intellect they were not disturbingly above or below the average of their countrymen, who regarded them, with some truth, as being in all bodily gifts the finest stock in Europe. By exercise, temperance and plebeian alliance, the spindle-shanked lord of Fielding had become the ancestor of an invigorated race. They had shed their brutality and extravagance; their eccentricities were of a harmless sporting kind; they were forward in good works; they habitually had family prayers.[2] Of two rich men, or two clever men, England was not ashamed to prefer the gentleman, and the preference operated for the

---

[1] All statistics contain an element of guess-work. But the best opinion seems to be that in the mid-fifties, England had rather more than 3½ million acres, with crops running to 40 bushels. The yield over all was 26¼ bushels.

[2] Lord Hatherton used to say that in 1810 only two gentlemen in Staffordshire had family prayers: in 1850 only two did not.

benefit of many gentlemen who were both poor and stupid. Mr. Podsnap is not a bad man: in the one crisis he has to face he acts with right decision. But Dickens's heart is with little Mr. Twemlow, who never made a decision in his life and would probably have got it wrong if he had. If they had stood against each other for a borough constituency in the South it is not improbable that the ten-pound householders would have chosen Mr. Twemlow. England is large, there is room, and a future, for Sir Leicester and the Iron-master, but Mr. Podsnap is a belated and sterile type.

Mr. Gladstone had two names for this peculiar habit of mind. Once he called it 'a sneaking kindness for a lord'; at another time, more characteristically, 'the shadow which the love of freedom casts or the echo of its voice in the halls of the constitution'. The philosophic historian may take his choice, and it is easier to frame a defence or an indict-ment of the Victorian attitude to aristocracy than to under-stand why, in a money-making age, opinion was, on the whole, more deferential to birth than to money, and why, in a mobile and progressive society, most regard was had to the element which represented immobility, tradition, and the past. Perhaps the statement will be found to include the solution. The English *bourgeoisie* had never been isolated long enough to frame, except in the spheres of comfort and carnal morality, ideals and standards of its own. It was imitative. A nation, hammered into unity by a strong crown, had ended by putting the power of the Crown into commis-sion, and the great houses in succeeding to the real authority, had acquired, and imparted to the lesser houses, something of the mysterious ascendancy of the royal symbol. For a hundred years they ruled, and almost reigned, over an Eng-land of villages and little towns. The new urban civilization was rapidly creating a tradition of civic benevolence and government, but it had no tradition of civic magnificence. To be anything, to be recognized as anything, to feel himself as anything in the State at large, the rich English townsman, unless he was a man of remarkable gifts and character, had still to escape from the seat and source of his wealth, to learn a new dialect and new interests, and he was more likely to magnify than to belittle the virtues of the life into which he and his wife yearned to be admitted, the life, beyond wealth, of power and consideration on the land. From time immemorial a place in the country had been the crown of a merchant's career, and from the first circle the impulse was communicated through all the spheres down to the solid centre of the ten-pound franchise and the suburban villa. Within the limits thus marked out by instinctive deference, the electorate was free, and not, on the whole, ill qualified to make a general choice between parties and policies. It could see that Peel was wanted in 1840, that Palmerston was wanted in 1854, and whatever the House of Commons might say, that he was the man for 1858, that the House of Commons must be reformed in 1830 and the Corn Laws repealed in 1846. Through its educated stratum, which was proportionately large as the electorate was still small, through the still costly newspapers written for that stratum, through the opportunities which the orders of the House still gave to private members,[1] it could maintain a fairly even pressure on Parliament, and the work of Parliament was correspondingly increased. Parliaments in the eighteenth century and in the French wars were not in the first instance legislative bodies: they met to ventilate grievances, vote taxes, and control the executive. From about 1820 the age of continual legislation begins, and, as it proceeds, the ascendancy of the business end of Parliament over the debating end, of the Cabinet over the back benches, is more and more strongly affirmed. But between the two Reform Acts the executive and deliberative elements in Parliament were still in reasonable equipoise: Mr. Gladstone's punctilious phrase that the Government would seek the advice of the House, was not quite a formality in an age when the Government commanded

---

[1] This is of great importance for the character of Victorian Parliaments. After the disappearance of Speeches on Petitions in 1843, questions to Ministers steadily increased. The Government had only Mondays and Fridays, and on the motion for adjournment to Monday any member could raise any question, the result being, as Disraeli, said a conversazione. (The present system of numbered questions goes back to a proposal for regulating the conversazione made in 1860.) Moreover, every Monday and Friday before Easter, on the motion for going into Committee of Supply, the same liberty existed. As a result, I find in one fortnight, besides several useful little Bills introduced or advanced, the following subjects reviewed by the Commons, often in great detail, on the initiative of private members (sometimes, of course, by arrangement with the Government): Corruption at Elections, Criminal Appeal, Civil Service Economy, Defective Anchors, the Shrubs in Hyde Park, Publication of Divorce Reports, Church Rates, Indian Finance, the Ballot, Naval Operations in China (by the Admiral commanding, at great length), Flogging, Manning the Navy, Competitive Examination, and the Export of Coal.

less than half the time of the House, and the fact that a
large minority, sometimes a majority, of the Cabinet were
Peers relieved the congestion of debate by spreading it over
two Houses. As a branch of the legislature, the House of
Lords is of limited utility, and it could neither compel
nor avert a change of Ministry or a Dissolution; but it
was an admirable theatre for the exposition or criticism
of policy, and Peel, a House of Commons man through and
through, came late in life to the opinion that public business
might be advantaged if the Prime Minister were relieved of
the management of the Commons and set to direct operations
from the security of the Upper House.

XIII

In the great peace of the fifties the lines of force released
in the earlier decades, lines best remembered by the names
of Arnold, Newman, and Carlyle, come round into pattern.
It is about this time that the word Victorian[1] was coined to
register a new self-consciousness. 'Liverpool below, Oxford
on top,' was said of Mr. Gladstone, and it might be said more
generally of the English intelligence of the fifties. Work
shapes the mind, leisure colours it; the grim discipline of the
years of peril was relaxed: life was richer, easier, and friend-
lier. To turn from the stark, forbidding dogmas of James
Mill on Government to the humorous wisdom of Bagehot's
English Constitution, with its large allowances for the idleness,
stupidity, and good nature of mankind, is to enter another
world of thought, at once less logical and more real, and the
contrast not unfairly represents the change that had come
over England in thirty years.

In the general movement of the English mind few episodes
are so instructive as the revulsion which in the fifties reduced
the Economic Evangelicalism of 1830 from dominant philosophy to middle-class point of view and so prepared the way
for the teaching of Pater and Arnold, the practice of Morris
and Toynbee, the recognition, after years of derision or
neglect, of Ruskin and Browning. 'Nothing', Bagehot once
wrote, 'is more unpleasant than a virtuous person with a
mean mind. A highly developed moral nature joined to an

[1] The first example I have noted is in E. P. Hood, *The Age and its Architects*,
1851.

undeveloped intellectual nature, an undeveloped artistic nature, and a very limited religious nature, is of necessity repulsive,' and in the fifties England was becoming keenly aware of the narrowness and meagreness of her middle class tradition. A process very like that which was stratifying the proletariate into the Respectable and the Low, was creating out of the upper levels of the middle class a new patriciate, mixed of birth, wealth, and education, which might be Liberal or Conservative in politics, Christian or nothing in religion, but was gradually shedding the old middle-class restraints on enjoyment and speculation. And of this readjustment of classes and values, if the basis was security and prosperity, the principal agents were the Universities and the public schools.

In 1831 Brougham had defined The People as 'the middle classes, the wealth and intelligence of the country, the glory of the British name'. In 1848 a pamphlet appeared under the title *A Plea for the Middle Classes*. It was concerned with their education. The Barbarians and the Populace were provided for. Strenuous work, and what seemed to economists a formidable expenditure, were giving popular education in England a dead lift to a level not much below Prussia, on paper, and, on paper, well above France and Holland, the three countries from which much of the inspiration had come. It was the education vote, indeed, which opened the eyes of the public to the cost of the social services, and there was a growing doubt, which the Newcastle Commission of '58–'60 confirmed, of the value received for the money spent. Nominally, out of two and a half million children only one hundred thousand or so slipped through the net. The leaving age had been forced up to eleven and the school life lengthened to four years. But the cellar and the pedlar still flourished, a substantial proportion of the children were still not taught to write and only a tiny fraction got very much beyond. Robert Lowe, introducing payment by results, with the catchword 'if dear efficient, if inefficient cheap', succeeded for the first and last time in interesting the English public in an education debate without the sectarian spice. Nor can it be doubted that his policy was right. If he levelled down the best schools, he levelled up the worst, and so made sure that when compulsion came in the seventies those who were compelled to go to school would learn something when they got there, to write a letter, to make out a bill and hem a shirt. It was not much, but in the thirties it would have seemed a visionary ideal. That the ideal had been even so imperfectly realized, that the late Victorian democracy was not altogether unfit for its responsibilities, was in the main the work of one man, and if history judged men less by the noise than by the difference they make, it is hard to think of any name in the Victorian age which deserves to stand above or even beside Kay-Shuttleworth's.

In the early nineteenth century England had possessed in seven or eight hundred old grammar schools an apparatus for giving the middle classes an education as good as public opinion required for the class above and below, and by a disastrous miscalculation she let it run down. Not that it was wholly wasted. A good country Grammar school neither over-taught nor over-gamed, with a University connexion and a strong local backing, gave probably as sound an education as was to be had in England: such was Wordsworth's Hawkshead and the King's School at Canterbury where Charles Dickens looked wistfully through the gates at the boyhood he had never known, and Tiverton and Ipswich and many more. Some of them, like Tonbridge and Sherborne, Bedford, Manchester, and King Edward's Birmingham, climbed up to public-school level. Others contrived to make decent provision for the sons of minor gentry or superior tradesmen of their neighbourhood. But they were not always locally available and the deficiency was supplied by the private school of all grades, from Mr. Squeers, through Mr. Creakle, up to Dr. Strong, or by a new, and very characteristic, Victorian invention, the proprietary school of which University College School was the model, Marlborough and Clifton the most eminent examples.

In 1861 the whole system of secondary education was brought under review by the Taunton Commission. Below the schools which were in touch with the Universities all was chaos; those which aimed lowest seem to have done best: they could produce good clerks, though hardly better than the best National Schools. Above them the rank and file of the secondary schools, under-staffed by untaught ushers, were turning out at fifteen or so the boys who were to be the executive of the late Victorian industries and professions, the ascendant element in the late Victorian electorate, in a word the worst educated middle class in Europe. And, if the education of the middle-class boy was bad, the education of the girl was worse. For the better classes it was a domestic industry staffed in the first place by the mother, who might delegate the routine to a governess, and by visiting masters. Those families who could afford an annual stay in London added some intensive teaching by specialists in music, drawing, and the languages. The domestic system involved the employment of untrained gentlewomen as teachers, and the figure of the governess, snubbed, bullied, loving, and usually quite incompetent, is a standby of Victorian pathos. Lady Blessington first introduced it into literature, it reached its apotheosis in *East Lynne*. The silliness and shallowness of the boarding school is an equally constant topic of Victorian satire, but like the boys' schools, they were of all degrees. Browning's aunts had an admirable establishment at Blackheath, and George Eliot was excellently taught at her Coventry boarding school. London was ringed with such institutions, through which the drawing-master and the music-master wearily circulated on foot from Battersea over the river to Chiswick and up by Acton to Hampstead and Highgate. Below the boarding-school class was that unfortunate stratum just too high to make use of the charity school, the National school or the British Day. For them there was rarely anything better than a superior dame's school in a parlour or a very inferior visiting governess.

The demand for a better sort of woman was not a new one: Swift had urged it vehemently in eighteenth-century England, Montesquieu in France. But the curriculum was still dominated by the economic uniformity of women's existence and the doctrine of the Two Spheres. Every girl was prospectively the wife of a gentleman, a workman, or something in between. For the few unmarried there was the small annuity or dependence, as companion, governess or servant, in house or shop. Education, therefore, meant a grounding of morals and behaviour to last all through life, and a top dressing of accomplishments intended partly to occupy the girl's mind, partly to attract the men, and, in the last resort, to earn a living by if all else failed. For the intelligent girl in a sympathetic home there was a most stimulating provision of books, travel, and conversation. But this was no part of the curriculum at Chiswick or Cloisterham and it would have been thrown away on Dora Spenlow. Economically the two spheres had hardly begun to intersect. Intellectually, the overlap was steadily increasing, and it was for this common province of taste, criticism, intelligence, and sympathy that wise mothers trained their daughters, sensible girls trained themselves and the more fortunate husbands trained their brides.

Tennyson, always the most punctual exponent of contemporary feeling, published *The Princess* in 1847, a year in which many minds were converging on the problem. With the express approval of Queen Victoria a Maid of Honour planned a College for Women, King's College undertook to train and examine governesses, and Bedford College started with classes in a private house. From these three movements all the higher education of women in England has proceeded, but within our period it did not proceed very far. The Taunton Commission found that the secondary education of girls was still in a miserable condition. At Cheltenham and North London College where those distinguished but unfortunately named ladies, Miss Beale and Miss Buss, held sway, the country had models capable of a rich development, but the age of development begins exactly in 1865. Cambridge, with qualms, had just allowed girls to sit for Local examinations: London was still refusing to let them sit for matriculation. The collision of the Two Spheres is a Late Victorian theme, almost a Late Victorian revolution: in our period only the first mutterings of the revolution can be heard.

That the education of girls, as codified by eighteenth-century manners and moralized by nineteenth-century respectability, tended to a certain repression of personality in the interests of a favourite sexual type, can hardly be denied. But in the Victorian age this type was moulded by the pressure of an uncompromising religion: if the convention was that eighteenth-century man preferred his women fragile, and nineteenth-century man liked them ignorant, there is no doubt at all that he expected them to be good ; and goodness, in that age of universal charity, imported the service of others, and if service then training for service. Children and the sick had always been within the lawful scope of women's activities, and in a generation not less scientific than benevolent, the evolution

THE
FALL OF DELHI.

We have received the following telegram from our own correspondent at Trieste :—

"TRIESTE, MONDAY, OCT. 26.

" The steamer Bombay arrived from Alexandria at half-past 10 a.m. to-day. She left Alexandria on the 20th inst.

" The Calcutta and China mails left Alexandria on the 19th per French steamer. The Bombay portion was to be despatched on the 21st, with intelligence from Bombay to the 3d inst.

" Delhi was assaulted on the 14th of September, and was in possession of our troops on the 20th. Full particulars not yet known. Our loss on the 14th was 600 killed and wounded.

" General Outram's force reached Cawnpore on the 14th, and General Havelock crossed the Ganges on or before the 19th.

" From Lucknow the accounts are favourable, and confident hopes are entertained that the garrison will be relieved.

" At Agra all was quiet up to the 19th.

" The dâks were stopped between Lahore and Mooltan. Cause unknown. The Punjab was otherwise tranquil.

" The intelligence from the Bombay Presidency is favourable, though a few cases of disaffection had occurred in the army in Scinde. At Kurrachee the 21st Bombay Native Infantry had been disarmed, and about 20 men of the regiment had been convicted and executed.

" At Hyderabad, in the same province, a company of native artillery had been disarmed.

"Portions of Her Majesty's 4th and 95th had arrived at Bombay.

" Prices of imports had generally advanced.

" Bank rates of interest unaltered.

" Government paper had rallied.

" Freights steady.

" Exchanges, 2s. 1⅝d."

From The Times, *27 October* 1857

of the ministering angel into the professional teacher, nurse and doctor was inevitable. Often obscured by agitation for subordinate ends—the right to vote, to graduate, to dispose of her own property after marriage—the fundamental issue of feminism was growing clearer all through the century, as women, no longer isolated heroines but individuals bent on a career, drew out into the sexless sphere of disinterested intelligence, and Mary Wollstonecraft's conception of autonomous personality took body; a process which may be truly named Victorian if only for the horror with which Victoria regarded it. 'I want', said Bella Rokesmith to her husband, 'to be something so much worthier than the doll in the doll's house.' In the profusion of Dickens, the phrase might pass unnoticed. Twelve years later Ibsen made it the watchword of a revolution.

XIV

Compared with the uncertain aims and methods of middle-class and female education, the growth of the Universities and public schools has all the appearance of a concerted evolution aiming at the production of a definite type.

The institution of serious examinations, at Cambridge in 1780, at Oxford in 1802, had created at the two Universities fields of keen intellectual emulation. The distinction of pass and honours not only set up an objective for the ambitious, but united them in an intellectual aristocracy where form was studied as eagerly as, in later days, athletic gifts.[1] By tradition Cambridge was mathematical and Oxford was classical, but Oxford had an honours school in mathematics before Cambridge established the classical tripos, and the awe-inspiring double first, whatever it may signify in feminine fiction, properly meant a first in the two final schools: it was correctly used of Peel and Gladstone. For men who took their reading seriously, the standard was high and the classical impression lasting. Except Brougham, who was educated at Edinburgh, it is not easy to recall any public man of eminence who could have talked science with Prince Albert ; but many of them were competent scholars, several were excellent scholars, and the imprint of a thorough, if narrow, classical education

[1] Peel's translation of *suave mari magno: suave*, it is a source of melancholy satisfaction, was remembered all his life. Hogg and Shelley (in Hogg's *Life*) seem to me the first undergraduates, recognizable as such, on record.

is visible in Hansard whenever the speaker is Peel or Lord John Russell, Gladstone or Derby. It was equally diffused over Whigs and Tories, and the Radicals, who on principle might have been expected to be averse to a purely literary discipline, numbered by accident in their ranks the most illustrious classical scholar and the most exacting classical tutor of the age—George Grote and the elder Mill.

Both at Oxford and at Cambridge the career of the passman was little more than the prolongation of his school days without the discipline. In fact, as Freeman put it, prospective parsons and prospective lawyers, young men of rank and fortune, were provided for; if they had any intellectual ambitions they were admirably provided for; if they had not, the Universities had little to give them, and outside the circle of the Church, the Bar, and the landed gentry, they had nothing to give at all. In their internal discipline they were overgrown with a picturesque tangle of privileges, distinctions, and exemptions; founders' kin and local fellowships, servitors and sizars, gentlemen commoners and fellow commoners: New College and King's took their degrees without examination,

πάντων πλὴν ἵππων ἀδαήμονές ἐστε κυνῶν τε
καίτοι γ' οὔθ' ἵππων εἰδότες οὔτε κυνῶν,

and the tuft, the golden tassel on the cap, survived until 1870 at Oxford as a mark of noble birth. The governing oligarchy of heads of houses stood aloof from the general body of masters; and the fellows, except where personal influence drew together groups of disciples, stood aloof from the undergraduate. Compared with the eighteenth century the intellectual life was intenser, manners and morals were more refined. Compared with the later nineteenth century, studies and sports were far less standardized, manners and morals were still barbaric. There was much unscientific cricket and rowing, a fair amount of riding and hunting, occasional street fighting, some wenching, and much drinking. But there is universal agreement that the state of the Universities was steadily improving as the juniors became less childish and the seniors less remote.

The Universities were definitely Anglican. At Cambridge a man could not graduate, at Oxford he could not matriculate, without signing the Thirty-Nine Articles.[1] The Commons

---

[1] To which, incidentally, Wesleyans took no exception.

in 1834 passed a Bill enabling dissenters to graduate. The Lords threw it out. Practically, it was not a matter of much consequence, as dissenters were not, as a rule, of the class whom Oxford and Cambridge served, and a new private venture called the London University was already at their disposal. It was strongly Radical in origin and affinity, it was entirely secular, and its curriculum was very much wider than that of the old Universities. The foundation of the University of London marks the entry of a new idea; the conception of a University as training for a specific profession, for medicine, law, engineering, or teaching, was in England a novelty to which the examples of Germany and Scotland both contributed. In 1845 Macaulay had to explain to a house of Oxford and Cambridge men that in Scotland, as in London, there were no Proctors, and that the academic senate had no power to deal even with such enormities as getting drunk in the street or attending a Nonconformist place of worship. But as a seat of instruction University College rose at once to the first rank, and there are few pictures of the young Victorian mind so attractive as the pages in which Hutton set down his memories of Long and de Morgan, and their brother sophists, and of his walks with Bagehot up and down Regent Street in search of Oxford Street and truth. Liberal, accessible and utilitarian, it might have been expected that the example of the Londoners would have been widely and speedily followed. That it was not, that the northern colleges emerged late and slowly from their original obscurity, shows how alien to the middle classes was the idea of higher education not connected with practical utility or social distinction, and how much was lost with the disappearance of the Nonconformist academies of the eighteenth century.[1] A feeble effort to provide the north with inexpensive culture was made by the Dean and Chapter of the richest of English cathedrals, but the historian of Victorian England will not often have occasion to mention the University of Durham.

On the world outside their walls the ancient Universities exercised an exasperated fascination: they were clerical;

[1] Owens College, founded in 1851, begins to count from about 1860. Readers of *Endymion* will remember how the younger Thornbury was diverted from Mill Hill and Owens to Radley and Oxford. Of another Manchester father, Disraeli told the Queen that he sent his sons to Oxford to be made into gentlemen 'but unfortunately they only became Roman Catholics'.

they were idle; they were dissipated; they reflected those odious class distinctions by which merit is suppressed and insolence fostered; their studies were narrow, their teaching ineffective. And on every count of the indictment the reformers found themselves supported by eminent friends within the gates, by Thirlwall at Cambridge and by Tait and Jowett at Oxford. The Commission of 1850–2 and the Acts of 1854 and 1856 only accelerated, and consolidated, a process of internal reform which had proceeded somewhat faster at Cambridge than at Oxford, partly because for ten years the activities of Oxford had been diverted to religious agitation, while Cambridge had had the good sense to profit by her Chancellor's experience as an undergraduate of Bonn.

The object of the Commission was to clear away the constitutional obstructions to internal development and to make the Universities more accessible to the middle classes, more useful to the pass-man, and more serviceable to pure learning. But in principle the Universities affirmed their essence, against Germany and Scotland, as places not of professional but of liberal education in a world which still acknowledged that public life, in the Church, in Parliament, or on the County Bench, was not only a more distinguished, but a better life than the pursuit of wealth by industrious competition. If we imagine Victorian England without Oxford and Cambridge, what barrier can we see against the encroaching tide of utility and material standards? Even in their alliance, their too close alliance, with the aristocracy there were elements of advantage. The Clergyman was rarely an instructed theologian, but he was not a seminarist. The scholar growing up among men destined for a public career took some tincture of public interests; the professional man, the Barrister, the Politician, the Civil Servant, and the gentleman unclassified, acquired the same double impress of culture and manners; and the Universities broke the fall of the aristocracy by civilizing the plutocracy.

The founders of the London University showed insight into the needs of their time by attaching schools to each of their two colleges. The old Universities were fed by the public schools, by the grammar schools, and by the private tutor who was commonly a clergyman; the preparatory school for young boys was in existence, and one of them,

The nation has just sustained the greatest loss that could possibly have fallen upon it. Prince ALBERT, who a week ago gave every promise that his valuable life would be lengthened to a period long enough to enable him to enjoy, even in this world, the fruit of a virtuous youth and a well-spent manhood, the affection of a devoted wife and of a family of which any father might well be proud,—this man, the very centre of our social system, the pillar of our State, is suddenly snatched from us, without even warning sufficient to prepare us for a blow so abrupt and so terrible. We shall need time fully to appreciate the magnitude of the loss we have sustained. Every day will make us more conscious of it. It is not merely a prominent figure that will be missed on all public occasions ; not merely a death that will cast a permanent gloom over a reign hitherto so joyous and so prosperous ;—it is the loss of a public man whose services to this country, though rendered neither in the field of battle nor in the arena of crowded assemblies, have yet been of inestimable value to this nation,—a man to whom more than any one else we owe the happy state of our internal polity, and a degree of general contentment to which neither we nor any other nation we know of ever attained before.

Twenty-one years have just elapsed since Queen VICTORIA gave her hand in marriage to Prince ALBERT of Saxe-Gotha. It was an auspicious event, and reality has more than surpassed all prognostics, however favourable. The Royal marriage has been blessed with a numerous offspring. So far as it is permitted to the public to know the domestic lives of Sovereigns, the people of these islands could set up no better model of the performance of the duties of a wife and mother than their QUEEN ; no more complete pattern of a devoted husband and father than her CONSORT. These are not mere words of course. We write in an age and in a country in which the highest position would not have availed to screen the most elevated delinquent. They are simply the records of a truth perfectly understood and recognized by the English people.

From The Times, 16 *December* 1861

at sigl
told M
the U
ledge.
said tl
and f
Austr:
the re
increa
to get
and o
well-e
brancl
and C:
Civil
beatei
annex
Servic
The
could
world.
ruling
absolu
tocrac
ship:
great
new i
teentl
purita
by pu
this id
the U
autho:
counti
defect
flower
respec
have t
dialec

¹ But
of this
Sophocl

Temple Grove at East Sheen, was famous. Some details have been preserved of the life lived by the boys: hands, face 'and perhaps the neck', were washed daily; feet once a fortnight, heads as required; a vernal dose of brimstone and treacle purified their blood, a half-yearly dentist drew their teeth, it was the custom under flogging to bite the Latin Grammar. Not a bad preparation, one may think, for Long Chamber where boys of all ages were locked up from eight to eight 'and cries of joy and pain were alike unheard'. But the system was not yet stereotyped, and much education was still received at home or in the study of the neighbouring rector. Apart from the ceremonial of Eton and Christ Church for the aristocracy, a public-school education was no necessary part of the social curriculum. Of Victorians born in good circumstances, neither Macaulay nor Tennyson, Newman, or Disraeli, got their schooling that way, and at the University or in after-life it made no difference. The Old Giggleswickian was not yet a named variety.¹

Indeed, at the beginning of the century, the public schools had been in some danger of extinction, and if the grammar schools had been equipped for their task, it is very probable that our higher education would, to our great advantage, have developed on a less expensive, less exclusive, basis. Eton existed on prestige, but Westminster, Winchester, and Harrow had barely 200 boys between them. Charterhouse had a sudden brief popularity, and Rugby was coming up steadily under James. The opening, first of the Oriel fellowships and then of the Balliol scholarships, set a new goal for ambitious schoolmasters, and the record of Butler's pupils put Shrewsbury in a conspicuous eminence. But practical parents disliked the purely classical curriculum; sensitive parents were dismayed by the tales of squalor, cruelty, and disorder which were told of almost every school; and religious parents hesitated to entrust young boys to institutions which gave only a formal security for piety and morals.

Arnold reconciled the middle classes to the public school. He shared their faith in progress, goodness, and their own

¹ The first Old —an I have noticed is, as might be expected, an Old Rugboean in 1840. A man born in the fifties told me that until he was twelve he was intended for the local grammar school, as the family could only support one son at Eton. A discovery of coal on the estate altered the position. He had to begin by learning English in place of the N. Riding dialect which was his native speech.

would have thought Sidney Herbert rather barbarous:[1] Ariosto, one fears, would have set him down as a prig—and to its defects must be in large measure ascribed the imprecision of late Victorian thought and policy which contrasts so ominously with the rigorous deductions of the early Victorians. Yet in the far distance I can well conceive the world turning wistfully in imagination, as to the culminating achievement of European culture, to the life of the University-bred classes in England of the mid-nineteenth century, set against the English landscape as it was, as it can be no more, but of which nevertheless some memorials remain with us to-day, in the garden at Kelmscott, in the hidden valleys of the Cotswolds, in that walled close where all the pride and piety, the peace and beauty of a vanished world seem to have made their last home under the spire of St. Mary of Salisbury.

XX

In surveying a period of history it is sometimes useful to step outside and see what happened next. Of late Victorian England the most obvious characteristics are the Imperialism of Beaconsfield and Chamberlain and the counterthrust of Gladstonian Liberalism; the emergence of a Socialist and, in a lesser degree, of a Feminist movement as calculable forces; the decay of the religious interest and the supersession of the aristocracy by the plutocracy, a process masked by the severe and homely court of Victoria, but growing precipitate, after the agricultural depression, with the influx of South African money and American brides. Early Victorian had become a term of reproach when Victoria had still ten years to reign.

It was the good fortune of England in the years we have been surveying to confront a sudden access of power, prosperity, and knowledge, with a solidly grounded code of duty and self-restraint. In the fifties and sixties, the code still held good, but the philosophy on which it was based was

[1] But Aristophanes has given the best definition of the type that I know, 'an insider who enjoys his privileges and is regular in his duties to the outsiders'.

μόνοις γὰρ ἡμῖν ἥλιος καὶ φέγγος ἱλαρόν ἐστιν,
ὅσοι μεμυήμεθ' εὐ-
σεβῆ τε διήγομεν
τρόπον περὶ τοὺς ξένους
καὶ τοὺς ἰδιώτας.

visibly breaking up. It had rested on two assumptions which experience had shown to be untenable: that the production of wealth by the few meant, somehow, and in the long run, welfare for the many; and that conventional behaviour grounded on a traditional creed was enough to satisfy all right demands of humanity. At our distance in time we can see the agnostic and feminist turn impending: we can understand the connexion, peculiar to England, between the socialist and aesthetic movements of the next age. But life was too leisurely and secure for agitation. The reforms of the forties satisfied the aspirations of the poor and the consciences of the rich, until a new tide set in and carried us forward again with the Education Act of 1870 and the legislation of Disraeli's Government, with which Young England, now grown grey, redeemed the promise of its far-off fantastic youth. In the fifties the main current of Utilitarianism was running in the channels which the great administrators had dug for it: the springs of religious feeling opened by the Evangelicals had been led over the new fields which Newman, Arnold, and Carlyle—miraculous confederacy—had won or recovered for English thought; and Economic Evangelicalism was no more than a barren stock. The first Victorian generation had built with the sword in one hand and the trowel in the other: in the fifties the sword was laid aside and the trowel was wielded, quietly, unobtrusively, anonymously, by civil servants and journalists, engineers and doctors, the secretaries of Trade Unions and the aldermen of manufacturing towns. Early in the thirties, Nassau Senior had boldly declared, against the current Malthusianism, that if the influx of Irish labour could be checked and the outflow of English labour assisted the population question could be left to settle itself. Now his words seemed to be coming true. A race so tenacious of its immemorial village life that in 1830 a Sussex family could hardly be persuaded to seek its fortune in Staffordshire, or a Dorset family that Lancashire existed, was flocking by the hundred thousand in quest of the Golden Fleece, or the land where the gates of night and morning stand so close together that a good man can earn two days' wages in one. By 1860 the whole world was the Englishman's home and England was at peace.

Released from fear, the English mind was recovering its

power to speculate, to wonder and to enjoy. The dissolvent elements in Early Victorian thought, romance and humour and curiosity, the Catholicism of Oxford, the satire of Dickens, the passion of Carlyle, the large historic vision of Grote and Lyell and Arnold, were beginning to work. One of the last survivors of the mid-Victorian time spoke of those years as having the sustained excitement of a religious revival. Excitement was Lord Morley's word also, and all through the fifties we are aware of the increasing tension of thought. The Christian Socialists rose in ill-directed but fruitful revolt: the Pre-Raphaelites struck out for a freedom which they had not strength to reach. Tennyson in *Maud*, Dickens in *Hard Times* turned savagely on the age that had bred them. We miss the precise objectives, the concentrated purpose of the earlier age. Science and poetry, business and adventure, religion and politics are not yet divided into separate, professional avocations; but they are thrown together in an irregular, massive synthesis, of which the keynotes still are competence and responsibility, a general competence not always distinguishable from a general amateurishness, a universal responsibility sometimes declining into a universal self-importance. Not for a long time had the English character seemed so upright, or English thought so formless, as in that happy half generation when the demand for organic change was quiescent, the religious foundations were perishing and the balance of land and industry was slowly toppling.

We are nearing the years of division. In 1859 the last of the Augustans was laid by Johnson and Addison, and the Red House was begun at Bexley: in 1860 Ruskin issued as much of *Unto this Last* as Thackeray dared to print, and how great a part of late Victorian thought is implicit in five books of those same years, in the *Origin of Species*, Mill on *Liberty* and *Essays and Reviews*: in Fitzgerald's Omar and Meredith's *Richard Feverel*. We are approaching a frontier, and the voices that come to us from the other side, *Modern Love* and *Ecce Homo*, Swinburne's first poems and Pater's first essays, are the voices of a new world, of which the satirist is not Cruickshank but du Maurier, the laureate not Tennyson but Browning, the schoolmaster not Arnold but his son. The late Victorian Age is opening.

He has left none like him—none who can rally round him so many followers of various opinions, none who can give us so happy a respite from the violence of party-warfare, none who can bring to the work of statesmanship so precious a store of recollections. It is impossible not to feel that Lord PALMERSTON's death marks an epoch in English politics. "The old order changeth, yield-" ing place to new." Other Ministers may carry into successful effect organic reforms from which he shrunk. Others may introduce a new spirit into our foreign relations, and abandon the system of secret diplomacy which he never failed to support. Others may advise HER MAJESTY with equal sagacity, and sway the House of Commons with equal or greater eloquence; but his place in the hearts of the people will not be filled so easily. The name of Lord PALMERSTON, once the terror of the Continent, will long be connected in the minds of Englishmen with an epoch of unbroken peace and unparalleled prosperity, and cherished together with the brightest memories of the reign of Queen VICTORIA.

From The Times 19 *October* 1865

3 X